A THESAURUS OF
BRITISH ARCHAEOLOGY

A THESAURUS OF BRITISH ARCHAEOLOGY

LESLEY ADKINS
& ROY A. ADKINS

DAVID & CHARLES
Newton Abbot London

BARNES & NOBLE BOOKS
Totowa, New Jersey

This Book is Dedicated to our Parents

British Library Cataloguing in Publication Data

Adkins, Lesley
  A thesaurus of British archaeology.
  1. Archaeology—Great Britain—Terminology
  I. Title   II. Adkins, Roy A.
  936.1   DA90

  ISBN 0-7153-7864-3
  ISBN 0-389-20245-2 (United States)

Typeset by Typesetters (Birmingham) Limited
Edgbaston Road, Smethwick, Warley, West Midlands
and printed in Great Britain
by Redwood Burn Limited, Trowbridge, Wiltshire
for David & Charles (Publishers) Limited
Brunel House   Newton Abbot   Devon

First published in the USA 1982 by
Barnes & Noble Books
81 Adams Drive, Totowa, New Jersey, 07512

Contents

Preface and Acknowledgements 6

Notes for Readers 7

1 The Palaeolithic Period 9

2 The Mesolithic Period 21

3 The Neolithic Period 27

4 The Bronze Age 45

5 The Iron Age 74

6 The Roman Period 99

7 The Saxon Period 143

8 The Medieval Period 167

9 Archaeological Techniques 205

10 Miscellaneous 242

Bibliography 285

Index 297

Preface and Acknowledgements

This book was written in an attempt to fill a gap in the existing range of archaeological reference books. We felt that there was an increasing need for a dictionary-type of book devoted to British archaeology, and thought that a thesaurus would be more flexible in use than a dictionary. This book is essentially a thesaurus of technical terms and jargon frequently found in archaeological books and journals. It deals only with archaeology; very little historical information has been included. Consequently there is some imbalance between the period chapters which reflects a general imbalance in the archaeology between these periods.

Grateful thanks are due to Dr A. G. Crocker, Professor B. W. Cunliffe, Dr T. M. Dickinson, Dr H. S. Green, R. Jackson, A. MacGregor, J. S. McCracken and S. Needham for reading and commenting on portions of the text. Thanks are also due to Professor K. Branigan and A. D. F. Streeten for their help and advice. We should also like to thank Paul Ashbee, Alaric Toy, G. H. Kenyon and Leicester University Press for their permission to reproduce the illustrations on pages 31, 173 and 270 respectively.

There was not room to acknowledge all our sources of reference; the bibliography represents only a fraction of the works that were consulted. We would therefore like to acknowledge here our debt to the authors of all the works which we used during the compilation of this book.

Notes for Readers

This book is intended primarily as a work of reference for British archaeology, covering the Palaeolithic to Medieval periods. It attempts to explain the various specialised terms used by archaeologists, and alternative terms and illustrations are given wherever possible. In order to keep the book to a reasonable size, we decided to cover only England, Scotland and Wales, and not to include Ireland. For the same reason, Post-Medieval and Industrial Archaeology have not been included.

The book may be used as a dictionary by looking up particular terms in the index which will provide the relevant page numbers. For example, the term 'lewis-hole' occurs on page 112. If the terms used in this explanation are not understood, they can be looked up in the index. Alternative terms have been placed in brackets; for example — beehive rotary quern (beehive quern, rotary quern). Scales in accompanying figures are only given as an indication of size. It must be borne in mind that similar objects or features may vary in size. All measurements are given in metric units, except for measurements of areas which are given in acres. New county boundaries and names have been used.

At the end of most sections sources for further reading are given; these are by no means comprehensive but should guide the reader to other works since many of the sources recommended give extensive bibliographies.

Where radiocarbon dates are too early to be calibrated they have nevertheless been used since it was felt that these dates provided some indication, albeit inaccurate, of the time spans involved.

Abbreviations Used in Text

cm	centimetre(s)
km	kilometre(s)
m	metre(s)
pl	plural
sing	singular
sl	slang

For an explanation of the terms ad, AD, bc, BC, bp and BP, see page 232.

Conversion Table

1 inch	2·5 centimetres
1 foot	30·5 centimetres
1 yard	91·0 centimetres
1 mile	1·6 kilometres
1 centimetre	0·4 inches
10 centimetres	3·9 inches
20 centimetres	7·9 inches
50 centimetres	1 foot 8 inches
1 metre	1 yard 4 inches
10 metres	10 yards 2 feet 8 inches
50 metres	54 yards 2 feet 1 inch
1 kilometre	⅝ mile

Chapter 1

The Palaeolithic Period

Introduction

The **Palaeolithic** period is usually divided into the **Lower Palaeolithic**, the **Middle Palaeolithic** and the **Upper Palaeolithic**. **Lower Palaeolithic** describes the earliest flint tools in Britain (Clactonian, Acheulian and Levalloisian traditions); **Middle Palaeolithic** the fine flake tools of the Mousterian tradition; and **Upper Palaeolithic** the blade cultures of the last glaciation. The **Upper Palaeolithic** consists of the **Earlier Upper Palaeolithic** and the **Later Upper Palaeolithic** divided by the period known as the **Full Last Glacial**, when the advance of the glaciers probably made most of Britain uninhabitable, or habitable only in the summer months.

Other than flint artifacts, evidence of Palaeolithic occupation is extremely scarce. The only wooden implement to survive is a spear-point from *Clacton-on-Sea*, Essex. Apart from a skull fragment of Lower Palaeolithic date from *Swanscombe*, Kent, and the Upper Palaeolithic burial in *Paviland Cave*, West Glamorgan, no human remains definitely dated to the Palaeolithic have been found in Britain. Bone and antler tools are known only from the Upper Palaeolithic. The available evidence therefore gives a much more unbalanced picture of the Palaeolithic period than is the case with later periods; this imbalance being further accentuated by the small total amount of material in relation to the time-span of the Palaeolithic.

Reading: British Museum 1968; Mellars, P. A. 1974.

Dating and Environment

The effective range of radiocarbon dating is at present around 60,000 to 70,000 years, which barely extends to the last glaciation.

Although it is possible to date some Palaeolithic sites by uranium series dating, attempts to construct a chronological framework for the Palaeolithic have to rely on the geological evidence for glacial and interglacial periods. **Glacial periods (glacials, glaciations)** were periods within an 'ice age' when a lowering of temperature caused the polar ice sheets to advance towards the equator. **Interglacials** were periods of warmer climate between glacials. **Interstadials** were warmer phases within the glacial periods themselves. The Palaeolithic extends throughout the glacials and interglacials of the latter part of the last ice age **(Great Ice Age)**, which falls within the latter part of the period known geologically as the **Pleistocene**. The Pleistocene and the subsequent **Holocene** (the period of time from the end of the Pleistocene up to the present) make up the geological period known as the Quaternary.

Because of the difficulties involved in correlating geological and climatic phases over wide geographical areas, archaeological chronological frameworks are usually related to the local geological succession of events. The sequence of glacials and interglacials recognised in Britain is shown in Table 1, and provides a relative time-scale into which archaeological deposits can often be fitted. Dating for the British sequence is extremely approximate, and the dates given in the table are only tentative indications of the time-scales involved. Table 2 correlates the British sequence with those in other parts of the world. Again the dates are to be taken only as a guide.

Recent research on **deep-sea cores** (sample cores of rock drilled from ocean floors) using oxygen isotope analysis has radically altered the traditional view of the Pleistocene. This research has shown that instead of three or four glaciations during that period, there may have been as many as seventeen. The three main methods by which the evidence from deep-sea cores can be dated are radiocarbon dating (for the upper core), uranium series dating, and magnetostratigraphy; and the resulting evidence can provide a chronological framework for the sequence of glacials and interglacials. It is, however, difficult to correlate this framework with the evidence on land, much of which is at present being reconsidered, and so the traditional frameworks have not yet been replaced, although it is likely that they will be revised in the near future.

Table 1

The time range of Palaeolithic Industries in Britain relative to the sequence of Glacials and Interglacials (after Mellars 1974 and Evans 1975)

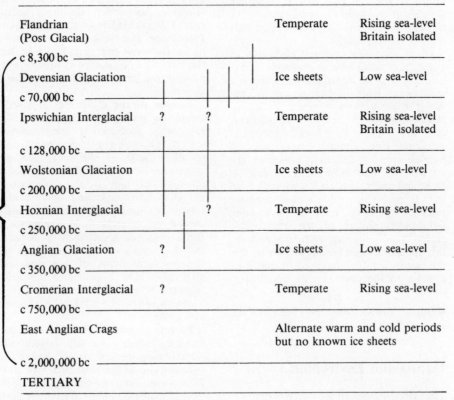

PLEISTOCENE		Acheulian	Clactonian	Levalloisian	Mousterian (Middle Palaeolithic)	Upper Palaeolithic		
	Flandrian (Post Glacial)						Temperate	Rising sea-level Britain isolated
	c 8,300 bc							
	Devensian Glaciation						Ice sheets	Low sea-level
	c 70,000 bc							
	Ipswichian Interglacial	?		?			Temperate	Rising sea-level Britain isolated
	c 128,000 bc							
	Wolstonian Glaciation						Ice sheets	Low sea-level
	c 200,000 bc							
	Hoxnian Interglacial			?			Temperate	Rising sea-level
	c 250,000 bc							
	Anglian Glaciation	?					Ice sheets	Low sea-level
	c 350,000 bc							
	Cromerian Interglacial	?					Temperate	Rising sea-level
	c 750,000 bc							
	East Anglian Crags						Alternate warm and cold periods but no known ice sheets	
	c 2,000,000 bc							
	TERTIARY							

N.B. The dates quoted are very tentative and serve only as an approximate guide to the time-spans involved.

Table 2

Correlation of the main stages of the Pleistocene in various parts of the World (after Evans 1978)

Britain	N Europe	Alps	N America	Others
Flandrian				Post Glacial or Holocene
Devensian (glaciation)	Weichselian	Würm	Wisconsin	Last Glaciation
Ipswichian (interglacial)	Eemian		Sangamon	Last Interglacial
Wolstonian (glaciation)	Saale	Riss	Illinoian	Penultimate Glaciation
Hoxnian (interglacial)	Holstein		Yarmouth	Penultimate Interglacial or Great Interglacial
Anglian (glaciation)	Elster	Mindel	Kansan	Antepenultimate Glaciation
Cromerian (interglacial)	Cromerian		Aftonian	Antepenultimate Interglacial
East Anglian Crags		Gunz	Nebraskan	Several alternate warm and cold stages
TERTIARY				

N.B. This is intended as a guide to the terms used and not as a statement of fact, since correlations of glacials and interglacials in various parts of the world are by no means certain.

For the Late Last Glacial period in particular, pollen analysis provides an additional dating framework to the traditional geological one. By examining the relative abundance of different tree species and the ratio of tree pollen to non-tree pollen (the **TP:NTP ratio** or the **AP:NAP ratio**) it has been found that the history of arboreal vegetation can be divided into zones reflecting changes in the composition of forest due to climatic changes. This technique has been used to construct a relative dating system that reaches as far back as the Late Last Glacial (see Table 3). Several schemes of zonation (defining zones) have been worked out, either using evidence from pollen (**pollen zones**) or by using macroscopic plant remains. The latter method was used by Blytt in 1876 and by Sernander in 1908, and this scheme of zonation is often referred to as the **Blytt and Sernander zones**. The use of these zones as a method of dating has been largely superseded by the radiocarbon method.

As well as providing a means of relative dating, pollen analysis provides evidence for the environment at various times during the Palaeolithic. This evidence shows that the development of vegetation during the interglacials (Cromerian, Hoxnian and Ipswichian) followed a similar pattern, consisting of four major phases of woodland development and degeneration reflecting climatic changes. The first phase is characterised by birch and pine woodland with a certain amount of open grassland, followed by a phase in which warmth-loving trees such as oak, alder, hazel and yew also appear. This is followed by the appearance of fir and hornbeam in the woodland. The final phase sees a thinning out of woodland, and an increase of grassland, while birch and pine become dominant. Although this broad pattern occurs in all three interglacials, the detailed composition of the vegetation at various times can be sufficiently distinctive for individual sites to be fairly accurately

11

assigned to a specific phase of a particular interglacial on the basis of pollen analysis.

In contrast to the interglacials, there is virtually no evidence for the environment during the glacial periods since conditions then were unsuitable for the preservation of organic material. It seems certain, however, that in areas not covered by glaciers the environment was one of treeless, sub-arctic tundra.

Reading for Dating and Environment: Bowen, D. Q. 1978; Evans, J. G. 1975; Megaw, J. V. S. and Simpson, D. D. A. 1979; Mellars, P. A. 1974; Schwarcz, H. P. 1980.

Table 3

The archaeological phases and pollen and vegetational zones for the Devensian Glaciation (after Evans 1975, Evans 1978, and Megaw and Simpson 1979)

Period	Archaeological phases	Approx dates bc	Pollen zones	Blytt and Sernander zones	Vegetation
		POST-GLACIAL			
		——— 8,300 ———			
			III	Younger Dryas	Tundra
Late	Later	9,000			
Last	Upper		II	Allerød	Birch woods
Glacial	Palaeolithic	10,000			
			I	Older Dryas	Tundra
		11,000			
		——— 13,000			
Full Last Glacial	?				
		——— 25,000			
Middle Last Glacial	Earlier Upper Palaeolithic				
		——— 50,000			
Early Last Glacial	?Mousterian and ?Acheulian and Levalloisian Survivals				
		——— 70,000			

DEVENSIAN GLACIATION

IPSWICHIAN INTERGLACIAL

N.B. The dates quoted are tentative and serve as a guide to the periods of time involved.

Economy

Throughout the Palaeolithic period, men in Britain lived by hunting animals, birds and fish, and by gathering wild vegetable foods; the changes in climate causing changes in the animals and vegetables available for exploitation. No evidence for the types of vegetation exploited has survived, nor is there a great deal of definite evidence for the types of animal hunted at various stages of the period. For the Lower Palaeolithic, remains of elephant, rhinoceros, wild ox, bear, horse, red deer and fallow deer have been found in association with Clactonian flint tools on a few sites; and at other sites remains of elephant, wild ox, horse and red deer have been found in association with Acheulian flint tools. The animal remains found in association with Levalloisian flint tools at some sites (particularly at *Crayford*, Kent, and *Brundon*, Suffolk) suggest that some hunting groups were specialising in hunting mammoth.

There is extremely little reliable evidence for the animals hunted during the Middle Palaeolithic; nor is there much more evidence for the Earlier Upper Palaeolithic, although during the latter period the woolly rhinoceros, horse, giant Irish deer, elk and bison seem to have been some of the animals hunted. There is more reliable evidence for the Later Upper Palaeolithic which suggests that horse was one of the main animals being hunted; remains of the reindeer, giant Irish deer and woolly rhinoceros, as well as those of smaller animals (such as arctic fox, hare, and some species of birds) have also been found in association with Later Upper Palaeolithic flint tools.

It should be borne in mind that there is no indication of the relative importance of meat and vegetable food to the people of the Palaeolithic period, and it is quite possible that some hunter-gatherers lived more by gathering than by hunting.

Where available, caves were used for shelter. No evidence of other types of shelter has survived in Britain.

Reading for Economy: Evans, J. G. 1975; Megaw, J. V. S. and Simpson, D. D. A. 1979; Mellars, P. A. 1974.

The Lower Palaeolithic

Although it seems likely that groups of people using handaxes were present in Britain during the Anglian Glaciation (probably during an interstadial), the earliest occupation for which there is definite evidence occurs during the succeeding Hoxnian Interglacial. This is provided by the **Clactonian industries** (named after the site at *Clacton-on-Sea*, Essex) which consist of simple flint tools made by flaking with powerful blows from a **hammer stone**. Hammer stones, which are very battered through much use, have been found on Clactonian sites; when hammer stones were insufficiently used to produce this battering they are indistinguishable from any other suitable stones. This method of flaking produced distinctive flakes with prominent bulbs and cones of percussion. The anvil flaking technique was probably used as well.

The range of Clactonian tools consists of bifacially worked core tools, and flakes which were often shaped by secondary working. The core tools fall into three main types: **pebble chopper-cores (pebble chopping tools)**, **biconical chopper-cores (biconical chopping tools)**, and **proto-handaxes**.

Although many Clactonian flakes have secondary working, the nature of the flaking does not seem to follow any tool-making tradition. In the past, attempts have been made to classify them, but they were largely unsuccessful, and the flake tools are generally regarded as non-specialised.

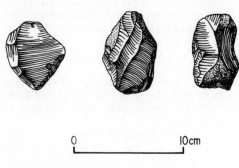

0   10cm

Examples of Clactonian Flakes

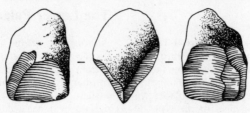

Pebble Chopper-core

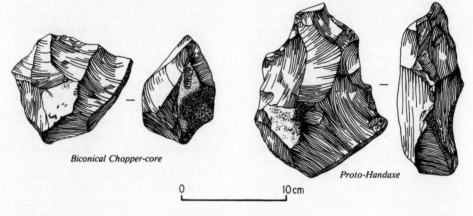

Biconical Chopper-core

Proto-Handaxe

0   10 cm

Clactonian Core Tools

Wooden Spear-point from Clacton-on-Sea, Essex

0   10cm

In addition to flint tools and waste flakes, a wooden spear-point, three utilised bones and a bone tool are also known (recovered from the site at Clacton). These are all that survive to give any indication of the use of organic materials by early man in Britain; animal bones have, however, been found with Clactonian industries at several sites.

The number of Clactonian sites in Britain is so small that little can be deduced from their distribution, other than their general riverside location.

A second group of Lower Palaeolithic industries are the **Acheulian industries** (named after the site at *Saint-Acheul*, France), which seem to appear in Britain around the middle of the Hoxnian Inter-glacial. They are typified by the **handaxe (biface, boucher, coup de poing)**, the

dominant tool in all Acheulian assemblages. Geological evidence shows that these industries cover a wide time-span. Several attempts have been made to classify and date various stages of the British material: Wymer has suggested (Wymer, J. J. 1968) four stages called **Early Acheulian, Middle Acheulian, Late Middle Acheulian** and **Late Acheulian**. Other schemes have also been suggested (see Collins, D. 1978, 47ff).

There are many types of Acheulian **handaxe** and the main ones are shown in the accompanying figure. Although termed handaxes, these tools were probably used as all-purpose tools and not as axes. Some of the thin ovate and cordate handaxes of the later Acheulian industries may have been hafted.

As well as handaxes, a great number of flakes have been found in Acheulian assemblages. These are of two types: **primary flakes** resulting from the roughing-out of a handaxe with a hammer stone, and **finishing flakes** which are removed in the final trimming of a handaxe using the **bar**

hammer technique (striking the flint with a length of wood or bone rather than with a hammer stone). Finishing flakes are distinguishable by being thinner than primary flakes and having diffuse bulbs of percussion and very small striking platforms. Apart from waste flakes, both primary and finishing flakes have been found with secondary working; as with the flakes in Clactonian assemblages, these seem to be non-specialised tools shaped without regard to a particular flintworking tradition.

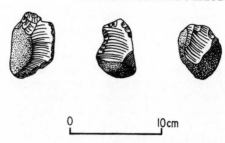

Examples of Acheulian Flakes with Secondary Working

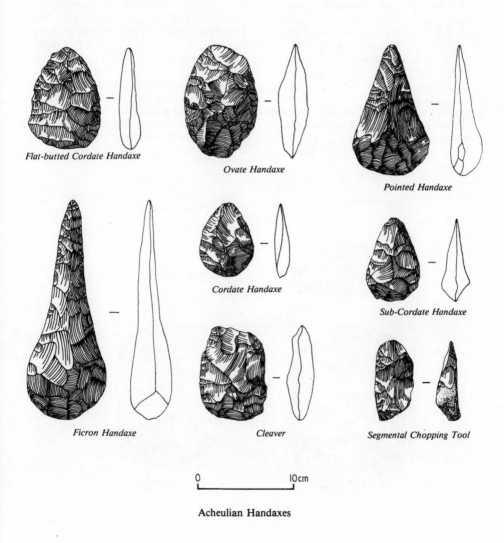

Flat-butted Cordate Handaxe

Ovate Handaxe

Pointed Handaxe

Ficron Handaxe

Cordate Handaxe

Sub-Cordate Handaxe

Cleaver

Segmental Chopping Tool

Acheulian Handaxes

15

Chopper-cores similar to those of the Clactonian industries are sometimes found in Acheulian assemblages; a few with carefully shaped straight cutting edges have also been found. It has been suggested that chopper-cores were used for chopping bones. Acheulian handaxes are found over much of southern and eastern England. Most come from south-east of a line from the Wash to the Bristol Channel. It has been suggested that the Clactonian and Acheulian traditions represent two completely separate cultural groups: the Clactonian groups exploiting heavily forested areas, the Acheulian groups appearing in the more open conditions of the mid-Hoxnian to exploit open areas.

The differences between the Clactonian and Acheulian industries in Britain are relatively clear-cut and there appears to be some separation in time between these industries, with the Clactonian largely preceding the Acheulian. **Levalloisian** flint tools (named after the site at *Levallois-Perret*, Paris, France) are found in assem-blages unassociated with other types of flint tools; they are also found in small numbers in some of the assemblages of the later Acheulian industries. There is no sharp division between these Acheulian and Levalloisian industries, and the latter are often considered to be a specialised technique forming part of the Acheulian industries from the time of the penultimate (Wolstonian) glaciation onwards. Because of this, Levalloisian flint tools are usually referred to as products of the **Levallois technique (Levalloisian technique)**, and are not always considered to constitute a separate and distinct industry. The Levallois technique was a method of manufacturing flakes of a specific size and shape. This was done by roughing out a core from a piece of flint in order to form a fairly flat face and a carefully prepared striking platform. From this prepared core a characteristic flake **(Levallois flake)** was struck. The most common type of Levallois core is known as the **tortoise core**.

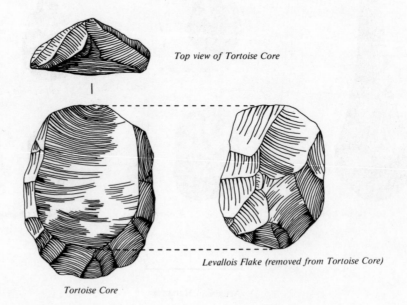

Top view of Tortoise Core

Levallois Flake (removed from Tortoise Core)

Tortoise Core

0   10cm

Some **prismatic cores** were also used to produce long, narrow flakes, and were usually prepared with a striking platform at each end so that flakes could be struck from both ends. Flakes were sometimes shaped by further flaking around the edges.

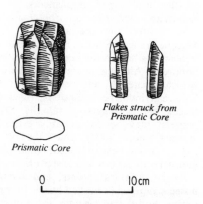

Flakes struck from
Prismatic Core

Prismatic Core

0   10cm

Reading for Lower Palaeolithic Artifacts: Mellars, P. A. 1974; Wymer, J. J. 1968; Wymer, J. J. 1977b.

The Middle Palaeolithic

Evidence for the Middle Palaeolithic in Britain comes from the **Mousterian industries** (named after the site at *Le Moustier*, France). The industries from the earliest sites (probably dating to the very beginning of the last glaciation) are characterised by distinctive **bout coupé handaxes**. These are distinguished from cordiform handaxes by the angular outline of their base.

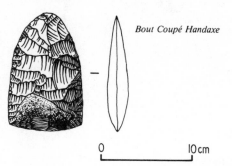

Bout Coupé Handaxe

0   10cm

There is, as yet, little evidence for the association of other flint artifacts with these handaxes, but elongated and pointed flakes were found at the site at *Creffield Road, Acton*, Greater London. This stage of the Middle Palaeolithic in Britain is sometimes called the **Paxton stage** after the site at *Little Paxton*, Cambridgeshire, where bout coupé handaxes have been found.

Later Middle Palaeolithic industries in Britain are characterised by more rounded and smaller handaxes similar to those of the **Mousterian of Acheulian tradition (MAT)** of south-western France, and this term is sometimes used for the British industries. Again there is little evidence for other artifacts associated with these handaxes, although **side scrapers, points, backed knives, denticulated flakes** and **discoidal cores** have been found.

Mousterian Point

Side Scraper   Discoidal Core

Backed Knife

0   10cm

Middle Palaeolithic Implements

The Middle Palaeolithic industries date to the last glaciation (Devensian glaciation). It is most likely that Britain was only occupied at the beginning and end of this glaciation and during warmer periods within it; the evidence from sites in Britain suggests very brief, and perhaps only seasonal, occupation.

Reading for Middle Palaeolithic Artifacts: Mellars, P. A. 1974.

The Upper Palaeolithic

There were two main phases of the Upper Palaeolithic: the **Earlier Upper Palaeolithic** (corresponding to the Middle Last Glacial period), and the **Later Upper Palaeolithic** (corresponding to the Late Last Glacial). These two phases were separated by the Full Last Glacial, during which conditions in Britain would have been so hostile that any occupation by man was probably confined to brief summer visits, and apart from the burial in *Paviland Cave*, West Glamorgan, there is in fact no indication of man's presence in Britain at this time. The burial at Paviland, which had been sprinkled with red ochre, was of a young man, but was originally thought to be female, and is often referred to as the **Red Lady of Paviland**. This burial has a radiocarbon date of 16,510± 340 bc which is towards the end of the Full Last Glacial.

The Earlier Upper Palaeolithic

There are about a dozen well recorded sites of this period in Britain, and at least another twenty that have produced some material of this date. Most of these sites are caves, although it is likely that many open sites have been destroyed or still lie undetected.

The flint industries of this period usually include relatively large leaf-shaped implements **(leaf points)** which have similarities to the leaf-shaped implements of the **Solutrean** industries on the Continent (named after the site at *Solutré*, near Mâcon, France). For this reason the British implements have often been termed **Proto-Solutrean**. Although a connection between British material and the Continental Solutrean industries cannot be ruled out, recent dating suggests that the British material may be considerably earlier. It appears more likely that the British industries are related to the Blattspitzen industries of central and eastern Europe.

Apart from leaf points, **end scrapers, nosed scrapers** and **busked burins (busqued burins, burins busqués)** are also found, as well as waste flakes.

In addition to flint artifacts there are also a few **bone pins** of this period as well as a few pieces of bone that have had patterns and pictures scratched onto them.

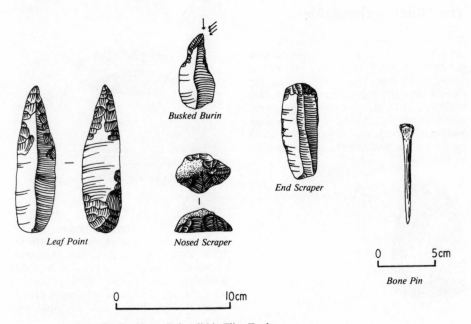

Busked Burin

End Scraper

Leaf Point

Nosed Scraper

0   5cm

Bone Pin

0   10cm

Some Earlier Upper Palaeolithic Flint Tools

The Later Upper Palaeolithic

There are at least twenty-five well recorded sites of this period in Britain. The majority of these are caves, but there is evidence for open sites in southern and eastern England. The distribution of sites shows two distinct regions of occupation: northern Britain (particularly the southern and eastern foothills of the Pennines), and south-western Britain. There appears to be no difference between these regions in material assemblages, however, and they are more likely to reflect different hunting grounds or migration routes.

Of the flint tools from these sites the most characteristic are the **backed blades**, which were often flaked to an angular shape **(angle-backed blades)**. Two specific types of the angle-backed blade are the **Creswell point (Creswellian point)** and the **Cheddar point**. The Creswell point has a single angle on the blunted edge whereas the Cheddar point has an angle at both ends of the blunted edge, producing a trapezoidal tool. It was once thought that the differences between the Creswell point and the Cheddar point reflected different cultural groups, but a more recent analysis (Campbell, J. B. 1977) has cast doubt on this.

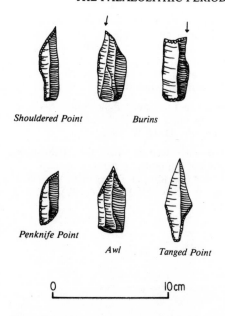

Shouldered Point   *Burins*

Penknife Point

Awl   *Tanged Point*

0   10 cm

Examples of Later Upper Palaeolithic Flint Tools

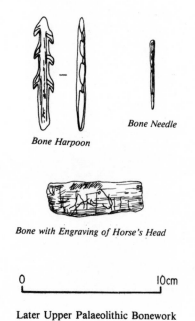

Bone Needle

Bone Harpoon

Bone with Engraving of Horse's Head

0   10 cm

Later Upper Palaeolithic Bonework

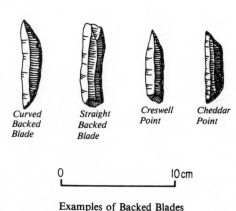

Curved Backed Blade   *Straight Backed Blade*   *Creswell Point*   *Cheddar Point*

0   10 cm

Examples of Backed Blades

Other types of flint tool of this period include steeply retouched **awls**, various **burins** and **end scrapers, penknife points, shouldered points**, and occasionally **tanged points**.

Finds of bone implements are more common for this period than for preceding ones and consist mainly of **bone points, bone needles, bone harpoons** and a few **engraved bones** with patterns or pictures on them. Two **bâtons-de-commandement** are known from *Gough's Cave*, Cheddar, Somerset. These are pieces of bone or antler, perforated at one end and often decorated. Their exact purpose is unknown, but may be symbolic.

Reading for Upper Palaeolithic Artifacts: Campbell, J. B. 1977; Megaw, J. V. S. and Simpson, D. D. A. 1979.

General Reading for the Palaeolithic Period: Campbell, J. B. 1977; Megaw, J. V. S. and Simpson, D. D. A. 1979; Mellars, P. A. 1974; Wymer, J. J. 1968; Wymer, J. J. 1977b.

0   10cm

Bâton-de-Commandement

Chapter 2

The Mesolithic Period

Introduction

The majority of the evidence for the **Meso-lithic** period in Britain comes from flint-work, and consequently any attempts at differentiating cultural groups have to be based largely on differences between various flint assemblages. This has some-times led to the distinctions between cultural groups resting on relatively minor differences between the respective flint assemblages, and it has been argued that this situation presents a too fragmentary, and possibly false, picture. The recent trend has been away from defining specific cultural groupings, and more towards a wider view of the Mesolithic as a whole, divided into the **Earlier Mesolithic** and the **Later Mesolithic**. The division between these two periods probably occurs in the earlier seventh miillennium BC.

For some years the accepted view of the Mesolithic consisted of the **Maglemosian culture** (corresponding to the Earlier Mesolithic) which was superseded by a number of regional cultures — **Sauve-terrian, Tardenoisian, Obanian** and **Horsham** (corresponding to the Later Mesolithic). The Maglemosian culture probably still presents a true picture of the Earlier Mesolithic; doubt has arisen, how-ever, about the distinctions between some of the later cultural groups recognised in Britain, and also about the closeness of the links with the Continental cultures in the Later Mesolithic.

Reading: Jacobi, R. M. 1976; Mellars, P. A. 1974.

Flintwork

The Earlier Mesolithic

The flint industries in Britain which are dated to the Earlier Mesolithic period have much in common with the Maglemosian industries (named after the site at *Maglemose*, Denmark). These British industries have therefore been termed **Maglemosian.** They were first thought to be confined to the lowland areas of southern and eastern England, but recent evidence shows a more widespread distribution over both lowland and upland England, with some possible sites in Scotland and Wales. These Earlier Mesolithic industries are characterised by various types of imple-ment. **Microliths** were common and were used throughout the Mesolithic. They were very small worked flint flakes and blades. In the Earlier Mesolithic they tended to be relatively large and simple in form, and are sometimes labelled the **broad-blade industries**. The **obliquely-blunted point** is a particularly common form. Large **isosceles triangle** microliths and **elongated points**, with one edge blunted, are also frequently found. Most of the microliths were probably used as tips and barbs for arrows.

A very distinctive form of flint imple-ment is the **tranchet axe** or **adze**. This is a heavy flint axe sharpened by removing a large flake **(transverse flake, tranchet flake)** from the edge by means of a blow struck transversely to the axis of the axe. Some of the longer axes are sometimes called **Thames picks**, because many of this type have been dredged from the River Thames. Axes and adzes were probably hafted by means of an antler sleeve, although other methods of hafting were possible (see Neolithic flint and stone axes). Other types of flint artifact in use at this period include **end-scrapers** on blades and flakes, **gravers (burins)** and **awls**.

Reading for Earlier Mesolithic Flintwork: Jacobi, R. M. 1976; Mellars, P. A. 1974; Wymer, J. J. 1977a.

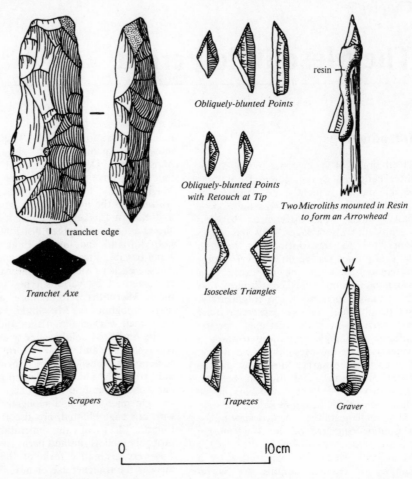

resin

Obliquely-blunted Points

Obliquely-blunted Points
with Retouch at Tip

Two Microliths mounted in Resin
to form an Arrowhead

tranchet edge

Tranchet Axe

Isosceles Triangles

Scrapers

Trapezes

Graver

0   10cm

Some Types of Earlier Mesolithic Flint Implements

The Later Mesolithic

The Later Mesolithic flint industries are distinguished by the appearance of new forms of microliths, sometimes labelled **narrow-blade industries**. They tend to be smaller, and have a wider range of shapes than those of the Earlier Mesolithic. Microliths in the form of small **scalene triangles (micro-triangles)** became common, as well as other geometric forms such as **trapezoids** blunted on three edges, **crescents**, and narrow **rods** blunted along one or both edges. These flint implements have parallels in the **Sauveterrian industries** (named after the site at *Sauveterre-le-Lemance*, France) on the Continent, and so the British industries have often been labelled **Sauveterrian**. They also have parallels in the **Tardenoisian**

industries (named after the site at *La Fère-en-Tardenois*, France), in particular the **transverse arrowhead (petit-tranchet arrowhead)**. Assemblages consisting solely of the geometric forms are most common in the northern half of Britain. As well as these geometric forms, there were also assemblages consisting of a mixture of geometric and larger non-geometric types, like those of the Earlier Mesolithic. These assemblages are found mainly in southern and eastern England.

Within this grouping of mixed assemblages, one clear sub-group stands out, defined by the occurrence of a distinctive microlith known as a **Horsham point** (named after the site at *Horsham*, Sussex). This sub-group has sometimes been labelled the **Horsham culture**, although this term is

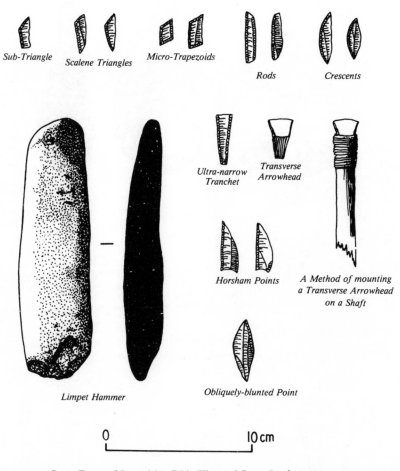

Sub-Triangle   Scalene Triangles   Micro-Trapezoids

Rods   Crescents

Ultra-narrow   Transverse
Tranchet   Arrowhead

Horsham Points   A Method of mounting
a Transverse Arrowhead
on a Shaft

Limpet Hammer   Obliquely-blunted Point

0   10 cm

Some Types of Later Mesolithic Flint and Stone Implements

now rarely used; it is largely confined to Kent, Surrey and Sussex.

There is evidence of further assemblages of flint from the shell-midden sites along the western coast of Scotland. These belong to the **Obanian industries** (named after the site at *Oban*, Strathclyde). These industries are very poor in flint and stone work. Apart from the characteristic long, sub-rectangular pebbles known as **limpet hammers (limpet picks)**, which were probably used for removing shellfish from rocks, the most common flint implements are crudely worked scrapers and heavily **scaled** pieces (**éclats écaillés**), the latter being pieces of flint with retouching that resembles the imprint of fish scales.

Other flint artifacts of the Mesolithic period include **cores, microburins** (a distinctive form of waste flint formed in the process of making microliths; they were not true implements), and **pebble maceheads with hour-glass perforations**, although the latter reappear in both Neolithic and Bronze Age contexts. **Picks** were pointed core tools, often crudely made, which were probably used for a variety of purposes. It is unlikely that they were hafted.

Reading for Later Mesolithic Flintwork: Green, H. S. 1980; Jacobi, R. M. 1976; Mellars, P. A. 1974; Wymer, J. J. 1977a.

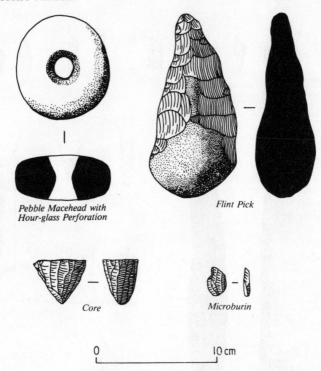

Pebble Macehead with
Hour-glass Perforation

Flint Pick

Core

Microburin

0   10 cm

Examples of Mesolithic Flint and Stone Artifacts

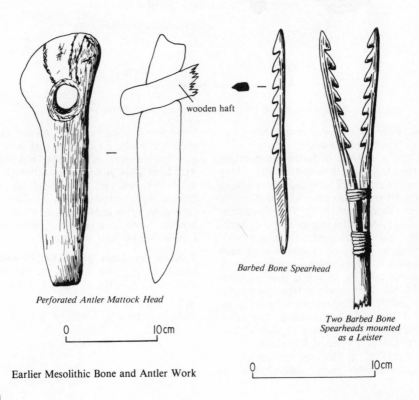

wooden haft

Barbed Bone Spearhead

Perforated Antler Mattock Head

0   10cm

Earlier Mesolithic Bone and Antler Work

Two Barbed Bone
Spearheads mounted
as a Leister

0   10cm

Bone and Antler Work

The Earlier Mesolithic

The dating of many stray finds of antler and bone implements to the Earlier Mesolithic relies heavily on comparison with excavated examples from *Star Carr*, North Yorkshire, and from *Thatcham*, Berkshire. Implements of this period consist mainly of **barbed spearheads** of antler and bone, some of which may have been mounted in pairs to form **leisters** which were used for catching fish (unbarbed bone spearheads have also been found at *Thatcham*, Berkshire), **perforated antler mattock heads, bone awls, bone pins, antler chisels** or **wedges**, and **perforated antler sleeves** for hafting axes and adzes. At *Star Carr*, North Yorkshire, several **red deer frontlets** (part of the skull) were found with antlers still attached. These were probably used as head-dresses, either for hunting, or for some ceremonial purpose.

Reading for Earlier Mesolithic Bone and Antler Work: Clark, J. G. D. 1954; Lacaille, A. D. 1954; Mellars, P. A. 1974.

The Later Mesolithic

There is not so much evidence for bone and antler work in the Later Mesolithic, although this may be due to differential preservation. Much of the bone and antler work of this period comes from the shell-midden sites on the western coast of Scotland, and from stray finds from northern Britain. Flattened **harpoon heads** with barbs along both edges are known, as well as **bone awls, bone pins** and **limpet scoops**. The term 'limpet scoop' has at times been applied to objects of bone, antler, and stone, although the stone objects are now usually called **limpet hammers** (see stone and flintwork). It is possible that these implements were used for scooping limpets out of their shells, but they may have been used for other purposes. **Perforated antler mattock heads** continued to be used. Chisel-like objects of antler are also known. It is likely that some forms of bone **fish hook**, and bone or wood **fish gorges** were used throughout the Mesolithic.

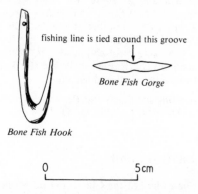

fishing line is tied around this groove

Bone Fish Gorge

Bone Fish Hook

0   5 cm

Reading for Later Mesolithic Bone and Antler Work: Clark, J. G. D. 1954; Lacaille, A. D. 1954; Mellars, P. A. 1974.

Wood

Much of the evidence for wooden artifacts of Mesolithic date comes from *Star Carr*, North Yorkshire, and dates to the Earlier Mesolithic. At this site birch was used to form a **brushwood platform**, providing a relatively dry and firm area on part of the lakeside marsh. The remains of a **wooden handle** were recovered in the perforation of an antler mattock, and remains of a **wooden paddle**, probably for use with a

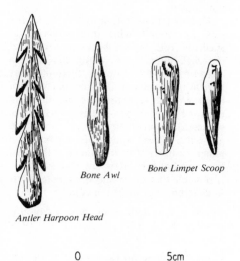

Bone Awl

Bone Limpet Scoop

Antler Harpoon Head

0   5 cm

Later Mesolithic Bone and Antler Tools

dugout canoe, were found. Rolls of **birch bark** have also been found which were probably used to provide resin with which flints, such as arrowheads, could be glued to their shafts.

Several **dugout canoes** have been dated to the Mesolithic; some undated ones may also belong to this period. Wood was probably also used for **bows** and **arrowshafts**, for **spear** and **harpoon shafts**, for **hafts** for axes and adzes, and for **handles** for other implements.

Reading for Wood: Clark, J. G. D. 1954; Coles, J. M. et al 1976.

Beads and Pendants

Beads and pendants of various materials were used throughout the Mesolithic. **Perforated animal teeth** and **bone beads** were used. At *Star Carr*, North Yorkshire, beads or pendants of **amber** and **shale** were also found. At *Cnoc Sligeach*, Oronsay, Strathclyde, a number of **cowrie shells** with double perforations have been found, which were probably used as beads or pendants. Perforated shells are also known from other shell-midden sites.

Reading for Beads and Pendants: Clark, J. G. D. 1954; Lacaille, A. D. 1954.

Environment

The ending of the Glacial period by an improvement of climate, due to a rise in temperature, occurred at *c*8000 BC. This improvement was gradual, and probably not constant, and its indirect effects on man were much more significant than the improvement in climate itself — the earlier melting of the glaciers causing a rise in sea level which eventually led to the separation of Britain from the Continent in the mid seventh millennium BC. It has been suggested that the differences in flintwork of the Later Mesolithic, between Britain and the Continent, may be attributed to this separation at the end of the Earlier Mesolithic. The isostatic uplift in northern Britain was also caused by the melting of the glaciers.

The end of frost weathering allowed deeper soils to form and the open tundra-like vegetation was gradually replaced by woodland. In addition the open-country species of animals were replaced by woodland species.

Reading for Environment: Evans, J. G. 1975.

Settlement and Economy

The changes in environment gradually forced man to change his mode of life. The hunting of herds of a few species of animals changed to the hunting of individual animals from a wide variety of species, because herds of animals were much less frequent in the woodland.

Fishing and the gathering of vegetable foods were also part of the Mesolithic economy, although there is little evidence to suggest the degree of importance attached to these food sources.

Throughout the Mesolithic the economy was based on hunting and gathering, probably carried on by small bands of hunters moving about a particular territory. The settlement sites which have been properly investigated appear to have been occupied intermittently, perhaps seasonally. They were probably camping sites with temporary shelters made from organic materials, although only the barest evidence for these shelters has survived. Pits have been found on some sites, but their use is not known.

An apparent exception to this way of life was the **strandlooping** (the gathering of shellfish from the seashore) carried on at the shell-midden sites along the western coast of Scotland. However, these sites may have also formed part of a seasonal cycle of hunting and gathering over different territories. Several possible cycles have been suggested, consisting of hunting and gathering in deep woods, along rivers, and along seashores at various times of the year, but none has been definitely proved, and it is possible that different cycles were in use in different regions of the country.

Reading for Settlement and Economy: Bradley, R. J. 1978; Evans, J. G. 1975; Mellars, P. A. 1974.

General Reading for the Mesolithic Period: Megaw, J. V. S. and Simpson, D. D. A. 1979; Renfrew, C. 1974.

Chapter 3

The Neolithic Period

Introduction

In 1954 Professor Piggott (Piggott, S. 1954) set out a scheme for this period envisaging two main groupings: the **Primary Neolithic**, consisting of settlers from the Continent moving into the south and east of Britain with the colonisation of the north and west taking place, partly by diffusion from southern Britain, and partly by the direct arrival of groups of chambered-tomb builders; and a **Secondary Neolithic** resulting from the fusion of indigenous Mesolithic cultures and colonising Neolithic ones. The duration of the Neolithic was envisaged as about 400 years. The Primary Neolithic was seen to consist of the **Windmill Hill culture**, which was the earliest phase, while colonisation of the north and west gave rise to the **Clyde-Carlingford culture**, the **Boyne culture** and other related groups. The **Peterborough culture**, the **Rinyo-Clacton culture**, the **Ronaldsway culture**, the **Dorchester culture** and the **Bann** and **Sandhill cultures** belonged to the Secondary Neolithic.

Since 1954, however, the evidence of radiocarbon dating has shown that the duration of the Neolithic was about 2,000 years starting around 4500 BC, and that colonisation probably did not expand from the south and east, but was widespread at an early date. The term **Secondary Neolithic** is now envisaged as a development of the Primary Neolithic, and the whole Neolithic period is now often divided loosely into the **Earlier Neolithic** and the **Later Neolithic** with an imprecise division between them somewhere in the latter half of the fourth millennium BC.

Reading: Piggott, S. 1954; Smith, I. F. 1974.

Economy

Almost by definition the Neolithic economy was based on agriculture. The first Neolithic colonists found much of Britain wooded and began to clear small areas for cultivation. Some of these clearings appear to have been temporarily used and then abandoned, allowing trees to recolonise the area. The sequence of forest clearance, crop cultivation, abandonment and forest regeneration is called a **landnam**; the terms **Brandwirtschaft (slash-and-burn, burn-beating)** and **swidden agriculture** are often used inaccurately as synonyms. **Swidden** is a term used for a form of agriculture whereby a clearing is cultivated for a few years until the fertility of the soil is reduced and then abandoned in favour of a fresh clearing. **Brandwirtschaft (slash-and-burn, burn-beating)** is the burning of vegetation and the use of the ashes to enhance the fertility of the soil. It is a technique that usually forms part of a system of swidden agriculture, but although there is evidence for its use on the Continent, no convincing evidence for it has been found in Britain.

On lighter, better drained soils, larger and more permanent clearances were made. Mixed agriculture was practised: wheat was grown (mainly the **emmer** variety, with some **einkorn**) and there is also evidence for the cultivation of **naked barley**. Criss-cross plough scratches have been found, probably made by a simple plough, perhaps drawn by oxen. It has been suggested that such a plough was used for the initial breaking up of the soil, and that subsequent tillage was done by wooden **hoes** or **spades**. Harvesting of wheat was probably done with single-piece **reaping knives (single-piece sickles)**, although **composite reaping knives** made of small flint flakes set in a wooden tool may also have been used. Barley was probably often harvested by uprooting. True balanced sickles were not used until the Bronze Age.

The ears of corn could have been stored whole, but it is more likely that they were threshed and winnowed, and only the grain was stored — probably in pits (**grain storage**

pits). Daub with impressions of withies has been found in some of these, which has been suggested as evidence for the lining of pits. When required, the grain was ground into flour with grain rubbers.

The majority of animals kept by early Neolithic farmers seems to have been cattle, with some sheep or goats, or both, and pigs. Some hunting was done, but this added relatively little to the total food production. Cooking was probably done by roasting over an open fire, or by boiling in a hole in the ground or in a wooden trough by using **pot boilers**, which were stones heated in a fire and then dropped into water to heat it. Clay ovens have been found in several houses in the late Neolithic settlement at *Rinyo*, Orkney.

By the late Neolithic there seems to have been a change of emphasis from a mixed agriculture towards a more pastoral one. There is less evidence for cereals, while the number of animals, particularly pigs, increased. In some areas forest regeneration took place in the clearances: this seems to have been connected with the increase in pig-breeding since pigs are forest-dwelling animals. Hunting still played a minor role in the economy, although there is evidence, from both coastal and inland sites, of the exploitation of various forms of shellfish.

Reading for Economy: Clark, J. G. D. 1960; Evans, J. G. 1975; Piggott, S. 1954; Simpson, D. D. A. 1971; Smith, I. F. 1974.

Houses and Settlements

There is little definite evidence for early Neolithic settlement. Isolated farms seem to have been the usual pattern. The farmhouses were usually rectangular, about 8m × 5m, built of timber, and probably having a thatched gabled roof. Evidence rarely survives of the farmhouses or other structures apart from scattered postholes, and pits filled with domestic rubbish, which were probably originally grain storage pits.

There is a little more evidence for later Neolithic settlements. Isolated farmsteads continued to be used, and were often similar to early Neolithic ones. Pits and 'occupation floors' still provide much of the evidence for settlement, although there is little evidence to suggest that many pits were still being used for grain storage.

In the Orkneys, the easily split Caithness flagstone was used for building at several sites; much more evidence of Neolithic settlement has therefore survived there, as at *Skara Brae* and *Rinyo*. Both these settlements appear to have been villages and the usual type of house seems to have been approximately 4m to 6m square with rounded corners. The method of roofing is uncertain, but it is possible that a turf roof was supported on timbers, or even on whalebones. Caithness flagstone was also used to make beds, boxes, cupboards and hearths, so that these items, which were normally made from organic materials, have actually survived.

Reading for Houses and Settlements: McInnes, I. J. 1971; Smith, I. F. 1974.

Causewayed Camps (Causewayed Enclosures, Interrupted Ditch Enclosures)

These sites date to the early and middle Neolithic. They are roughly circular areas enclosed by between one and four concentric ditches with banks on their inner sides. The ditches were dug in irregular segments with 'causeways' of undisturbed earth between them. It is not known whether the banks were originally continuous or also 'causewayed'. There is little evidence for any fence or palisade on top of the bank. Other than sporadic pits and postholes, the interior of these enclosures is usually devoid of features. In most cases pottery, animal bones, human bones (occasionally inhumation burials) and burnt material are found in the ditches, sometimes deliberately buried.

These enclosures were situated both in valley bottoms and on hill-tops; in the latter case they sometimes cut across the contours of the hill rather than following them, rarely taking full advantage of the natural defensive features of the site. Various functions have been suggested for these sites including settlement, defence, and use as cattle compounds; more likely functions include meeting places for trade and/or cult ceremonies, or areas where the exposure of dead bodies was practised. The true functions or combination of functions of these sites are not known; it is possible that different sites performed different functions but there is direct evidence for an attack at the site of *Crickley Hill*, Gloucestershire.

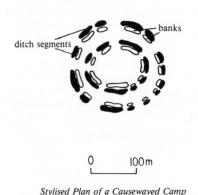

Stylised Plan of a Causewayed Camp

Reading for Causewayed Camps: Drewett, P. C. 1977; Piggott, S. 1954; Smith, I. F. 1971.

Henges

This term is used to denote various ceremonial sites which have certain features in common. They are almost all circular or near-circular in plan, and can range from about 9m to over 450m in diameter, with an average diameter of over 60m. The circular areas are usually defined by a bank and internal ditch, although some have an external ditch, or a ditch on both sides of the bank. The bank and ditch can be quite small, or very large as at *Avebury*, Wiltshire, where the ditch is 21m across and 9m deep in places. The banks and ditches are interrupted by an entrance or entrances, and it is on these that attempts to clarify henges are usually based. **Class I henges** have one entrance and **Class II henges** more than one entrance. Henges with a pair of diametrically opposed entrances are the most common type of class II henge.

Stone circles occur in only a few henge monuments (mainly class II henges), but circular settings of timber posts have been found on a large proportion of excavated

sites. Other features found in henge monuments include circles of pits, central stones, cairns or burials, stone or timber entrance posts, and outlying stones or timber posts. The great variation between henges caused by differing combinations of some of these possible features means that no two henges are exactly alike.

Present dating evidence suggests that class I henges were being built from the late fourth millennium BC to the late third millennium BC, while the building of class II henges began about the middle of the third millennium BC and continued into the second. Henges therefore span the transition between the late Neolithic and the early Bronze Age. It has been suggested that henges developed from causewayed camps and, in turn, stone circles developed from henges, but further evidence is needed before this can be conclusively demonstrated.

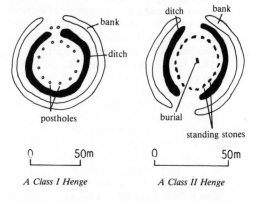

A Class I Henge   *A Class II Henge*

Some henges contained timber buildings, probably temples, eg *Durrington Walls*, and *Woodhenge*, Wiltshire.

Reading for Henges: Atkinson, R. J. C. et al 1951; Forde-Johnston, J. 1976a.

Stone Circles

Circles of standing stones were being built from the late fourth millennium BC to the late third millennium and therefore span the transition between the late Neolithic and early Bronze Age. Over such a period of time the forms and functions of these circles would be likely to change. Even with meticulous excavation, it is often difficult to date these circles, and few of them have so far been reliably dated. But attempts at classification of these circles combined with the available dates have produced some indications of the changing forms and functions.

Early Stone Circles (c3370 to 2670 BC)

It is likely that the earliest stone circles, built in the late Neolithic, developed out of the same tradition of enclosing circular areas that is seen in causewayed camps and henges; there may have been a development from causewayed camps to henges and then to stone circles. Many of the early circles have closely set stones with a clearly defined entrance.

Outside most of these circles stood **monoliths** (single standing stones) some of which may have been aligned on the rising or setting sun at midsummer or midwinter. Traces of burning and fragments of human bone are often found within the circles; these seem to be dedicatory deposits rather than the remains of cremation burials.

One exceptional group of circles, which must have originated in the Later Neolithic, surrounded both the Clava passage graves (see Clava group), and the ring cairns in the Inverness area. These circles have stones rising in height towards the south-west (where the Clava passage graves have their entrance). Some of the Inverness monuments, which were surrounded by a stone circle, appear never to have contained burials; they may have more in common with shrines than with tombs. It has been suggested that they were used for ceremonies involving the sun and the dead (see also Bronze Age stone circles).

Reading for Stone Circles: Burl, A. 1976; Burl, A. 1979; Grinsell, L. V. 1970.

Stonehenge see Chapter 4.

Silbury Hill

Silbury Hill, Wiltshire, is a huge, unique, man-made mound, built around 2600 BC. It has an apparent volume of about 354,000 cubic metres, of which about 106,200 cubic metres consist of a natural ridge upon which the mound was built. The remaining 247,800 cubic metres were quarried from the area surrounding the mound to form a ditch, originally about 38m wide and 9m deep. The hill is 39m high and was built as a series of circular platforms, each 4m to 5m high. The hill must have resembled a stepped cone during construction; the steps, except for the topmost one which is still visible, were then filled in to give the mound smooth-sloping sides. The purpose of the mound is still unknown, but the most likely theory seems to be that it was used for burial.

Reading for Silbury Hill: Vatcher, F. de M. and L. 1976.

Cursuses (cursūs; *sing*: cursus)

Cursuses were long narrow enclosures, often just under 100m wide, but sometimes several miles long. They were bounded on each side by a bank and external ditch, and closed at the ends by a continuation of this bank and ditch. Little else is known about these earthworks, but their association with long barrows and their frequent proximity to henge monuments suggests that their function was primarily religious.

Reading for Cursuses: Atkinson, R. J. C. et al 1951; Atkinson, R. J. C. 1955.

Burial

During the Neolithic long barrows and round barrows, either chambered or un-chambered, were used for burial.

Unchambered Tombs

Unchambered round barrows of a Neolithic date are rare except in northern England. They contain primary inhumation burials of Neolithic date.

Earthen long barrows (unchambered long barrows) occur mainly in areas where there was little or no stone suitable for building chambered tombs. The radiocarbon dates so far obtained suggest that earthen long barrows may have been earlier than chambered long barrows, but both types of barrow were being constructed in

the period *c*3700–2500 BC. The differences
between the two types probably arose from
the adaption of the current burial rite to
whatever building materials were available.
Earthen long barrows were long banks of
chalk and earth, or sometimes just earth,
usually between 20m and 120m long. They
were normally originally rectangular or
trapezoidal in plan, with a height varying
between about 1m and 7m. The mound of
the barrow was usually made of material
from **quarry ditches**, which usually flanked
the long sides of the mound and sometimes
curved inwards at the ends; it was unusual
for quarry ditches to continue round the
ends of the barrows. Exceptionally long
earthen long barrows, eg the one at *Maiden
Castle*, Dorset, which is 545m long, are
sometimes known as **bank barrows**. In
northern England and Scotland **unchambered long cairns** occur which seem to
have been a local variation of the earthen
long barrow.

The orientation of earthen long barrows
was approximately east-west, although the
exact orientation in certain cases may have
been related to the axis of the hill on which

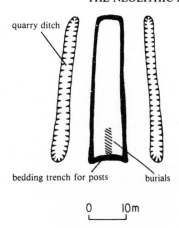

quarry ditch

bedding trench for posts   burials

0   10m

Plan of an Earthen Long Barrow

they were sited, or to other artificial landscape features, such as cursuses. Evidence
from excavations suggests that the mounds
covered elaborate timber structures at the
eastern end, often with a **façade** and a
timber **mortuary house**, the roof of which
has collapsed. A burial deposit of one or

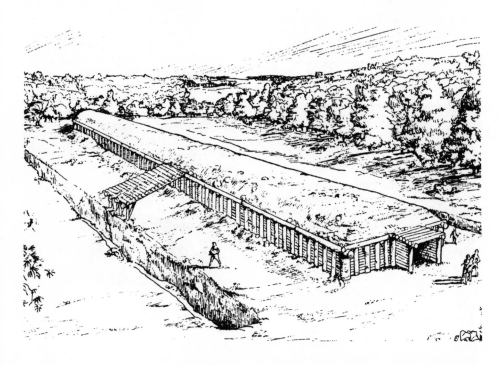

Reconstruction of the Earthen Long Barrow, when first built, at Fussell's Lodge, near Salisbury, Wiltshire

several interments (eg one barrow had at least fifty-one interments) was usually placed on the floor within the mortuary house. The interments were mainly articulated or disarticulated inhumations, usually without grave goods, and the condition of some of the disarticulated bones suggests that the bodies had previously been exposed elsewhere (probably on a platform on stilts). This may have taken place within a **mortuary enclosure (long mortuary enclosure)** — a sub-rectangular area enclosed by a discontinuous ditch and internal bank.

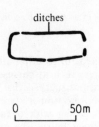

ditches

0   50m

*Plan of the Long Mortuary Enclosure
at Dorchester, Oxfordshire*

Cremations do not seem to occur in primary contexts in earthen long barrows, but in the Yorkshire area partially burnt interments are often found which may have been charred during the firing of the mortuary house.

Reading for Unchambered Tombs: Ashbee, P. 1970; Grinsell, L. V. 1979; Smith, I. F. 1974.

Chambered Tombs

Chambered tombs consist of round and long barrows and other forms of barrow which contained a burial chamber. A **burial chamber** strictly means the actual chamber in which the burials were deposited, but it is often used in a more general way to describe the whole of the buried stone structure within a chambered tomb. The walls of the passages and chambers were constructed either of **orthostats** (large stone slabs) or of **drystone walling** (composed of stones laid on top of each other without any bonding material such as mortar), or frequently a combination of both. The roof consisted of one or more stone slabs (**cap-**

stones), resting directly on the top of the orthostats. **Corbelling** could also be used to give greater headroom and reduce the space covered by the capstone. The **corbels** (stone slabs) were laid on top of the walls and successive layers built up until the remaining gap could be bridged by a single capstone.

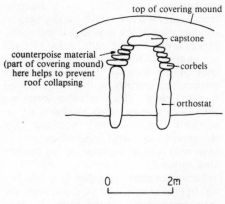

Diagram of Roofing using the Corbelling Technique

The terms **dolmen** and **cromlech** are now seldom used as archaeological terms, but were once used to describe any megalithic burial chamber including **portal dolmens**. Portal dolmens consist of a massive capstone, supported on two **portal stones** which form an entrance and a third stone which is usually shorter. The entrance is often blocked by a fifth stone slab. These chambers would originally have been covered by mounds which have since been robbed and eroded away, leaving only the stone burial chamber.

0   1m

A Portal Dolmen

Chambered tombs can be divided into the following two main types:

Passage graves These have a passage, usually about 1m wide and less than 1m high, leading to a wider and higher chamber which could be rectangular, square, polygonal, or circular. They were normally set in a circular mound or cairn.

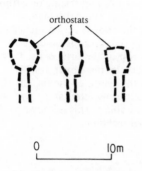

Some Typical Plans of the Chambers and Passages of Passage Graves

Gallery graves These have a parallel-sided gallery which is either straight or 'elbowed' and is usually wider, higher and longer than the passages of passage graves. Gallery graves were usually set in long mounds or cairns. **Transepted gallery graves** have side chambers **(transepts)** opening off the gallery. Passage graves could also have side chambers opening off the chamber or the passage. Some tombs can be interpreted as either passage graves or gallery graves.

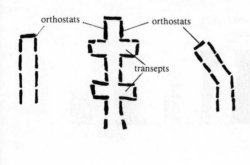

Plans of the Chambers of some Gallery Graves

Chambered tombs have been divided into numerous regional groups as a useful means of organising the available information, although there is little evidence that such groups represent different religions, burial rites or groups of people. Not all known tombs can be easily fitted into these groups. The main groups are:

Severn-Cotswold group (Cotswold-Severn group) There is much variation in the details of these tombs but all consist of gallery graves set within straight-sided long mounds or cairns which were trapezoid, or sometimes almost rectangular, in plan. They have a stone **façade** at one end with either a **portal** leading from the **forecourt** into the chamber, or a **dummy portal (false portal)** built as part of the façade. In chalk areas this type of barrow has a **kerb (retaining kerb)** around the sides, but the western

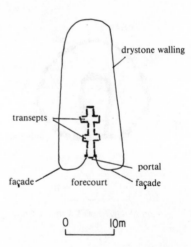

Plan of a Severn-Cotswold Chambered Tomb

barrows of this group have a drystone wall instead. These walls seem to have been composed of an inner wall of rough blocks and an outer wall of more regular slabs with an intermediate rubble core. In a few instances there is evidence that **extra-revetment material** (mainly rubble) was heaped up against the outer wall at some stage, apparently to support it. It is possible that this material was contemporary with the drystone wall, but it is more likely that it was a later addition. These tombs were used for collective burial over a period of some years. When the last burial was deposited, the forecourt was deliberately blocked with rubble and the tomb was left alone. The extra-revetment material may have been added at this stage.

Medway group A small group of long barrows which have a single chamber at one end of the mound.

Peak group Comprises a small group of passage graves set in round barrows, distributed over the Derbyshire Dales, south of the High Peak.

Scilly/Penwith group A group of round cairns with close-set retaining walls or kerbs and usually a parallel-sided chamber entered from the east or south-east. The entrance leads straight into the chamber and so these tombs are sometimes called **entrance graves**.

Clyde group Consists largely of long cairns, usually rectangular or trapezoid in plan, with a gallery often divided into segments by stone slabs **(septal slabs)** half (or less) the height of the walls. These tombs are sometimes called **segmented gallery graves**. The gallery narrows at each septal slab, usually because of the deliberate overlapping of the wall slabs **(imbrication)** at these points. The gallery was often roofed by capstones resting on orthostats to give a low roof about 1m high. In the larger galleries the roof is raised higher than this by resting the capstone on drystone walling built on top of the orthostats. Entrance to the gallery in the larger tombs is usually through the centre of the façade which was often built using alternating orthostats and drystone walling. This is known as the **post-and-panel technique**.

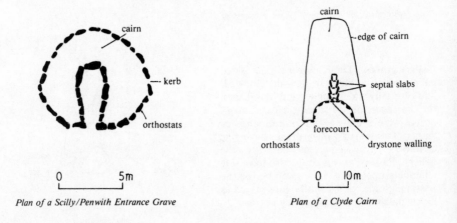

Plan of a Scilly/Penwith Entrance Grave

Plan of a Clyde Cairn

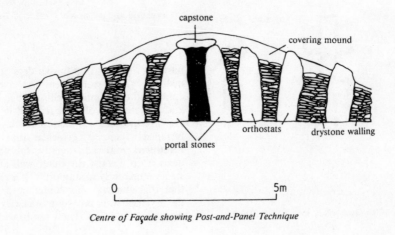

Centre of Façade showing Post-and-Panel Technique

Orkney-Cromarty-Hebridean group (O-C-H group) This is the main group of Scottish passage graves. There is great variation in the details of the plans of their chambers and covering cairns. The small, simple tombs are polygonal in plan, usually about 1·5m in diameter. They were entered by a short narrow passage. This type of chamber is usually covered by a round cairn about 8m in diameter. Other tombs follow this general form but had much larger chambers, while some had the entrance to the passage, and the entry from passage to chamber, marked by pairs of transversely set stone slabs.

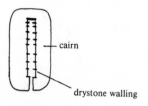

Plan of a Stalled Cairn

Maes Howe group A small group of passage graves also confined to the Orkney Islands. The chambers are large, square or rectangular, built in drystone walling, usually without orthostats. Small cells open off the main chamber, which was entered by a long passage. The chambers are covered by a large round cairn.

Bargrennan group A small group of tombs which have a relatively small chamber entered from a passage, usually under a round cairn. There could be more than one such chamber under each cairn. Their distribution overlaps with the Clyde group. They have similarities with both the Clyde and the O-C-H groups, and may be a hybrid of these two types.

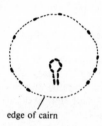

edge of cairn

Plan of an O-C-H Group Passage Grave

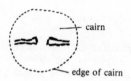

Plan of a Bargrennan Group Passage Grave

Plan of a variant form of Passage and Chamber found in O-C-H Group Tombs

There are many other minor variations of this type of tomb, in particular the **stalled chamber (stalled cairn)** where lateral slabs divide the chamber into stalls and help to support a high roof. They are only found in the Orkney Islands.

Clava group A small group of passage graves which usually have round chambers built in drystone walling with a high corbelled roof. These chambers were set centrally in large round cairns edged by a heavy stone kerb and entered by a passage. The cairns were surrounded by a stone circle, usually 3m to 5m from the stone kerb.

35

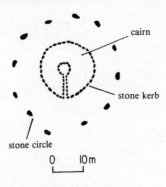

Plan of a Clava Group Passage Grave

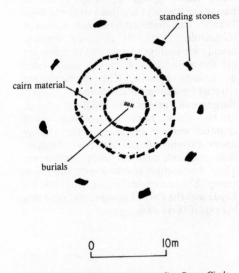

Inverness Ring Cairn with surrounding Stone Circle

Flint Mines

Flint mines were dug to obtain better quality flint from deeper in the chalk, which was used mainly for the production of axes: other smaller tools could be made from the waste flint from axe production. Flint knappers made rough-out axes and other tools in hollows around the tops of the shafts. Some of the mines may have been started in the Mesolithic period, and some may have continued into the Bronze Age, although flint-mining was certainly at its peak during the Neolithic. It is not known whether flint-mining and flint axe production was a full-time occupation, or whether it was carried on by local farmers during slack periods in the agricultural year.

Flint mines can be roughly grouped into three types: open-cast pits, simple shafts, and galleried shafts. All three types are often found on the same site. Mines were dug using ox-scapula shovels, antler picks and wedges, and flint and stone axes. The antler picks were hammered into fissures in the chalk and then used as levers. Stone and flint axes could be used to break up particularly hard chalk. Pit-props do not seem to have been used. Erosion of the tops of shafts has probably destroyed any evidence of pit-head constructions, although some sort of wooden platform may have been built over part of the top of the shaft. It is probable that chalk-rubble and flint were hauled up in baskets on ropes, and that access to the shafts was gained by simple ladders (possibly notched tree-trunks), but no evidence of these has survived. The shafts were probably lit by simple lamps consisting of a wick floating in oil contained in a cup carved out of chalk.

Reading for Flint Mines: Evans. J. G. 1975; Piggott, S. 1954.

Related to the Clava group tombs are the ring cairns of the Inverness area. **Ring cairns** are banks of stones (or sometimes earth, in which case the structure is known as a **ring barrow**), enclosing an area in which burials were placed. The ring cairns of the Inverness area were surrounded by the same type of stone circle that encloses the Clava tombs (see also stone circles and Bronze Age burial).

Reading for Chambered Tombs: Grinsell, L. V. 1953; Grinsell, L. V. 1979; Smith, I. F. 1974.

Stone Axe Factories

Axes of other types of stone were made at **stone axe factories**, which were usually situated at outcrops of rock, where suitable fragments could be found amongst the scree. Only one site (*Mynnydd Rhiw, Gwynedd*) has so far produced evidence of mining. Many of the rocks used for making

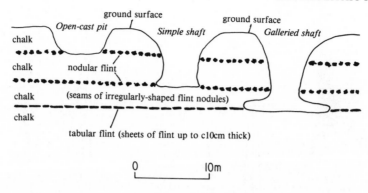

Types of Shaft used in Flint Mining

axes are fine-grained with fracturing characteristics almost as good as those of flint; stone axes could also be made from less suitable rocks by grinding and polishing.

The main axe factories are found in the Lake District, Cornwall, north Wales and Northern Ireland, although the sources of many stone axes have not yet been identified. Factory sites are usually easily identifiable by the presence of debris from the manufacture, and axes from each factory can be identified by petrological examination.

Stone Axe Trade

Although less sharp than flint axes, stone axes were not so easily blunted, or so liable to break. They were traded widely, particularly in southern England, probably as completely finished articles, although some unfinished rough-outs may also have been traded. Some axes were even imported from Northern Ireland and from the Continent. It is not yet certain whether flint axes were also objects of trade since few flint axes have been identified as products of specific flint mines.

Reading for Stone Axe Factories and Trade: Piggott, S. 1954; Smith, I. F. 1974.

Flint and Stone Artifacts

Flint and Stone Axes

Not all the flint and stone 'axes' produced by the flint mines and stone axe factories were used in the same way. Most were made as axes for felling and dressing timber, some were used in mining, and others were shaped for use as **adzes, chisels** and **gouges**. They were probably hafted differently according to the way in which they were used. Adzes may have been hafted in antler sleeves but it is more likely that they were hafted on a **knee-haft (knee-shaft haft)**. All these flint tools can be flaked only, flaked and partly ground or partly polished (usually on the working edges), or else fully ground or fully polished. Apart from unfinished rough-outs, stone axes are always ground and may also be polished. Often the sides of an axe are blunted, or ground round or flat, to help prevent the haft from splitting when the axe-head is fitted into a slot in the haft. Flint and stone axes appear to have been used throughout the Neolithic. Most of them vary in shape and size, although there are a few distinctive forms.

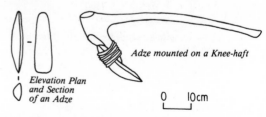

Adze mounted on a Knee-haft

Elevation Plan and Section of an Adze

A Stone or Flint Adze and a possible method of Hafting

37

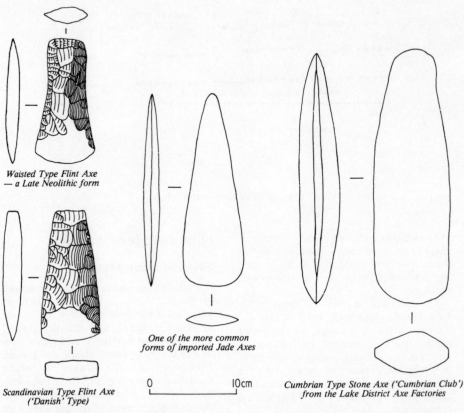

Waisted Type Flint Axe — a Late Neolithic form

Scandinavian Type Flint Axe ('Danish' Type)

One of the more common forms of imported Jade Axes

0   10cm

Cumbrian Type Stone Axe ('Cumbrian Club') from the Lake District Axe Factories

Some of the more distinctive forms of Neolithic Stone and Flint Axes found in Britain

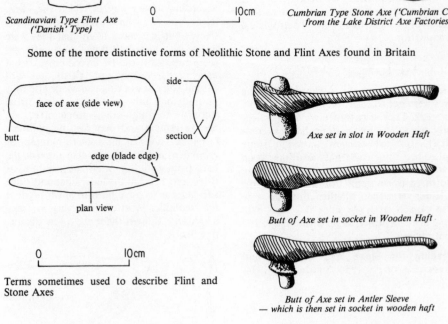

side

face of axe (side view)

section

butt

edge (blade edge)

plan view

0   10cm

Terms sometimes used to describe Flint and Stone Axes

Axe set in slot in Wooden Haft

Butt of Axe set in socket in Wooden Haft

Butt of Axe set in Antler Sleeve — which is then set in socket in wooden haft

0   10cm

Possible Methods of Hafting Neolithic Flint and Stone Axes (only axes set in a slot in a wooden haft have so far been found in Britain)

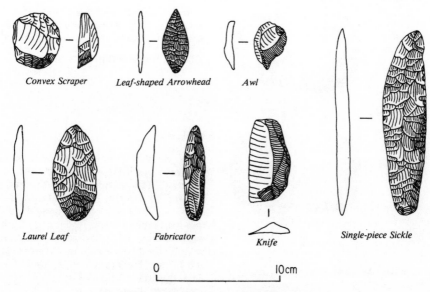

Convex Scraper *Leaf-shaped Arrowhead* *Awl*

Laurel Leaf *Fabricator* *Knife* *Single-piece Sickle*

0   10cm

Some Distinctive Neolithic Flint Tools

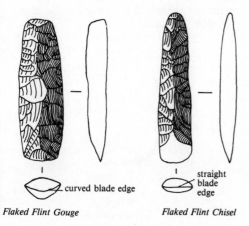

curved blade edge

straight
blade
edge

Flaked Flint Gouge *Flaked Flint Chisel*

Other Flint and Stone Artifacts

During the early Neolithic there seems to have been very little regional variation in the forms of the flint artifacts being used — **leaf-shaped arrowheads, convex scrapers** and a range of very distinctive **narrow-flake tools**. There is much uncertainty about the development of flint artifacts during the late Neolithic, but several changes occurred during the third millennium BC; in many areas **transverse arrowheads** made from flint flakes began to be used, and narrow-flake tools were replaced by broader forms. At the end of the Neolithic **perforated stone maceheads** began to appear.

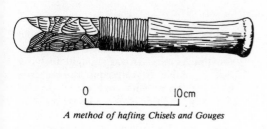

0   10cm

A method of hafting Chisels and Gouges

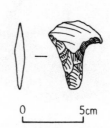

0   5cm

*Transverse Arrowhead (Chisel-ended Arrowhead,
Petit-tranchet Derivative Arrowhead, P.T.D. Arrowhead)*

39

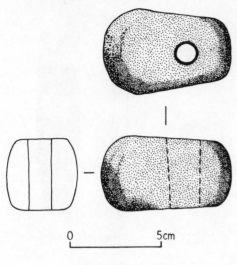

0   5cm

Perforated Stone Macehead

Reading for Flint and Stone Artifacts:
Adkins, R. A. and Jackson, R. 1978;
Bordaz, J. 1970; Clark, J. G. D. 1960;
Evans, J. 1897; Green, H. S. 1980; Pitts,
M. 1980; Smith, I. F. 1974.

Carvings on Stones
see Chapter 4.

Grain Rubbers (Saucer Querns)

Grain was ground into coarse flour by using
a grain rubber. This consisted of a saucer-
shaped lower stone on which the grain was

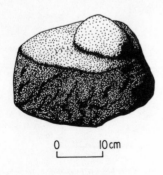

0   10cm

A Grain Rubber

spread, and a bun-shaped upper stone
which was rubbed over the grain in order to
grind it, probably using a circular motion.

Reading for Grain Rubbers: Curwen, E. C.
1937.

Pottery

Early Neolithic pottery was once termed
Western Neolithic, Neolithic 'A' and
Windmill Hill pottery. It is the earliest
known pottery in Britain, dating from
c3300 BC, and was once thought to be
imported from Europe. The pottery is plain
with rounded bases and plain rims. Some
have perforated or solid lugs for suspension
and lifting. The fabric is fine, hard, sometimes burnished, and usually tempered with
coarse grit. There were regional styles such
as **Hembury, Windmill Hill, Grimston,
Heslerton, Lyles Hill, Abingdon** and
Mildenhall ware. Pottery seems to have
been traded, since Hembury pottery was
made in Cornwall and is found throughout
southern England.

0   10cm

Windmill Hill Ware

**Late Neolithic pottery (Peterborough
pottery)** was once termed **Secondary
Neolithic pottery**. It was thought to have
been a native development of pottery,
based on basketwork and contemporary
with early Neolithic pottery, but is now seen
as a later development. Most of it is thick
walled, round bottomed, coarse, and profusely decorated with impressed whipped
cord, finger tipping, bird bone, stamped,
combed, and grooved ornamentation.

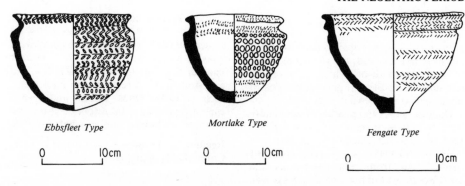

Ebbsfleet Type

0   10cm

Mortlake Type

0   10cm

Fengate Type

0   10cm

Peterborough Pottery

There were three main styles: **Ebbsfleet pottery** first appears, then **Mortlake pottery** and then **Fengate pottery**. The styles were contemporary in their latter stages. Ebbsfleet pottery was originally plain or sparsely decorated, but later was more profusely decorated, with a poorer and coarser fabric. Mortlake pottery was thicker and more heavily ornamented. The bases were still rounded but the rims were more pronounced. Fengate pottery had flat bases and an urn-like appearance. In northern Britain, pottery similar to Peterborough ware has been termed **impressed ware**.

Grooved ware (Rinyo-Clacton ware) was used all over Britain. The pots had flat bases and were bucket or flower-pot shaped, with thick walls. They were decorated with incised or grooved lines, pointillé ornament and applied decoration. The pottery was made from *c*3000 to *c*2000 BC.

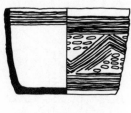

Grooved Ware Pottery

0   10cm

Reading for Pottery: Cunnington, M. E. and Goddard, E. H. 1934; Manby, T. G. 1974; Megaw, J. V. S. and Simpson, D. D. A. 1979; Smith, I. F. 1974; Wainwright, G. J. and Longworth, I. H. 1971, 235–306.

Pottery Spoons

Pottery spoons of Neolithic date have been found. They range from narrow-handled ones to those with thick handles and bowls.

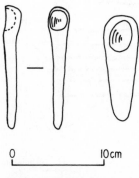

0   10cm

Neolithic Pottery Spoons

Reading for Pottery Spoons: Piggott, S. 1935.

41

Wood

Many articles were probably made of wood, but have not survived; the surprising range of Neolithic woodwork which has nevertheless survived in Britain, gives some idea of the extent to which wood was used.

Dugout canoes and **paddles** of wood have been found; in marshy areas timber was used to construct **trackways**. At least two types of trackway were used: **corduroy roads**, made from split tree-trunks and brushwood, held in position by pegs driven into the ground, and **plank tracks** made from wooden planks supported on pegs.

Wood was used extensively in buildings, as shown by the evidence of postholes on settlement and burial sites. Examples of wooden **hurdles** have also survived, as have **handles** for flint tools and **hafts** for flint and stone axes. A few wooden implements such as **forks, clubs, dishes**, and even a **carved figure**, have been found; also a few examples of **bows** and **arrowshafts**.

Reading for Wood: Coles, J. M. et al 1976; Coles, J. M. et al 1978.

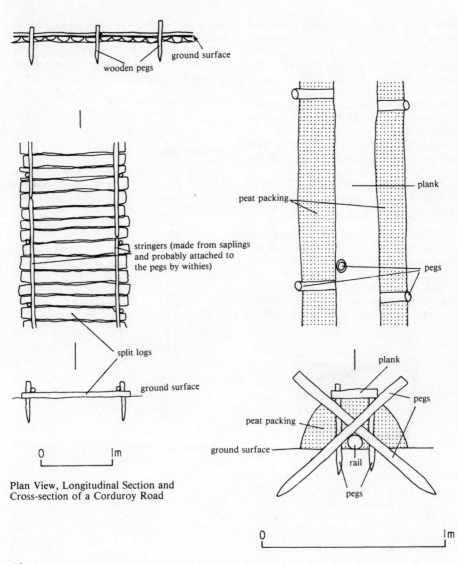

Plan View, Longitudinal Section and Cross-section of a Corduroy Road

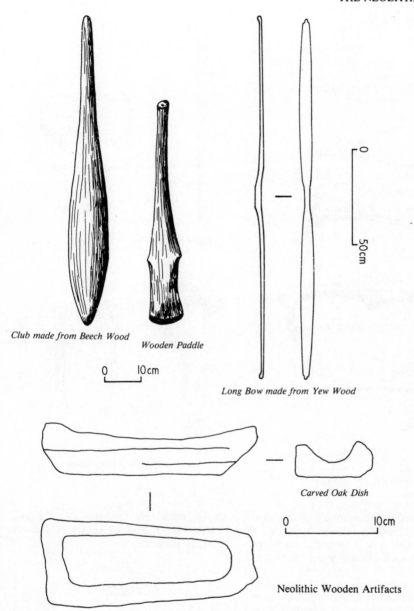

Club made from Beech Wood

Wooden Paddle

0   10cm

Long Bow made from Yew Wood

0

50cm

Carved Oak Dish

0   10cm

Neolithic Wooden Artifacts

Chalk

Chalk cups were probably used as simple oil lamps and are often found in flint mines. Perforated chalk blocks were probably used as weights; smaller pieces of chalk, with a perforation and sometimes an incised design, seem to have been used as pendants. Chalk figurines, phalli and chalk balls, which were often found with phalli, were probably connected with a fertility cult.

Models of stone axes carved from chalk were found at Woodhenge, Wiltshire. Chalk plaques with incised decoration are known, and three decorated chalk drums (chalk carved in the form of a squat cylinder) were found with a burial under a barrow at Folkton, North Yorkshire.
Reading for Chalk: Wainwright, G. J. and Longworth, I. H. 1971, 262.

Bone and Antler

Many kinds of bone and antler artifacts were used during the Neolithic. **Antler picks** and **rakes, ox-scapula shovels** some with **antler handles,** and **bone wedges**, were used for digging and mining.

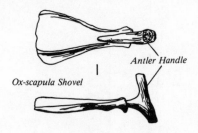

Ox-scapula Shovel

Antler Handle

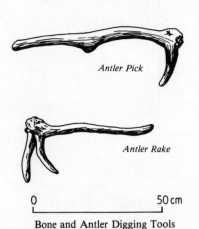

Antler Pick

Antler Rake

0   50 cm

Bone and Antler Digging Tools

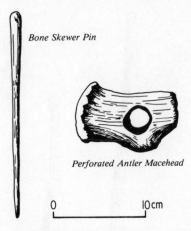

Bone Skewer Pin

Perforated Antler Macehead

0   10cm

Later Neolithic Bone and Antler Artifacts

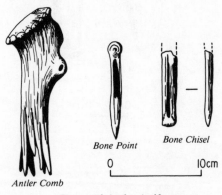

Bone Point

Bone Chisel

Antler Comb

0   10cm

Bone and Antler Artifacts

Antler combs were probably used to strip hair from hides, and **bone points** were probably used as awls to pierce them for sewing. **Bone chisels** and **gouges** may also have been used in the processing of skins and hides. In the Later Neolithic **bone pins** became more numerous; bone **skewer pins** are often found with burials, and in some instances seem to have been used for fastening bags containing cremations. **Perforated antler maceheads (perforated antler hammers)** also appear in the Later Neolithic, and at *Skara Brae*, Orkney, a wide range of bone and antler artifacts has been found, including several types of **pins, pendants** and **beads.**

Reading for Bone and Antler: Clark, J. G. D. 1952; Piggott, S. 1954; Whittle, A. W. R. 1977.

Jet

Jet or shale **belt fasteners (belt sliders, sliders)** and jet beads are known from Later Neolithic contexts.

Jet Belt Fastener

0   5cm

Reading for Jet: McInnes, I. J. 1968.

General Reading for the Neolithic Period: Megaw, J. V. S. and Simpson, D. D. A. 1979; Renfrew, C. 1974.

Chapter 4

The Bronze Age

Introduction

The **Bronze Age** is characterised by the first use of copper and bronze. The period used to be divided into the **Early Bronze Age** (*c*2300–1400 BC), the **Middle Bronze Age** (*c*1400–1000 BC) and the **Late Bronze Age** (*c*1000–700 BC). It has now been redefined as the **Earlier Bronze Age** (*c*2300–1200 BC) and the **Later Bronze Age** (*c*1200–700 BC).

Within the Bronze Age various cultures and metalworking industries have been recognised. The Beaker culture dates from *c*2300 BC and is represented by pottery, burials and some settlement. The Wessex culture dates from *c*1700 BC and is represented by burials accompanied by rich grave goods. Since it is only represented by these burials, it is not a culture in the strictest sense. It is contemporary with many sites that have produced food vessels. The Deverel-Rimbury culture dates from *c*1400 BC and is mainly represented by burial sites accompanied by Deverel-Rimbury pottery, and some settlement sites. The Bronze Age has also been divided into phases based on evidence from metalwork industries.

Reading: Burgess, C. B. 1974; Burgess, C. B. 1980; Megaw, J. V. S. and Simpson, D. D. A. 1979.

Settlement Sites and Agricultural Economy

Beaker people have been described as nomadic and pastoral, since very few domestic sites of this period are known (as with all the Earlier Bronze Age period), while there is evidence for the hunting of red deer and collecting of shellfish. A more settled economy is indicated, however, by finds of grain rubbers, paired postholes which may have been corn-drying racks, and oval settings of postholes and stone packing which may have been huts or enclosures. There have been finds of bone implements and animal bones (particularly at *Northton*, Isle of Harris, Western Isles) which may indicate a settled pastoral economy. Grain impressions (mainly barley) have also been found on some Beaker vessels. Two rectangular enclosures are known from *Belle Tout*, Sussex, within which were several timber-built structures. A few drystone oval structures are known in Scotland, which may have been revetment walls for pits in the sand.

Later evidence for settlement in southern Britain is associated with Deverel-Rimbury pottery. The settlements are often enclosed ones consisting of rectlinear banks and ditches surrounding circular huts. The ditches may have been foundation trenches for fences. Some of these settlements were once considered to be cattle enclosures, since early excavations revealed no trace of internal occupation, although more recent excavations have revealed buildings. They are often associated with Celtic fields and **cross ridge dykes, spur dykes** and **ranch boundaries (linear ditches, linear earthworks, triple dykes)** which are ditches and banks dividing up the countryside and which continued in use into the Iron Age (see Chapter 5). **Reaves** are low stone banks used as field boundaries. They are about 1m to 2m wide and up to 80cm high and are usually covered by vegetation; they are found on Dartmoor, Devon. Settlement was preferred in valleys, near rivers, and along coastal plains. Some nucleated or village-like settlements are known in southern England (eg *Itford Hill* and *Plumpton Plain*, Sussex) consisting of trackways, huts and enclosures.

In the West Country there is evidence for moorland settlement on what would have been open grassland and scrub. On the southern and western valleys of Dartmoor, enclosures **(pounds)** are known, consisting of stone walls inside which are huts. These huts would have had thatched conical roofs supported by an inner ring of posts and a central post, with an outer stone-built wall similar to Iron Age double-ring round-houses. There were also unenclosed settlements and isolated huts. All three types of settlement were associated with reaves and predated the formation of blanket bog. There is also evidence for extensive field systems in other parts of Britain, although as yet there is little evidence for settlement.

Later Bronze Age settlement includes '**mini-hillforts**' (such as *Thwing*, Humberside), consisting of a large hut site surrounded by a large bank and inner and outer ditches. There is also growing evidence for pre-Iron Age settlement of hill-forts, consisting mainly of palisades and ditches surrounding huts and pits (such as *Mam Tor*, Derbyshire), and there is also evidence for some cave occupation, and for unenclosed settlement sites, associated with Post Deverel-Rimbury tradition pottery.

The environment of the Earlier Bronze Age was characterised by weather which was warmer and drier than that of today. There was continued clearance of land for agriculture, and cultivation extended onto higher and marginal land. There was an increase in birch and ash trees. In the Later Bronze Age there was a deterioration of climate which continued into the Iron Age, leading to the widespread formation of blanket bog.

Throughout the Bronze Age there is evidence for mixed farming. Cattle (*Bos longifrons*) and sheep bones are found, as well as some goat, horse (probably domesticated as there are finds of horse harness) and pig. Sheep were kept for wool as well as for meat. At *Harrow Hill*, Sussex, there was a sub-rectangular enclosure in which about one hundred cattle skulls were found; this may have been an enclosure for slaughter. Arable farming is attested by finds of grain rubbers, grain impressions on pottery, finds of grain in pits (mainly hulled barley and emmer wheat), and bronze sickles. Plough marks are occasionally found, including cross-ploughing marks at *Gwithian*, Cornwall. Spade marks have also been discovered (eg *Gwithian*, Cornwall), providing evidence that the spade was used in cultivation. The hunting of deer was also practised.

Reading for Settlement Sites and Agricul- tural **Economy**: Bowen, H. C. and Fowler, P. J. 1978; Bradley, R. J. 1978; Burgess, C. B. 1980; Fleming, A. 1978; Megaw, J. V. S. and Simpson, D. D. A. 1979; Selkirk, A. and W. 1979; Thomas, A. C. 1970.

Ritual

Many bronze implements have been found in rivers and bogs which may have been ritual deposits. The **Wilsford shaft** near *Stonehenge*, Wiltshire, is a pit at least 33m deep and 2m in diameter, which contained several items of Bronze Age date. A C^{14} date of 1,380± 90 bc has been obtained from wood from the shaft. The shaft may have had a ritual purpose. Other features which probably had a ritual significance are stone circles, standing stones, henges and carvings on stones. There is much evidence for ritual in the burial practices of the Earlier Bronze Age, but virtually nothing is known of the underlying beliefs.

Reading for Ritual: Burgess, C. B. 1980; Megaw, J. V. S. and Simpson, D. D. A. 1979.

Burial

During the Bronze Age, there is an increasing tendency towards single burial, a trend which began in the Later Neolithic. Many Bronze Age burials were covered by a round barrow or cairn. The **bowl barrow** is the most common type of round barrow and is a simple round mound, usually with a surrounding ditch and sometimes a bank, found all over Britain. A **bell barrow** has a berm between the mound and the surrounding ditch, and occasionally an outer bank. A **disc barrow** has a small central mound on a wide platform surrounded by a ditch and an outer bank. Bell and disc barrows are also termed **bermed barrows**. A **saucer barrow** has a low mound surrounded by a ditch and outer bank, with no berm. A **pond barrow** is a circular depression surrounded by an outer bank and can contain cremations, inhumations, and dismembered inhumations, as well as empty pits, and may have had other ritual functions besides burial. The size of the barrows can vary considerably and does not reflect the wealth of the burial. **Ring ditches** are circular or near-circular ditches, usually

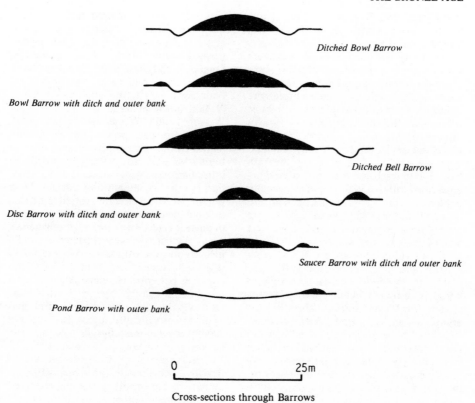

Ditched Bowl Barrow

Bowl Barrow with ditch and outer bank

Ditched Bell Barrow

Disc Barrow with ditch and outer bank

Saucer Barrow with ditch and outer bank

Pond Barrow with outer bank

0   25m

Cross-sections through Barrows

seen as crop-marks from the air. Most excavated ring ditches have been found to be the remains of ploughed-out barrows.

The internal structure of barrows varies, but often includes a mound of turf or earth covering a central burial, which was placed either in a pit, or occasionally on the old land surface. Grave-pits were sometimes lined with wood or stone slabs; inhumations and some cremations were sometimes placed on wooden planks or in coffins built from wooden planks **(composite coffins, plank coffins)**, or else in coffins made from hollowed-out tree-trunks with lids **(mono-xylous coffins, dugout coffins, tree-trunk coffins)**. Some hollowed-out coffins resembled boats **(dugout canoe coffins, boat-shaped hollowed tree-trunk coffins, canoe-shaped dugout tree-trunks)**. Cremations contained in small wooden boxes are also known. Sometimes the barrows covered pre-mound stakeholes or postholes. Barrows are found mainly in southern Britain, and bell, disc, saucer and pond barrows (sometimes described as

'fancy' or 'exotic' barrows) are largely confined to Wessex. Flat graves and cairns were more common in northern Britain.

Beaker burials are found in Britain dating from *c*2300 BC. These consisted of single crouched inhumations covered by small bowl barrows accompanied by beakers. Some beaker burials were cremations. In southern Britain the burials were placed in oval pits covered by barrows. In north-east England some very large barrows are known. A few barrows covered more than one interment, and some barrows covered circular settings of stakeholes or postholes or banks of stone. In northern Britain the burials were often placed in stone-lined graves or cists and were either flat graves or were covered by cairns. Beaker burials are often found as secondary interments in Neolithic long barrows, especially those of the Severn-Cotswold and Clyde groups. A few beaker burials were accompanied by a variety of grave goods such as copper daggers, awls, basket-shaped earrings and discs of gold, barbed and tanged arrowheads and daggers of flint, stone bracers and battle axes, jet or shale conical buttons, and bone, jet or shale belt-rings.

Burials accompanied by food vessels are known mainly in north-east Britain, some of which were accompanied by a few grave goods. In the Highland Zone the burials are usually contained in flat graves with stone cists, and elsewhere in pits or graves covered by mounds. In North Yorkshire and Humberside, for example, the inhumations are contained in deep pits beneath large round barrows. The pits are sometimes lined with wood or contain tree-trunk or plank coffins. In north-east England and Scotland burials with food vessels are mainly single inhumations and in the west mainly single cremations.

Wessex culture burials are found from *c*1700 BC and stand out because of the richness of a few of the burials. This type of burial is restricted mainly to the Wessex region. The **Wessex I group (Bush Barrow group** — named after *Bush Barrow*, Wiltshire) is the earlier phase and includes both male and female burials, some of which are very rich. The interments were mainly crouched or extended inhumations, but there were some cremations. Grave goods include Armorico-British daggers, flat axes, amber beads and spacer beads, halberd pendants, grape cups, stone battle axes and a variety of gold objects. The **Wessex II group (Aldbourne-Edmonsham group** — named after *Aldbourne*, Wiltshire, and *Edmonsham*, Dorset) con-

sists mainly of cremation burial of both males and females under barrows. Grave goods include Camerton-Snowshill daggers (named after finds from *Camerton*, Somerset, and *Snowshill*, Gloucestershire), bone tweezers, Aldbourne cups, bronze and bone pins, and shafthole battle axes. There is also much material common to both Wessex I and Wessex II burials. Both groups also had poorer burials accompanied by only a few objects; some of these burials were placed in flat graves between other barrows. Most Wessex I and II male burials were accompanied by daggers. Most burials were covered by round barrows, often in **linear cemeteries** (laid out in a line), in **nuclear cemeteries (nucleated cemeteries)** where the barrows were clustered around a **primary barrow (founder's barrow),** or in **dispersed cemeteries** (which have no apparent pattern). The most common type of Wessex culture barrow is the bowl barrow, although disc, saucer, bell and pond barrows are also found. Bell barrows usually covered male burials; disc barrows usually covered Wessex II female burials.

Urns are commonly found in non-Wessex burials, occasionally accompanying inhumations but mostly containing cremated human remains, either as a primary or as a secondary burial under a barrow, some of which are grouped in cemeteries. There are a series of **dagger graves** in Scotland which are mostly crouched inhumations in cists accompanied by daggers, although there are some extended inhumations. Some

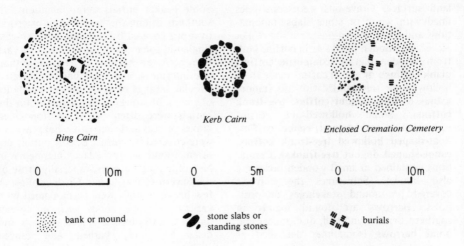

Ring Cairn

Kerb Cairn

Enclosed Cremation Cemetery

0   10m

0   5m

0   10m

⬚ bank or mound

⬤ stone slabs or standing stones

burials

barrow burials in Britain have no accompanying grave goods and so it is not possible to say whether these are a later form of burial. In northern Britain urned and unurned cremations are sometimes found in flat cemeteries, occasionally surrounded by circular funerary enclosures such as banks of earth or stones, ditches, and stone circles (**enclosed cremation cemeteries**). Also found in northern Britain, and having their origins in the Neolithic period (see Chapter 3), are **ring cairns** which consist of a bank of cairn material surrounding an open area in which burials were deposited; a few burials were placed in the bank. Some ring cairns have stone circles in the interior (**embanked stone circles**). Some cairns have massive kerbs and are termed **kerb cairns**. Various combinations of stone circles, banks and barrows were occasionally used for burial (see also stone circles).

The custom of accompanying burials with grave goods declines from *c*1400 BC. In south-east Britain there is cremation in flat cemeteries (**urnfields**) in Deverel-Rimbury urns (named after *Deverel*, Dorset, and *Rimbury*, Dorset) with very few other grave goods; some of the cremations were unurned. Flat cemeteries could contain over one hundred burials. Single or multiple cremation in barrows also continued, mainly in south-west Britain, sometimes as secondary burials in earlier barrows. Elsewhere established burial methods disappear and little is known of burial rites in the Later Bronze Age (see also stone circles for burial).

Reading for Burial: Ashbee, P. 1960; Burgess, C. B. 1976; Burgess, C. B. 1980; Grinsell, L. V. 1979; Lynch, F. 1972; Megaw, J. V. S. and Simpson, D. D. A. 1979; Ritchie, J. N. G. and MacLaren, A. 1972.

Stone Circles

Stone circles were built from the Later Neolithic period onwards (see Neolithic stone circles), although the most impressive examples are seen in the Earlier Bronze Age. Some of these circles were over 100m in diameter. Some of the stone 'circles' were built as flattened circles or ovals. Many seem to have a preferred number of

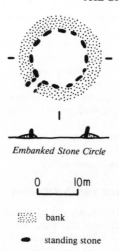

Embanked Stone Circle

0   10m

▒▒▒ bank

● standing stone

stones depending on the region, such as twelve in the Lake District and ten in north-east Scotland. Regional differences in the construction of circles are also seen. In Wales, Yorkshire and the Derbyshire Peak District the stones were often set into a bank, sometimes with burials of children at the centre of the ring (**embanked stone circles**) (see also burial). Two, three or complexes of several circles are seen together in south-west Britain (eg at *Avebury*, Wiltshire). Some circles, particularly in the Welsh Marches and Cumbria, have avenues of standing stones leading up to them. **Concentric circles** have one circle inside another and are rare. Stone circles were added to many henges at this period.

Recumbent stone circles (RSC) also belong to this period. They are similar to the Inverness circles (see Chapter 3) and occur mainly in north-east Scotland. The stones of these circles rise in height, usually towards the south-west, and the two tallest stones flank a large prostrate stone (**recumbent stone**). These circles sometimes surrounded a ring cairn containing a cremation. Circles of this period in north and west Britain often enclosed burials in barrows, cairns or cists, although this phenomenon is rare in southern Britain.

Most stone circles were probably erected in the Earlier Bronze Age, and there is no evidence that stone circles were erected after *c*1200 BC. The later circles tend to be smaller, using smaller stones, and are often oval or sub-circular in plan. Ovals of six or eight stones are found in central Scotland, as well as **four-posters** (four stones set at the corners of a rectangle about 4m by 5m, often containing a cremation burial in an urn). On Dartmoor, Devon, circles were built around cairns and were approached by long rows of stones. Stone circles are rare in northern Scotland, but multiple rows of small stones approaching round cairns are found. Burials and stone circles seem to have been closely associated in this period, and there is much evidence for cremation burials around stone circles.

Measurement and Astronomy

In the last few years the research of Professor Thom into the functions of some stone circles and the mathematics required in their laying-out has stimulated a great deal of speculation and research, although not all maintaining his standards.

From measurements taken from stone circles, Thom has worked out a unit of measurement (the **megalithic yard** which is 2·72ft or 0·829m). He suggested that this unit was used all over Britain and Brittany, and was kept constant by the issuing of measuring rods from a national centre. Further research, however, has revealed minor regional variations in this unit of measurement, possibly indicating that it was based on a simple body measurement (in the same way that the 'body-yard' is based on the distance from the nose to the end of an outstretched arm).

Research into the possible astronomical functions of stone circles has not met with overwhelming success. In some instances plausible alignments have been demonstrated between stones in stone circles, distant landmarks, and the rising or setting of the sun, moon, or some of the brighter stars, but the evidence that any of the circles were observatories or computers is inconclusive. Surveyors of stone circles are severely hampered by the fact that in most circles stones have moved, fallen or been completely removed, so that accurate alignments are very difficult to prove. It seems most likely that many circles had alignments to heavenly bodies for religious rather than 'scientific' reasons, and that the function of the circles was primarily religious and ceremonial.

Reading for Stone Circles: Burl, A. 1976; Burl, A. 1979; Thom, A. 1967; Thom, A. 1971.

Standing Stones

Apart from stone circles, standing stones were erected singly **(monoliths)**, in pairs, or in long lines sometimes called **stone rows**. Monoliths may have been used to mark boundaries and trackways, although they often appear to have had a religious function. They are sometimes associated with barrows and cairns as well as with stone circles, and are sometimes interpreted as phallic symbols. Stone rows are likewise sometimes associated with stone circles, barrows and cairns, while others may have been used as boundary markers. Ritual deposits of stone and flint tools, and also Beaker burials, are sometimes found at the foot of standing stones. Such stones are very difficult to date; they are usually attributed to the Bronze Age, but some were probably erected during the Neolithic, and many were probably erected much later.

Reading for Standing Stones: Burl, A. 1976; Burl, A. 1979; Grinsell, L. V. 1970.

Henges see Chapter 3.

Stonehenge

The site of *Stonehenge*, Salisbury Plain, Wiltshire, is worth mentioning in a little detail because it is unique in terms of architectural sophistication. It was built in several phases; the first phase was begun in the Later Neolithic *c*2800 BC (or possibly earlier as indicated by C[14] dates obtained from recent excavation), with the building of a bank and external ditch with a single entrance together with the Aubrey Holes and the erection of the **heel stone**. The **Aubrey Holes** are circular pits 1m wide and 1m deep, laid out in a circle with a diameter of *c*86·5m. They appear to have been filled in soon after they were dug, possibly as part of some religious ceremony. At *c*2100 BC, approximately eighty bluestones were erected to form two concentric circles. **Bluestones** (so-called because of their colour when freshly broken) are of various types of rock from the Presely Mountains in south-west Wales, but mostly of a type of rock known to archaeologists as **spotted dolerite**. The bluestone circles were never completed, and a large gap was left on their west side. At this time the original entrance was widened and the nearer part of the Avenue was built.

At *c*2000 BC the building of the lintelled circle and horseshoe of large sarsen stones was begun; **sarsen stones (sarsens)** being sandstone boulders found on the chalk downs of Wiltshire. This circle and horseshoe replaced the bluestone circles, which were dismantled. The sarsens were dressed to shape with heavy stone mauls; the sides of the lintels were dressed to fit the curves of the circle and were joined end-to-end by tongue-and-groove joints; lintels were held in place on top of the uprights by mortise-and-tenon joints. The horseshoe was formed with five sarsen trilithons. A **trilithon** is the name given to two upright stones joined at the top by a stone lintel; trilithons are only found at Stonehenge.

At some time after the sarsens were erected, just over twenty of the previously dismantled bluestones were also dressed and erected in an oval setting within the horseshoe. The **Y holes** and **Z holes** which formed a double circle around the sarsen circle were dug *c*1550 BC and were probably intended to take the remaining bluestones, but the project was abandoned before all the holes were dug and no stones were set up; the oval setting of bluestones was also demolished. The bluestones from the oval setting were reset into a horseshoe shape within the sarsen horseshoe, and the remaining unshaped bluestones were used to form a close-set circle between this horseshoe and the sarsen circle. At *c*1100 BC the Avenue was extended over the hill to the east and then south-eastwards towards the River Avon, which suggests that Stonehenge was still in use at this late date, although it is not known when it finally fell into disuse.

Reading for Stonehenge: Atkinson, R. J. C. 1978; Atkinson, R. J. C. 1979.

Carvings on Stones

Cup marks are simple, roughly hemispherical depressions carved on stone, probably by using a pecking technique. They are found on some standing stones, on the stones of some stone circles, on some natural boulders and rock outcrops, and on

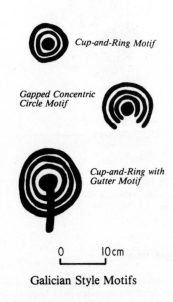

Cup-and-Ring Motif

Gapped Concentric Circle Motif

Cup-and-Ring with Gutter Motif

0   10 cm

Galician Style Motifs

the stones of some burial chambers and cists. They date to the Later Neolithic and the Bronze Age. They have also been found on stones from Iron Age sites, although these stones may have been re-used. Cup marks may have had a religious significance. **Single grave art** is the term given to carvings on cists, urn covers, and other stones associated with Later Neolithic and Earlier Bronze Age barrows and cairns. A wide range of motifs and combinations of motifs are found, often associated with cup marks. Most of the carvings occur in northern Britain, but they are also found in Ireland and on the Continent. The **cup-and-ring, cup-and-ring with gutter** and **gapped concentric circles** are sometimes known as the **Galician style** of rock art because of their similarities to the carvings of Galicia (north-west Spain). Most other motifs belong to the group called **passage grave art** since many examples come from passage graves in northern Ireland and northern Britain.

Carved stone balls appear in the Later Neolithic and were probably made throughout the Bronze Age. Various types have been recognised; their distribution is almost entirely confined to Scotland and their use is unknown.

A Carved Stone Ball

0   5cm

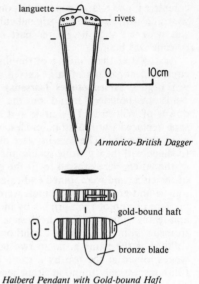

Armorico-British Dagger

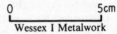

gold-bound haft

bronze blade

Halberd Pendant with Gold-bound Haft

0   5cm

Wessex I Metalwork

Reading for Carvings on Stone: Simpson, D. D. A. and Thawley, J. E. 1972; Marshall, D. N. 1976–7.

Metalwork

Much evidence for the Bronze Age is derived from its bronzework, which can be divided into various industries and phases, although implements can occur in more than one phase.

Beaker Culture

The introduction of copper implements and copper working into Britain can be attributed to the Beaker culture. Copper implements are found mainly in Beaker burials and include **tanged flat daggers (tanged daggers, tanged knives)** some of which had a single rivet hole or notch in the tang and are called **single-riveted tanged daggers**. Other beaker metalwork includes **pins, awls, tubular beads, halberds** (found mainly in the Highland Zone), and **broad-butt flat axes (broad-butted flat axes)**.

Migdale-Marnoch Tradition

Around 2000 BC, bronze made from copper alloyed with tin began to be used. This early phase of bronze working is termed the **Migdale-Marnoch tradition** (named after *Migdale*, Highland, and *Marnoch*, Grampian), and in its later stages it overlaps with metalwork from the Wessex culture. **Pins, awls, tubular beads, basket-shaped earrings (ear-pendants)**, plain, ribbed or ridged **rings** and **bracelets, narrow-butted flat axes, riveted flat daggers (flat riveted daggers)** usually with three stout rivets, and **hollow cones** belonging to this tradition have been found.

Wessex Culture

The **Wessex culture** dates from the seventeenth century BC and the metalwork is found mainly as grave goods. In **Wessex I** (the earlier phase) **Armorico-British daggers (Bush Barrow daggers)** are found, so-called because of their similarities to ones in Armorica (Brittany). These daggers are flat and triangular in shape. They usually have six slender rivets and sometimes a projecting tongue **(languette)** and lateral grooves. Traces of wooden and leather sheaths have survived with some of them, as well as dagger pommels of wood, one decorated with thousands of minute gold pins. Also found are **halberd pendants** (miniature copies of hafted bronze halberd blades), flat axes (including some miniature ones), and awls.

Wessex II dates from *c*1500 BC and the metalwork is characterised by **Camerton-Snowshill daggers** which are ogival in shape, with a midrib, and two or three large rivets. Some are ornamented, and some have traces of a wooden sheath. **Knife-daggers** are blades less than about 10cm in length, which usually have two rivet holes. Pins are occasionally found including **crutch-headed pins, ring-headed pins** (composed of one or more rings), **bulb-headed pins (globe-headed pins)**, and **disc-headed pins**. Tanged **razors** have also been found.

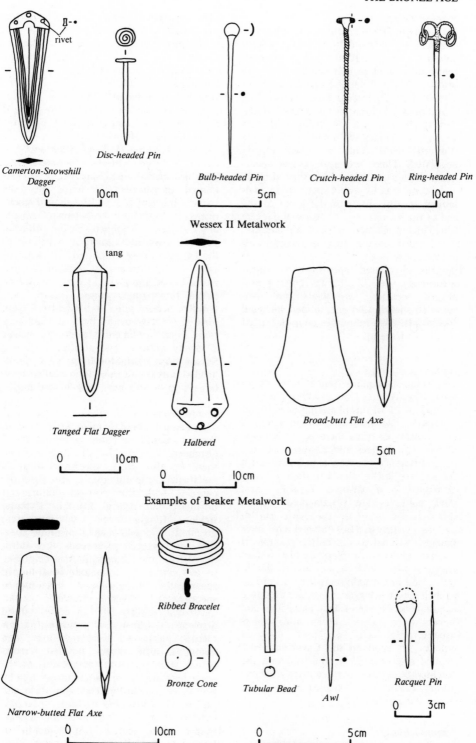

rivet

Disc-headed Pin

Camerton-Snowshill
Dagger

0   10cm

Bulb-headed Pin

0   5cm

Crutch-headed Pin

0

Ring-headed Pin

0   10cm

Wessex II Metalwork

tang

Tanged Flat Dagger

0   10cm

Halberd

0   10cm

Broad-butt Flat Axe

0   5cm

Examples of Beaker Metalwork

Ribbed Bracelet

Bronze Cone

Tubular Bead

Awl

Racquet Pin

0   3cm

Narrow-butted Flat Axe

0   10cm

0   5cm

Migdale-Marnoch Tradition Metalwork

53

Arreton Down Tradition

The **Arreton Down tradition** of metalwork (named after *Arreton Down*, Isle of Wight) dates to the sixteenth and fifteenth centuries BC and is represented widely in southern England, apart from Wessex, and extends into Yorkshire. The metalwork is found mainly in hoards and as single finds, and is characterised by thin-butted axes which have flanges and a wide cutting edge **(flanged axes)** and are occasionally decorated. There are also **tanged spear-heads** (with a lozenge or kite-shaped blade and a tang, usually with a single rivet), **end-looped spearheads** (with the loops at the end of the socket), and a variety of daggers which include Camerton-Snowshill daggers, three-ribbed daggers and other daggers with grooves or midribs. There are rare finds of **tanged-and-collared spearheads ('tanged spearheads with a separate collar')** and **pegged socketed spearheads (unlooped socketed spearheads)** and **looped socketed spearheads**. Also found are plain or lugged **chisels** (or **tracers**).

Acton Park Phase

The **Acton Park phase** (named after *Acton Park*, Clwyd) dates from c1500 BC. Some of the metalwork of this phase has been found in hoards. The metalwork is characterised by various types of **palstave**, which is a type of axe with flanges and a stop-ridge; the main difference between a palstave and a flanged axe is that the stop-ridge is more developed in a palstave. Typical Acton Park palstaves are ornamented with a shield-shaped motif on the blade **(shield-pattern palstaves)**. **Haft-flanged axes** have flanges confined to the hafted portion of the axe. **Dirks** and **rapiers** are also found. Daggers, dirks and rapiers are similar in form, and are usually classified according to their length. Daggers are under c20cm in length, dirks between c20cm and 35cm, and rapiers over c35cm. Dirks and rapiers usually only have two rivet holes or notches. In Scotland the **Caverton phase** (named after *Caverton*, Borders) and the **Auchterhouse phase** (named after *Auchterhouse*, Tayside) are concurrent with the Acton Park phase.

Taunton Phase

The **Taunton phase (Ornament Horizon, Taunton-Barton Bendish phase** — named after *Taunton*, Somerset, and *Barton Bendish*, Norfolk) dates from c1300 BC and is confined mainly to southern Britain. In Scotland this phase is represented by the **Glentrool phase** (named after *Glentrool*, Dumfries and Galloway). In northern Britain **wing-flanged axes** are found, whereas in southern Britain **low-flanged palstaves** and **south-western palstaves (high-flanged palstaves)** developed. There are also **Taunton-Hademarschen socketed axes, socketed chisels, hammers** and **punches, basal-looped spearheads, socket-looped spearheads** (the loops near the socket) and **side-looped kite-shaped spearheads** (the loops half-way between the blade and socket). **Knobbed sickles (button sickles), saws** and **rapiers** also belong to the Taunton phase. Imported and continentally inspired 'ornaments' include twisted, plain, ribbed and incised **torcs** and **armlets, coiled finger-rings, cones, Picardy pins (swollen-necked pins)** and **'Glentrool type' pins** (these have a nail head and are very rare). Local 'ornaments' developed, such as a variety of **torcs** and **armlets**, including **Sussex loops ('Brighton loops')** and **quoit-headed pins (quoit pins, loop-headed pins, large loop-headed pins, ring-headed pins)**.

Penard Phase

The **Penard phase** (named after *Penard*, West Glamorgan) dates from c1200 BC. Ornament Horizon objects continue and there is also much experimentation in metalworking in this phase, stimulated by contacts with the urnfield cultures of northern and central Europe. **Cylinder sickles (ring-socketed sickles)** were invented, and **leaf-shaped peg-hole (peg-socketed, pegged) spearheads** were introduced from the Continent. Also belonging to this phase are **triangular basal-looped spearheads (straight-based basal-looped spearheads)**, some circular **shields** (although possibly later in date), **tanged arrowheads, transitional palstaves (narrow bladed palstaves), socketed axes** and **hammers, bifid razors, pointed ferrules** (which were fitted on to the ends of the spearshafts and were sometimes secured by pegs or rivets), and **notched-butt dirks** and **rapiers**. The **Cutts** type of notched-butt dirk (named after *Cutts*, Ireland) has a leaf-shaped blade and is found mainly in Ireland; the **Lisburn** class (named after *Lisburn*, Ireland) has a straight blade.

Rixheim, **Erbenheim** and **Hemigkofen**
swords were imported from central and
western Europe, from which local swords
developed including the **Chelsea sword**
(named after *Chelsea*, Greater London)
which has a leaf-shaped blade and flat
section, and the **Ballintober sword** (named
after *Ballintober*, Ireland) which has a leaf-
shaped blade and a lozenge section. A few
Rosnoën swords (Lambeth swords,
Lambeth/Rosnoën swords — named after
Lambeth, Greater London, and *Rosnoën*,
France) are known. They have a straight
blade and a flat section and were probably
imported from France. Also imported were
Rixheim-Monza swords (named after
Rixheim, France, and *Monza*, Italy) which
are hook-tanged and rod-tanged.
U-shouldered swords were also developed
in this period.

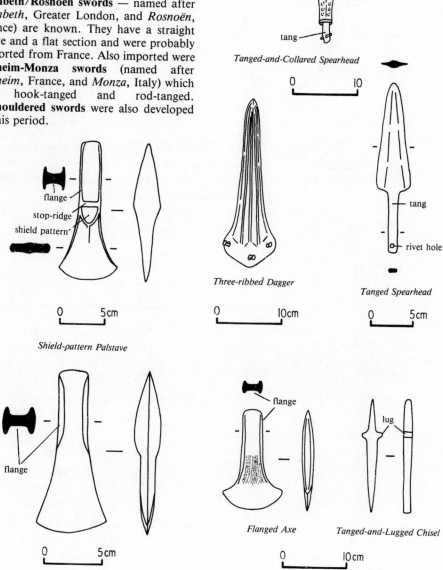

Tanged-and-Collared Spearhead

Three-ribbed Dagger

Tanged Spearhead

Shield-pattern Palstave

Haft-flanged Axe

Flanged Axe

Tanged-and-Lugged Chisel

Acton Park Phase Metalwork

Arreton Down Tradition Metalwork

55

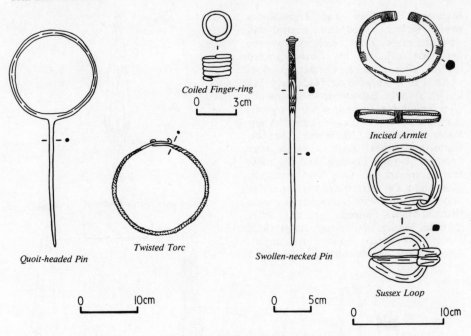

Coiled Finger-ring

0   3cm

Incised Armlet

Quoit-headed Pin

Twisted Torc

Swollen-necked Pin

Sussex Loop

0   10cm

0   5cm

0   10cm

Examples of Taunton Phase 'Ornaments'

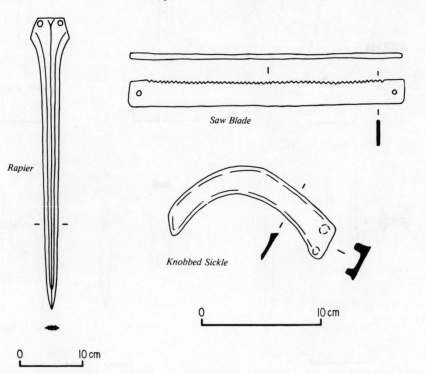

Rapier

Saw Blade

Knobbed Sickle

0   10cm

0   10cm

Examples of Taunton Phase Metalwork

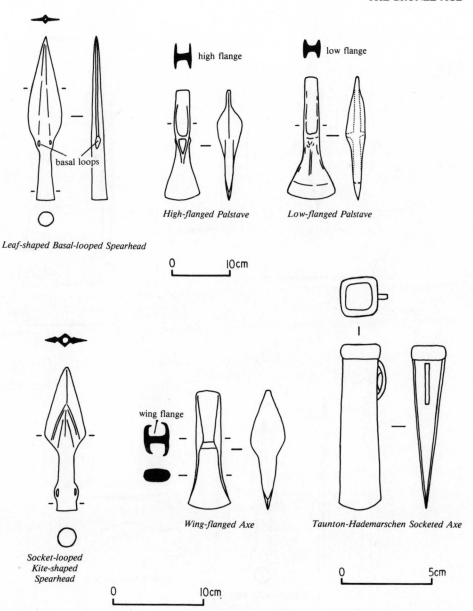

high flange

low flange

basal loops

High-flanged Palstave

Low-flanged Palstave

Leaf-shaped Basal-looped Spearhead

0   10cm

wing flange

Wing-flanged Axe

Taunton-Hademarschen Socketed Axe

Socket-looped
Kite-shaped
Spearhead

0   10cm

0   5cm

Examples of Taunton Phase Metalwork

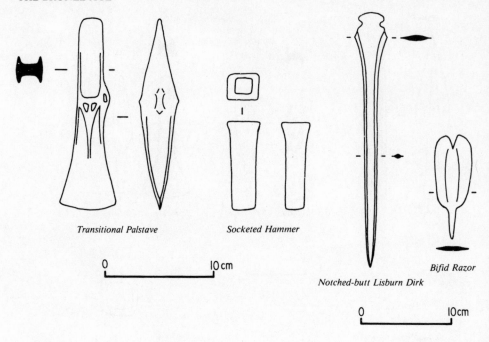

Transitional Palstave

Socketed Hammer

0   10 cm

Bifid Razor

Notched-butt Lisburn Dirk

0   10cm

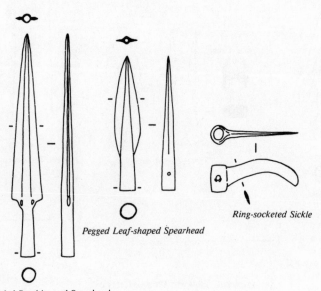

Pegged Leaf-shaped Spearhead

Ring-socketed Sickle

Triangular-bladed Basal-looped Spearhead

0   10cm

Penard Phase Metalwork

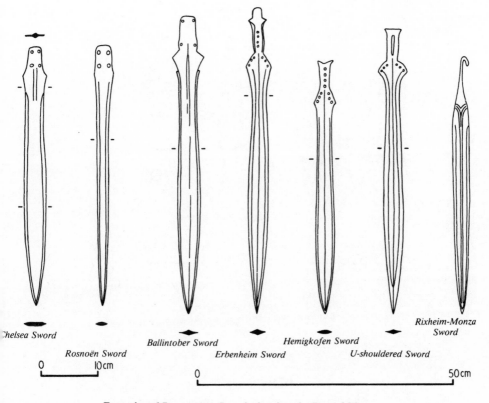

Chelsea Sword

Rosnoën Sword

Ballintober Sword

Erbenheim Sword

Hemigkofen Sword

U-shouldered Sword

Rixheim-Monza Sword

0   10cm

0   50cm

Examples of Bronze Age Swords dated to the Penard Phase

Wilburton-Wallington and Poldar Phases
From the tenth century BC a heavily leaded bronze alloy began to be used widely in southern Britain. This is termed the **Wilburton phase** (named after *Wilburton*, Cambridgeshire). Pegged types of spearheads became predominant, including **lunate-opening spearheads** and **stepped-blade spearheads**. Pointed ferrules gave way to **tubular ferrules. Wilburton leaf-shaped swords (V-shouldered swords)** developed, characterised by a straight terminal, a slotted tang, and two or four holes or slots in the V-shaped shoulders. There are also **long tongue-shaped chapes (tongue chapes), late palstaves**, socketed axes, notably **indented axes**, and horse equipment. The **Wallington tradition** (named after *Wallington*, Northumberland) is contemporary with the Wilburton phase in northern England; unadulterated tin-

bronze continued to be used, and also old metalwork forms such as dirks, rapiers, transitional palstaves and various types of spearhead. **Protected looped spearheads** and **single looped spearheads** developed, as well as various types of socketed axe. A few **flesh forks (flesh goads)** may belong to this phase. In Scotland this period is termed the **Poldar phase** (named after *Poldar Moss*, Central).

Ewart Park Phase
The **Ewart Park phase** — named after *Ewart Park*, Northumberland — **(Post Wilburton phase)** dates from the ninth century BC and is characterised by the general use of lead-alloyed metal, a wider range of products, and a proliferation of hoards — mainly founders' hoards of scrap metal or 'ritual' deposits. Horse and

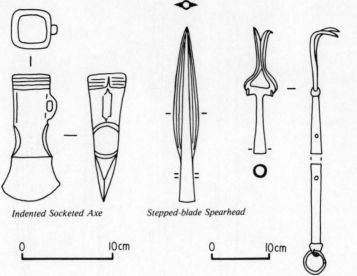

Indented Socketed Axe

Stepped-blade Spearhead

0   10cm

0   10cm

Flesh Fork (head and butt in
two parts)

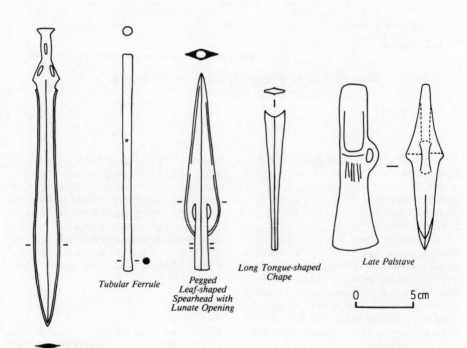

Tubular Ferrule

Pegged
Leaf-shaped
Spearhead with
Lunate Opening

Long Tongue-shaped
Chape

Late Palstave

0   5 cm

Wilburton Leaf-shaped Sword

0   10cm

Wilburton-Wallington Metalwork

wheeled vehicle equipment is found. The importance of the spear appears to decline, except in the Broadward complex. There are many regional differences, but some tools and weapons are common to most traditions, such as the **Ewart Park sword** which has two or three holes (rarely slots) in the hilt. Regional traditions include the **carp's tongue complex (carp's tongue sword complex, Bexley Heath tradition** — named after *Bexley Heath*, Greater London) which is seen in south-eastern England and is characterised by hoards of scrap metal, including **carp's tongue swords, bag-shaped chapes, triangular perforated knives, hog's back knives** and **'bugle-shaped objects'** of unknown use. There are also socketed axes, particularly the **south-eastern type** and **end-winged axes**, chisels, gouges and punches, pegged leaf-shaped spearheads, and many bronze objects of unknown use.

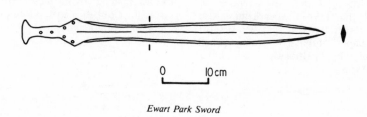

Ewart Park Sword

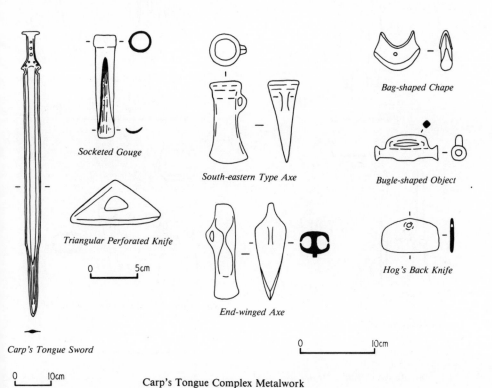

Socketed Gouge

Triangular Perforated Knife

South-eastern Type Axe

End-winged Axe

Bag-shaped Chape

Bugle-shaped Object

Hog's Back Knife

Carp's Tongue Sword

Carp's Tongue Complex Metalwork

61

The **Llantwit-Stogursey industry (Llant-wit-Stogursey group)** — named after *Llantwit Major*, South Glamorgan, and *Stogursey*, Somerset — is seen mainly in South Wales and the Bristol Channel area, and is characterised by hoards of tools, mainly three-ribbed **'South Welsh' socketed axes**. Also found are faceted socketed axes, socketed gouges, tanged chisels, late palstaves, and some weaponry.

The **Broadward complex (Broadward group, Broadward tradition)** is seen mainly in the Welsh Marches, the Thames Valley and parts of central-southern England. It is characterised by hoards of weapons, in particular the **barbed spearhead**. Also found are other types of spearhead, short tongue chapes, tubular ferrules, small tanged chisels, palstaves, and other occasional tools.

The **Heathery Burn tradition** (named after *Heathery Burn Cave*, Durham) is seen in northern England and is characterised by several types of socketed axe, in particular three-ribbed and plain styles of the **'Yorkshire' axe**. There are also late palstaves, socketed gouges and chisels, tanged chisels, knives with ribbed tangs, swords, plain rings, pegged spearheads, buckets, tongs, and horse and wheeled vehicle bronzes such as nave bands, strap distributors and phalerae.

In Scotland this phase is represented by the **Duddingston, Covesea** and **Ballimore Phases** (named after *Duddingston Loch*, Lothian, *Covesea Cave*, Grampian, and *Ballimore*, Strathclyde).

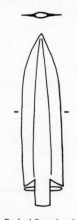

Barbed Spearhead

0   10 cm

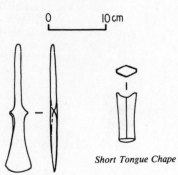

Short Tongue Chape

Tanged and Lugged Chisel

0   10 cm

Broadward Complex Metalwork

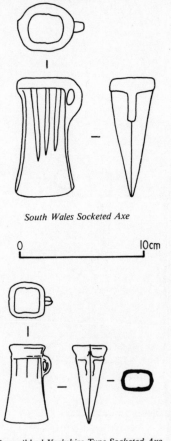

South Wales Socketed Axe

0   10 cm

Three-ribbed Yorkshire Type Socketed Axe

0   10 cm

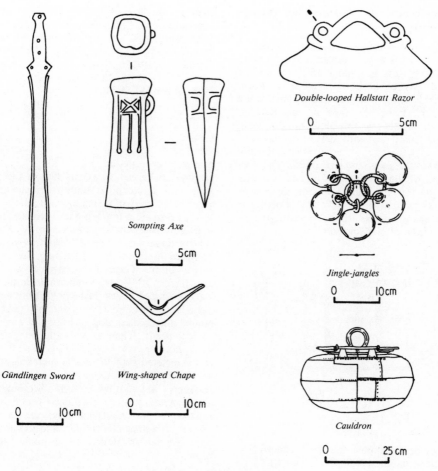

Double-looped Hallstatt Razor

0   5cm

Sompting Axe

0   5cm

Jingle-jangles

0   10cm

Gündlingen Sword   Wing-shaped Chape

0   10 cm   0   10cm

Cauldron

0   25 cm

Hallstatt C Metalwork

Hallstatt C Phase

From c700 BC **Hallstatt C** metalwork is found in Britain brought from the Continent, possibly by raiders, immigrants, gift exchange, itinerant smiths, or as trade goods or imports. This is termed the **Llyn Fawr phase**, named after *Llyn Fawr*, Mid Glamorgan. Most finds are swords, and are not usually found in association with other artifacts since they are often isolated finds from rivers. Ewart Park metalworking traditions were rapidly abandoned. Several Hallstatt C **Gündlingen swords** (named after *Gündlingen*, West Germany) are known. They have a pommel tang, broad and shallow butt, and long, narrow blade. **Thames type swords** developed during this phase. These are Ewart Park swords influenced by Gündlingen swords. Other bronzework from this period includes **winged chapes, cauldrons, razors** (mainly single or double-looped, although there are some twin-bladed crescentic ones), **horse harness mounts** including **phalerae** and **jingle-jangles (jangle-plates)** which are decorative horse mounts, and **swan's neck sunflower pins. Massive socketed axes (Sompting axes** — named after *Sompting*, Sussex) developed; they had a pronounced collar and were usually decorated with ribs and pellets. Iron begins to be used in this period, and soon replaced bronze as the main material for tools and weapons (see Iron Age metalwork).

Manufacture of Copper and Bronze Artifacts

Plano-convex circular **ingots (cakes)** of bronze are known. Copper flat axes were probably cast in simple open moulds of fired clay or in hollows in sand. From *c*2000 BC they were also cast in open stone moulds. From the time of the Arreton Down metalwork two-piece moulds were being used, probably mainly of clay and also of soft stone. Some bronze moulds are known for axes and palstaves. The two pieces of the mould were aligned correctly by the use of various location devices or markings and tied together. Cores for producing sockets **(hollow casting)** may have been of clay and sand.

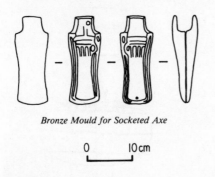

Bronze Mould for Socketed Axe

0   10 cm

Hafting

Many of the implements and weapons had wooden handles or hafts. These could be tied by thongs or cords to looped implements. Rivets and pegs were also used to secure handles.

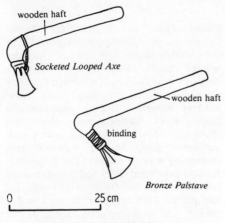

Socketed Looped Axe

Bronze Palstave

0   25 cm

Possible Methods of Hafting a Palstave and Socketed Axe

Reading for Metalwork: Burgess, C. B. 1968a; Burgess, C. B. 1968b; Burgess, C. B. 1974; Burgess, C. B. 1980; Burgess, C. B. and Coombs, D. 1979; Evans, J. 1881; Gerloff, S. 1975; Megaw, J. V. S. and Simpson, D. D. A. 1979; Rowlands, M. J. 1976; Smith, M. A. 1959.

Gold

In the Beaker period gold basket-shaped **earrings** are known, as well as **discs** of sheet gold, and gold-capped **studs** for securing stone bracers. Also belonging to the Earlier Bronze Age are a few **lunulae** — collars of sheet gold found mainly in Ireland. A gold **cape** or **tippet** was found at *Mold*, Clwyd; it was once thought to have been an ornament for a pony. There is sheet-gold work associated with Wessex I material including lozenge-shaped plates, belt-hooks, pommel mounts, gold-bound amber pendants, gold-bound amber discs and gold-bound shale conical beads. There is virtually no gold work apart from a single sheet-gold ribbed cup associated with Wessex II material. In the Later Bronze Age a few gold **dress fasteners** are known from Scotland, although many more have been found in Ireland. A few gold **bar torcs** are also known, as well as penannular bracelets and rings similar in design to examples in bronze.

Reading for Gold: Burgess, C. B. 1980; Eogan, G. 1967; Megaw, J. V. S. and Simpson, D. D. A. 1979; Taylor, J. J. 1970.

Flint and Stone

Flint continued to be used in the Bronze Age for various tools, and there is evidence that flint mines also continued from the Neolithic into the Earlier Bronze Age. Flint was gradually superseded by bronze, although it was still utilized in the Later Bronze Age. The main flint tools include **plano-convex knives (slug knives)**, associated particularly with Yorkshire vases. They were typically leaf-shaped, elongated, and retouched over the whole of the convex surface. Mainly associated with the Beaker culture are flint daggers, arrowheads and scrapers. The **daggers (knife-**

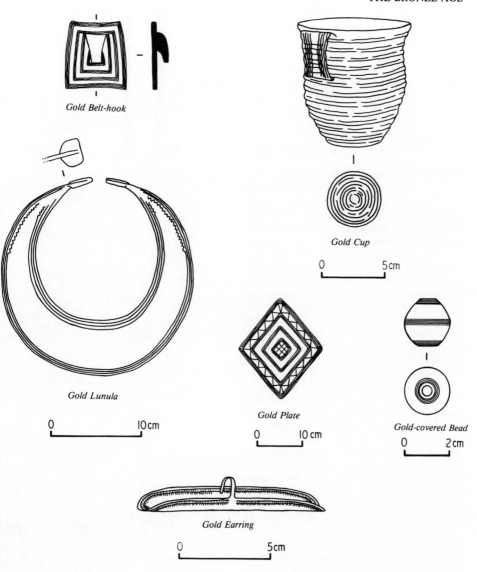

Gold Belt-hook

Gold Cup

0   5 cm

Gold Lunula

0   10 cm

Gold Plate

0   10 cm

Gold-covered Bead

0   2 cm

Gold Earring

0   5 cm

daggers) are finely flaked and sometimes have notches to hold bindings in place. The arrowheads are **barbed and tanged arrowheads**; the tangs usually project beyond the barbs, although some are squared off **(Breton type arrowheads, Breton arrowheads)**.

Stone artifacts include a few perforated **maceheads** continuing from the Later Neolithic. There are also perforated **axehammers** and perforated **battle axes** **(shafthole axes)** which have late Beaker to Wessex II associations. Battle axes have been subdivided into **Woodhenge, Calais Wold, Wilsford, Herd Howe, Codford St Peter, Loose Howe, Scotsburn, Snowshill** and **Crichie groups**. A more simple classification of **Early, Intermediate** and **Developed groups** is also used. Axe-hammers are larger (usually more than 15cm long) and coarser than battle axes. As with Neolithic stone axes, evidence for the trading of battle axes and axe-hammers is provided by petrological examination to determine the original source of the stone.

There are also **saddle querns** including fragments of Niedermendig lava from Germany which may have been part of querns. So-called **'sponge-finger stones' (spatulae)** of soft rock have been found; they are elongated with rounded ends and have a ground and polished surface. Similar Earlier Bronze Age tools in bone and antler have been interpreted as either pottery-working tools, leather-working tools, net rules, or part of an archer's equipment; they are often found in male graves associated with either leather-working tools or archers' equipment. Stone **bracers (wrist-guards)** are also known from Beaker contexts. They can be waisted with two perforations at each end; rectangular and flat with one, two or three perforations at each end; or flat and narrow with rounded ends and one perforation at each end. They are thought to have been worn on the wrist as a protection from the recoil of a bowstring in archery, and would have been attached to an organic lining such as leather. Stone **pot boilers** continued to be used in cooking. There are also some **whetstones**; a few from Wessex II contexts are perforated **(whetstone pendants)** and may have been worn on a belt as status symbols or as amulets. From a Wessex I grave came a stone **macehead**. It is egg-shaped and smoothly polished and probably had a plain wooden handle, although it is often incorrectly reconstructed with the dentated bone mounts which accompanied it. Carved stone balls are also known. **Stone moulds** for the manufacture of bronze tools and weapons are known, including simple **'open' stone moulds (single-valve stone moulds)** and **two-piece moulds (bivalve moulds)**.

Reading for Flint and Stone: Burgess, C. B. 1980; Megaw, J. V. S. and Simpson, D. D. A. 1979; Roe, F. E. S. 1966; Roe, F. E. S. 1979.

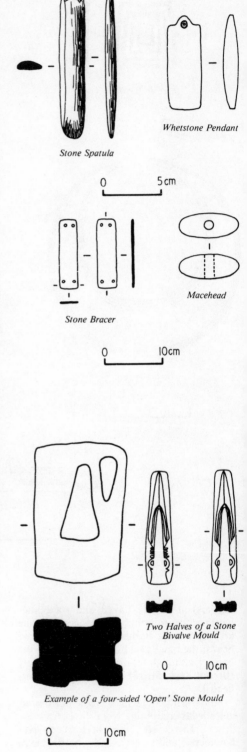

Whetstone Pendant

Stone Spatula

0   5 cm

Macehead

Stone Bracer

0   10 cm

Two Halves of a Stone Bivalve Mould

0   10 cm

Example of a four-sided 'Open' Stone Mould

0   10 cm

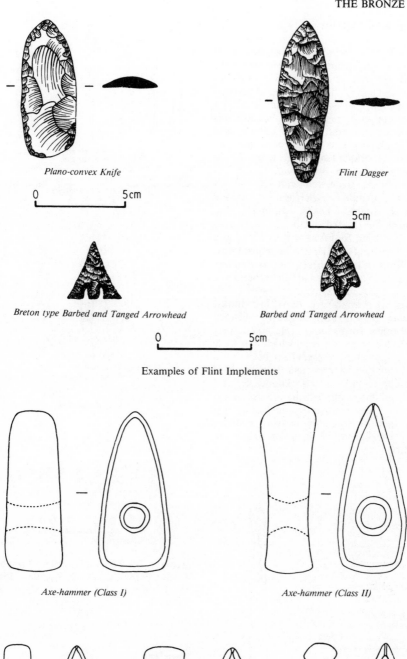

Plano-convex Knife

Flint Dagger

0   5cm

0   5cm

Breton type Barbed and Tanged Arrowhead

Barbed and Tanged Arrowhead

0   5cm

Examples of Flint Implements

Axe-hammer (Class I)

Axe-hammer (Class II)

Early Battle Axe

Intermediate Battle Axe

Developed Battle Axe

0   10cm

67

Bone and Antler

In the Beaker period bone **belt-rings (belt fasteners, ring pendants, pulley rings)** are known as well as **spatulae** of bone and antler which may have been used as pottery-working tools, for softening and burnishing leather, or in archery. Small bone **combs** pointed at one end are also known, and were probably used in the decoration of pottery. A unique **ladle** of horn was found inside a beaker at *Broomend*, Grampian. Bone objects associated with the Wessex culture include V-perforated **conical buttons, points, beads, pommels** and **plaques.** Perforated teeth for necklaces have also been found as well as antler and bone **maceheads,** antler and bone **pendants,** and horn **hilts. Dentated bone mounts** belonging to a wooden staff were found in a Wessex I burial. Associated mainly with Wessex II burials are bone **belt-hooks, tweezers, pins** (mainly simple ring-headed ones; other forms are rare), and a perforated leg bone of a swan which may have been a flute. Bone **daggers** have been found mainly in the Thames near London, and bone dagger hilts are also known. Several bone and antler implements are associated with the Later Bronze Age including long bone **spatulae** (possibly weaving swords), antler **cheekpieces,** and antler **toggles** or **handles.**

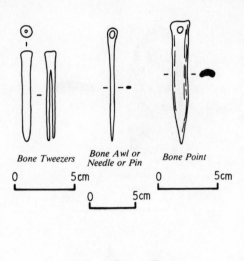

Bone Tweezers   Bone Awl or Needle or Pin   Bone Point

0   5cm   0   5cm

0   5cm

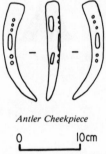

Antler Cheekpiece

0   10cm

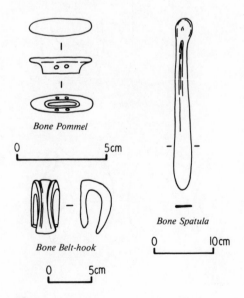

Bone Pommel

0   5cm

Bone Belt-hook

0   5cm

Bone Spatula

0   10cm

Dentated Bone Mounts

0   10cm

Reading for Bone and Antler: Annable, F. K. and Simpson, D. D. A. 1964; Britnell, W. J. 1976; Gerloff, S. 1975; Hardaker, R. 1974.

Amber

Amber objects are mainly found in association with the Wessex culture and include variously shaped **beads** and **spacer beads (spacer plates), cups, dagger pommels, rings, pendants, conical buttons** with V-perforations, and gold-bound amber **discs** and **pendants.**

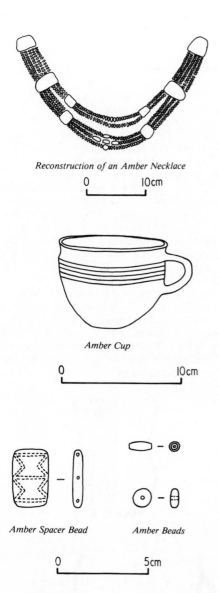

Reconstruction of an Amber Necklace

0   10cm

Amber Cup

0   10cm

Amber Spacer Bead   *Amber Beads*

0   5cm

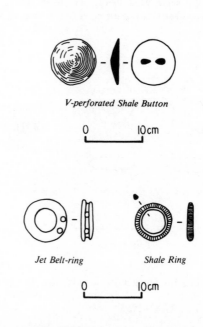

V-perforated Shale Button

0   10cm

Jet Belt-ring   *Shale Ring*

0   10cm

rings. A **bowl**, possibly of shale inlaid with gold in the form of a boat (**boat-bowl**), is known from Wales. A **macehead** of polished shale or jet inlaid with gold studs was found with a Wessex I burial. **Armlets (bracelets)** of triangular or D-section are known from Later Bronze Age settlements.

Jet can be difficult to distinguish from shale. It seems to have been used mainly in the Earlier Bronze Age for beads, spacer beads, and belt-rings.

Reading for Shale and Jet: Annable, F. K. and Simpson, D. D. A. 1964; Burgess, C. B. 1980.

Clay

Fired clay was used for pottery, clay slabs, briquetage, moulds, loomweights and spindle whorls. **Clay slabs (perforated clay plaques)** are flat rectangular plaques of fired clay with a thickened edge and irregular internal perforations. Their function is uncertain, but may have had something to do with cooking.

Reading for Clay: Burgess, C. B. 1980; Megaw, J. V. S. and Simpson, D. D. A. 1979.

Reading for Amber: Annable, F. K. and Simpson, D. D. A. 1964; Gerloff, S. 1975.

Shale and Jet

Shale objects are known from various parts of Britain, and are mainly dated to the Earlier Bronze Age. They include **beads** of various shapes including gold-covered beads and **spacer beads**, V-perforated **conical buttons**, **belt-rings**, **pendants** and

Faience Beads

Faience is a sintered 'glass' and not a proper glass. Beads made of faience date to the Earlier Bronze Age in Britain. They are found mainly in Scotland and Wessex, and are associated with the Wessex culture. They used to be interpreted as evidence of trade with the Mycenean culture of the Aegean, but recent spectrographic analysis of these beads has led to the suggestion that the British beads were made locally. The main forms of faience bead found in Britain are the **segmented bead, star bead (star-shaped bead)** and **quoit bead (quoit-shaped bead)**.

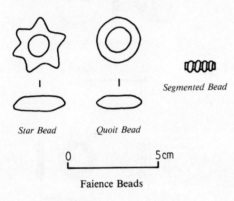

Star Bead   Quoit Bead

Segmented Bead

0   5 cm

Faience Beads

Reading for Faience Beads: Newton, R. G. and Renfrew, C. 1970; Stone, J. F. S. and Thomas, L. C. 1956.

Glass Beads

There is a little evidence that true glass beads (as opposed to faience) were being imported into Britain as early as the second millennium BC. These beads come mainly from badly documented excavations which gave no illustrations or detailed descriptions, and most of the beads have since been lost. They seem to have been made mainly of undecorated blue or greenish-blue glass in a simple shape. Most of these beads were found in funerary deposits and some appear to have a connection with the Wessex culture.

Reading for Glass Beads: Guido, C. M. 1978.

Pottery

Beakers (drinking cups) first appear in the Neolithic but are mainly dated to the beginning of the Bronze Age. They appear to be later than Neolithic grooved ware, and earlier than food vessels but overlap considerably with both. Beakers are found over much of western Europe. Abercromby divided the British beakers into **A, B** and **C beakers**, later classified as **long-necked, bell** and **short-necked beakers**, but this classification has been largely superseded. Through the variations in decoration and form, D. L. Clarke suggested seven major waves of immigration from the Continent, although Lanting and Van der Waals have since seen the development of British beakers from European beakers with one major intrusion of **All Over Cord beakers (AOC beakers)**. Beakers are fine, well-fired drinking vessels covered with zoned geometric ornament, and are generally found in burials. Their incised decoration is sometimes filled with white paste. There are also some handled mugs.

Long-necked Beaker

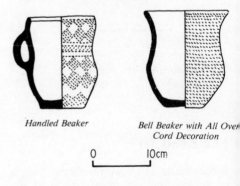

Handled Beaker

Bell Beaker with All Over Cord Decoration

0   10 cm

Food vessels are generally contemporary with and later in date than beakers. **Yorkshire vase food vessels (Yorkshire vases)** are most common and occur mainly in eastern England associated with inhumation burials; they are rare in southern England. The pottery is coarse and thick with flat bases, decoration (particularly on the shoulder and rim), and classically with perforated lugs. **Irish bowl food vessels** are bowl-shaped and are found mainly in Ireland, but a few do occur in Scotland. They are usually associated with burials, both inhumations and cremations.

Yorkshire Vase Food Vessel

0   5cm

During the Earlier Bronze Age cremation became the predominant burial rite, and **cinerary urns** became an important feature in containing the burials. Urns are generally parallel to and later in date than food vessels. The pottery is heavy and coarse with a variable cover of decoration. There are various forms of urn: **collared urns (overhanging-rim urns, crowned urns)** are most common, **tripartite urns** have an overhanging rim separated from the body by a concave neck, **cordoned urns** are tall vessels with applied cordon decoration found mainly in Scotland, **biconical urns** occasionally have cordon decoration and are found mainly in south-east Britain, **bucket urns** are often undecorated, and **encrusted urns** have applied decoration, similar to some **enlarged food vessels**. Encrusted urns and enlarged food vessels are often described as **food vessel urns**.

Miniature cups (pygmy cups, incense cups) are usually associated with cremations in urns. They are regarded as accessory

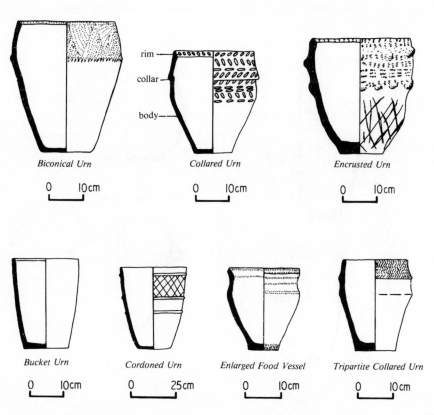

Biconical Urn

0   10cm

rim ——
collar ——
body ——

Collared Urn

0   10cm

Encrusted Urn

0   10cm

Bucket Urn

0   10cm

Cordoned Urn

0   25cm

Enlarged Food Vessel

0   10cm

Tripartite Collared Urn

0   10cm

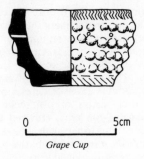

Grape Cup

Aldbourne Cup

vessels and probably had a ritual function. They were often perforated with one or more small holes. There are two well-defined types of miniature cup: **grape cups** which were small cups decorated all over with small balls of applied clay, and **Aldbourne cups** which are later in date and have a wide mouth and a straight body, decorated with geometric incised and pointillé decoration.

Deverel-Rimbury pottery is found mainly in south-east Britain in cremation burials and settlement sites dating from *c*1400 BC. There are three main types of vessel: **bucket urns, barrel urns** and **globular urns. Cornish urns** are found in Cornwall and are large heavily decorated urns, often with strap handles (ribbon handles).

The tradition of cremation appears to cease by the Later Bronze Age and funerary vessels are no longer seen. From the eleventh century BC **Post Deverel-Rimbury tradition pottery** is seen, having a wider range of forms than Deverel-Rimbury pottery. The pottery consists of thin-walled plain jars and bowls, together with much coarse ware. From the eighth century BC increased decoration is seen.

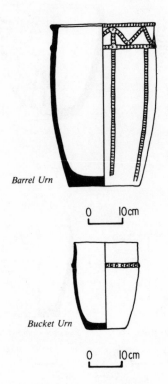

Barrel Urn

Bucket Urn

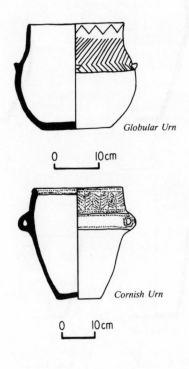

Globular Urn

Cornish Urn

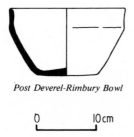

Post Deverel-Rimbury Bowl

0   10cm

Reading for Pottery: Abercromby, J. 1912; Annable, F. K. and Simpson, D. D. A. 1964; Barrett, J. 1976; Barrett, J. 1979; Burgess, C. B. 1980; Clarke, D. L. 1970; Gibson, A. M. 1978; Lanting, J. N. and Van der Waals, J. D. 1972; Longworth, I. H. 1961; Megaw, J. V. S. and Simpson, D. D. A. 1979; Simpson, D. D. A. 1968.

Wood

Wood was widely used for a variety of objects. The use of ash, oak, hazel, pine, beech, elm, willow and apple is recorded from various sites and finds. Objects of wood include dagger sheaths, dagger handles, sword sheaths, rapier sheaths, spearshafts, a possible club, bows, bowls, boxes, handles and hafts for various implements, planks, stave-built tubs, coffins (see burial), stakes and ladders. Wood was also used in the construction of huts (eg for the posts and wattle) and for building boats and trackways. **Trackways** include ones made of hurdles of interwoven brushwood, or brushwood held in place by long stakes and piles, and of longitudinal planks and branches with some transverse pieces of wood and brush. **Boats** include **logboats** made from hollowed-out tree-trunks (**dugout canoes**): McGrail advocates the term 'logboat' as a replacement for the term 'dugout canoe' since dugout vessels are not always canoes. There are also plank-built boats.

Reading for Wood: Coles, J. M. et al 1978; Green, H. S. 1978; McGrail, S. 1978.

Textiles and Leather

There is evidence for textiles from finds of weaving implements including cylindrical (bun-shaped) and pyramidal **loomweights** of baked clay; pyramidal ones are later in date. There are also a few **spindle whorls** of baked clay, chalk, and stone, and a possible bone weaving comb from *Shearplace Hill*, Dorset. Postholes have been found associated with loomweights at *Itford Hill*, Sussex, and may originally have held the posts of an upright loom. Remains of textiles have been recorded from inhumation and cremation burials including wool and possibly linen, and there is also some evidence for woven grasses and basketwork. Flax seeds have been found, which may indicate the use of linen. Textile fragments sometimes survive in the corroded surface of metalwork.

Traces of leather scabbards occasionally survive adhering to dagger blades. Possible leatherworking tools have been found, including bronze awls, and burnishers of bone and stone.

Reading for Textiles and Leather: Burgess, C. B. 1980; Henshall, A. S. 1950; Megaw, J. V. S. and Simpson, D. D. A. 1979.

General Reading for the Bronze Age: Burgess, C. B. 1980; Megaw, J. V. S. and Simpson, D. D. A. 1979.

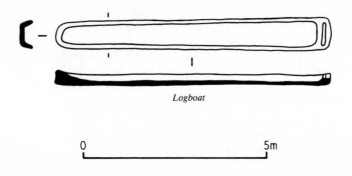

Logboat

0   5m

Chapter 5

The Iron Age

Introduction

The Iron Age period in Britain dates from c700 BC and is characterised by the use of iron, overlapping at first with Bronze Age traditions. Iron tools and weapons are first seen in the Hallstatt C culture, which has been placed in the Bronze Age chapter, since most of the material is a continuation of Bronze Age traditions, although Hallstatt C is generally regarded as the beginning of the Iron Age. In 1931 C. F. C. Hawkes divided the Iron Age into **Iron Age A, B** and **C**; Iron Age A represented Hallstatt immigrants, and B and C early and late La Tène immigrants. Iron Age B was considered to be the result particularly of **Marnian invasions**. Hallstatt is named after the site *Hallstatt* in Austria, La Tène after the site in Switzerland, and Marnian after the Marne district in France. This system has since been continually modified and invasion theories largely discounted. The Iron Age is now generally seen as consisting of indigenous regional groups, influenced by contact with the Hallstatt and La Tène cultures of the Continent, with some immigration, such as the Arras culture (of immigrants from France) in Humberside, and the Belgic immigration into southern England from the mid second century BC. The Iron Age is conventionally considered to end with the Roman invasion in AD 43, although Iron Age traditions persisted long after this date, particularly in Scotland.

Reading: Cunliffe, B. 1978.

Settlement Sites

Unenclosed Settlements

There are many unenclosed settlements consisting of huts, pits and postholes. Circular huts **(round-houses)** are found in many parts of Britain from the Early Iron Age. They probably had wattle and daub walls, thatched conical roofs (usually turfed roofs in northern Britain), porches and drainage gulleys. All that usually survives of these structures are rings of postholes or stakeholes **(post-ring** or **post-circle)** which carried upright timbers, or circular gulleys **(ring-groove)** in which upright timbers could be placed with stones packed around them. Timbers could also be placed on stone pads. A **single-ring round-house (simple ring-post house)** had a wattle and daub wall (or drystone wall where suitable stone was available) which supported the roof; a **stake-wall round-house** had this outer wall composed partly of stakes. Some single-ring round-houses also had a central support for the roof. A **double-ring round-house** had an outer wall of wattle and daub, and an inner circle of upright timbers which supported the roof. A few rectangular

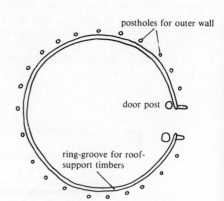

Plan of a Double-ring Round-house

buildings are also known. Internal features found in huts consist of drainage gulleys, hearths, and occasionally ovens. Settings of two, four, five and six postholes also occur. A two-posthole structure may represent a drying rack. The four, five and six-posthole structures are most likely to have been raised granaries. Other possibilities are small shrines, or platforms for the exposure of the dead; some are close to hillfort ramparts and so may have been watch-towers.

Other unenclosed settlements were protected or fortified in some way:

Oppida (sing **oppidum**) were nucleated settlements occupied in the late Iron Age. They vary in size and type. Large areas were often demarcated by **dykes** (large banks and ditches). Oppida are characterised particularly by finds of coinage and much imported material. They may have been tribal centres.

Courtyard houses are known particularly in Cornwall. They had a central courtyard surrounded by rooms and a thick stone wall with a single entrance. They sometimes had **souterrains (fogous)** which are underground chambers and passages of stone. Courtyard houses were sometimes situated within rounds. They were occupied into the Roman period.

Caves were sometimes occupied in the Iron Age period.

Crannogs are found in southern Scotland. They consisted of a circular timber-framed hut about 16m in diameter built on a natural or artificial island (the latter created from ballast, stakes, piles or brushwood) at the edge of a loch, joined to the mainland by a wooden causeway. They were occupied into the Roman, and sometimes to the Medieval, period. There were similar sites in Somerset on the edge of lakes, termed **lake villages** eg *Meare* and *Glastonbury*.

Blockhouses occur in the Shetland Isles and consisted of a wide section of wall with an entrance passage and lateral chambers. They were often associated with timber-framed buildings. They often preceded brochs; stone-built huts such as at *Jarlshof*, Shetland, also preceded some brochs.

Brochs are found mainly in northern Scotland and the Western and Northern Isles (particularly the Orkneys and Shetlands), singly or in groups. A broch was a circular tower about 10m in internal diameter, with a drystone wall about 5m thick and up to 10m high. The walls had a slight batter on the outer face. From the first-floor level the wall was usually in two sections about 1m apart, tied together by rows of stone lintels forming superimposed galleries. These were reached by stone staircases. There may have been an upper rampart walk. The ground-floor wall often

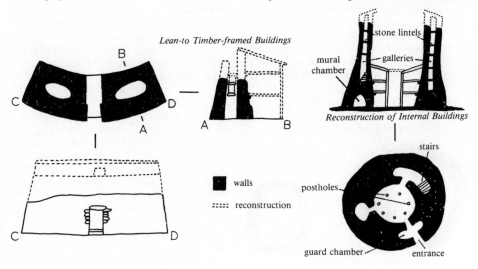

Lean-to Timber-framed Buildings

stone lintels

mural chamber

galleries

Reconstruction of Internal Buildings

walls

reconstruction

stairs

postholes

guard chamber

entrance

Plan, Elevation and Section of a Blockhouse

Section and Plan of a Broch

0   10m

0   5m

had galleries and chambers with corbelled roofs. There was usually one entrance to the broch through a narrow passage, often with guard chambers. Excavations have revealed traces of timber-framed lean-to huts in the interior. Ledges on the inner wall may have supported an upper floor or gallery. Brochs may have had wooden roofs. They seem to have been built from the second century BC and to have been occupied into the Roman period.

Wheelhouses are also found in northern and north-west Scotland. They were circular, stone-built huts about 9m in diameter, with the interior divided by radial stone piers projecting from the wall, leaving the centre clear for a hearth. In **aisled wheelhouses (round-houses)** the piers are free-standing but connected to the wall by stone lintels. The piers may have supported wooden or turf roofs.

Duns are distributed from south-west Scotland to the Inner Hebrides and northern Scottish mainland. They were fortified homesteads and were circular or oval in plan with drystone walls 3m to 6m thick. They may have been preceded by timber-laced forts. **Galleried duns** had walls about 4m thick with an entrance, mural cells, galleries, and stairs, and were similar to brochs. They were about 3m high and up to 20m in internal diameter. There were timber structures in the interior. **Galleried promontory duns** had a wall built across the neck of an inland or coastal promontory, the steep sides of which were defended by smaller walls. Larger duns resemble small hillforts, with a thick stone wall enclosing a large area. Some have vitrified timber-laced walls. They were occupied from the late Iron Age to the Roman period.

Small forts, duns and brochs in Scotland have been termed the **castle complex**.

Plan of an Aisled Wheelhouse

0   10m

Plan of a Dun

0   10m

Enclosed Settlements (Enclosures)

There were also many enclosed settlements in the Iron Age in Britain, consisting of one or more huts surrounded by one or more banks and ditches, and occupied over a long period, eg *Little Woodbury*, Wiltshire.

Scooped enclosures are groups of huts terraced into the hillside and enclosed by a bank or wall; they are found in northern Britain.

Rounds occur widely in Cornwall and Devon and consist of a bank and ditch surrounding an area rarely more than 3 acres in extent and containing timber structures.

Raths are similar to rounds and occur in south-west Wales. Both raths and rounds were occupied into the Roman period. The distinction between hillforts, raths, rounds and enclosed hut sites is not always clear.

Hillforts are fortified enclosures of varying size found in many parts of Britain. They were either **univallate**, having one rampart and ditch, or **multivallate**, having more than one rampart and ditch. The term hillfort can describe the following:

Contour fort A hillfort with defences following the contours of the crest of a hill.

Cross-defence A hillfort where a rampart cut off and defended a hill-top promontory.

Promontory fort This is either a cross-defence or a cliff-castle.

Cliff-castle A promontory projecting into the sea, the neck of which was defended by one or more series of banks and ditches. They occur mainly in south-west Britain.

Hillforts occur from the Later Bronze Age; their origins are not clear. They may have developed due to internal warfare and through pressure on land arising from a climatic change in the Earlier Bronze Age, or from small cattle enclosures; they could also have developed through increased contacts abroad where hillforts were also being constructed. They were probably used for a variety of purposes such as meeting places, refuges, cattle enclosures, permanent settlement sites and religious foci.

Hillfort settlement Few hillfort interiors have been excavated. Some of the excavated ones show signs of occupation, with religious shrines, huts and storage pits. It is not certain if in all cases this occupation was permanent, but in some cases it is likely to have been.

Ramparts Various stages can be seen in the development of ramparts. The earliest and simplest was a timber palisade **(palisade enclosure, stockaded enclosure)** — single or double rows of close-set timbers embedded in a foundation trench, without ditches or banks. **Vertically faced ramparts** consist of various forms, for example **box-style ramparts** had a front and rear row of vertical timbers, held together with horizontal timbers, enclosing a rubble and earth bank. Others had an earthen bank to the rear, while some were **timber-laced** (reinforced with a timber framework). Some ramparts had no rear timbers. Stone was sometimes used for the facing of the ramparts, often in conjunction with timber-lacing; this was particularly common in northern Britain. Some ramparts were completely of stone, particularly in Wales. Many timber-laced ramparts are **vitrified** (fused into a glassy mass) where the forts have been set on fire. Forts with this type of rampart are known as **vitrified forts**; they are common in Scotland. **Chevaux-de-frise** is found in forts of Scotland and Wales and consists of stones about 50cm to 1m in height, placed close together outside fort walls to make access more difficult. In southern Britain **dump ramparts (glacis ramparts)** replaced earlier fortifications in the third to first centuries BC. Ditches were

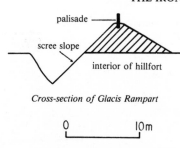

Cross-section of Glacis Rampart

0   10m

deeper, and ramparts built at a sloping angle, sometimes with scree slopes and a palisade on the top of the rampart. The **Fécamp** style of rampart has a large rampart of dump construction, and a very wide flat-bottomed ditch. It is found in northern France and the term has been used to describe some ramparts of hillforts of the first century AD in southern England. Except in the case of dump ramparts, there was usually a **berm** (flat space of ground) between the front of the rampart and the inner edge of the ditch. Sometimes there was a low bank on the outer edge of the ditch called a **counterscarp bank**.

There were one or sometimes two entrances in hillforts. The **single-portal entrance** is the earliest type and sometimes had ditches turned inwards. The **dual-portal entrance** had a double doorway, sometimes set further back in the rampart.

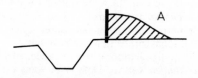

Cross-section of Rampart without Rear Timber Facing

Cross-section of Box-style Rampart

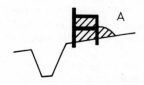

Cross-section of Box-style Rampart with additional Sloping Bank and Timber-lacing

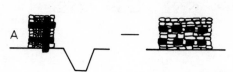

Cross-section and Front View of a Timber-laced Rampart

A   interior of hillfort

▮   timbers

0   10m

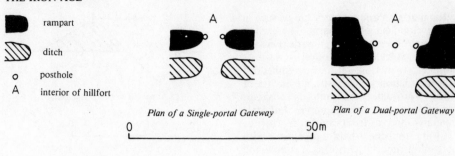

rampart

ditch

o   posthole

A   interior of hillfort

Plan of a Single-portal Gateway

Plan of a Dual-portal Gateway

0   50m

Plan of a Long Earthwork
added to the Entrance

Plan of Hornworks

Plan of an Inturned Corridor Entra

0   100m

0   50m

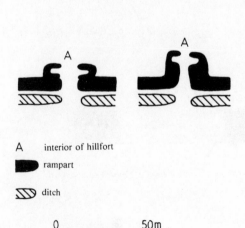

A   interior of hillfort

rampart

ditch

0   50m

Plans of Two Types of Guard Chamber

Inturned corridor entrances became common in forts of southern Britain: the ramparts were turned inwards to form a long corridor approach with the main gate set at the end. In some hillforts a pair of **hornworks** was added. These were extra ramparts containing an outer gate for additional protection. Occasionally there was multivallation at the entrance, such as at *Maiden Castle*, Dorset. A long earthwork, parallel to the entrance, was also added to some hillforts. In the hillforts of western Britain **timber guard chambers** developed and were often later replaced by **stone guard chambers**. These controlled traffic through the gateways. One type had the chambers built immediately behind the ramparts, and another type had the chambers built at the end of long corridor entrances.

Features such as ramparts and entrances vary widely in date according to individual sites. Many hillforts were abandoned before the Belgic invasions in southern Britain, and some were abandoned before the Roman invasion, while others seem to have been strengthened at this time and suffered attack by the Romans.

Reading for Settlement: Ellison, A. and Drewett, P. C. 1971; Feacham, R. 1977; Forde-Johnston, J. 1976b; Guido, C. M. 1974; Hamilton, J. R. C. 1962; Hamilton, J. R. C. 1966; Hamilton, J. R. C. 1968; Harbison, P. 1971; Harding, D. W. 1974; Jesson, M. and Hill, D. 1971; MacKie, E. 1965; Megaw, J. V. S. and Simpson, D. D. A. 1979.

Agricultural Economy

There is evidence for the depopulation of some upland areas in the Iron Age as soils became impoverished and bogs and moorlands spread. This may have been due to a climatic deterioration or to the activities of man, such as forest clearance, or a combination of both.

In the Lowland Zone there is evidence for both arable farming and pastoralism, but in the Highland Zone there seems to have been a greater emphasis on pastoralism. Evidence for **arable farming** comes from finds of reaping hooks and sickles, quernstones for grinding grain, pits (rare in the Highland Zone) and possible raised granaries for the storage of grain. Large, usually irregular, depressions up to 70m long have been found in the chalk in southern England and have been termed **working hollows.** They may have been quarries, or were possibly used for threshing. Charred grain and impressions of grain on pottery also sometimes survive. Emmer gave way to spelt as the most common type of wheat, and naked barley gave way to hulled barley, both of which can be sown in the winter. Celtic fields defined by lynchet banks survive in many parts of Britain. They were cultivated by plough or spade.

Animal bones provide the evidence for **pastoralism.** Cattle (*Bos longifrons* variety) were most common, and then sheep (a variety similar to Soay sheep). Other less common domesticated animals were the pig, horse and dog. Transhumance was probably practised in some areas. **Pastoral enclosures** continued in use from the Bronze Age. These were small rectangular ditched enclosures, and may have been used for the control of livestock, although some have produced evidence for occupation. In Wessex **'banjo' enclosures** date from the third century BC and consist of a circular ditched enclosure approached from a long entrance. Pastoral enclosures and banjo

Plan of a 'Banjo' Enclosure

enclosures are often associated with **ranch boundaries. Linear ranch boundaries** consisted of long stretches of bank and ditch which divided the land into well defined areas. Short lengths of bank and ditch (**cross ridge dykes** and **spur dykes**) ran across upland ridges and spurs in south-east England. Cross ridge dykes were once seen as **covered ways (sunken droveways)** connecting areas of grazing land either side of a ridge. The purpose of these ranch boundaries may have been political, but it seems more likely that they were land divisions within a settled community of mixed farming. In the Midlands there are **pit alignments** of closely spaced pits which may have been boundaries; the nature of these boundaries is not known.

Hunting and gathering only played a small part in the economy. Bones of deer and fish have been found in small quantities, as well as those of small mammals and birds. Shellfish were widely collected.

Reading for Agricultural Economy: Bradley, R. J. 1971; Cunliffe, B. 1978.

Storage Pits

By the fifth century BC grain storage in large underground pits had become common. These pits were once interpreted as pit-dwellings. Grain can be stored for several years in sealed, airtight pits. Pits were beehive, bottle, barrel, cylindrical, or bath-shaped, and were up to 2m deep. They could be lined with wickerwork or clay, although this was unusual in chalk areas, and they probably had lids of cob or compressed earth. Pits often had a secondary use as rubbish pits, or for the burial of skeletons. They may have had other uses, such as the storage of other foods, or as vats for tanning.

Reading for Storage Pits: Bowen, H. C. and Wood, P. D. 1967; Coles, J. M. 1973, 39–45; Reynolds, P. J. 1974.

Querns

Two types of quern were in use during the Iron Age. They were used for grinding corn into flour. The **saddle quern** was the earliest type and consisted of a lower stone **(saddle stone)** on which the corn was placed, and an upper stone **(rider)** which was pushed to-and-fro on top of this. In some areas saddle querns continued in use into the Roman period, but they were generally replaced by the **beehive rotary quern (beehive quern, rotary quern)**. These querns consisted of a thick lower stone with a socket for the spindle, and a hemispherical ('beehive-shaped') upper stone with a socket for a handle. These querns were heavier and thicker than Roman rotary querns (see Roman querns for method of working).

Reading for Querns: Curwen, E. C. 1937; Stanford, S. C. 1974, 185–7.

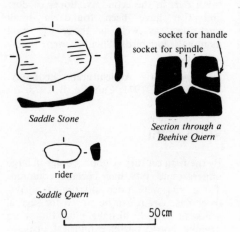

Saddle Stone

socket for handle
socket for spindle

Section through a Beehive Quern

rider

Saddle Quern

0   50 cm

Textiles

Wool was probably mainly sheared by knives, as shears only appear from the late Iron Age. Spinning and weaving are known from the following evidence. **Spindle whorls** of stone, baked clay, potsherds, shale, bone and lead have been found.

Spindle Whorl of Baked Clay

0   3 cm

Loomweights of clay, stone, chalk and cob are known. Loomweights of cylindrical form made from baked clay occur from the Bronze Age into the Iron Age and were then replaced by a triangular variety with perforations across the corners. Triangular bone **weaving tablets** have been found. Implements of bone which may have been **shuttles** are known, although they are often also described as gouges or pegs. **Weaving combs** are common; they were made from relatively flat pieces of bone, antler, or occasionally horn. Not many examples are known abroad. They were once thought to have been used for beating up the weft thread in weaving, but this is not now generally accepted, and they could have performed a variety of functions. Bone and bronze **needles** have been found. Nets were used, since a few **netting needles** are known, as well as lead and stone **net weights (net sinkers)** for weighting down fishing nets.

Impressions of textiles and basketry have been found on Iron Age pottery. All evidence for cloth in the Iron Age is of woollen cloth. Examples of basketwork and rush matting have been found.

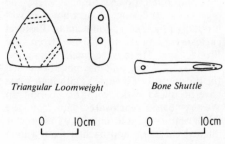

Triangular Loomweight

Bone Shuttle

0   10 cm   0   10 cm

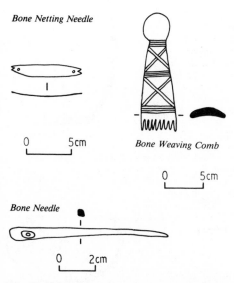

Bone Netting Needle

0 5cm

Bone Weaving Comb

0 5cm

Bone Needle

0 2cm

Reading for Textiles: Bulleid, A. and Gray, H. St. G. 1911; Cunliffe, B. 1978; Henshall, A. S. 1950; Hodder, I. and Hedges, J. W. 1977.

Pottery

Pottery was hand-made by the ring-coil method and was fired in bonfire kilns. Many regional stylistic zones (**style zones**), based particularly on pottery, are recognised by Cunliffe (Cunliffe, B. 1978). In northern Britain very little pottery is found, apart from the extreme north and west of Scotland.

In the seventh century BC finer wares than those of the Bronze Age are found, with finger-tip and cordon decoration. **Situlae-type pottery** is found, copying bronze vessels and consisting mainly of **bipartite situlae** and **bipartite bowls** found in south-east Britain. The pottery is basically similar

throughout south-east Britain, but there are many regional differences. A characteristic fine ware which occurs mainly in Wessex has a haematite slip, giving it a reddish colour. Bowls are most common, with horizontal rilling on the shoulders (**furrowed bowls**). Haematite slip was also added to jars with incised decoration; these had a wider distribution than the bowls. Style zones for this early Iron Age pottery include the **Ultimate Deverel-Rimbury culture** (south-east Britain) eighth to sixth centuries BC, **Early All Cannings Cross group** (Wessex) eighth to seventh centuries BC, **Later All Cannings Cross group** (Wessex) seventh to sixth centuries BC, **Kimmeridge-Caburn group** (south coast of Britain) eighth to sixth centuries BC, **West Harling-Staple Howe group** (eastern England) eighth to sixth centuries BC, and the **Ivinghoe-Sandy group** (Buckingham-shire-Bedfordshire) seventh to sixth centuries BC.

In the fifth and fourth centuries BC pottery styles changed, influenced by La Tène pottery from France, and particularly by the **vases carénés** (vessels with a sharp angular profile and, usually, a pedestal base) and **vases piriformes** (vessels with a high rounded shoulder and a pedestal base). Well made angular bowls and jars appear, often in a fine black burnished ware, sometimes with a pedestal base. This pottery is found mainly in south-east Britain. In Wessex haematite bowls with applied cordons and pedestal bases are found. Style zones for this period include **All Cannings Cross-Meon Hill group** (Wessex) fifth to third centuries BC, **Park Brow-Caesar's Camp group** (south-east Britain) fifth to third centuries BC, **Long Wittenham-Allen's Pit group** (Upper Thames) fifth to second centuries BC, **Chinnor-Wandlebury group** (Chilterns) fifth to third centuries BC,

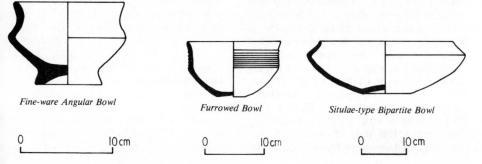

Fine-ware Angular Bowl

0 10cm

Furrowed Bowl

0 10cm

Situlae-type Bipartite Bowl

0 10cm

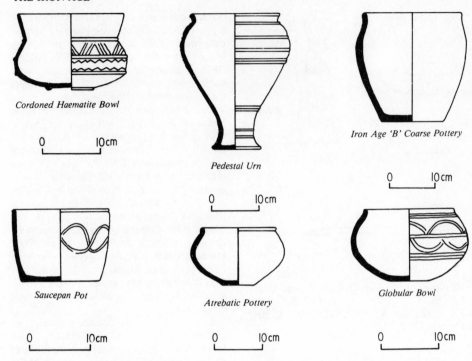

Cordoned Haematite Bowl

0   10cm

Pedestal Urn

0   10cm

Iron Age 'B' Coarse Pottery

0   10cm

Saucepan Pot

Atrebatic Pottery

Globular Bowl

0   10cm

0   10cm

0   10cm

Darmsden-Linton group (eastern England from the Wash to the Thames) fifth to third centuries BC, **Fengate-Cromer group** (Norfolk) fifth to third centuries BC, **Breedon-Ancaster group** (East Midlands) fourth to third centuries BC, and the **Arras group** (north Humberside) fourth to first centuries BC.

From the fourth century BC plain coarse pottery occurs **(Iron Age 'B' coarse ware)**. The pottery is not distinctive, and consists mainly of plain jars, bowls, barrel jars, and large globular jars.

From the third to first centuries BC pottery styles developed, with several regional groups. There were two main groups: firstly the **saucepan pot** is found from Sussex to the Cotswolds, and is a vertical-sided pot often with a beaded rim and rectilinear or curvilinear decoration. It is termed the **Southern British saucepan pot style (saucepan pot continuum)** and includes the style zones of **Caburn-Cissbury style** (Sussex), **St Catherine's Hill-Worthy Down style** (Hampshire), **Yarnbury-Highfield style** (Wiltshire), **Hawk's Hill-West Clandon style** (Surrey), **Southcote-Blewburton Hill style** (Berkshire Downs-Reading), **Glastonbury-Blaise Castle Hill**

style (Somerset), **Croft Ambrey-Bredon Hill style** (Herefordshire-Cotswolds), and the **Lydney-Llanmelin style** (south-east Wales coast). Secondly, in the Midlands and eastern Britain highly decorated jars and globular bowls occur from the second to first centuries BC **(open bowl continuum** and **jar continuum)**. The jar continuum of eastern England (once termed **South Eastern B** or **Southern Third B**) includes the following style zones: **Sleaford-Dragonby style** (between the rivers Welland and Humber), **Mucking-Crayford style** (Thames estuary), and the **Late Caburn-Saltdean style** (Sussex). The open bowl continuum of the Midlands includes the following style zones: **Stanton Harcourt-Cassington style** (Upper Thames), **Hunsbury-Draughton style** (Northamptonshire), **Chilterns and East Anglia**, and **Trent Valley**. Other groups — of the second to first centuries BC — include the following style zones: **Maiden Castle-Marnhull style** (Dorset), **Danes Graves-Staxton style** (Humberside), and the **Glastonbury style** (south-west England).

In the first century BC the potter's wheel was introduced, and at this date **Aylesford-Swarling pottery** (a form of Belgic pottery) is found in south-east Britain. This pottery is a high quality wheel-thrown ware, characterised by pedestal urns, cordoned and grooved bowls, and open-mouthed omphalos-based jars. In Wessex **Atrebatic pottery** is found, characterised by globular jars with narrow mouths, and jars with high shoulders. Some have a distinctive bead rim. In Dorset **Durotrigian pottery** is found, characterised by jars, tankards and cups.

From the first century BC fine tableware was imported from Gaul, including terra rubra and terra nigra wares, Arretine ware, samian, and Gallo-Belgic butt and girth beakers. Also imported to Britain was wine in amphorae.

Reading for Pottery: Cunliffe, B. 1978.

Pottery spoons or **scoops** are also known in the Iron Age.

Reading for Pottery Spoons: Brewster, T. C. M. 1963.

Use of Natural Resources

Salt

Salt extraction was carried out along the coasts in the Iron Age. Briquetage has been found, as well as the characteristic 'red hills'.

Leather

Leather was probably used for articles such as horse harness, footwear, scabbards, shields, vessels, bags and clothing.

Wood

Wood was widely used for huts, defences and a large variety of articles including wheels, axles, dugout canoes, rafts, stakes, planks, basketwork, hurdles, trackways, wattle, scabbards, ladders, chopping blocks, mallets, loom-frames, plough handles, ard beams, pestles, doors, draughtsmen, stoppers, statuettes, handles and hafts, pegs, tubs, bowls, ladles, iron or bronze-bound buckets, and tankards. Tankards had bronze handles and could be completely or partially covered in bronze sheet or bands. They were about 15cm high.

Ladle of Oak

0   10cm

Clay, Chalk and Stone

Clay was used for pottery, sling stones, spindle whorls, beads, loomweights, briquetage and ovens.

Chalk was used for loomweights, spindle whorls and figurines.

Stone was used for net weights, sling stones, querns, spindle whorls, loomweights, whetstones and crude lamps.

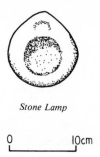

Stone Lamp

0   10cm

Bone and Antler

Bone and antler were used for antler picks or levers, dice, rings, weaving combs, needles, netting needles, rubbers (or polishers — highly polished pieces of bone probably used in burnishing), pendants, finger-rings, beads, awls, borers, hammers, cheekpieces, toggles, handles, weaving tablets, spindle whorls, ornamented plaques, notched pins, pins and potters' tools. There are also worked tibiae of sheep and goats which may have been shuttles, gouges or pegs, and various tools made from the metatarsi and metacarpi of sheep and goats; their exact purpose is not known. There are also worked scapulae, and various bones with perforations and notches. Perforated teeth have been found which may have been used as pendants or as necklaces.

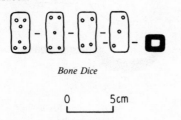

Bone Dice

0   5cm

Shale

Shale was worked in the area around *Purbeck*, Dorset, and was used mainly to make armlets. Shale vessels, spindle whorls and decorated discs are known. The lathe was used in shale working from the late Iron Age.

Jet, Amber and Coral

Jet was used for bracelets, beads, finger-rings and pendants.
Amber was used for inlay decoration, beads and finger-rings.
Coral was used for inlay decoration and beads.

Reading for Use of Natural Resources: Bulleid, A. and Gray, H. St. G. 1911; Bulleid, A. and Gray, H. St. G. 1917; Clarke, D. V. 1970; Coles, J. M. et al 1978; Corcoran, J. X. W. P. 1952; Cunliffe, B. 1978; Gray, H. St. G. and Cotton, M. A. 1966; Kennett, D. H. 1977; Wainwright, G. J. 1971; Wheeler, R. E. M. 1943.

Glass

There is evidence that during the first century BC opaque red glass was imported into Britain as a raw material and used to decorate bronzework; but there is little evidence for the importation of finished glass objects before the Roman invasion. The earliest known import of Roman glass-ware is a set of twenty-four glass gaming counters found in a Belgic burial at *Welwyn Garden City*, Hertfordshire, and dated to the first century BC (see Roman gaming counters). The only evidence for the importation of glass vessels before the Roman invasion comes from fragments of cast glass vessels found at a few sites in south-eastern England, eg *Hertford Heath*, Hertfordshire. Strabo (iv, 5, 3), referred to the importation of glass vessels to Britain from Gaul (about forty years before the Roman invasion) but the evidence hardly supports this statement. Iron Age glass beads, bangles, rings, and the heads of pins are also found.

Reading for Glass: Cunliffe, B. 1978.

Metals

Lead

Lead does not occur frequently among Iron Age remains except for a few articles such as spindle whorls and net sinkers.

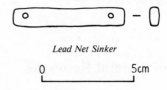

Lead Net Sinker

0   5cm

Silver and Gold

Until the first century BC the extraction of silver was limited, but from that date it was used for coinage, and in an alloy with gold to make **electrum** for torcs and arm-rings.

Gold was used for torcs, arm-rings and coinage.

Bronze and Tin

Bronze remained the main material for tools and weapons until the fifth century BC. It still continued in use for a variety of other objects such as bowls, cauldrons, sword and dagger scabbards, shields, brooches, pins, harness and chariot fittings, needles, tweezers, mirrors, awls, armlets, rivets, helmets, chains, studs, and various bindings. The cire perdue method of manufacture was often used. Crucibles used for bronze working have been found, as well as clay moulds, and bone tools for fashioning the wax models.

Tin was exported to the Continent, according to classical writers, and was also used in bronze working.

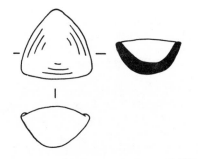

Clay Crucible for Bronze Working

0 ⊢————————⊣ 10cm

Iron

Iron was used for various tools and weapons from *c*600 BC, although it did not become a major material until about the fifth century BC and was never very common in northern Scotland. Bowl furnaces were used for smelting iron. **Currency bars** are a form of iron ingot and were widespread in southern Britain during the second and first centuries BC. There are four regional varieties: **sword-shaped, spit-shaped, ploughshare-shaped** and a few found in Cambridgeshire which are **bayleaf-shaped (spear-shaped, leaf-shaped)**. They probably represented a medium of exchange or barter.

Iron tools include **socketed reaping hooks** (sometimes referred to as sickles; the term sickle should be used where the blade lies either side of the handle like a question mark, and reaping hook where the blade lies to one side of the handle. A sickle was balanced and could be swung), **sickles, bill hooks, ploughshares, tongs, hammers, axe-hammers, axes** (socketed and looped, or socketed and unlooped; shafthole axes are rare and date to the late Iron Age), **adzes, awls, gouges, knives, saws** and **files**.

Iron fittings include **nails** (rare), **iron dogs** (clamps, cleats, clips, staples), **latchlifters, rings, studs** and **bucket bindings**. Iron was also used for items such as jewellery and personal ornaments, harness and chariot fittings, weapons, slave chains, cauldron chains, tripods for suspending cauldrons **(cauldron hangers)** and fire dogs. **Fire dogs** consisted of two uprights which supported a bar and were probably used mainly as spits for cooking over hearths. They often had animal-like heads (possibly heads of oxen). They are found mainly in south-east Britain from the first century BC.

Reading for Metals: Allen, D. F. 1967; Brailsford, J. 1975; Bulleid, A. and Gray, H. St. G. 1917; Manning, W. H. and Saunders, C. 1972; Piggott, S. 1971; Spratling, M. G. 1979.

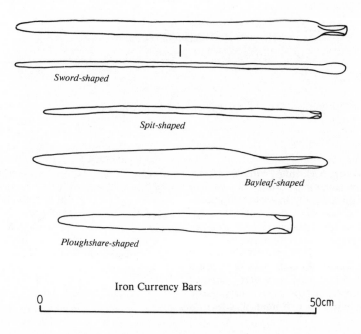

Sword-shaped

Spit-shaped

Bayleaf-shaped

Ploughshare-shaped

Iron Currency Bars

0 ⊢————————————————————⊣ 50cm

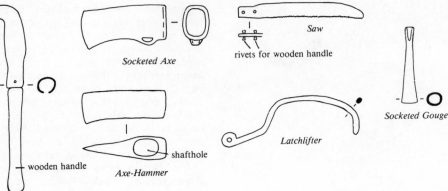

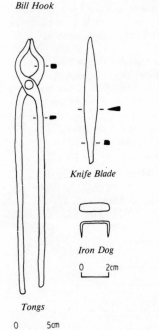

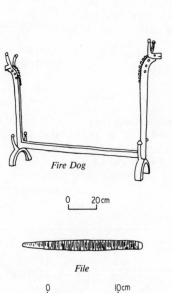

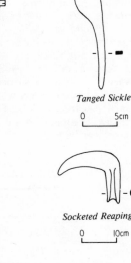

Examples of Iron Artifacts

Jewellery

Torcs (torques, neck-rings, collars) of gold, electrum or sometimes bronze are known, and are found mainly in eastern England. They are of twisted, rod, tubular, beaded, or collar-like form — twisted ones could be made from one to over sixty twisted wires. The terminals of torcs are plain or decorated loops. **Wraxall class torcs** are a group of torcs found in western Britain; they were made of bronze, were hinged and had a **joggle joint (catch joint)** mechanism.

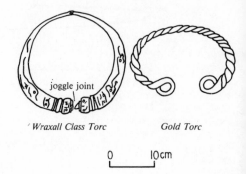

Wraxall Class Torc   Gold Torc

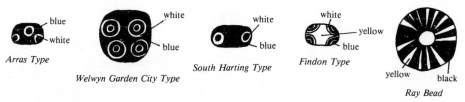

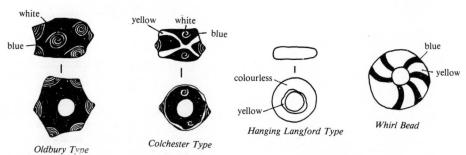

Beads imported from the Continent or influenced by Continental Styles

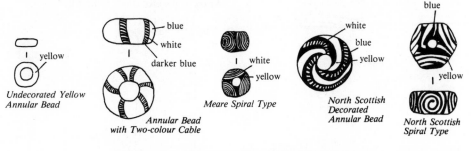

Beads made in Britain or influenced by British Styles

Note: The colour-scheme on some types of bead is varied; the colours indicated above are only a guide.

Some of the Main Types of Iron Age Glass Beads in Britain

Torcs were probably worn round the neck by some of the nobility.

Necklaces could be made from beads of bone, glass, jet, coral, baked clay, marble or amber. Bone, teeth, and flint pendants have also been found. The importation of glass beads, which had begun during the Bronze Age, increased during the Iron Age; some of these imported beads were copied in Britain, and different styles and patterns of decoration developed. Relatively few of these beads have been closely dated, and there is also continuity between periods, so that some types of bead are found in both Iron Age and Roman contexts. C. M. Guido has recognised a number of imported and indigenous beads. Some of the main types are illustrated above.

There is little evidence for pre-Roman **glass bangles (glass armlets)** in Britain, despite such articles being relatively common on the Continent. A few fragments are known from sites along the south and south-west coasts, such as *Hengistbury*, Hampshire, and *Poole*, Dorset. Shale and jet bracelets or armlets are also known. **Massive armlets** of bronze are known from northern Britain, dating from the first century AD; they are penannular in shape, with expanded and perforated terminals. **Spiral snake bracelets** of bronze are also known. They terminate in snakes' heads. **Spiral knobbed bracelets** of bronze have knobbed terminals. There are also hinged bracelets of bronze, as well as various **La Tène bracelets** of bronze or

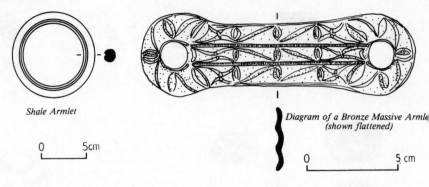

Shale Armlet

0   5cm

Diagram of a Bronze Massive Armlet (shown flattened)

0   5 cm

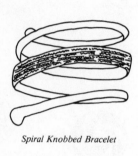

Spiral Knobbed Bracelet

0   10cm

iron, known mainly from Humberside. They were usually plain, ribbed or knobbed. Some have a mortise-and-tenon fastening. Gold arm-rings have also been found.

Finger-rings were of bronze, or sometimes of iron or bone, and rarely of gold, amber or jet. They were usually spiral in form and date to the late Iron Age. They were also worn as **toe-rings**. An imported silver ring is known.

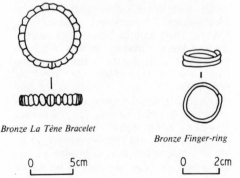

Bronze La Tène Bracelet

0   5cm

Bronze Finger-ring

0   2cm

Swan's neck pins were made of bronze or iron. In Scotland distinctive swan's neck pins with **sunflower (disc) heads** are found. **Ring-headed pins** were made of bronze or iron and were derived from swan's neck pins. **Projecting ring-headed pins** are known, mainly from Scotland.

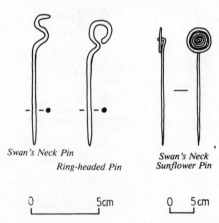

Swan's Neck Pin

Ring-headed Pin

Swan's Neck Sunflower Pin

0   5cm

0   5cm

Brooches take over from pins as a dress fastening from about the fifth century BC onwards. They were made mainly of bronze, but there are some iron ones. A few **Hallstatt brooches** are known, although most are **La Tène brooches** dating from the fifth century BC to the Roman period. **Involuted brooches** are curved in shape, and **flat bowed brooches** have the bow and pin parallel. A few brooches are known which were imported from Spain in the fourth century BC **(Iberian brooches)**. **Penannular brooches** were also worn. Bronze **loop fasteners** for clothing are known, as well as bronze **looped studs, dumb-bell buttons** and bone and bronze **toggles**.

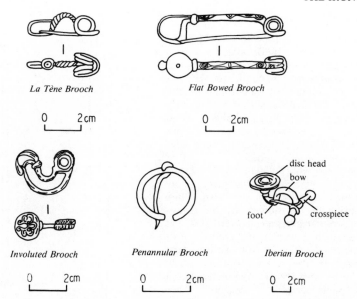

La Tène Brooch

0   2cm

Flat Bowed Brooch

0   2cm

Involuted Brooch

0   2cm

Penannular Brooch

0   2cm

Iberian Brooch

disc head
bow
foot   crosspiece

0 2cm

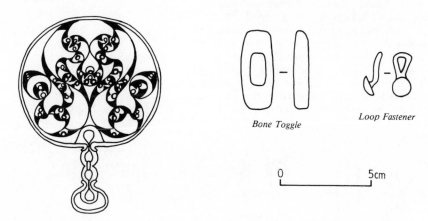

Bone Toggle

Loop Fastener

0   5cm

Back of an Engraved Bronze Mirror

0   10cm

The earliest **mirrors** date to the first century BC and were circular, plain and made of iron, with iron handles and bronze mounts. Most mirrors, however, were made of bronze, with engraved decoration; kidney-shaped mirrors are common.

Combs of bone and **tweezers** of bronze or iron have been found, and a few toilet sets similar to Roman examples are known.

Reading for Jewellery: Brailsford, J. 1975; Brailsford, J. and Stapley, J. E. 1972; Bulleid, A. and Gray, H. St. G. 1911; Guido, C. M. 1978; Kilbride-Jones, H. E. 1937–8; Kilbride-Jones, H. E. 1980; MacGregor, M. 1976; Megaw, J. V. S. 1971; Simpson, M. 1968; Stead, I. M. 1979; Stevenson, R. B. K. 1976; Wheeler, R. E. M. 1943.

Weapons and Armour

From about the sixth century BC **Hallstatt daggers** are found in Britain; **La Tène I daggers** appear in the fourth century BC. Dagger blades were made of iron. The hilt guard and pommel bar were usually of iron in Hallstatt D daggers, and of bronze in La Tène daggers. Hilts were probably of wood or bone. **Dagger sheaths** were made completely of wood, or of wood bound with bronze or iron, or sometimes of iron or bronze lined with wood. There were a variety of bronze chapes. The sheaths were suspended from belts by **twin loop suspension** or occasionally by the Continental **strap suspension**. Towards the end of the fourth century BC the production of the dagger declined. Iron **swords** first appeared in the seventh century BC in association with Bronze Age material, but were superseded by daggers. They reappeared in the third century BC. These swords were of iron with bronze hilt guards. The scabbards were of bronze or iron, often with elaborate designs, and sometimes of wood or leather. Iron and bronze scabbard chapes and bindings have been found. The scabbards had strap suspension. Socketed **spearheads** of iron are known from late Iron Age contexts, and were probably used as javelins. An iron spearhead decorated with bronze mounts is known. Tanged **arrowheads** of iron dating from the first century BC have been found. Baked clay and

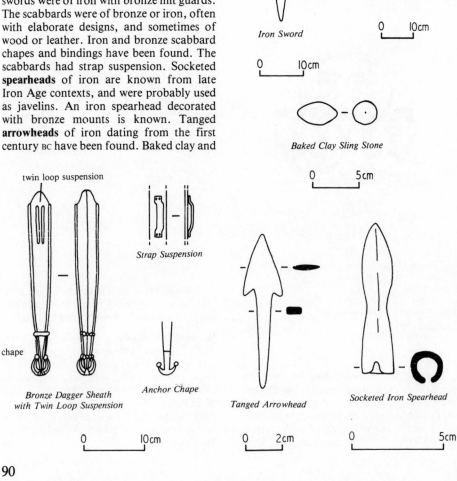

Iron Sword

Sword Scabbard

0   10cm

0   10cm

Baked Clay Sling Stone

0   5cm

twin loop suspension

Strap Suspension

chape

Bronze Dagger Sheath with Twin Loop Suspension

Anchor Chape

Tanged Arrowhead

Socketed Iron Spearhead

0   10cm

0   2cm

0   5cm

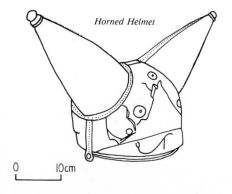

Horned Helmet

0   10cm

stone **sling stones (sling bullets, sling shots)** were also used. Bronze **helmets** of late Iron Age date are known. One example is a parade helmet with horns that was found in the Thames. Another has a neck guard, similar to Roman examples. Bronze **carnyxes** (sing **carnyx**) are known. These were war trumpets with animal heads, and seem to be late Iron Age in date. Rectangular **parade shields** of bronze have been found. They would originally have had a backing of wood or leather. Circular and elongated bronze shield bosses and bronze bindings have been found which would have decorated shields of leather or wood.

Reading for Weapons and Armour: Brailsford, J. 1975; Jope, E. M. 1961b; Piggott, S. 1950; Piggott, S. 1959.

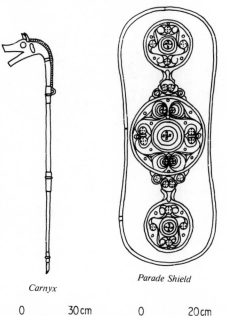

Carnyx

Parade Shield

0   30cm

0   20cm

Carts and Chariots

The first evidence for carts and chariots dates to *c*700 BC. They were made mostly of wood, with iron and bronze fittings. Carts have been found in burials. A chariot was pulled by two horses or oxen harnessed to a yoke. Various iron and bronze cart fittings have been found. The wooden rims of the wheels **(felloes)** were made from one piece of wood, probably steamed into shape; the ends were probably secured by iron plates. In the Hallstatt period the wheels were protected by iron strips **(strakes)** nailed to the felloes, but from the La Tène period single-piece iron tyres **(hoop tyres)** were shrunk onto the felloe while red hot. Circular iron or bronze **nave hoops (nave bands, nave bindings, hub rings)** and **hub linings** protected the outside and inside of the wheel hub (nave) to prevent it from splitting.

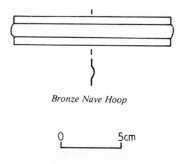

Bronze Nave Hoop

0   5cm

Axle-caps of iron bound the ends of the axles; they were perforated to allow linch pins to pass through the axles and keep the wheels in place. Some linch pins were very elaborate, with decorated bronze terminals. **Vase-shaped linch pins** are found, as well as **crescent-shaped linch pins** which were a Belgic variant. A possible linch pin of antler has been found. Wooden ones may have been used. **Yoke mounts (yoke terminals)** protected the ends of the yoke. **Pole tips (pole sheaths)** of bronze or iron probably protected the end of the cart pole, or possibly the ends of the yoke, and usually took the form of a cylinder closed at one end. **Chariot horn caps** were of hollow bronze and may have decorated the ends of shafts of wood or horn. Some have been described as axle-caps.

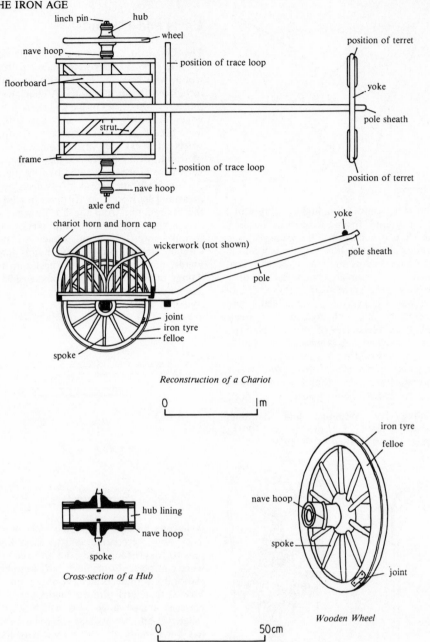

Reconstruction of a Chariot

0   1 m

Cross-section of a Hub

Wooden Wheel

0   50 cm

Various fittings for leather horse harness (**harness mounts**) have been found, dating from *c*700 BC onwards. **Bridle bits (horse bits)** were of iron or bronze. **Terret rings** were of iron or bronze. They may have been attached to the yoke or pole of the cart (possibly by lashing) and the reins passed through them. **Cheekpieces** were of bronze, antler or bone. They were probably attached to the bridle bit. **Strap distributors (strap buckles, strap unions, strap junctions, strap links)** were of bronze and took various forms. They may have been used to allow harness straps to cross at right-angles. **Harness loops** are small rings of bronze and were probably used to link narrow straps on a horse's head. Larger **harness rings** may have been used instead of

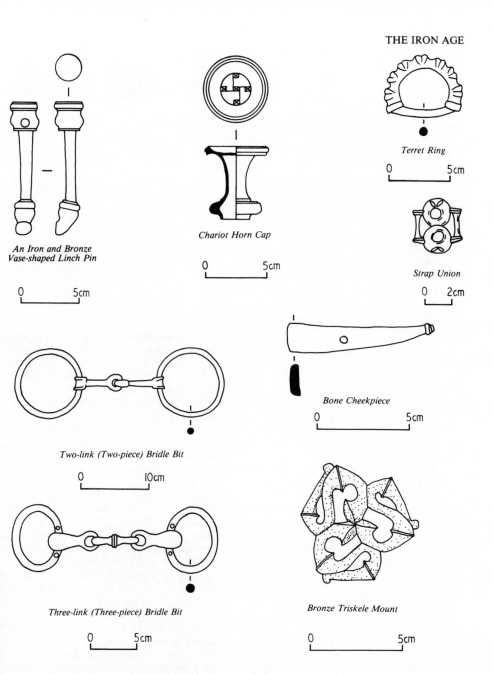

An Iron and Bronze
Vase-shaped Linch Pin

0   5cm

Chariot Horn Cap

0   5cm

Terret Ring

0   5cm

Strap Union

0   2cm

Two-link (Two-piece) Bridle Bit

0   10cm

Bone Cheekpiece

0   5cm

Three-link (Three-piece) Bridle Bit

0   5cm

Bronze Triskele Mount

0   5cm

terret rings. Bronze openwork discs with triskele designs **(triskele mounts)** were attached to harness as hanging decoration. A unique **pony cap** (once thought to be a chamfrein) was found at *Torrs*, Dumfries and Galloway **('Torrs Chamfrein')**. The cap has horns attached to it which are believed to have been added in recent times (the horns were probably originally part of a warrior's helmet, or mounts for drinking horns). The cap was made of bronze; it would probably have been attached to the harness and used on ceremonial occasions. **Horseshoes** of iron dating to the late Iron Age have been found.

Reading for Carts and Chariots: Atkinson, R. J. C. and Piggott, S. 1955; Fox, C. 1946; Kilbride-Jones, H. E. 1980; MacGregor, M. 1976; Roe, D. A. 1960; Stead, I. M. 1979.

Coinage

A few **Greek coins** of the fifth to second centuries BC have been found in Britain, but can rarely be attributed to definite Iron Age levels. Coins are rarely found in north and west Britain. The earliest coins date to the second to first centuries BC; they were imported from the Continent, and consist of six series termed **Gallo-Belgic A-F**. The first coins were gold **staters** which portrayed stylised representations of the head of Apollo and a horse and chariot. **Gallo-Belgic A** coins are termed **Bellovacian**. **Gallo-Belgic B** coins were struck from Bellovacian dies defaced on one or both

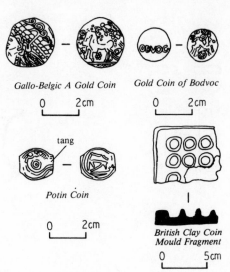

Gallo-Belgic A Gold Coin

0   2cm

Gold Coin of Bodvoc

0   2cm

tang

Potin Coin

0   2cm

British Clay Coin Mould Fragment

0   5cm

0   200km

Tribes of Britain

sides. **Gallo-Belgic C** coins are not very common in Britain, although coinage began to be struck in Britain from the first century BC based on these coins. **Gallo-Belgic D** coins consist of **quarter staters** only, the designs of which are barely recognizable. **Gallo-Belgic E** coins consist of uniface gold staters (blank on one side) and represented the largest wave of coinage into Britain. **Gallo-Belgic F** coins mark the end of gold coinage struck in Gaul; they are rarely found in Britain.

Coins were made in Britain from the first century BC **(British coins)** and have been classified as **British A-R** and **X-Z**. The blanks were cast in clay moulds which were then individually struck between dies. British A-R were uninscribed gold coins; X-Z consisted of gold, silver, and bronze coins. The British Q coin portrayed a distinctive triple-tailed horse. Gold, silver and bronze coins were later minted by various tribes in southern Britain, almost all bearing legends giving the name of the issuer, and sometimes the mint. Classical influences are seen in the designs of these coins, and they were issued until the Roman invasion.

From the mid second century BC various tribes can be recognised in Britain, largely through coin evidence, but the borders of their territories cannot be precisely defined.

Potin coins (speculum coins, tin coins) — bronze coins with a high proportion of tin in their composition — are found in Kent and the Thames Valley. They have Gallic prototypes, but it is not known by and for whom they were made. They seem to represent small change during the period from the early first century BC into the Roman period. They have a stylised head of Apollo on the obverse, and a stylised bull on the reverse. They were cast in strips, probably in moulds of baked clay, and were then cut up, retaining the **tangs** (the superfluous metal which joined the coins in strips).

Armorican coins are found in Britain, suggesting trade with France. A few of the coins are of gold, but most are of base silver, attributable to the Coriosolites tribe of Brittany. Other miscellaneous coins from Gallic tribes have also been found in Britain. Gold **'bullets'** (bullet-shaped coins) have been found in Scotland. These were primitive coins from the Marne district of France.

Reading for Coinage: Allen, D. F. 1962; Allen, D. F. 1971; Allen, D. F. 1980; Cunliffe, B. 1978; Milne, J. G. 1948.

Art

Early Celtic art (once termed **La Tène art**) consists particularly of stylised and geometric motifs. Bronze objects especially were decorated, including weapons and personal ornaments. The art style has its origins on the Continent, where this style of art was common from the fifth to first centuries BC when it declined, although an insular variety of the art style continued in Britain.

Reading for Art: Brailsford, J. 1975; Fox, C. 1958; Kilbride-Jones, H. E. 1980; MacGregor, M. 1976.

Sculpture, Statuettes and Figurines

Wooden statuettes and chalk figurines have been found; a small bronze statuette, probably imported from Spain, is known; and several first century BC bronze figurines of animals, especially boar figurines which may have had a ritual significance, have been found in Britain. There are bronze statuettes of figures, probably of classical origin, and also some first century BC bronze masks about 5cm high. A granite **tricephalos** from Scotland is a sculptured

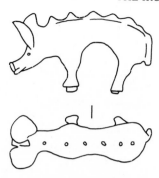

Bronze Boar Figurine

0   5cm

stone depicting a head; it has a hollow in the top and dates approximately to the third to first centuries BC.

Reading for Sculpture, Statuettes and Figurines: Foster, J. 1977; Megaw, J. V. S. and Simpson, D. D. A. 1979.

Imports

Britain had close contacts with the Continent throughout the Iron Age, and many objects were imported to Britain, particularly from Gaul and northern Italy. Such imports may have been trade goods, gifts, or personal belongings of travellers; it is usually impossible to say exactly how a particular item found its way into Britain. Personal objects such as jewellery, harness fittings, weapons and pottery were often imported. A number of luxury objects were brought in, although some of them do not have definite Iron Age associations and may have been imported by collectors more recently; they include many bronze vessels, such as a ribbed bucket of the sixth century BC from Italy, a fragment of a 'Rhodian flagon' of the seventh to sixth centuries, an Etruscan oenochoe (jug) of the sixth to fifth centuries, an Etruscan trefoil-mouthed flagon of the fifth century and jugs of the fourth century BC. There are also several finds of Greek pottery dating from the seventh century BC. Definite imports of luxury goods date mainly from the first century BC and include an Italian bronze oenochoe, an Italian bronze patella (pan), bronze vases and wine strainers from Gaul or Italy, Roman silver cups, tableware

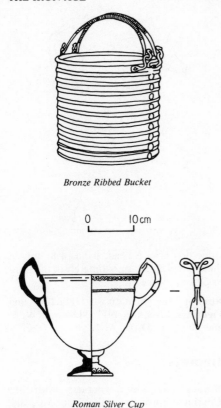

Bronze Ribbed Bucket

0   10 cm

Wooden Figurine

0   20 cm

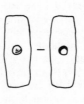

Roman Silver Cup

0   5 cm

including samian and Gallo-Belgic wares, a silver medallion of Augustus, glass vessels, glass gaming pieces, and amphorae of wine. Brooches, and a bronze statuette with eyes inset with glass beads, were imported from Spain. (See also Iron Age and Roman pottery, glass, jewellery, weapons and burial).

Reading for Imports: Harbison, P. and Laing, L. 1974; Laver, P. G. 1927.

Religion

According to classical writers the religious sites of the Iron Age were places such as rivers, bogs, springs and woods. There is little archaeological evidence for these sites apart from the many finds, some very rich, which have been found in rivers and bogs, some deposited as hoards. These may have been votive offerings. Amongst the finds

Reconstruction of Bronze Votive Shields

0   10 cm

are small bronze **votive shields** and **votive swords**. **Wooden figurines** have been found.

Chalk figurines are known, often with carved belts and swords; they are usually found decapitated. Bronze **spoons** or **scoops** are often found in pairs, sometimes with inhumations, or in bogs. They may have had a ritual function. A few **shrines** have been found, resembling the later Romano-Celtic temples in form. They were built in wood such as the rectangular post-built structure found at *Heathrow*, Greater London. Classical writers give some

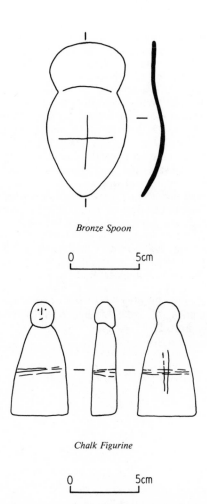

Bronze Spoon

0   5cm

Chalk Figurine

0   5cm

cremations which were urned or unurned, and were placed under small **barrows** surrounded by a shallow ditch. They were often grouped in cemeteries (eg *Ampleforth Moor*, North Yorkshire) and were sometimes situated at the site of an older barrow. They continued in use until the fifth century BC. It seems likely that the ashes of most cremations were scattered, or buried without urns, barrows or accompanying grave goods.

Inhumations are also rare in the Early Iron Age, although this method of burial superseded cremation from the fifth century BC. Structures of four postholes have been interpreted as supporting platforms for the exposure of the dead, whose bones may have been subsequently scattered. Numerous articles have been recovered from rivers, and these may have been grave goods accompanying bodies or bones thrown into the water. Several inhumations have been found in disused storage pits, a few accompanied by grave goods. Disarticulated human bones have been found in rubbish deposits, and this supports the idea of exposure of the dead. Isolated shallow graves have also been found in the ditches and ramparts of hillforts of the first century BC but these may be ritual burials. In western and northern Britain inhumation burials are found in stone **cists** which are sometimes found in cemeteries. The bodies are contracted and have accompanying grave goods. In southern and eastern Britain there are some isolated burials. **Warrior burials** are seen from the second century BC; these are male inhumations, accompanied by weapons, in shallow graves without barrows. There are some rich **female burials** accompanied by many personal grave goods usually buried in cists, some beneath cairns of stone 1·2–1·5m high. A few female cremations in urns are known. There are also **spoon burials**; these are inhumations accompanied by bronze spoons or scoops. In Humberside **Arras type burials** are found, similar to those in France. They consist of small barrows grouped in large cemeteries of 100–200 barrows with crouched, or sometimes extended, bodies. Some barrows were surrounded by square or round ditched enclosures. There were a few grave goods. Some bodies were buried in wooden coffins, and some were buried with **mortuary carts (cart burials)**. These burials

evidence about a Druidic cult, and some evidence of the gods worshipped can be obtained from those traditions which persisted into the Roman period. A number of **shafts** and deep **pits** have been found which may have had a religious function; some may have originally been wells, although some are too narrow to have had this function.

Reading for Religion: Cunliffe, B. 1978; MacGregor, M. 1976; Piggott, S. 1968; Ross, A. 1967; Ross, A. 1968.

Burial

In the Early Iron Age there is a scarcity of evidence for burials, although cremation was probably mainly practised following Bronze Age traditions. There are a few

are characterised by the deposition of the body and the cart, either whole or dismantled, in a rectangular pit under a barrow, accompanied by cart and harness fittings, personal ornaments, food offerings, occasional ritual sacrifice, and the burial of the horses eg at *Danes Graves*, Humberside. Cart burial is rare in other parts of Britain. These cemeteries continued in use until the Roman period. In south-west England inhumation accompanied by grave goods often continued to the Roman period eg at *Maiden Castle*, Dorset, where a **war cemetery** (composed of the victims of a battle) has been found dating to the Roman invasion.

In south-east England cremation became the predominant method of burial from the first century BC. **Aylesford-Swarling** cemeteries of cremation burials, and sometimes inhumations, are found (named after the type-sites of *Aylesford* and *Swarling*, Kent). The ashes were placed in urns in small pits. Some had few or no grave goods, while others had many. **Bucket burials** are a common feature, with the cremations placed in wooden buckets or situlae, with many grave goods. North of the Thames are a few **Welwyn burials** which were rich, aristocratic graves, where the cremations were placed in large grave-pits. The pits contained many grave goods, including goods imported from the Continent, such as tableware and wine amphorae. Some barrow burials of this date have also been found such as that at *Lexden*, Essex, where a burial in an oval pit with many rich grave goods was covered by a large barrow.

Reading for Burial: Cunliffe, B. 1978; Ellison, A. and Drewett, P. C. 1971; Stead, I. M. 1979; Whimster, R. 1977.

General Reading for the Iron Age: Cunliffe, B. 1978; Megaw, J. V. S. and Simpson, D. D. A. 1979.

Chapter 6

The Roman Period

Introduction

Britain was invaded in AD 43 by the Romans. There had been previous contacts with the Roman world, mainly through trade, and Julius Caesar had led military expeditions into Britain in 55 and 54 BC. After AD 43 many changes took place in Britain, particularly as a result of **romanization** — the adoption of Roman civilization. In AD 410 due to the situation abroad the emperor Honorius directed Britain to see to its own defence. This date is conventionally seen as the end of Roman Britain, although it is clear that a Roman way of life continued for many years until the Saxon invasions in the mid fifth century (see Introduction to Chapter 7).

Reading: Frere, S. S. 1978.

Military sites

Fortresses were permanent bases for legionary troops. They were constructed of timber or stone, the later ones generally in stone, and normally covered c50 acres. They had a rampart and ditches, and internal buildings including the **principia** (headquarters-building) which included a **sacellum** (shrine) and an underlying strongroom; **praetorium** (commandant's house); **officers' houses; barrack blocks** which took up the most space inside the fortresses and housed about eighty men, normally in 10 eight-man units — **contubernia; valetudinarium** (hospital); **horrea** (granaries which were substantial buttressed buildings, raised above the ground level for ventilation); **bath-houses; fabricae** (workshops); and a **basilica exercitatoria** (drill hall). There were also **ovens** and **latrines. Amphitheatres** were positioned outside fortresses (see amphitheatres).

Forts (castella) were permanent bases covering c2½–10 acres and normally

housed a single unit. By the Flavian period (AD 69–96) they were usually rectangular in plan, with rounded corners, a rampart **(vallum)** and ditch **(fossa)**, and four gateways flanked by towers. Multiple ditches became more common in the later Roman period. They were usually V-shaped with a rectangular slot at the bottom.

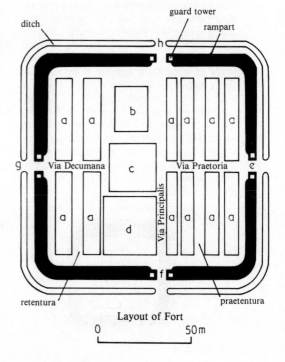

Layout of Fort

0   50 m

a *Barracks*
b *Horrea (Granaries)*
c *Principia (Headquarters-building)*
d *Praetorium (Commandant's Quarters)*
e *Porta Praetoria (Main Gate)*
f *Porta Principalis Dextra (Right-hand-side Gate)*
g *Porta Decumana*
h *Porta Principalis Sinistra (Left-hand-side Gate)*
retentura Area behind principia (literally 'rear tents')
praetentura Area in front of principia (literally 'forward tents')

99

Ramparts were usually made of turf, earth, or puddled clay, with timber revetments. Internal buildings were of timber, although stone tended to replace timber after cAD 100. The internal layout of forts and fortresses was very similar. Bath buildings were usually sited outside the fort.

Gyrus: a possible gyrus has been found at *The Lunt* Roman fort, near Coventry. This was a circular arena 32m in diameter and with a sunken floor 80cm below ground level with a single entrance. There were large recesses for posts for a surrounding wall. It may have been used for training horses for the army or as a weapon-training ground.

Saxon Shore forts were built from the mid third century, along the southern and eastern coasts of Britain, as a response to the threat of raiders. They were characterised by stone walls with tile bonding courses and external towers, eg *Portchester*, Hampshire. A **bonding course** was a horizontal layer of a regularly shaped material such as tiles or bricks to reinforce walls of irregularly shaped stone such as flint. Saxon Shore forts were associated with a series of signal stations.

Fortlets housed small military patrols, and were situated at strategic points where some watch or control was necessary. They usually had one rampart and one or two ditches and a single gate. There were a few internal buildings such as barrack blocks.

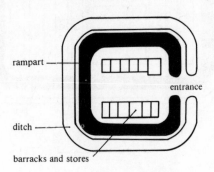

Plan of a Fortlet

0   20m

Camps (castra) were marching camps, or occasionally semi-permanent quarters. They were also constructed as part of training manoeuvres. The troops lived in tents, the arrangement of which gave rise to the layout of buildings in forts. The camps consisted of a ditch (**fossa**) with an earthen bank and palisade formed by stakes (**pila muralia**). The camps were usually rectangular in plan. The gateways could be protected by a **tutulus** (a short stretch of bank and ditch fronting the gateway), or by a **clavicula** (a curved extension of the bank and ditch).

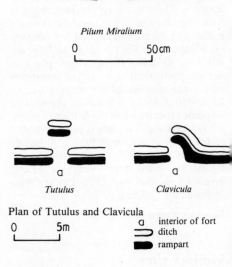

Pilum Miralium

0   50cm

Tutulus   Clavicula

Plan of Tutulus and Clavicula

0   5m   interior of fort
                      ditch
                      rampart

Signal stations usually consisted of a wooden tower surrounded by a circular ditch and bank, although **beacon stands** (stone platforms on which fires were lit) have also been found. Some fortlets served as signalling stations. Stone towers were also built along the north-east coast in the fourth century as part of the Saxon Shore defences against raiders, and were surrounded by a stone wall and ditch.

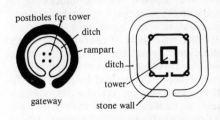

postholes for tower

ditch
rampart
ditch
tower
stone wall
gateway

Plan of a Signalling Tower

Plan of a Saxon Shore Signalling Tower

0   50m

Reading for Military Sites: Collingwood, R. G. and Richmond, I. 1969; Gentry, A. P. 1976; Hobley, B. 1971; Johnson, S. 1976; Webster, G. 1969.

Hadrian's Wall and the Antonine Wall

Hadrian's Wall

Hadrian's Wall was constructed across the north of England from *Wallsend*, Tyne and Wear, to *Bowness-on-Solway*, Cumbria, as a northern frontier to the province. Construction began in AD 122. The frontier defences first consisted of a line of forts, with a wall to the north 122km long. The wall was c3m thick **(broad wall)** and was probably 4·5m high with a parapet and battlements. The wall was built in stone, in short lengths, by centuries (military units), and these lengths were marked by inscribed stones **(centurial stones)**. The western section of the wall was constructed in turf **(turf wall)**, possibly because limestone for mortar is not so readily available in this area. **Fortlets (milecastles)** were built every Roman mile (1,620yd or 1,481m), with two turrets between each milecastle; these were built in turf along the turf wall and in stone elsewhere. The milecastles accommodated patrol troops and had internal buildings of stone or timber, and north and south gates. The turrets were c5m square and had an upper storey. They were used as look-out posts. In front of the wall was a V-shaped ditch c8m wide and c3m deep.

This first phase of the wall was altered before completion: the forts were transferred to the wall, and the wall was completed as a **narrow wall** 2·25m wide. To the south of the wall there was a ditch **(vallum)**, which probably served as a boundary marker. A line of fortlets and turrets was built along the Cumberland coast, linked by a palisade and ditch. There were also outpost forts. The wall underwent a complex history of alteration, withdrawal and re-use.

Antonine Wall

Construction of the Antonine Wall began cAD 140, initially to replace Hadrian's Wall as a frontier in a more northerly position across the Forth-Clyde isthmus. The wall was built of turf and clay on a stone base 4·5m wide. The rampart was probably at least 3m high with a wooden parapet and a ditch to the north. The wall was built in sections, which were marked by **distance slabs**. The forts along the wall were smaller and more closely spaced than those along Hadrian's Wall. The fort ramparts were usually of turf, with main buildings in stone and the rest in timber. There were also fortlets, but no turrets. **Beacon platforms** made of turf have been found projecting from the south side of the wall; they probably formed a system of long-distance signalling. Like Hadrian's Wall, the Antonine Wall underwent a series of changes.

Reading for Hadrian's Wall and Antonine Wall: Breeze, D. J. and Dobson, B. 1978; Bruce, J. C. 1978; Potter, T. W. 1979.

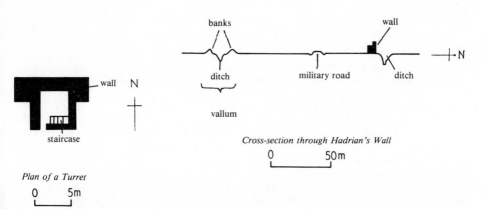

banks

wall

ditch

military road

ditch

N

wall N

staircase

vallum

Cross-section through Hadrian's Wall

0   50m

Plan of a Turret

0   5m

Settlements

A **colonia** was a settlement founded as part of government policy for Roman citizens, who were usually discharged soldiers. Towns could also be promoted to the status of a colonia. A **municipium** was a chartered town, lower in status than a colonia. Many deliberately planned towns were **cantonal capitals** – capitals of the **civitates** (administrative regions). **Centuriation** is the division of land into regular plots outside a colonia, but this practice has not been convincingly demonstrated in Britain.

A large number of settlements (**vici**) grew up for various reasons eg mining settlements, trading centres, or settlements around mansiones, forts and fortresses. Some larger settlements were fortified and are sometimes termed **small towns**.

Some areas eg the Fenlands and Salisbury Plain, seem to have been administered as **imperial estates** for agriculture and mining; the Fenlands were first drained in the Roman period by an elaborate system of drainage channels and dykes. Other settlements continued little changed from the Iron Age. There were single farms, hamlets and ranches. Some sites were enclosed with a bank and ditch. In south-west Britain rounds and courtyard houses continued from the Iron Age, while in Wales raths and hillforts were still used as enclosed settlements. Native settlements also continued in Scotland.

Reading for Settlements: Collingwood, R. G. and Richmond, I. 1969; Phillips, C. W. 1970; Rodwell, W. and Rowley, T. 1975; Wacher, J. S. 1974.

Towns

Houses

Houses experienced a development similar to that of villas. Simple rectangular timber-framed houses were constructed in the first century. Some had corridors and additional rooms, as well as tessellated floors and wall-paintings. In the second century these were increasingly replaced by stone-built houses. By the addition of further ranges of rooms, some developed into **winged houses** (similar to the winged corridor villa) and **courtyard houses** (similar to the courtyard villa), some of which were very large. These stone-built houses often had many refinements such as baths, hypocaust heating, mosaics and wall-paintings. There is no conclusive evidence that they had an upper storey. Various types of house were in use at any one time, the size and design of houses reflecting the status and wealth of the owner or tenant.

Public Buildings

Town Walls and Gateways A few towns were surrounded by an earth rampart and ditch in the first and early second centuries; many towns, however, built these at the end of the second century. The gateways were probably of timber and there is some evidence from the ramparts for timber-lacing, timber revetments and towers. Some earth ramparts were faced with stone, and had stone gateways.

Walls of stone were built from the early third century. These were 1·2–3m thick, and had a rubble core. There were usually one or two ditches. Stone walls were sometimes inserted in front of an earlier earth rampart. Gateways were of stone, with one or more portals and occasionally towers. Most towns and villages had such fortifications by the fourth century, enclosing up to 330 acres. In the late fourth century external towers were added, for better deployment of artillery.

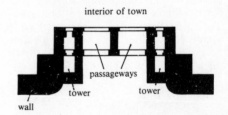

interior of town

passageways

tower   tower

wall

Plan of a Gateway

0   10m

Forum (pl Fora) All large towns had a forum. These varied in size, but consisted of a large square for public meetings and markets, usually surrounded on three sides by a colonnaded portico with shops and offices. A **basilica** often occupied the fourth side, often with an elaborate

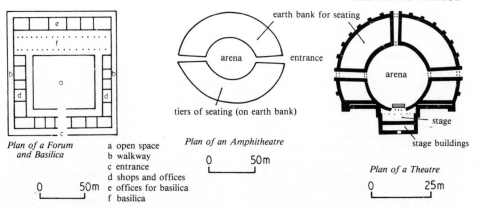

Plan of a Forum
and Basilica

a open space
b walkway
c entrance
d shops and offices
e offices for basilica
f basilica

Plan of an Amphitheatre

0   50m

0   50m

Plan of a Theatre

0   25m

entrance on the opposite side of the square. The basilica consisted of a long aisled hall, used for the administration and jurisdiction of the town, and small rooms used for offices.

Market Hall (Macellum) This was usually similar in design to a forum: it was an open square for a market surrounded by porticos containing shops.

Shops Various types of shop have been identified. They were at first timber-framed, but later were of stone. Burnt-out shops of the first century have revealed merchandise such as glass, mortaria and samian pottery.

Theatres These had a D-shaped audi-torium **(cavea)** with tiers of seats in a semi-circle surrounding an arena **(orchestra)** which was fronted by the stage **(pulpitum)**. There were often stage buildings **(scaena)** behind the stage. The earthwork banks supporting the tiers of seats were revetted in timber or later in stone, and the structure was open to the sky. Theatres are some-times found in towns, and also in rural settings, where they seem to have been associated with religious sites. **Theatre masks** of clay are known. These may have been worn in classical theatre, or in ritual ceremonies.

Amphitheatres These were elliptical arenas surrounded by tiers of seating on earthen banks, probably reached by external staircases. The banks were revetted in timber or later in stone. Amphitheatres were open to the sky, although the seating may have been sheltered by awnings. They were usually positioned outside towns, and were used for various amusements. Military amphitheatres **(ludi)** were used for training as well.

Circuses None have been found in Britain, although pictures of circuses some-times occur, eg on mosaics, pottery, and glass vessels.

Reading for Towns: Collingwood, R. G. and Richmond, I. 1969; Liversidge, J. 1968; Marsh, G. D. 1979; Thompson, F. H. 1976; Wacher, J. S. 1974.

Water Supply, Drainage and Baths

Water Supply

Large masonry **aqueducts** consisting of an arched structure were rare in Britain. Romano-British aqueducts were open channels of stone, underground stone channels, or lead, wooden or ceramic **pipes**. These supplied towns and forts with water, some of which was stored in large stone or lead **tanks**; the overflow was often used to flush latrines and sewers. Water was also commonly obtained from **wells**. A **force-pump** has been found at *Silchester*, Hampshire, and was probably used for raising water.

Drainage

Some towns are known to have had a system of underground **sewers**, consisting of masonry channels fed by lateral ones. Manholes have been found with square stone manhole covers. The sewers were usually flushed with waste water from aqueducts and public baths. Drains were also made as timber-lined and covered channels; vaulted drains constructed from tiles and mortar were also used. Some towns had open drains in the streets for rain water. The effluent was probably discharged into the nearest river, or into cess pits.

Latrines

Public lavatories have been found in towns, often in association with public baths. They consisted of a sewer over which were placed seats of stone or wood, and which was flushed with waste water, usually from the baths. In front of the lavatories was a gutter containing running water for washing. This type of lavatory system is also known in military contexts. Private houses and villas rarely had a flushed lavatory but usually had a wooden seat fixed over a pit.

Baths

Bath suites are found in public baths and also in villas, town houses, inns and forts. They were often free-standing buildings to avoid the risk of spreading fire. They were similar to Turkish baths, consisting of a series of rooms with graded heat, heated by hypocausts. Many rooms were apsidal, and baths often had wall-paintings and mosaics. Bath suites can vary in size and there is no standard pattern, but most contained a **frigidarium** (cold room with a cold plunge bath), a **tepidarium** (warm room with a warm bath), and a **caldarium** (hot room with a hot bath). Bath suites could also contain an **apodyterium** (changing room), a **palaestra** (exercise yard), a **latrina** (latrine), and a **sudatorium (laconicum, sweating room)** — a room, usually circular, with a very hot dry temperature and no bath. Other rooms are often found, which could have been **unctoria** (massage rooms). **Iron beams** have been found which probably supported a boiler over the stokehole for the hypocaust heating. Boilers would have produced a damp heat.

Reading for Water Supply, Drainage and Baths: Collingwood, R. G. and Richmond, I. 1969; Wacher, J. S. 1971; Wacher, J. S. 1974.

Temples and Religion

Many religions were practised in Roman Britain; classical gods, native gods and ones from the Near East were worshipped, and the Imperial Cult and Christianity were practised.

There is some archaeological evidence for **Christianity** in Roman Britain. The **Chi-Rho monogram** ☧ (the first two letters of the Greek word Christos) was a Christian symbol, and is found on various items such as tableware (especially pewter), mosaics, lamps, spoons, wall-paintings, lead tanks, and rings, and also as graffiti. AO or AW ('Alpha Omega' — the first and last letters of the Greek alphabet signifying the 'beginning and the end' of the Revelation of St John) is also seen, sometimes in conjunction with the Chi-Rho. These symbols are found on various articles such as **lead tanks** which may have been water tanks used for baptism.

Other inscriptions are found which may be interpreted as Christian. Many pagan representations were adopted as Christian symbols, especially in mosaics, such as ones depicting the god Orpheus. **Word squares** have been found such as the one scratched on a piece of wall-painting from *Cirencester*, Gloucestershire:

ROTAS
OPERA
TENET
AREPO
SATOR

'The sower Arepo guides the wheels carefully'. This word square was probably a Christian cryptogram for the following:

A
P
A
T
E
R
A|PATERNOSTER|O
O
S
T
E
R
O

Pater noster = 'Our Father' and AO = 'alpha omega'.

Some possible churches have been found, such as at the fort at *Richborough*, Kent, which was associated with an hexagonal structure lined with plaster; from parallels abroad this structure may have been a font. Some Christian burials have been found (see burial).

Classical temples are rare; these had a **cella** (internal room with a shrine) surrounded by a portico of columns, often raised on a **podium** approached by steps. A **pediment** with sculpture was supported on the columns.

pediment and pediment sculpture

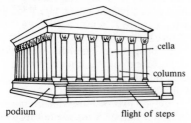

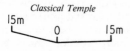

Classical Temple

The most common temple was the **Romano-Celtic temple** which was usually square or rectangular, sometimes circular or polygonal, with a cella lit by clerestory windows. This was usually surrounded by a portico or enclosed ambulatory, probably with windows. These temples were situated both in the country and in towns.

A **mithraeum** was a temple for the worship of Mithras and usually consisted of a central aisle with benches on each side, an apse or recess for the main shrine at one end, and a narthex or ante-chamber at the other.

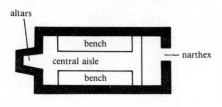

Plan of a Mithraeum

Diadems and **crowns** of sheet bronze have been found which were probably part of a priest's regalia. **Votive tablets (votive plaques)** of bronze and silver inscribed with a dedication to a god are known, as well as curses inscribed on lead or bronze tablets or plates. Small figurines and models are also found which may have had a religious function. Stone **altars** have been discovered. They usually consist of a capital, sometimes decorated, a central shaft with an inscribed dedication, and a base. The altars were dedicated to classical gods, native gods, foreign gods or personified spirits. Altars are found mainly on military sites.

Inscriptions are found on a variety of objects. They were usually carved in formal capital letters and painted. **Cursive writing** was used for everyday writing and is found on writing tablets and as graffiti.

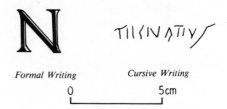

Formal Writing   *Cursive Writing*

Reading for Temples and Religion: Barley, M. W. and Hanson, R. P. C. 1968; Collingwood, R. G. and Richmond, I. 1969; Collingwood, R. G. and Wright, R. P. 1965; Lewis, M. J. T. 1966; Liversidge, J. 1968; Muckelroy, K. W. 1976.

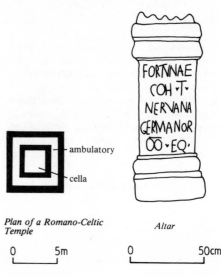

Plan of a Romano-Celtic Temple   *Altar*

105

Monumental Arches

Monumental arches (triumphal arches) are rare in Britain. They are known only from *Verulamium (St Albans)*, Hertfordshire, *Richborough*, Kent, and *London*. They were probably erected for commemorative and triumphal reasons.

Monumental Arch

0   5m

Reading for Monumental Arches: Blagg, T. F. C. 1977.

Mansiones

Mansiones were posting stations or inns. They were situated along roads, in towns and in minor centres, and consisted of various rooms for accommodation (including bath suites), and stabling. **Mutationes** were smaller centres providing a change of horse. Both types of building are difficult to identify. These posting stations often attracted settlement and so could develop into small towns.

Reading for Mansiones: Wacher, J. S. 1974.

Villas

The term villa refers to a country house or farm; it is often restricted to describe such buildings constructed in stone or brick, or the country houses of the rich. There were various types of villa; the design and building materials usually reflecting the needs and tastes of the owner, as well as the geographical area, rather than the period. They are found mainly in Lowland Britain, and many had refinements such as mosaic or tessellated floors, wall-paintings, hypocaust heating and bath suites. There seems to have been an expansion of villas in the second century, a decline in the third century and a revival in the late third and fourth centuries, when particularly fine ones were built. There seems to have been a gradual breakdown in villa occupation towards the end of the Roman period.

Some of the early examples replaced Iron Age buildings. The simplest type of villa was a row of two or more interconnecting rooms (once termed a **cottage house**) which first appear in the mid first century. These villas usually had stone footings and were probably half-timbered, and roofed in slate or tile. There may have been an upper storey. Some had mosaics and wall-paintings and were obviously the homes of landowners rather than of tenant farmers.

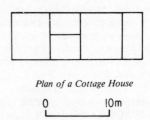

Plan of a Cottage House

0   10m

The **winged corridor house** developed from *c*AD 100 and was very common in Britain. The simplest type had a corridor with rooms behind, and two wings. They often had mosaic floors, bath suites, hypocausts, additional rooms and outbuildings, and could be very elaborate.

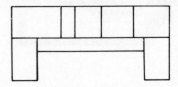

Plan of a Winged Corridor Villa

0   10m

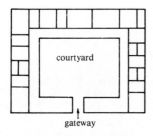

Plan of a Courtyard Villa

0   50m

Courtyard villas had a rectangular court-yard with rooms on at least one side (sometimes on all four sides) with a main gateway. They sometimes developed from winged corridor villas and were the richest type. They usually had many refinements and were often part of a large farming estate.

Aisled houses (aisled villas or basilicas) seem to have belonged to the poorer classes (probably farm labourers). The simplest were rectangular buildings divided by posts into a nave and two aisles, but they were sometimes divided by internal partitions. This type could have bath suites, mosaics and hypocausts, and were often the outbuildings of a more wealthy type of villa. They were probably shared with the farm animals. Some aisled buildings had a specific agricultural or industrial, rather than a domestic, use.

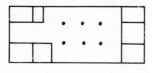

Plan of an Aisled Villa

0   10m

Some villas seem to have been occupied by Roman officials; the villa at *Folkestone*, Kent, for example, may have been occupied by a commander of the British fleet, and the villa at Fishbourne, near *Chichester*, Sussex, seems to have been a palatial residence for a local dignatory. Some villas were associated with imperial estates.

Villa outbuildings are often found, although their specific purpose is not always known. Barns, stables, corn-drying ovens, threshing floors, granaries and byres are known. **Corn-driers (corn-drying ovens)** are usually found as T- or Y-shaped channels lined with chalk or stone, with some sign of burning at one end, and remains of grain. This structure consisted of a long flue along which warm air passed, and a stokehole. Above this there may have been a wooden floor on which corn was placed to dry. A roofed building may have covered this. More elaborate types are found. Recent experiments have shown that these corn-driers may actually have been malting floors.

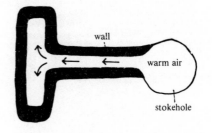

Plan of a T-shaped Corn-drying Oven

0   Im

Reading for Villas: Morris, P. 1979; Richmond, I. 1969; Todd, M. 1978; Wacher, J. S. 1978

Hypocausts

Hypocausts were underfloor heating systems, either **pillared** or **channelled**. In pillared hypocausts the floor was supported on **pilae** — stacks of tiles, or occasionally stone slabs or monoliths. Hot air circulated under the floor from a furnace stoked outside the building. In channelled hypocausts

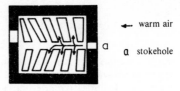

Plan of a Channelled Hypocaust

0   3m

the hot air circulated in channels, often set in a radial arrangement, the centre of the floor sometimes being supported on pilae **(composite hypocaust)**. The channels were formed either by building up the support for the floor, or by digging into the ground, and could be lined with chalk or stone. Hot air and smoke escaped through flues of box tiles set in the wall and plastered over. Flues were also constructed by using iron hold-fasts and spacers of clay, or possibly by

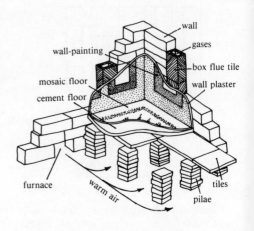

'Cutaway' view of a Pillared Hypocaust

0   50cm

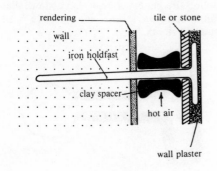

Method of Use of Clay Spacers

0   10cm

Clay Spacer

0   5cm

tegulae mammatae. Ashes would have been raked or shovelled from between the pilae from time to time. An alternative form of heating was the portable **brazier**.

Reading for Hypocausts: Davey, N. 1961; Money, J. H. 1974; Williams, J. H. 1971.

Floors

Floors could be of various materials such as rammed clay, chalk or gravel, **opus signinum** (a very hard waterproof cement, coloured red by the addition of crushed tile), herringbone bricks, flagstones (rare due to the lack of suitable stone), timber, mosaics, or opus sectile. Floors of **opus sectile (floor inlay, cut-stone floors)** were rare in Britain. They consisted of patterns made up from large pieces of stone, such as marble, which were cut into various shapes. **Mosaics** were floors composed of small cubes **(tesserae)** of variously coloured materials such as tile, chalk, greensand, sandstone, limestone, shale, marble, pottery and occasionally glass. They are found in both urban and rural houses. **Tessellated floors (opus tessellatum)** used tesserae of one colour, or more than one, to produce geometric patterns. Other mosaics had designs depicting, for example, Christian, mythological, sporting or marine themes. The tesserae were laid in mortar over guide-lines; complicated patterns were prefabricated. There seem to have been regional schools of mosaicists. From cAD 100–200 there was a demand for mosaics in towns. From cAD 300–370 there was a revival, this time for villas as well; most mosaics are dated to this period.

Reading: see next section.

Walls

From the mid first century AD many villas had wall-paintings, but they are difficult to date and reconstruct. The walls of most types of villa were plastered. Background colours were applied to the plaster and the design, which may have been previously incised on the wall with a stylus, was then painted on. The colours were obtained from various materials, including red and yellow ochres, powdered charcoal, iron oxide and copper silicate. Walls could also be lined with marble or mosaics. There is also some evidence for relief decoration, and decorative mouldings in stucco. There is little evidence for decorated ceilings.

Readings for Floors and Walls: Cunliffe, B. 1971; Liversidge, J. 1969; Liversidge, J. 1977; Neal, D. S. 1976; Pratt, P. 1976; Rainey, A. 1973; Sear, F. 1976; Smith, D. J. 1969.

Windows

Walls do not usually survive high enough for windows to be preserved and so most evidence for windows comes from cellars. These windows seem to have had sloping sills and splayed sides and were rounded or square at the top. They could be glazed, the glass panes being held in place by cement. **Iron grilles** probably did not hold glass in place, as was once thought: they were probably set in windows without glass, or else in front of glass panes, as a security measure. Wooden shutters may have been used.

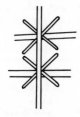

Part of a Window Grille

0   20cm

Reading for Windows: Harden, D. B. 1961; Liversidge, J. 1968.

Tiles and Roofs

Tile and brick production was a seasonal activity. The prepared clay was pressed into wetted wooden moulds and turned out when partially dry. Some tiles were then stamped or combed to form a key for wall plaster. The tiles and bricks were left to dry out completely and were then fired in parallel-flue kilns or tile clamps.

Flue tiles (tubuli) were used in hypocausts. Their outer surface was scored or impressed with patterns so that wall plaster would adhere firmly.

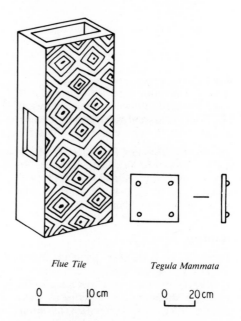

Flue Tile   *Tegula Mammata*

0   10 cm   0   20 cm

Tegulae mammatae were large flat tiles with four raised bosses **(mammae)** on each corner. They may have been used in hypocausts instead of flue tiles.

Flat tiles of various sizes were common and used for a variety of purposes such as bonding courses in walls. **Imbrices** (sing **imbrex**) and **tegulae** (sing **tegula**) were used for roofs. The tiles were not secured by nails but may have been fixed by mortar. The roofs were probably extended well beyond the walls since there is no evidence for eaves guttering. Hexagonal slabs of stone fixed with nails and diamond-shaped slates were also used for roofing; thatched straw or reeds may also have been used. All roofs probably had a timber framework.

109

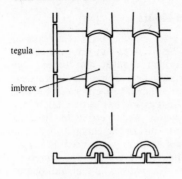

Part of Roof of Tegulae and Imbrices

Hollow **voussoirs** were used in baths to form a vaulted roof which conducted warm air. Roof finials and ridge pieces of stone, and clay antefixes have also been found.

Reading for Tiles and Roofs: Brodribb, G. 1979a; Brodribb, G. 1979b; Davey, N. 1961; Lemmon, C. H. and Hill, J. D. 1966; Lowther, A. W. G. 1948; McWhirr, A. and Viner, D. 1978; Williams, J. H. 1971.

Gardens

There is evidence for planned formal gardens in Roman Britain, consisting of walkways with flower beds and hedges. The villa at Fishbourne had a series of water pipes, feeding basins or fountains in various parts of the garden. There were probably ornamental statues as well.

Reading for Gardens: Cunliffe, B. 1971.

Furniture

There is very little evidence for furniture in Roman Britain apart from that portrayed on contemporary sculpture and carved tombstones.

Couches Those with foot and head rests were used, probably made mainly of wood. A leg from a couch was found at *Silchester*, Hampshire; it was made from Kimmeridge shale.

Chairs Examples made in wickerwork with sides and a high back are popular on statues and carved relief.

Stools Four-legged stools were probably in use. Folding stools made in iron with bronze fittings and leather seats have been found.

Tripods Folding tripod stools were also in use; they were made of iron.

Tables There were small three-legged round tables, probably made of wood in most cases. Many examples of legs in Kimmeridge shale have been found, some with animal reliefs. Round table tops of Kimmeridge shale have also been found.

Although there is little evidence in Britain, large wooden benches, tables, cupboards, shelves and beds must have been common. Stone bench ends have been found. There is evidence of stone furniture inlay, probably for table tops. Cushions and mattresses must have been used with couches and other furniture, but there is very little evidence for upholstery apart from some leather, wool, and a few fragments of cloth.

Reading for Furniture: Cunliffe, B. 1971; Liversidge, J. 1955; Liversidge, J. 1969.

Roads

There was a widespread system of roads in the Roman period, the Roman army being responsible for the initial network of communications. Main roads were usually straight, and were laid out by surveyors, but many roads would only have been tracks, with little or no metalling. Main roads were constructed on a solid base of rammed clay, chalk, gravel or other local material, with a camber (**agger**) and side ditches. Where the area was marshy, the road was laid on timber corduroy foundations. Paved roads are sometimes found, and wheel ruts occasionally survive. Rivers were probably crossed by fords wherever possible, but there are a few traces of bridges, such as stone abutments and piers. Most bridges were probably either constructed completely in wood, or as a wooden roadway supported on stone piers. **Milestones** were placed along roads and were inscribed with the relevant distance and the name of the emperor; they were of stone, usually cylindrical in shape and 120–180cm in height.

Reading for Roads: Collingwood, R. G.

and Wright, R. P. 1965; Johnston, D. E. 1979; Liversidge, J. 1968; Margary, I. D. 1973; Sedgley, J. P. 1975; Taylor, C. C. 1979.

Carts and Harness

Carts (see also Iron Age carts and chariots)

Chariots went out of use in the early Roman period in Britain, but carts remained similar to those used in the Iron Age. They were made of wood with metal fittings. Finds include wooden wheels, as well as iron **linch pins** which were of two basic types: crescentic-headed and spatulate-headed, with or without a loop. **Hub rings (nave bands, nave bindings, nave hoops)** and **hub linings** of iron are found, as well as **pole tips** and **axle-caps**.

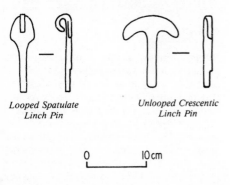

Looped Spatulate Linch Pin   *Unlooped Crescentic Linch Pin*

0   10 cm

Harness

Much Roman harness was similar to that used in the Iron Age. Metal fittings included **bridle bits (snaffles)** of iron or bronze, **curb-bits** (attached to the bridle and worn under a horse's neck), and **terret rings**. There were also **harness loops** of bronze, **phalerae** (bronze roundels which decorated elaborate saddle cloths and straps; some were worn by soldiers on breast armour), **cheekpieces** of bronze and iron, and an iron **headstall** which was found at *Newstead*, Borders. It was decorated with enamelled medallions. There are also examples of headstalls of bronze and iron. **Spurs** are known, although they are not common. They were made of bronze, iron, or bronze with iron pricks or rivets.

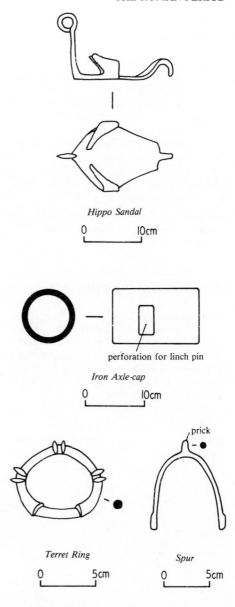

Hippo Sandal

0   10 cm

perforation for linch pin

Iron Axle-cap

0   10 cm

prick

Terret Ring   *Spur*

0   5 cm   0   5 cm

Hippo sandals made of iron have been found. They were probably worn by draught animals for temporary protection, or to prevent them slipping on wet surfaces. **Horseshoes,** similar to modern ones, were used during the period, but few have been definitely attributed to the Roman period.

Reading for Carts and Harness: Kilbride-Jones, H. E. 1980; Liversidge, J. 1968; Manning, W. H. 1976; Shortt, H. de S. 1959.

Water Transport and Lighthouses

Coracles, canoes and barges were probably used on rivers. Some carvel-built ships have been found. There is also evidence for docks and jetties of timber, and stone bases probably for cranes for unloading cargo.

Two Roman lighthouses are known in Britain, one on each side of Dover harbour. They were octagonal in plan, with 3·6m-thick walls of rubble faced with ashlar and bonding courses of tile. They may originally have been 25m high.

Reading for Water Transport and Lighthouses: Liversidge, J. 1968; Wheeler, R. E. M. 1929.

Architectural Remains

Many architectural remains have been found, belonging to both public and private buildings. These include stone column bases, drums and capitals, and mouldings. Fine stone was sometimes used, occasionally imported from the Mediterranean. **Lewis holes** enabled heavy stones to be lifted by the prongs of a lewis or lewison (lifting tackle).

Reading for Architectural Remains: Cunliffe, B. 1971.

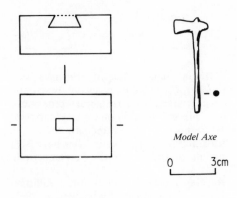

Model Axe

0   3cm

Lewis Hole

0   50cm

Sculpture

Various statuettes in bronze and clay have been found, often of classical deities or animals. Pipeclay figurines were cast in moulds and are mainly figures of Venus. Many of them were used as votive offerings or charms. There were also small carvings in jet, stone, shale and amber. Large statues carved in stone or cast in bronze were made, usually of eminent figures or deities, and inscribed pedestals for statues are sometimes found. A number of model objects have been found; they are mainly of bronze, but sometimes of iron, silver, lead or bone. The axe is the most common model, but there is a variety of other types including wheels, spears, stools and bells. They may have had a ritual function.

Reading for Sculpture: Green, M. J. 1975; Toynbee, J. M. C. 1964; Wheeler, R. E. M. 1930, 43–9.

Milling

Rotary querns (rotary hand-mills) consisted of a lower stone **(nether stone)** with a central spindle set in it, usually of metal, and an **upper stone** which fitted over the spindle and was supported by the **rynd** (of metal or wood) which rested on top of the spindle. The upper stone was turned by means of a wooden handle; experiments have shown that it was easier to use a reciprocating motion rather than a rotary one. The faces of the stones sloped downwards and were dressed with radial striations to help the grain and flour move towards the edges of the stones and out of the mill. Various types of coarse stone were used to make these querns including Andernach lava imported from the Rhineland. The native beehive quern continued to be used as well. Corn could also be ground in larger rotary querns, some large enough to be turned by donkeys, though these are rare. Like portable querns, they consisted of an upper and lower stone. Large circular masonry platforms have been found which probably belonged to these large rotary querns.

Millstones have been found belonging to watermills and mechanically driven mills; as have iron shafts or spindles which rotated the stone. Stone spindles have also been

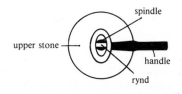

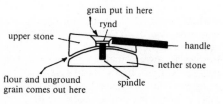

Section and Plan of a Rotary Quern

0   20 cm

found, either belonging to the wooden waterwheels or to the stones. Stones with slots for spokes were the core of the hubs for waterwheels. Mill races have also been found.

Reading for Milling: Curwen, E. C. 1937; Liversidge, J. 1968.

Natural Resources

Various natural resources were mined or quarried including gold, galena (for lead and silver), tin, copper, iron, coal, stone, gravel, clay, sand and chalk.

Gold was mined at *Dolocauthi*, Dyfed. It was used mostly for coinage, and also for jewellery.

Lead (usually as the ore galena) was mined mainly in the Mendips. It was poured into moulds, probably of clay, usually after the extraction of silver, to form ingots **(lead pigs)** with official stamps. Lead was used for a variety of articles such as spindle whorls, weights and seals. Sheet lead was widely used for items such as tanks, piping, lining of baths, containers and coffins. Lead plates with curses have also been found. Lead was also used in the production of pewter.

Silver was obtained from lead by the cupellation process. Flat ingots of silver have been found, both **bar-shaped** and **double-axe shaped**. Silver was used to make various types of vessels (such as bowls, dishes, jugs, skillets and goblets), coinage, thimbles, votive tablets, spoons, jewellery and pins. It was also used in niello and inlay decoration.

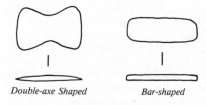

Double-axe Shaped   *Bar-shaped*

Silver Ingots

0   10 cm

Pewter is an alloy of lead and tin. The pewter industry was based in the West Country using tin from Cornwall and lead from the Mendips. It was popular as a substitute for silver from the third century, and was used particularly for table services, some articles of which have fish symbols and Chi-Rho monograms and so may have had a Christian significance. Stone moulds for the casting or beating of pewter vessels have been found.

Tin was mined in Cornwall and was used as an alloy with copper to make bronze, and later as an alloy with lead to make pewter.

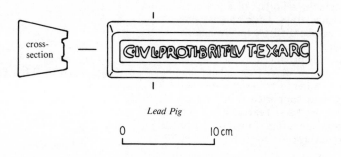

Lead Pig

0   10 cm

113

Copper ores were mined or collected from the surface. Copper was most commonly used as an alloy with tin to produce bronze. It is possible to work bronze cold, but it was generally cast. Lead was added to increase its fluidity. Bronze was usually cast in stone moulds, although larger items were produced by the lost-wax method. Sheet bronze was also used for the production of some vessels. Bronze was used for many objects such as personal goods, statues, coins, tableware, chariot and harness equipment, fish hooks, small bells and votive tablets. **Brass** was produced by the addition of zinc to copper.

Iron ores were mined, usually by the open-cast method, and smelted in bowl furnaces and shaft furnaces. The latter were introduced by the Romans. Iron was used to make a wide range of weapons, tools and fittings.

Various stones were quarried and inscriptions have been found on some quarry faces. **Lime-kilns** have been found which were square or oval and built of stone. They burnt limestone or chalk to which sand was added for mortar; it could also be used for plaster and stucco work. **Coal** was usually obtained in open-cast mining and was sometimes used in smelting and heating (although **charcoal** was the main fuel for smelting).

The **Kimmeridge shale industry** was carried out in Dorset. Various objects were made from shale such as table tops, table legs, bracelets, plates, trays, spindle whorls, counters and carvings. Many objects were made on a lathe and flints were used to carve the shale. **Coal money** is the name given to the circular pieces of shale which are the cores from lathe-turned bangles.

Jet was probably collected off the beaches at *Whitby*, North Yorkshire, and was probably worked in the area, mainly in the third and fourth centuries. It was used to make pins, finger-rings, bangles, beads, pendants, spindle whorls, dice, distaff handles, carvings, trays, knife handles and counters. It can be difficult to distinguish jet from shale.

Salt was usually produced by the evaporation of seawater or water from inland salt springs. The water was evaporated in shallow clay pans supported over hearths on cylindrical fire bars. Fragments of the pans and bars are often found and are known as **briquetage**.

Rope and **basketwork** have been found in Roman contexts.

Leather often survives in waterlogged deposits. It seems to have been widely used by the Romans for a variety of objects such as tents, horse harness, saddles, clothing, shoes, bags, shield covers, scabbards and chamfrons. Military **tents** were made from overlapping leather panels and resembled ridge tents. **Saddles** were probably of leather, some with pairs of horns for strengthening. Such horns of bronze have been found at *Newstead*, Borders. Most Roman **footwear**, including women's and children's shoes, had soles of several layers of leather with hobnails. Soles of wood are rare. A **carbatina** was a sandal made from one piece of leather stitched at the heel. It had a soft sole and an openwork upper fastened by a lace. A **soccus** was a shoe made from a leather sole without hobnails, and a separate leather upper. A **caliga** was the traditional legionary sandal with hobnails and a separate leather upper, consisting of numerous thongs. A **calceus** was a shoe with hobnails and a separate leather upper secured by thongs. A **solea** was a simple sandal with a thong between the toes and a sole with hobnails.

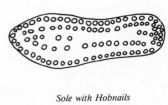

Sole with Hobnails

0   10 cm

Carbatina

0   10 cm

114

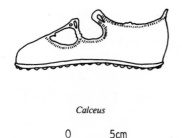

Calceus

0   5cm

Numerous **wooden articles** have been found in waterlogged deposits. They include:

Barrels: these were probably used for conveying liquids. A secondary use for barrels was in the lining of pits and wells.

Buckets: wooden with metal fittings.

Wooden Bucket

0   20cm

Pipes: these carried fresh and waste water and consisted of lengths of hollowed, roughly hewn timber joined by iron collars.

Tent pegs: were made of wood.

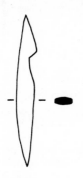

Wooden Tent Peg

0   20cm

Chests: usually only the metal fittings survive. Also made of wood were handles for all kinds of tools and implements, boxes, bowls, soles for shoes, combs, bobbins, spindles, cart wheels, oars and yokes.

Various articles of **bone and antler** are known such as weaving combs, toilet combs, pins, needles, spoons, ligulae, bracelets, knife handles, buttons, sword hilts, tablet weaving plates, hinges, dice, amulets, pendants and counters.

Reading for Natural Resources: Brown, D. 1976; Charlesworth, D. and Thornton, J. H. 1973; Davey, N. 1961; Dix, B. 1979; Elkington, H. D. H. 1976; Jackson, D. A. 1973; Lawson, A. J. 1976; Liversidge, J. 1968; McIntyre, J. and Richmond, I. 1934; Manning, W. H. 1976; RCHM 1962; Robertson, A. et al 1975; Robinson, H. R. 1975; Sherlock, D. 1976; Waterer, J. W. 1976; Webster, G. 1955.

Textiles

The evidence for Romano-British textiles is as follows: Wool was sheared using iron **shears** which varied in size and which were used for a variety of purposes, besides shearing sheep. Iron **carding combs** have been found. They were probably set in a wooden handle. **Distaffs** were usually of wood. Some ornamental ones had moulded

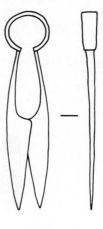

Shears

0   10cm

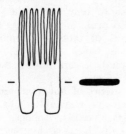

Iron Carding Comb

0   20 cm

handles made from amber, jet, bone or shale into which was set an iron pin. **Spindles** were of bone or wood and were up to 30cm long, with thickening to hold the spindle whorl. **Spindle whorls** were made from potsherds, baked clay, shale, metal and jet.

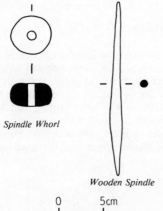

Spindle Whorl

Wooden Spindle

0   5cm

After spinning, the wool was probably wound into a ball, or onto bone or wooden bobbins. It was then woven on warp-weighted looms. **Loomweights** of baked clay, limestone and chalk have been found.

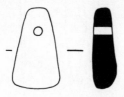

Baked Clay Loomweight

0   10cm

Some of these may have been used as net weights or to weigh down thatch on buildings **(thatch weights)**.

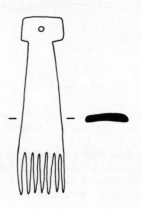

Weaving Comb

0   5cm

The weft thread was probably pushed into place by wooden or bone **weaving swords (spathae)**, although none has yet been identified in Britain. Some antler and bone **weaving combs** similar to those used in the Iron Age have been found, and may have been used for this purpose. **Tablet weaving** was carried out, attested by finds of triangular and square bone and bronze plates.

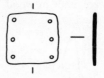

Tablet-weaving Plate

0   10cm

Long **needles** of bronze, possibly used for knitting, have been found. **Needles** for sewing were usually of bone, and sometimes of bronze or iron. **Netting needles** (a rod forked at both ends) of bronze and iron were used to make nets. **Thimbles** of bronze and silver are known.

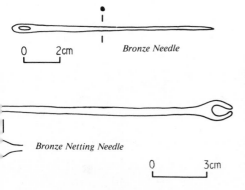

Bronze Needle

0   2cm

Bronze Netting Needle

0   3cm

Agricultural Economy

There is evidence in Roman times for the growing of cereals including wheat, barley and oats; beans, peas, turnips and flax are also known to have been grown. Cattle, sheep and pigs are known to have been kept, and the agricultural economy appears to have been based on mixed farming.

Reading for Agricultural Economy: Wacher, J. S. 1978.

Many remains of woollen textiles have been found. Other textiles were rare but included silk, linen and cotton. A glass **linen rubber** used for smoothing linen has been found.

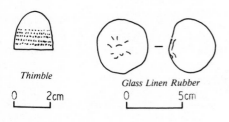

Thimble

Glass Linen Rubber

0   2cm

0   5cm

Reading for Textiles: Wild, J. P. 1970a.

Fasteners

Button-and-loop fasteners have been found; they were made of bronze, and were sewn or fixed to a garment. Some were enamelled. The head probably fitted through a buttonhole or a loop. They have also been interpreted as harness fittings. **Buttons** of horn and bronze are known **(dumb-bell buttons)**; clothes were also fastened by brooches and long pins.

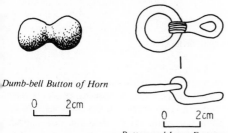

Dumb-bell Button of Horn

0   2cm

Button-and-Loop Fastener

0   2cm

Reading for Fasteners: Kilbride-Jones, H. E. 1980; Wild, J. P. 1970b.

Iron Tools

Iron was widely used for tools, and many Roman types differ little from hand-made tools of recent years. There was a wide range, including those used by the blacksmith, carpenter, joiner, farrier, shoemaker, farmer and other workers. Many had wooden handles.

Carpenters' and joiners' tools included **axes** of various shapes, **adzes, axe-adzes, hammer-adzes, hammers** of various forms, **nail claws**, a wide range of **chisels** (solid, socketed and tanged examples are known, the blades varying from thin to widely splayed), **socketed gouges** and **carpenters' planes** where the basic body was wood, usually with an iron sole and four rivets. The cutting edge was always of iron. The wooden case does not usually survive. There were two types of **saw**: one was a hand saw with one handle, the other was a bow saw or frame saw which was held at each end. The latter are rarely found complete. **Compasses, rasps** and **files** are also known.

Blacksmiths' tools included **tongs, sets** (strong chisels for cutting hot or cold metal and usually struck with a hammer), **anvils, punches** (used on hot metal; they could be round, square or any other desired shape and they could also be tanged), **files** and **drifts**.

Cobblers' tools included **cobblers' feet (lasts)**, and **awls**.

Building tools included **plasterers' trowels, plasterers' floats** (flat wooden boards with a handle used for smoothing plaster; examples made completely from iron are rare), **dividers** (also made from bronze), **wedges** (for use in quarries), **picks** and **crowbars**.

Agricultural tools included **forked hoes,**

117

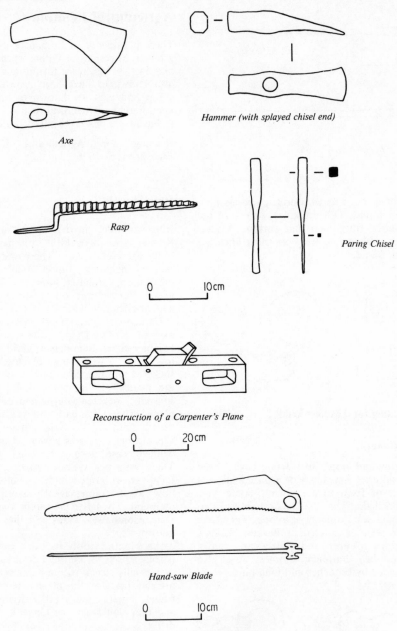

Axe

Hammer (with splayed chisel end)

Rasp

Paring Chisel

0   10cm

Reconstruction of a Carpenter's Plane

0   20cm

Hand-saw Blade

0   10cm

Some Examples of Carpenters' Iron Tools

turf cutters, **spade-shoes (spade-irons)** which were iron rims which fitted on spades of wood and were either straight or round-mouthed, **peat spades** used mainly in Scotland; **pitchforks** either tanged or socketed, **rakes, mattocks, ploughshares, spuds** which were probably used for cleaning mud from the share and mould-board of the plough, **reaping hooks** — late Iron Age and early Roman ones seem to be socketed and later ones tanged, **sickle blades** which unlike reaping hooks could be swung, **scythes** which were swung with two hands, and **shears**.

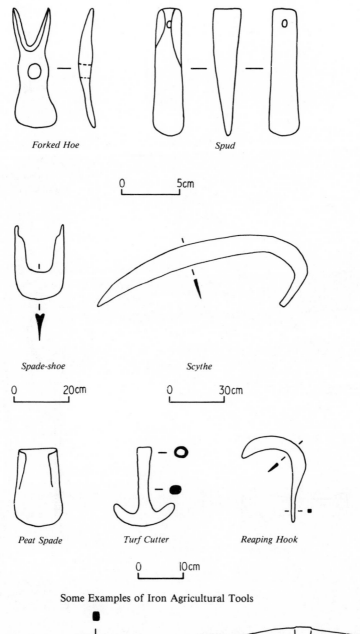

Forked Hoe   Spud

0   5cm

Spade-shoe   Scythe

0   20cm   0   30cm

Peat Spade   Turf Cutter   Reaping Hook

0   10cm

Some Examples of Iron Agricultural Tools

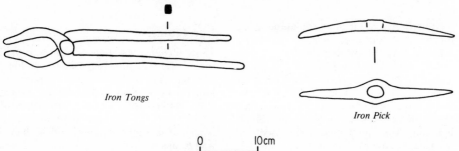

Iron Tongs   Iron Pick

0   10cm

119

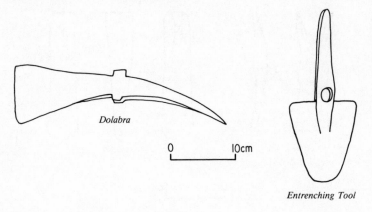

Dolabra

0   10cm

Entrenching Tool

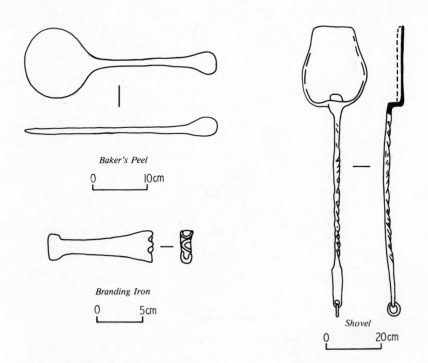

Baker's Peel

0   10cm

Branding Iron

0   5cm

Shovel

0   20cm

Military tools included **dolabrae** (sing **dolabra** — pickaxes usually used by soldiers), and **entrenching tools**.

Also found are **shovels** with long handles and small blades used for raking ashes. A **baker's peel** was found at *Housesteads*, Northumberland, and was used to place loaves in and out of a hot oven. Small **branding irons** may have been used for marking woodwork.

Iron Fittings

These included **T-staples** which were used for a variety of purposes, such as holding box flue tiles and other tiles in position, **joiners' dogs** (iron dogs, clamps, cleats, clips, staples) used to hold two pieces of wood together — some large ones held blocks of masonry together, and **U-shaped wall hooks**.

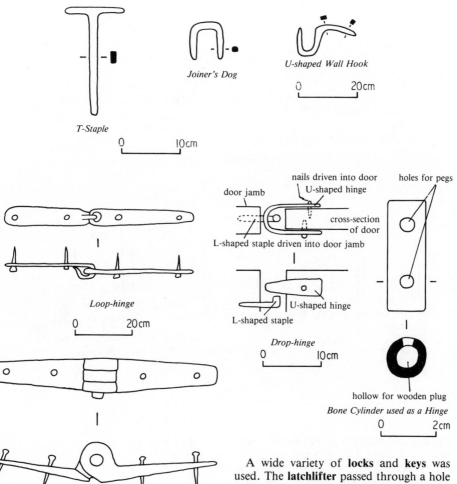

Joiner's Dog

U-shaped Wall Hook

0   20cm

T-Staple

0   10cm

nails driven into door

door jamb

U-shaped hinge

holes for pegs

cross-section of door

L-shaped staple driven into door jamb

Loop-hinge

0   20cm

U-shaped hinge

L-shaped staple

Drop-hinge

0   10cm

hollow for wooden plug

Bone Cylinder used as a Hinge

0   2cm

Strap-hinge

0   5cm

Three main types of **hinge** are known:
Drop-hinge This had two parts: a U-shaped hinge attached to a door which slotted over an L-shaped staple in the door jamb. It could also be used for gate hinges.
Loop-hinge This had two parts and was used on lids.
Strap-hinge (pivot-type hinge) This was for both vertical and horizontal use.
Perforated **bone cylinders** are known which have been interpreted as hinges: they were plugged with wood to provide a wooden spindle at one end and a matching socket at the other, so that two or more cylinders could be interlocked. They could have been used on wooden cupboards and boxes.

A wide variety of **locks** and **keys** was used. The **latchlifter** passed through a hole in a door and raised a latch. These first appeared in the Iron Age. The **tumbler lock** was opened with a T or L-shaped **lift key** of iron. A more elaborate form pushed the bolt along with a **slide key** of iron or bronze. A **lever lock (rotary lock)** was similar to a modern lock and was opened by turning a key. Padlocks were also used, the most complex being the **barb-spring padlock**.

Iron fittings also included **split pins**, **collars** for wooden pipes, **ring-headed pins**, **studs**, **hooks**, **ferrules** (probably used to protect the ends of sticks, spears and so on), **chains** and **manacles**. There were two basic types of **nail**: square-sectioned with a flat or round head, or rectangular-sectioned with a triangular head. **Iron beams** have been found which are 1m to 2m long and seem to have supported boilers for bath-houses (see bath buildings).

121

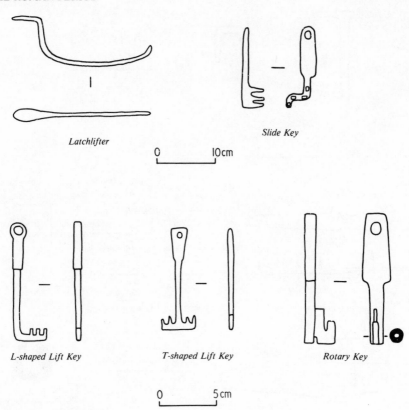

Latchlifter

Slide Key

0   10cm

L-shaped Lift Key   T-shaped Lift Key   Rotary Key

0   5 cm

Reading for Iron Tools: Corder, P. 1943; Frere, S. S. 1972, 149–50; Manning, W. H. 1970; Manning, W. H. 1976; Piggott, S. 1955; Rees, S. E. 1979; Wacher, J. S. 1971; Wheeler, R. E. M. 1930.

Domestic Artifacts

Silver, bronze, and iron vessels were used. Pewter vessels became common in the late third and fourth centuries. Bowls, dishes, jugs, ewers, frying pans, beakers, cups, plates, handled wine strainers, and sauce-pans **(paterae)** are known. There were also bronze oil flasks for use in the cleansing process at the baths. Very elaborate vessels were probably non-functional and some may have had a sacrificial purpose. **Gridirons (craticula)** were iron grids used to support pots over charcoal fires. **Spoons** were made of bone, iron or silver. Folding spoons are known. Some spoons had pointed stems used for eating shellfish. Iron

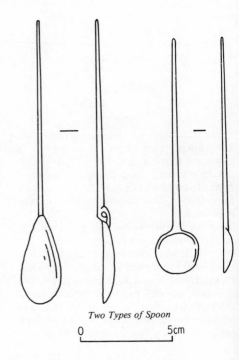

Two Types of Spoon

0   5cm

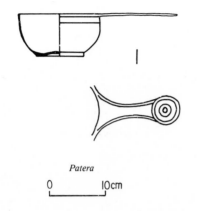

Patera

0   10cm

There seems to have been an organised industry in whetstones. They were usually rectangular in shape, but size and form varied widely.

Reading for Domestic Artifacts: Manning, W. H. 1976; Peacock, D. P. S. 1971; Wheeler, R. E. M. 1930.

Weapons and Armour

Weapons

Weapons were generally made of iron. The **gladius** was a short sword, usually used by legionaries. A **spatha** was a longer sword, usually used by auxiliary troops. Both types were hung from a belt or a baldric in a scabbard or sheath of wood covered with leather and metal. They had handles (**hilts**) of bone, ivory, or possibly wood. The **dagger (pugio)** was rarely used as a weapon. It seems to have largely gone out of use by the early second century. Its scabbard was often highly decorated. The **pilum** was a throwing spear or javelin consisting of a long wooden shaft and slender iron spearhead. Some had lead-weighted spearheads (**plumbatae**). **Barbed spearheads** are rare; some may have been brought to Britain by auxiliary troops.

knives were used and ranged from large cleavers to small folding knives. Blades were usually pointed with tangs, though large examples were often socketed. Handles were of bone, metal or wood; some were very ornate. **Whetstones (hones)** were made of stone and were used for sharpening knives and other edge tools.

Two types of **artillery** machine were used by the Romans. The **catapulta** (or **onager** — ass, or **scorpion**) was usually mounted on wheels; large stone balls (**ballista balls**) were placed at the end of an arm which was wound back and then released for firing. **Ballistae** were smaller machines, similar in action to cross bows. They fired thick wooden arrows tipped with iron bolt-heads. A **carro-ballista** was a ballista mounted on a cart. Both types of artillery had a range of about 350m.

Ferrules were used to protect the butts of wooden spearshafts. Archers are attested by rare finds of **arrowheads** which were usually socketed, barbed or leaf-shaped and made of iron. **Sling bolts** (or **bullets**) were fired by units of slingers using acorn-shaped lead bullets (**glandes**) or ones of baked clay. **Calthrops** of iron were thrown in the path of the enemy, especially cavalry, as an impediment to movement.

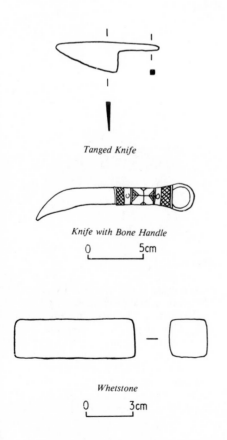

Tanged Knife

Knife with Bone Handle

0   5cm

Whetstone

0   3cm

Armour

Three types of **body armour** were worn.

123

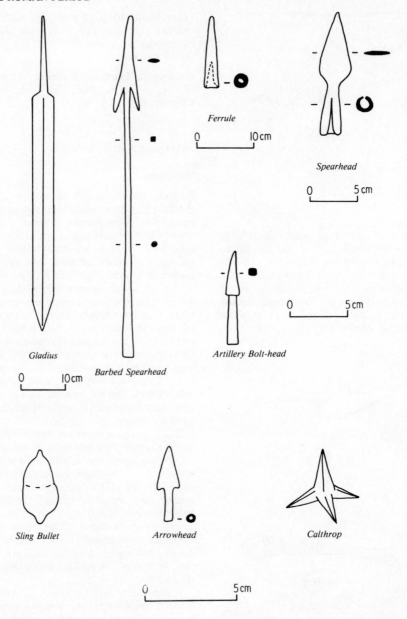

Ferrule

0   10 cm

Spearhead

0   5 cm

Artillery Bolt-head

0   5 cm

Gladius

0   10 cm

Barbed Spearhead

Sling Bullet   Arrowhead   Calthrop

0   5 cm

Lorica segmentata consisted of a cuirass of iron strips; **lorica hamata** was iron mail; **lorica squamata** was an armour of variously shaped scales of bronze or iron.

Helmets were of various types. A **jockey-cap** was a helmet with a peak-like projection to protect the back of the neck. The **Coolus** type of jockey-cap was made of bronze with a knob for a crest, cheekpieces and a flattened neck guard. **Imperial-Gallic** helmets were made of iron with 'eyebrow' decoration, cheekpieces and a neck guard. **Cavalry sports' helmets (parade helmets)** were made of iron or bronze and covered the whole face; some were very elaborate. The helmets were probably lined with a woollen fabric glued to the inside.

Shields were of two types. The **clipeus** was an oval shield used by auxiliaries; the **scutum** was a curved rectangular shield

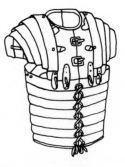

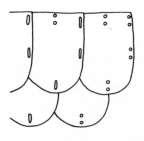

Lorica Hamata

Lorica Squamata

Lorica Segmentata

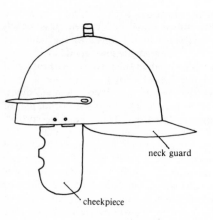

neck guard

cheekpiece

Coolus Type of Jockey Helmet

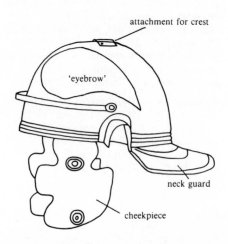

attachment for crest

'eyebrow'

neck guard

cheekpiece

Imperial-Gallic Type of Helmet

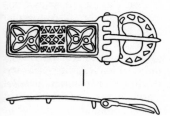

Enamelled Bronze Belt Plate and Buckle

Belt Stiffener
Stud for attachment
to leather belt

Eye Guard

125

about 1·5m high, used by legionaries. Shields were made of wood bound with iron or bronze. They were covered on the outside with leather and metal fittings, including a **boss (umbo)**. On the inside was a hand grip.

Horse armour has also been found, including leather masks **(chamfrons)**. Two elaborate ones decorated with tooled and studded ornament were found at *Newstead*, Borders. **Eye guards** of metal have been found; some were attached to the harness and some to chamfrons.

Many fittings for leather **belts** have been found, especially in military contexts. They were usually of bronze, often very ornate, with niello and enamelled decoration. Belt or strap **terminals** were used, as well as belt **buckles** which were often attached to **belt plates** or **belt ends**. **Belt stiffeners (belt mounts)** of bronze are also found. Some distinctive belt fittings, which are probably late Roman in date, were once thought to be evidence of Germanic mercenaries in Britain in the late Roman period: see Saxon Introduction, and Saxon belt fittings.

Reading for Weapons and Armour: Buckland, P. 1978; Christison, D. et al 1898–9, 213–8, 246; Connolly, P. 1975; Cunnington, M. E. and Goddard, E. H. 1934, 173, pl liii; Hawkes, C. F. C. and Hull, M. R. 1947; Robinson, H. R. 1975.

Glass

Glass is known to have been used for vessels, window panes, gemstones, rings, heads of bronze pins, gaming counters, bangles and beads. A glass linen rubber is also known.

Vessel Glass

By the time of the Roman conquest of Britain, glassblowing was common in the Roman world and was gradually superseding other methods of manufacturing glass vessels. By the second century nearly all glass vessels were blown. Although some glass-making sites are known in Britain, it is likely that most Roman vessel glass was imported from the Continent. Very little Roman glass has been found on pre-Conquest sites.

A wide range of vessels was produced

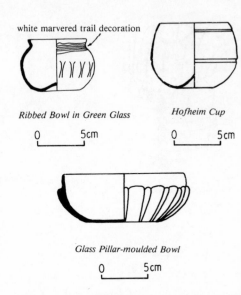

white marvered trail decoration

Ribbed Bowl in Green Glass

0   5cm

Hofheim Cup

0   5cm

Glass Pillar-moulded Bowl

0   5cm

during the early Roman period, including **fine ribbed bowls** and **cameo glass vessels** which seem to disappear in the late first century. Cameo glass was made by blowing the vessel with at least two skins of different colours **(cased glass)**. It is not known exactly how this was done in Roman times, but it is possible that the technique of **cupping** was used. This technique consists of blowing the outer skin of glass, and, while it is still hot, blowing the inner skin inside it and marvering it to weld the two skins together. Often the outer skin was opaque white, overlying a darker colour or colours. When the vessel was cold, much of the outer surface was cut away to reveal the inner, differently coloured glass; and the remaining part of the outer glass was cut into a figured scene in relief, with a lapidary wheel.

A rare type of vessel was the **gold-band glass** vessel. These were made by sandwiching a thin band of gold foil between two skins of clear glass, these skins being cast and ground so that they fitted together exactly with the gold foil trapped between them.

Coloured glass was used for high quality vessels (mainly tableware) but this was superseded by the use of colourless glass for such wares around the end of the first century. **Facet-cut** colourless glass came into use at that time and continued in use into the fourth century. Facet-cutting was the decoration of a vessel by cutting the surface into closely set facets (often diamond-shaped). Glass vessels for everyday use were usually made of bluish-green glass until the fourth century when greenish-yellow glass began to be used.

During the first century a few vessels were still made by casting, notably the **pillar-moulded bowls**. These were made in a variety of colours, but brightly coloured and polychrome bowls seem to have stopped being made about the middle of the first century, although the bluish-green ones continued until the beginning of the second.

A distinctive early form of blown vessel is the **Hofheim cup** — a small hemispherical cup with wheel-cut lines. It seems to have gone out of production by about AD 75.

Decorated mould-blown vessels are rare in Britain, but very distinctive, and included **circus cups** and **gladiator beakers** which portray chariot racing and gladiatorial contests, often with the names of the competitors. There are also **negro-head beakers** and **almond-knob beakers**.

From the first to the third centuries many vessels were decorated with **pinched projections**.

In the second and third centuries, **snake thread decoration** was used, although it was not very common in Britain.

Square bottles began to be made around the time of the Conquest and continued in use into the third century. **Rectangular, hexagonal, octagonal** and **cylindrical**

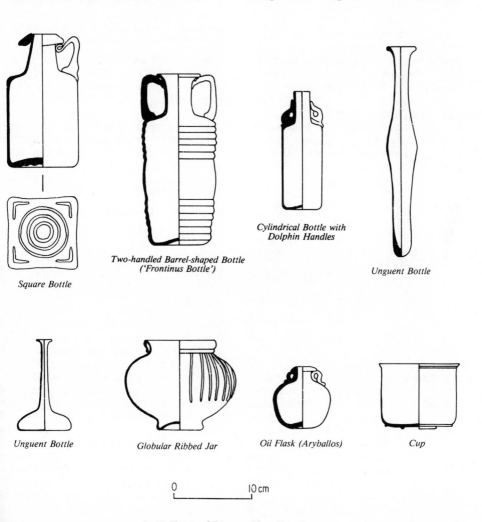

Square Bottle

Two-handled Barrel-shaped Bottle ('Frontinus Bottle')

Cylindrical Bottle with Dolphin Handles

Unguent Bottle

Unguent Bottle

Globular Ribbed Jar

Oil Flask (Aryballos)

Cup

0   10 cm

Some Types of Roman Glass Vessel

127

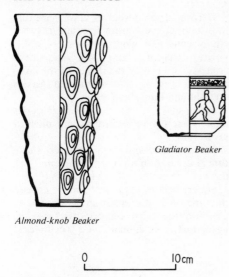

Gladiator Beaker

Almond-knob Beaker

```
0                    10 cm
```

bottles were also made. **Unguent bottles** are found throughout the Roman period. **Barrel-shaped bottles** were made in the fourth century. These often had an abbreviated form of **'Frontinus'** on the base and are sometimes called **Frontinus bottles**. Cylindrical bottles with dolphin handles, and long narrow **unguent bottles** also date to the fourth century.

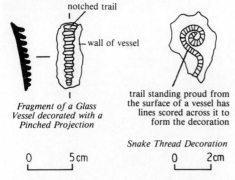

notched trail

← wall of vessel

Fragment of a Glass Vessel decorated with a Pinched Projection

trail standing proud from the surface of a vessel has lines scored across it to form the decoration

Snake Thread Decoration

```
0        5 cm          0      2 cm
```

In the fourth century vessels began to be decorated with applied blobs of different colours and with complex trails marvered into the surface. The high quality wares were decorated with, for example, hunting or biblical scenes, either engraved, or portrayed by the cameo technique. However, many glass vessels of the fourth century were very thin and some were not finished off properly. By about AD 400 the use of Roman glass virtually ceased in Britain, although pieces are found in Saxon graves after this date.

Reading for Glass: Harden, D. B. 1969; Price, J. 1976; Price, J. 1978.

Window Glass

Window glass first occurs in the first century. Most Roman window glass was made by casting, but some of it was made by the cylinder method. Cylinder glass probably dates from the third century. Only one piece of crown glass is known to date to the Roman period in Britain; it was found in a fourth century context at *Chichester*, Sussex. Window glass was often quite thick and usually had a blue-green tint, although some nearly colourless window glass has also been found. There is little evidence for the size of window panes in Britain; one has been found as large as 60cm square.

Reading for Window Glass: Harden, D. B. 1961; Harden, D. B. 1969.

Enamelling

Enamelling was used in the decoration of metal objects such as jewellery (especially bronze brooches), skillets, cups, studs, belt mountings, and mountings for caskets. Cloisonné jewellery has been found but is rare before the fifth century.

Reading for Enamelling: Butcher, S. A. 1976.

Pottery

Fine Wares

Much fine ware was imported into Britain from the Continent, in particular **samian pottery (terra sigillata, red gloss pottery, red coated pottery)** which was a fine tableware imported on a large scale. It was usually red with a glossy surface formed by a slip of fine clay, the red colour being obtained by firing in an oxidizing atmosphere. Some black samian is found, fired in a reducing atmosphere. Plain vessels were wheel thrown, and relief-decorated ones made in moulds, impressed with decorative scenes. Samian is a useful dating key because of the potters' stamps and the changing style of decoration, form and fabrics, which varied from centre to centre.

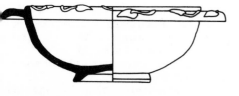

Samian Bowl with decoration en Barbotine

0   5cm

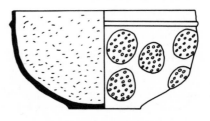

Lyon Ware Raspberry Cup

0   5cm

Samian Bowl with Moulded Decoration

0   10cm

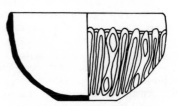

Central Gaulish Colour-coated Cup
with Hairpin and Teardrop Decoration

0   3cm

The pots were made in a limited number of forms, classified by **Dragendorff (Dr** or **Drag), Knorr and Walters, Curle, Ludovici** and **Ritterling**. Types of vessels include dishes, cups, bowls, jars, mortaria, candlesticks, inkwells and jugs. Samian was made in Italy from the first century BC **(Arretine ware)**; this is rarely found in Britain. The industry was taken over by potteries in southern Gaul in the first century AD. The vessels from these potteries were plain or simply decorated, with trailing scrolls and leaves, mainly en barbotine. The industry passed to central Gault in cAD 100. Highly decorated vessels, especially with human and animal figures, were made using rouletting and relief moulding techniques. East Gaulish potteries took over cAD 150; standards declined and production ceased cAD 250. Samian was also made in small quantities at *Colchester*, Essex.

Imitation samian (pseudo-samian) was made in Britain. The pottery styles imitated samian ones, but the decoration was impressed and not moulded. The samian gloss was imitated by using a red colour coat.

Other fine wares imported, particularly in the first century, came mainly from Gaul, the Rhineland and Italy. Some fine wares were manufactured in Britain. **Gallo-Belgic wares** describes pottery made in France in the first century especially **terra nigra** (a fine, polished grey-black ware), **terra rubra** (a cream to buff pottery with an orange colour coat), and **mica-dusted pottery** (see mica-dusting). White or buff Gallo-Belgic wares were probably made in Britain. There were also other imported colour-coated wares:

Pompeian red pottery was made in France and consisted of shallow plates with a thick internal red slip. 'Pompeian' describes the colour.

Lyon ware was a very thin-walled, cream-coloured pottery, with colour coats from red to dark brown. Small cups and beakers are distinctive, decorated with roughcast sand and en barbotine, including **raspberries** which were small discs of applied clay.

Central Gaulish colour-coated pottery had a yellow or light-brown fabric and a brown colour coat. Especially common

129

were cups and beakers with **hairpin** and **teardrop** decoration, and with roughcast decoration.

South Gaulish colour-coated pottery had a buff to orange fabric and a brown colour coat; especially common were cups and beakers with roughcast decoration.

Lower Rhineland colour-coated ware (Rhenish ware) had a fine, hard white fabric with a dark-brown colour coat, or else a buff, red or brown fabric. Especially common were decorated cups and beakers, including **motto beakers** which had white barbotine scrolls and words forming phrases such as 'Bibe' (drink up) and 'Vivas' (good health).

Spanish colour-coated ware had a buff to brown fabric with a brown or orange colour coat and consisted of a wide range of vessel shapes with barbotine decoration.

North Italian colour-coated ware had a grey fabric, in particular **eggshell ware** — pottery with an extremely fine, thin fabric.

North Italian red slip ware was a fine orange slip-coated ware found in Britain mainly in the fifth and sixth centuries.

Lead glazed ware had a fine yellow-white fabric and a green glaze. It was first made in Gaul and was once termed **St Rémy ware**.

Reading for Fine Wares: Arthur, P. and Marsh, G. 1978; Greene, K. 1979; Hartley, B. R. 1969; Oswald, F. and Pryce, T. D. 1920.

Coarse Wares

Imported coarse wares included amphorae and mortaria. But most coarse wares and some fine wares were made in various production centres in Britain, fired in bonfire, single-flue or parallel-flue kilns:

Alice Holt (Farnham) pottery was made in the *Farnham* district of Surrey from the mid first to the fourth centuries, and consisted mainly of grey and cream sandy cooking pots.

Lower Nene Valley ware (Nene Valley ware, Castor ware) was characterised by a

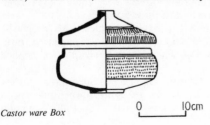

Castor ware Box

0   10cm

fine, whitish-grey fabric with dark colour coating. **Hunt cups** are common with rouletting and animals en barbotine. **Castor boxes** are also distinctive. Imitation samian, painted parchment ware and mortaria are also common.

Oxford potteries produced wares mainly from the third century, in particular parchment wares (a buff pottery), imitation samian and mortaria.

New Forest potteries produced wares from the mid third century, in particular red slipped bowls, slipped and white parchment wares and fine tablewares in a stoneware. Indented beakers are common.

Brockley Hill potteries near London were an important centre for mortaria, in a pink to buff fabric, from the mid first century. The potteries had declined by the mid third century.

North Kent Marshes potteries produced BB2 wares, London ware, poppy-head beakers, and grey wares from the mid first to fourth centuries.

Severn Valley ware was a light buff-orange pottery made from the mid first to fourth centuries. Some has been found on Hadrian's Wall.

Crambeck ware was made from the mid fourth century in North Yorkshire, especially dishes, bowls, and mortaria of buff ware ornamented with a reddish-brown paint.

Colchester potteries manufactured Gallo-Belgic forms, imitation samian, fine wares and barbotine beakers similar to those of the Nene Valley, from the mid first to fourth centuries.

Pevensey ware was made in Sussex from the late fourth century. It had a very hard dark orange/red fabric with a deep red-orange colour coat.

Dales ware is found in Derbyshire, Lincolnshire and Humberside from the second to fourth centuries and consisted of coarse shell-tempered hand-made cooking pots.

Derbyshire ware was made from the mid second to late fourth centuries and had a hard gritty fabric. The vessels were often designed to hold lids and can be confused with Medieval vessels. The fabric had a pimply surface, sometimes described as 'goose flesh petrified'.

Knapton ware was made in Humberside in the fourth century. Crude hand-made cooking pots of native origin were common, heavily tempered with calcite mineral grits.

Huntcliff ware was a calcite-gritted ware also made in Humberside, used particularly for cooking pots.

Trent Valley ware was a rough, dark-grey, shell-gritted fabric made in the mid-late first century. Especially common were tall cooking pots and jars similar to some Dales ware.

Parisian stamped wares, found in North Yorkshire, Humberside and Lincolnshire, were beakers and jars, often cordoned or rouletted, made in various hard, grey fabrics. They were burnished externally and decorated with impressed stamps.

Savernake wares were light-grey flint-gritted vessels made in Wiltshire in the mid first to late second centuries.

Wessex grog tempered wares were hand-made pots copying black burnished wares from the late third century.

Patch Grove ware is found in north-west Kent and was produced from the mid first to late second centuries.

East Midland burnished wares consisted of grey-brown bowls and jars found mostly in the north-east Midlands. They date to the late third and fourth centuries.

Calcite-gritted (shell-gritted) wares were made in the Midlands from the late third century and had a coarse fabric heavily tempered with particles of shell or calcite.

London ware was an early imitation of terra nigra and was made in southern England.

Black burnished ware is divided into black burnished 1 and 2 (BB1 and BB2). BB1 was a black, gritty, partly burnished, hand-made ware. It was bonfire fired. Cooking pots were most common and often had lattice decoration. BB2 was a grey-black, partly burnished, wheel-thrown ware and was finer than BB1. Lattice decoration was also used. BB1 was made from the first century in the *Poole*, Dorset, region and at *Rossington Bridge*, South Yorkshire. BB2 was made from the mid first century in *Colchester*, Essex, and north-west Kent.

Pottery Forms

Mortaria (sing **mortarium**) were large strong bowls with a flange for easy gripping, and a spout; they were used for the preparation of food. Grit could be added to the inside to roughen and strengthen it **(trituration)**. Rims varied considerably. In the first and second centuries there was often a maker's stamp.

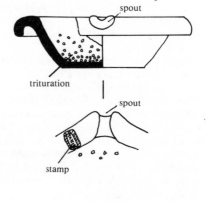

Mortarium

0   10cm

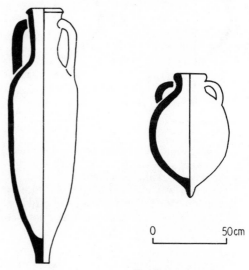

Two Types of Amphora

0   50cm

0   20cm

Amphorae were large two-handled containers mainly used for the transport of liquid and perishable commodities, such as wine and olive oil. They usually had a pointed base to enable easy stacking. They were brought into Britain from the late Iron Age to the post-Roman period, probably full of imported goods. **Tituli picti** (painted inscriptions) were painted on some amphorae to indicate the source, type and quantity of the commodity. Many amphora styles are known by **Dressel numbers**, after H. Dressel's classification, or by **Camulodunum numbers**, from the classification of amphorae found at *Colchester* (*Camulodunum*), Essex.

Flagons were used for holding liquids. They had narrow necks and globular bodies with one or more handles and a screw, ring or flanged neck, or a disc rim. **Hofheim flagons** were imported to or made in Britain for the army cAD 43–70. They had cylindrical necks, and outcurved lips with a triangular section, with one or two handles. **Lagenae** were large two-handled flagons at least 0·5m high. A **jug** was a flagon or handled jar with a spout.

handled jar with a wide mouth. A **storage jar** was a large jar for storage (eg of grain); some smaller jars were probably used for storage as well.

Beakers were drinking vessels of various forms such as **butt beakers, girth beakers, folded beakers (indented beakers), motto beakers** (see Lower Rhineland ware), **ovoid beakers** (some of which had handles and were termed **handled beakers**) and **hunt cups**. A **pedestal beaker** was a beaker with a pedestal base. A **poppy-head beaker** was shaped like the seed-head of a poppy and was often decorated en barbotine.

Bowls had a variety of forms such as **wide-mouthed, carinated, segmental (hemispherical), tripod**, and **campanulate**. A **spouted strainer** was a bowl, usually biconical, with a projecting tubular spout with an internal strainer, possibly for straining wine. A **Castor box** was a type of bowl with a lid (see Lower Nene Valley ware).

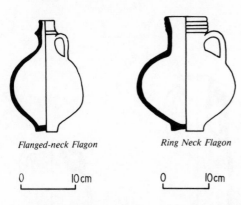

Flanged-neck Flagon   Ring Neck Flagon

0   10cm   0   10cm

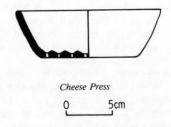

Cheese Press

0   5cm

Jars could be narrow- or wide-mouthed. **Cooking pots** were coarse ware jars for cooking and the preparation of food. A **face urn** was a jar with a human face in appliqué decoration and was often used as a funerary vessel. A **honey jar** was a double-

A **cheese press (cheese wring)** had holes and ridges on the base and sometimes on the lids, and may have been used for cheese making. **Tazze (incense cups)** often have signs of burning on their interior. They may have been used as lamps or in religious rites.

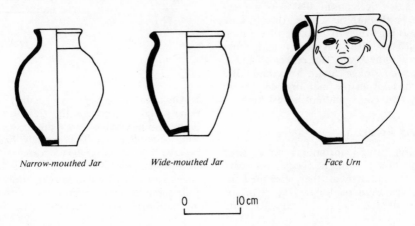

Narrow-mouthed Jar   Wide-mouthed Jar   Face Urn

0   10cm

Girth Beaker

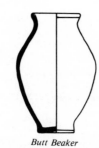

Folded Beaker

Ovoid Handled Beaker

Butt Beaker

Poppy-head Beaker

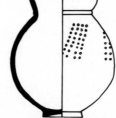

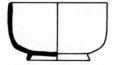

Segmental Bowl

Tripod Bowl

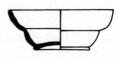

Campanulate Bowl

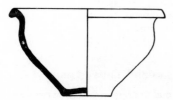

Wide-mouthed Bowl

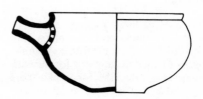

Bowl with Spouted Strainer

0   10cm

Unguent Flask

Tazza (with frilled cordons)

Unguent flasks were possibly used as containers for ointment or perfume. Other pottery forms include **dishes (pie dishes, dog dishes), plates (platters), triple vases (flower vases), tankards (mugs)** and **lids**.

See also Chapter 7 for Romano-Saxon pottery.

0   5cm

0   5cm

133

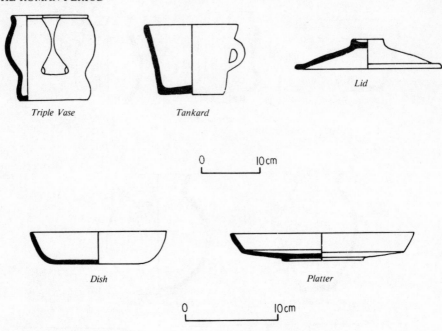

Triple Vase

Tankard

Lid

0   10cm

Dish

Platter

0   10cm

Reading for Coarse Wares and Pottery Forms: Cunliffe, B. 1971; Hull, M. R. 1958; Kaye, W. 1914; Swan, V. G. 1978; Webster, G. 1976.

Lighting

Rooms could be lit by torches, candles or lamps. Most **lamps** were of pottery and consisted of a small chamber to contain the oil, with a filling hole, a nozzle for the wick and sometimes a handle. Some had more than one nozzle. They were made in two-piece moulds. Many had elaborate designs and a maker's stamp. Lamps could also be made in bronze, lead or iron. Some were made for suspension. Open lamps of pottery or metal are also found; they are not now thought to have been used as lamp-holders. Pottery **lampfillers** have also been found; some were once thought to be children's feeding bottles. Candles were also used. **Candelabra** and **candlesticks** of pottery, bronze and iron have been found.

Reading for Lighting: Bailey, D. M. 1976; Collingwood, R. G. and Richmond, I. 1969; Wheeler, R. E. M. 1930.

Finials and Votive Lamps

Several pottery artifacts have been found which were once interpreted as chimney

Pottery Candlestick

0   5cm

Votive Lamp

0   5cm

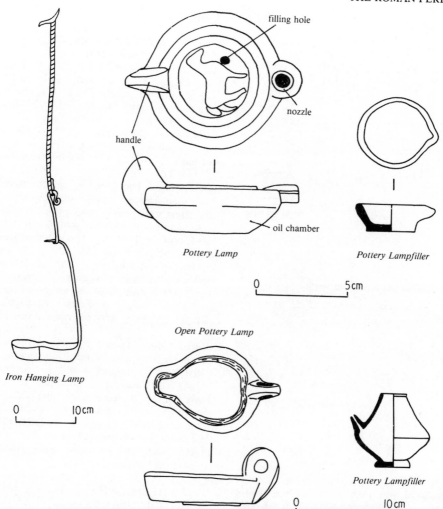

filling hole

nozzle

handle

Pottery Lamp

oil chamber

Pottery Lampfiller

0   5 cm

Open Pottery Lamp

Iron Hanging Lamp

0   10 cm

Pottery Lampfiller

0   10 cm

pots. They are now seen as two groups: **finials** (or **ventilators**) which were pierced at the top; and **votive lamps** (or **lamp chimneys**). The latter were probably associated with religious rites. Both types have openings cut in the side.

Reading for Finials and Votive Lamps: Lowther, A. W. G. 1934; Lowther, A. W. G. 1972.

Weights and Measures

A **balance (libra)** was used for weighing. This consisted of a **balance arm** of bronze, iron, or occasionally bone, from which two scale pans of bronze were suspended.

Folding balance arms are known. The goods to be weighed were placed on one scale pan and weights of lead, stone, bronze, iron, or bronze-covered lead were placed on the other scale pan until the two pans balanced. A **steelyard (statera)** consisted of a balance arm with a scale pan for the goods to be weighed suspended from one end. A **steelyard weight** was moved along the arm until it balanced; the weight of the object was measured from marks along this balance arm. The arm could often be suspended from different hooks, so as to cover different ranges of weight; the weights were marked on one or two faces of the balance arm and corresponded to the hook used. Combined balance and steelyards are known.

135

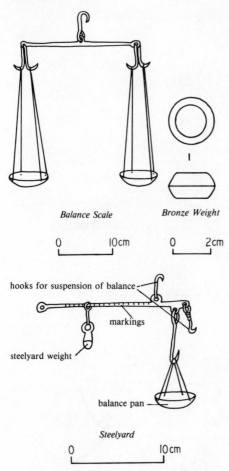

Balance Scale   *Bronze Weight*

0   10cm   0   2cm

hooks for suspension of balance

markings

steelyard weight

balance pan

Steelyard

0   10cm

A bucket-shaped vessel of bronze (**modius**) measured corn; folding bronze **rulers** have been found and ox bones divided into units of measurement. Bronze and iron **dividers** are known, and also lead, bronze, or bronze-covered lead **plumb-bobs**.

Corn Measure

0   15cm

Reading for Weights and Measures: Wheeler, R. E. M. 1930.

Coins

Coins underwent a complicated history of change and reform, particularly due to heavy inflation in the later Empire. They were struck in official mints and usually carried a mint mark. There were three classes of coinage: gold *AV* , silver *AR* , and bronze *Æ* .

Gold Coins The **aureus** was the main gold coin. A **solidus** was introduced in cAD 309. A **tremis** was one third of a solidus, popular after AD 370.

Silver Coins The **denarius** was the main silver coin. **Denarii** became very debased so that some were merely silver-plated bronze coins, and eventually they went out of use in the mid third century. The **antoninianus** was introduced in AD 214, and carried a radiate crown on the emperor's head. It was equivalent to about 1½ denarii. Coins with heads of emperors wearing radiate crowns are often called **radiates. Barbarous radiates** are later and inferior copies of radiates.

Bronze Coins These consisted of bronze and brass coins and included the **sestertius** (**'first brass'**), **dupondius** and **as** (**'second brass'**) and **semis** and **quadrans** (**'third brass'**). Coins of reduced size appeared in the third and fourth century (**minims**), some only 4mm in diameter (**minimissimi**). The **follis** was introduced in AD 295 as a bronze coin alloyed with silver which became very popular.

1 aureus = 25 denarii
1 denarius = 4 sestertii
1 sestertius = 2 dupondii
1 dupondius = 2 asses
1 as = 2 semisses
1 semis = 2 quadrantes

The obverse side of coins usually portrayed the emperor's head, and the reverse usually commemorated an event or virtue.

Reading for Coins: Casey, P. 1980; Collingwood, R. G. and Richmond, I. 1969; Reece, R. 1970.

Purses

Arm-purses of bronze worn on the forearm are found mainly in military contexts.

Reading for Arm-purses: Liversidge, J. 1968.

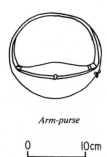

Arm-purse

0 _____ 10cm

Dodecahedra

Several dodecahedra have been found. Their purpose is not known, although many theories have been put forward, such as surveying instruments or lucky charms.

Dodecahedron

0 _____ 5cm

Reading for Dodecahedra: Wheeler, R. E. M. 1930, 110–11.

Musical Instruments

There is little evidence for musical instruments apart from literature, mosaics, and sculpture. The cithara, lyre and lute were probably played, as well as various wind instruments. **Bone whistles** and **flutes** have

Bronze Mouthpiece

0 _____ 2cm

been found and also mouthpieces of bronze and iron, probably belonging to the **tuba** — a straight trumpet up to 1·2m long.

Reading for Musical Instruments: Liversidge, J. 1968.

Games

Gaming boards for various types of game have been found, including a kind of backgammon and a war game. They were made of stone, tile, bone or wood and were usually divided into squares by incised lines. **Dice** were made from bone,

Dice

0 ____ 2cm

occasionally lead or jet. **Game pieces (counters)** were made of bone, horn, jet, glass and potsherds. Bone ones often have graffiti on one face. Glass counters were usually plano-convex in section; some were decorated, although the most common ones were undecorated in black, white or transparent green. Besides their use in games, some of them may have been used as a form of 'tally' in mathematical calculations (see also Iron Age gaming counters).

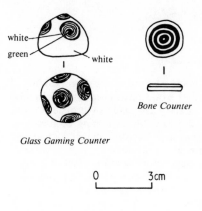

Glass Gaming Counter

Bone Counter

0 _____ 3cm

Reading for Games: Liversidge, J. 1968; Turner, R. C. 1979.

Toilet and Surgical Instruments

Toilet articles are common finds; some may have had a surgical use. They include **nail cleaners, tweezers, ear picks** (or **scoops**) and **tooth picks**, found singly or in sets, and usually made of bronze. Iron and bronze **strigils** were hollow scrapers used for removing from the skin the oil which was applied after bathing. **Razors (novacula)**

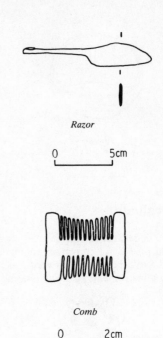

Razor

0   5cm

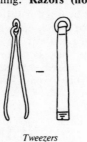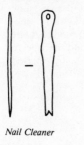

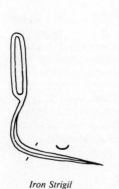

Nail Cleaner   *Tweezers*   *Ear Scoop*

Comb

0   3cm

0   2cm

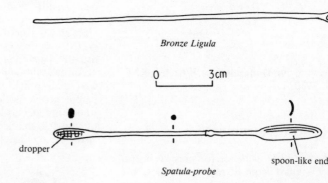

Bronze Ligula

0   3cm

dropper

Iron Strigil   *Spatula-probe*   spoon-like end

0   5cm

0   3cm

were made of bronze and iron. **Combs** of bone and wood have been found. **Ligulae** (sing **ligula**) were made of bronze or bone and were used for extracting cosmetics or medicine from narrow unguent bottles.

Surgical instruments also included **spatula-probes** (or **spathomelae**) of bronze: the broad end was used for applying ointments and the swollen end as a probe, depressor or dropper.

Bronze **artery forceps** and **rectractors**, and **scalpels** of bronze or iron have also been found. Evidence for medicaments

occurs as **oculists' stamps** which were used to mark cakes of eye ointment. They were made of clay or stone.

The ivory sticks of a **fan** were found at *York*; the connecting material may have been leather. **Mirrors** of polished bronze and silver are known. There were plain rectangular mirrors in a wooden frame, as well as discs, some of which had soldered handles. Some disc mirrors had handles across the back. Circular **lid mirrors** consisted of two mirrors shaped like lids which fitted together when not in use; this type

Oculist's Stamp

0   2cm

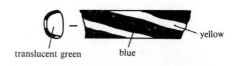

translucent green   blue   yellow

Side View and Section of a fragment of a Type 1 Glass Bangle

0   3cm

was rare in Britain. Mirrors of silvered glass are known but rarely survive. They were held in a lead frame and were probably imported from the glasshouses of *Cologne* in the third and fourth centuries.

Reading for Toilet and Surgical Instruments: Lloyd-Morgan, G. 1977a; Lloyd-Morgan, G. 1977b; RCHM 1962.

Jewellery

Bracelets were made from gold, silver, bronze, jet, shale, glass, bone or ivory. They ranged from plain types to designs such as snake representations and twisted wire forms. **Glass bangles** have been divided into three types: **type 1** is not very common and is mainly restricted to a small area of Scotland. It has oblique bands of opaque red and yellow, or blue and yellow, laid over a core of different coloured glass which is only visible on the inside of the bangle. Sometimes additional decoration was added to the outside (such as eye motifs) and marvered flush with the surface. **Type 2** has between one and three narrow cables (usually blue and white) fused lengthwise into a translucent core (normally blue or green). **Type 3** consists of a number of sub-types. They basically consist of a single-coloured core in opaque white or yellow with no decoration, or of blue, amber, yellow or white trails inlaid into white, blue or green cores.

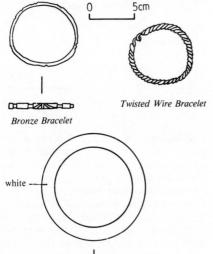

0   5cm

Twisted Wire Bracelet

Bronze Bracelet

white

Side View, Top View and Section of an Undecorated Type 3 Glass Bangle

0   5cm

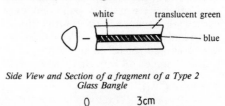

white   translucent green

blue

Side View and Section of a fragment of a Type 2 Glass Bangle

0   3cm

blue   white

Side View and Section of a Type 3 Glass Bangle

139

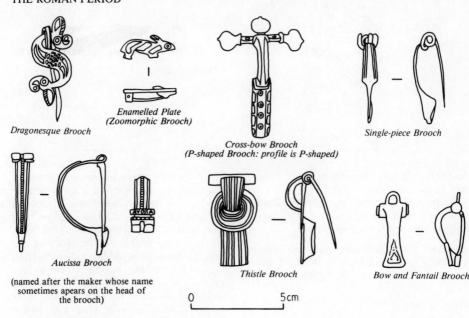

Dragonesque Brooch

Enamelled Plate
(Zoomorphic Brooch)

Cross-bow Brooch
(P-shaped Brooch: profile is P-shaped)

Single-piece Brooch

Aucissa Brooch

(named after the maker whose name
sometimes apears on the head of
the brooch)

Thistle Brooch

Bow and Fantail Brooch

0   5cm

Brooches (fibulae) are common finds; they were used to fasten clothes and were made of bronze or occasionally of iron. Some had enamelled decoration. They ranged from simple types made from a single piece of bronze wire to very elaborate ones which were used in pairs and were particularly common in the fourth century. **Pins** made from bone, jet, silver and bronze were also used for fastening clothing or as hairpins. Some had very elaborate heads.

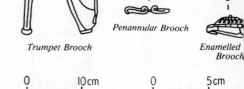

Trumpet Brooch

Penannular Brooch

Enamelled
Brooch

0   10cm   0   5cm

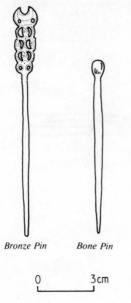

Bronze Pin   Bone Pin

0   3cm

Beads for necklaces were made from glass, coral, marble, bronze, pottery, stone, amber, bone, jet, shale and shell. Necklaces were also made from gold wire or chain. **Pendants** are also known. Three broad groups of **glass bead** were in use in the Roman period in Britain: Iron Age types, Roman types, and exotic beads from many parts of the Roman Empire. The Iron Age types of bead continued to be used until the middle of the second century, but subsequently there were very few brightly decorated beads. Precious and semi-precious stones were preferred for jewellery, and small, relatively plain monochrome glass beads were preferred to the more garish Iron Age types. Late Roman

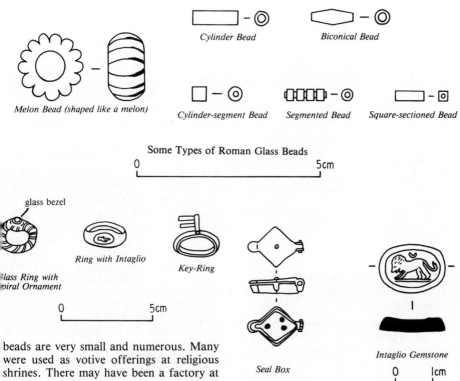

Cylinder Bead

Biconical Bead

Melon Bead (shaped like a melon)

Cylinder-segment Bead   Segmented Bead   Square-sectioned Bead

Some Types of Roman Glass Beads
0   5cm

glass bezel

Ring with Intaglio

Key-Ring

Glass Ring with
Spiral Ornament

0   5cm

Seal Box

0   2cm

Intaglio Gemstone

0   1cm

beads are very small and numerous. Many were used as votive offerings at religious shrines. There may have been a factory at *Woodeaton*, Oxfordshire, producing beads solely for offering at the nearby shrine. There were probably a few small bead factories in Britain, although no definite site has yet been found. Some exotic beads found their way to Britain throughout the Roman period, although they were more numerous in the later Roman period. Little research has yet been done to trace the origins of these exotic beads.

Earrings are rare, although examples of gold, pewter and bronze have been found. **Rings** of various designs are found, made of gold, silver, gilded or plain bronze, iron, jet and glass (often with spiral ornamentation in yellow or white). Some had bezels inset with semi-precious stones, glass, intaglios or cameos. Some rings were made from twisted wire. Bronze **key-rings** are also known. **Intaglios** were semi-precious stones or glass precisely engraved with designs such as scenes from mythology. They were intended for making an impression in wax or clay. The wax seals were often protected by **seal boxes** made of bronze, with holes in the side through which a cord was passed. They also had one or more air holes. Seals were often used in conjunction with writing tablets.

Reading for Jewellery: Collingwood, R. G. and Richmond, I. 1969; Guido, C. M. 1978; Henig, M. 1974; Kilbride-Jones, H. E. 1937–8; Kilbride-Jones, H. E. 1980; Liversidge, J. 1968; Mackreth, D. 1973; Stevenson, R. B. K. 1976; Wheeler, R. E. M. 1930.

Writing Implements

Writing tablets of wood were used. One side was filled with wax with a raised border of wood. Two or more tablets were usually attached by a string or leather thong and sealed with wax. A **diptych** consisted of two tablets bound together, a **triptych** of three tablets, and a **polyptychon** more than three tablets. Writing was done with a **stilus** (**stylus**) of bronze, iron, or bone — one end was sharp, and one was flat to erase mistakes. Writing sometimes survives on tablets where the stilus scored the wood through the wax. Writing was also done on thin wooden tablets with ink using reed or

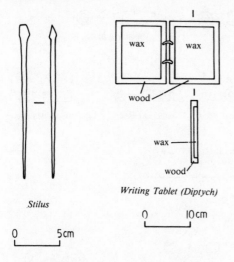

Stilus

Writing Tablet (Diptych)

0   5cm

0   10cm

metal pens with split nibs. **Inkwells** were made of bronze or pottery (particularly samian pottery).

Reading for Writing Implements: Bowman, A. K. and Thomas, J. D. 1974; Southwark and Lambeth Archaeological Excavation Committee 1978, 397–401.

Burial

Inhumation and cremation were both practised at the time of the Roman invasion; cremation became more common until the mid second century when inhumation gradually took over. Burials were placed outside towns, in cemeteries, which were often alongside roads and sometimes enclosed by a wall.

Cremation

The ashes of the dead were placed in containers — generally pottery or glass vessels or lead canisters **(ossuaria)**. They could also be placed in cists of tiles, stone or wooden planks, or placed in masonry mausolea or under barrows. **Barrows** are most common in south-east England. They could be up to about 13m high. Many had a flat top which may have carried a tombstone or wooden marker. **Tombstones** were usually decorated and carried an inscription — often including DM (Dis Manibus = to the spirits of the departed) and HSE (hic situs est = buried here). They are mostly found in military contexts. Wooden markers may have been used, but if so have not survived.

Inhumation

The poor were probably buried in shrouds or sacks, or in wooden coffins, the iron fittings of which sometimes survive. Wealthier people were buried in stone sarcophagi, lead coffins, lead-lined wooden coffins, or lead-lined stone coffins. Lead coffins were usually only inner coffins. Coffins were often placed in **mausolea** (which were rectangular or sometimes circular masonry buildings, usually internally decorated), or else in vaulted tomb chambers. Coffins could also be buried, placed under barrows or put in tile or stone cists. Stone sarcophagi could be plain and, where intended for burial, were sometimes roughly finished. Lead coffins and linings were often decorated. Stone sarcophagi could also be very elaborate and were most common in the third century. One feature of inhumation, which seems to have been a Christian practice, was to cover the body in the coffin with liquid plaster (gypsum or lime), thereby helping to embalm the body. Burials were accompanied by grave goods until the gradual acceptance of Christianity led to a decline in their use.

Reading for Burial: Dunning, G. C. and Jessup, R. F. 1936; Jessup, R. F. 1959; Liversidge, J. 1968; Reece, R. 1977; Toller, H. 1977.

General Reading for the Roman Period: Birley, A. R. 1964; Collingwood, R. G. and Richmond, I. 1969; Frere, S. S. 1978; Liversidge, J. 1968; Wacher, J. S. 1978.

Chapter 7

The Saxon Period

Introduction

The **Anglo-Saxon** period (**Saxon, Dark Ages, Migration, Migration and Early Medieval, Early Medieval, Medieval**) dates from the breakdown of Roman rule and Roman institutions in Britain in the fifth century, and lasted until the Norman Conquest in 1066. 'Anglo-Saxon' is a convenient label for the whole period, but the first settlers included **Angles** (from southern Denmark, settling in East Anglia and northern England), **Saxons** (from Germany, settling in the Thames Valley and Wessex), **Jutes** (from northern Denmark, settling in Kent and the Isle of Wight), and **Frisians** (from north Holland). There was also influence from the **Franks** (from Gaul: France and Belgium), particularly in Kent. The first Germanic people to settle in Britain were once thought to have been **foederati** and **laeti** (barbarian settlers on the Continent with an hereditary obligation of military service in the Roman army) coming to Britain from the fourth century onwards, as mercenaries in the Roman army. Their presence in Britain was thought to be indicated by distinctive brooches, buckles and belt fittings. However, this theory is no longer widely accepted. The first Saxons in Britain are now thought to have come in the early to mid fifth century, first as raiders and subsequently settling in the country (see also belt fittings).

The early settlers were divided into tribal groups, but by the ninth century there were four kingdoms: Wessex, Mercia, East Anglia and Northumbria. The latter three fell to the Vikings in the ninth century, only to be united under a single English king in the tenth, and ruled again by the Scandinavians in the eleventh century. The **Vikings** (literally 'sea farers') came from Scandinavia (Denmark, Norway and Sweden). Many places have names such as 'Danes' Camp' but have yet to be proved as camps of the Danes. Viking incursions and settlement were probably widespread as is suggested by the evidence of place names of Scandinavian origin, Viking art (mainly sculpture), Viking artifacts, a few burials, and coin hoards dating to the time of the raids.

The Saxon period is often divided into **Early Saxon** (450–650), **Middle Saxon** (650–850) and **Late Saxon** (850–1066). The Early Saxon period is often termed **pagan Saxon** (Christianity only being revived in Saxon areas of Britain from the late sixth century). The term **sub-Roman** is occasionally used to describe the fifth century.

Scotland, Wales and Cornwall were little influenced by Saxon and Viking incursions, although there was a major Viking settlement in the Northern Isles. The inhabitants of these areas are sometimes described as **Celts** or **Celtic-speaking people** and the areas **Celtic Britain**. In these areas this period is also referred to as **Early Christian**, and the archaeological evidence for the period is difficult to recognise since Iron Age traditions continued, making sites and finds difficult to date closely. The **Picts** (**Picti**) inhabited eastern and northern Scotland (**Pictland**), and the **Scots** (**Dalriadic Scots, Scotti**) who were of Irish descent inhabited western Scotland (**Dalriada**). There was also some Irish settlement in Wales and Cornwall.

Much of the history of this period is known from documentary evidence, and is supplemented by archaeological evidence, particularly coins.

Reading: Alcock, L. 1971; Dickinson, T. M. 1977; Thomas, A. C. 1971a; Wilson, D. M. 1976a.

Agricultural Economy

There is evidence for the cultivation of

spelt, rye, wheat, hemp, flax, woad and barley. Barley was the most important crop. Animals reared included pig, cattle, ox, sheep and goat. The horse was kept, but not for food. Bones of wild and domestic birds have also been found, and there is evidence for the exploitation of freshwater and marine fish, and shellfish.

Reading for Agricultural Economy: Wilson, D. M. 1976a.

Settlement

In the Celtic areas of Britain, Iron Age type settlement continued; raths, rounds, duns, souterrains, brochs, crannogs, and wheel-houses all continued to be used. **Nuclear forts** were built in Scotland and consisted of a central enclosure **(citadel)** linked to a series of outer enclosures bounded by stone walls constructed on the natural defences of a rock outcrop. **Defensive enclosures** were often built within Iron Age hillforts and were not necessarily built on a rock outcrop, although they are very similar to nuclear forts. Iron Age hillforts were refortified in various parts of Celtic Britain at this time.

In the Northern Isles there were also Viking houses of long-house form. These were rectangular in plan with stone and turf walls and a turf roof. The walls were often slightly bowed **(bow-sided houses**; they are sometimes described as **boat-shaped)**.

In Anglo-Saxon England most settlement sites were rural and did not usually occupy former Roman sites, except in some towns. Some royal sites are known, with large halls and outhouses, and on other sites there is evidence for workshops, outhouses, pits, pens and **sunken-featured buildings (Grubenhaüser**: sing **Grubenhaus, grubhuts** (sl), **cabanes, pit-huts, hut hollows)**. The latter consist of a pit, usually with a post-hole at each end. They were once thought to be huts with the pit bottom forming the floor of the hut, but they are now considered to have had raised wooden floors. Some may have been huts, while others are believed to have been weaving sheds or other types of workshop. They seem to have gone out of use in the seventh century. There is also evidence for framed rectangular buildings of posthole construction, with wattle and daub walls. They appear to

be mainly later in date than Grubenhaüser, and were sometimes bow-sided. Their posts could be set in postholes or on stone pads or beams. They are similar in plan to Medieval long-houses, and some larger ones are called **halls (timber halls)**. Floors were of clay, cobbles, stone, earth, or in some cases possibly of wood. Hearths are not often found, and so braziers may have been used.

Many villages are mentioned in the Domesday book and are therefore probably at least as early as late Saxon in date. Of these villages, many have continued to be occupied to the present day and have offered little opportunity of examining them for the presence of Saxon remains; deserted Medieval villages, which offer greater opportunities for examination, have as yet produced little evidence of former Saxon settlement.

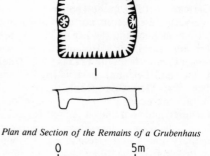

Plan and Section of the Remains of a Grubenhaus

0   5m

Reading for Settlement: Hamilton, J. R. C. 1956; Laing, L. 1975; Rahtz, P. 1976; Thomas, A. C. 1971a; Wilson, D. M. 1976a.

Towns

There is increasing evidence, particularly in the form of metalwork and pottery, for the continuity of settlement of some Romano-British towns into the Saxon period. Evidence for continuity of use of buildings is still not very abundant. From about the seventh century, coastal and riverine trading and industrial towns were developing (such as *Southampton*, Hampshire). Industries included metalworking, bone working, woodworking, textile production, leatherworking, and pottery manufacture, and there is evidence for extensive trading contacts with the Continent. In the ninth and tenth centuries new fortified towns were established in Wessex **(burhs)** which are mentioned in the Burghal Hidage (a document dating to the early tenth century). They had defences of dump construction ramparts and ditches, probably surmounted by a timber palisade. Other towns were also fortified, mainly with earth ramparts and one or more ditches. Many towns seem to have had a planned layout. *York* is the only Viking town in Britain for which there is substantial evidence. No towns were established in Celtic Britain.

Reading for Towns: Biddle, M. 1976.

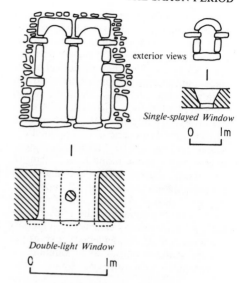

exterior views

Single-splayed Window

0   1m

Double-light Window

0   1m

Mills

At first grain was hand-ground in rotary querns, but later **watermills** constructed of wood were used for grinding grain, and millstones belonging to these mills have been found. By the eleventh century watermills were common in England. There is no evidence for windmills in Britain before the twelfth century.

Reading for Mills: Wilson, D. M. 1976a.

Churches

Most early churches were probably of timber, although little evidence of them has survived. Most early masonry churches were of a simple plan consisting of a nave, and sometimes a chancel, porticuses (in a cellular plan church) or transepts (in an integrated plan church), and a tower. **Porticuses (porticūs:** sing **porticus)** were lateral chambers. Some churches had side aisles in the nave. Cellular plan churches consisted of individual compartments connected by small archways or doorways; integrated

plan churches had an open plan. Chancels were apsidal or square-ended in plan, and some churches had small crypts and upper galleries. Square towers were placed between the nave and chancel or at the west end. Round towers at the west end are found in East Anglia. It is unlikely that the towers were built as refuges from Viking marauders as was once thought. The upper storeys of towers were used as belfries. Windows could be single-splayed or double-splayed, and there are some double windows with a central shaft. Doorways were usually rounded at the top, although some doorways and windows had triangular-shaped heads. Walls were constructed of ashlar, coursed stone, coursed rubble, oblique or herringbone coursing, or random rubble, while floors were of mortar or plaster. Window glass (some coloured) has been found on several sites, and many churches were probably plastered both inside and out.

Reading for Churches: Cherry, B. 1976; Christie, H. et al 1979; Morris, R. 1979; Taylor, H. M. 1978.

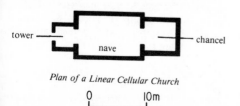

tower — nave — chancel

Plan of a Linear Cellular Church

0   10m

Monasteries

Monasteries were built in Celtic Britain from at least the sixth century, and were often sited within abandoned hillforts or in

145

coastal or inland promontory forts. In England, monastic sites were built from at least the seventh century. They can be difficult to recognise, particularly on town sites where the churches no longer exist, since monasteries at this period had no standard plan and early buildings would have been of wood. A church, refectory, dormitory (usually a single cell for each monk), guest house and domestic buildings would probably be found in most monasteries. Some monasteries seem to have been enclosed by a ditch and bank (**vallum, vallum monasterii**), or some other type of enclosure. The presence of an early monastery can sometimes be indicated by finds of inscriptions, evidence for literacy (such as writing implements), and exotic pottery. **Double houses** were communities of men and women ruled over by an abbess.

Reading for Monasteries: Cramp, R. J. 1976; Thomas, A. C. 1971a; Thomas, A. C. 1971b.

Burials

In the pagan Saxon period burials were mostly in cemeteries, but individual burials, mainly in barrows, also occurred. Some burials were deposited in earlier barrows. In northern and eastern England there were cremation cemeteries. The cremations were placed in pots and had few accompanying grave goods. In other parts of the country there were inhumation cemeteries (mainly extended burials) and mixed cremation and inhumation cemeteries. The inhumations had many accompanying grave goods, usually weapons for men and jewellery for women. Other grave goods included drinking vessels, glass vessels, buckets, bone pins, cosmetic brush holders (see needlecases), coins, spoons, spindle whorls, hanging bowls, combs, bone draughtsmen, buckles, purse-mounts, tweezers, strapends, belt mounts, latchlifters, keys, toilet sets consisting of miniature iron or bronze shears, knives, tweezers and ear-scoops, girdle-hangers, and pottery vessels. In the seventh century the number of grave goods decreased, and the cemeteries were laid out more regularly, with bodies orientated east-west. This change may have been due to a gradual adoption of Christianity.

In Celtic Britain, Christian burials occur from an early date. Some of these were commemorated by inscribed stone slabs or pillars (see stone sculpture). In Scotland **long cist cemeteries** occur. These consist of inhumations with no grave goods placed in long stone cists. They may have been Christian burials.

Ship burials and **boat burials** — burials placed in ships or boats — are found. There are some very rich burials; the richest and most famous being the **Sutton Hoo ship burial** from *Sutton Hoo*, Suffolk. Here there was a group of burials under barrows, the largest containing a seventh-century ship burial, probably of a king. The ship had been dragged up from the estuary of the river Deben, and the body and grave goods placed in it. The whole ship and burial deposit was covered with a barrow. No body was found; it appears to have been destroyed by the acid soil. The grave goods were extremely rich and largely unique. They included much gold jewellery set with garnets, millefiori and enamel (such as jewelled shoulder clasps and a purse lid), a gold buckle, and a sword with a jewelled gold pommel and hilt. The other grave goods included imported silver, mainly dishes, drinking horns and wooden vessels decorated with silver gilt panels, a bronze Coptic bowl (from Egypt), bronze hanging bowls with enamelled escutcheons, a 'sceptre' comprising a fine whetstone with bronze attachments, an imported Swedish parade helmet, an iron axe-hammer with an iron shaft, an iron stand, spears, chain mail, leather shoes, a leather bag, a maplewood lyre, a large circular shield, and iron-bound wooden vessels.

From the eighth century in England the majority of burials was in Christian cemeteries or churchyards. These burials were extended inhumations with no grave goods. Only a few Viking burials are known (recognisable by their grave goods — often swords), and it has been suggested that the Vikings adopted the Christian burial method and used existing churchyards. Only two Viking cemeteries are known — a group of barrow burials at *Ingleby*, Derbyshire, and a group of burials at *Kildale*, North Yorkshire. Viking graves are also known from the Northern Isles.

Reading for Burial: Bruce-Mitford, R. 1972; Bruce-Mitford, R. 1975; Bruce-Mitford, R. 1978; Meaney, A. 1964; Nash-

Williams, V. E. 1950; Rahtz, P. et al 1980; Thomas, A. C. 1971a; Thomas, A. C. 1971b; Wilson, D. M. 1976a.

Dykes

In the seventh and eighth centuries, expansion of English power led to the construction of artificial boundaries between the English and Welsh in order to avoid border disputes. These consisted of several dykes (linear earthwork boundaries), the longest and most famous being **Offa's Dyke** which ran from the mouth of the Wye to the mouth of the Dee. There were also linear earthworks in other parts of the country, some of which may have represented boundaries between various kingdoms.

Reading for Dykes: Fox, C. 1955; Ordnance Survey 1966; Stanford, S. C. 1980.

Mortar Mixers

Three Middle Saxon mortar mixers have been found at *Northampton*. Plaster, mortar and concrete are formed by the mixing of lime, or similar material, with an aggregate (usually sand or gravel) and water. Limestone was first burnt in a kiln, producing quicklime. This was then slaked (mixed with water) in a trough or pit to produce lime putty. Sand or gravel was then mixed with this lime putty to produce plaster, mortar or concrete. The Northampton mortar mixers were hollow basins 2m to 3m in diameter, lined with wattle work. A central post supported a beam from which a number of paddles were suspended. This beam was rotated by people or animals.

Reading for Mortar Mixers: Williams, J. H. 1979, 118–33.

Metals

Gold and Silver

Little is known of the mining or extraction of metals in the Saxon period. Gold and silver were probably imported. Gold was used for jewellery (such as rings), and for coinage. Silver was used for coinage, jewellery, sword hilts, pins, double-linked chains (found only in Scotland), decorative mounts and chalices. Various gold and silver objects have been found in Scandinavia which were taken there from Britain in Viking raids. A large silver hoard, originally from Ireland, was found at *Cuerdale*, Lancashire, buried in a lead-lined chest. This was probably taken in a Viking raid. Several silver hoards have been found in Celtic areas containing such things as rings, armlets, necklaces and scrap silver (see also Sutton Hoo).

Lead and Pewter

Pewter was occasionally used for brooches and rings. Lead was rare in the pagan Saxon period but was used in the later period for vessels, spindle whorls, loomweights, balance weights, figures, glazing strips and

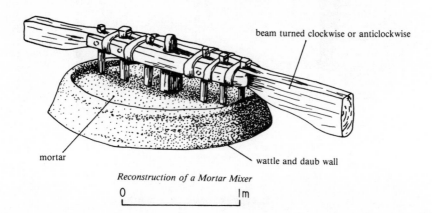

beam turned clockwise or anticlockwise

mortar

wattle and daub wall

Reconstruction of a Mortar Mixer

0   1m

147

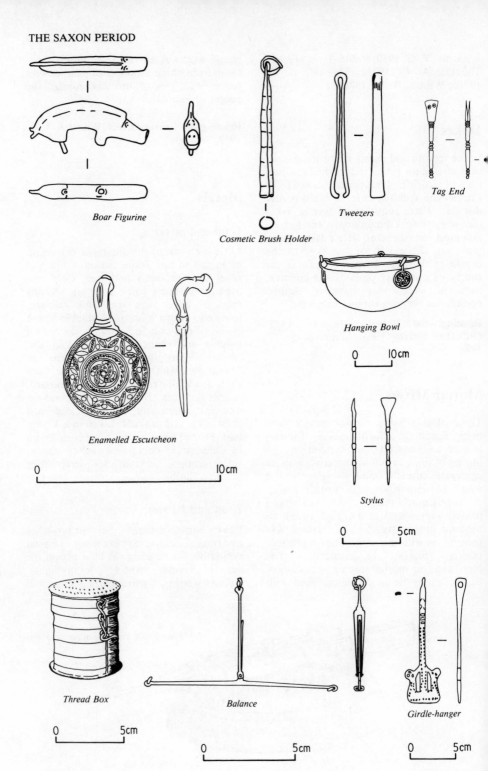

Boar Figurine

Cosmetic Brush Holder

Tweezers

Tag End

Hanging Bowl

0   10cm

Enamelled Escutcheon

Stylus

0   10cm

0   5cm

Thread Box

Balance

Girdle-hanger

0   5cm

0   5cm

0   5cm

Examples of Saxon Bronze Artifacts

roof flashings. Lead mortuary crosses and name-plates of late Saxon date are also known. Fragments of lead have been found from lead working.

Bronze

There is some evidence of bronze working from excavations in most areas of Britain — mainly copper found in crucibles. Bronze was used for a variety of objects including buckles, strap-ends, brooches, hooked fasteners, rings, tweezers, balances, scale pans, weights, styli, rivets, studs, boar figurines, bells, tag ends, coins, pins, needles, bowls, hanging bowls, buckets, scabbard chapes, cheekpieces and stirrups.

Some late Saxon **balances** have folding arms. **Styli** were probably used to write on wax tablets; the thick end would have been used as an eraser. Some **tag ends (tags)** have decorated plates and zoomorphic terminals. They were split to receive a strap or ribbon and may have been used as book markers; some may have been used as strap-ends. There are also **'needle cases'** of bronze, consisting of a tapering tube of sheet bronze closed by a ring at the narrow end and open at the broad end. Needles would have fallen out and so they probably actually held hair or bristles and were used as **cosmetic brushes. Thread boxes (work boxes)** occur frequently in women's graves of the seventh century. They were made of sheet bronze and contained organic material (mainly thread and cloth) and occasionally needles. They had a lid and were suspended from a chain. **Hanging bowls** are found in both Celtic and Saxon contexts (the latter are often graves); they were bowls suspended by three or four rings, often with ornate **escutcheons**. T-shaped pieces of bronze **(girdle-hangers)**, imitating keys, were hung from châtelaines. There is evidence for pits for casting church bells. (See also Sutton Hoo.)

Iron

Little is known about how iron ore was obtained in the Saxon period, although there is evidence for the use of shaft furnaces and smelting in most areas of Britain. Iron could be embellished by tinning (applying a coating of tin), applying bronze or copper to the surface, or inlaying

with other metals. It could also be used in pattern-welding. Iron was used for a variety of objects including weapons, tools and fittings. Other objects included tweezers, weaving swords, buckles, needles, snaffle-bits, horseshoes, stirrups, prick spurs, knives, latchlifters, keys, locks, padlocks, and purse-mounts. **Purse-mounts (strike-a-lights, firesteels)** probably had a dual purpose as the framework of a tinder-pouch and as the steel from which to strike a spark.

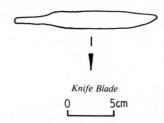

Knife Blade

0   5cm

Iron **knives** of the early Saxon period were often tanged, single-edged and of wedge-shaped cross-section. Folding knife blades are known, dating mainly from the tenth century.

Smiths' tools included iron hammers, cold chisels, tongs, pritchels and files, but no anvils have yet been found.

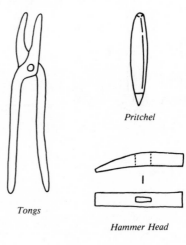

Pritchel

Tongs

Hammer Head

Blacksmiths' Tools

0   10cm

Carpenters' tools included iron axes, adzes, hammers, boring-bits, chisels, gouges, draw-knives, planes (similar to

149

Roman planes), saws, and wedges. Some
axes may have been tools and weapons,
including T-shaped axes and the francisca,
possibly used as a throwing axe.

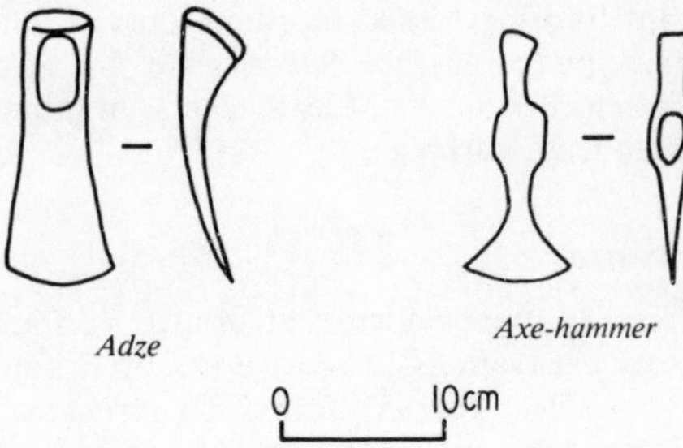

Adze

Axe-hammer

0   10 cm

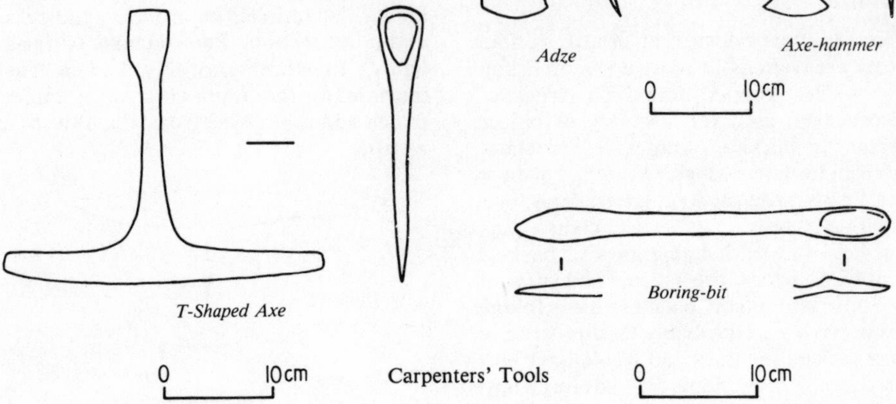

T-Shaped Axe

Boring-bit

0   10 cm   Carpenters' Tools   0   10 cm

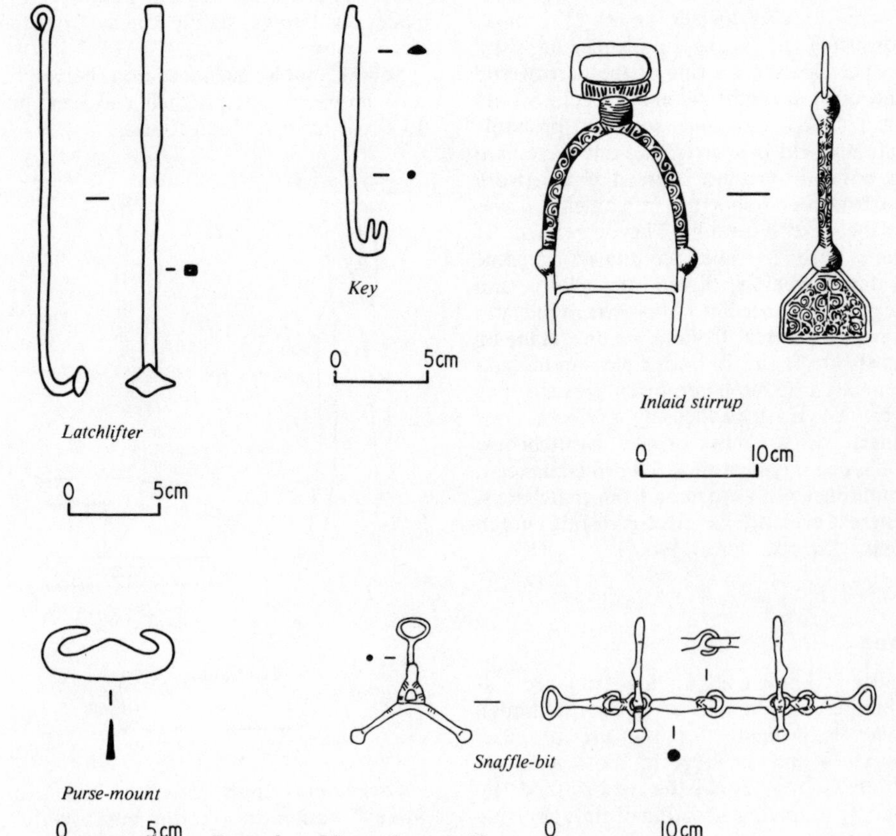

Key

0   5 cm

Inlaid stirrup

0   10 cm

Latchlifter

0   5 cm

Purse-mount

Snaffle-bit

0   5 cm   Examples of Saxon Iron Artifacts   0   10 cm

Agricultural tools included iron plough shares, scythes and spade-shoes (see also Sutton Hoo).

Reading for Metals: Brown, D. 1974; Brown, G. B. 1915; Fowler, E. 1968; Graham-Campbell, J. and Kidd, D. 1980; Hawkes, S. C. 1973; Henderson, I. 1979; Kilbride-Jones, H. E. 1980; MacGregor, A. 1978; Rodwell, W. 1979; Wilson, D. M. 1976b.

Weapons

Spearheads

Spearheads are the most common type of Saxon weapon found. The spear usually had a shaft of ash, although there were many forms and sizes of spearhead. The earliest spearheads were barbed and these are first seen in the Roman period. Spearheads with angular blades are the most common. Those of the later Saxon period tended to be larger, with moulded or grooved sockets to strengthen the junction between the blade and socket.

Swords

In the pagan Saxon period swords are found mainly in graves of men, while in the Viking period they are found mainly in graves and in rivers. Early swords **(spathae)** were two-edged weapons with a flat blade and tang, while later swords had a fuller (once termed a blood-channel) down the length of each face of the blade. Hilts can be very elaborate and have been used as the basis of classifications of swords. The **hilt** consists of the pommel, pommel bar, guard and grip. **Grips** were of wood, bone, horn, leather or metal. The earliest swords had straight **pommel bars**; these became slightly longer and curved from the ninth century. **Pommels** were often **cocked-hat shaped** or **boat shaped. Ring swords** had an attachment to the pommel **(ring-pommel)** to take a ring or bead, and date to the sixth century. The **lobed pommel** was popular from the ninth century. **Scabbards** were of leather-covered wood, occasionally with a metal chape. **Blades** of swords often carried the maker's name or mark, and were often **pattern-welded**, particularly from the ninth

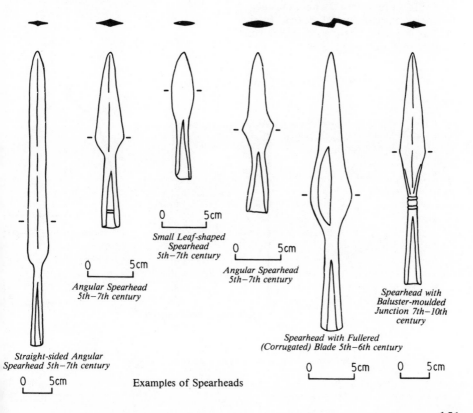

Small Leaf-shaped
Spearhead
5th–7th century

0   5cm

Angular Spearhead
5th–7th century

0   5cm

Angular Spearhead
5th–7th century

0   5cm

Straight-sided Angular
Spearhead 5th–7th century

0   5cm

Spearhead with Fullered
(Corrugated) Blade 5th–6th century

0   5cm

Spearhead with
Baluster-moulded
Junction 7th–10th
century

0   5cm

Examples of Spearheads

century. Pattern-welded swords were once described as **damascened**, but damascening was an oriental process which was not used in the manufacture of Saxon swords. In pattern-welded swords, strips of iron and steel were forged, twisted and welded together. The blade of the sword was then polished and the differing bands of iron and steel formed distinctive patterns.

Scramasaxes: sing **scramasax** (seaxes: sing **seax**) were single-edged swords or daggers, resembling an enlarged knife. In England scramasaxes date from the sixth century. Some have inlaid patterns and inscriptions. They had pommels, although these rarely survive. Scabbards were mainly of wood or leather, with bronze or silver fittings.

Other Weapons

The Saxon **shield (buckler)** was circular or oval in form, made of wood and sometimes covered with leather. The centre was pierced and was covered by an iron **boss (umbo)** attached to a grip. Early bosses were squat in form, but later became taller, developing into **sugar-loaf bosses**. In the late Saxon period kite-shaped shields with rounded tops were introduced.

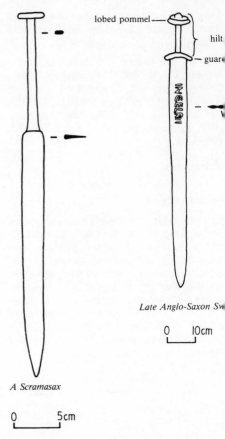

lobed pommel

hilt

guard

Late Anglo-Saxon Sword

0   10cm

A Scramasax

0   5cm

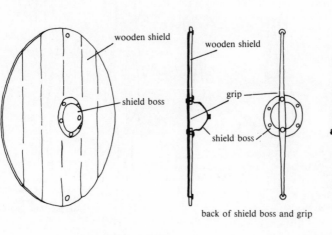

wooden shield

shield boss

wooden shield

grip

shield boss

back of shield boss and grip

Reconstruction of a Shield with a Low Conical Boss and Long Grip

0   20cm

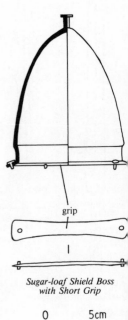

grip

Sugar-loaf Shield Boss with Short Grip

0   5cm

Bows and arrows: only one bow has been found but hazelwood arrowshafts are known, and arrowheads are occasionally found. Only two **helmets** have been found and these were probably imported. Two examples of iron **chain mail** have also been found. The **francisca** was a throwing axe probably used in battle.

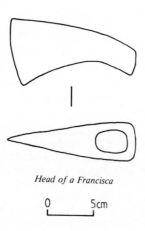

Head of a Francisca

0   5cm

Reading for Weapons: Anstee, J. W. and Biek, L. 1961; Davidson, H. R. E. 1962; Evison, V. I. 1963; Evison, V. I. 1976; Swanton, M. J. 1973; Wheeler, R. E. M. 1935; Wilson, D. M. 1965; Wilson, D. M. 1976b.

Coins

Roman coins have been found in contexts dating to the fifth and sixth centuries, but most of these seem to have been heirlooms made into pendants. From the end of the sixth century, trade brought in gold coins from the Merovingian Franks called **tremisses (trientes)** which had replaced the Roman solidus. These coins became smaller and were subsequently debased by adding silver and copper. The first Anglo-Saxon coins were struck in *c*650; they were made of gold and are found mainly in south-east England. They are also called **tremisses (thrymsas)**. From the 690s these coins

became very debased and were then replaced by silver coins (**sceattas, sceats, proto-pennies, pennies**). These coins are found mainly in south-east Britain. They were individually cast in clay moulds and then struck. They continued in use to at least the mid eighth century. Some have runic inscriptions.

From the late eighth century silver **pennies** were issued in Britain with a design based on the Frankish denarius. These were struck on wider and thinner flans stamped out from sheets. These coins had a larger surface area with a portrait and name of the ruler as part of the legend. They rarely have runic inscriptions. In the ninth century copper **stycas** were minted in Northumbria, also bearing the names of the rulers. A number of coin hoards of the late ninth century have been found in Britain which were probably hidden during Danish raids. In 991 the **Danegeld** (a political bribe in the form of a levy) began to be paid to the Scandinavians, and consequently thousands of Anglo-Saxon coins have been found in Scandinavia. **Long cross pennies** were first struck by Aethelraed II in 997.

Reading for Coins: Blunt, C. E. 1960; Dolley, R. H. M. 1964; Dolley, R. H. M. 1976; Dolley, R. H. M. 1978; Kent, J. P. C. 1975.

Jewellery

Jewellery of this period consisted of finger-rings, beads, brooches, armlets and bracelets, earrings and pendants. Other decorative ornaments included belt buckles and other belt fittings, pins, and wrist clasps.

Spirally wound bronze **finger-rings** are fairly common. Silver, gold, jet, amber and glass rings have also been found.

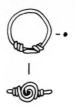

Bronze Spirally Wound Finger-ring

0   2cm

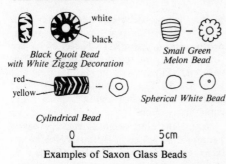

white
black

Black Quoit Bead
with White Zigzag Decoration

Small Green
Melon Bead

red
yellow

Cylindrical Bead

Spherical White Bead

0   5cm

Examples of Saxon Glass Beads

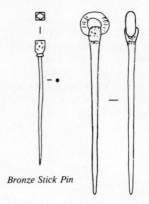

Bronze Stick Pin

Bronze Ring-headed Pin

0   5cm

Beads for necklaces were of bone, amber, crystal, silver, iron or glass. Little study of Saxon glass beads has been done; what evidence there is comes mainly from pagan Saxon burial sites and there is relatively little evidence for the use of glass beads in the later period. Some of the main types of Saxon glass bead are shown in the illustration.

Pendants were of jet, amber or gold. Some were made from coins. Thin gold circular pendants (**bracteates**) are found in women's graves in Kent. They have a loop for suspension and are embossed with human and zoomorphic designs. Silver necklaces have been found in Scotland.

Earrings of silver, bronze and gold are known, some with inset jewels.

Bracelets were made of shale, silver, bone, jet and glass. Bronze bracelets are rare. There was an apparent revival of **glass bangles (glass armlets)** in Ireland and in a few places in England, although they are still rare in this period. They had gone out of fashion in the late Roman period.

A variety of bronze, silver and bone **pins** are known, from simple round-headed ones to decorated ones. **Ring-headed pins** are common in Celtic Britain; they have pins which can swivel. **Stick pins** have fixed heads. Pins were used in the hair and for fastening clothing. **Linked pins** consist of a pair of pins linked by a chain.

In Anglian women's graves pairs of small bronze clasps (**sleeve clasps, wrist clasps**) are often found, and which seem to have been used to fasten cuffs together like a decorative hook and eye.

Brooches were the most common type of Anglo-Saxon jewellery and were of bronze, silver, pewter or occasionally gold. They were often used to fasten clothing and sometimes occur in pairs connected by a

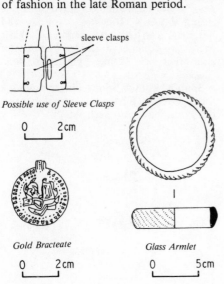

sleeve clasps

Possible use of Sleeve Clasps

0   2cm

Gold Bracteate

0   2cm

Glass Armlet

0   5cm

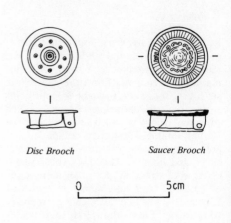

Disc Brooch

Saucer Brooch

0   5cm

chain. There are many types of brooch, some very plain and some extremely ornate, but they are basically either disc, circular or bow brooches.

Disc brooches were cast in one piece of bronze, silvered or tinned, with a geometrical pattern. They date from the late fourth century. **Applied disc brooches (composite disc brooches, applied brooches)** consisted of an upper decorative sheet fixed to a base plate. The pins were mostly of iron. Similar to disc brooches are **saucer brooches**. These are a common type and were sometimes cast in one piece, or else a thin sheet of bronze was applied to a base plate (**applied saucer brooch, applied brooch**). They were often decorated with geometric, spiral or animal patterns. There are some very ornate disc brooches inset with precious stones. They are found mainly in Kent and are later in date than saucer brooches, and were often made of silver or gold.

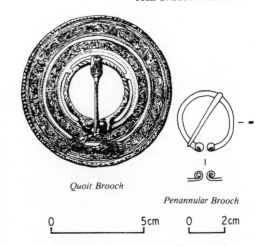

Quoit Brooch

Penannular Brooch

Circular brooches include **ring brooches (annular brooches)**, and **penannular brooches (broken ring brooches)**, some of which have decorated terminals. **Quoit brooches** have much rich decoration, but

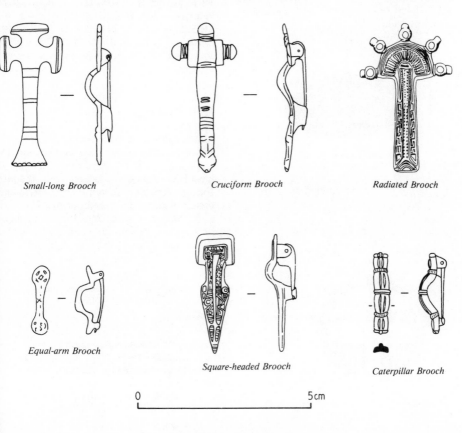

Small-long Brooch

Cruciform Brooch

Radiated Brooch

Equal-arm Brooch

Square-headed Brooch

Caterpillar Brooch

Some Types of Bow Brooch

they are rarely found. They are penannular brooches to which a decorated plate ('quoit') has been added. They date to the early fifth century.

Bow brooches include **small-long brooches** of which there are many shapes, and **cruciform brooches** which can be up to 15cm long. They are found in Anglian areas of England: the foot is shaped into the head of an animal which becomes very stylised. The 'foot' was actually worn at the top. They date to the fifth to seventh centuries. **Florid cruciform brooches** were very ornate. Other types of bow brooch are the **square-headed brooch (great square-headed brooch), radiated brooch (radiate head brooch)** and **equal-arm brooch (equal-armed brooch). Caterpillar brooches** date to the eighth to ninth centuries and are rarely found.

There are various other types of brooch, such as the Viking **trefoil-shaped brooches** and **tortoise brooches**, which were shaped like the humped shell of a tortoise. These have openwork patterns and are often found in pairs.

Many types of brooch are found in Celtic Britain, particularly penannular brooches, some of which are very large and elaborate with long pins. They are similar to ring-headed pins. Viking trefoil-shaped brooches and tortoise brooches have also been found in Celtic Britain.

Much jewellery was embellished with millefiori and semi-precious stones, as well as by tinning, gilding, silvering and niello. Cloisonné and champlevé enamel were used, and also cloisonné ornament using an inlay of precious stones and glass: jewellery decorated by this method is sometimes termed **polychrome jewellery. Chip-carving** was a form of ornament derived from woodworking. The brooches were cast in moulds which had been carved with designs.

Reading for Jewellery: Åberg, N. 1926; Aldsworth, F. 1979; Avent, R. 1975; Brown, G. B. 1915; Bruce-Mitford, R. 1972; Dickinson, T. M. 1979; Evison, V. I. 1978; Fowler, E. 1963; Jessup, R. F. 1974; Kilbride-Jones, H. E. 1937–8; Leeds, E. T. 1945; Leeds, E. T. 1946; Leeds, E. T. 1949; Leeds, · E. T. and Pocock, M. 1971; Stevenson, R. B. K. 1976; Wilson, D. M. 1976b.

Belt Fittings

Many distinctive belt buckles, strap-ends and other belt fittings are known, mainly from graves, which were once thought to have been brought to Britain from the late fourth century onwards by Germanic mercenaries in the Roman army. They are now considered to be late Roman in date. Many have designs in chip-carved work. They are found mainly in south-east Britain.

Tortoise Brooch

Penannular Brooch (mainly found in Celtic Britain)

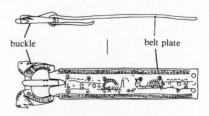

Bronze Buckle with Stylised Dolphin Heads and Buckle Plate

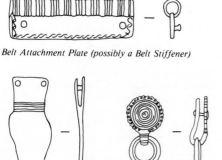

Belt Attachment Plate (possibly a Belt Stiffener)

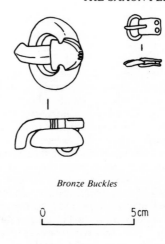

Bronze Buckles

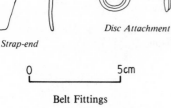

Strap-end

Disc Attachment

0   5cm

Belt Fittings

0   5cm

There are various types of Saxon bronze buckle, some with plates, and also bronze belt mounts, dating from the fifth century.

Reading for Belt Fittings: Evison, V. I. 1968; Hawkes, S. C. and Dunning, G. C. 1961; Simpson, C. J. 1976.

Textiles

Spindle whorls were made from baked clay, stone, pebbles, amber, chalk, lead, coal, jet, glass or bone. **Loomweights** were made of coarse baked clay and were hand-made. **Annular loomweights (quoit-shaped loomweights)** are pagan Saxon in date; they were made as rings. **Intermediate loomweights**

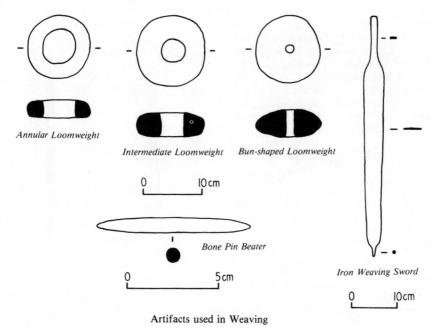

Annular Loomweight

Intermediate Loomweight   Bun-shaped Loomweight

0   10cm

Bone Pin Beater

0   5cm

Iron Weaving Sword

0   10cm

Artifacts used in Weaving

157

have smaller central holes. **Bun-shaped loomweights (doughnut-shaped loomweights)** were made as discs and had a pierced central hole. Lead loomweights have been found, and rows of loomweights burnt *in situ* have been excavated, possibly indicating a loom which collapsed after burning. Postholes, possibly for the uprights of a loom, have also been found. The warp-weighted loom was at first used, but towards the end of the Saxon period the horizontal loom seems to have been introduced: this would explain the lack of loomweights in this period. Bone **pin beaters (thread pickers)** may have been used for beating down individual threads in the weft of the cloth. **Weaving swords (weaving batons)** were probably mainly of wood, although iron and bone examples have been found. **Needles** of iron, bone and bronze were used, and fulling pits have been found. **Linen smoothers** of glass, and possibly of stone, are known. The cloth was mainly woollen, although some silk and linen were used. Braid has been found, as well as thread for sewing, and thread boxes. Baskets, twine, rope and string are also known.

Reading for Textiles: Dunning, G. C. et al 1959, 23–5; MacGregor, A. 1978; Wilson, D. M. 1976b.

Leather

Tanning pits for the preparation of leather have been found as well as leather shoes (usually of turnshoe construction), laces, belts, garments, bags, sheaths, gloves and bookbindings. Purses, pouches, wallets and bags are known from graves, especially those of women. Bronze fittings belonging to these purses have also been found.

Reading for Leather: MacGregor, A. 1978; Richardson, K. M. 1961.

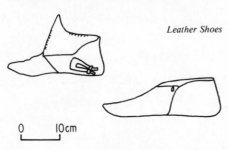

Leather Shoes

0   10cm

Wood

Wood was widely used, particularly for buildings and boats and for a variety of objects including casks, buckets, coffins, bowls, spoons, lyres, combs, cups, shingles, flutes, caskets, boxes, sword sheaths and sword grips. Some wooden objects were lathe-turned, and some were of stave construction. Wood was also used to line pits and wells, either with planks or barrels, or with a woven wicker lining. (See also Sutton Hoo.)

Reading for Wood: MacGregor, A. 1978; Wilson, D. M. 1976b.

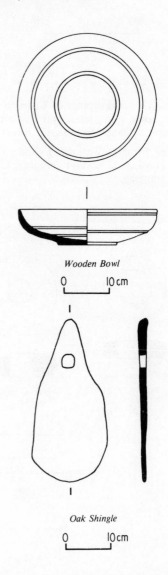

Wooden Bowl

0   10 cm

Oak Shingle

0   10cm

Bone and Antler

Bone and antler objects include comb cases, combs, pins, needles, beads, inlaid caskets, casket fittings, spindle whorls, skates, handles, chessmen, counters, thread pickers, plaques, bracelets, buckles, bobbins (or possibly toggles), writing tablets, sword hilts, weaving swords and horn drinking vessels. Bone dice are known from Scotland, and some late Saxon bone spoons have been found.

Combs include single-sided, double-sided and handled combs. Single-sided are late Saxon in date, and include triangular single-sided combs. Double-sided combs were made throughout the Saxon period. **Comb cases** carried either single-sided or double-sided combs. There are often incised designs on the plates of composite combs.

There is a wide range of **pins**, and some are regarded as pin beaters. There were dress or hairpins, some of which have 'hipped' shafts and date to about the sixth to ninth centuries. **Pig fibula pins** occur

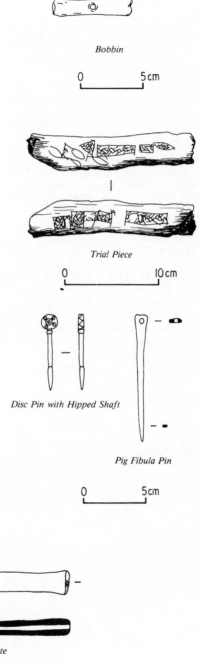

Bobbin

0   5 cm

Trial Piece

0   10 cm

Disc Pin with Hipped Shaft

Pig Fibula Pin

0   5 cm

Bone Comb and Case

0   5 cm

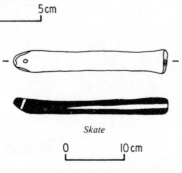

Skate

0   10 cm

Examples of Saxon Bone Artifacts

throughout the Saxon period. They are a Scandinavian type and may have been used as netting needles or dress pins. Some bone pins have carved animals' heads.

There is evidence for bone working at many sites. The lathe was used, and the tools used in bone and antler working were probably similar to those used in carpentry. Compass-cut ring-and-dot patterns were often used, particularly on combs. **Trial pieces** are often found, which seem to have been used for trying out patterns for the decoration of various objects. (See also Sutton Hoo.)

Reading for Bone and Antler: Addyman, P. V. and Hill, D. H. 1969; Collis, J. R. and Kjølbye-Biddle, B. 1979; MacGregor, A. 1976; MacGregor, A. 1978; Williams, J. H. 1979.

Ivory

Combs, gaming pieces, rings and a seal matrix of ivory have been found. The rings vary from about 10cm to 15cm in diameter and may have been bracelets or more probably part of a bag. Such rings are often found with girdle-hangers and work boxes which could have formed part of a châtelaine. Ivory was obtained through trade, and came mainly from the elephant and sometimes from the walrus.

Reading for Ivory: MacGregor, A. 1978; Myres, J. N. L. and Green, B. 1973.

Amber and Jet

Amber was used for beads, pendants, spindle whorls and rings. Rough-outs and half-finished articles as well as complete objects have been found. Jet was used for pendants, rings, bracelets, spindle whorls and chessmen. The lathe was used in the manufacture of some amber and jet articles.

Reading for Amber and Jet: MacGregor, A. 1978.

Stone

Stone was used in buildings, and also for articles such as spindle whorls, quernstones (particularly of Mayen lava in the late Saxon period), net sinkers, millstones, whetstones, gaming boards, lamps, grave markers, crosses and other incised or sculptured commemorative stones. Many **whetstones (hones)** were schist hones, which can be traced to a source in southern Norway. Some were perforated for suspension from a belt. Chalk was sometimes used for mortars. There is evidence for much organised quarrying and trade of stone over a considerable distance, as well as trade in manufactured stone articles. Viking steatite

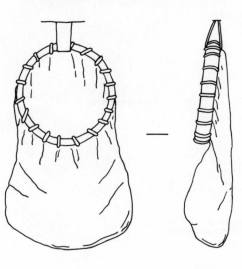

Reconstruction of a Bag using an Ivory Ring

0   10cm

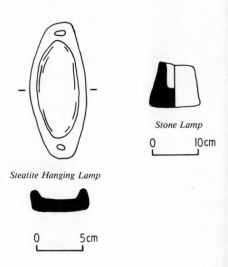

Stone Lamp

0   10cm

Steatite Hanging Lamp

0   5cm

bowls, loomweights and lamps are found in the Northern Isles, and occasionally in England. (See also Sutton Hoo.)

Reading for Stone: Addyman, P. V. and Hill, D. H. 1969; Evison, V. I. 1975; MacGregor, A. 1978.

Stone Sculpture

Pictish stones are found in Scotland. These are stones that have been shaped and carved: **Class I stones (Pictish symbol stones)** are rough pillars or boulders depicting animals and simple or elaborate geometric patterns and objects. They date to around the fifth to seventh centuries, and are non-Christian. **Class II stones (Pictish cross-slabs)** depict a wide range of Christian symbols and are later in date than Class I stones; some may have been tombstones. Some stones have ogam inscriptions, particularly in western and northern Scotland. Pictish symbols also occur on portable artifacts.

In Cornwall and Devon there are inscribed memorial stones — some in ogam, some with Latin letters but Irish names, and some with both. Some may have been inscribed by Irish immigrants. Stone crosses are also known in this area.

In Wales there are simple inscribed stones dating to the fifth to seventh centuries. The stones are unshaped or roughly shaped slabs and pillar stones, and the inscriptions are in Latin or ogam, or both; they were usually set up as tombstones or memorials. Dating to the sixth to eleventh centuries are unshaped or roughly shaped slabs and pillar stones, decorated with incised crosses and normally uninscribed. They were probably memorial stones. There are also sculptured crosses and cross-slabs dating to the ninth to eleventh centuries. Stone crosses were set up in many parts of Saxon England; some were erected on a stone base. They are not common in southern England. The Vikings continued this tradition of carving, adapting Saxon sculpture, although Saxon styles persisted.

There are a few stones with runic inscriptions (**rune-stones**). They are seldom found *in situ*. Some **pillow-stones** have runic inscriptions, and may have been placed under the head of a body in a grave; stones with runic inscriptions are most frequently

A Class II Pictish Stone

0   50cm

Sixth-century Tombstone from Cornwall with Ogam and Latin Inscriptions

0   50cm

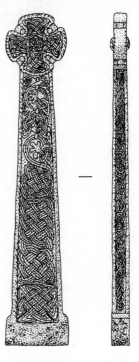

Late Saxon Carved Cross

0   50cm

161

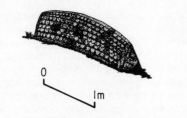

0
|m

Hog's-backed Tombstones

0 |m

memorial. Most of these runic inscriptions were probably Christian. Flat **grave covers** are also found, and are sometimes described as **coffin slabs**. **Hog's-backed tombstones (hog-back tombstones, hog-back stones, hog-back grave covers)** are memorial stones of the tenth century, found mainly in northern England. They resemble buildings (possibly shrines) with walls and curved roofs covered with shingles. Some have carved animals at the

ends. They may have been grave covers, or grave markers.

Reading for Stone Sculpture: Bailey, R. N. 1980; Lang, J. T. 1978; Macalister, R. A. S. 1945; Nash-Williams, V. E. 1950; Thomas, A. C. 1971a.

Ogam and Runes

Ogam (ogham) is a stroke alphabet which developed in southern Ireland in the late third or fourth century and is often found on inscribed stones in Celtic Britain. The letters were arranged along a guide-line which was usually the edge of a stone.

Runes are a type of alphabet which was also supposed to have magical properties. The Germanic runic alphabet was the **futhark** and the Old English runic alphabet was the **futhorc** — a modified version introduced by Saxon settlers. Runic inscriptions are found from the fifth century onwards, particularly in Kent and eastern England. The Scandinavians later introduced Scandinavian runic alphabets also called futharks. Runes are found on tombstones, tools, weapons, crosses, coins, rings and combs.

Reading for Ogam and Runes: Elliott, R. W. V. 1959; Jackson, K. 1950; Macalister, R. A. S. 1945; Page, R. I. 1973.

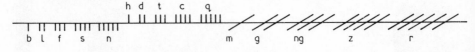

The Ogam Alphabet

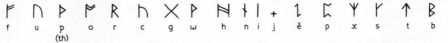

| f | u | p (th) | o | r | c | g | ɯ | h | n | i | j | ĕ | p | x | s | t | b |

Runic Alphabet (Futhorc) from an Inscribed Scramasax found in the Thames at Battersea

| e | ŋ=ng | d | l | m | œ | a | œ | y | ea |

Art

The chronology of the Saxon period is often based on the typology of ornament styles, particularly those appearing on metal objects and stone sculpture. Decoration was often zoomorphic. The main styles include the **quoit-brooch style** which developed in Britain in the early fifth century and used semi-naturalistic animal motifs. **Salin's style I (Style I)** developed on the Continent in the fifth century, probably from Roman styles, and is also found in Britain. It is characterised by stylised animals. It was replaced by **Salin's style II (Style II)** in the late sixth century, which used intertwined motifs. From the ninth century art styles developed, particularly using classical vine-scroll and plaited-band ornament on stone. These designs later incorporated animals. From c900 Viking art began to influence Anglo-Saxon art with various styles coming from Scandinavia, although Saxon styles persisted. The acanthus ornament became a distinctive decorative feature in the late Saxon period.

Reading for Art: Bailey, R. N. 1980; Evison, V. I. 1965; Haseloff, G. 1974; Wilson, D. M. 1976a.

Glass

Glass was used for vessels, window glass, ornament in jewellery, spindle whorls, linen smoothers, rings and bangles. **Linen smoothers** were of dark glass and were probably imported.

Glass Vessels

Many glass vessels of the period c400–700 have survived since they were often deposited as grave goods. The earliest vessels of this period are **stemmed beakers** which continued from the late Roman period into the fifth century. During the fifth century **claw beakers** developed from copies of late Roman glasses decorated with hollow dolphins, and they continued in use well into the seventh century. **Bell beakers** also date to the fifth century and **cone beakers** date mainly to the fifth and sixth centuries although a few have been found in seventh-century graves. **Drinking horns** are very rare in Britain (although more common on the Continent); they seem to have developed from cone beakers. In the seventh century **bag beakers, pouch bottles** and **squat jars** appear, though these vessels are mainly confined to Kent. A few **bottles, bowls** and **palm cups** have been dated to this period.

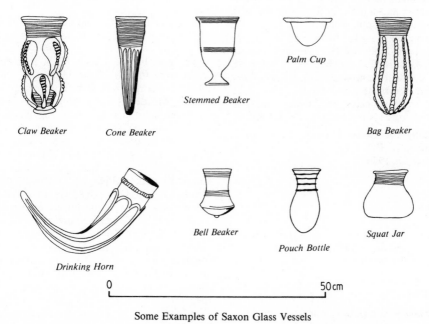

Palm Cup

Stemmed Beaker

Claw Beaker   Cone Beaker

Bag Beaker

Drinking Horn

Bell Beaker

Pouch Bottle

Squat Jar

0   50 cm

Some Examples of Saxon Glass Vessels

163

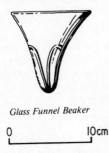

Glass Funnel Beaker

0   10cm

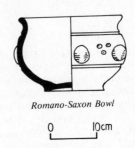

Romano-Saxon Bowl

0   10cm

The coming of Christianity stopped the rite of burying grave goods with the dead and so relatively little is known about late Saxon vessels. The claw beakers degenerated into a type with only a few flat claws, and the palm cup developed into the **funnel beaker**. More evidence about late Saxon glass has been gained from recent excavations on settlement sites, but little has yet been published.

Window Glass

There is little evidence for the use of window glass during the Saxon period, although more knowledge is being gained from current excavations. The available evidence suggests that in some cases glass was being used for windows in monastic churches as early as the seventh century (including coloured window glass), while by the ninth and tenth centuries glass was also being used in some domestic buildings. All the window glass for this period appears to have been made by the cylinder method. Some of this glass may have been imported, but at least one monastic site (*Glastonbury Abbey*, Somerset) has produced evidence that window glass was being made in Britain towards the end of this period.

Reading for Glass: Harden, D. B. 1961; Harden, D. B. 1971; Harden, D. B. 1978; Hunter, J. 1980.

Clay

Baked clay was used for pottery vessels, lamps, spindle whorls, loomweights, and moulds for brooches.

Pottery

Romano-Saxon pottery was wheel-made. It is found from the late Roman period and consists mainly of jars and bowls with bosses. It was once considered to be evidence of Saxon occupation in the late Roman period, but is now thought to be Roman.

Early Saxon pottery dates from *c*400–650. Corrugated **amphorae**, possibly for wine and olive oil, and other fine tablewares, were imported to Celtic areas of Britain from the Mediterranean and Africa from the fifth to seventh centuries. In Cornwall **Gwithian-style pottery** is found in the late sixth century; this is a hard well-made type of pottery. In the late sixth century **grass-marked wares** appear in Celtic areas. This pottery is similar to Irish pottery of this period and probably represents Irish immigrants; it is coarse and has grass impressions on the underside. It was traded to other areas of Britain from Cornwall.

Early Saxon settlers did not make wheel-thrown pottery but used hand-made pottery consisting of small plain cooking pots which were brown, grey or black in colour. They were fired in clamp kilns, and some have simple decoration including lugs and bosses. Most early Saxon pottery, however, is found in cemeteries, either as cinerary urns or as small accessory vessels accompanying inhumations. Unlike domestic wares, these pots often had a fine fabric and seem to have been hand-made by specialist potters. Plain urns probably date from this period although they are difficult to date. Urns with simple linear patterns are found in the fifth century, but begin to give way in the later fifth century to urns with boss ornament (**Buckelurnen**), which became more and more highly decorated. At the end of the sixth century, stamps and bosses were the predominant form of decoration. Some wheel-thrown pottery was also used as accessory vessels in in-

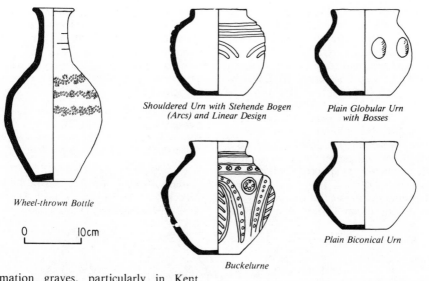

Wheel-thrown Bottle

Shouldered Urn with Stehende Bogen (Arcs) and Linear Design

Plain Globular Urn with Bosses

Plain Biconical Urn

Buckelurne

0   10cm

0   10cm

humation graves, particularly in Kent. These included bottles (sometimes incorrectly called Jutish bottles), jugs, bowls, spouted pitchers and jars. They may have been imported from the Continent. With the spread of Christianity, funerary vessels disappeared: they are not found from the seventh century onwards.

Middle Saxon pottery dates from *c*650–850, is found mainly on domestic sites and is hand-made. In East Anglia, however, pottery termed **Ipswich ware** was made on a slow wheel; it was fired to a high temperature and is usually grey in colour. This pottery had a wide distribution. Cooking pots are most common, but small bowls and dishes, some with spouts for wooden handles, and spouted pitchers are often found. Many pots have sagging bases. Lugs are common on pitchers and bowls. Most of the pottery is plain but there is some

stamped decoration. Slow wheel pottery is found in Northumbria and is termed **Whitby-type ware** and **Ipswich-type ware**.

Late Saxon pottery (Saxo-Norman pottery) dates from *c*850–1150. Fast wheel-thrown pottery became widespread in various centres in England, and there are many regional types of pottery named after the kiln or type-site such as **York-type ware, Cheddar-type ware, Torksey-type ware, Otley-type ware, Leicester ware, Northampton ware, Nottingham splashed ware, Derby-type ware, Chester-type ware, Portchester-type ware** and **Michelmersh ware**. The most distinctive types of pottery for this period are Thetford-type ware, St Neots-type ware, Stamford-type ware and Winchester ware. **Thetford-type ware** (named after *Thetford*, Norfolk) has a hard, grey, sandy fabric. The pottery was wheel-thrown and fired in fully developed kilns, and consists of tall cooking pots and jars, bowls and pitchers (some spouted), storage jars, dishes, costrels and barrels. **St Neots-type pottery** (named after *St Neots*, Cambridgeshire) has a soft, shell-tempered fabric. It was thrown on a fast wheel, but was not well fired. The pottery consists of tall cooking pots and jars, bowls (some with spouts), spouted pitchers, plates and lamps. **Stamford-type ware** (named after *Stamford*, Lincolnshire) occurs widely in

Ipswich Spouted Pitcher

0   10cm

165

the Midlands and north-east England from *c*900. It has a very fine buff fabric. Many types of vessel were produced such as spouted pitchers, jars, cooking bowls, lamps and lids, and from the late eleventh century the jug reappeared in England. Some of the pottery was glazed with a yellow or pale-green glaze. In southern England **Winchester ware** (named after *Winchester*, Hampshire) is best known. Glazed, wheel-thrown pottery in a hard sandy fabric was produced at Winchester, consisting mainly of spouted pitchers, with cups, bowls, lids, jars, jugs, tripod pitchers and bottles (imitating leather prototypes: such a copy of an artifact in a different material is called a **skeuomorph**). The tripod pitchers appear to be hand-made. Most of this pottery dates to the eleventh century, when hand-made pottery continued to be produced in England. Pottery, including amphorae, was also imported from the Rhineland and France.

Reading for Pottery: Evison, V. I. 1979; Evison, V. I. et al 1974; Haslam, J. 1978; Hurst, J. G. 1976; Myres, J. N. L. 1977; Thomas, A. C. 1968.

General Reading for the Saxon Period: Alcock, L. 1971; Brown, D. 1978; Thomas, A. C. 1971a; Wilson, D. M. 1976a.

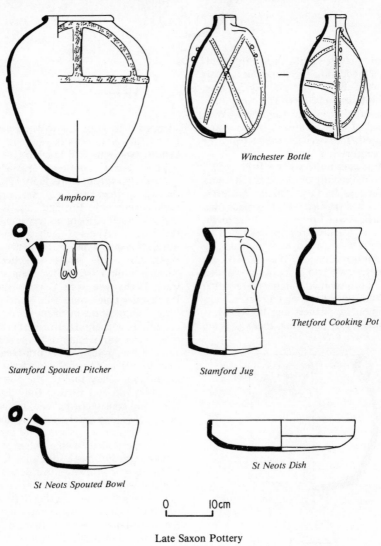

Amphora

Winchester Bottle

Stamford Spouted Pitcher

Stamford Jug

Thetford Cooking Pot

St Neots Spouted Bowl

St Neots Dish

0   10cm

Late Saxon Pottery

Chapter 8

The Medieval Period

The **Medieval period (Middle Ages)** dates conventionally from the Norman invasion in 1066 to approximately 1500.

Towns

There was an increase in the development of towns in the Medieval period, and from the thirteenth century old towns were enlarged and new ones developed. Towns could contain a variety of features including houses, shops, town walls, inns, castles, cathedrals, churches, monasteries, market places, market crosses, and wharves. Some ports were sited inland on navigable rivers. Town defences comprising a rampart and ditch or a stone wall were often built, and probably served as a barrier for tolls as well as for safety. Some Roman walls were used as the basis for defence, and some Saxon walls continued in use. Many defences were built from the early thirteenth century to the fourteenth century, particularly stone walls with D-shaped mural towers or turrets from which missiles could be discharged. Walls were often crenellated, and some had two rows of **arrow loops (arrow slits, loopholes, meurtrières)** which were narrow windows for firing arrows: usually an upper row for firing from the wall walk, and a lower one for firing from ground level. The gradual development of firearms in the later Medieval period led to the provision of **gun loops (gun ports, shot holes)** in town walls for firing cannons. Their external appearance is a circular hole, often with a vertical slit below and above. Inside was a splayed embrasure on which the gun was rested. Gateways were also an important part of town walls; they often consisted of a stone tower with a single passageway with wooden gates and a portcullis.

Excavations in towns often reveal cobbled yard surfaces, stone, chalk and wood-lined cess pits, wells (often near cess pits), rubbish pits, and houses aligned along streets. Evidence for various industries is often encountered, including pottery manufacture, metalworking, bone working and leather working. Many towns had a planned street system in the form of a grid, or else they developed along a single market street.

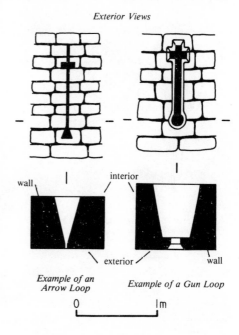

Exterior Views

wall

interior

Example of an Arrow Loop

exterior

wall

Example of a Gun Loop

0   1m

Reading for Towns: Barley, M. W. 1975; Kenyon, J. R. 1978; Platt, C. 1976; Turner, H. L. 1971.

Deserted Villages

Deserted Medieval Villages (DMVs) are villages which have been totally deserted. The reasons for this are not entirely understood but may have been a combination of economics, Black Death, and the bad weather which caused some upland villages to be deserted. Villages were sometimes moved elsewhere, eg through emparking, leaving behind deserted villages. Villages which have been partially deserted are called **shrunken villages**. When deserted, the tumbled walls became overgrown and survive as earthworks, and the roads which had been worn lower than the surrounding land survive as **hollow ways**. A **toft** consisted of the land on which a house was built **(house platform)** and the adjoining backyard, and a **croft** was a piece of land adjoining a house used for pasture or arable; often they became gradually higher than the surrounding land and roads, and can survive as distinctive earthworks.

Unlike urban sites where rubbish was frequently deposited in pits, very few rubbish and cess pits are found on village sites; the rubbish was probably spread on the fields as a fertiliser.

Villages are often classified according to their plan such as a **street-village**, with houses fronting one or both sides of a street; a **cross-roads village**, where the houses were centred at a cross-roads; and a **bridge-head village**, where houses were centred near a bridge. Some villages had one or more greens. No standard plans are recognizable in villages, although there are some instances where villages were planned. The houses in villages were often longhouses. Also associated with villages and farms are corn-drying kilns and malting kilns, both of similar construction. Timber barns were used, and large stone barns were built from the thirteenth century. Dovecotes are also known. Water-storage pits have been found, and also late Medieval saw-pits. Evidence for industry such as pottery manufacture and iron-working is often found in villages.

Reading for Deserted Villages: Beresford, G. 1975; Beresford, M. W. and Hurst, J. G. 1971.

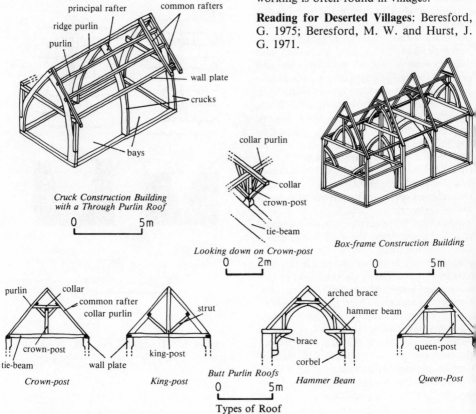

principal rafter

common rafters

ridge purlin

purlin

wall plate

crucks

bays

*Cruck Construction Building
with a Through Purlin Roof*

0   5 m

collar purlin

collar

crown-post

tie-beam

Looking down on Crown-post

0   2 m

Box-frame Construction Building

0   5 m

purlin   collar

common rafter

collar purlin

strut

arched brace

hammer beam

crown-post

king-post

brace

queen-post

tie-beam   wall plate

corbel

Crown-post

King-post

Butt Purlin Roofs

0   5 m

Hammer Beam

Queen-Post

Types of Roof

168

Houses

Most information for Medieval houses comes from surviving examples rather than from archaeological remains. The earliest houses were probably mainly **cob-walled** — cob was usually made of clay mixed with sand, straw and gravel — or **timber-framed (half-timbered)** consisting of timber supports with wattle and daub infilling. **Wattle and daub** consists of branches or thin laths **(wattle)** woven together and covered with mud or clay **(daub)**. The houses had floors of clay, stone, cobbles or stone flags, and roofs of thatch or shingles. Stone only began to be used in building houses from the late twelfth century when there was much rebuilding in stone, with stone or tiled floors, cobbled yards, and roofs of tile or slate. There was also much development in carpentry techniques. The simplest type of timber-framed house was of **cruck** construction consisting of a series of pairs of timbers set in or on the ground and meeting at the top. The crucks acted as the principal frame and as the main trusses for the roof. The other method of building was the construction of a box-frame with a triangular roof. Triangular types of roof are found on both timber and stone buildings. **Jettied houses** are timber-framed houses which occur from the thirteenth century, particularly in towns. A **jetty** was an overhanging storey which provided a larger room.

Single roofs consisted of rafters supported by bracing members, and **double roofs** consisted of rafters supported by purlins. Single and double roofs may be divided into **bays** by **trusses**. The most common types of truss were the **crown-post, king-post, queen-post** and **hammer beam**. Single and double roofs may also be classified as rafter roofs, butt purlin roofs or through purlin roofs. **Through purlin roofs** have the purlins carried on the backs of the blades of the principal rafters which cannot therefore be used as common rafters; such roofs are usually found in association with cruck construction. In a **butt purlin roof** the principal rafters were in line with the other rafters and so acted as common rafters. The purlins were not actually butted but ran through the principal rafters by mortise-and-tenon joints. Some roofs had aisle posts where the buildings were aisled. They are not usually found in cruck-framed buildings.

The **hall** was the basis of many houses, both in town and country. The earliest type of hall house is the **upper hall house (hall and cellar house)**. The hall was on the upper floor and was open to the roof. It was the main room **(greater chamber)** of the house. Below was a lower room **(lesser chamber, undercroft, crypt)**. This type of house was built in stone from the late twelfth century and such houses are often known as **Jews' houses** because many of the wealthy people that owned such houses were Jews. The undercroft could be used for shops or for storage, and often had a stone vaulted ceiling. It was reached by steps down from the street, while the hall was reached by an outside staircase. Further rooms could be added to the hall, in particular a **solar (great chamber, soler, solarium** — literally a room above ground-floor level) which was a private bed-sitting room over a cellar.

By the fourteenth century, the hall was built at ground-floor level. It had no upper storey since it was open to the roof with a central hearth for heating. There was a two-storied block at each end which formed an **H-plan house (end hall house, hall and cross wings, double-ended hall)**: the domestic and service wings were kept separate, with the solar at the opposite ('upper') end of the hall. The cellar under the solar gradually became a living room or storeroom **(wardrobe)**.

Halls were at first aisled, but improvements in roof construction dispensed with aisles by raising the whole system of the roof support on tie-beams. Halls gradually acquired timber ceilings, chimneys and fireplaces. The earliest fireplaces were arched and in the late twelfth century the **hooded fireplace** appeared which had a stone smoke hood projecting from the wall. It went out of fashion by the late fourteenth century, to be replaced again by the arched fireplace. Square-headed fireplaces are also seen from the fifteenth century.

Windows were similar in design to those seen in churches. **Oriels (oriel chambers)** are a feature of the fifteenth century and were projections or built-out galleries with windows. They were built at the upper end of the hall.

Kitchens may have been in the hall in some early Medieval houses although detached kitchens are known. They were probably detached as a fire precaution.

Kitchens gradually became incorporated in the main building by the fifteenth century.

Many large houses had a **chapel** or **oratory**. Early chapels were probably of wood, and many chapels were at first-floor level with a vaulted undercroft, but detached ground-floor chapels are also known. From the fifteenth century ground-floor chapels became common, with very tall chancels and large east windows. Chapels were sometimes placed in towers.

Other rooms included the **gardrobe (privy)**: this was a toilet. Some had flushing water, and some were contained in gardrobe towers with a shaft passing to a cess pit. **Gatehouses** were occasionally built as a defensive measure and were two-storey buildings with a passageway.

In the late fourteenth and fifteenth centuries, particularly in Scotland and the Borders, **tower houses** were common. These were stone towers of three or four storeys with substantial stone walls. They are sometimes wrongly termed pele-towers. **Bastel-houses (bastles, pele-towers)** were houses of two to three storeys, with the lower floor for animals, and the upper for domestic use, reached by an outside staircase. They had pitched roofs and were not tower-like in appearance.

In the fifteenth century the hall gradually became less important. With the advent of fireplaces, a ceiling could be inserted since the smoke did not have to escape through the roof, and houses gradually became compact blocks of smaller rooms.

The houses of the poor probably consisted of living rooms on the ground floor with sleeping accommodation in a loft. In the country, poorer people lived in **long-houses** which consisted of two rooms and a central cross-passage. One room was used for animals and the other was for domestic use. The term 'long-house' is often used even when there is no proof that one room was used for animals, and the term **'of long-house form'** has been advocated for these examples. Some had stone foundations or low stone walls. They were probably built mainly of wood. Remains of cob-walled and turf-walled long-houses have also been found. Central hearths were used.

Reading for Houses: Beresford, G. 1979; Braun, H. 1968; Brunskill, R. W. 1978; Cordingley, R. A. 1961; Meirion-Jones, G. I. 1973; Wood, M. 1965.

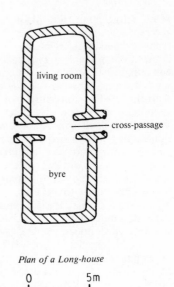

Plan of a Long-house

0   5m

Inns

Courtyard inns had the main buildings set back from the street and ranged round a courtyard, and were mainly timber-framed. **Gatehouse inns** consisted of a rectangular block of rooms with a gateway through the building leading to a courtyard with minor rooms and stables behind. They were built mainly in stone.

Reading for Inns: Pantin, W. A. 1961.

Almshouses

Almshouses (spital houses, spittle houses, maisons-dieu, bedehouses, hospitals) are found mainly in towns. They were independent institutions set up by benefactors, and were used as hostels and hospitals. Some had a large infirmary hall with a chapel at one end but later halls tended to be divided into separate rooms, and almshouses with separate dwellings and a chapel often grouped around a quadrangle became more popular, although many of the latter are Post-Medieval in date.

Reading for Almshouses: Godfrey, W. H. 1955.

Castles

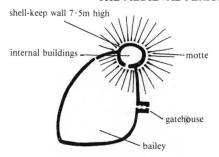

shell-keep wall 7·5m high

internal buildings

motte

gatehouse

bailey

Plan of a Shell-keep Castle

0   100 m

The earliest castles were **motte-and-bailey castles** which were erected after the Norman Conquest to gain control of the country quickly. The **motte** was a flat-topped conical mound of earth, partly erected from material from a surrounding ditch, which initially supported a wooden watchtower overlooking the bailey. Wooden watchtowers were sometimes later replaced by stone keeps. The **bailey (ward)** was an adjacent area containing timber buildings and was surrounded by a ditch. Motte-and-bailey castles continued to be built into the thirteenth century. A **ringwork (castle of enceinte, ringwork-and-bailey castle)** was an enclosure within a bailey which contained a keep and sometimes took the place of a motte. The inner enclosure is sometimes called an **inner bailey** and the surrounding enclosure an **outer bailey**.

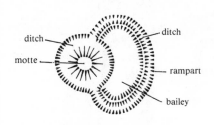

ditch

ditch

motte

rampart

bailey

Plan of a Motte-and-Bailey Castle

0   100 m

From the late eleventh century castles began to be built in stone, and had a stone keep surrounded by a bailey and stone wall **(keep-and-bailey castles)**. Some keeps were built on mottes, although they were usually built on level ground. The **keep (keep-tower, tower-keep, donjon)** was the main building of the castle and could be used for refuge. The earliest keeps were rectangular in plan and had one entrance on the first floor approached by stairs. They were usually three storeys high, and sometimes contained a chapel. From the late twelfth century keeps were circular, oval or polygonal in plan with no projecting angles so that they could be more easily defended.

Some castles had **shell-keeps** consisting of a circular or oval wall often built up around or on top of a motte, with living accommodation built against the inner face of the wall, with a central courtyard. Wing walls were sometimes built down the slopes of the motte. Some shell-keeps were built on ground level. Shell-keeps are rare in Scotland.

Later castles were larger, with a more regular layout. The period of Edward I saw the climax of castle building, particularly in Wales. There was more emphasis on towers and fortified gatehouses on the outer stone wall, and large surrounding moats were dug to prevent the walls being undermined by siege operations. The gateway had a **portcullis** (a wooden or iron grille) and a drawbridge over the moat. **Barbicans (outworks)** were outer fortifications protecting a gateway; they sometimes terminated in another gateway. From the thirteenth century there was a growing practice of building an outer castle wall, forming an inner and outer bailey, with mural or flanking towers. The innovations in castle building originated in the Near East. Keeps gradually went out of use, replaced by domestic quarters in the inner bailey, and in the mural towers and gatehouses of the inner-bailey wall.

Early castles had arrow loops, and gun loops were gradually incorporated in the walls (see town walls). **Machicolations (murder holes)** were openings in the ceiling of a gateway through which missiles could be thrown. They were also built into projecting timber platforms **(hoarding, brattices)** which were later built in stone,

171

and were constructed on the outside of
parapets of towers and walls (**machicolated
parapets**). Wall walks often had a crenellated parapet consisting of **embrasures
(crenels, crenelles)** which were the
openings, and **merlons** which were the solid
parts. Crenellated parapets were called
crenellations or **battlements**. From the
thirteenth century the embrasures were
often protected by wooden shutters. **Put-
log holes** are holes in masonry walls thought
to have been used for horizontal wooden
poles (**put logs**) used in scaffolding.

Reading for Castles: Brown, R. A. 1976;
Cruden, S. H. 1960; Forde-Johnston, J.
1977; Fry, P. S. 1980; Kenyon, J. R. 1978;
Renn, D. 1973; Toy, S. 1966.

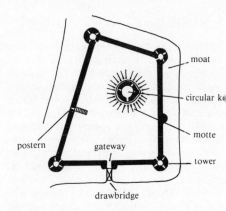

Plan of a twelfth-century Keep-and-Bailey Castle

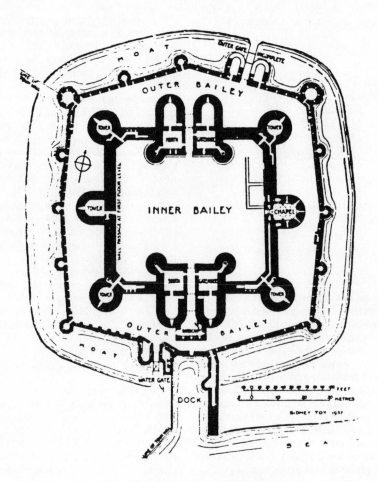

Plan of Beaumaris Castle, Anglesey, Gwynedd

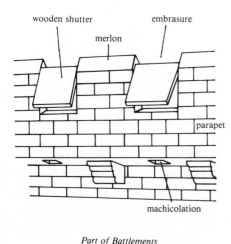

wooden shutter
merlon
embrasure
parapet
machicolation

Part of Battlements
0   1m

Monasteries

From about the late eleventh century there was a monastic revival. There were several different orders, the main ones being Benedictine, Augustinian and Cistercian. Friars appeared in the thirteenth century and became established mainly in towns. The head of a monastery was either an abbot or prior and hence the religious house was an **abbey** or **priory**, although it is not possible to draw a sharp distinction between the two titles. Monasteries gradually adopted standardised plans during the Medieval period. The monastery buildings were grouped around a central rectangular cloister court, and although the plans of each monastery varied and underwent continual change, some buildings had a fixed position relative to the overall plan. The buildings consisted of a **gatehouse, church, cloister** (a courtyard with a surrounding covered walk), **chapter-house** (the building where monastic business was conducted) always on the eastern side of the cloister and usually rectangular in plan or rectangular with an apse at the east end although polygonal examples are known, and the **frater** (refectory) which was always on the south side of the cloister and was often raised on an undercroft with a vaulted roof. The west side of the cloister was

varied in its use: it was often used for the abbot's or prior's lodgings. In Cistercian houses the lay brothers' dormitory could be on this side, often placed over cellars (**cellarium**), with the abbot housed elsewhere. The Carthusian order lived in separate cells, and had very small churches; their monasteries did not follow a standardised plan.

Other buildings had no fixed arrangement, and included the **dorter** (dormitory, often raised over an undercroft), **kitchens, reredorter** (containing latrines, often set over a stream), **lavatorium** (lavatory — a place for washing), **infirmary** (**farmery**) which was usually on the eastern side of the monastery and often consisted of a long aisled building lit by clerestory windows, **gatehouse, library** and **treasury**. The **slype** (wide roofed corridor) was usually positioned between the chapter-house and south transept. A **grange** was an independent monastic farm managed by lay brothers. It could contain barns, living quarters, halls and a chapel. Many monasteries were destroyed during the Dissolution of the Monasteries in the sixteenth century.

Reading for Monasteries: Butler, L. A. S. and Given-Wilson, C. 1979; Dickinson, J. C. 1961; Platt, C. 1969.

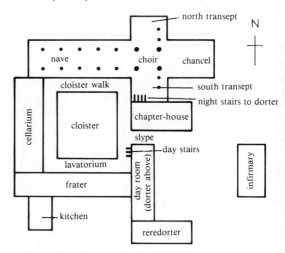

Simplified Plan of the Layout of a Monastery
0   50m

Churches

From the time of the Norman Conquest many secular and monastic churches and cathedrals were rebuilt and enlarged in stone, and new ones built. A **cathedral** is the principal church of a diocese containing the bishop's throne; there is no architectural distinction between a cathedral and a church. The styles of architecture seen in churches are also to be found in other buildings, particularly stone-built houses. Many monastic churches were destroyed during the Dissolution of the Monasteries in the sixteenth century.

The earliest churches are **Norman Romanesque (Norman, Anglo-Norman, Romanesque)**. These are cruciform in plan with a nave, an apsidal or square-ended chancel, and a central, square or round tower. Occasionally there were subsidiary towers. Some circular naves are known in parish churches. Romanesque architecture is characterised by round-headed and moulded arches, window openings and doorways, and by barrel vault ceilings. Some windows had two lights separated by a central shaft — **lights (days)** are the openings of a window between shafts or mullions. Windows and arches could be decorated with carved mouldings, often using chevron (zigzag) ornament. The interior of churches was covered in decorative wall plaster. These early churches were often rebuilt or enlarged by adding aisles to the nave with square, cylindrical or, later, compound pillars.

Prosperity in the twelfth century led to a change in architectural styles. The **Transitional phase (Transitional Gothic)** dates from c1170 to c1220, during which there was a change from the Romanesque style to **Gothic architecture (Gothic style, Pointed style)**, so-called because it did not owe its influences to a classical style, as did the Romanesque. There was a change from round-headed arches and windows to those which rose to a point. The use of pointed arches, rib-vault ceilings and more slender proportions enabled higher walls to be built and wider spaces to be vaulted. Churches grew larger and more imposing. **Bell towers** at the west end of the church became common and some detached bell towers are known. In early churches the **crossing**, where the nave, chancel and transepts met, was poorly lit. Later churches had **lantern towers** at the crossing formed by the walls of the crossing being built higher to contain windows.

Early English Gothic (First Pointed) is the first pure Gothic phase and dates from c1220 to c1290. It is characterised by tall, narrow pointed windows **(lancet windows)**, usually without tracery, although plate tracery is seen in the later period. In **plate tracery** patterns were formed by cutting away the solid stone above the lights rather than by carved stone bars springing from the mullions as in later tracery **(bar tracery)**. Some windows were divided by narrow perpendicular columns **(mullions)**. Window frames for glass were inserted into the window jambs and mullions. **Low side windows (lepers' windows)** were set low down in the outer wall of the choir or chancel, usually on the south side. **Squints (hagioscopes)** are small windows allowing a view of the altar from places in the church where it could not otherwise be seen. They are also found in some houses, giving a view to the chapel from adjoining rooms. Much decoration was used in English Gothic architecture, particularly stylised foliage and mouldings. **Spires** began to be placed on towers, some of which were covered

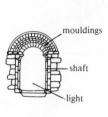

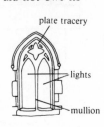

bar tracery

Norman Window

0   1m

Early English Window

0   1m

Decorated Gothic Window

0   2m

Perpendicular Window

0   2m

174

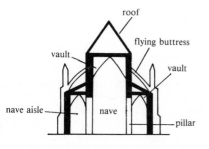

roof

flying buttress

vault

vault

nave aisle

nave

pillar

Cross-section through a Church

0   10m

Vaults

Vaulting was a means of roofing an area with a stone roof. The earliest type was the **barrel vault (tunnel vault)** which was a semi-circular vault similar to a long stone arch. It needed buttresses to stabilise it, and was unsuitable for spanning wide areas. A

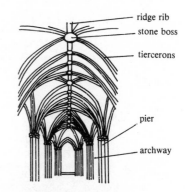

ridge rib

stone boss

tiercerons

pier

archway

Tierceron Vault (looking down nave aisle)

with lead. Lead was at times also used for roofs. **Flying buttresses (arch buttresses)** began to be used which were in the form of an arch designed as a counterthrust to the weight of the nave vaulting. Solid buttresses had been used in earlier periods.

The Early English style gradually developed into the **Decorated Gothic (Second Pointed, Middle Pointed)** which dates from c1290 to c1350. More ornate architecture is seen in this period including an increased number of lights and more elaborate tracery in windows. Vaulting becomes more complex. **Sedilia** (two or three seats) are seen in the south wall of the chancel near the altar. The **piscina** (a basin used by the priest for ritual washing) is often found near the sedilia.

From the late fourteenth century the **Perpendicular Gothic style (Third Pointed)** developed; this lasted until the sixteenth century. The pointed arch became flatter, and arches and windows were often framed by a rectangular outline. There were towers of very great height, and rich decoration, including intricately carved timber roofs and ceilings.

Most **burials** were in churchyards. Bodies were placed in shrouds, in stone or wooden coffins, or chalk cists. Later graves often cut into earlier ones, perhaps indicating that gravestones or markers were not widely used. Some burials are found in straight rows, however, and the absence of grave-stones suggests that wooden markers were sometimes used. Stone grave covers and coffins are also known.

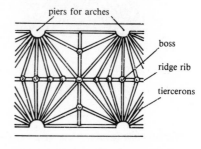

piers for arches

boss

ridge rib

tiercerons

Part of a Tierceron Rib-vault (looking up at ceiling)

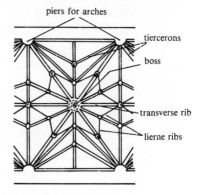

piers for arches

tiercerons

boss

transverse rib

lierne ribs

Part of a Lierne Vault (looking up at ceiling)

0   5m

Reading for Churches: Clapham, A. W. 1934; Morris, R. 1979; Smith, E. et al 1976.

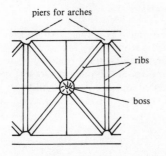

Part of a Quadripartite Rib-vault (looking up at ceiling)

Part of a Fan Vault (looking up at ceiling)

0   5m

groined vault (groin-vault, cross-vault) was formed by two intersecting vaults. Some intersecting barrel vaults are known.

Ribbed vaulting (rib-vault, Gothic vault) was a new feature in Gothic architecture and was composed of intersecting cells divided by masonry ribs. Each bay was divided into various sections by ribs (such as **quadripartite rib-vault**, four parts; **sexpartite rib-vault**, six parts) and was strengthened by stone arches. From the late thirteenth century more complex plans were used: **tierceron ribs** subdivided each section of a rib-vault to form a **tierceron vault**, and in the fourteenth century more ribs were used to form a stellar pattern **(lierne vaults)**. In the fifteenth century the number of ribs multiplied forming **fan vaults**, used mainly in ecclesiastical architecture. Carved stone bosses decorated the intersections of ribs.

Reading for Vaults: Morris, R. 1979.

Bridges

Both large bridges crossing rivers and small bridges crossing moats were initially of wood, mostly oak. A few stone bridges were built in the twelfth and thirteenth centuries, but most were built in the fourteenth and fifteenth centuries. Stone bridges were built on arches; the piers were about 5m apart. The piers often incorporated triangular projections **(cutwaters)** from which the arches were built, or else the projections were carried up to the top of the parapet to provide recesses for pedestrians when vehicles were passing. Most Medieval bridges were very narrow — about 3m to 4m wide.

Reading for Bridges: Rigold, S. E. 1975; Robins, F. W. 1948.

Mills

Watermills were built in both town and country. Those in towns were mainly for corn-milling. In the thirteenth century the cloth industry in the countryside was transformed by the use of **fulling mills** using water power. Abandoned watermills sometimes display characteristic earthworks such as the remains of the mill pool and mill race.

Windmills were only found in the country. The earliest type of mill was the **post-mill** which was supported on a central post set in two intersecting beams **(cross-**

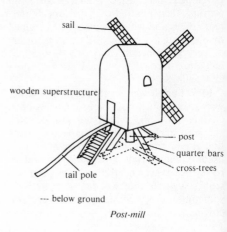

Post-mill

0   5m

trees) and strengthened by **tie-beams (quarter bars).** The mill stood on top of a mound partly constructed from the material from a surrounding ditch. These mounds are sometimes mistaken for prehistoric barrows. The body of the mill could be rotated to enable the sails to be turned into the wind. There is some documentary evidence for Medieval **tower mills,** although none survive or have been excavated. Unlike post-mills, only the cap and sails were turned into the wind, while the body remained stationary.

Reading for Mills: Beresford, M. W. and St Joseph, J. K. S. 1979; Cossons, N. 1975; Salmon, J. 1966.

Moated Sites

Moated sites vary greatly in size, shape and complexity. Most of them are found in Lowland Britain on badly drained soils, and date mainly to the thirteenth and fourteenth centuries. They consist of a central platform, usually rectangular and partly or completely surrounded by a **moat** which was a flat-bottomed ditch usually more than 3m wide. Moats were usually intended to contain water and were sometimes served by inlet and outlet leats or channels. They could be crossed by permanent bridges, drawbridges or causeways. There are sometimes stone revetments to one or both sides of the moat. On the central platform stood a domestic house (sometimes the manor house), occasionally with outbuildings and gardens. The moated site was often associated with other moat complexes used as fishponds or to contain gardens or buildings. Moated sites are often confused with a variety of other earthworks, some later in date, including fishponds and mill ponds. The purpose and origin of moated sites are not clearly understood but they may have been a response to social unrest and colonisation of new land at this period.

Reading for Moated Sites: Aberg, F. A. 1978.

Fishponds

Fishponds date from the Medieval period to the present century. They may consist of single rectangular ponds or complexes of ponds (**fish stews, stewponds**). They are

sometimes associated with moated sites, and are themselves at times confused with moated sites. They were also a common amenity on monastic sites. They were used to keep fish alive for food during the winter months.

Reading for Fishponds: Beresford, M. W. and St Joseph, J. K. S. 1979, 67–9; Taylor, C. C. 1978.

Pillow Mounds

Pillow mounds are 'pillow-shaped', rectangular in plan — about 10m to 20m long and 5m to 10m wide — and usually with a shallow surrounding ditch. They are flat-topped and usually no more than 0·5m high. They have been identified as warren earthworks used for farming rabbits. Little is known about the use of artificial warrens.

Reading for Pillow Mounds: Beresford, M. W. and St Joseph, J. K. S. 1979, 68–72; Taylor, C. C. 1974.

Emparking

The practice of emparking was carried out from the thirteenth century to set up deer parks for hunting which were mostly about 150 to 300 acres in extent. They were enclosed by extensive banks and ditches which often survive as distinctive earthworks.

Reading for Emparking: Platt, C. 1976.

Salt

Salt was obtained from the sea at **salterns.** Where the sea has subsequently retreated, the salterns are now up to 25km inland. Evidence for these former salterns is seen in traces of charcoal and pottery in fields. Salt-boiling kilns have also been found.

Reading for Salt: Beresford, M. W. and St Joseph, J. K. S. 1979.

Use of Metals

Gold was used for objects such as rings, brooches, coins and seal matrices; **silver** was used for spoons, strap-end hooks, buckles, seal matrices and coins.
   Pewter was used for pilgrims' signs, brooches, saucers, spoons and occasionally buckles. **Lead** was used for weights,

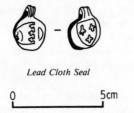

Lead Cloth Seal

0   5cm

ampullae, pilgrims' signs, window leading (cames), cloth seals, and crosses. Lead **crosses** were often placed with the dead (particularly plague victims).

Bronze and **brass** were used for articles such as sheath chapes, belt chapes, buckles, buttons, lace tags, mounts, studs, heraldic pendants, pilgrims' signs, brooches, rings, seal matrices, purse frames, tweezers, thimbles, pins, bodkins, needles, keys, hinges, doorknockers, tap handles, figures, vessels, candlesticks, crucifixes, church bells, rumbler bells, book clasps, balances, and spurs. **Lace tags (bootlace tags, tag ends)** were used to bind the ends of laces. There is some evidence from excavations for Medieval bell-founding. **Bells** were cast in founding-pits; these pits are sometimes found, as well as associated bronze slag and remains of the baked clay mould. Bells were cast by the lost-wax method: a clay model of a bell was made which was covered in wax. This was then surrounded by an outer skin of clay **(clay cope)** with reinforcing bands of iron. The wax was then melted out and the molten metal poured in. The clay

Latten is an alloy similar to brass and was used for steelyard weights, seal matrices, spoons and monumental brasses. It was made by melting ground calamine ore with charcoal and copper. **Monumental brasses** were popular from the early thirteenth

century to *c*1650. Figures were engraved on 'brass' (actually latten) and then the surface was burnished and the engraved lines often filled with a black or coloured substance. Shields were occasionally filled with enamel. **Palimpsests** are brasses which have been re-used and different inscriptions added; the old figures are sometimes modified. Another type of palimpsest is when the plain reverse of a brass is used, leaving the original side undamaged.

Tin Tin mines have been found in the West Country. Tin was mined particularly by **streaming**; the upper layers were dug away to expose the ore-bearing layers, and running water from artificial leats was washed over these to separate out the tin-bearing ores. Shaft mining seems to be later in date. Tin was used in the production of pewter and bronze, and also for tinning.

Iron Waste material is sometimes found around iron-mining shafts. Evidence for Medieval iron smelting has also been found, including slag heaps, smelting furnaces and dumps of charcoal. Iron was used for objects such as weapons, armour, tools, padlocks, keys, spurs, horseshoes, snaffle-bits, curb-bits, stirrups, curry combs, purse frames, buckles, hooks, fish hooks, chains, nails, bolts, vessels, chest handles, strap-hinges, hinge-pivots, trivets, staples, ferrules, bucket handles and various other fittings.

Reading for Use of Metals: Cameron, H. K. 1974; Down, A. 1978, 164–9; Hatcher, J. 1973; London Museum 1940; Macklin, H. W. 1975; Morris, R. 1979, 78–9; Platt, C. and Coleman-Smith, R. 1975; Williams, J. H. 1979.

Enamel

Enamel was used to decorate heraldic pendants, candlesticks, bronze figures, crucifixes, brooches and monumental brasses.

Reading for Enamel: British Museum 1924; London Museum 1940.

Coins

The earliest Medieval coinage consisted of silver **pennies**. They were struck from hand-

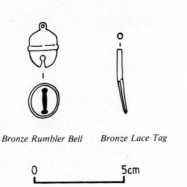

Bronze Rumbler Bell   *Bronze Lace Tag*

0   5cm

made dies which were replaced when worn out. In 1180 **short cross coinage** was introduced in England which depicted a small cross. It is found in Scotland from 1195 to 1250. In the mid thirteenth century this was replaced by **long cross coinage** which depicted a cross with longer arms. At this date gold coinage was introduced. In 1279 a silver fourpence coin **(groat)** was minted, as well as **halfpennies** and **farthings**. A **half groat** was later minted. Silver pennies were often called **sterlings**.

In the late thirteenth century there was a shortage of coins and much foreign coinage was brought to Britain, and counters, jettons and tokens were used. Pennies were also cut in half or quarters to provide a small denomination.

Reading for Coins: Metcalf, D. M. 1977; Platt, C. 1978.

Jewellery

Jewellery consisted mainly of brooches and rings. **Rings** were of bronze, silver or gold and were sometimes set with precious stones. **Posy rings** (inscribed rings) of gold are known. Some **brooches** were circular **(ring brooches, annular brooches)** ranging from plain forms of a simple ring of metal to highly decorated forms. There are also **penannular brooches** and **disc brooches**. Brooches were often used for fastening

Plain Circular Brooch

0   5cm

clothes. They were made of bronze or pewter; decorative brooches of gold and enamel are also known.

Reading for Jewellery: London Museum 1940.

Belts and Straps

Belts and straps were made of leather. **Strap-end buckles** and **belt-end buckles** often consisted of a buckle and two metal plates **(buckle plates)**. The belt was inserted between the plates and held by rivets or between the two prongs of a fork-shaped central piece. There were also single buckles and double buckles and a variety of belt **chapes**. Buckles fitted on one end of a strap or belt and chapes on the other end. Buckles and chapes were of bronze, iron or pewter. Strap-end hooks and decorative mounts of bronze and silver are also known.

Reading for Belts and Straps: London Museum 1940.

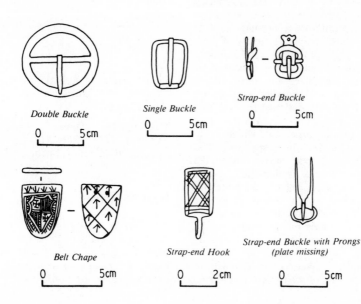

Double Buckle

0   5cm

Single Buckle

0   5cm

Strap-end Buckle

0   5cm

Belt Chape

0   5cm

Strap-end Hook

0   2cm

Strap-end Buckle with Prongs (plate missing)

0   5cm

Heraldic Pendants and Discs

Pendants formed part of Medieval horse furniture. They were usually of bronze or copper with heraldic designs in enamel or niello. Non-heraldic ones are sometimes found. They could be attached to horse harness or worn across a horse's forehead. Heraldic bronze **discs**, sometimes with enamel work, plain relief or impressed designs, were also used as harness ornaments. Some had projecting studs which fastened them to leather, and some were probably inset into the leather. Others show signs of attachment to a metal surface and so probably decorated articles such as mazer bowls.

Reading for Heraldic Pendants and Discs: London Museum 1940.

Flask-shaped Ampulla with Scallop-shell Decoration

```
0            10cm
```

Heraldic Pendant

```
0      5cm
```

Pilgrims' Signs

Pilgrims' signs (signacula) were distributed at various shrines and were worn on clothing as proof of a pilgrimage and as talismans. They were made mostly of poor quality pewter, or of lead or brass, and were cast in stone moulds. They consisted of **badges** and **ampullae**, the latter being miniature flasks with handles worn round the neck. They were designed to hold holy oil or water, and were often surrounded by circular openwork ornament, which made handles unnecessary for suspension. The flask shape developed into a chape-like shape; many have a scallop-shell design. Most ampullae were sealed by pinching and hammering the mouth closed. They are known from the late twelfth century, but pilgrims' badges were more common by the early fifteenth. Several forgeries were made during the nineteenth century. The two most important places of pilgrimage in England were *Canterbury*, Kent (the shrine

Chape-shape Ampulla

```
0                    5cm
```

of St Thomas à Becket) and *Walsingham*, Norfolk (the shrine of Our Lady of Walsingham).

Reading for Pilgrims' Signs: London Museum 1940; Spencer, B. W. 1968; Spencer, B. W. 1971; Spencer, B. W. 1975.

Seal Matrices

Seal matrices (dies) (sing **seal matrix, die**) are found, usually made of latten, silver, or occasionally gold, lead, pewter, ivory, jet or wood. They usually had a handle and were mostly circular or pointed oval in shape.

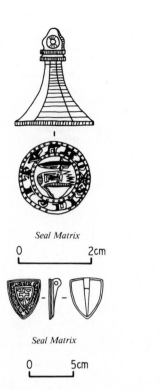

Seal Matrix

0   2cm

Seal Matrix

0   5cm

Steelyard Weight

0   5cm

They were used to make impressions in wax as seals for attesting documents or closing letters.

Reading for Seal Matrices: London Museum 1940; Tonnochy, A. B. 1952.

Weights and Measures

The most common instrument for weighing in the Medieval period was the equal-armed **balance** which consisted of a balance arm of bronze with bronze scale pans and weights. Some balances had folding arms. From the thirteenth century the **steelyard** was used. **Steelyard weights** were made of latten by the cire perdue method: when the core was extracted, the necessary weight was made up by the addition of lead. The weights are globular in shape and have two, three or four shields, usually with heraldic devices. **Tumbrels (coin balances)** are known: these are balances designed to weigh coins; coins of the correct weight or more would tip up the balance and slide off.

Reading for Weights and Measures: Dru Drury, G. 1926; London Museum 1940; Mayhew, N. J. 1975.

Metal Vessels

Cooking vessels were mainly of pottery in the early Medieval period, but vessels of cast and sheet bronze became increasingly popular in the later Medieval period. Bronze **jugs** are found, some with three legs and some with a flat base and spout. Three-legged bronze **ewers** with a tubular spout are common. The tubular spout often ends in an animal's head. **Cauldrons** of bronze were usually round-bottomed; some had three legs and angular handles and could be suspended over, or stood directly in, a fire. **Skillets** of bronze with three legs and a projecting flat strip handle were used from the thirteenth century. **Chafing dishes** in metal were common from the fifteenth century and were used for holding charcoal to keep food hot at table. **Strainers** of bronze are also known. **Bowls** were often made of wood, or in the later Medieval period in pewter. Bowls made from other metals or metal and wood were for special purposes such as **mazer bowls**. A mazer was a popular type of drinking vessel — the sides and bottom of the bowl were made of maple-wood with a silver band round the top. One type of copper bowl is shallow, with a narrow, flat, everted rim, and is engraved on the inner surface with biblical scenes, figures of classical mythology or figures of virtue and vice. These date to the twelfth and early thirteenth centuries and were probably imported from the Rhineland.

Medieval secular plate rarely survives; it would have included mazers, and rose-water dishes made of silver. Ecclesiastical plate rarely survives because of the Reformation, but would have included much goldsmith's work. **Chalices** have been found — early ones have two handles, later

181

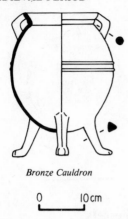

Bronze Cauldron

0   10 cm

ones have no handles but have a knop and a high foot. **Patens** are also known, as well as **plates** and **saucers** of pewter. Pewter saucers are mostly found with pewter chalices and were placed in priests' coffins from *c*1280 to 1350.

Reading for Metal Vessels: Lewis, J. M. 1973; London Museum 1940.

Cooking Utensils

Forks were not generally used. **Spoons** of the eleventh to thirteenth centuries are rare. A few silver ones are known with an animal's head gripping the bowl at the base of the stem; there are also some spoons of bone and horn, and a few bronze examples.

Spoons of the fourteenth and fifteenth centuries have pear-shaped bowls, slender stems and **knops** of various designs. **Maidenhead spoons** have knops in the form of a female bust, possibly the Virgin Mary. Spoons recognised from the later Medieval period are mostly of pewter and latten, although they were probably usually made of wood, bone or horn. Silver spoons are occasionally found.

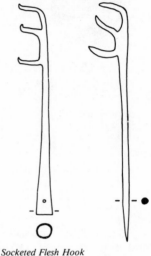

Socketed Flesh Hook

Tanged Flesh Hook

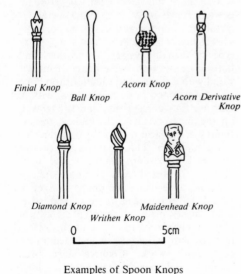

Finial Knop

Ball Knop

Acorn Knop

Acorn Derivative Knop

Diamond Knop

Writhen Knop

Maidenhead Knop

0   5 cm

Examples of Spoon Knops

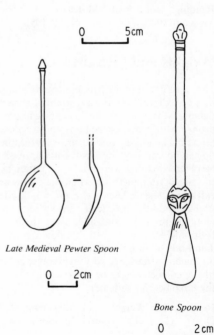

0   5 cm

Late Medieval Pewter Spoon

0   2 cm

Bone Spoon

0   2 cm

182

Flesh hooks were commonly used in cooking. They had an iron hook with two or three prongs, with either a socket or a tang for the attachment of a wooden handle. It is not clear if there is a chronological difference between the two types.

Knives: see tools.

Reading for Cooking Utensils: London Museum 1940.

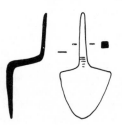

Iron Trowel

0   10 cm

Tools

Many tools used in the Medieval period are identical or very similar to tools in use in recent times, and often differ little from those dating from the Iron Age.

Agricultural tools included iron mattocks, picks, spades, scythes, reaping hooks, sickles, rakes, bills and pitchforks. **Spades** were wooden with a metal sheath similar to Roman examples. Blades made completely of metal appear in the later Medieval period and could be rectangular, rounded or pointed. Carpenters' tools included iron axes, saws, chisels, hand-drills, spoon augers, mallets and hammers. Also found are iron trowels, calipers, dividers, tongs, punches and shears.

There are various types of Medieval **axe**. A **woodman's axe** is similar to Romano-British axes but lacks a hammer end. The most common type of **carpenter's axe** was a T-shaped axe, and there were also straight-sided triangular axes with a tubular socket. **Bearded axes** have a strong downward projection of the blade. Some axes are characterised by a **looped socket** where the tail of the axe was bent over to form the socket. These were easy to produce and were probably a general all-purpose tool. A 'Medieval-type' **battle axe** evolved in the thirteenth century; earlier battle axes are similar to the Saxon francisca.

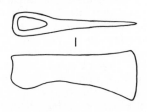

Woodman's Axe

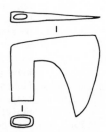

Carpenter's Axe with Tubular Socket

winged socket

Bearded Axe

T-shaped Carpenter's Axe

Axe with Looped Socket

Battle Axe

0   20 cm

183

Many **knives** probably had a dual role as domestic knives and weapons. The tanged knife continued in use, and the strip tang became popular from the fourteenth century. A tang was inserted into a piece of wood or bone for a handle, and a strip tang had a piece of bone or wood either side of the tang attached by rivets. **Knife-daggers** occur mainly in the fourteenth and fifteenth centuries; the triangular section of a scramasax-type blade is retained but the blade becomes much longer. The hilts are usually simple, although elaborate ones dating to the fifteenth century are known. Many leather sheaths for knives and knife-daggers have been found.

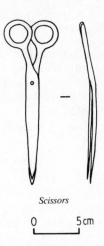

Scissors

0   5 cm

Reading for Tools: Beresford, G. 1975; Gailey, A. and Fenton, A. 1970; London Museum 1940.

Armour and Weapons

Armour

In the early Medieval period **chain mail armour** was worn which was made of inter-linked iron rings and comprised a **hauberk** which was a type of knee-length mail or reinforced shirt with a mail hood. **Conical helmets** were also worn. These had a **nasal** (a protruding piece to protect the nose) which gradually went out of use. From the early thirteenth century a helmet called the **helm (great helm, heaume)** was also worn. Helms were at first flat-topped but later became conical; early helms had no movable visor, but later ones did. From the fourteenth century a new type of helmet **(bascinet, basinet)** with a hinged visor, some long and pointed, was used. Helmets were worn with a cape of mail **(aventail, tippet)**. German armourers preferred the helmet known as the **sallet (salet, salade)** some of which had a long neck guard. In the late fifteenth century the helmet known as the **armet** was made consisting of a hemispherical skull hinged to two side plates, with a removable visor.

Plate armour was gradually added to mail armour from the fourteenth century, and by the fifteenth all armour was plate armour, mostly imported from Italy and Germany. **Jousting** (single combat) and **tournaments** (group combat) became

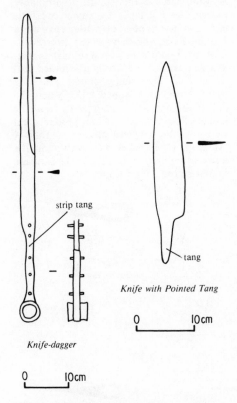

strip tang

Knife-dagger

tang

Knife with Pointed Tang

0   l0 cm

0   l0 cm

Pruning knives are found from the tenth century onwards. They could have been used for purposes other than agricultural. **Scissors** seem to have been made from the thirteenth century, although **shears** were still commonly used and were similar to modern-day examples. They were normally made of iron, but were sometimes of latten. Late Medieval shears have a pronounced loop at the junction of the two arms.

184

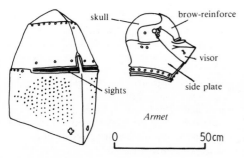

Great Helm

Armet

0   50cm

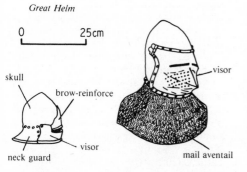

Sallet

Pig-faced (Snout-faced) Bascinet

0   25cm

0   50cm

popular in the fifteenth century and required a different type of armour with reinforcing plates. Horses were also protected by armour.

Early Medieval shields were long and kite-shaped; these gradually became smaller and triangular in shape. Small wooden circular shields **(bucklers)** are known which were used in fencing.

Bows and Arrows

A **long bow** consisted of a bow of wood about 1·8m long, and a bowstring, and fired arrows. A **cross bow** fired **cross-bow bolts (quarrels)** which were heavier than arrows, and consisted of a bow attached crosswise to a wooden **tiller (stock)**. The bowstring was drawn back, at first manually, but later special devices were employed as the cross bow became stronger. The cross-bow bolt was held in place in the cross-bow nut, with the bowstring held by the projections on the cross-bow nut. When the trigger was released, the nut rotated and the bowstring was released firing the cross-bow bolt. These bows were

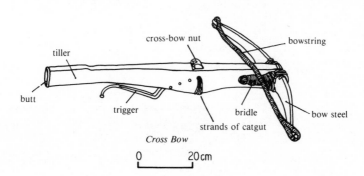

Cross Bow

0   20cm

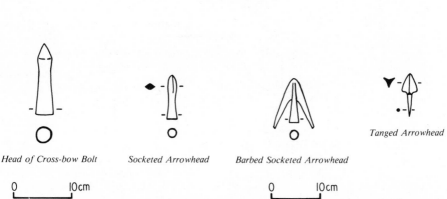

Head of Cross-bow Bolt

Socketed Arrowhead

Barbed Socketed Arrowhead

Tanged Arrowhead

0   10cm

0   10cm

185

of wood in the early Medieval period, but composite bows of wood, horn or bone, and sinew are known from the twelfth century, and bows of steel from the late fourteenth. Bone and antler **cross-bow nuts (nuts, release nuts, tension pins)** are sometimes found.

A variety of Medieval **arrowheads** are known. Barbed arrowheads tended to be used mainly for hunting; barbless ones were used more particularly for warfare. Socketed arrowheads were more common than tanged arrowheads. Leather **wrist-guards (bracers)** were worn as protection against the recoil of the bowstring.

Swords

The swords in use from the eleventh to thirteenth centuries were **cruciform swords** which had various types of **pommel** including **lobed pommels** (a Viking survival lasting to the thirteenth century), **flattened hemispherical pommels** (late twelfth to thirteenth centuries), **brazil nut pommels** (developed from flattened hemispherical pommels and usually associated with long straight quillons, dating to the thirteenth and fourteenth centuries), **disc pommels, spherical pommels** (twelfth to fourteenth centuries — a very common type), **wheel pommels** (late thirteenth century, a development from the disc pommel), **trefoil pommels**, and **multilobed circular pommels** (a development from the plain disc pommel dating from the thirteenth to mid fourteenth centuries). **Quillons** were straight or sometimes curved, and were plain and stout. The **sword blade** was quite wide with a fullered groove down the centre, sometimes with an inscription.

Swords of the fourteenth and fifteenth centuries consisted of cruciform and 'hand-and-a-half' swords. Cruciform swords of this date have a tapering blade with a diamond section; the wheel pommel is most common, lasting to the late fifteenth century. Other types of pommel are seen but are uncommon, such as **lozenge**

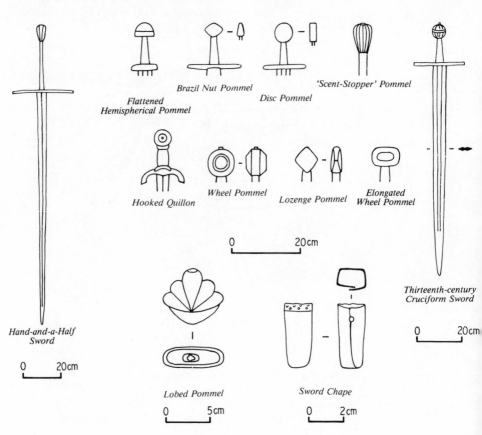

Flattened Hemispherical Pommel

Brazil Nut Pommel

Disc Pommel

'Scent-Stopper' Pommel

Hooked Quillon

Wheel Pommel

Lozenge Pommel

Elongated Wheel Pommel

Hand-and-a-Half Sword

0   20cm

Thirteenth-century Cruciform Sword

0   20cm

0   20cm

Lobed Pommel

0   5cm

Sword Chape

0   2cm

pommels (early fourteenth century) and elongated wheel pommels (late fourteenth century). An elaborate disc pommel appeared in the fifteenth century, and the spherical pommel became more popular from the mid fifteenth. Quillons were fairly short and stout in the fourteenth century but became longer and more slender from the early fifteenth. In the mid fifteenth century quillons became curved, some with sharp projections, and occasionally with floriated tips. A few examples curve upwards with a sharp hook at the ends. Plain straight quillons disappear. The ricasso appeared at the end of the fifteenth century; this was a short blunt portion of blade just below the hilt. These swords continued in fashion even after 'hand-and-a-half' swords went out of fashion.

Hand-and-a-half swords (bastard swords) became popular from the mid fourteenth century. They had longer blades and hilts and heavier pommels, and could be used with one or two hands. The quillons are often long and slender with sharply hooked ends. In the early fifteenth century the 'scent-stopper' pommel became very popular. Blades often had a flattened hexagonal section. Sword sheaths were of leather with bronze chapes. Falchions were single-edged swords with curved wide blades, although very few examples are known.

Daggers

Military daggers included rondel daggers and quillon daggers; civilian daggers included baselards, single-edged knife-daggers (see knives) and kidney daggers, although there are exceptions to this rule. The blades were usually made of iron, and grips were probably mainly of wood or bone. Rondel daggers date from the fourteenth to the sixteenth century and have a pommel and guard in the form of flat discs set at right angles to the tang. The term rondel dagger is also used for all forms of dagger with a circular or near-circular guard but with any sort of pommel. Quillon daggers date from the thirteenth century and were like miniature swords. Kidney daggers (ballock daggers) were made from the early fourteenth century and occur throughout the Medieval period. They are found mainly in civilian contexts, and had single-edged blades. The 'kidneys' are

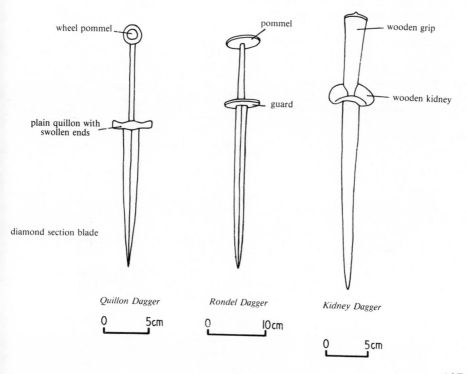

wheel pommel

plain quillon with swollen ends

diamond section blade

pommel

guard

wooden grip

wooden kidney

Quillon Dagger

0   5cm

Rondel Dagger

0   10cm

Kidney Dagger

0   5cm

normally of wood, riveted onto a flat metal plate. Metal 'kidneys' seem to be foreign. **Baselards (basilards)** were also a civilian weapon and could vary considerably in size. They were used from the late fourteenth century to the late fifteenth and have an H-shaped hilt. Dagger sheaths were of leather, sometimes with bronze chapes.

Spearheads

Hunting spears usually had wings at the base of the blade **(winged hunting spears)** and remained in use throughout the Medieval period. Slender and solid **military spearheads** are early Medieval in date, and needle-like ones are later. Late Medieval spearheads have the socket carried well up into the body. A **lance** was a long, stout spear with a shaft about 3m long with a small leaf-shaped blade. Besides the spear there was a wide range of other hafted weapons, mainly of the late Medieval period. They were mostly weapons of foot-soldiers and were derived from agricultural tools. **Halberds** were derived from axes, and had protruding hooks and spikes. **Guisarmes (glaives, scythe-knives)** are similar to scythes, usually with the addition of spikes, and were fixed to a shaft about 2m long. Other hafted weapons included **bills, military forks** and **pole axes** (a long shaft with an axe; battle axes had short shafts). Blades of pole axes became increasingly longer. **Pikes** had long narrow lance-like heads and shafts of about 3m to 6m long. **Military forks (martels-de-fer)** were also used. The primitive wooden club developed into the **mace** which consisted of a knobbed or flanged iron head set on a short wooden shaft.

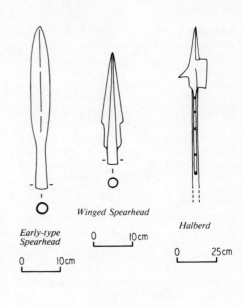

Early-type Spearhead
0   10cm

Winged Spearhead
0   10cm

Halberd
0   25cm

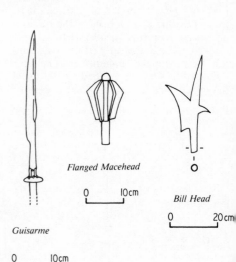

Guisarme
0   10cm

Flanged Macehead
0   10cm

Bill Head
0   20cm

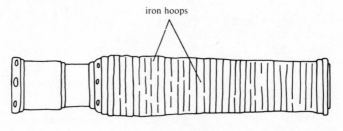

iron hoops

Fifteenth-century Cannon made from long flat hammered Iron Bars girded by Hoops

0   1m

Cannons

Cannons were used from the fourteenth century; the term **bombard** is often used for very early large cannons. The early cannons were made of bronze; later ones were smaller with longer barrels, and were made of flat overlapping iron bars welded together and connected by iron hoops which were shrunk on. Cast-iron cannons were not made until the Post-Medieval period. Early cannons were breech-loaded: they had an iron chamber for gunpowder wedged behind the cannon ball. They were less effective and accurate than cross bows, and had to be cleaned after every firing. Ammunition consisted of iron quarrels, and later stone shot (cannon balls) fired by gunpowder. The **bed** — the support or base of the cannon — was of wood. Small hand guns were also used.

Reading for Armour and Weapons: Blackmore, H. L. 1976; Blair, C. 1958; Borg, A. 1979; Clephan, R. C. 1911; Department of the Environment 1976; Dunning, G. C. 1974b; London Museum 1940; MacGregor, A. 1975–6; Mann, J. 1962; Maxwell-Irving, A. M. T. 1970–1; Norman, A. V. B. and Pottinger, D. 1979; Payne-Gallwey, R. 1903.

Horse Furniture

Horseshoes

Early Medieval horseshoes were light in form, with countersunk nail holes (which produced a wavy edge to the shoe), and calkins. This type is not found after the thirteenth century. They can be difficult to distinguish from similar Romano-British forms. Later horseshoes are heavier and broader and the calkins are often very pronounced, although they disappear from the

sixteenth century. Fullered horseshoes occur from the late Medieval period.

Stirrups

Stirrups were made of iron. Looped stirrups (ring stirrups) and square stirrups with a flattened foot-rest are known in the early Medieval period. Stirrups became more elaborate from the fourteenth century, with a tendency towards an asymmetrical projection on one side. In the fifteenth century there is little change apart from the frequent addition of a small triangular 'tongue' in the centre of the footplate.

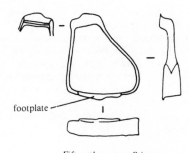

footplate

Fifteenth-century Stirrup

0   10cm

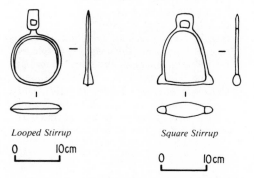

Looped Stirrup

0   10cm

Square Stirrup

0   10cm

Spurs

Prick spurs had a variety of types of points and terminals. Early spurs had straight arms which became curved by the thirteenth century. **Rowel spurs** may have been introduced to England in the late thirteenth century; the earliest ones are similar in form

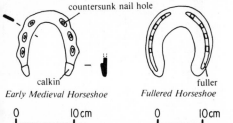

countersunk nail hole

calkin

Early Medieval Horseshoe

0   10cm

fuller

Fullered Horseshoe

0   10cm

189

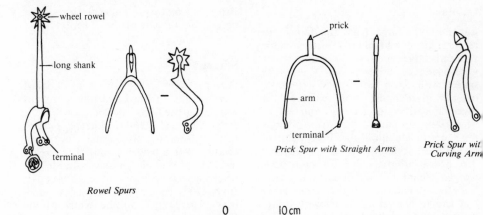

Rowel Spurs

Prick Spur with Straight Arms

Prick Spur with Curving Arms

0   10 cm

to prick spurs, with small rowels usually with six or seven points. In the late fourteenth century the many-pointed wheel rowel became common, and the body of these rowel spurs was curved. In the fifteenth century the shank increased in length due to the use of horse armour and the body became more elaborate. Spurs were usually made of iron, and sometimes of bronze.

Horses' Bits

Few horses' bits can be accurately dated. **Snaffle-bits** and **curb-bits** were both used and were usually made of iron. Snaffle-bits seem to have been used for animals such as pack-horses and consisted of a simple mouthpiece, usually of two links, with a ring at each end **(side-rings, cheekpieces)** for the attachment of the reins. Elaborate examples of snaffle-bits are also found. **Curb-bits** are rare before the thirteenth century. Early ones have fairly plain bars, with a straight bar projecting downwards, joined by a transverse bar at the bottom.

They become more elaborate in the fifteenth century and, towards the end of the fifteenth century, pairs of **bridle bosses** accompanied the more elaborate curb-bits and concealed each end of the mouthpiece.

Reading for Horse Furniture: London Museum 1940.

Keys

Medieval keys are difficult to date closely. There are many varieties of door keys, chest keys and casket keys, which were made mainly of bronze in the earlier period, and of iron in the later period. Barrel-padlocks are known to have been used and there are finds of barrel-padlock keys. Medieval slide keys and latchlifters have also been found and are similar to Roman examples.

Reading for Keys: London Museum 1940.

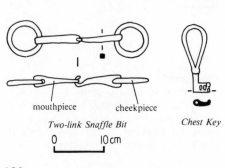

mouthpiece   cheekpiece

Two-link Snaffle Bit   Chest Key

0   10 cm

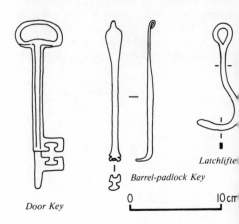

Latchlifter

Barrel-padlock Key

Door Key

0   10 cm

190

Purses

Sack-shaped bags or purses tied at the neck with string and sometimes knotted at the base were probably used throughout the Medieval period and later. They are rarely found, although they are often depicted in representations. A **gypcière** was a large flat wallet of leather or cloth worn like a satchel, or else fastened by one or two loops to the belt. They remained in use right through and beyond the Medieval period. **Metal-framed purses** consisted of a metal frame supporting a bag and are sometimes wrongly termed gypcières. Only the metal bar of bronze or iron usually survives, with a loop for attachment to a belt. There were usually one or two **pendents** to which the purse material was attached to form one or two pockets. They came into fashion from the mid fifteenth century and most of them date from *c*1475 to 1550.

Reading for Purses: London Museum 1940.

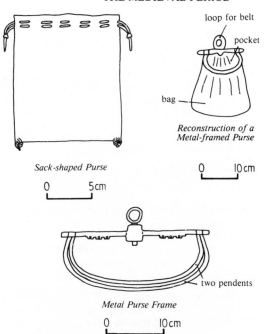

Reconstruction of a
Metal-framed Purse

Sack-shaped Purse

Metal Purse Frame

Lighting

The most common form of lighting was the open **cresset-lamp** which could be of stone or pottery. Some pottery ones were funnel-shaped for insertion in a wall-bracket, and double-shelled examples are known dating from the twelfth century. These open lamps were filled with oil with a wick floating on the surface. **Candlesticks** were in use throughout the Medieval period and ranged from fine ecclesiastical ones to the simple rush-light held in an iron holder. Candles were either impaled on a spike (**pricket-spike**) or held in a loop or socket. Earlier candlesticks had three legs and a pricket-spike, but some later ones were influenced by candlesticks from the Near East and had a cylindrical base. Candlesticks often had a drip-pan and were usually made of latten or iron. Ornate candlesticks had designs in bronzework or enamel, and were mostly imported from *Limoges*, France. **Lanterns** appear in manuscripts from the thirteenth

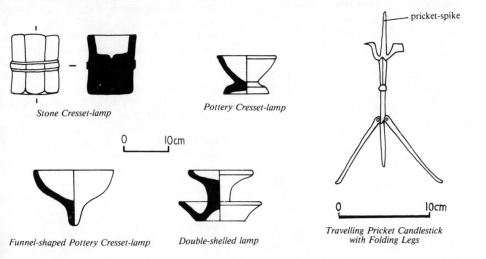

Stone Cresset-lamp

Pottery Cresset-lamp

Funnel-shaped Pottery Cresset-lamp

Double-shelled lamp

Travelling Pricket Candlestick
with Folding Legs

191

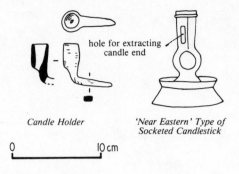

hole for extracting candle end

Candle Holder

'Near Eastern' Type of Socketed Candlestick

0   10 cm

century and were sometimes made completely of metal with a small opening in one side for the light, or else had panels of horn or glass. The latter were more common in the later Medieval period (see also glass lamps).

Reading for Lighting: British Museum 1924; Curle, A. 1925–6; Jope, E. M. et al 1950; London Museum 1940.

Stone

Stone was used for cresset-lamps, quernstones, mortars, rubbing stones, whetstones, moulds for casting brooches, millstones and coffins. **Whetstones (hones)** were made from micaceous schist in the early Medieval period. They were often perforated for suspension from the belt. Incised stone cross-slab grave covers were used. Part of a slate gaming board with lines shallowly incised has been found; it was probably used for nine men's morris.

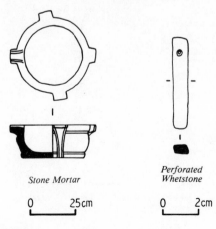

Stone Mortar

Perforated Whetstone

0   25 cm   0   2 cm

Reading for Stone: Dunning, G. C. 1977; London Museum 1940; Platt, C. and Coleman-Smith, R. 1975.

Amber and Jet

Amber and jet were used for chessmen and beads. There is evidence for the manufacture of amber beads in the form of raw amber, spoiled beads and finished and unfinished examples.

Reading for Amber and Jet: Mead, V. K. 1977.

Bone, Antler and Ivory

Bone and antler **combs** were single-sided or double-sided, and simple or composite. Composite combs were made from tooth segments riveted together between two or more connecting plates; simple combs were made from a single piece of bone, antler or ivory. Comb cases are also known. There is often incised decoration on combs.

Bone and antler were also used for spindle whorls, gaming pieces including chessmen, handles, needles, bodkins, dice (mostly with ring-and-dot decoration), skewers, combs, pin beaters, awls, hairpins, end-blown flutes, tuning pegs (instrument pegs) for stringed musical instruments, skates, cross-bow nuts and tools. Bone **skates** used in ice-skating were usually made from the metapodials of horses and cattle; they were fastened to the instep and the ankle by cords passed through holes in the skates. As they had no cutting edge, it was necessary to propel oneself along with a stick. This type of skate was in use from prehistoric to comparatively modern times and is known in Britain from the eighth century onwards. Evidence of bone and antler working has come from various sites, and includes prepared pieces of bone for buttons. Inkwells of horn are also known.

Ivory was used for caskets, writing tablets coated with wax, combs, statuettes, chessmen, and handles.

Reading for Bone, Antler and Ivory: British Museum 1924; Durham, B. 1977; Fry, D. K. 1976; Galloway, P. 1976; Lawson, G. 1978; MacGregor, A. 1976; Megaw, J. V. S. 1968; Platt, C. and Coleman-Smith, R. 1975; Williams, J. H. 1979.

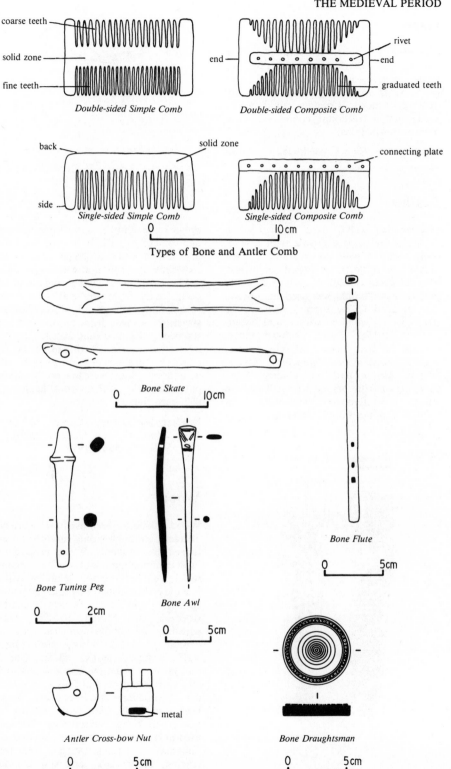

coarse teeth

solid zone

fine teeth

Double-sided Simple Comb

end

rivet

end

graduated teeth

Double-sided Composite Comb

back

solid zone

side

Single-sided Simple Comb

connecting plate

Single-sided Composite Comb

0   10 cm

Types of Bone and Antler Comb

Bone Skate

0   10 cm

Bone Tuning Peg

0   2 cm

Bone Awl

0   5 cm

Bone Flute

0   5 cm

Antler Cross-bow Nut

metal

0   5 cm

Bone Draughtsman

0   5 cm

193

Games

Chessmen of bone, jet and ivory are known, and **draughtsmen** have also been found, as have counters and dice for a type of backgammon and gaming boards for nine men's morris. Counters could also be used as **jettons** (reckoning counters) in commercial transactions.

Reading for Games: Bell, R. C. 1960; London Museum 1940.

Leather Shoe of Turnshoe Construction

0   10cm

Leather

Leather was widely used. It was often decorated by being engraved with a blunt tool, stamped with metal stamps (often heraldic in subject), embossed, or incised with a sharp knife. It was sometimes painted. Cuir bouilli was used for objects not intended to be supple, such as the covering of wooden chests and cases. Leather articles found include shoes, sheaths, straps, belts, inkwells, cases, costrels, book covers, pouches, caskets, bottles, gloves and wristguards. Most surviving **sheaths** belong to small civilian knives or knife-daggers and were often decorated. Some military sword and dagger sheaths are known, sometimes decorated and sometimes set in elaborate metal bindings. Small knife or dagger sheaths were sometimes incorporated with larger ones.

Many offcuts of leather and shoes have been found from shoemaking and shoe repair. Shoes were mainly of **turnshoe construction** — made from a one-piece upper stitched at the instep and attached to a sole by leather thongs or thread. They were either slip-on shoes or tied round the ankle with thongs. Some were low boots. Tanning pits used in the preparation of leather have also been found.

Reading for Leather: Carver, M. O. H. 1979; Platt, C. and Coleman-Smith, R. 1975; Williams, J. H. 1979.

Leather Knife Sheath

0   5cm

Wood

Wood must have been used for a variety of artifacts, although it only survives in water-logged environments. It was probably the most common material for vessels, many of which were lathe-turned. Wooden artifacts include bowls, dishes, boxes, cups, platters, spoons, tankards, mazers, spindles, stoppers, lids, barrels, handles, combs, whistles, tally sticks (notched sticks for counting), spades, bows, gaming pieces, staffs, shingles, casks, ladders, bucklers and lavatory seats. Medieval logboats are also known and worked fragments and offcuts of wood have also been found. Buckets were stave-built with iron handles and reinforcing bands. Wood was also widely used in the construction and decoration of buildings, the lining of pits and wells, fencing, basketwork, and ship building.

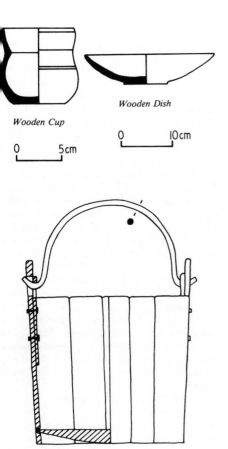

Wooden Dish

Wooden Cup

0 ____ 5cm

0 ____ 10cm

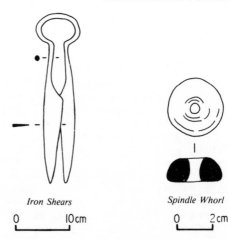

Iron Shears

0 ____ 10cm

Spindle Whorl

0 ____ 2cm

spindles are known. Long wooden **distaffs** over 1m long are known to have been used, although none have yet been found. Dyeing is attested by finds of seeds of plants used for dyeing, as well as possible dyeing vats. Bone implements which may have been pin beaters used in weaving have also been found. Finds of textiles are mainly of wool. Some silk and lace have been found, and also rope and string. Evidence for textiles is also seen in finds of needles, thimbles, scissors, and pins of bronze wire with coiled heads. The horizontal loom was probably used (see Chapter 7).

Reading for Textiles: Crowfoot, E. 1975.

Stave-built Bucket with Iron Handle and Fittings

0 ____ 10cm

Various woods were used, particularly oak for barrels, casks and building materials, and birch and ash for vessels.

Reading for Wood: Butler, L. A. S. 1974; Dunning, G. C. 1937; Dunning, G. C. 1974b; McGrail, S. and Switsur, R. 1979; Platt, C. and Coleman-Smith, R. 1975.

Textiles

Iron **shears** for shearing wool have been found. The wool was carded and teased by pairs of hand cards which were small square boards with handles, set with little metal hooks. **Spindle whorls** were of bone, baked clay, stone, lead or chalk, and wooden

Window Glass

During the early Medieval period the cylinder method continued to be used for making window glass, but at some stage the crown method was introduced, probably from Normandy. From the thirteenth century onwards both types of glass were in use in Britain. By the twelfth century glass was beginning to be common in church windows, and in the thirteenth century it was beginning to be used in the windows of better-class houses. By the end of the Medieval period glass windows were probably normal in these houses.

Stained Glass Windows

Stained glass windows were in use throughout the Medieval period, and are usually classified according to their style and date.

They are mainly found in churches and cathedrals.

Twelfth Century

The main types of window belonging to this period include **pattern windows (decorative windows)** which consisted of simple geometrical patterns using both coloured and colourless glass. A later development of this type of window was the **grisaille window** which consisted of clear glass windows with patterns painted on with grey paint; the patterns were often of foliage. **Figure windows** portrayed well-known figures such as kings and apostles, often with their names worked into the design. **Medallion windows** were made up of a number of 'medallions' of various shapes showing incidents and groups of figures. Each medallion was surrounded by a thin border of patterned glass called **strapwork**. The background to the medallions was decorated with a contrasting colour of leaf-patterns and the whole was surrounded by a wide border of leaf-shape patterns, occasionally including geometric shapes.

Jesse windows (Tree of Jesse windows) portrayed the genealogy of Christ. At the base, a vine issued from a reclining figure of Jesse and formed a series of oval spaces, each with a seated figure of a king with the figure of a prophet on each side. The end of the series was the Holy Mother, with Christ above her surrounded by the end branches of the vine. **Rose windows** were large round windows in cathedrals. Little glass from twelfth-century windows has survived.

Thirteenth Century (**Early Gothic**)

During this period all the earlier types of stained glass window continued to be made, although there seems to have been a little more emphasis on detailed drawing and realism. Towards the end of the century grisaille windows with small medallions set in them **(medallion and grisaille windows)** began to appear. The medallions were of various shapes such as quatrefoils, oblongs with trefoil tops, and circles, and often contained single figures. Also at this time **heraldic windows** portraying shields bearing coats of arms began to appear.

Fourteenth Century (**Middle Gothic, Decorated**)

Windows became much larger and were divided by stone mullions into lights with trefoil or cinquefoil heads surmounted by tracery lights. Iron armatures were superseded by saddle bars as window supports.

Grisaille windows became more detailed, so that the types of leaves forming the patterns were recognizable, and the leaf designs were enhanced by staining. Small shields or roundels, or emblems such as the Keys of St Peter, were sometimes added, while the complicated strapwork designs were superseded by simpler patterns of quarries. Medallion and grisaille windows developed into windows showing panels and single figures on grisaille, and Jesse windows became larger with more realistic vines. Tracery lights contained a variety of designs, including leaf patterns, saints and grotesque beasts. Heraldic windows continued to develop as well. The most typical windows of this period were **figure and canopy** and **subject and canopy** windows, in which the figure or subject (often a biblical scene) was set beneath a canopy. The canopies resembled those depicted on tombs and brasses, and gradually developed into complex designs occupying much of the upper part of the window. The figure and canopy and subject and canopy panels were usually placed half-way up the light, with the rest of the light being filled with grisaille.

Fifteenth Century (**Late Gothic, Perpendicular**)

The windows of this period are a gradual development from those of the previous period, but drawing skills tended to take precedence over glazing skills with an emphasis on what was being portrayed: the leadwork no longer formed part of the design but was merely functional. **Quarry windows** were a very popular extension of grisaille windows. The quarries were diamond-shaped and individually decorated in the centre by a variety of small motifs such as flowers, birds, insects and heraldic devices. As in the previous period, quarries were used as a background for figures, shields and roundels. Figure and canopy windows continued to develop and were the most common windows of this period, and subject windows were also very popular with the subjects arranged in a line across the lights, each with its own canopy. In the latter half of the century the subjects were not confined to a single light, but were spread over two or three, and the canopy was often omitted. Jesse windows declined in popularity but tracery lights became very important and heraldic windows were also very popular.

Reading for Window Glass: Baker, J. 1960; Morris, R. 1979.

Glass Vessels

It is only in recent years that Medieval glass has been systematically collected and recorded during excavations, and so although evidence of Medieval glass vessels is at present scarce, it is likely to become more plentiful in the near future.

Little is known about glass vessels of the early Medieval period apart from a few Islamic vessels imported from the East. In the thirteenth and fourteenth centuries, however, good quality clear-glass vessels were imported from Italy, while green-glass vessels of varying quality were imported from Italy and northern Europe. The most distinctive of these imports were **stemmed glasses** and **bowls**. The stemmed glasses had long stems and shallow bowls and often had elaborate decoration on the stem and base of the bowl. The bowls had notched foot-rings and were often decorated with prunts, zigzag trails and blobs.

Another distinctive though rare group of vessels was made from glass of a mustard-yellow colour, and consisted mainly of **goblets** with a wide stem and rim, and blue trail on the bowl which appears green against the yellow of the bowl.

Colourless Stemmed Glass with Self-coloured and Dark-blue Decoration

0   10cm

Colourless Glass Bowl with Notched Footring and Blue Trails and Blobs

0   10cm

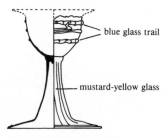

blue glass trail

mustard-yellow glass

Goblet in Mustard-yellow Glass

0   5cm

Syro-Frankish glasses are another group of vessels also dating to the thirteenth and fourteenth centuries. They were once thought to have been made in Syria, but were probably made in Venice. They are distinguished by the use of red, white and yellow enamelling, by the depiction of heraldic figures and animals, and often by inscriptions in Gothic letters.

Imported vessels were usually good quality tablewares of soda-lime glass, and domestic vessels of forest glass. Domestic vessels of forest glass were also made in Britain from the thirteenth century. Forest glass was usually green in colour and of lower quality than soda-lime glass. Vessels such as lamps, urinals, bottles and distilling apparatus were produced (see also pottery for distilling apparatus). **Lamps** had no means of suspension on the actual glass and were probably held in a metal ring which was either supported by a bracket or suspended from chains or wires. **Urinals** were used for medical diagnosis and were of two forms; the commonest form was hemispherical with a straight neck and a wide rim with an upturned edge; the less common form was a bag-shaped vessel.

Glass Hanging Lamp

0   10cm

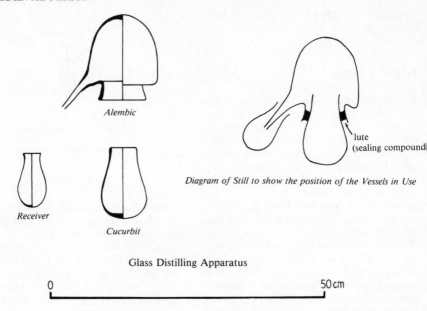

Alembic

Receiver

Cucurbit

lute
(sealing compound)

Diagram of Still to show the position of the Vessels in Use

Glass Distilling Apparatus

0   50 cm

They continued in use until the seventeenth century. **Bottles** were made from the fourteenth century to the seventeenth and often had a characteristic **writhen** neck formed by blowing the bottle in a ribbed mould and twisting it slightly. An important group of vessels was used for distilling purposes, mainly by alchemists. Glass tubing, some of which was writhen, was also made for use in alchemy. **Linen smoothers** were also made from forest glass.

By the fifteenth century there was increased manufacture from the local glasshouses, as well as an increase in imports of forest glass, mainly from the Low Countries and Germany, and of soda-lime glass from Italy, particularly from Venice.

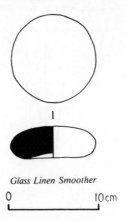

Glass Linen Smoother

0   10 cm

Some distinctive imports began to appear in Britain during the late fifteenth century and included **bottles** with a very high kick, **straight-sided cups** with a high kick, and **goblets** with **lattimo** decoration (a white trail, usually marvered into the body of the vessel). Elaborately decorated bowls and beakers were also imported.

Reading for Glass Vessels: Charleston, R. J. 1975; Harden, D. B. 1961; Harden, D. B. 1971; Moorhouse, S. 1972.

Clay

Clay was used for pottery, cresset-lamps, spindle whorls, piece moulds, crucibles, bricks, floor tiles, roof tiles and other roof furniture. **Pipeclay figures** have been found, and also **cake-moulds** of terracotta which were used in cooking for stamping cakes.

Reading for Clay: London Museum 1940.

Floor Tiles and Bricks

Tiles were made from the end of the twelfth century and were most common in the thirteenth and fourteenth. Three main colours were produced: self-coloured (using different clays), and yellow and green coloured by glazing. Tiles were only fired

Examples of Inlaid Tiles

0   10cm

once in a parallel-flue kiln. The use of decorated floor tiles was confined to Lowland England and they went out of use in domestic buildings by the sixteenth century.

Tile mosaic is the use of variously shaped tiles to produce a pattern. Plain mosaic tiles were glazed dark green and yellow, or sometimes brown and yellow. Decorated tile mosaic used variously shaped tiles which were impressed to form a pattern; a more elaborate version was to fill up the depressions with white-firing clay. Mosaic tiles were most commonly used in conjunction with square tiles in elaborate pavements. They had to be cut by hand or else shaped in wooden moulds; their manufacture was discontinued in the mid fourteenth century. Some tiles were scored to look like groups of mosaic shapes. They are called **pseudo-mosaic tiles**.

The majority of floor tiles were either square inlaid or printed tiles, although it is often difficult to distinguish between the two types. **Inlaid tiles** date from c1230. They were impressed with a carved wooden stamp, and the resulting depressions were filled with a white-firing clay. The edges of the design are clear-cut, unlike **printed tiles**, which are generally later in date and continued in use in some areas to the sixteenth century. They were cheaper and easier to produce than inlaid tiles since they were stamped with a die dipped in a white slip, resulting in designs which were often smeared. There were various areas of manufacture, for example, *Penn*, Buckinghamshire. Both inlaid and printed tiles were glazed.

Other kinds of tile were made at the same time as printed and inlaid tiles. **Relief tiles** were made from the thirteenth century. The design was impressed with a die so that the pattern was raised, or occasionally countersunk into the tile **(counter relief tiles)**. Clay was not used to fill the depressed area and so the tiles became worn quickly. They were glazed and of one colour. **Line-impressed tiles** were decorated using stamps (probably of wood) with very thin raised lines, and resemble tiles incised freehand with a sharp tool. They were made in a single colour, and were used from the late thirteenth to the sixteenth centuries. **Incised tiles (linear decorated tiles)** were decorated by scoring a freehand design with a sharp tool. **Sgraffiato tiles** are rare: the whole surface of the tile was covered in white clay and the design was incised down into the tile body.

Water pipes and bricks were also made of baked clay. From about the twelfth to thirteenth centuries, bricks were made approximately 25–35cm long, 15cm wide and 3–5cm thick, and are known as **great bricks**. Bricks with a more standardized size were made from the thirteenth century, as well as some tile-like bricks.

Reading for Floor Tiles and Bricks: Eames, E. S. 1968; Eames, E. S. 1980; Harley, L. S. 1974; Ward Perkins, J. B. 1937; Wright, J. A. 1975.

Roof Furniture

Roof furniture of baked clay appeared in southern Britain from the thirteenth century, probably due to a change in roofing materials from thatch to tiles and slates. Most **chimney pots** were conical with the top pierced by a hole, and there were usually two holes in the sides. The tops could be incised, and the sides decorated. Most chimney pots were unglazed and were made on a slow wheel. They can be recognized by their smoke-blackened interior. Decorative pottery **roof finials** are also found. These decorated gable ends and were originally decorative ventilators until chimneys came into use. Some were zoo-morphic in character and some were attached to ridge tiles **(attached finials)**. **Ridge tiles** and **louvers (louvres, smoke turrets)** are also known. A louver was a form of pottery roof ventilator with side openings which fitted over a hole in the roof or was sometimes attached to a ridge tile. It allowed fumes from an open hearth to escape. **Roof tiles** were made of fired clay or of slate. Oak shingles have also been found.

Reading for Roof Furniture: Dunning, G. C. 1961; Dunning, G. C. 1968; Dunning, G. C. 1974a; Platt, C. and Coleman-Smith, R. 1975; Wood, M. 1965.

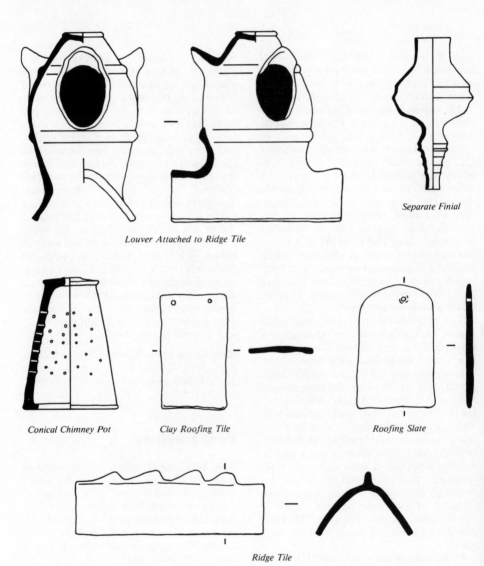

Separate Finial

Louver Attached to Ridge Tile

Conical Chimney Pot   *Clay Roofing Tile*   *Roofing Slate*

Ridge Tile

0   50 cm

Pottery

From the eleventh to the thirteenth century pottery was made in a shell or grit-tempered fabric on a slow wheel and was fired in clamp kilns. Most common are large wide-mouthed cooking pots with sagging bases, as well as some tripod and spouted pitchers and jugs. Stamped decoration, applied strips and frilling were used.

From the thirteenth century the pottery industry revived, with various regional potteries producing a wide range of vessels made on fast wheels and fired in developed kilns. Decoration became increasingly lavish, with painted designs and trailed slips in different colours, and applied ornament including human and animal figures. Lead glazes became common, especially in the later period. From c1300 onwards off-white or buff wares developed in Surrey, with a patchy green glaze (**Surrey white wares**).

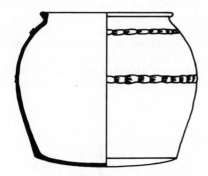

Thirteenth-century Cooking Pot

0   10 cm

Polychrome Parrot-beak Jug

0   10 cm

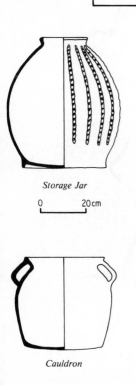

Storage Jar

0   20 cm

Dish

Platter or Bowl

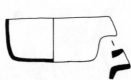

Bowl with Tubular Socket for Handle

Tripod Cauldron

Tripod Pipkin

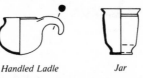

Cauldron

Handled Ladle

Jar

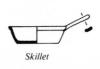

Skillet

0   50 cm

201

From the fifteenth century Surrey white wares have a thick green and yellow glaze; the term **Tudor green** usually describes those dating from the sixteenth century. **Cistercian wares** were made in northern England from c1450–1550 and usually had a red fabric and a dark-brown glaze. From the twelfth century much pottery was imported, particularly from France, and included fine polychrome jugs and pitchers. The main types of vessel seen in this period are **cooking pots** which commonly have feet, and sometimes spouts for handles, and are usually unglazed. There are also **cauldrons** used for the preparation and serving of food, **tripod cauldrons, skillets** (flat frying pans, with a handle probably intended for a wooden extension), **pipkins** (saucepans with a single handle probably intended for a wooden extension), **tripod pipkins, handled ladles** (probably used as dipping ladles), **dishes** (often glazed on the interior), **dripping pans (fish dishes** — flat dishes with a handle), **chafing dishes, bowls, storage jars,** and **jars**.

Jugs are the most common form of vessel found in Medieval deposits. There was a wide range from simple to highly decorated forms including **baluster jugs** whose height was about three times its diameter, **puzzle jugs** — a pitcher or jug pierced in various places and supposed to be a challenge for drinkers, **knight jugs** which were tubular spouted jugs with representations of horses and knights, **standard jugs, 'face-on-front' jugs (face jugs)** which became common in

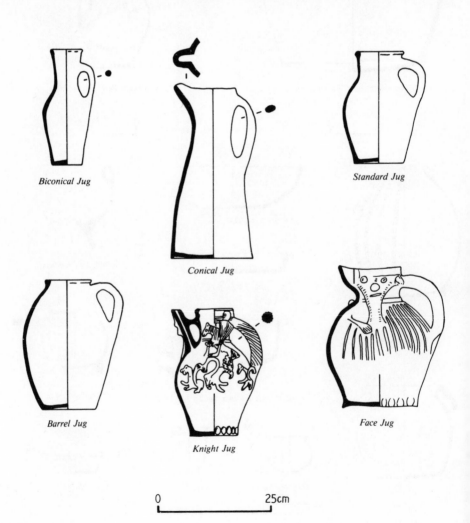

Biconical Jug

Conical Jug

Standard Jug

Barrel Jug

Knight Jug

Face Jug

0   25cm

the fourteenth and fifteenth centuries with faces usually of bearded men modelled on the front or sides, **parrot-beak jugs, conical jugs, biconical jugs (carinated jugs)** and **barrel jugs**.

Curfews were large pottery covers put over open fires at night to avoid sparks, with holes in the sides to keep the fire alight. They are fire-blackened inside. Also made of pottery were **lids, money boxes, urinals, chamber pots, mortars** — some imported from France, **beehive bases, mugs, cruets** used in churches to hold wine and water for Mass, **cups** which were introduced towards the end of the fifteenth century, **torches, pitchers** — common vessels used for containing water, usually with a larger capacity than jugs, **tripod pitchers**, and **ewers** which were pitchers with pouring lips. **Aquamaniles** were vessels

holding water for washing hands and were usually made in the shape of an animal. **Costrels** were pilgrim bottles, usually with a flattened shape and suspended by two loops. There were two main shapes: barrel and cylindrical. Also found are **cisterns (bunghole jars, bunghole pitchers), bottles, ring vases, lamps** (see lighting), **crucibles** and **posset pots**, which were two-handled cups with a cover and a spout dating mainly to the seventeenth and eighteenth centuries and used for drinking posset.

Pottery **distilling equipment** was similar to that of glass (see glass vessels) and included **alembics, cucurbits, distilling bases** and **receivers**. Type 1 alembics were used with cucurbits as in glass stills, and Type 2 alembics rested on the flanges of a distilling base.

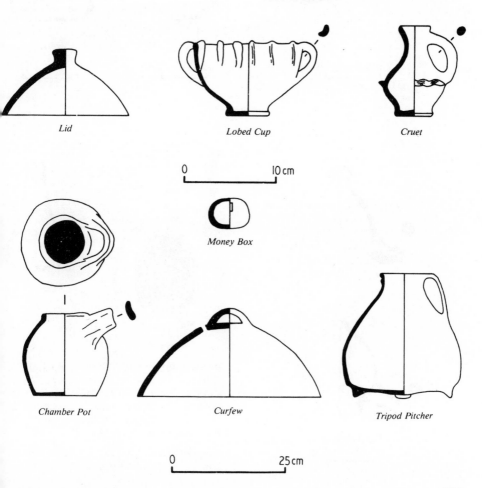

Lid

Lobed Cup

Cruet

0   10 cm

Money Box

Chamber Pot

Curfew

Tripod Pitcher

0   25 cm

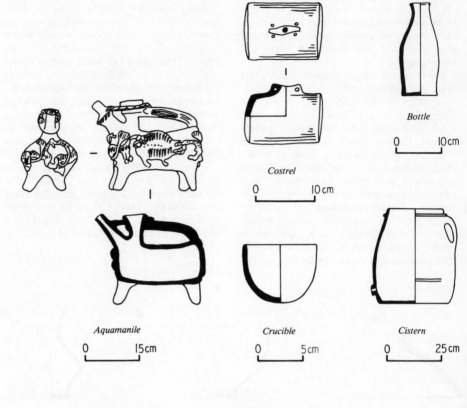

Costrel

0 _____ 10 cm

Bottle

0 _____ 10cm

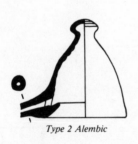

Aquamanile

0 _____ 15cm

Crucible

0 _____ 5cm

Cistern

0 _____ 25cm

Type 2 Alembic

Type 1 Alembic

0 _____ 10cm

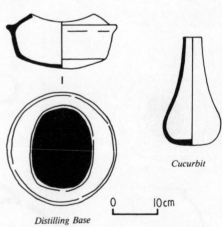

Distilling Base

Cucurbit

0 _____ 10cm

Reading for Pottery: Barton, K. J. 1979; Dunning, G. C. et al 1959; Evison, V. I. et al 1974; Farmer, P. G. 1979; Haslam, J. 1978; Lewis, J. M. 1968; Moorhouse, S. 1972; Platt, C. and Coleman-Smith, R. 1975; Rackham, B. 1972.

General Reading for the Medieval Period: London Museum 1940; Platt, C. 1978.

Chapter 9

Archaeological Techniques

Methods of Locating Sites and Surveying

In the widest sense **fieldwork** covers all aspects of archaeology in the field, including surveying and excavation, but it is often restricted to mean fieldwalking. **Field-walking** is a method of looking for sites and finds by walking over the ground (with the owner's permission). Many archaeological sites can be found by this method, but it takes experience to distinguish between the various types. To ensure complete coverage of an area by fieldwalking, a method of **system walking** is used. On a large scale, this means marking on a map the area to be searched, dividing that area into smaller areas, perhaps by a grid system, and then walking over each area in turn, recording sites and finds within the relevant area on the map. On a smaller scale this method can be used to locate the approximate boundaries of a site where there is a scatter of pottery and other remains on the surface: a grid is laid out and each square searched, with the finds plotted onto a plan of the area. The overall plan of the scatter of debris therefore gives an idea of the location and extent of the site.

Although always needing to be verified by other means, many sites can be initially discovered by **documentary research**. The study of early charters and maps can provide a great deal of information about sites, particularly those of Saxon and Medieval date. Such research can also help to determine the date of a site originally detected by other means. For example, if a mound located by fieldwalking is found to be marked on a map drawn in AD 1700, this map would provide a *terminus ante quem* for the construction of the mound.

Aerial photography (air photography): Since flying time is expensive, photography is the most practical method of recording patterns seen from the air for later study and analysis. Such patterns may pass unnoticed from the ground, and so aerial photography is primarily a method of finding new sites, although it can also be of use in providing a better understanding of known ones.

Aerial photographs (APs, air photographs) are either vertical or oblique. **Vertical APs** are taken from directly above a site; the distortion of the image is reduced to a minimum in such photographs so that they can be converted relatively easily into a map of the site. They can also be taken as **stereoscopic pairs** which reveal the relief of

Diagram of a pattern of crop marks in a field of barley as seen from ground level

The same crop marks as seen in an oblique aerial photograph

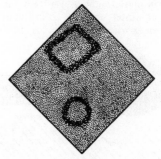

The same crop marks as seen in a vertical aerial photograph

0   100m

Crop Marks viewed from Different Angles

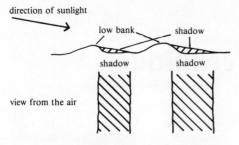

direction of sunlight

low bank   shadow

shadow   shadow

view from the air

the position of the banks is indicated by the shadows

*Diagram showing how low relief features cast shadows
in low winter sunlight to form Shadow Marks*

0   1m

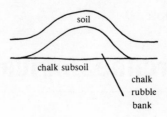

soil

chalk subsoil

chalk
rubble
bank

after flattening by ploughing this becomes:

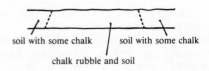

soil with some chalk   soil with some chalk

chalk rubble and soil

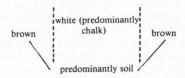

brown   white (predominantly chalk)   brown

predominantly soil

*Diagram showing the formation of a Soil Mark and its
appearance from the air*

0   1m

an area and give a three-dimensional effect when viewed through a stereoscope. Special equipment and suitable aircraft are needed to take vertical APs. **Oblique APs** are taken at an angle to a site. They do not require special cameras and can be taken from most light aircraft, and often they convey a better impression of the site than a single vertical AP. However, the image of the site and its surroundings is often very distorted because of the angle from which the photograph was taken: without the aid of expensive and complicated equipment to convert the oblique projection of the photograph to a vertical projection (a process known as **rectification**), it is impossible to draw a map of the site or even locate it accurately.

The patterns observed from the air are caused by shadow marks, soil marks or crop marks, or combinations of all three. **Shadow marks** show up low relief in conditions of winter sunlight, or in the morning or evening when the sun is low in the sky.

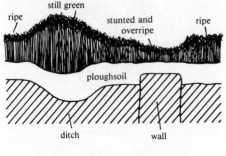

still green

ripe   stunted and
overripe   ripe

ploughsoil

ditch   wall

*Diagram showing the effect of
Buried Features on a Growing Crop*

0   1m

They are often enhanced when the earthworks have a light covering of snow. **Soil marks** are visible as different soil colours or tones in ploughed fields. For example, a bank built of chalk rubble and subsequently flattened by ploughing will appear from the air as a white stripe against the background of the ordinary ploughsoil. **Crop marks** are produced by sites which are completely buried and which affect the growth of the crops growing above them. For example, crops growing above a wall have less soil and moisture available than crops growing above an adjacent ditch, so that the ones over the wall will be stunted and ripen sooner than those over the ditch. This difference in ripeness is visible as patches of different colour within the crop. Some crops are more sensitive than others in this respect. Barley is particularly good for producing crop marks, while grass only produces them in a severe drought.

Shadow marks, soil marks and crop marks can also be produced by geological features (such as ice wedge cracks), recent features (such as pipe-lines), and biological features (such as fungus rings), so that the analysis and interpretation of aerial photography needs experience and skill. **Fungus rings (fairy rings)** are rings of darker coloured grass in pastures and meadows caused by fungi in the soil. Several types of fungi can cause this effect, particularly **Marasmius oreades (fairy ring champignon)**. The fungi stimulate the production of nitrates in the soil which fertilise the grass and produce a circular crop mark. Without excavation it is very difficult to distinguish between a fungus ring and a crop mark produced by a ring ditch.

Infra-red Photography Infra-red is a wavelength of light invisible to the human eye, but which can be detected on special photographic film. The amount of infrared light reflected from a plant depends on the ripeness of the plant, and so infra-red photographs of growing crops contrast areas of ripe and less ripe plants and make crop marks clearly visible that may be hardly visible in ordinary photographs. **False-colour infra-red photography** is a technique that uses different colours to emphasise the contrast between features in an infra-red photograph. The colours bear no relation to the natural colours of the area photographed.

Dowsing is the same procedure as water-divining and can be used to locate buried archaeological features. The success or failure of the method depends on the talent and skill of the **dowser**, who usually uses some form of simple instrument such as a Y-shaped piece of wood which is held in the hands and whose movements indicate the position of the features as the dowser walks over them. Once the position of a site has been located, it can also be surveyed by dowsing. A grid is laid out over which the dowser walks, so that the results of the survey can be plotted on to a scale plan of the area.

Bosing Like dowsing, this is a method that relies heavily on the talent and skill of the operator. A heavy object, such as a weighted wooden mallet or a metal weight, is struck against the earth while the operator listens to the sound produced. Undisturbed ground produces a dull note whereas a filled-in ditch or pit often produces a more resonant sound. The method is limited by the ability of the operator to distinguish between the various sounds and the fact that it is usually only successful on sites where there is bedrock or compact subsoil fairly near the surface. The results are generally recorded in relation to a gridded area and plotted onto a scale plan.

Probing A **probe** is a metal rod (usually steel or an alloy such as duralumin) about 2cm in diameter and usually at least 1m long, with a T-handle on one end and a sharpened point at the other. The probe is pushed firmly into the earth as far as possible and its depth of penetration measured. It is then removed and the procedure is repeated nearby. The presence of buried features such as a wall or a ditch is revealed by the different depths of penetration of the probe. For the most meaningful results, probing is used systematically over an area marked out with a grid.

Augering An **auger** is very similar to a probe, except that it has a large 'corkscrew' end which can be twisted down into the earth. By twisting it in to a constant depth and then bringing it up and examining the soil held in the coils of the 'corkscrew', an idea of what lies below can be gained. Some types have a hollow shaft so that when the auger is brought up to the surface it contains a core of soil representing a vertical section. A **Hiller borer** is a special type of auger used mainly for collecting samples of peat.

Resistivity Meter Soils conduct electricity mainly through water containing mineral salts within the soils. The amount of resistance to the flow of electricity through the soil (the **resistivity** of the soil) can be measured by a resistivity meter. Resistivity in the soil varies considerably, and these variations generally reflect differences in the dampness of the soil. Since buried features like ditches and pits hold a greater amount of moisture, they have a low resistivity, whereas solid features have a high resistivity. By conducting a systematic **resistivity survey** and plotting the results in a convenient form, the buried features on a site can be detected. A resistivity meter is used by inserting metal probes into the soil, passing a current between them through the soil, and measuring the resistance of the soil to the current on the resistivity meter. The probes are then moved to another position on the site grid, and the process is repeated, and so on. This method works best where there are well-drained subsoils (such as gravel or chalk), since too much water in the soil can greatly reduce the variations in the soil resistivity.

Pulsed Induction Meter (PIM) This instrument works by applying pulses of magnetic field to the ground from a transmitter coil. These pulses induce currents in metal objects and magnetic fields in some soils, which are then detected by a receiver coil. The instrument is of little use in detecting anything other than metal, and is thus of extremely limited use in the detection and interpretation of sites.

Soil Conductivity Meter (SCM) This consists of a radio transmitter and a receiver, set at right angles to one another at each end of a bar 1m long, which is carried from a shoulder strap so that the bar is horizontal. The transmitter and the receiver operate continuously and the conductivity of the soil below the instrument is measured. Variations in this conductivity, caused by buried features, can then be plotted and interpreted. Although in many ways similar to the pulsed induction meter, the soil conductivity meter is of greater use in detecting sites since it can detect features such as pits and ditches as well as metal objects.

Magnetic Methods of Detection As well as iron objects and features of fired clay, such as kilns and hearths, pits and ditches filled with domestic rubbish can sometimes be detected by magnetic methods. The thermo-remanent magnetism of fired clay produces a local distortion in the earth's magnetic field which can be detected by suitable instruments; some pits and ditches can also be detected due to differences in their magnetic susceptibility and that of the surrounding subsoil. These distortions of the earth's field are called **magnetic anomalies** and to detect them various instruments can be used:

The **proton magnetometer (absolute magnetometer)** has a small bottle of water or alcohol within an electrical coil. The intensity of the magnetic field is determined by the behaviour of the protons (nuclei of the hydrogen atoms) in the water or alcohol in the bottle, and the rest of the instrument amplifies the signal produced in the coil and gives a reading of the intensity of the magnetic field. By conducting a systematic survey, magnetic anomalies can be plotted. Another instrument is the **proton gradiometer**. This has two detector bottles between 1·5m and 3m apart, and instead of measuring the absolute intensity of the magnetic field at one point, it measures the difference in magnetic intensity between the two bottles. The difference will only be significant when one of the bottles is near a magnetic anomaly. A similar instrument is the **differential proton magnetometer**. This works in much the same way except that instead of moving both bottles to take different readings, one bottle moves and the other remains stationary. The **fluxgate gradiometer** operates on a different principle, using strips of mu-metal as detectors, and gives a continuous information read-out. All types of gradiometer have the advantage of not being disturbed by electric cables, steel-framed buildings, nearby electric trains and so on, which create problems for proton magnetometers.

The unit of measurement of the strength of magnetic fields is the **oersted** (previously known as the **gauss**, a term still used by many archaeologists and American scientists). A smaller unit is the **gamma**.

100,000 gamma = 1 oersted (gauss)

Surveying

Standing monuments and sites, particularly earthworks, may be **surveyed** (measured and recorded) in order to obtain a permanent record of the site, sometimes as a preliminary to excavation. There are various means of recording — from making sketch plans using one's pace as a measure, to more accurate plans using a variety of instruments, the most basic being measuring tapes and ranging rods. A level can be used to make drawings of the contours of the area by taking readings of successive points (see also excavation). Besides measured drawings, photography and making written notes are important parts of surveying (see also trial trenching).

Reading for Methods of Locating Sites and Surveying: Brothwell, D. and Higgs, E. S. 1969; Clark, A. J. 1975; Coles, J. M. 1972; Council for British Archaeology 1970; Fitter, R. and M. 1967; Foard, G. 1978; Goodyear, F. H. 1971; Hampton, J. N. et al 1977; Taylor, C. C. 1975; Wilson, D. R. 1975; Wood, E. S. 1979.

Excavation

Excavation is the unearthing and examination of an archaeological site. The processes of excavation destroy the evidence, so that a completely excavated site is a completely destroyed site. In order to obtain the maximum amount of information, an excavation must be carried out skilfully and carefully, and detailed records of all the evidence must be made.

A distinction is usually made between research excavation, rescue excavation and salvage excavation. In a wide sense all excavations are 'research' excavations, but the term **research excavation** usually describes excavations of sites which are not under threat of destruction. **Rescue excavations** are excavations of sites which are under threat of destruction, and an excavation conducted to recover as much evidence as possible from a site whose destruction has already begun is known as a **salvage excavation** (for example, the rapid examination of a trench being dug by a mechanical digger).

Techniques of Excavation

Trial trenching (trial excavation, test pit, sondage) is a method of examining a site by digging small trenches on various parts of it in order to ascertain the nature, exact location, depth and extent of the site, usually as a preliminary to a full-scale excavation.

There are several ways of laying out an area to be excavated. The method or

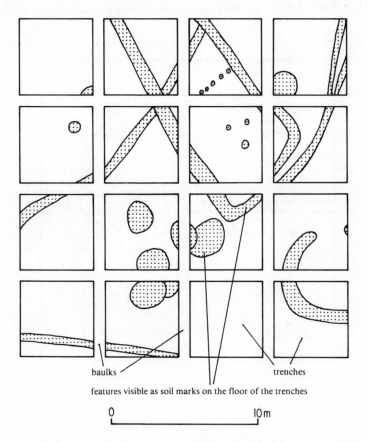

baulks

trenches

features visible as soil marks on the floor of the trenches

0   10 m

Plan of an Excavation using the Box System

combination of methods chosen depends on the nature of the site. The **box system (grid method)** consists of laying out a regular series of square (or sometimes rectangular) trenches separated by strips of untouched earth called **baulks (balks),** usually between 50cm and 100cm wide. As the trenches are excavated, the sides of the baulks provide sections through layers and features which have been excavated. After the sections have been recorded, the baulks can then be excavated separately. This system provides a fairly comprehensive view of the stratigraphy of the site as a whole, and for this reason the box system, or adapted forms of it, is used mainly on sites with deep and complex stratigraphy. Another method of excavation is **area excavation (extensive excavation, open excavation)** which consists of excavating a large area with very few or no baulks. This method emphasises the horizontal relationship between features at the expense of not having a visible record of the overall stratigraphy of the site in the

form of a baulk. Consequently, the method is usually used on sites where overall stratigraphy is virtually non-existent.

The **quadrant method** is often used on approximately circular sites, such as round barrows. This involves the excavation of four quadrants of the site leaving baulks between the quadrants. This can also be used for excavating approximately circular features (for example, pits) within a site itself, although baulks are not left in very small features.

The **planum method** of excavation is sometimes used on sites with a relatively stone-free soil and which are devoid of solid features such as walls or cobblestone floors. The method involves the removal of a layer of arbitrary thickness (a **spit**) from the whole site. The new surface thus revealed is recorded and the process repeated until the site had been completely excavated. By superimposing the plans of the successive arbitrary layers, a picture of the structure of the site is formed. Finds are recorded three-

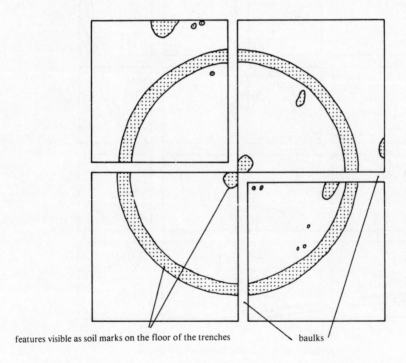

features visible as soil marks on the floor of the trenches   baulks

Plan of an Excavation using the Quadrant Method

0   10m

dimensionally so that they can be related to the features. This method is not commonly employed over an entire site, but is often used to deal with specific features. For example, it might be used to excavate a grave where only a silhouette of the skeleton survives.

Most excavations are conducted by recording and then removing each layer in the order in which they are discovered, leaving baulks to preserve evidence of stratigraphy wherever necessary. Nearly circular features such as pits can be excavated by the quadrant method, while other features usually have sections cut through them; when these sections have been recorded, the remaining fill in the features is excavated. **Fill** is a general term used to describe soil and silt which have accumulated in 'hollow' features such as ditches and pits.

Features

Feature is a general term describing pits, ditches, gulleys, postholes, walls and so on which are rarely recognizable as such when they are first uncovered. Many features represent the remains of structures. The use of the term 'feature' reduces the danger of a wrong identification in the initial stages of excavation.

Postholes: a posthole is a hole dug to take the lower end of a post. The post is set into the hole and earth is placed around it to make it stand firm. Stones are sometimes wedged around the post in the hole with the earth filling **(post packing)**. If the post is not later removed, it will eventually decay *in situ* leaving a **post pipe (post cast)** in the fill of the posthole. This usually appears as a darker stain of soil or a loosely filled area ('pipe'). **Stakeholes** are similar to postholes, but are usually smaller and are

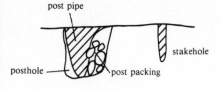

Diagrammatic Section through a Posthole and a Stakehole

formed by stakes which have been driven into the ground, rather than being set in prepared holes in the ground.

Pits were used for various purposes such as **rubbish pits, cess pits, storage pits** and **quarry pits**. The purpose of some pits cannot always be ascertained. Silted up **ditches** and **gulleys** are often found. These were usually dug for drainage, but some were used for other purposes such as marking a boundary line, or for defence. **Beam slots (timber slots)** were trenches dug to contain **sleeper beams (sill-beams, cill-beams, ground sills)** which were horizontal wooden beams used as foundations for buildings. Sleeper beams sometimes rested directly on the ground surface rather than being sunk in a trench. A **construction trench (foundation trench, bedding trench)** is a trench dug to receive the foundations of a structure (often a stone wall). These trenches are usually wider than the foundations to be built, and the gaps left between the sides of the trench and the foundations are later filled in.

When buildings were left derelict, they were often demolished so that the materials could be re-used. Walls were dismantled to ground level and sometimes a trench was dug around the foundations to remove these as well. The trench was subsequently filled in or silted up. The only evidence for the previous existence of walls in such cases is this **robber trench (ghost wall)**.

A **silhouette** is a stain left in the soil, usually by organic material such as pieces of wood, bodies and so on, after these objects have completely decayed.

Stratigraphy

The **stratigraphy** of a site is the succession of layers and features **(stratified deposits)**. If there has been no disturbance (such as by ploughing), the upper layers or features are later in date than layers or features below; similarly, if a layer or feature cuts into another layer or feature, the former is later in date. However, no site is completely undisturbed, since even the action of earthworms can cause the downward movement of finds through the soil, making them appear too early in date (see also Methods of Dating). **Sections** can provide visual evidence of stratified deposits. They are the vertical faces of baulks across the site or across features, and display any changes in

211

Sequence of events

Key (with actual dates of events)

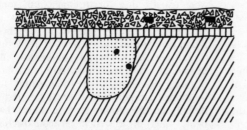

Pit dug — coins give *terminus post quem* of 1820. Soil
and turf form — no dating evidence. Debris from
demolished building spread over turf — coins give
terminus post quem of 1920

modern soil and turf

rubbish deposited in pit
in 1940

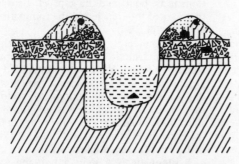

Second pit dug, cutting first pit. Original layers become
mixed in the heaps of debris around the side of the pit.
Rubbish deposited — coins give *terminus post quem* of
1939. Rubbish covered with thin layer of debris from
heaps around the pit

debris from building
demolished in 1937

soil and turf buried by
demolition debris

fill of pit dug and filled in
in 1850

chalk subsoil

▲   coin dated 1939

■   coin dated 1920

●   coin dated 1820

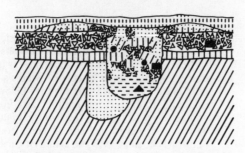

Pit filled in — latest coin gives *terminus post quem* of
1939. Soil and turf form — no dating evidence.
Note: there is now no dating evidence for the first pit

0   1m

Simplified Diagrammatic Sections showing some of the Methods and Problems of Stratigraphy

soil colour and texture. Usually the different coloured and textured deposits form **layers** representing material laid down on the site by various means (for example, a layer of cobbles representing a yard surface). A **tipline** is a layer which is formed by dumped material (usually rubbish) slipping down the side of a feature (such as a pit or mound). This results in a sloping line in the section. A series of tiplines in a feature can often provide evidence about how the feature became filled in and how long the process took. An **occupation layer** can cover a site and contain finds demonstrating that the layer was formed while the site was occupied by people.

Horizontal stratigraphy has little to do with stratigraphy; the concept assumes that graves in a cemetery were laid out systematically, expanding in one direction to form a linear cemetery, with the earliest graves at one end and the latest graves at the other. If some of the grave goods can be dated to check this hypothesis on a cemetery, a process of seriation can be conducted on the grave goods from all the burials.

Finds

Because stratigraphy can provide information about the structural and chronological relationships between features on a site (see also Methods of Dating), the position of finds in a stratified sequence is very important. The position of a find on a site and its relationship to its immediate surroundings is known as its **context**. A find not discovered in a buried context (for example, an object lying on the surface of a ploughed field) is known as a **stray find**. If several finds are found together in the same context (for example, in an undisturbed grave) they are said to be in **association** with each other. Such finds are regarded as contemporary and so are useful for cross-dating. A set of objects found in association with each other is called an **assemblage**.

The term **find** is used to describe a portable artifact (such as a roofing tile) as opposed to a stone wall which is a feature. Important finds are termed **small finds**, and are usually given special treatment such as three-dimensional recording and separate labelling and storage. The importance of finds is largely relative to the site on which they are found; for instance, all finds might be treated as small finds on a site producing very few finds. **Conservation** is often needed on finds (especially metal ones) which are very fragile or begin to decay more rapidly after being unearthed, and is the process of stopping or slowing down this decay by cleaning and preserving the finds using a variety of physical and chemical treatments in a laboratory.

Recording

A number of techniques are used for recording on excavations. Detailed plans are drawn at suitable scales at various stages during the excavation. The plans are sometimes related to a **base line** (a line between two suitable fixed points on the site), although they are usually related to a grid laid out over the whole site. The **grid** consists of an imaginary network of squares, the corners of which are usually marked by pegs or stakes. Each peg is usually marked with coordinates which fix its position in relation to the grid. These coordinates are usually the distances of the peg from a fixed point (the **origin** of the grid). For example, a peg might be mapped as being 30m north and 10m west of the origin. By using the grid system, any point on the site can be given accurate coordinates which can be plotted onto plans.

There are several techniques of making scale plans of a site once a base line or a grid has been established. One technique is the **offset method (offset planning)**, where points are located by measuring the perpendicular distance from the point to a measured base line or to a line between two points on a grid. An alternative method is **triangulation** where each point is located by measuring its distance from two known fixed points. The distances are marked with compasses on a scale plan, and the point is plotted where the compass arcs cross.

For very detailed planning a **planning frame (grid frame, drawing frame)** is often used. This is a square or rectangular rigid frame, often of light metal tubing, with string forming a network of squares. The frame is laid over the area to be planned, and its corners are located on the plan by triangulation or offset. Details within each square of the planning frame can then be drawn on squared paper, or on a transparent paper or plastic on top of the squared paper.

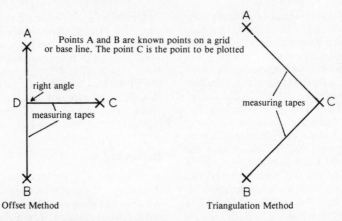

Points A and B are known points on a grid or base line. The point C is the point to be plotted

Offset Method

Triangulation Method

Comparison of the Offset and Triangulation Methods of plotting a point: in the Offset Method the distances AD *and* DC *are measured, and in the Triangulation Method the distances* AC *and* BC *are measured*

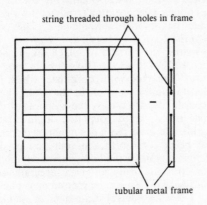

string threaded through holes in frame

tubular metal frame

Plan View and Side View of a Planning Frame

0   1m

Apart from drawing plans of the excavation at various stages, the heights and depths of the features are also recorded by means of a **level**. There are various types of level, but they all basically consist of a telescopic sight which has adjustments, and spirit levels which enable the instrument to be made level when mounted on a tripod. A suitable fixed point **(datum point, bench mark)** on the site is chosen, which is used throughout the excavation in order to compare all results. It is usual to find out the height of this point above the **Ordnance Survey Datum (Ordnance Datum, OD)** which is a fixed point established by the Ordnance Survey at *Newlyn*, Cornwall, equivalent to the mean sea level. When the height of a point on the site is to be measured, the level is set up, and a **levelling staff (staff)** — a staff marked with a metric or imperial scale — is held vertically on top of the datum point. A reading is taken by looking through the telescopic sight of the level and noting the figure observed on the staff. The staff is then moved to the point on the site whose height is to be measured ('levelled') and a second reading is taken by moving the telescopic sight of the level on its swivel base until the staff can be sighted. The difference between the two readings is equivalent to the height of the point on the site above or below the datum point. If the second reading is greater than the reading of the datum point, it is lower in depth than the datum point, and vice versa.

Another method of recording is the drawing of sections **(section drawing)**. This is usually done by using a spirit level to set up a level piece of string between two points **(datum line)**. This line is used in the same way as a base line in offset planning: points are plotted by measuring vertically up or down to the datum line and then measuring along the datum line. By recording the location and the height of the two ends of the datum line, the section drawing can be correlated with the other records of the site.

It is often useful to record the overall stratigraphy of a site by the use of a **matrix (Harris-Winchester matrix)**. This consists of a diagrammatic representation of the stratigraphic relationship between all the layers and features on a site. On a small, simple site this is usually unnecessary, but can be of great help when dealing with large sites with extremely complex stratigraphy.

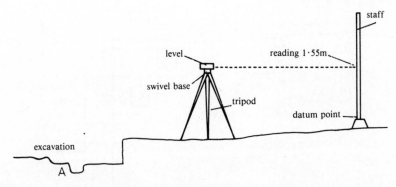

The level is set up, the staff held vertically over the datum point and a reading (1·55m) is taken

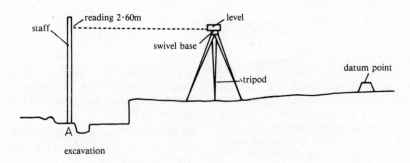

The staff is moved and held vertically over point A (the point to be levelled), the level is swung around on its swivel base, checked to see that it is still level, and another reading (2·60m) is taken. The difference in readings is 1·05m, and the reading at point A is greater than the reading at the datum point, showing that the height of point A is 1·05m below that of the datum point

Finding the height of a point relative to the Site Datum Point (not to scale)

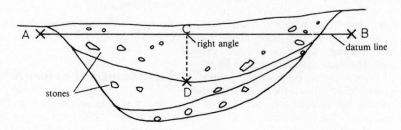

To plot point D the distances CD and AC are measured

A Method of Section Drawing

0   50 cm

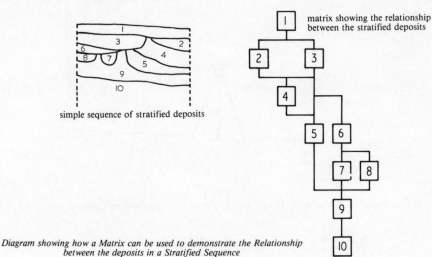

simple sequence of stratified deposits

matrix showing the relationship between the stratified deposits

Diagram showing how a Matrix can be used to demonstrate the Relationship between the deposits in a Stratified Sequence

A very important method of visual recording on excavations is the use of **photography**. Both monochrome and colour films are used to record sections, features and overall views of the site. A specialised use of photography is **photogrammetry**. This is a technique used for map-making from aerial photographs which has been adapted for use on excavations. By moving a camera along a rigid framework to keep the camera at a constant height above the site, a series of photographs with a 60 per cent overlap is taken. These photographs can then be converted into detailed plans of the site by using the same machines employed in making maps from aerial photographs. Less accurate drawings can be produced directly from vertical photographs. Photogrammetry is of particular value where there are large features too fragile to be planned by normal means.

Apart from visual methods of recording, many written notes are made about the various features, layers and finds discovered. These are often augmented by the use of **feature sheets, finds sheets, context sheets** and other printed forms for recording relevant information; they act as checklists of information to be recorded and help to organise the records of a site more efficiently.

All finds (including small finds) on a site must also be recorded, noting the feature and layer from which the finds came. The exact location and the height **(three-dimensional recording)** are usually noted for small finds. It is usual to keep all finds from a particular layer or feature separate from other finds in a labelled polythene bag, or box.

Reading for Excavation: Barker, P. 1977; Coles, J. M. 1972; Harris, E. C. 1979; Webster, G. 1974.

Experimental Archaeology

The purpose of experimental archaeology is to attempt to reconstruct and study ancient practices, such as methods of agriculture, the making of artifacts and the building of structures. Other processes can also be tested such as the length of time a ditch takes to silt up, and what evidence is left of a structure after it has been deliberately burnt down.

Reading for Experimental Archaeology: Coles, J. M. 1973; Coles, J. M. 1980.

Environmental Evidence

The study of ancient animals and plants in relation to their environment is called **palaeoecology**. Environmental factors affecting man are usually grouped under climate, geology, soil, vegetation and animal life. The evidence for past environments comes from three main sources: plant remains, animal remains, and soils and sediments.

Plant remains

The study of ancient plant remains is known as **palaeobotany**. **Palaeoethno-botany** is the study of plant remains associated with ancient man, such as the remains of plants which were gathered or grown for food. **Archaeobotany** is the study of plant remains recovered from archaeological sites. The main types of plant remains and the techniques of using them as evidence of past environments are as follows:

Pollen Analysis (palynology) In anaerobic and acid conditions, grains of pollen often survive; these can be identified and counted under a microscope and a picture of the former vegetation in the area from which they came can be constructed from their types and relative abundance. The results of pollen analysis are usually presented as a form of histogram called a **pollen diagram**, in which the vertical axis represents the column of soil or sediment from which the pollen was extracted, and the horizontal axis represents the relative abundance of the various species or groups of pollen grains. Sometimes the results of such pollen analysis are presented in terms of the number of each type of pollen grain, rather than in terms of what percentage of the

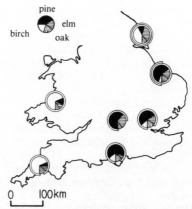

Note: The rings around the main diagrams represent hazel calculated as a percentage over and above the other species

Pie Dish Diagrams used to present the results of analysis of Pollen, dated to part of the Boreal Period, in Southern Britain

whole sample each type of pollen represents. This is known as **absolute pollen analysis** and the results are presented in graphs called **absolute pollen diagrams**. Another method of presenting the relative abundance of various types of pollen from a site is the **sector diagram (pie dish diagram, pie diagram, pie chart)**, which uses segments of a circle to represent different pollens, the size of each segment reflecting the relative abundance of each

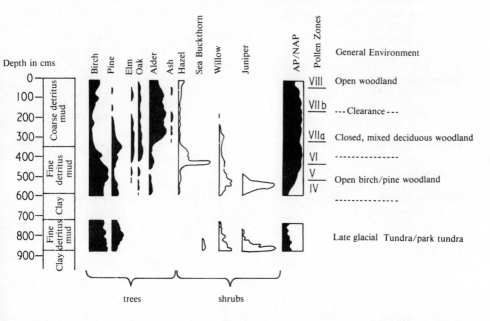

A Pollen Diagram

217

type. This kind of diagram is usually used to compare results from several sites to illustrate regional differences at a particular point in time. For some sites **three-dimensional pollen diagrams** are constructed. These involve samples from exactly contemporary horizons from several widely separated points in a peat bog. The results of pollen analysis of these samples are compared and this gives a more accurate indication of the location of areas affected by particular types of land use and the size of the area involved.

Pollen analysis has two distinct uses — dating, and the reconstruction of former vegetation.

Dating Pollen analysis was first used on a large scale on the peat bogs of Scandinavia and Britain. The results showed that over the past 10,000 years the arboreal vegetation consisted of several well-marked zones **(pollen zones)** reflecting changes in the composition of forest (see Table 4). The study of the ratio of tree pollen to non-tree pollen subsequently enabled these zones to

be defined more closely and to be extended as far back as the latter part of the Pleistocene (see also Chapter 1). The major vegetational changes reflected by these zones were considered to be caused by changes in climate, and so an archaeological find in a peat bog could be dated by comparing the results of the pollen analysis of the peat associated with the find with the known scheme of pollen zones. As a dating method, pollen analysis has been largely superseded by radiocarbon dating.

Reconstruction of Former Vegetation The most recent pollen zone was once taken to reflect a deterioration in climate since it was characterised by an increase in the pollen of birch, hornbeam and herbs, and a decrease in the pollen of elm **(elm decline)**. However, more precise identification of pollen has shown that there was an increase in 'weeds of cultivation' such as plantain, with rare finds of cereal pollen, and that this change was due to forest clearance and cereal cultivation by man and not to a climatic deterioration. More recently,

Table 4
A Table of Some of the Zonation Schemes in Britain (after Evans, J. G. 1978)

Recent zones and climate	Blytt and Sernander zones	Pollen zones	Vegetation	Archaeology
Flandrian zone III	Sub-atlantic	VIII	Rise of ash, birch, beech	Historical period
	Sub-boreal	VIIb	and hornbeam	
Decreasing warmth				Iron Age
			Increase of open land	Bronze Age
			Elm decline	Neolithic
Flandrian zone II	Atlantic	VIIa	Mixed oak forest plus	
Climatic optimum			alder	
Flandrian zone I	Boreal	VI	Mixed oak	Mesolithic
		V	forest plus hazel and pine	
Increasing warmth	Pre-boreal	IV	Birch and pine	
Late-Devensian zones				
III Cold	Younger Dryas	III	Tundra	
II Amelioration	Allerød	II	Birch woods	Upper
I Cold	Older Dryas	I	Tundra	Palaeolithic

radiocarbon dating has provided a more accurate time-scale for pollen sequences. Samples for pollen analysis are now taken from lake sediments and soils as well as peat bogs, and although interpretation of the results is often complicated by the need to distinguish between pollen from local vegetation and wind-blown pollen from all over the general area, pollen analysis is the main method of constructing a picture of the former vegetational history of both large and small areas.

In anaerobic conditions, such as in peat bogs or waterlogged pits and ditches, **macroscopic plant remains** often survive. These may range from seeds, parts of leaves and twigs to whole tree-trunks. They provide an indication of the local environment of a site, although it has to be considered how the remains arrived on the site, since materials brought onto the site by animals and man (for example, as firewood) may not reflect the local environment. If the remains of the plants were only produced at a particular season of the year (for example, nuts), this can indicate that the site from which they came was only occupied at that season of the year.

Smaller plant remains are usually collected by **flotation**, whereby the plant remains are separated from the sediments that contain them by breaking up the samples in a tank of water **(flotation tank)**. The sediments sink and the **flot** (plant remains and other debris) floats, and can be collected in sieves. A more sophisticated technique is the **froth flotation** method in which the sample is broken up and paraffin added. The paraffin coats the plant remains, causing them to float more easily. A detergent is then added to the mixture, which is then agitated, causing a froth to develop in which the plant remains float. The plant remains can then be skimmed off the surface of the mixture.

Charcoal is burnt organic material, usually wood or grain. Because it contains a high percentage of carbon, it is not susceptible to microbial decay and frequently survives on archaeological sites. The plants from which charcoal has been derived can usually be identified. Like macroscopic plant remains, charcoal can give an indication of local vegetation, although the plants may have been brought onto the site from some distance, and this possibility must be taken into account in the interpretation of

the evidence. Grain charcoal **(carbonised grain)** can often provide evidence about arable farming.

Plant impressions are formed by plant remains (mostly seeds or grain) which have become incorporated in a plastic material and are subsequently destroyed leaving their impression: for example, grain may be incorporated in the surface of a clay pot and is then destroyed when the pot is fired, leaving impressions of the grain. Articles of fired clay such as pottery and tile, as well as tufa and stalagmite, are the most usual sources of plant impressions. As with other plant remains, the reliability of their evidence as an indicator of the environment depends on the way in which the plant remains became incorporated in the impressed material and on the type of impressed material itself. Combined with the evidence from carbonised grain, grain impressions have provided information about prehistoric arable farming in Britain.

Phytoliths (plant opals) are microscopic silica structures which occur in the cells of certain plants (particularly grasses). They are sometimes found on archaeological sites, particularly in layers of ashy material in pits and hearths, but the conditions under which they survive are not well known. They can be identified by their size and shape, although some forms are found in more than one species of plant. More research is needed before phytoliths can provide much useful evidence of former environments.

Diatoms are microscopic algae which live in water. They have a cell wall of silica which often survives in sediments, sometimes as a thick deposit known as **diatomaceous earth**. Diatoms can be identified by the size and form of their cells, and since most species are each confined to a particular habitat (freshwater, estuarine or marine), they can be used as an indicator of salinity at the time they were incorporated in the ancient sediments.

Dendrochronology (tree-ring analysis) is usually used as a method of dating (see methods of dating), but it can provide environmental evidence as well. Trees lay down a growth ring each year and in some species of tree the thickness of these rings is influenced by fluctuations in temperature or rainfall (if the tree is not affected by other influences such as nearby standing water). Provided that the tree can be dated, the pattern of varying thicknesses of rings through the trunk of a tree can provide a useful indication of the variations in climate during the life of that tree.

Reading for Plant Remains: Bannister, B. 1969; Dimbleby, G. W. 1967; Evans, J. G. 1978; Fletcher, J. 1978.

Animal Remains

The study of animal remains from archaeological contexts is known as **archaeozoology**; such remains on a site may be derived from several sources, all of which present problems when used as environmental evidence. The three main ways in which animal remains may be deposited on a site are as the remains of human food, as the remains of animal food, and as the remains of animals living there. But most carnivorous animals, including man, are selective in what they hunt for food, which makes it difficult to use food remains as environmental evidence. It can also be difficult on some sites to distinguish between human food debris and that of other carnivorous animals. The remains of animals living on the site provide slightly better environmental evidence, although there are still problems because the nature of the site, or even small parts of it, can influence the types of animals living there. This makes it difficult to derive general theories from specific groups of animal remains. For example, cave sites often have a great abundance of carnivore remains but this is not reliable evidence of a general abundance of carnivores.

Various types of evidence from animal remains can indicate that a site was only occupied at a particular time of the year. The season of the year can be indicated by the presence of the remains of migratory animals or a study of otolith growth rings. The presence of insects which only occur at particular seasons and the age range of animals can also give an indication of season. Each species of deer sheds its antlers at a relatively precise time of year, and so a study of antlers from a site can provide evidence of seasonal occupation. For sites with middens of marine shells, oxygen isotope analysis of the shells can be used to determine the time of the year when they were collected. The main types of animal remains are as follows:

Large Mammals

In Britain the majority of large mammal remains consist of bones, although under exceptional conditions animal tissue is preserved, particularly as leather (tanned animal tissue) in waterlogged deposits. In the analysis of animal bones all the animals from which the bones have come are first identified; a count of the minimum number of each type of animal is then made, usually by counting the numbers of one specific bone from each type of animal. Environmental reconstruction can then be attempted, based on the present-day habitats and geographical ranges of the animals. This is not always a good guide since the present-day geographical ranges of many animals are controlled by man, but often there is no other guide, and even this is not available for extinct species. Also, many large mammals can adapt themselves to a wide range of habitats. Because of the various problems, it is desirable to examine as large a collection of bones as possible so that the results are at least statistically valid. Further study of an assemblage of bones can provide other information such as the distribution of sexes and age ranges of a particular species indicating, for example, whether that species was domesticated or wild.

Small Mammals

In Britain small mammals consist mainly of rodents, with some insectivores such as hedgehogs and smaller carnivores such as polecats and weasels. Since such animals are unlikely to have been used regularly as human food, their remains can provide reasonable environmental evidence. In an excavation, smaller bones are usually collected by sieving soil on site, by examination of soil samples, or by flotation. Teeth and skull fragments are the most easily identified; most other bones are difficult to recognise. As with large mammals, small mammal remains can provide information about climate and vegetation; they are less reliable indicators of vegetation than large mammals, but more reliable indicators of climate since, being able to survive in small pockets even in heavily farmed areas, their present geographical ranges are fairly reliable reflections of their past geographical ranges.

Human Bones

The study of human bones and teeth can provide information about ancient diseases and diet, but little research has been carried out on the effects of other environmental factors upon the human skeleton. The study of diseases in antiquity is known as **palaeopathology**. There are several instances of **trepanation (trepanning, trephining, trephination)** — the practice of cutting out a piece of the skull. In modern times this was done to relieve pressure on the brain, although in antiquity it may have been carried out for other reasons. Examination of the edges of the skull where the piece was removed can usually indicate whether the bone started to regenerate (and the patient survive) after the operation. The **cephalic index** defines the relationship between the length and breadth of a skull so that skulls are said to be **brachycephalic** (round-headed) or **dolichocephalic** (long-headed), or somewhere in-between. It was once thought that some groups of people had predominantly one shape of head, and burials were sometimes attributed to a particular culture merely on the shape of the skull. However, further research has shown that the cephalic index varies greatly in any group of people and so it is no guide to the cultural group from which it came.

Bird Remains

Bird remains may consist of bones, egg-shell, guano, pellets, and sometimes even feathers, claws and beaks. Guano and pellets are evidence of the presence of living birds, while finds of bird bones and egg-shell on archaeological sites usually indicate which species were being exploited by man. Migratory species of birds can indicate at what time of year a site was occupied. Bird remains have not been studied as much as mammal remains because they are often difficult to identify.

Remains of Reptiles and Amphibians

In Britain these mainly consist of the bones of snakes, frogs and toads. They are rarely found on archaeological sites and are rarely used as environmental evidence.

Fish Remains

Fish remains consist of bones, scales and otoliths. Fish skeletons break up very easily and the most easily identifiable parts are the jaw bones and teeth; other bones are difficult to identify. Scales rarely survive but can be used to identify the species. **Otoliths** are part of a fish's balancing mechanism; they rarely survive, but can usually be used to identify the species of fish from which they came. Because they

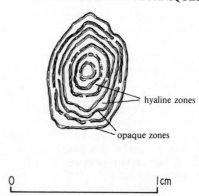

hyaline zones

opaque zones

0   1 cm

An Otolith from a Plaice showing Hyaline Zones and Opaque Zones. The Hyaline Zone represents Winter Growth, while the Opaque Zone, which is made up of small Growth Increments, represents Spring and Summer Growth

have annual growth rings, they can also be used to determine the age of the fish and the season at which it was killed.

Because fish occupy a wide variety of habitats, they can be used in the study of ancient river systems and as indicators of the types of environment exploited by man and the season during which a site was occupied. Fish remains have rarely been found in Britain, possibly because they have been overlooked in excavations; the recent increase in the use of sieving on excavations has greatly increased their discovery.

Insects

Insect remains rarely survive except in anaerobic deposits such as peat, mud, and the bottom of ditches and wells. The most common find is the hard exterior skeleton of beetles, but many other fragments of insects may be preserved. The remains are usually collected by froth flotation in a laboratory, but their identification is difficult since the distinguishing feature of the species may not be present on the surviving fragments. Insects are particularly useful as indicators of climate since they react to climatic changes much more rapidly than plants. Insects can also provide information about the environment of a region, but they are more usually used to complement information from pollen analysis in the reconstruction of local environments. Since many species of insect are associated with specific crops or other organic products used by man, they can often be used as evidence of a particular economy or industry. For example, insects that thrive on flesh, and one particular species which is a pest in tanneries, can provide evidence of tanning on a site.

Molluscs

Usually only the shells of molluscs survive, and only in calcareous conditions. The shells are collected, identified, and the results usually presented in the form of a histogram similar to a pollen diagram. The shells are usually collected by **wet sieving** (sieving with the aid of water to wash away the unwanted material).

Marine and Estuarine Molluscs Marine and estuarine molluscs occur in various coastal deposits such as beach sands and estuarine clays. The four main groups are gastropods (such as the whelk), bivalves (such as the mussel), scaphopods (a small group of tusk-shaped shells) and cuttlefish. Gastropods and bivalves are most common; these can be identified and sorted into estuarine, sandy-shore and rocky-shore species and can thus provide information about ancient coastlines. Where molluscs have been exploited for food by man, the shells which have accumulated in middens or in occupation layers can provide evidence of the nature of the coastline that was being exploited, and give some indication of the type of economy. The study of the size and form of shells in a large collection, such as a midden, can provide additional information. For example, a decrease in shell size over a period of time might indicate over-exploitation of that species.

Freshwater Molluscs Little work has been done on freshwater molluscs in association with archaeological deposits, although they frequently occur in water-logged features such as wells, ditches and pits, where they can indicate whether the site was waterlogged throughout the year or was subject to periodic wet and dry periods. They are not very useful as indicators of climatic change, but they can provide information about changes in lakes and rivers. Some freshwater molluscs such as mussels were collected by man for food and so can sometimes provide information about economy.

Land Molluscs (slugs and snails) Land molluscs survive in a wide variety of situations, the main ones being buried soils, fills of archaeological features, slopewash

deposits, blown sand and loess, tufa and travertine, and freshwater deposits. They can provide evidence of local environment based on knowledge of present-day habitats, giving information about vegetation, humidity, soil stability, and some of the effects of man upon the environment. Land molluscs can also give information about climate, based on knowledge of present-day geographical ranges, but in this respect they are not as useful as insect remains.

Other Animal Remains

Remains of other animals do survive under favourable conditions, and can often provide some evidence of ancient environments, although they are of less importance.

Reading for Animal Remains: Chaplin, R. E. 1971; Cornwall, I. W. 1956; Dawson, E. W. 1969; Evans, J. G. 1972; Evans, J. G. 1978; Ryder, M. L. 1969; Shackleton, N. J. 1969.

Soils and Sediments

The study of soils is called **pedology**. The study of fossil soils is called **palaeopedology**. Various types of soils and sediments contain preserved plant and animal remains and so they have an important influence on the evidence for past environments. The examination of some types of soil also provides additional information, usually about climate and the effect of man on the landscape.

Soil is initially formed from rock by a combination of physical and chemical weathering.

Physical Weathering

Physical weathering includes the breaking off of rock fragments from a surface due to the repeated expansion and contraction of the rock because of alternating high and low temperatures (**insolation**). Frost action also breaks up rock, and river and sea action can erode valleys and coastlines. Rock surfaces can also be eroded by fine particles carried by the wind, by glaciers, by material carried by glaciers (forming glacial deposits), and by the debris moved by solifluction. Soil erosion can also be caused by farming, in particular through tillage and overgrazing. Various types of sediment can be formed by physical weathering, and these are usually classified as aquatic, aeolian or terrestrial. **Aquatic sediments** range from mud to coarse sands and gravels. **Aeolian sediments (wind-blown sediments)** consist mainly of wind-blown sand **(coversand)** and wind-blown silt **(loess)**. Coversands are formed by **saltation**, a process in which sand is transported and dropped by successive gusts of wind. Loess consists of small particles of silt capable of being carried considerable distances without strong gusts of wind. **Terrestrial sediments** are formed in a number of ways:

Slopewash deposits These are formed by material slipping down and accumulating at the base of a slope; this can happen in cold conditions where melting ice cannot soak into the frozen subsoil and so flows downhill, carrying along soil and rubble. This is termed **solifluction (solifluxion)**. **Ploughwash (hillwash)** is formed in a similar way to solifluction deposits, although in this case drainage is obstructed by a degeneration of the structure of the soil, often due to tillage or overgrazing. **Scree** is also found on and at the base of slopes. This is angular rock debris caused by fragments of rock becoming detached through weathering and rolling down a slope or cliff. It cannot strictly be classed as a slopewash deposit. **Breccia** is scree which has become consolidated in a matrix of calcite.

Glacial deposits The main glacial deposit is **boulder clay (till)**, formed by the glacial erosion of rock. It consists of boulders and pebbles of varying shape and size mixed with finer material. Other glacial deposits include **outwash sands** and **outwash gravels** which are laid down at the edge of a glacier.

Precipitates In Britain the main precipitate deposits are tufa and stalagmite. These are calcareous deposits formed by the evaporation of water carrying lime in solution which leaves a precipitate of calcium carbonate. In caves, evaporation is slow and results in a hard precipitate called **stalagmite**. In the open air, evaporation is faster, resulting in a softer deposit known as **tufa (travertine)**. The term **travertine** is sometimes reserved for deposits formed by hot springs.

Cave deposits Scree, breccia and stalagmite are common in caves. **Cave earth** is found only in caves and consists of the build-up of animal and human occupation debris, weathering from the sides and roof of the cave, and material blown in from out-side. Under normal conditions, chemical weathering reduces similar material to a soil, but in a cave chemical weathering is reduced, resulting in a cave earth.

Organic sediments The most common organic sediment is peat. This is formed under anaerobic (usually waterlogged) conditions which inhibit the breakdown of organic material. The three main types of peat (named after their main constituents) are sphagnum peat (consisting mainly of sphagnum moss), brushwood peat, and reedswamp peat (consisting mainly of the remains of reeds).

Chemical Weathering
Rainwater absorbs carbon dioxide to form a weak carbonic acid. Plants and dead plant remains also give off various acids, particularly humic acid. These acids dissolve various mineral components in rocks, which may be carried away by water percolating through the ground. The process of minerals being washed away is known as **leaching**; chemicals dissolved in this way are often precipitated to form tufas, stalagmites and **iron pans** (hard layers of minerals, most of which are iron compounds). **Hydrolysis** — a chemical reaction between water and rock — also causes the breakdown of rocks; the action of acids and hydrolysis creates **clay minerals** which are an important constituent of soil. **Humus**, which consists of decomposed and partly decomposed organic material, combines with the clay minerals and particles of silt and sand to form **soil crumbs**, the space between the soil crumbs being filled with air or moisture. The breakdown of this structure is the first stage of soil degradation. The processes of weathering and soil formation cause various **horizons** (bands of differing soils) to develop; the sequence of horizons is known as the **soil profile**.

Physical and Chemical Features of Soils
The relative sizes of particles (texture) in a sediment are an indication of its origin. For example, gravels are laid down by rapidly flowing water, and sands are laid down by water that is slow moving. Soils can be described according to the percentages of clay, silt and sand they contain. For example, **loam** consists of approximately equal parts of clay, silt and sand. The amount of **sorting** in a sediment can also give an indication of its origin: a **well-sorted** sediment consists of particles of roughly equal size, while an **unsorted** sediment is a

mixture of variously sized particles. Other physical features indicating the origin of a sediment are the shape of the particles (rounded particles have undergone a much longer period of transport than angular ones), the surface of the particles, and the overall form of the sediment and its relation to the topography.

Since the breakdown of minerals in a rock to form soil takes place in several stages, examination of the mineral components in a soil can indicate how much weathering has taken place, and may therefore provide information about climate. Examination of minerals in a sediment which may have been transported some distance (such as boulder clay) can provide information about the origin of the sediment. Examination of the humus content of a soil or sediment can reveal buried soil horizons which may not otherwise be detected.

The **pH** value of the soil (the measure of the amount of alkalinity or acidity) is an indicator of the type of remains likely to survive in that soil. For example, a high pH value of 8·5 indicates a very alkaline soil in which bones and mollusc shells are likely to be preserved. The pH scale runs from 0 to 14; 7 is neutral; values less than 7 indicate acidity and over 7 alkalinity.

The phosphate content of the soil comes from decayed bone and dung, and so **phosphate analysis** can be used to identify the former presence of bone in archaeological features. It can also be used to identify the occupation layers in archaeological deposits, and to find the location and extent of settlement sites.

The colours of the various soil horizons can provide information about the humus and iron content and so can indicate features such as buried topsoil horizons and iron pans. Colour can be defined by reference to a colour chart. The most widely used chart is the **Munsell colour chart**, which defines soil colour by a code of numbers and letters and a descriptive name, for example '10 YR 3/4 Dark Yellowish Brown'.

Examples of Soil Types Several types of soil in Britain can provide important evidence about climate and the effect of man on the landscape, although the present soil type in an area is no guide to the past soils of that area.

Brownearth soils form on neutral or slightly acid subsoils and consist of a weathered horizon (containing minerals — mainly iron oxides) on top of the parent rock; this weathered horizon is itself covered by a deep humus horizon. These soils are characteristic of mixed deciduous woodland which maintains this type of soil; forest clearance can lead to the degradation of this soil and to the formation of podsols, sols lessivés and gleys. Continued ploughing of a brownearth soil can lead to the formation of a rendsina soil.

Rendsina soils commonly form on chalk and limestone. They consist simply of a humic horizon directly overlying the parent rock. Soil-dwelling animals (particularly earthworms) are often abundant in this type of soil. The burrowing of these animals can cause the downward movement of material too large to pass through an earthworm's gut, to form a **stone line**, and a stone-free **turf line**. Cultivation destroys turf and stone lines and mixes the humic horizon, and so examination of ancient rendsina soils can often indicate whether or not the land was cultivated.

Podsols form on very acid subsoils (often sand) and in areas of high rainfall. These soils have a shallow horizon of humus overlying a leached horizon from which the humus and iron have been washed downwards to form a thin layer (often an impervious hardpan) above the parent rock. Podsols are characteristic of heaths and moorland.

Gleys are waterlogged soils in which there is a grey, or mottled grey and orange, horizon beneath the top (humus) horizon. The grey colour is caused by iron compounds in an anaerobic condition (caused by the waterlogging); this changes to an orange colour where the horizon is not totally anaerobic.

Sols lessivés are a type of brownearth soil in which particles of clay have been washed out of the upper horizon to form a clayey horizon below. Like podsols, sols lessivés seem to result from the clearance of woodland by man.

Plant remains, animal remains, soils and sediments are found in a wide variety of contexts. For convenience, these can be divided into natural contexts and archaeological contexts.

Natural Contexts

Marine sediments may be either coastal,

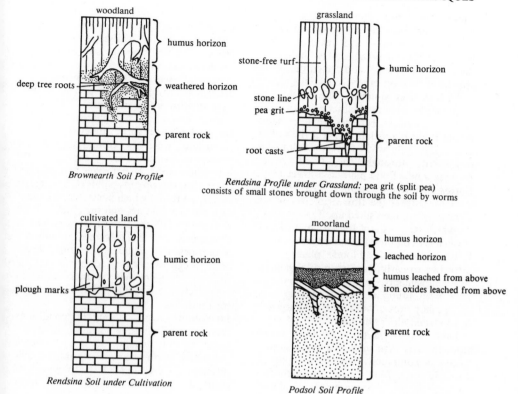

Brownearth Soil Profile

Rendsina Profile under Grassland: pea grit (split pea) consists of small stones brought down through the soil by worms

Rendsina Soil under Cultivation

Podsol Soil Profile

Some Soil Profiles

0 ⊢─────────────────────────────┤ 50 cm

offshore or deep-sea sediments. Offshore sediments in the seas around Britain are beginning to provide information about Pleistocene chronology and climate in much the same way as deep-sea cores (see Chapter 1). Deposits such as estuarine clays, ancient land surfaces and peat beds may be preserved below the present sea-level, in shallow basins and estuaries.

Ancient coastlines are preserved either by **tectonic uplift** (upward earth movement), or by a fall in sea-level; processes which are often linked to the effects of glaciation and its aftermath. Tectonic uplift can be caused as a reaction to the removal of the weight of ice when a glacier melts. This is known as **isostatic recovery** and it can lift ancient coastlines above sea-level so that they are preserved. The other main process by which coastlines have been preserved is by the **eustatic** fall in sea-level during the Pleistocene. This was a gradual world-wide

fall in sea-level caused by former interglacial sea-levels not being reached in subsequent interglacials. The ancient beaches preserved by these processes are known as **raised beaches** and they are sometimes associated with ancient marine caves containing human occupation debris.

Coastal blown sand is wind-blown sand which may form in any area where there is sand without a surface cover of vegetation, together with dry conditions. Dunes form where sand collects around obstacles in its path, and a system of blown sand and sand dunes develops. A sand-dune system may preserve evidence of the local environmental history, particularly if the deposition of sand has not been constant, in which case buried soils may occur within as well as under the sand, giving evidence of phases when sand deposition ceased. Often human occupation debris, middens, or even parts of settlement sites may be buried under blown-sand deposits, and layers of blown sand may be interposed between various occupation and environmental layers enabling a better understanding of the archaeological and environmental sequences than on other terrestrial sites.

Ancient river systems The remains of these may be preserved either as terraces or as buried channels. **Terraces** are the remains of old flood plains left above a river after an increase in the water flow causes it to cut downwards through the flood plain, forming a new flood plain at a lower level. **Buried channels** are formed when a rise in sea-level reduces the flow of a river which eventually becomes silted up. The processes by which terraces and buried channels are formed are complex and varied, and not yet fully understood. Flood plains were attractive to early man; many Palaeolithic flint implements, particularly handaxes, have been found in river-terrace gravels, while many sites of later date are known to have existed alongside rivers.

Lakes, like rivers, provided many attractions to early man such as a water supply, means of communication and a supply of fish and water fowl. Lakes also provide a catchment for environmental evidence, particularly pollen, which may survive even after the lake has dried up.

Glacial features The effects of glaciation consist of erosion and deposition of material and are important to the inhabitants of previously glaciated areas since the erosion and deposition of material can drastically change the form of the landscape and the type of soils. Glaciers consist of ice sheets and valley glaciers. **Ice sheets** are vast masses of ice, covering large areas, which erode the land surface leaving it relatively smooth and uniform. **Valley glaciers** form in highland regions where they flow through existing valleys with the effect of widening and deepening them to form **U-shaped valleys**. **Corries** can form at the heads of these valleys; they are deep, steep-sided, rounded hollows. There are many glacial features which have formed due to the deposition of material, all of which may have an influence on local environment. Deposited material includes **outwash sands** and **outwash gravels** which are laid down immediately adjacent to the limit of the ice, usually over an extensive area.

Periglacial features Compared with the effects of glaciation, the effects of erosion

and deposition just outside the area of glaciation (periglacial area) had relatively little effect on the landscape. Apart from erosion and deposition by solifluction, and the formation and deposition of loess and coversand (see physical weathering), the other main features of the periglacial area were **cryoturbation structures**, such as ice wedges, involutions and pingos.

Ice wedges will form under permafrost conditions, when the ground shrinks and cracks; in warmer weather the cracks fill with water which later freezes and enlarges the cracks; this process builds up a wedge of ice in the ground which melts with the onset of a warmer climate, and the cracks fill up with debris. Where several cracks occur, a characteristic pattern is formed, usually like a network of irregular polygons. These patterns can be mistaken for archaeological features in aerial photographs, while in cross-section ice wedges can be mistaken for postholes.

Involutions form in milder conditions than ice wedges; they form in the upper layers of the ground. It is not known precisely how they form, but it appears that differential freezing and thawing of materials push up sediments to form bulbous flask-shaped forms. They form surface patterns similar to but much smaller than those formed by ice wedges. Where the soil cover is thin in upland areas, these patterns may appear as **stone rings** (rings of unweathered stones), while on slopes they may appear as stripes.

The remains of **pingos** usually consist of rings of soil and rock which can be mistaken for ring cairns or henges. The rings are formed by a lens of ice beneath the ground which forces soil and rock upwards as it expands, until the soil and rock slip off to form a ring that is left when the ice melts. **Dry valleys** were formed by solifluction acting along planes of weakness in the underlying rock. They are characteristic of chalk and limestone areas. In southern Britain the sediments deposited in the bottom of these valleys consist of an initial deposit of scree and solifluction debris containing one or more buried soil horizons; this is overlain by tufa (which can also contain buried soil horizons) and which in turn is covered by hillwash. Archaeological remains are often associated with hillwash, which was probably caused by tillage or overgrazing; Mesolithic artifacts have been recovered from the tufa deposits in dry valleys. These dry valley deposits are largely calcareous and preserve good molluscan evidence of former environments.

Peat bogs form under two differing types of conditions: **ombrogenous peat (blanket peat)** forms under conditions of high rainfall and takes no account of topography, but spreads blanket-like irrespective of the terrain. In most ombrogenous bogs several layers are visible, often including one or more **recurrence surfaces**. These are horizons formed by the renewed growth of peat after the drying out of the bog surface, and they indicate a return to wet conditions after a lengthy dry period. **Topogenous peat** formation is controlled by topography. It forms in basins, filled-in lakes and other places where drainage is impeded. Topogenous peat relies mainly on ground water for its growth, and so is not a good indicator of climate.

Caves There is a variety of naturally formed underground shelters, and it is convenient to distinguish between them according to the methods of their formation. **Sea caves** are carved out of cliffs by the sea; they are usually associated with raised beaches. **Inland caves** are usually ancient underground river systems, parts of which have been broken into by subsequent erosion. Sometimes weathering and erosion enlarge the mouth of a cave to form a **rock shelter**. Deposits found in caves are often classified as **autochthonous deposits** (formed *in situ* in the cave) and **allochthonous deposits** (brought into the cave from outside). **Fissures** in rock sometimes contain human occupation debris, but this has usually been transported into the fissure from elsewhere; fissures were not normally inhabited.

Archaeological Contexts

Many archaeological sites have banks and ditches; and buried soil beneath banks, sediments in ditches, and sometimes the bank itself provide contexts from which environmental evidence can be obtained.

Banks Soils buried beneath banks are usually either **acid soils**, in which pollen is likely to survive, **basic soils**, in which bones and mollusc shells are likely to survive, or **neutral soils**, in which it is unlikely that a significant amount of any environmental evidence will survive, with the exception of charcoal which can survive in all three types

of soil. In rare cases, a buried soil is anaerobic, in which case a whole range of environmental evidence may survive, including macroscopic plant remains and insects. These categories of soil and the respective environmental evidence that is likely to survive within them apply not only to buried soils, but also to many other types of soils and sediments (see also pH).

When a buried soil is protected by an overlying earthwork, it is not affected by the erosion to which the surrounding soil is subject. This erosion lowers the unprotected area around an earthwork, so that the buried soil is left at a higher level than the modern soil (sometimes as much as 1m higher). This process is known as **differential weathering**. Remains of ancient soil and subsoil horizons only survive in such protected situations. Apart from buried soils, timber used in the construction of an earthwork may survive under or within an earthwork and so provide evidence about the types of wood used in its construction.

Ditches Sediments in ditches can provide useful environmental evidence. Large ditches are particularly useful since the environmental evidence accumulated in their fill is more likely to reflect a regional rather than a local environment. The sediments in a ditch accumulate in several stages. After the ditch is dug, frost weathering of the sides causes a build-up of coarse debris in the bottom of the ditch. The turf adjacent to the sides of the ditch is undercut by frost weathering and lumps of turf also fall into the ditch and are incorporated in the coarse fill at the bottom. This is called the **primary fill (primary silt, rapid silt)**, and experiments suggest it takes between ten and twenty years to form. This results in the ditch being wider and shallower with less steep sides, so that the rate of weathering decreases. This stage of more gradual weathering results in a **secondary fill (secondary silt, slow silt)**. Eventually the rate of weathering slows down sufficiently for a soil to form. Sometimes no further deposition takes place and so the ditch remains in this state. Often the soil over the ditch becomes buried by ploughwash from nearby agriculture, and if the agriculture is sufficiently intermittent further soil horizons may develop over the ditch during periods when there is no nearby tillage. These deposits covering the initial soil

227

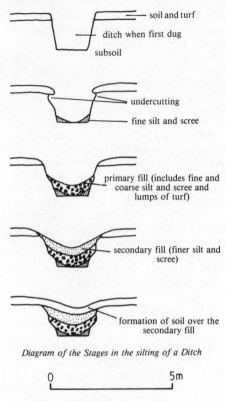

soil and turf

ditch when first dug

subsoil

undercutting

fine silt and scree

primary fill (includes fine and coarse silt and scree and lumps of turf)

secondary fill (finer silt and scree)

formation of soil over the secondary fill

Diagram of the Stages in the silting of a Ditch

0   5m

horizon in the ditch are known as the **tertiary fill (tertiary silt)**. Where a ditch is very deep or is in a low-lying situation, part of its fill may be waterlogged, and so anaerobic. This often provides additional environmental evidence which can be used to complement and check the evidence from the aerobic parts of the fill.

Apart from banks and ditches, a variety of other features occurs on archaeological sites. Most **pits** on archaeological sites were used for refuse or for storage, often of grain or other foodstuffs; many storage pits were later used as rubbish pits or for burial. Storage pits which were not re-used for some other purpose silted up in a similar way to ditches. If conditions are favourable both molluscan and insect remains can survive in pits, and the latter can often indicate what was stored there. Cess pits are often waterlogged and can therefore preserve a range of organic remains, including internal parasites of humans and animals. **Wells** and **shafts** usually have a partially waterlogged fill similar to deep

ditches, and provide similar types of evidence.

Postholes are difficult to use as sources of environmental evidence because their fill may be composed of debris from a great variety of sources, and it is usually difficult to distinguish clearly between the various components of the fill. Similar difficulties apply to other types of feature such as bedding trenches, beam slots, and graves.

Middens are rubbish heaps consisting mainly of human food debris with other waste products. Shellfish remains are common in middens, often in large quantities since even a single meal of shellfish generates a large amount of waste. Bird and fish bones also occur frequently. By sampling, or sometimes by complete excavation, middens can provide evidence of the diet, economy and size of the community, as well as information about the types and relative importance of the animals and habitats being exploited. They can also provide evidence of whether the site was occupied throughout the year or only seasonally. **Shell middens** composed almost entirely of the debris from shellfish occur at Mesolithic coastal sites where shellfish appear to have been the main element of the diet for at least part of the year. They are also found on town sites of other archaeological periods, where shellfish were being eaten in large quantities as a delicacy.

Lynchets often preserve buried soils which can yield environmental information. These soils may be the remains of the pre-lynchet soil horizon, or may represent standstill phases during the formation of the lynchet itself. Further information can often be obtained from molluscan remains from the lynchet deposits themselves.

Reading for Soils and Sediments: Evans, J. G. 1978; Limbrey, S. 1975.

Techniques of Analysing Artifacts

There are several reasons why it is often desirable to analyse an artifact. For instance, the identification of the constituents of a piece of metal or glass can provide evidence about the development of technology, while the minerals in a piece of pottery can indicate the source of the clay from which it was made. No single method of analysis can be relied upon to identify all the constituents of an object, and there are methods which only determine the presence or absence of a few elements. Consequently, more than one method is often used to analyse an artifact.

One specific problem with methods which only analyse the surface of an object is **surface enrichment**; this occurs in metal alloys. For example, a coin made of an alloy of silver and copper may have a higher concentration of silver on its surface than at its centre. This obviously means that an analysis of the surface of such an alloy is no guide to the composition of the alloy as a whole. The processes whereby alloys suffer surface enrichment are not fully understood.

Another problem of analysis is that objects often have a **patina**. This is a surface layer which has been altered by interaction with the immediate environment in which the object has lain, so that its colour and physical composition are different from the interior of the object. The term is mainly used to describe such surface layers on objects of flint, bronze and glass. The patina on flint is often bluish or white, but can be yellowish-brown to red, and is usually due to contact with iron compounds in ground water. The patina on bronze is usually dark green and is a relatively stable form of corrosion; however, livid green spots which are often found on bronze are a virulent form of corrosion known as **bronze disease (chloride corrosion, copper corrosion)**.

One purpose in analysing an artifact is to find out what **trace elements** — elements in minute proportions — are present. They occur naturally in the raw materials used for most artifacts, and examination to find out what trace elements are present, and in what proportions, can lead to the identification of the source(s) of the raw material from which the artifact was made.

One method of artifact analysis is **physical examination**. A great deal can often be learnt about an object merely by looking at it with the naked eye **(macroscopic examination)**, or with the aid of a microscope **(microscopic examination)**. For example, the main inclusions in a sherd of pottery can be identified in this way. It is often useful to take a photograph at high magnification (a **photomicrograph**) of part

of an object in order to display details of its form and structure.

To help standarise subjective observations during physical examination, colour and hardness can be referred to by standardised scales. The colour of an object can be matched with a colour on a **Munsell colour chart** which is capable of providing a very precise coding for each colour. For hardness the **Moh scale** is most commonly used. This is a scale of 1 to 10, corresponding to ten different minerals. If the sample can be scratched by one of these minerals, it is softer than that mineral, and so by trial and error the sample's position on the scale can be worked out. For more precise measurements of hardness there are other methods such as the **Brinell hardness number**. This is mostly used to express the hardness of metals and is determined by pressing a small hardened steel ball for a fixed time, and with a constant pressure, into the surface of the metal being tested. The hardness of the metal is then determined by the diameter of the depression left in the surface by the steel ball.

It is often useful to take **X-ray photographs (radiographs)** of an object. Such radiographs are no different from those taken for medical purposes in hospitals. A heavily corroded metal object, for example, can be identified from the radiographs taken of it before the removal of the corrosion. In recent years, techniques have been developed for taking microscopic radiographs **(X-ray microscopy)** which are usually used in the examination of biological and metal remains. Similarly, by using **infra-red photography**, it is possible to gain a picture of the surface of an object that is encrusted without removing the encrustation.

Petrological examination is a method used mainly for examining objects of pottery and stone. A thin slice is cut from the object, fixed to a glass slide and ground down until it is only $0.02mm$ thick; this is called a **thin section**. The thin section is then examined under a microscope in various lighting conditions, and the minerals in the sample are identified. In this way, distinctive combinations of minerals in the stone or fired clay can be detected which can often be correlated with minerals in a rock or clay in a particular area and thus the source of the material defined. Another method of examining the minerals in pottery is **heavy mineral analysis**. In this method a sample of pottery is crushed and the resulting powder floated on a viscous liquid so that the particles of clay and sand float and only the heavy minerals sink to the bottom. These heavy minerals can then be collected and identified under the microscope, and can give an indication of the source of the materials used in the pottery.

Chemical analysis consists of dissolving a sample from an artifact in an acid and testing the resulting solution with various chemicals to determine the elements of which the artifact is composed. This method is mainly used on metal artifacts, its use being restricted by the necessity of taking a large sample of the artifact and the fact that it is a time-consuming method. Most often, chemical analysis is used to establish the presence or absence of a specific element, rather than as a full analysis of the constituents of an artifact.

Metallographic microscopy is the microscopic examination of metal objects. A sample from an object is highly polished and then etched to reveal its internal structure; it can then be examined under a metallurgical microscope which uses reflected light to emphasise the structure of the prepared surface. **Transmission electron miscroscopy** is used to examine the structure of metals, ceramics and stone. In this method a beam of electrons is transmitted through a sample of an object; by a system of lenses, a magnified image of the sample is projected onto a fluorescent screen and this image is recorded on a photographic plate behind the screen. The sample must be extremely thin so that it can be penetrated by the beam of electrons. Wear marks on stone tools and surface marks on pottery can be examined in this way by making a replica of the surface marks in thin plastic or carbon film, and using this film as a sample from an object. **Scanning electron microscopy** is also used to examine the surface structure of an object; it has the advantage over transmission electron miscroscopy of a greater depth of focus at high magnification and an ability to cope with much larger samples. The technique consists of moving a narrow beam of electrons across the surface of the specimen **(scanning)** causing some electrons to be back-scattered and some secondary electrons to be emitted; these are then recorded and counted. Since the number of

the back-scattered and secondary electrons is determined by the angle at which the beam hits the surface of the specimen, the changing counts of back-scattered and secondary electrons as the beam moves over the surface represent the structure of that surface.

Optical emission spectrometry For this method of analysis a sample, drilled out of the object, is ignited in an electric arc. The light emitted from this arc varies according to the elements present in the sample and, by passing this light through a prism, a spectrum is formed and photographed. This spectrum is characteristic of the elements present, and the percentage of the sample that each element forms can be determined. The method is mainly used for analysis of metal objects, but is also used on other artifacts such as pottery.

X-ray fluorescence spectrometry In this method the object is bombarded with X-rays, causing it to fluoresce and emit secondary X-rays which are characteristic of the elements present. These secondary X-rays are examined with a spectrometer and from this the elements present in the object are determined. Since the X-rays do not penetrate very far, the method is really an analysis of only the surface of an object, unless the object is very thin or relatively transparent to X-rays. A special version of this technique is the use of an **X-ray milliprobe**. In this case the primary X-rays are focused in a narrow beam onto a very small area of the object, providing an analysis of a small part of the surface, rather than the whole of the surface.

Neutron activation analysis (gamma-ray spectrometry) In this process an object, or sample of an object, is irradiated with neutrons in a nuclear reactor. This converts some of the atoms in the object into radioactive isotopes which are unstable and decay, emitting radiation characteristic of the elements present. This radiation is analysed by using a spectrometer, and the elements thus identified. This method has the disadvantage that the radioactivity of the object may make it unsafe to handle for some years, and so it has to be stored in a place which is shielded against radiation.

Infra-red absorption spectrometry is used for identifying chemical compounds and minerals in an artifact, thus helping to determine the nature and source of the material from which the artifact was made.

A sample from the artifact is crushed and then subjected to infra-red radiation; some of this radiation is absorbed, and by measuring the amount of absorption of each wavelength of radiation, the minerals and chemical compounds in the sample can be identified.

Atomic absorption spectrometry is a method of analysing the chemical composition of metals and some non-metals such as flint. A sample from the artifact is dissolved and the resulting solution is atomised in a flame. A light is shone on this flame from a hollow cathode lamp made from or lined with the element to be analysed, so that the light has a wavelength corresponding to the emission wavelength of the element; the amount of light absorbed by the sample as it is atomised in the flame provides an estimate of the amount of the element in the sample. The disadvantage of the technique is that this procedure has to be repeated with a different hollow cathode lamp for each element analysed, but usually the results are more accurate than those obtained by optical emission spectrometry.

In **electron microprobe analysis (electron probe microanalysis)** accelerated electrons are focused onto a spot $0 \cdot 001$mm in diameter. As this hits the sample, X-rays are produced which are characteristic of the elements present in the sample. These X-rays are then examined using a spectrometer, and thus the elements are identified. Although the sample examined is small, it can be studied in great detail.

Beta-ray back-scattering is a method used mainly for determining if lead is present in a glass or a glaze. A sample is bombarded with Beta-rays and the number of rays which are scattered back from the sample is measured. Elements with high atomic numbers (such as lead) scatter back the Beta-rays, while elements with low atomic numbers absorb them. Since lead is usually the only element with a high atomic number found in glass and glazes, the results can be compared with those from glasses of known lead content, and so the amount of lead in the sample can be estimated.

X-ray diffraction analysis is used to determine crystal forms and thus to identify minerals present in an object. The object, or sample of an object, is exposed to X-rays, and the characteristic pattern in which the X-rays are diffracted is recorded; from this the minerals present can be determined.

Reading for Techniques of Analysing Artifacts: Aitken, M. J. 1974; Brothwell, D. and Higgs, E. S. 1969; Council for British Archaeology 1970; Goodyear, F. H. 1971; Hodges, H. 1964; Tite, M. S. 1973; Tylecote, R. F. 1962.

Dates and Dating

Dates can be of several types, but all dates are **relative dates** since they are all measured relative to some point in time. The term is more usually applied when an object or event is known to be later or earlier in time than another object or event, but the elapse in time between them, and their positions in a conventional framework for measuring time, are not known. For example, if A is older than B, both are dated relative to each other, but if it is known that A is 500 years older than B, then both A and B have **chronometric dates**, because the amount of time which has elapsed between them is known. An object or event has an **absolute date** when the amount of time which has elapsed from the point of origin of a conventional framework for measuring time is known. Absolute dating is therefore a specific form of chronometric dating. The most common framework for measuring time is the BC/AD system (before Christ, and *anno domini* — 'in the year of Our Lord') which measures time in solar years before and after the Birth of Christ. The Birth of Christ is regarded as an instantaneous moment in time and thus there is no 0 BC or AD 0, since the Birth of Christ is the origin of the conventional framework, and all dates are measured in years before or after it. Another framework for measuring time is the BP (before present) system, which also uses solar years. The year AD 1950 is conventionally used as the standard reference year for this system, so that the date 5000 years BP means 5,000 years before AD 1950. In the strict sense, the BP system gives chronometric dates, but the convention of having a standard 'present' in AD 1950 means that any date BP is effectively an absolute date.

Reading for Dates and Dating: Michels, J. W. 1973.

Methods of Dating

The dating of sites and artifacts is of great importance in archaeology, and new methods are constantly being developed. The main ones currently in use and relevant to British archaeology are as follows:

Radiocarbon dating (carbon-14 dating, C-14 dating) All living things contain traces of a radioactive isotope of carbon (C^{14}). While an organism is alive, the C^{14} is kept in a fixed proportion to ordinary carbon, but after death this proportion is no longer maintained because the amount of C^{14} diminishes. Because of the decay of C^{14}, the radioactivity of a dead organism diminishes to one half the original amount in approximately 5,700 years, to one quarter in 11,400 years, and so on. Thus, by determining the proportion of C^{14} to ordinary carbon in a sample of dead organic material, the approximate date of death of the sample can be calculated. Three potential sources of error must however be taken into account. Firstly, since the 'date' calculated is never exact because the amount of C^{14} in the sample cannot be measured with absolute accuracy, the date is always accompanied by a ± figure, which has the mathematical significance of a **standard deviation**. This is a statistical expression of the uncertainty of measurement of the proportion of C^{14} in the sample. For example, a date of 2145 BC ± 105 indicates that there is a 2:1 chance that the real date lies between 2145 + 105 BC and 2145 − 105 BC. Secondly, the time taken for half the quantity of C^{14} to decay (the **half-life**) is at present conventionally assumed by archaeologists to be 5,568 ± 30 years, but recent research has shown the half-life to be closer to 5,730 ± 40 years. The conventional half-life will continue in use until a new one is internationally accepted. Thirdly, C^{14} dates are calculated on the assumption that the amount of C^{14} available to be absorbed by living organisms (and thus the initial proportion of C^{14} to ordinary carbon in living organisms), has remained constant throughout the time-span covered by the method. It has been found that this assumption is not justified; for example, C^{14} dates are sometimes as much as 600 years too young in the third millennium BC.

Methods of calibrating C^{14} dates are available, particularly by comparison with dates determined by dendrochronology using the **bristlecone pine**, an extremely long-living tree native to parts of North America. Tables of correction factors have been published, but none has been universally accepted and research is still continuing. To circumvent the problem, uncalibrated dates are usually shown in **radiocarbon years** signified by the use of lower-case letters (bp, bc, or ad) while calibrated dates are shown in upper-case letters. For example, 2490 ± 50 bc is an uncalibrated date expressed in radiocarbon years, while 2490 ± 50 BC is a calibrated date expressed in solar years.

Dendrochronology (tree-ring dating) Each year trees lay down a growth ring underneath the bark and, because variation in the thickness of these rings in many trees depends largely on variations in climate, cross-sections through many trees show a pattern of thick and thin rings, each representing a year's growth. By matching the pattern of rings between several trees and pieces of timber, a pattern covering a considerable period of time can be constructed.

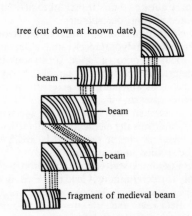

tree (cut down at known date)

beam —

beam

beam

fragment of medieval beam

Diagram showing the principle of building up a Chronological Sequence by matching the Tree-Rings of various trees

Once a pattern has been established and securely tied in to known dates, timber of unknown date can be dated by matching it with part of the established pattern of rings. A pattern that cannot be tied to known dates is called a **floating chronology**. This method of dating is limited since any particular pattern is only valid within a small distance of the place of origin of the wood used to establish the pattern. Also, not every type of tree varies the thickness of its rings, so not every piece of wood can be dated by this method. The pattern of rings can be upset by very local conditions, such as a tree being near free-standing water. Finally, a rapidly fluctuating climate (such as Britain's) is not conducive to a good tree-ring pattern. Consequently dendrochronology is not widely used in Britain, and is mainly employed for dating medieval timbers.

Archaeomagnetic dating (thermo-remanent magnetism) When clay is heated above a certain temperature, the magnetism of any magnetic oxides of iron in the clay is obliterated, but returns on cooling, its direction and strength being determined by the earth's magnetic field. Thus the clay retains a record of the strength and direction of the earth's magnetic field at the time of cooling after the clay was last fired. This is the fired clay's **archaeomagnetism (thermo-remanent magnetism)**. Since the earth's magnetic field fluctuates with time, the difference in direction and strength between the earth's present magnetic field and that of the clay can be measured, if the clay has not been moved since it was fired (for example, the base of a kiln or oven still *in situ*). By carrying out this procedure on sites whose dates are known, a pattern of the fluctuations of the earth's magnetic field can be built up with which results from sites of unknown date can be compared and so dated. Due to fluctuations in the earth's magnetic field with area as well as with time, each pattern of fluctuations is only valid for a limited geographical area.

Thermoluminescent dating (TL dating) Minerals (particularly quartz crystals) found in most clays store energy acquired by absorbing any nuclear radiation to which the clay is exposed. If the clay is heated above 500°C (such as a pot when it is fired), the stored energy is given off as light. This emission of light, additional to the ordinary red-hot glow when a substance is heated, is called **thermoluminescence**. As soon as a piece of pottery has lost its stored energy during firing, it once more begins to accumulate energy. By laboratory examination of the pottery and the soil in which it was found, the actual energy stored in the minerals in the pottery and the rate at which the minerals have absorbed energy since the pot was last heated can be determined, and therefore the time which has elapsed since the pottery was last heated above 500°C.

Fluorine analysis, uranium dating and **nitrogen analysis** are all methods of giving relative dates to bones. **Fluorine analysis** determines the amount of fluorine in bones and, because buried bones accumulate fluorine from ground water, older bones contain more fluorine than younger ones buried in the same place. Similarly, bones tend to absorb uranium from ground water and **uranium dating (uranium analysis, radiometric assay)** is the measurement of the amount of uranium in bones from the same place in order to determine which are older. **Nitrogen analysis** determines the amount of nitrogen left in bones. Once a bone is buried its nitrogen content is gradually lost, so that among bones from the same place, older bones will have the lower nitrogen content. These three methods can only be used for relative dating because the rate at which bone absorbs fluorine and uranium, and loses nitrogen, is dependent on extremely localised factors, such as the type of deposit in which the bones were buried.

Stratigraphy This deals with the relationship between various archaeological layers and features. Its use was adopted from geology and relies on the principle that where one layer or feature overlays or cuts through another, the upper one is later in date if there has been no disturbance. Such superimposed layers and features are said to be **stratified**, and material in undisturbed layers and features is said to be **in situ**. Disturbance by roots, animals, worms and so on, can be difficult to detect. The greater the disturbance (such as many pits cutting into each other), the more likelihood of objects of different dates being mixed together. With careful interpretation, stratigraphy can provide relative dating for objects contained within the stratified layers and features. For example, material in the fill of a pit sealed by a later turf line must be earlier in date than material in that turf line, provided there has been no disturbance; the turf line therefore provides a **terminus ante quem** for material in the pit (a point in time before which the material was deposited). If the turf line then became buried, for example by a later demolition layer, the objects in the demolition layer would probably be later in date than the turf line, and the turf line would provide a **terminus post quem** for material in the demolition layer (a point in time after which the material was deposited).

Cross-dating This is a method of providing a relationship between two cultural groups. If an object from one culture is found in definite association with objects of another culture, the latter culture must be contemporary with or later than the former. A series of such associations usually indicates that the two cultures are at least partly contemporary. This is a method of relative dating.

Seriation This is an extension of typology. Once the variations in an object have been classified, the various classes can often be shown to form a developmental series. This can be used as a framework for relative dating, and can often be augmented by obtaining dates for some of the classes by other methods of dating. Its use as a dating method is based on the assumption that the variations in the object only occur with time and not as a result of other factors, but as this is not always so it has to be used with great caution.

Oxygen isotope analysis In recent years much evidence of climatic change during the Pleistocene has been recovered from deep-sea cores by oxygen isotope analysis, and in the near future this is likely to have a significant effect on the present view of the Pleistocene in Britain and on the dating of the Palaeolithic period (see Chapter 1). Oxygen isotope analysis is based on the fact that, when water evaporates, the oxygen isotopes O^{16}, O^{17} and O^{18} are given off at different rates. The ratio between these isotopes in the water varies according to the amount of evaporation taking place, and so is an indicator of the temperature of the water. Fossilised organisms which once lived in the sea and absorbed oxygen from the water preserve in their remains the ratio between the oxygen isotopes which existed while they were living. Since the remains of these organisms make up the sedimentary rocks from which deep-sea cores are drilled, by measuring the ratio between the oxygen isotopes at various points in a core an estimate can be made of the fluctuations of temperature that occurred while the sediments were being laid down. By obtaining dates for various parts of the core, the glacials, interglacials, stadials and interstadials of the Pleistocene can be dated, and their duration and intensity estimated.

There are three main methods of dating parts of deep-sea cores: radiocarbon dating (for the upper part of the core only), uranium series dating, and magnetostratigraphy. **Uranium series dating (uranium series disequilibrium dating)** is based on the uranium nuclides U^{238} and U^{235}, which decay through a series of shortlived isotopes, finally becoming stable lead. Since uranium is present in water, but the daughter isotopes are virtually absent, carbonate organisms and inorganic carbonates take up uranium but none of its daughter isotopes. Provided that the sample has been unaffected by external influences, the extent to which daughter isotopes in the sample have formed from the original uranium indicates the age of the sample. This method has proved very successful at dating fossil corals from deep-sea cores.

The method known as **magnetostratigraphy** is similar in principle to archaeomagnetic dating. Volcanic rocks preserve a record of the strength and direction of the earth's magnetic field at the time the rocks cooled **(thermo-remanent magnetism)**. Similarly, sedimentary rocks may also preserve a record of the earth's magnetic field through the alignment of the grains of sediment as they settle through the water **(detrital remanent magnetism)**. By plotting the various changes in the earth's magnetic field from the remanent magnetism of the various layers of volcanic and sedimentary rock, and by obtaining dates for significant changes in the earth's magnetic field, a framework can be built up into which results from samples from other sites can be fitted and dated. (See also pollen analysis for dating.)

Reading for Methods of Dating: Aitken, M. J. 1974; Bowen, D. Q. 1978; Brothwell, D. and Higgs, E. S. 1969; Council for British Archaeology 1970; Council for British Archaeology 1971; Fleming, S. 1976; Fletcher, J. 1978; Michels, J. W. 1973.

Hedgerow Dating

This technique is mainly relevant to the Medieval and Post-Medieval periods. It is based on the theory that, in a hedge originally planted with only one species of shrub, another different species of shrub becomes established every hundred years **(Hooper's hedgerow hypothesis)**. In practice the average number of species in a 30m length of a reasonably complete and fairly well managed hedge is said to give the approximate date of the hedge in hundreds of years.

Reading for Hedgerow Dating: Evans, J. G. 1975; Taylor, C. C. 1975.

Glass Layer Dating

This is a method of dating glass based on the hypothesis that the layers in the weathering crust on pieces of ancient glass are laid down annually. Subsequent research, however, has shown that this is not the case. A much greater knowledge of weathering processes is necessary before any further attempts can be made at evolving a technique for dating glass by weathering-crust layers.

Reading for Glass Layer Dating: Hurst Vose, R. 1980; Newton, R. G. 1971.

Data Analysis

With the amount of evidence available to archaeologists continually increasing, various methods of data analysis are being developed in order to cope with this situation. The first step in most methods of data analysis is to **quantify** the data: this means expressing the evidence in terms of variable quantities which are usually known as **attributes** of the **units** being considered. For example, if the evidence being examined is a collection of handaxes, each handaxe may be considered as a unit and the attributes chosen would usually be the main dimensions of each handaxe or the presence or absence of various characteristics; if the evidence consists of assemblages of material, such as a number of grave groups, each grave group would be a unit and the attributes chosen would usually be the types of object that could be recorded as present or absent in each unit. The results of quantification are usually expressed as a **data matrix** which is a table of the **scores** (dimensions, or the presence or absence of characteristics or items, expressed numerically) of the various attributes for each unit. One serious problem in the formation of a data matrix is that both the units and the attributes are selected by the person quantifying the data, and information may be lost and the results misleading if the units and attributes are unwisely chosen. It is often convenient to present the information contained in a data matrix in a visual form, either as a final presentation of the evidence (such as in a pollen diagram) or as a means of organising the data before further analysis.

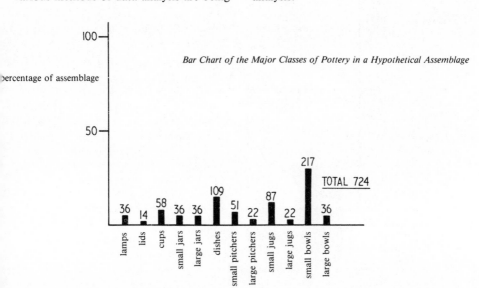

Bar Chart of the Major Classes of Pottery in a Hypothetical Assemblage

The simplest visual representation of quantified data is a **bar chart**, where each bar represents a count of units. Usually a bar chart represents a single row of figures of a data matrix, so that many bar charts are needed to represent a complete matrix. These can be arranged in a single diagram, but although this allows detailed comparison between separate aspects of different assemblages, such a diagram is usually very complex and comparisons between whole assemblages are very difficult. One method of making such comparisons easier is to replace each bar chart by a line joining the top of the bars, and plotting these lines in a single diagram. Often, however, the differences between assemblages will be small and so these lines will be close together and the diagram difficult to interpret. One solution to this problem is the **cumulative graph**: each bar is added to the previous ones and the top of each new bar made in this way is plotted on a graph. This gives a much clearer impression of the overall relationship between the assemblages being compared, but it has the disadvantage of giving a disproportionate visual effect between the beginning and the end of the cumulative sequence. A small number of categories of data can be expressed visually as percentages in a sector diagram (see pollen analysis).

Histograms are similar in appearance to bar charts, but use rectangular columns instead of bars. The total area of each column represents the frequency with which observed values of some variable quantity (for example, the length of each handaxe in a collection) have fallen within a particular range of values. The extent to which a histogram presents a meaningful picture depends largely on how wisely the ranges of values are chosen. Several histograms can be made into **cumulative frequency polygons** and plotted on the same diagram for purposes of comparison. This is done in a similar way to the formation of cumulative graphs, and cumulative frequency polygons resemble cumulative graphs in appearance.

Another method of presenting data visually is the **scatter diagram**, which usually involves the plotting of two attributes (for example, length and width) of a number of objects, as dots on a two-dimensional coordinate system. This results in a number of dots scattered over the diagram, which can display both the relationship between each object and the relationship between the two attributes plotted. For example, in the figure the flint flakes (represented by the dots) fall into two distinct clusters: a group of shorter, narrower flakes and a group of larger, broader flakes, suggesting two distinct groups of flakes differentiated by

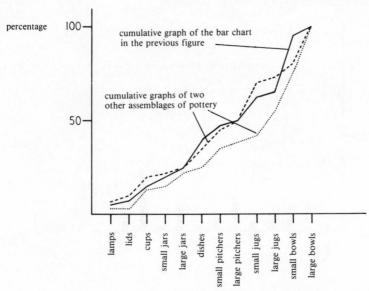

Cumulative Graphs of three Hypothetical Assemblages of Pottery

umber of pottery vessels

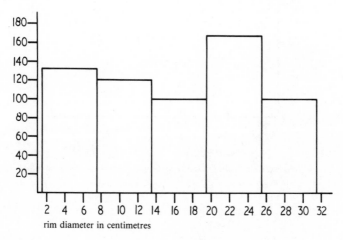

rim diameter in centimetres

umber of pottery vessels

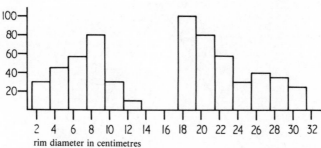

rim diameter in centimetres

Two Histograms portraying the same data but using different Ranges of Values

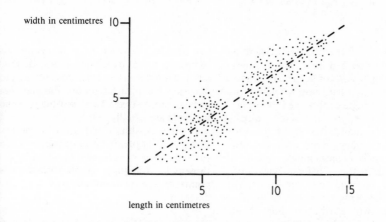

width in centimetres

length in centimetres

Scatter Diagram plotting length against width for a Hypothetical Assemblage of Flint Flakes

237

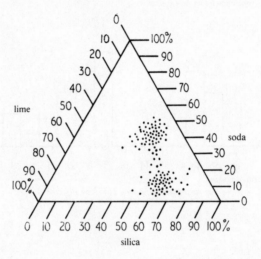

thickness in millimetres

diameter in millimetres

Scatter Diagram plotting thickness against diameter for a Hypothetical Collection of Bronze Bracelets

lime / soda / silica

Use of a 3-Pole Triangular Graph to display the results of an Analysis of a Hypothetical Collection of Pieces of Glass

size. In addition, all the dots are close to a straight line (the dashed line), which shows that the two dimensions of length and width in this group of flakes are closely related. In the example the angle of this line is approximately 45 degrees to the axes, which indicates that usually the shape of the objects does not vary greatly with size. In the figure above is a contrasting example of a scatter diagram for a different group of objects. This diagram does not show any evidence of clustering or of a relationship between the two attributes. For three attributes it is possible to draw a three-dimensional scatter diagram using perspec-

tive drawing or some form of symbols to represent three dimensions; for a small amount of data it is even possible to plot diagrams for four attributes, but for comparing more than two attributes other methods are usually employed.

If three attributes add up to a constant sum (for example, the proportions of silica, soda and lime in various pieces of glass), a **three-pole triangular graph (ternary diagram)** can be used in a similar way to a scatter diagram.

Reading for Data Analysis: Doran, J. E and Hodson, F. R. 1975; Orton, C. 1980.

Classification

One method of coping with a large amount of data is classification. The division of a large number of objects (for example, glass beads) into smaller groups makes it easier to summarise the data, and the groups themselves may provide further evidence. For example, the area over which a group of similar beads has been found may give some indication of where the beads were made.

Until recently, virtually all classifications of objects were done by the technique of **typology**. This is the sorting of objects into **types** on the basis of similarities in form and decoration, so that one type of glass bead, for example, might be annular with a yellow ray design on a blue background, while another type might be a plain tubular red bead. The effectiveness of this technique obviously depends on the knowledge and ability of the person using it. Although many classifications constructed by this method have proved sound and useful, the subjective nature of the technique has led to a search for more objective, (particularly mathematical) methods; such classification, based on mathematical methods, is known as **numerical taxonomy**. The techniques used to establish a numerical taxonomy are known collectively as **cluster analysis**. This attempts to group objects together according to the degree of similarity between them. Various mathematical methods have been devised to measure such similarity, and there are also various techniques of producing groups **(clusters)** from such measurements. **Agglomerative techniques** group together the most similar objects and then repeatedly add new, slightly less similar, ones to existing groups; **divisive techniques** start with the complete collection of objects to be classified, and repeatedly subdivide the collection into smaller groups. The results of cluster analysis are often shown in the form of a **dendrogram**, but the significance of the groupings depends on the nature of the original data. Some applications of numerical taxonomy have been criticised on both mathematical and archaeological grounds, but numerical taxonomy can be of use, particularly where the quantity of data to be classified is very large.

Reading for Classification: Doran, J. E. and Hodson, F. R. 1975; Everitt, B. 1975.

identification number of each artifact

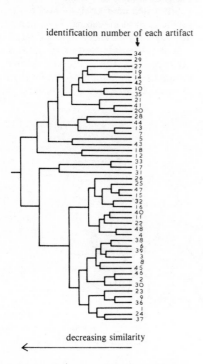

decreasing similarity

A Dendrogram portraying the results of a Cluster Analysis on a Hypothetical Collection of 48 Flint Tools

Spatial Analysis

This is the study of spatial patterns in archaeological data. The **distribution** of sites or objects is the pattern of their locations and such a distribution (for example, of hillforts) is usually studied by plotting the locations onto a map to form a **distribution map**, which then provides a visual impression of the distribution pattern. This gives an indication of the spatial relationship of the sites or objects to each other, and also of their relationship to the natural environment. Distribution maps are a very useful visual presentation of spatial patterns, but care is needed in their interpretation since, for example, a clustering of finds in a small area may indicate a concentration of settlement, or it may indicate the area covered by a keen local archaeological fieldworker.

Much spatial analysis consists of **locational analysis**, which is a set of techniques used in geography to study the relationships between sites, and between individual sites and their environment. One of these techniques is **nearest-neighbour analysis**, which analyses the degree to which a distribution pattern is dispersed by calculating the average distance of each point in the pattern from its nearest neighbour. This result is then divided by the average distance that would result if the pattern was randomly distributed (a random distribution may be worked out by statistical methods). The resulting figure is the **nearest-neighbour index**, which is usually denoted by the symbol R, and varies from 0·00 (a completely clustered pattern) to 2·29 (a completely uniform pattern). An index of 1·00 indicates a random distribution. Care must be taken in using this technique since it should only be used on a complete pattern of sites of the same date and similar function. The size of the area for analysis is also important since the density of the distribution pattern will depend on the size of the area chosen. The method is also liable to distortion by the 'boundary effect', which tends to give a nearest-neighbour index which is too large, because some sites may have their nearest neighbours just outside the area being analysed.

Central place theory attempts to explain the distribution of sites in terms of the goods and services they provide for the surrounding region. It is assumed that a 'central place' (such as a large town) serves a circular area, and that all other such centres in a region are equal in size and function, giving a pattern of adjoining hexagons with a 'central place' in the centre of each hexagon. (Hexagons are usually used in place of circles to avoid the gaps and overlapping which occur in a pattern of circles.) It is also possible to relate sites of less importance to this pattern. The basic theory has been much modified and has greatly increased in complexity. The application of this theory is limited by the need to assume that the terrain, population and transport costs are uniform, although it can be a useful model in the interpretation of some settlement patterns.

Another method of analysing the relationship between sites is the use of **Thiessen polygons**. These are constructed by drawing lines, perpendicular to and bisecting lines joining sites. The polygons formed by these lines each enclose one site and the area enclosed by the polygon is nearer to that site than to any other site. Such polygons can serve as models for the territory controlled by each site, market areas for centres of production, and so on. The method assumes that all sites are contemporary and of the same status, although there are statistical methods which can make allowances for the differing status of the sites being considered.

Site catchment analysis assumes that the further a natural resource is from a site, the less likely it will be exploited by people from that site; beyond a certain distance the cost of exploiting the resource becomes uneconomic. The catchment area is defined by drawing an arbitrary circle around the site,

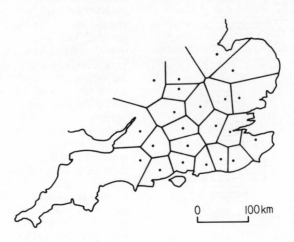

0   100km

Thiessen Polygons constructed around a Hypothetical Distribution of Sites in Southern Britain

and then calculating the proportions of natural resources (such as arable land and pastoral land) within the circle. The results can indicate the nature and function of the site. The radius of the circle is often set at 5km for agriculturalists and 10km for hunter-gatherers. These areas may not be realistic, nor do they take account of the terrain. Also, the values of the resources to the people living on the site may not be the same as those of today.

The **rank-size rule** states that if sites are ranked in descending order of size, the nth site will be $\frac{1}{n}$ the size of the largest. For example, the fourth site will be one quarter the size of the first. This theory is no longer widely accepted.

Trend surface analysis is a means of producing a generalised map from observed distributions. The resulting map looks like a contour map, but instead of representing variations in height, the 'contours' represent variations in the number of sites or finds. For example, a map might be drawn to represent the distribution of products from a pottery-manufacturing site. Since the distribution of artifacts consists of a number of isolated points, statistical methods are used to plot the 'contours'. Such a map portrays the broad trends and also local variations in the distribution. It can be used for sites and finds distributed over a large area, and also on a small scale to examine the distribution of finds over a particular site.

Reading for Spatial Analysis: Doran, J. E. and Hodson, F. R. 1975; Hodder, I. and Orton, C. 1976.

Models

Models are idealised representations of real situations, and are used to obtain a better understanding of the reality. A model may be a physical model of a site, object, or part of the landscape; eg a reconstruction of an Iron Age hut is a model. The term model, however, is more usually applied to a theoretical rather than a physical model. A distribution map and a scatter diagram are examples of simple models, while a more complex model might be a theory proposing various phases of invasion and settlement. Models vary greatly in the extent to which they represent real situations; a very specific and realistic model (such as a reconstruc-tion of an Iron Age hut) may only be applicable to a small number of sites, perhaps only to one, whereas a more general model (such as the division of pre-history into the three ages of stone, bronze and iron) will have a much wider application.

A special form of model is the **computer simulation**. A computer is given data (real or invented) and programmed to produce a model from the data. A model derived from invented (usually random) data is usually used to examine the general relationships within the model itself.

Reading for Models: Clarke, D. L. 1972; Doran, J. E. and Hodson, F. R. 1975.

Use of Mathematics and Computers

A great deal of mathematics (mainly statistics) is used in data analysis. Apart from the specific forms of analysis already mentioned, many other statistical tests and techniques are occasionally used. Some of these have only come into general use with the advent of the electronic calculator, computer and microprocessor; they were previously considered impractical because of the amount of arithmetic that was involved. In this respect, the use of computers has greatly increased the scope of data analysis in recent years, so that new techniques are still being developed and the mathematical analysis of archaeological data is still in a relatively experimental stage.

As well as being used for mathematical calculations and for simulation studies, computers are also beginning to be used for archaeological **data banks** where information is stored within the computer; use is made of the computer's fast working speed to gain rapid retrieval of information thus stored.

Reading for Use of Mathematics and Computers: Doran, J. E. and Hodson, F. R. 1975; Orton, C. 1980.

General Reading for Archaeological Techniques: Barker, P. 1977; Brothwell, D. and Higgs, E. S. 1969; Champion, S. 1980; Coles, J. M. 1972; Doran, J. E. and Hodson, F. R. 1975; Evans, J. G. 1978; Orton, C. 1980; Taylor, C. C. 1974; Wood, E. S. 1979.

Chapter 10

Miscellaneous

Introduction

Archaeology is the study of man's past by means of material remains. In the historic period these remains can be related to groups of people known from historical sources (for example, the Vikings), but in the prehistoric period the only evidence for groups of people comes from the material remains themselves. To help overcome this problem, the concept of cultures was developed. A **culture** describes all the material remains which are commonly associated with each other in a particular area and at a particular point in time, and which therefore seem to represent a particular group of people. Ideally there should be different sorts of remains (for example, artifacts, settlement sites, burials), and different types of remains (for example, flint axes, flint scrapers, flint knives) recurrently found associated with each other. However, the term 'culture' is often used loosely to describe a collection of remains that appears to represent a distinct group of people but does not meet all the requirements of the strict definition of the term. The term **facies** has been used to describe aspects of a culture or industry which appear to be a sub-set of the culture or industry, although the term is now seldom used. An **industry** is a group of different types of tool which are contemporary, of the same material, and are commonly found in association with each other (such as the Llantwit-Stogursey industry). The term **tradition** is used to describe a style which gradually evolved over a period of time. The term is also used loosely to mean 'industry'. **Independent invention** describes the same idea (for example, the same techniques or artifacts) invented independently by more than one group of people, instead of being spread from one group of people to another **(diffusion)**.

Archaeological Periods in Britain

Largely for convenience, the past is divided into various periods. Firstly, the past is divided into the historical period and the prehistoric period. The **historical period (historic period)** is that portion of the past of which an account **(history)** can be given based on evidence from written records. The earlier portion of the past, before the existence of written records, is **prehistory (prehistoric period)**. The term **protohistory** is sometimes used for the transition period between the prehistoric and historic periods denoting a phase for which few written records are available, and for which most evidence is derived from archaeology. In Britain AD 43 (the Roman invasion) is conventionally accepted as the boundary between the prehistoric and historic periods. Prehistory was originally subdivided by the **Three Age system** — first formulated by Christian Jurgensen Thomsen (1788–1865) to classify the collections in the National Museum of Denmark. Prehistory was divided into a **Stone Age**, a **Bronze Age** and an **Iron Age** on the basis of the predominant material out of which tools and weapons were made. The system was gradually elaborated by dividing the Stone Age into the **Old Stone Age (Palaeolithic)** and the **New Stone Age (Neolithic)** — a **Middle Stone Age (Mesolithic)** was subsequently added; the Palaeolithic was later divided into the **Lower, Middle** and **Upper Palaeolithic**, and finally a **Copper Age (Chalcolithic)** was inserted between the Neolithic and the Bronze Age to denote a period when copper was being used for tools and weapons. The terms 'Copper Age' and 'Chalcolithic' are not used in British archaeology since evidence for such a distinct period has not been found in Britain.

Hoards

A **hoard** is a collection of material (usually of metal) deposited in the ground. Such collections are classified into several types according to the probable reasons for their deposition: a **personal hoard** is a collection of personal property, a **founder's hoard** contains scrap metal and cakes of metal for use in making new tools, a **merchant's hoard** contains new objects ready to be traded, and a **hoard of loot** is a collection of stolen property. All these types of hoard were buried for safe-keeping and were not recovered. The **votive hoard (votive deposit)**, however, consists of offerings to a god or gods, often deposited over a long period of time. A **coin hoard** (consisting of coins) may be a personal hoard, a votive hoard or a hoard of loot. The value of a hoard as an assemblage of associated artifacts depends on its nature; for example, a merchant's hoard would contain objects made and in use at the same point in time, while a votive hoard could contain objects differing in date by several centuries.

Burial

The disposal of human remains is known as **burial**; the associated religious customs are known as **burial rites**. Very little evidence of such rites usually survives, but the most common was the deposition of objects with the burial. These objects included tools, weapons, pottery vessels, ornaments and food, and are known as **grave goods**. Sometimes boats and carts were deposited as grave goods (see boat burials and cart burials). Animals and possibly humans were sometimes sacrificed and buried with the dead.

Buried human remains are called **interments**, and consist of cremations and inhumations. **Cremation** is the burning of human remains which were then usually deposited in some kind of container (such as a pottery urn, glass vessel or a bag made from organic material), and subsequently buried. **Urned cremations** were buried in urns; **unurned cremations** were not. **Inhumation** is the burying of an unburnt human corpse, and was done in several ways: the body could be laid out in an approximately straight line (**extended inhumation, extended burial**); the leg joints could be bent by an angle less than 90 degrees (**flexed inhumation, flexed burial**); or the leg joints could be bent through an angle greater than 90 degrees (**crouched inhumation, crouched burial**). A **contracted inhumation (contracted burial)** had the knees brought right up against the chest.

Instead of being interred, a corpse could be exposed to the elements by laying it on the ground, or on a platform above the ground (**exposed burial, exposure**). If the skeleton was later collected and buried, the bones tend to be jumbled together, showing that the skeleton had been disturbed after the flesh holding the bones together had rotted away (**disarticulated skeleton**). An **articulated skeleton** shows that the body was buried before the flesh had decomposed, and not subsequently disturbed.

Interments were sometimes buried in or under **barrows** (mounds of earth) or **cairns** (mounds of stones); the term **tumulus** (pl **tumuli**) is used to denote a burial mound irrespective of the material from which it was made. A **composite barrow** was made from stones and earth. The first interment in a barrow or cairn is the **primary interment (primary burial)**. Contemporary interments that are interpreted as being of less important people than the primary interment (for example, servants buried with a king) are sometimes called **satellite interments (satellite burials, subsidiary burials, subsidiary interments)**. The term **subsequent primary interment (subsequent primary burial)** is sometimes used to describe a burial which was deposited shortly after the primary burial, and was apparently of equal importance to it. Interments inserted into a barrow at a later date, often with a different burial rite, are known as **secondary interments (secondary burials)**; if there is a great difference in date between the deposition of primary and secondary burials (for example, Saxon burials deposited in a Bronze Age barrow), the secondary burials are often called **intrusive interments (intrusive burials)**.

An inhumation might be buried in a grave in the ground without a covering mound; this is termed a **flat grave**. Flat graves, barrows and cairns can all occur singly, or can be in groups called respectively **flat cemeteries, barrow cemeteries** and **cairnfields**. Cremations rarely occur as

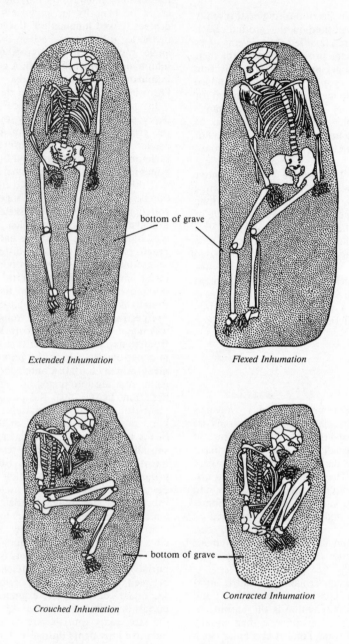

Extended Inhumation

Flexed Inhumation

bottom of grave

Crouched Inhumation

Contracted Inhumation

bottom of grave

0   1m

Examples of Inhumation Posture

isolated burials: they are more often found as secondary burials in barrows and cairns, or sometimes in flat cemeteries (see also urnfields and cremation cemeteries).

Agriculture

A distinction is often drawn between the Highland Zone and the Lowland Zone of Britain. The **Highland Zone (Highland Britain)** is made up of areas of Palaeozoic rocks (the most ancient group of rocks in Britain) which are hard mountainous regions with high rainfall, whereas the **Lowland Zone (Lowland Britain)** is made up of areas of younger rock which give rise to low-lying land and gently rolling hills with a lower rainfall. It was once thought

The Highland and Lowland Zones of Britain

that, particularly in the prehistoric period, arable agriculture was confined to the Lowland Zone and pastoral agriculture to the Highland Zone. Recent evidence has shown that this is not so, and it appears likely that any suitable land was used for arable agriculture, irrespective of geographical position, so long as climatic, social and economic conditions were favourable.

Evidence for pastoralism can be indicated by the bones of animals used for food, by the evidence for leather working and textiles, and by earthworks which appear to be the remains of stock enclosures. Arable agriculture can be indicated by various specialised tools, by evidence from plant remains and pollen, and by a significant alteration of the landscape.

Assuming that the ground has been cleared of woodland and undergrowth, the first stage in growing a crop was the breaking up of the ground to form a seed bed. There is very little evidence of how this was done in Britain before the use of ards, but various implements may have been used: antler picks are known to have been used in digging ditches and flint mines, and so may have been used in agriculture. **Digging sticks** (pointed sticks stabbed into the ground to break up the soil) may have been used, and it is possible that some of the larger perforated stone maceheads were used as weights for digging sticks. Wooden hoes may have been used as, probably, were wooden spades. Spade marks and spade-cut furrows have been found at several sites, and turves in some barrows are of a shape and size that indicate they were cut with wooden spades. Evidence of **lazy bed** cultivation has also been found. This is the digging of land with a spade to form ridges (usually between 0·5m and 2·5m wide) with the furrows between them normally 0·3m to 1m wide.

Even after the introduction of ards, manual tools would still have been used, in some cases to supplement the work done by the ard, and also to cultivate land where ards could not be efficiently used.

Ploughs and Ards

The main difference between a **plough (heavy plough)** and an **ard (light plough)** is that a plough had a mouldboard capable of

245

turning over the earth, whereas an ard had no mouldboard and could only break up the soil. The earliest evidence for ploughing is the **ard marks (plough marks, plough scratches)** which were discovered beneath South Street long barrow, *Avebury*, Wiltshire. These marks, the remains of furrows cut by an ard, have been dated to the early third millennium BC. They form a criss-cross pattern that appears to be evidence for **cross-ploughing** (the ploughing of an area twice — the second time with the furrows at right angles to those formed by the first ploughing). It is likely that this was done in order to break up the soil more effectively. Plough marks dating to the Bronze Age, the Iron Age and the Roman period have been found on various sites in Britain.

Ards

Early ploughing was probably done with a form of bow ard or crook ard, both of which were made of wood. The remains of several bow ards of Iron Age date have been found, but no evidence for the use of a crook ard has yet been discovered. The **bow**

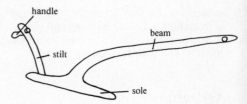

(beam and sole made from a single piece of wood)

Diagram of a Crook Ard (side view)

0 |m

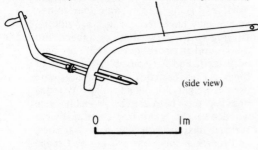

beam (to which oxen were harnessed to pull the ard)

(side view)

0 |m

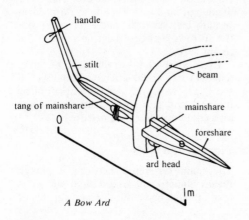

handle

stilt

tang of mainshare

0

beam

mainshare

foreshare

ard head

|m

A Bow Ard

ard (beam ard) consisted of a stilt and share inserted through a hole in the base of the plough beam. The **crook ard (sole ard)** consisted of a plough beam and horizontal sole made from a single piece of wood, with a stilt attached to the rear of the sole. In Britain, the earliest known remains of ards are sandstone bars **(stone ard points, stone ard shares)** which appear to be the points of shares. Stone ard points are found only in the Orkney and Shetland Islands, although they are also known from other parts of Europe. At least one of the British stone ard points has been dated to around 2000 BC, but they may have been used for a long time before and after this date. It is not known exactly how stone ard points were attached to the ard itself. A few bone implements are known which may also have been used as shares.

During the Iron Age socketed and tanged iron shares were introduced. **Socketed shares (flanged shares)** were of several types but all appear to have fitted over a wooden foreshare, or in some cases possibly over the end of the stilt. Socketed shares developed during the Iron Age and the Roman period, becoming longer, larger and more solid. They were probably used on a form of bow ard. There were three main types of **tanged share:** ones with spatulate blades which date to the Iron Age, **bar shares,** and bar shares with two wings beaten out to grip the wooden part of the share, which date to the Roman period. Tanged shares were also probably used on a form of bow ard.

Iron **coulters** (knives mounted in front of shares to cut the sod vertically before the share cut it horizontally) were probably introduced around the middle of the Roman period. It is likely that these were initially used on bow ards.

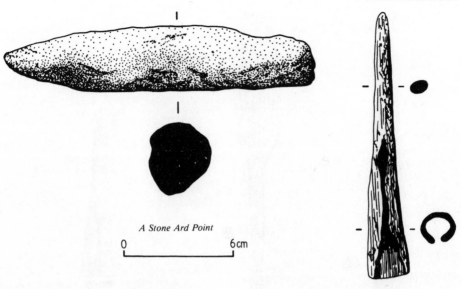

A Stone Ard Point

0 _____ 6cm

Socketed Iron Share of Iron Age Date

0 _____ 5cm

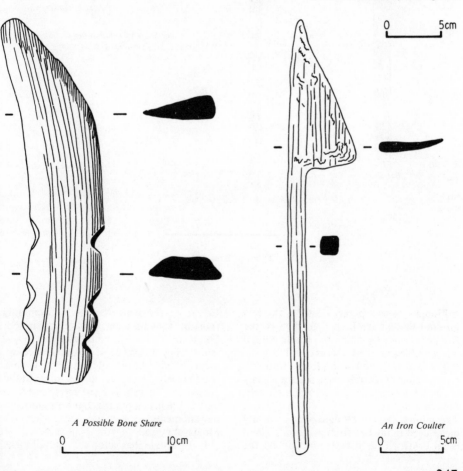

A Possible Bone Share

0 _____ 10cm

An Iron Coulter

0 _____ 5cm

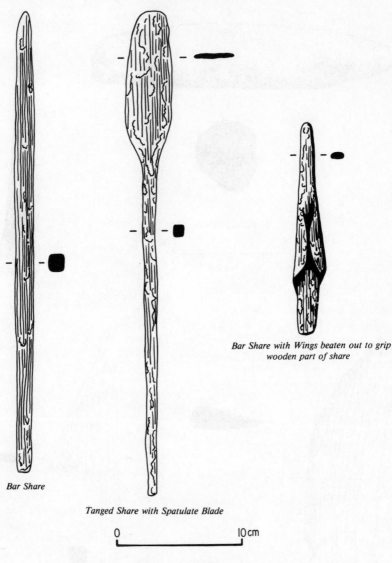

Bar Share with Wings beaten out to grip wooden part of share

Bar Share

Tanged Share with Spatulate Blade

0   10 cm

Types of Iron Shares

Ploughs with shares fitted with **ears (ground-wrests)** are known to date to the Roman period. By tilting the whole plough it is possible that these shares could turn the soil to one side, and so a plough with this type of share probably represents an intermediate type between an ard and a plough.

Ploughs

The **plough (heavy plough)** was probably introduced in the late Roman period. There is no evidence for its introduction by the Belgae in the Iron Age as is commonly thought. It had a share, coulter and mouldboard, and was capable of cutting the sod and turning it right over. With the development of the heavy plough, heavy soils (particularly clays) could be successfully cultivated. There was some later modification of the heavy plough, but no significant developments took place until after the Medieval period.

It is possible that some ards and ploughs

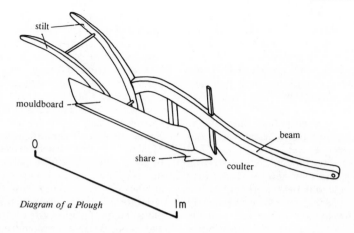

Diagram of a Plough

0   1 m

were pulled by people, but the evidence of finds of yokes and ox-goads suggests that from at least as early as the Bronze Age a pair or pairs of oxen were used. At some time during the late Saxon period the **horse collar** was introduced which was a rigid padded collar that fitted around a horse's neck and rested on its shoulders. This was an improvement in harnessing which did not tend to strangle the horse as previous methods did. The horse collar enabled horses to pull ploughs, although oxen continued to be used.

Harvesting was probably done with flint knives or 'sickles' in the Neolithic period. In the Bronze Age, bronze reaping hooks were introduced, and were replaced in the Iron Age by iron reaping hooks and, later, balanced iron sickles. Scythes were introduced during the Roman period.

Fields

Probably by at least 2000 BC systems of **pre-historic fields (Celtic fields)** were established over large areas of England. These were usually either small square fields or long rectangular ones between about ½ acre and 1½ acres in area. In some places long rectangular fields appear to have replaced small square fields and therefore may be a later development. Celtic fields are usually recognised by the lynchets which enclose them. Stone walls, fences, hedges and ditches were all used to enclose these fields, and on sloping ground **lynchets** built up against, and eventually over these field boundaries: with repeated ploughing, soil moved downhill and built up against the field boundary forming a **positive lynchet**, while below the boundary, in the next field, the same process removed soil to form a **negative lynchet**. These fields were usually laid out (at least to some extent) across the contours of a slope, so that lynchets formed on all four sides of the field, rather than just two. In upland areas irregular **curvilinear plots** are known. It is not known for certain whether these were cultivated or whether they were used in pastoral farming; there is evidence, however, that some were ploughed, and in some areas they appear to have been replaced by rectangular fields.

As well as fields for arable farming there

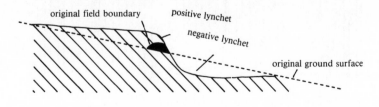

Diagrammatic Section through a Lynchet

0   10m

is also evidence for prehistoric pastoralism in the form of **ranch boundaries**. These are systems of long continuous banks and/or ditches which were probably used for controlling livestock. They appear to date from at least the Later Bronze Age (see also Bronze Age economy and Iron Age economy).

During the Roman period, many of the Celtic fields continued to be cultivated, but there is evidence that some of the field boundaries were broken down to form larger fields, and some new long fields were laid out. These **long fields** were four or five times as long as they were wide and were up to 2½ acres in area. They were usually arranged in blocks of parallel fields. Some large fields up to 12 acres in area are known, and there are also some very large enclosures of up to 50 acres in area which may be of Roman date and which were probably connected with stock raising.

There is very little evidence for any distinctive fields during the Saxon period, and yet it is during this period that the transition from the various types of field in use in the Roman period to the Medieval field system must have taken place. It is likely that the Saxons took over and used the fields that were in use when they arrived and that these were gradually modified. There are no

traces of fields or enclosures being used solely for stock raising in this period.

The most distinctive remains of Medieval fields are those of ridge and furrow. **Ridge and furrow (rig and furrow)** consists of long parallel ridges of soil separated by linear depressions (furrows). The ridges are usually at least 5m across **(broad rig)**; narrower ridges under 5m across **(narrow rig)** are usually straight low ridges of Post-Medieval date. Ridge and furrow is formed by using a heavy plough capable of turning the sod. First a furrow is ploughed and then another one is ploughed close to it in the opposite direction, then a third one is ploughed on the other side of the first one, and so on. Because the plough always turns the sods in one direction, they are always turned inwards towards the centre of the ridge. Over a period of many years, repeated ploughing in this way builds up a ridge leaving a depression (furrow) on either side.

It is not known for certain why ridge and furrow was formed; in many areas it provided good drainage on heavy soils, and it may have been adopted on well-drained soils out of habit rather than necessity. Much Medieval ridge and furrow is not straight, but when seen in plan is in the form of a reversed 'S' or sometimes a

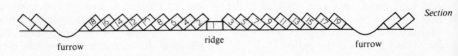

furrow ridge furrow *Section*

slices cut and turned over by the plough (the numbers give the order in which the slices were cut)

direction of plough

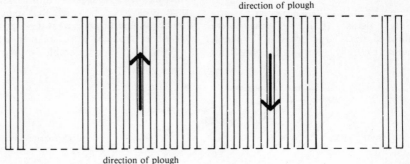

Plan V

direction of plough

Diagram to show how Ridge and Furrow was formed

0 5m

stretched 'C'. This twisting of the ridges appears to have been caused by the need to start to turn a large team of oxen which was pulling the plough before the end of the furrow was reached to avoid trampling or ploughing up adjacent land. At the end of the strips of ridge and furrow were **headlands (plough headlands)**. These were narrow strips of land where the plough and team of oxen could turn round and which provided access to the strips. Because these headlands were rarely ploughed they remained higher than the surrounding land whose height was gradually lowered by continuous cultivation. Earth cleaned off the plough on the headlands added to their height and often headlands remain as slight earthworks after all other traces of ridge and furrow have been destroyed.

Another distinctive form of remains of Medieval fields is **strip lynchets**. These are terrace fields usually seen on steep hillsides. They are made up of two parts: the flat strip of the field itself (the **tread**) and the steep scarped edge or lynchet called the **riser**. They are often as much as 200m long. The lynchets are formed in the same way as those of Celtic fields.

Ridge and furrow and strip lynchets usually formed part of the Medieval **open field system** which is known from historical sources. This was a system where several large, open fields were divided into strips which were all individually owned but which were farmed as a co-operative effort by all the owners and tenants of the strips.

Although by about AD 1300 much of England was being cultivated by the open field system, there were many parts of the country where enclosed fields continued to be used. This continued use tended to be confined to small and isolated communities. Where forested land was cleared for agriculture, however, the irregular fields so formed were often enclosed (usually with a bank and hedge or a stone wall). Such cleared areas were known as **assarts**, and the process of clearance known as **assarting**. In the later Medieval period fields again began to be enclosed in many parts of the country. This new enclosure of fields was for creating pasture land, mainly for sheep to meet a growing demand for wool.

Reading for Agriculture: Bowen, H. C. 1961; Bradley, R. J. 1978; Evans, J. G. 1975; Rees, S. E. 1979; Taylor, C. C. 1975.

Textiles

Textiles were in use in Britain from at least the Bronze Age onwards. Wool was available and flax was grown, and it is possible that nettles were also used to provide fibres. Hemp was probably introduced in the Roman period.

Bast fibres (the long chains of cells which carry food from the roots to the rest of the plant) could be extracted from flax, nettles and hemp, and then spun into thread. This extraction was done by first combing **(rippling)** the bundles of plants to remove the seed pods. The plants were then soaked in water so that much of the unwanted plant material was partially rotted and the bark was loosened — a process known as **retting**. The stems were then beaten with a wooden sword or mallet to remove the bark and separate the fibres from the woody core; this process is known as **scutching**. The fibres were then combed **(hackled, heckled)** to remove all unwanted material. The resulting fibres **(flax lint)** were then ready for spinning.

Wool was sheared with knives or shears. It could then be **teased** (the foreign bodies removed with a comb or with the fingers) and washed, possibly using **lye** (a solution of wood ash) as a degreasing agent. It was then combed until it was soft **(carded)**, when it was ready for spinning.

Spinning and Weaving

The fibres were placed on a **distaff**, which was usually a wooden stick 20cm to 30cm long, held in one hand. A strand of fibre was pulled out, twisted, and fastened to a **handspindle (spindle)** fitted through the centre of a **spindle whorl**. The fibre could then be spun, with the spindle whorl acting as a flywheel. The spinning wheel replaced the handspindle from the late Medieval period onwards. The spun fibre could then be wound into balls, or onto bobbins. It was then knitted, using knitting needles, or woven on looms. The most common loom in antiquity was the **vertical loom (upright loom, warp-weighted loom)**. This basically consisted of two wooden uprights with a horizontal beam across the top, and a **shed rod** further down to separate even and odd numbered warp threads and so create a **natural shed (shed)**. A **heddle rod** could

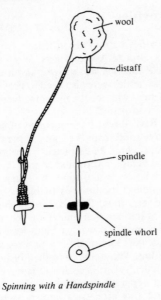

wool

distaff

spindle

spindle whorl

Spinning with a Handspindle

0   10 cm

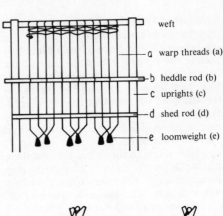

weft

a   warp threads (a)

b   heddle rod (b)

c   uprights (c)

d   shed rod (d)

e   loomweight (e)

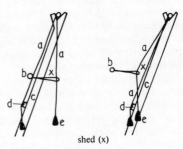

shed (x)

Warp-Weighted Loom

0   1m

bring the odd numbered warp threads backwards and forwards to alternate the shed and thereby enable the weft to be passed through as a single movement. The warp threads were weighted by **loomweights**.

A **horizontal loom** was probably used from the end of the Saxon period. It had a box-like frame and the warp threads were stretched horizontally between a warp beam and a breast beam; loomweights were not used. By using a **shedding mechanism** alternate warp threads could be lowered and raised so that the weft threads could be passed through in a single movement.

Tablet weaving (card weaving) was used to make braids. A pack of thin triangular, circular, rectangular or hexagonal tablets, pierced with two, three, four or six holes at the corners or edges, were threaded with warp threads. The weft would be threaded through the shed and the tablets turned once to create a new shed.

Finishing Processes

The cloth (especially woollen cloth) underwent a number of finishing processes: first any extraneous matter and knots were picked out of the cloth and any necessary

repairs made. It was then **felted** so that the cloth was thickened and the fibres adhered together to minimise the gaps in the weave. (True **felt** was made by beating, rolling and pressing unwoven animal hair or wool until it became a compact mass; oils may have been used to help the fibres mat together.) One method of felting was to **scour** the cloth (wash it in hot water) and then trample it underfoot. This caused the cloth to shrink considerably. A more thorough felting process was **fulling**. This consisted of cleaning and degreasing the cloth, usually with a solution of decayed urine or a solution of **fuller's earth** (a fine white clay) which absorbed much of the natural oils in the wool. The cloth was then trampled underfoot.

Cloth could be **bleached**, usually by exposure to sunshine and rain, or it could be dyed. It was more usual, however, to dye the thread before weaving, so that different colours could be used to weave patterns in the cloth. Dyes were produced from a great variety of plants. The method of extraction varied from plant to plant, but usually involved the crushing, soaking, boiling, or fermenting the dye-producing part. Initially the choice of plants for dyes was restricted to those native in Britain, but in later periods plants were specially imported. Most dyes were liable to run and so they were made fast by the use of a **mordant** such as alum.

Reading for Textiles: Baines, P. 1977; Henshall, A. S. 1950; Hodges, H. 1964; Patterson, R. 1956; Taylor, F. S. and Singer, C. 1956; Wild, J. P. 1970a.

Hides and Leather Working

Skins and hides were used for various types of coverings and containers from at least the Upper Palaeolithic period onwards. The term **hide** is sometimes reserved for the skins of large animals such as cattle and horses, and **skin** for the skins of smaller animals, with the term **pelt** used to describe untreated skins irrespective of the size; however, all three terms are often used indiscriminately to describe both treated and untreated skins of all sizes of animal.

In a hot dry climate it is possible to use raw animal skins, once they have been dried out, without serious deterioration, but in Britain skins would be likely to decay very rapidly if left untreated. After the removal of the skin from the animal, the layer of fat underneath the skin is scraped off. In the earlier prehistoric period this was probably done with a variety of flint, stone and bone tools, but from at least the Roman period onwards this was done with a two-handled knife (similar to a draw-knife but with a curved blade), called a **fleshing knife (beaming knife)**. The skin would usually be spread over a **beam (bench)**, often a section of a tree-trunk, so that it could be scraped easily. If the hair and outer surface of the skin **(epidermis)** were also to be scraped off **(scudding)**, the skin might be soaked and pounded. Alternatively the hair and epidermis might be loosened by treating it with urine or quicklime or other strong alkalis. The removal of the fat and epidermis leaves the **corium (derma)**, which is composed mainly of a fibrous material called **collagen**.

After this preparation, skins can be treated in several ways to prevent further decay: such treatment is known as **dressing**.

Smoking is one method of treating a skin by hanging it over a slow-burning wood fire; the skin then absorbs resinous material from the smoke which retards decay. It is possible that the skin would be thoroughly chewed before smoking to remove any remnants of fat and to make the skin supple; this method of dressing skins is known to have been used by Eskimos. Another method of preserving skins is by **oil-dressing (chamoising)**: an oil or oil-bearing material such as tallow, egg yolk or animal brains is thoroughly rubbed into the skin. An oil-dressing was also often used on leather to help prevent it becoming stiff and cracked. **Salt-dressing** was the use of salt for the preservation of skins: dry salt could be rubbed into the surface of the skin, or the skin could be soaked in brine. **Alum-dressing (tawing)** was the application of alum (sometimes with salt) by similar methods to those used for salt. Alum-dressing made the skin white and stiff. These processes had little permanent chemical effect on the skin; the materials with which the skin was impregnated in order to preserve it could be washed out and the skin rapidly decay.

The term **leather** is often used to describe skins that have been dressed, although it is sometimes reserved for skins treated with an irreversible preservation process such as tanning and some forms of oil-dressing. **Tanning (vegetable tanning)** is the process whereby **tannins** (chemical compounds found in many trees and shrubs; oak bark was virtually the only source of tannins used in Britain) react with the materials of the skin and so change its chemical composition. This was done by soaking the skins in a mixture of water and chopped oak bark in pits **(tanning pits, tan pits)** or sometimes in vats. To obtain a soft or more elastic leather, skins were made to swell before tanning by being suspended in an infusion of animal dung (dog dung being the most effective). This process, called **plumping (bating)**, was performed before scudding.

Some untanned leathers were used for special purposes: **parchment** was made from sheepskins (and sometimes from goat and ass skins) split into thin sheets called **shivers**. It was attached to a special frame, dried out, cleaned, smoothed and degreased. It was used mainly for writing on, or sometimes as a window-covering, when it would be oiled to make it more translucent. **Vellum** was made in the same way as parchment, but it was made from unsplit calfskin and some selected sheepskins, and was much finer in texture than parchment. The coarser hides of large animals, if dried out untanned, became very hard and inflexible. This type of skin was called **rawhide** and was used where hardness and inflexibility were advantageous. Leather was sometimes dyed.

Leather Working

Most leather artifacts were made by cutting out pieces of leather to shape and sewing the pieces together. Ordinary types of knife are not very useful for such cutting out since the point of the knife rapidly becomes blunt; usually a crescentic-bladed **half-moon knife** was used so that the wear was more evenly distributed along the curved blade edge. This type of metal knife was probably used from the Bronze Age onwards; before this, flint tools would have been used. Because of the toughness of leather, the holes for sewing were pierced with an **awl**. Awls of bone and metal and suitably shaped flint tools are commonly found. Rawhide and leather that had not been oil-dressed could be moulded to shape by a process known as **cuir bouilli** (literally 'boiled leather'): the leather was soaked in water, moulded into shape and then heated until it was dry. Once dry it would retain its shape unless soaked in water; to prevent this it could be made water-resistant by dressing it with oil or resin. An alternative method was to scald the soaked and moulded leather in near-boiling water before drying it out. The hardness of the finished article depended on the degree of heat used to dry it; too high a temperature made it very brittle.

Apart from dyeing, leather could be decorated by painting or gilding. It might also be decorated with various patterns cut, impressed or burnt into it (**tooling**). Leather could be stamped with a metal punch with a design on the end in order to form a pattern, or **embossed** by using dies or moulds to raise the design above the rest of the surface. The term **engraving** is sometimes used to mean the impression of a design into the surface of the leather using a blunt tool; the term **incised** is normally used if the design is cut into the leather. Designs could also be burnt into the surface with a

hot metal rod: this is known as **poker work**

Reading for Hides and Leather Working Hodges, H. 1964; Reed, R. 1972; Waterer J. W. 1956; Waterer, J. W. 1968.

Salt Working

From prehistoric times salt was extracted along the coastline. In the spring seawater was allowed to enter large **evaporation pans** (**salt pans, salterns**) along the shore; the liquid evaporated during the summer and in the autumn the crust of salt and earth was collected. This was roasted in an open fire to prepare the salt and earth mixture for the next stage when it was put in a solution in a large boiling pan of clay supported over a fire on clay bars. The water was then boiled off and the salt was collected and packed in moulds. Moulds were sometimes in two halves so that they could be re-used. So called **red hills** sometimes survive; these are mounds of burnt earth mixed with **briquetage** (the remains of clay bars, boiling pans and moulds) which are indicative of salt-working areas.

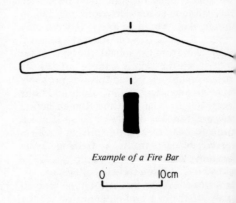

Example of a Fire Bar

0   10cm

Reading for Salt Working: Cunliffe, B 1978; Farrar, R. A. H. 1962; Riehm, K 1961.

Woodworking

Wood has always been a very important material for the manufacture of a great variety of things from timber buildings to plates and bowls. Although relatively few wooden articles survive, they can provide evidence of the methods used in their manufacture, and this information can be supplemented by the evidence of the tools used in woodworking. The term woodworking covers a number of processes:

Gathering the Raw Material

This might only involve breaking or cutting a suitable branch from a tree, although it generally involved the **felling** (cutting down) of one or more trees, which was usually done with an axe. The felled tree was **headed (thinned out)** by having all its branches cut off to leave the main trunk (the **butt** or **stick**). Any branches that were big enough could be used in addition to the trunk. The trunk could be used without further preparation, or else **barked** (the bark removed). It could then be used in buildings or to make items such as logboats. For building it might be roughly squared up **(faced)** with an axe or adze before it was used. If it was to be used for other purposes it would probably be seasoned first. **Seasoning** was the drying out of the wood, and was done gradually so that it did not crack. In order to speed up the seasoning process, timber was often split or sawn longitudinally, and stacked to allow a good circulation of air around the wood.

Shaping

Some woods can be split horizontally. This is known as **cleaving** and was usually done by driving a series of wedges into the timber. Rough trimming **(hewing)** was usually done with an axe or an adze; often no other trimming was done for timber used in building. To produce planks an adze was used, but for other trimming either an axe or an adze could be used. Sometimes fire was used to hollow out part of a tree-trunk during the making of such things as logboats and tree-trunk coffins. Since the charred wood was usually cut away during further shaping of the boat or coffin, evidence of the use of fire for this purpose is very rare.

The faces of a piece of timber could be smoothed by shaving, and a number of tools could be used for this purpose. The simplest tool was the **draw-knife (draw-shave)** consisting of a knife blade with a handle at both ends. A more sophisticated shaving tool was the **plane** which consisted of a chisel-like blade set at an angle in a slot in a wooden body called a **stock**. There are a great variety of types of plane, the main ones being the **jack plane** which was used for initial rough smoothing, a **smoothing plane** which produced a relatively level surface, and a **trying plane (trueing plane)** used for the final levelling. Other planes might be used for special purposes including various forms of **moulding plane**. These had the edge of the blade specially shaped to cut mouldings.

The cutting of timber would usually be done with saws. Some saws had no set to their teeth (that is, the teeth were in the same plane as the rest of the saw blade), while **cross-cut saws** had a set: alternate teeth were bent outwards to one side, while the rest of the teeth were bent outwards to the other side. This cut a wider slot and made the saw easier to use. The blades of saws tended to buckle in use, and to prevent this they were usually held under tension either by being attached to a bow **(bow saw)** or by being set in a frame **(frame saw)**.

For making holes in wood the simplest form of tool was an **awl**, only capable of making small holes. An **auger** had a cutter (often spoon-shaped) at one end, and a cross-handle at the other by which the cutter could be made to turn and thus cut a hole in the wood. A particular form of auger known from the Medieval period is the **breast auger** which had an extension beyond the cross-handle on which the carpenter could lean to give extra pressure. Various forms of bow drill and pump drill could also be used (see flint and stone-working), while in the Medieval period the **brace** was used; this was a cranked shaft into which a selection of variously shaped interchangeable cutting **bits** (often similar to the cutting end of an auger) could be fitted. Other general purpose tools used in shaping wood were various types of knives, chisels and gouges, while from at least the Roman period onwards a **rule** was used for measuring (see Table 5).

It is likely that a form of lathe was in use in Britain as early as the Bronze Age. The simplest form was the **pole lathe** which was driven using the same principle as the bow drill: a cord or thong was tied to a flexible pole, passed around one of the spindles (the **drive mandrel**) and fixed to a pedal, so that pressure on the pedal made the drive

Table 5

Some basic tools probably used in Britain at various periods, represented by X in Period Column

Tool	Mesolithic	Neolithic	Bronze Age	Iron Age	Roman	Saxon	Medieval
Axe	X	X	X	X	X	X	X
Adze	X	X	X	X	X	X	X
Knife	X	X	X	X	X	X	X
Awl	X	X	X	X	X	X	X
Bow drill	X	X	X	X	X	X	X
Chisel		X	X	X	X	X	X
Cross-cut saw			X	X	X	X	X
Auger			X	X	X	X	X
Draw-knife				X	X	X	X
Rule					X	X	X
Smoothing plane					X	X	X
Jack plane					X	X	X
Moulding plane					X	X	X
Breast auger							X
Brace							X
Trying plane							X

mandrel rotate, while the flexibility of the pole returned the pedal to its original position once it was released. By repeated pressing of the pedal, discontinuous rotation of the drive mandrel could be achieved. The piece of wood to be turned was fixed between the end of the drive mandrel and the end of another free-running mandrel. Another method of driving a lathe was the **double pedal drive**, which was similar to the drive on a pole lathe, but instead of one end of the cord being fixed to a pole, it was fixed to another pedal. Alternate pressure on both pedals caused a reciprocal rotation of the drive mandrel.

Joining

The simplest method of joining pieces of wood is by **lashing** them together with thongs or ropes. Planks of wood could be **sewn** together by passing ropes or thongs through holes drilled in each plank. Simple interlocking joints such as the mortise-and-tenon joint were in use at least as early as the Bronze Age, and such joints were held together by wooden **pegs (dowels)** which were driven into holes in the wood. **Treenails (trenails)** were used in a similar way: these were tapering wooden pegs made

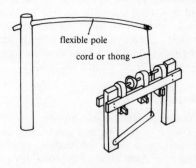

flexible pole

cord or thong

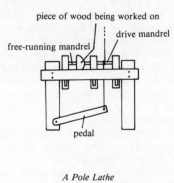

piece of wood being worked on

drive mandrel

free-running mandrel

pedal

A Pole Lathe

0   1m

by splitting rather than sawing a piece of wood. This made the resulting peg stronger and less liable to break. **Wrought iron nails** were introduced in the Iron Age.

A very specialised use of wood was the making of basketwork and wickerwork. This probably dates back to at least the Neolithic period, but very few examples of basketwork or wickerwork have survived from any period.

Reading for Woodworking: Coles, J. M. et al 1978; Goodman, W. L. 1964; Hodges, H. 1964.

Bone Working

Implements made from bone, and similar materials such as antler, horn and ivory, were shaped by cutting and abrasion. In later periods metal tools were used for this purpose, but before metal tools were known, flint and stone tools were used. Bone is difficult to carve with flint tools, although antler is more easily worked, and so a combination of flaking, gouging, sawing, splitting, scraping and abrading with stone was often used to shape these implements.

One technique used for making bone and antler artifacts (mainly during the Palaeolithic, Mesolithic and Neolithic periods) was the **groove-and-splinter technique**. This was the practice of using a flint implement to cut deep parallel grooves along the bone or antler through the hard outer wall and into the softer interior. The splinters of bone formed between the parallel grooves could be prised off and shaped into needles, awls, points and so on. This technique was also used to manufacture antler combs.

Reading for Bone Working: Clark, J. G. D. 1952; Clark, J. G. D. and Thompson, M. W. 1953; Oakley, K. P. 1972; Semenov, S. A. 1964.

Flint and Stone Working

The Raw Material

The most suitable materials for making stone tools are tough, fine-grained rocks, the best being **flint** or **chert** although other rocks were often preferred for axes, mace-

heads and so on. Good quality flint and chert are hard, and capable of producing a very sharp edge; they can be flaked easily since they have no preferential lines of fracture. When suitable quality flint or chert was not available, other rocks (usually quartzitic or basaltic) were used; although more resilient than flint, such rocks are more difficult to work and do not produce such a sharp edge.

Before the Neolithic period suitable stone for making tools was obtained from river and beach gravels and rock outcrops, but from the Late Mesolithic period onwards mines were dug to obtain suitable flint and, in at least one case, stone (see flint mines and axe factories).

Flint

Flint fresh from the parent rock (usually chalk in Britain) is covered with a rough whitish outer skin **(cortex)**, traces of which can still be seen on some flint tools. When unweathered, flint tools retain their natural colour of glossy black, grey or brown, and thin pieces are translucent. Under certain conditions, chemicals in the soil or water can weather the surface of flint to form a porous skin **(patina)** which is often bluish or white, but can be yellowish-brown to red due to staining by iron compounds.

Some flint and stone tools which have lain on the bed of a river have a surface encrustation, usually whitish in colour. This is often found on implements dredged from the river Thames and is sometimes known as **Thames patina**, or **race**. Where the edges of an implement have been smoothed by friction with sand and gravel over a long period of time (usually in river gravels) the implement is said to have been **rolled**. This abrasion by natural agencies **(rolling)** occurs mainly on Palaeolithic flint artifacts.

Reading for Flint: British Museum 1968; Oakley, K. P. 1972.

Types of Flint Fracture

Mechanical Fracture In theory, when a piece of flint is struck on its surface, the blow knocks out a solid **cone of percussion** with its apex at the point where the blow was struck. In practice a perfect cone is rarely achieved and so the normal mechanical fracture of flint consists of the detachment of flakes by striking a side of the flint on an edge where the junction

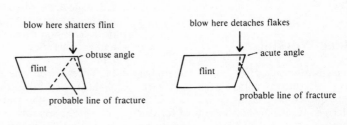

blow of exactly the right force delivered at the correct angle here should produce

— flint —

cone of percussion

Section through a Block of Flint before and after it is struck to produce a Cone of Percussion

0   10 cm

blow here shatters flint

obtuse angle

flint

probable line of fracture

blow here detaches flakes

acute angle

flint

probable line of fracture

Diagram to show some Fracturing Characteristics of Flint

0   50 cm

between two sides is an acute angle. As more flakes are detached, this angle approaches a right-angle, and a **critical angle** is reached, at which point further blows tend to smash the flint rather than detach flakes.

The parent block of flint from which flakes are struck is called the **core**. The edge on which the blow is struck to detach the flake is called the **striking platform (striking plane, flaking platform)**. The side of the detached flake which was part of the original surface of the core is known as the **dorsal surface**. The other side of the flake is known as the **ventral surface (main flake surface, positive flake surface, bulbar surface)**. On a mechanically struck flake the ventral surface displays some distinctive features, distinguishing it from flakes detached in other ways: just below the **point of percussion** (the point where the blow was struck), there is a swelling or bulb **(bulb of percussion)** which is a distorted segment of the complete cone of percussion. Below this, a **bulbar scar** sometimes occurs where a small chip of flint has been detached during the fracture. Below this **fissures** are often seen radiating from the point of percussion, and towards the bottom of the

flake there may be some concentric **ripples (conchoidal rings** or **waves)** radiating out from the point of percussion. Since these features tend to make the ventral surface of the flake resemble a mussel-shell, this type of fracture is known as a **conchoidal fracture**. All mechanically struck flakes should display at least two of these features; the bulb of percussion is almost always present.

On the core, the new surface (the **negative flake surface, flake bed, flake scar**) shows these features in reverse. The hollow left by the bulb of percussion is called the **negative bulb of percussion (bulb pit)**. A blow struck with a striker of resilient material (for example, bone) will often produce less pronounced features than a blow of equal force struck with less resilient material (eg stone). If the blow is too weak, or is struck at a bad angle, the flake may be detached by a **hinge fracture** which produces a short flake with a distinct thick rounded bottom edge that has the appearance of a thickened ripple. This is known as **step-flaking (resolved flaking)**.

Mechanical flaking is not always the product of intentional working by man. Flakes can be produced by other actions,

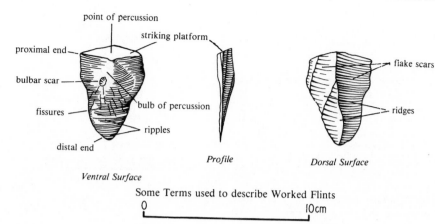

point of percussion

striking platform

proximal end

flake scars

bulbar scar

ridges

fissures

bulb of percussion

ripples

distal end

Profile

Dorsal Surface

Ventral Surface

Some Terms used to describe Worked Flints

0   10cm

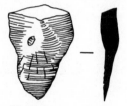

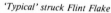

'*Typical' struck Flint Flake*

thickening characteristic of a hinge fracture

Flint Flake with Hinge Fracture

Comparison between a 'typical' struck Flint Flake and one with a Hinge Fracture

0   10cm

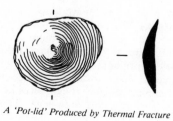

A 'Pot-lid' Produced by Thermal Fracture

Surface of a Flint showing Frost-pitting

Surface of a Flint produced by Starch Fracture

0   10cm

259

for example ploughs, waves and river action. These flakes can only be distinguished from ones intentionally struck by man through experience of handling and working flints.

Other Types of Fracture There are other causes of flint fracture which can easily be distinguished from mechanical flaking. **Thermal fractures** are the most common natural fractures, and are caused by changes in temperature — usually alternate freezing and thawing. Three main freaks of thermal fracture are commonly mistaken for flints worked by man:

Pot-lid fracture results in a flake that resembles a struck flake, and may even have shallow ripples.

Frost-pitting can sometimes produce flints that appear to have been fashioned into tools.

Starch fracture is a columnar fracture of the flint that produces flints superficially resembling blades and blade cores.

All these thermal fractures can be distinguished from mechanical fractures because they lack the features associated with conchoidal fracture.

Reading for Types of Flint Fracture: British Museum 1968; Hodges, H. 1964; Oakley, K. P. 1972; Wymer, J. J. 1968.

Methods of Flaking

The manufacture of implements from flint is known as **flint knapping** and the person who does it a **knapper (flint knapper)**. **Flaking** is the detaching of flakes of various sizes to shape an object. There are two methods of flaking: **percussion flaking** (striking a core or unfinished artifact) and **pressure flaking** (applying pressure to part of a core or unfinished artifact).

Percussion flaking can be divided into direct and indirect methods. In **direct percussion methods** the flint core can be held in the hand and struck with a suitable implement of stone, bone or wood. This is known as **hammer flaking (direct freehand flaking)** (see also bar hammer technique and hammer stones). The flint core can also be struck against another stone (**anvil stone**) which is known as **anvil flaking (block-on-block flaking, direct rest flaking)**.

In **indirect percussion methods** a punch, usually of bone or wood, is held against the flint core and struck. This is known as **punch flaking**.

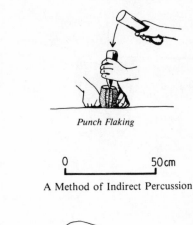

Punch Flaking

0   50 cm

A Method of Indirect Percussion

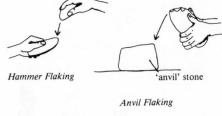

Hammer Flaking   'anvil' stone

Anvil Flaking

0   50 cm

Two Methods of Direct Percussion Flaking

Pressure flaking can be done either by holding the flint core in one hand and applying pressure on it with a suitable tool **(freehand pressure flaking)**, or by resting the core on the ground and applying pressure with a tool so constructed that the flint knapper can apply the weight of his chest or shoulder against the end of the tool. This is called **rest pressure flaking (impulsive pressure flaking)**.

The breaking up of a block of flint into suitably sized pieces for working is known as **quartering**. The initial shaping of a piece of flint into an approximation of the required shape is called **primary flaking (primary working)**, and the resulting approximate shape is called a **rough-out**. The trimming of the rough-out into a finished tool is called **secondary flaking (secondary working, retouch)**. In its crudest form, secondary flaking consists of the rough trimming of the edge of a tool to produce a mass of flake scars. Fine secondary flaking is often done by pressure flaking methods and several terms are used to describe it: **feather-edge flaking, fish** scale flaking, ripple flaking, shallow flaking and **free flaking**. A tool is said to have **invasive retouch** if secondary flaking has removed all evidence of primary flaking; if flakes have been removed in sequence the tool is said to have **serial flaking (fluted flaking)**. Retouch is described as **inverse** when blows are stuck on the dorsal surface in order to detach flakes from the ventral surface. **Collateral flaking** is where flakes have been detached from opposite edges of a tool so that the flake scars form a rib. The term **transverse flaking** is used where the flake scars run right across the width of the tool. **Channel flaking** describes one or more flake scars running right along the length of the tool. The term **oblique flaking** indicates that the flake scars run across the face of the tool at an angle to the edge. Tools with secondary working on one face only are said to have **unifacial flaking**; tools with secondary working on both faces have **bifacial flaking** and are sometimes known as **bifaces**.

Core tools are made by detaching flakes from a core of flint, and **flake tools** are made by detaching smaller flakes from a flint flake. **Blades** are long, narrow flakes, the edges of which are roughly parallel; they are usually **single-ridged** or **double-ridged** according to the number of ridges between previous flaking surfaces which are visible on the dorsal surface of the blade. Near the striking platform these ridges often become very pronounced and are sometimes called **spurs**. These are often trimmed off the core before fresh blades are struck and the new blades would then display **spur-trimming scars**.

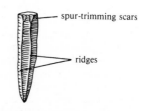

Blade with Spur-trimming Scars

As well as being fashioned into tools, cores may be trimmed in order to detach flakes more easily. These are known as **prepared cores**, a special case of the prepared core being the **blade core**. As blades are struck off the core, the angle between the striking platform and the sides of the core approaches a right-angle and prevents further blades from being detached. If the core is still sufficiently large, a flake can be struck off one end of the core at an angle, to provide a new striking platform from which blades can be struck. This is called **core rejuvenation** and the characteristic flake that is struck off the core is known as the **core rejuvenation flake (core tablet)**.

For grinding and polishing see stone working. See also Palaeolithic, Mesolithic, Neolithic and Bronze Age flintwork.

Reading for Methods of Flaking: Bordaz, J. 1970; Bordes, F. 1968; Hodges, H. 1964; Oakley, K. P. 1972.

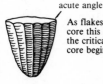

acute angle

As flakes are struck off the core this angle approaches the critical angle and the core begins to look like this

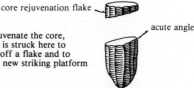

core rejuvenation flake

acute angle

To rejuvenate the core, a blow is struck here to knock off a flake and to form a new striking platform

Further flakes can now be struck from this side of the core

Core Rejuvenation

261

Stone

For most fine-grained rocks, percussion flaking was used to shape tools. Greater force was needed to detach flakes from stone than from flint, and there was no conchoidal fracture. Some rocks, however, were so tough that they could not be flaked and so were shaped by pounding with stone hammers which resulted in implements with a pitted (**pecked**) surface.

Because of the difficulties of shaping rocks other than flint and chert, the former were used mainly for large core tools such as axes and adzes. Because other stones do not have such a sharp natural edge as flint and chert, most stone tools have a ground, and sometimes a polished edge: most Neolithic stone axes and many flint axes are completely ground to shape, and many flint tools also have ground or polished edges.

Grinding could be done by rubbing the rough-out tool on a block of suitable stone (usually a sandstone); such stones, with the marks of grinding on them are sometimes called **polissoirs**. Polishing was probably done by rubbing the tool with a tough, flexible material (such as leather) impregnated with sand. Water was probably used as a lubricant in both grinding and polishing.

Perforations in stone implements were made by drilling, probably using a **bow drill** or a **pump drill**. The drill was probably made of wood or bone and may have been tipped with flint, or may merely have used sand as an abrasive. If the tip of the drill was solid, it would wear away during drilling and therefore the hole would tend to become narrower, forming a tapering perforation. By drilling through from the

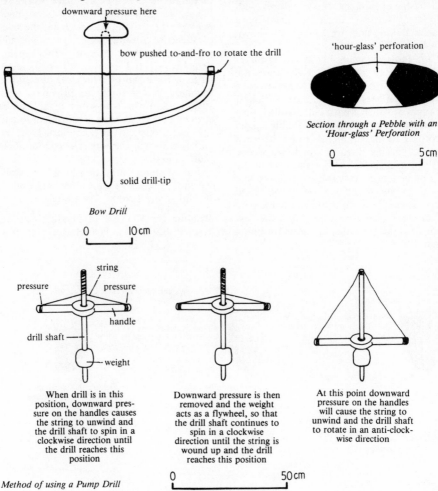

downward pressure here

bow pushed to-and-fro to rotate the drill

solid drill-tip

Bow Drill

0   10 cm

'hour-glass' perforation

Section through a Pebble with an 'Hour-glass' Perforation

0   5 cm

string

pressure   pressure

handle

drill shaft

weight

When drill is in this position, downward pressure on the handles causes the string to unwind and the drill shaft to spin in a clockwise direction until the drill reaches this position

Downward pressure is then removed and the weight acts as a flywheel, so that the drill shaft continues to spin in a clockwise direction until the string is wound up and the drill reaches this position

At this point downward pressure on the handles will cause the string to unwind and the drill shaft to rotate in an anti-clockwise direction

Method of using a Pump Drill

0   50 cm

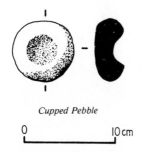

Cupped Pebble

0   10 cm

opposite side with a new drill, an **hour-glass perforation** was formed. If a hollow drill was used, the perforation should be cylindrical **(shafthole perforation)**. In later periods a hollow drill-tip of metal was probably used. Both types of drill may have had a weight attached: this is more likely on the pump drill where such a weight would have acted as a flywheel. Pebbles are sometimes found with a hollow on one or both sides **(cupped pebbles)** which resemble unfinished perforations, but these may have been used to apply downward pressure to bow drills.

Reading for Stone: British Museum 1968; Hodges, H. 1964; Oakley, K. P. 1972.

Working Floors

The place where a great deal of flint knapping has been done is known as a **working floor (chipping floor)**. This can often be identified by the many **waste fragments** of flint or stone **(débitage)**, which were not made into tools, and by broken or spoiled, unfinished tools. In making a flint implement as much as 90 per cent of the original block of flint may be wasted (although waste flakes can often be made into tools), and so a large amount of débitage is found on working floors.

Reading for Working Floors: Bordaz, J. 1970; Bordes, F. 1968; Wymer, J. J. 1968.

Some Specific Tools and Techniques

Notches on flakes and blades were sometimes used to hold a cord in place when the implement was lashed to a shaft. Blades and flakes with several notches along their edges are termed **denticulated** and may have been used for sawing. Notching was also an essential part of the **microburin technique** by which a blade was notched to weaken it and then snapped in two to form a microlith and a waste fragment (called a **microburin** because of its similarity to the tools known as burins or gravers). Microburins were produced during the manufacture of several types of microlith. **Backed blades (battered-back blades)** have one edge blunted by removing flakes nearly at right-angles to the face of the blade.

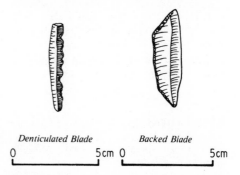

Denticulated Blade   Backed Blade

0   5 cm   0   5 cm

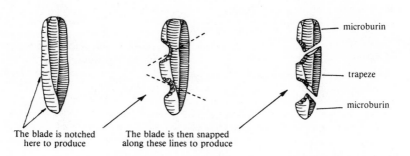

The blade is notched here to produce   The blade is then snapped along these lines to produce

— microburin

— trapeze

— microburin

Diagram to illustrate how Microburins were produced (in this case, as a by-product in the manufacture of a trapeze)

0   5 cm

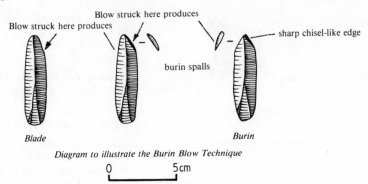

Blow struck here produces

Blow struck here produces

sharp chisel-like edge

burin spalls

Blade

Burin

Diagram to illustrate the Burin Blow Technique

0   5 cm

These blades may have been used as knives.

Burins (gravers) were made using the **burin blow technique** by which a blow (or blows) was struck on a blade (often prepared by preliminary retouching) to detach a narrow flake or flakes, called **burin spalls**, to form a sharp chisel-like edge. There are many types of burin and they are named according to their shape and the type of blade from which they were made. Burins were probably used for working bone and antler. The burin blow technique may also have been a means of resharpening awls. See also Palaeolithic, Mesolithic, Neolithic and Bronze Age flintwork.

Reading for Specific Tools and Techniques: Bordaz, J. 1970; Tixier, J. 1974.

Metalworking

The use of metals developed from the Bronze Age onwards; by the end of the Medieval period the main metals being used were iron, copper, lead, tin, silver and gold, and the main alloys were bronze, brass, latten, pewter, electrum and speculum.

Bronze

Copper ores were collected from surface outcrops or were mined; they were smelted in shaft or bowl furnaces to obtain molten copper which was formed into ingots. The ingots were then melted in crucibles (usually of clay), the dross was skimmed off the top, and the copper was stirred with green wooden sticks **(poled)** so that impurities did not make the copper too brittle. Tin was prepared in a similar way.

Copper is a very soft metal; the addition of tin to form **bronze** hardens the metal, while the addition of lead to bronze to form **lead bronze** makes it easier to cast. Some bronze has a small amount of antimony **(antimonial bronze),** and some bronze has a small amount of arsenic **(arsenical bronze).** Both these elements make bronze harder, but it is not known to what extent their inclusion in the bronze was accidental. **Brass** is an alloy of copper and zinc.

Bronze could be cast in moulds, molten bronze being poured into a mould to produce a solid object. **Open moulds (single valve moulds)** were simple moulds of clay or stone. More complicated solid objects could be made in **piece moulds (composite moulds)** which were frequently **two-piece moulds (bivalve moulds)** made of stone or bronze. Sometimes moulds were pierced with small channels **(air jets, vents)** to allow gases trapped in the mould by the molten metal to escape. These channels usually filled with the metal to form protrusions known as **casting jets.** Molten metal also tended to seep through the joins between the pieces of the mould; the protrusions of metal caused by this are known as **casting seams (casting flashes).** Casting jets, casting seams and any other extraneous metal joined to the casting were usually cut away during the finishing of the artifact after it had been removed from the mould. Piece moulds could also be used to produce simple hollow castings, such as implements with sockets; a core of clay, or clay and sand was suspended or held in place with pins inside the mould and was removed after casting.

Small solid objects could be cast by the **lost wax method (lost wax casting, cire perdue).** A wax model was made which was

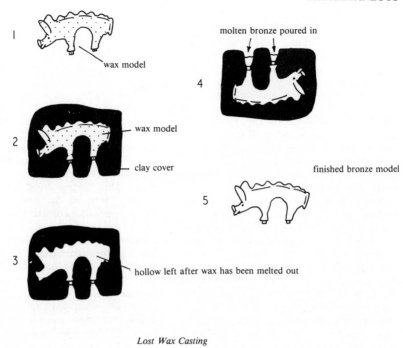

1 — wax model

2 — wax model / clay cover

3 — hollow left after wax has been melted out

4 — molten bronze poured in

5 — finished bronze model

Lost Wax Casting

0   10 cm

then covered in clay. The wax was melted out and molten bronze poured into the resulting hollow. After the metal had solidified, the outer clay cover was removed. Larger objects were made by **core casting (hollow casting)**. A rough shape of the object was made in clay and a wax model was then shaped round this which in turn was covered with clay and the wax melted out. The core was held in place by rods of bronze **(chaplets)**. Molten bronze was poured into the gap, resulting in a hollow object being made. The clay core was not always removed and so it can be difficult to distinguish these objects from solid objects made by lost wax casting. An alternative method of hollow casting was to model a figure in clay and then build up a piece mould around it in clay. This was cut off in pieces and the original model shaved down in size. The outer mould was reassembled around the model and molten bronze was poured into the resulting gap to form the casting.

Copper and its alloys can be shaped relatively easily by hammering **(cold working)**, but too much hammering alters the crystalline structure of the metal, making it harder and more brittle. To counteract this the metal is gently heated to a dull red heat and then allowed to cool. This process, which alters the structure of the metal, making it soft again, is called **annealing**. The heated metal could be cooled quickly by dipping it in cold water **(quenching)**. Vessels could be formed by hammering sheet metal against a concave mould **(sinking)** or a convex mould **(raising)**. Vessels could also be made by pressing sheet metal around a mould which was being rotated on a lathe; this is known as **spinning**. **Turning** is the process of rotating a cast vessel in a lathe and using sharp tools to remove irregularities from the surface of the vessel. Rings could be made by casting the rough shape of the ring and then hammering it against a tapering rod **(mandrel, mandril)** passed through the centre of the ring.

Objects, particularly vessels, were often finished off by being lightly hammered over the surface to remove any remaining irregularities **(planishing)** and then being polished with a fine abrasive. It is probable that edged tools and weapons were hammered to give them a hard cutting edge.

265

Molten bronze can be fused with bronze, and so additions to objects (such as handles on a vessel) could be joined by this method, known as **casting-on (running-on, burning-on)**. Pieces of bronze could also be joined together by soldering, but the most common method of joining pieces of bronze was by **riveting**. The rivets were short metal rods passed through corresponding holes in the pieces of bronze to be joined. The heads of the rivets might be cast, or else formed as the rivets were hammered down with specially shaped punch-like tools called **snaps**.

Apart from casting patterns in the surface of the bronze by the use of patterned moulds, bronze objects could be decorated by various methods of cold working and by the addition of other materials. Thin bronze could be decorated with designs raised in relief by hammering the back of the bronze with round-ended punches **(bossing tools)**; this method of decoration is known as **repoussé work**. The edges of the raised areas were often sharpened by outlining them with a **tracer** — a punch that produced a short indented line when struck. The tracer could also be used for other line decoration. Any design used to decorate bronze would usually be sketched in lightly first with scratches made by a hard pointed tool called a **scriber**. Stamps and punches could be used to impress designs on the surface of the metal; **pointillé** is a dotted decoration done with a small pointed punch. **Chasing** strictly only describes the parts of repoussé work done on the outer surface, but is often used loosely to describe any hammer and punch decoration.

Decoration which is formed by removing metal from the surface is termed **engraving** and is done with chisel-like tools called **gravers** and **scorpers** (the blade of a scorper is usually wider than that of a graver). These tools must be harder than the metal on which they are used: steel tools are usually used on bronze.

Bronze may be decorated by the application of other metals to its surface. In **overlay** work the surface of the bronze was raised into a series of sharp points by stabbing: the metal to be overlayed was then hammered onto these points. In **inlay** work, the decorative metal was hammered or melted into recesses in the bronze. Bronze objects could also be given a surface coating of metal so long as the melting point of that metal was lower than the melting point of bronze. This was known as **flashing (flushing)**.

Iron

In antiquity iron ore was mainly obtained through open-cast mining. The ore was cleaned to remove soil and rock particles, was washed and crushed, and then smelted in a furnace to obtain iron. **Bowl furnaces** and **shaft furnaces** were most commonly used. The simpler type was the bowl furnace, used in the Iron Age and the Roman period; it consisted of a shallow pit which was probably covered with a clay dome, with a hollow clay cone **(tuyère)** on one side through which a draught from a bellows was introduced, and an opening in the top to allow gases to escape. Bowl furnaces could only produce small amounts of iron at a time. Shaft furnaces were introduced in the Roman period and were more advanced than bowl furnaces, using bellows or a natural draught, and were capable of producing greater quantities of iron at a time.

Smelting is the process of heating the iron ore to separate the non-metallic constituents **(gangue)** from the iron compounds. The main fuel used was charcoal. At about 1200°C the **dross (slag, waste)** becomes fluid leaving a spongy lump of iron mixed with the remaining slag. This slag was expelled by forging, leaving a lump of raw iron **(bloom)**, which could then be forged into tools. At first only **wrought iron** could be produced; this was made by forging and was low in carbon. Wrought iron could be converted into a form of steel by heating it above 900°C and keeping it covered with carbon so that some of the carbon could be absorbed by the iron. The result was a hard but brittle metal which could be softened by annealing if it was cooled slowly, but would become hard and brittle again if quenched after heating. By heating to various temperatures and cooling at different rates, metals of different hardness could be produced. These processes are known as **tempering**. From the later Medieval period **cast iron** could be produced since it became possible to reach the melting point of iron (1635°C), although cast iron was occasionally produced by accident in earlier periods in Britain.

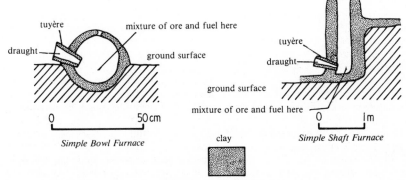

tuyère — mixture of ore and fuel here

draught — ground surface

tuyère

draught

ground surface

mixture of ore and fuel here

0 ___ 50 cm

0 ___ 1 m

clay

Simple Bowl Furnace

Simple Shaft Furnace

Sections through Furnaces

Iron cannot be shaped by cold working; it has to be heated until it is red hot before it can be hammered into shape **(forging)**. Because of this need to work iron while it is hot, **tongs** were necessary to grip the metal, and a hammer with a handle or haft was needed for hammering. Early anvils were probably blocks of stone. For cutting the iron, chisel-like tools called **sets (setts)** were used. These were used like chisels and were struck with a hammer. A **pritchell (pritchel)** was a hafted square-sectioned punch used for the initial punching of holes, which were finished off with a tapered rod of the required shape and size called a **drift**. Alternatively, in thin or soft iron, holes could be finished off with a **reamer** which was a tapered square-sectioned rod that was rotated in the hole.

Some tools were used in pairs; one part was fitted into a hole in the anvil and the other was hammered on top of it with the iron trapped in between. The main tools used in this way were fullers, flatters and swages. **Fullers** were like round-edged chisels and were used to make grooves or corrugations in the iron. **Flatters** were like stamps with flat faces and were used to smooth and flatten the surface of the metal. **Swages** were pairs of tools which had opposed semi-cylindrical faces which formed a cylindrical hole when placed together. They were used to reduce the diameter of cylindrical metal rods: different sets of swages were needed to produce rods with different size diameters.

Two pieces of iron can be **welded** by hammering them together while they are white hot; they can also be joined by rivets or by brazing. **Brazing** is a form of solder-ing using an alloy of copper and zinc called

brass spelter (hard solder) which is melted and fused with the pieces of iron to be joined. This did not produce a very strong joint but was useful for small and intricate jobs.

An iron object could be decorated by being inlaid or overlaid with various materials, or the surface of the object could be flashed with tin or brass spelter.

Gold

Gold was in use from the Bronze Age onwards. It was most commonly collected as a metal rather than as an ore, in the form of nuggets or gold dust which could be melted down in small crucibles. Gold usually occurs as an alloy with silver **(electrum),** or with copper, or both. The copper could be removed leaving electrum, and the silver could also be removed, but pure gold was too soft to work, and so an alloy of gold with copper or silver, or both, was preferable. The prepared gold could be beaten into a very thin **leaf (sheet)** without needing to anneal it. Much gold jewellery was formed by soldering fine gold wire to a base **(filigree),** or by soldering small granules of gold to a base **(granulation).** Surfaces of objects of various materials (such as metal and wood) could be covered in gold leaf **(leaf-gilding).** True **gilding** was the application of gold leaf to objects of copper or copper alloys so that the gold fused with the surface of the base metal, in much the same way that silvering was done.

Silver

Silver was rarely found in its native state but was usually obtained from the **cupella-**

267

tion of lead: when lead is heated in an ample supply of air it oxidises and the oxides are carried away in the furnace draught or absorbed by the immediate surroundings, particularly the crucible, to form **litharge** (mainly lead oxide), while the silver remains unoxidised. Pure silver was too soft for most purposes and so it was commonly alloyed with gold. It could be worked in a similar way to gold except that it had to be annealed after much hammering, and consequently silver leaf was rarely produced. Silver vessels could be made by hammering sheet silver into and around moulds. Silver could be inlaid with an alloy of copper and silver sulphide **(niello)** which produced a contrasting black pattern. **Silvering** is the coating of copper or bronze with silver so that the silver fuses with the surface of the bronze. Mercury was first rubbed onto the copper or bronze to form an amalgam, a silver amalgam (silver and mercury) was added, and the object was then heated to remove the mercury.

Lead and Pewter

The ore **galena** was the principal source of lead. It could be smelted and formed into ingots **(lead pigs)** or the silver could be first extracted by cupellation and the lead recovered by smelting the litharge. Lead was often worked unalloyed since its softness could be useful. It could be added to copper to form bronze, and to tin to form pewter. (See also glazes.)

Pewter was an alloy of lead and tin and was used particularly for tableware from the Roman period onwards. Pewter objects were usually cast in stone moulds.

Reading for Metalworking: Cleere, H. 1976; Hodges, H. 1964; Tylecote, R. F. 1962; Tylecote, R. F. 1976.

Enamel

Enamel is a vitreous material of various colours fused to a metallic surface as a means of decoration, and is usually flush with the surface of the metal. To achieve this, areas of the metal are cut out (or the metal objects cast with hollows) which are filled with glass powder and then heated so that the glass powder fuses to produce enamel. This was the most common type of

enamelling and is termed **champlevé (en taille d'épargne)**. An alternative method was to build up **cells (cloisons)** by soldering thin strips of metal (usually gold) onto a metallic surface; these cells were then filled with glass powder to form enamel. This technique is called **cloisonné enamel (cell enamel)**. Enamel can also be formed without a metal backing by providing a temporary backing during manufacture. This is termed **enamel in openwork (émaillerie à jour)**. **Émaux de basse taille (translucent enamels on sunk relief)** is a coating of translucent enamel spread over a metal backing cut in relief; this gives the appearance of areas of light and dark. **Painted enamel** is enamel spread thinly over metal articles, such as vessels, to produce elaborate pictures.

Reading for Enamel: British Museum 1924, 73–95; Hodges, H. 1964.

Glass

Constituents of Glass

Glass can be described as a downgraded silica. Pure fused silica is the ideal glass but this is difficult to make even with modern furnaces since it requires a melting temperature of around 2000°C. Since such a high temperature could not be obtained in ancient furnaces, an alkaline **flux** was added. The addition of a flux drastically reduces the durability of the glass and to counteract this a **stabiliser** (usually limestone) was also added. With the right proportions of additives, a reasonably durable glass with a relatively low melting point could be made. The **silica** (the glass **former**) was usually obtained from sand, flint or quartz. The flux was either **soda** obtained from **natron (nitrum)** which is a natural form of soda found in Egypt, or from the ashes of certain seaweeds, or else **potash** obtained from wood-ash (usually beech). Glass is sometimes classified as either a **soda-lime glass** or a **potash-lime glass (forest glass, Waldglas)**, depending on the combination of stabilisers and fluxes. All early glasses are soda-lime glasses, but during the Saxon and Medieval periods most of the glass in Britain is potash-lime glass.

Colourants and **de-colourants** The

impurities in the ingredients of ancient glass tended to colour it; blue-green caused by the presence of iron being the most common. To counteract the effects of such impurities and make the glass appear colourless, de-colourants could be added, the two most common being **manganese** and **antimony**. To produce coloured glass, various colourants could be added. The most common additives in antiquity were copper producing dark blue, dark green, ruby red or opaque red glass (depending on the conditions in the furnace), cobalt giving a deep blue glass, manganese a yellow or purple glass, antimony an opaque yellow and iron a pale blue, green or amber glass. The addition of colourants was not well understood or controlled. Substances were probably added without any understanding of their chemical properties.

It was also usual to add a quantity of scrap glass **(cullet)** to the **batch** (the amount of glass being made at one time). The addition of cullet lowered the temperature at which the batch fused together and provided a nucleus of relatively pure glass around which the new glass could form.

Reading for Constituents of Glass: Douglas, R. W. and Frank, S. 1972; Hurst Vose, R. 1980; Price, J. 1976.

Glassworking

There are four main categories of glassworking. In order of ascending skill required these are sintering, glass shaping, glass melting and glass making.

Sintering is the heating of silica until it coheres in a glass-like mass (such as faience), but is not fused into a proper glass. The individual grains of sand from which it is formed can be seen clearly under a microscope.

In **glass shaping** the glass was not fully melted, but was heated until it was soft enough to be pressed into the desired shape. **Glass melting** was the remelting and working of glass that had already been made from the raw ingredients and then allowed to solidify. Both glass shaping and glass melting could be done without the skill needed to make glass from the raw ingredients, using glass bought from glass makers.

Glass making was the actual fusing together of the raw materials to form glass. Before being heated to a high temperature in the furnace, the raw ingredients were first heated to a lower temperature, either in a special firing of the main furnace or in a **fritting oven (fritting furnace)**, to burn off some of the impurities. The process is known as **fritting**, and the resultant material as **frit**. The frit was then broken up, placed in a crucible, and heated as rapidly as possible to beyond the melting point in the **main furnace (founding furnace)**. This operation is **glass founding**. Before the glass was used, the temperature was allowed to drop to the temperature needed to work the glass, and impurities were skimmed off with a long-handled rake. Molten glass is sometimes termed **glass-metal**.

After the glass products were made, they were allowed to cool very slowly **(anneal)** in an **annealing oven (lehr, leer, lear)** to prevent the glass being shattered by stresses caused by the surface of the glass cooling more rapidly than the interior. The annealing oven may have been built against or on top of the main furnace. If cylinder window glass was being made, there may have been a separate **opening lehr** in which the cylinder could be allowed to uncurl on a flat surface and anneal.

Furnaces were nearly always wood-fired, although charcoal may have been used in some instances. Bellows were used, but the glass makers were usually still dependent on the prevailing wind to produce a draught in order to create a sufficiently high temperature. The **pots (crucibles)** were made of fireclay; their size and shape varied according to the period and the quantity of glass they were intended to hold. Roman pots could be quite large (one from *Silchester*, Hampshire, had a base diameter of 18cm and was probably about 30cm tall). Little is known of Saxon pots in Britain, but some Medieval ones seem to have been bucket or barrel-shaped and as big or bigger than Roman ones. The pots would usually be made at the glassworking site and fired in the main furnace; when in use the pots stood on a platform or bank within the furnace called a **siege**. Apart from flues and stokeholes, the furnace would have a number of **access holes (glory holes)** to allow access for collecting glass out of the pots and reheating the vessels while they were being worked on.

Evidence for Glassworking Furnaces

Glass beads must have been made in Britain during the Iron Age, although no glass-working sites of this date have been found. There is some slight evidence for glass-working in the Roman period. Cullet has been found at *Colchester*, Essex, and *Wroxeter*, Shropshire, crucible fragments at *Silchester*, Hampshire, and probable furnaces at *Caistor St Edmund*, Norfolk, *Wilderspool*, Cheshire, *Mancetter*, Warwickshire, and *Stocton Heath*, Lancashire. No site in any part of the Roman Empire has yet yielded sufficient evidence about a Roman glass furnace.

In the Saxon period evidence for glass-working is extremely rare. In the Medieval period it is also slight although documentary sources show that glassworking was carried out. A few glassworking sites are known, although the archaeological evidence has so far given little information about the furnaces. The only Medieval furnace about which there is adequate information is that at *Blunden's Wood*, Surrey, which has been dated to the second quarter of the fourteenth century. Here the main furnace was capable of heating four pots, each approximately 30cm high and 30cm in diameter. Adjacent to the furnace were two subsidiary furnaces; one probably served both as a fritting oven and an annealing oven, and the other was probably used for preheating the pots.

Reading for Glassworking: Douglas, R. W. and Frank, S. 1972; Hurst Vose, R. 1980; Price, J. 1976.

Glassworking Tools

Virtually no evidence of early glassworking tools has survived in Britain. Some were made of wood, others were of metal and would be difficult to recognise if fragments of them did survive. Few early glass-making sites have been identified in Britain. However, the basic methods of glassworking did not undergo radical change until the nineteenth century, and so it is reasonable to assume that the basic tools used in comparatively recent times were not much different from those used in earlier periods:

The **blowpipe** was an iron tube, usually with a slight thickening at the **gathering end** to facilitate the collection of the molten glass. They were usually about 1·2m long;

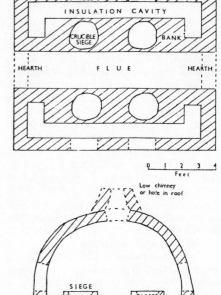

Reconstruction Plan and Section of Kiln A, Blunden's Wood, Surrey

the actual length depended on the height of the glassblower. The **punty iron (punty rod, pontil, puntee)** was a solid rod of iron about 1m long used to hold glass vessels (usually at the base) while being worked on. This left a characteristic thickening of glass on the base of the vessel called a **pontil scar (pontil mark)**. The **marver (marver block)** was a block of fine-grained stone with a smooth flat surface. The gob of glass was rolled on the marver (**marvered**) to shape it and to cool it sufficiently for it to be blown without distorting. **Shears** were used to trim the vessels while the glass was still malleable. **Pincers (pucellas)** were used to pull out blobs from the body of the vessel to produce raised decorative hollow knobs (**prunts**). A special form of pincers (**grozing iron**) was sometimes used for nipping off unwanted pieces from the edges of window glass after the glass had cooled. This technique was known as **grozing**. Long-handled **rakes** were used to skim off impurities floating on top of the molten glass in the furnace. **Moulds** were probably made of clay or wood. Wood was also used for various **shaping tools** that were held against the glass vessel as it was rotated on the end of the punty iron. Other shaping tools were made of iron. One resembled a pair of dividers, and another resembled sugar-tongs, with long blades instead of spoons. A **wooden fork** was used to carry finished vessels to the annealing oven.

Reading for Glassworking Tools: Douglas, R. W. and Frank, S. 1972; Harden, D. B. 1971; Hurst Vose, R. 1980; Kenyon, G. H. 1967; Price, J. 1976.

Manufacture of Glass Vessels

One of the earliest techniques of making glass vessels was that of building up molten glass on a **core**. A core (probably of clay and not of sand as once thought) was moulded around a metal rod. This core was then either dipped into molten glass (**core-dipping**), or had molten glass wound around it (**core-winding**). The outside of the vessel was marvered smooth and decoration and attachments such as handles could be added. When the vessel was cool the metal rod was removed and the clay core dug out.

Another early technique was that of building a vessel in a mould with sections of glass rods. Glass rods (**glass canes**) were produced either by pouring molten glass very slowly from a crucible which solidified into short lengths of glass rod, or more commonly by attaching a gather of glass to an iron post or an iron hook in a wall, and stretching out part of it into a rod by pulling part of the gather away on the end of a punty iron. The vessel was built up in a mould from sections cut from these glass canes, often using different coloured canes. The mould and glass were then heated until the glass sections fused together to form the vessel. When the vessel was removed from the mould it was polished on the outside and, where possible, on the inside surface as well.

A third early technique of vessel manufacture was that of **cold-cutting**. The vessel was shaped by cutting and grinding a solid block of glass using hard stones such as quartz or flint. Although it was possible to make vessels entirely by this method, it is likely that such vessels were cast to the approximate form and then finished off by cutting and grinding.

Another technique of vessel manufacture was that of **casting**, used to make open vessels such as jars, bowls and saucers. Casting could be done by the cire perdue method (see bronze working), or by placing powdered glass in a closed mould and heating the mould until the glass fused. Another method of casting was to use an external mould and an internal **plunger mould**. Molten glass would be poured into the external mould and the plunger pushed down into the molten glass to form the interior of the vessel.

These four techniques were used to make glass vessels before the invention of glass-blowing. After glassblowing became the predominant method of glass-vessel manufacture, these techniques fell into disuse except for special vessels, such as mosaic vessels.

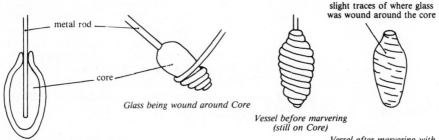

metal rod

core

Glass being wound around Core

Section through a Core-dipped Vessel before removal of metal rod and Core

slight traces of where glass was wound around the core

Vessel before marvering (still on Core)

Vessel after marvering with metal rod and Core removed

Core-Winding

0   10cm

Glassblowing was invented around 50 BC somewhere on the Syria-Palestine coast. By the time of the Roman invasion of Britain, glassblowing was common in the Roman world. Few glass vessels were imported into Britain before the Roman invasion, and so most ancient glass vessels found in Britain were made by glassblowing.

Molten glass will stick to hot iron and so iron tools used in glassworking had to be preheated; consequently an iron blowpipe had to be sufficiently long to prevent the glassblower being burned. To blow a vessel, the gathering end of the blowpipe was placed on the surface of the molten glass and twisted to collect a gather. The blow-pipe with the attached **gather (gob, paraison)** of glass was then lifted away from the pot, and continuously rotated to keep the gather attached to the end of the blow-pipe. This was then shaped by rolling it to-and-fro on a marver, and was expanded by the glassblower blowing down the blowpipe to form a bubble of glass. While not blowing down the blowpipe the glassblower had to keep his thumb over the end of the blowpipe to prevent the bubble from collapsing. One gather of glass might be enough for small vessels, but for larger ones the process of gathering, marvering and blowing might have to be repeated several times. For further shaping and decoration of the vessel, and for attaching handles and footrings and so on, the blown vessel was then attached to a punty iron with a small blob of molten glass **(pontil wad)**. The vessel was then **cracked off (knocked off)** the blowpipe by touching the vessel with a drop of cold water at the desired point to make it crack. The glass left on the blow-pipe (which is knocked off later) is some-times called the **welting-off ring**. This type of glassblowing is termed **free-blowing** or **blowing off-hand**. Vessels could also be made by blowing the gather into a mould to shape part or all of the vessel.

In more recent times glassblowing was carried out by a team of four men known as a **chair**. The master glassblower **(gaffer)** shaped the vessel while the blowpipe or punty was rolled back and forth on a chair with long parallel arms. Two assistants carried out further work such as attaching the footring. The fourth member (usually an apprentice) carried the finished vessels to the annealing oven. Such a team system was probably used from an early date; certainly many early vessels would require two or more craftsmen working on them at the same time.

Reading for Manufacture of Glass Vessels: Harden, D. B. 1968; Harden, D. B. 1969; Hodges, H. 1964; Hurst Vose, R. 1980; Price, J. 1976.

Techniques of Finishing Glass Vessels

Rims of vessels could be finished off in several ways: the rim could be cracked off and ground smooth when cold, or it could be rounded off by cutting with shears and heating in the furnace to form a **fire-rounded rim**. Alternatively the rim could be bent over to form a **flat rim** or a **tubular rim**. Sometimes the rim was cracked off and left rough as a **cracked-off rim**.

Bases could be formed by merely flattening the bottom of the vessel, or pushing it inwards to form a **concave base**, the concavity being known as the **kick**. A further development of the latter was to constrict the lower part of the vessel to form an **open base ring** or a **closed base ring**. Another method of making a base was to add a trail of glass to form a base ring (a **coil base**). A **pad base** was formed by adding another gather of blown glass to the base; this was then cracked off and the edges splayed out to form a ring on which the vessel stood. A true **base ring** was formed by adding a section of a cylinder of glass to the bottom of the vessel. Sometimes part of the vessel was pinched out to form a **cut-out ridge** or a **cut-out flange**. This method was also used to form a base ring, known as a **cut-out base**, of which the closed base ring is a particular form.

Section through Punty, Vessel and Blowpipe at the point when the Vessel has been attached to a Punty and is about to be cracked off from the Blowpipe

0   50cm

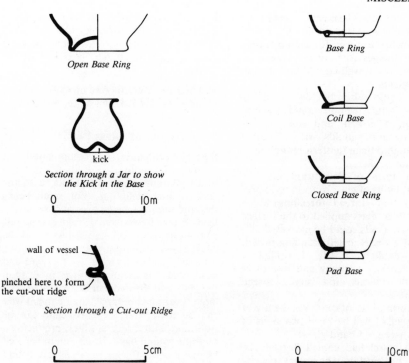

Open Base Ring

Section through a Jar to show the Kick in the Base

0   10m

wall of vessel

pinched here to form the cut-out ridge

Section through a Cut-out Ridge

0   5cm

Base Ring

Coil Base

Closed Base Ring

Pad Base

0   10cm

The body of a vessel could be **fire-polished** on the outside surface by reheating at the furnace until the outside surface was glossy. The interior of open vessels (and the exterior if desired) could be polished by using an abrasive wheel.

Handles were applied to the vessel from a separate gather of glass.

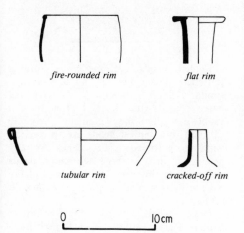

fire-rounded rim   flat rim

tubular rim   cracked-off rim

0   10cm

Some Types of Rim found on Glass Vessels

Reading for Techniques of Finishing Glass Vessels: Harden, D. B. 1969; Harden, D. B. 1971; Hurst Vose, R. 1980; Isings, C. 1957; Price, J. 1976.

Methods of Decorating Glass Vessels

There were several methods of decorating glass vessels; one was the use of different coloured glasses on the same vessel: **mosaic glass** vessels were made (in the early Roman period) from sections of different coloured glass canes which were placed in a mould and heated until they fused together, forming a multi-coloured vessel. **Millefiori** was a special type of mosaic glass, where the canes are arranged to look like stylised flowers. Different coloured glasses could also be used for decorative additions to the vessel; **self-coloured** describes additions which are of the same colour as the rest of the vessel.

Another form of decoration was the manipulation of the surface of the vessel; parts of the surface could be drawn out to form hollow projections called **prunts**. This type of decoration reached its peak with the elaborate prunts that gave claw beakers

273

their name (see claw beakers). Parts of the surface of the vessel could also be drawn out and pinched to form, for example, **fins**, **ridges** and **flanges** (see cut-out ridge), or parts of the vessel wall could be pushed in to form **indents**.

Vessels could also be decorated by blowing or casting them in moulds (such as pillar-moulded bowls), and some vessels were blown into moulds with elaborate patterns cut into them (**pattern-moulding** — see gladiator beakers).

Another form of decoration was the addition of **blobs** of glass to form solid projections, or **trails (thread, threading)** which were threads of glass applied to the surface of the vessel. Trails could be marvered into the wall of a vessel or left standing proud, when they could be further decorated by pinching, scoring, combing and so on (see pinched projections and snake thread decoration).

A rare form of decoration was the use of gold foil sandwiched between two skins of clear glass (see gold-band glass).

When a vessel had cooled it could be decorated by **cutting** which was usually done with an abrasive wheel. The decoration ranged from cutting a line below the rim of the vessel, to covering the surface of the vessel with close-set geometrical facets. **Engraving** was a surface technique which removed little of the glass and was usually employed on clear glass vessels to depict various types of scene. It was mainly done by an abrasive wheel, although some vessels were engraved with flint tools. A special use of cutting and engraving techniques was employed in the production of cameo glass (see cameo glass).

Glass vessels were also decorated by painting, although evidence of this rarely survives. See also Roman, Saxon and Medieval glass.

Reading for Methods of Decorating Glass Vessels: Harden, D. B. 1968; Harden, D. B. 1969; Harden, D. B. 1971; Hurst Vose, R. 1980; Isings, C. 1957; Price, J. 1976.

Manufacture of Glass Tubing

Glass tubing was made in a similar way to glass canes. A gob of glass was gathered on a blowpipe and blown and marvered into a short thick-walled cylinder. The end of this cylinder was attached to an iron post or iron hook on a wall and the cylinder was gradually stretched by the blowpipe being drawn away. To form the tube, the glass-blower blew gently into the blowpipe as he drew it away from the fixed end of the glass.

Reading for Manufacture of Glass Tubing: Hodges, H. 1964; Hurst Vose, R. 1980.

Manufacture of Glass Beads

Several techniques, or combinations of techniques, could be used to produce beads. **Wound beads** are produced by the core-winding technique. For small beads the core used is a metal wire about which a heat-softened glass cane is folded. The rest of the cane is cut off and the wire and the circle of glass are rotated and heated until a rounded bead is formed. As the wire and bead cool, the metal contracts more than the glass and the two can be separated. For larger beads a core larger than a metal wire can be used, and the glass cane can be wound around it several times, producing a **multiple wound bead**. Beads can be tapered by thinning out the glass cane as it is wound around the wire.

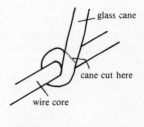

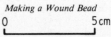

Making a Wound Bead

Folded beads are made by folding flattened glass canes around a wire in a similar fashion to wound beads. The long narrow beads thus formed often have a visible line where the two ends of the circle of glass join. **Spiral beads** are formed by winding softened glass canes spirally around a wire. **Tapered segmented beads** are made in this way, by thinning out the cane as it is wound to produce a tapered effect.

Drawn beads are made by working a gather of glass into a hollow funnel shape enclosing a bubble of air to form a hollow gob of glass. This is then **drawn** by fixing

Tapered Segmented Bead

0 _____ 1cm

one end of the gob and pulling the other, thus stretching the hollow gob into a hollow tube. This tube is then cut into sections to form beads. Bi-coloured beads can be made by this method by marvering the drawn-out tube and rolling it over molten glass of another colour and then cutting it into sections to form the beads. Bi-coloured beads can also be made by dipping the sections cut from the drawn tube into molten glass of a different colour. Instead of cutting the drawn tube, it can be pinched at the required intervals and broken into segments when cool.

Pressed beads are usually hexagonal, square or biconical, and are shaped by being pressed into moulds while still half-molten. **Blown beads** were made by blowing in the same way as vessels were blown. This type of bead is very rare in Britain. **Hand perforated beads** were formed by perforating drops of molten glass with a tool while the glass was still hot enough to be malleable. Such perforations were sometimes enlarged by filing.

scrabble	wave	eye motif
bands	chevrons	spirals
cable	rays	whirls
double swag	concentric rings	criss-cross or network

0 _____ 5cm

Some Patterns of Decoration found on Glass Beads

Decoration of Beads
Beads could be decorated by various patterns of different coloured glass being applied to the bead and either left standing proud, or more usually marvered into the surface of the bead while both the bead and the decorative glass were still hot. Some of the more common patterns of decoration are illustrated in the figure.

See also Iron Age, Roman and Saxon glass beads.

Reading for Manufacture of Glass Beads: Guido, C. M. 1978.

Manufacture of Window Glass

There were three main methods of making window glass, the earliest of which was casting. **Cast window glass** was made by pouring molten glass onto a flat surface, possibly an open wooden mould. When cold, one side of the glass was ground smooth; the resulting pane of glass had one glossy suface and one matt surface.

Crown glass (spun glass, bull's eye glass) was made by gathering a gob of glass on a blowpipe and blowing it as if for a vessel. This bubble was then transferred to a punty iron and separated from the blowpipe resulting in an open-ended 'bubble' which was then spun vigorously in the heat from the furnace until it flattened out into a disc of glass decreasing in thickness from the centre to the rim. When cool, the disc of glass was cut up into panes of glass or into small diamond-shaped panes called **quarries (quarrels)**. The thick centre portion of the disc (the **bull's eye**) was sold cheaply to be used where transparent windows were not essential.

Another way of making window glass was by the cylinder method. **Cylinder glass (muff glass)** was made by blowing a bubble of glass, as for crown glass, but instead of transferring it to a punty iron, the bubble was swung to-and-fro on the blowpipe as it was being blown. This resulted in a long cylindrical bubble. Both ends were cut off this cylinder and it was split along its length. This split cylinder was allowed to uncurl on a flat surface in an oven (**opening lehr**) to produce a flat sheet of glass.

Reading for Manufacture of Window Glass: Douglas, R. W. and Frank, S. 1972; Harden, D. B. 1961; Hurst Vose, R. 1980.

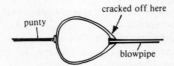

punty

cracked off here

blowpipe

First a large bubble of glass was blown and transferred to the punty iron

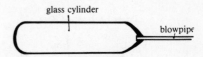

glass cylinder

blowpipe

First a long cylinder of glass was blown

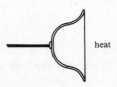

heat

The open end of the bulb was then widened to form a bell-like shape which was then spun in the heat from the furnace until, having been softened by the heat, the spinning caused it to open out into a large disc

The ends of the cylinder were removed and the cylinder was split longitudinally

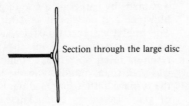

Section through the large disc

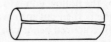

The split cylinder was then placed on a flat surface in an opening lehr and allowed to uncurl to form a flat sheet of glass

0   1m

Diagrams showing the principle of making Cylinder Glass

Stained Glass Windows

Stained glass windows are made of different coloured pieces of glass arranged to form a pattern or picture. The term is misleading since it often describes window glass coloured by methods other than staining. Staining was not used until the later Medieval period, and even then stained glass was used in conjunction with glass coloured by other methods. The glass in 'stained' glass windows was coloured in three different ways.

A batch of coloured glass could be made from which window glass of the same colour throughout was produced. This type of glass is sometimes termed **pot-metal**. A second method was the coating of colourless glass with a thin layer of coloured glass **(flashing)**. This produced **flashed glass (flash glass)** which was more transparent than pot-metal. Patterns could then be formed by **abrading**, which was the removal of parts of the coloured flashing.

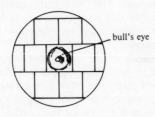

bull's eye

When cool, the disc of glass could be cut up into pieces of the required shape and size

0   1m

Diagrams showing the principle of making Crown Glass

The third method of producing coloured glass was by **staining**. This was done by painting the glass with a preparation containing silver sulphide or silver chloride. The glass was then heated in an oven, and the silver produced a yellow or orange colour. Staining was usually applied to colourless glass or to the colourless side of flashed glass, since it would react with the colourants in coloured glass. The dark lines on the glass depicting details of faces, folds in clothing and so on were made by painting on a preparation containing copper or iron oxides and powdered glass. This was then melted and fused with the glass by heating. This is sometimes called **glass enamelling**.

Fitting Stained Glass Windows

The window to be glazed was measured and the design that was to fill it was drawn out full size on a flat surface. Pieces of glass were then cut to shape by cracking the glass with a hot iron and trimming to the final shape by grozing. They were then positioned on the drawing and relevant details added by staining or by glass enamelling. Once all detail had been added, the glass pieces were joined together with strips of lead called **calmes (cames)** which had a groove down each side into which the glass fitted. The joins between these strips of lead were soldered together and waterproof cement was rubbed into the gaps between the lead and the glass. Because of the danger of such windows being blown in, large windows were assembled as a series of panels supported by ironwork. In the twelfth and thirteenth centuries this ironwork sometimes consisted of an iron armature made to follow the shape of the panels and was fixed to a wooden window frame, but the later method was to support the panels by a series of horizontal iron bars **(saddle bars)** and vertical bars **(stanchions)**.

Reading for Stained Glass Windows: Baker, J. 1960; Morris, R. 1979.

Techniques of Pottery Manufacture

Preparation of Clay

Clay is first obtained and then **weathered** (exposed to the weather to break it down into small lumps). **Tempering (grog,** gritting, filler, opening materials, backing, inclusions)** is added to the clay to prevent excessive shrinking of the pot and to give it stability; clays which are too **plastic** are sticky or greasy to handle and are unable to support themselves. Tempering also reduces the amount of clay required, and therefore the thickness of the pot and the firing time as well. A non-plastic material is added such as quartz sand, broken pieces of pottery **(grog** — a term also used more generally to describe all tempering materials), shell or flint.

Forming the Clay

The **clay paste** or **body** (the prepared clay) is formed into a pot **(clay shape)** in various ways:

Coil building (ring building) The base of the pot may be formed from a flattened lump of clay or from coils of clay. The walls of the pot are built up with coils of clay. This method was used in the prehistoric period, and also in later periods for very large pots. The coils were smoothed out, often on a **tournette (slow wheel)** which was a turntable rotated manually. This process can disguise the method of manufacture of the pot.

Slab forming (slabbing) The clay is rolled flat and shapes are cut out and assembled by pressing the edges together.

Moulding (press moulding) The pot is formed in a mould (usually a thick clay bowl thrown on a wheel and often decorated inside). When dry, the pot shrinks and can be easily removed from the mould (see also samian pottery).

Wheel throwing The pot is formed from a lump of clay rotated on a **fast wheel**. On a fast wheel a flywheel connected to the turntable is rotated by the foot or some other means which causes the turntable to revolve.

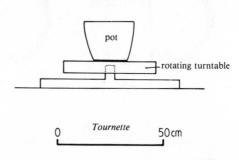

pot

rotating turntable

Tournette

0   50cm

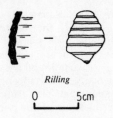

Rilling

0   5cm

Rilling consists of fine horizontal lines made by coarse particles in the clay when it is turned on a wheel. They are not indicative of wheel-thrown pottery as the same effect can be produced by a tournette.

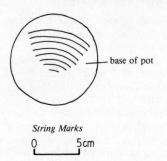

base of pot

String Marks

0   5cm

String marks (cheese-wire marks) are caused by string or wire used to detach the base of a pot from a wheel.

Surface Treatment of the Pot

One or more of the following decorative techniques can be carried out when the pot has dried slightly. **Appliqué decoration (applied decoration)** consists of sticking decorative clay forms to the surface of a pot with a thick slip. Handles can be similarly applied. A **cordon** is a raised continuous band round the vessel, applied in the same way as appliqué decoration. In **impressed decoration** patterns are impressed in the pot using, for example, shells, bird bones, finger tips and string. Potters occasionally stamped pots with designs and with their name **(potters' stamps)**. **Combing** and **comb stabbing** decoration uses a single or multiple point instrument drawn over or stabbed over the surface of the pot. **Frilling (pie-crust, finger-tip decoration)** is decoration made by impressing the finger tips along the rim or base of the pot.

Rouletting is done by holding a wheel against the pot while it rotates on the potter's wheel, producing a spiky pattern. In **roller stamping** the pottery has decoration applied by a patterned roller on which a design has been arranged in a small block. **Roughcast decoration (rustication, dusting)** is the decoration of a pot by sprinkling it with sand or pellets of wet clay. **Mica-dusted (mica-gilt)** pots are ones which have been sprinkled with mica or dipped in a thin micaceous slip to produce a sparkling effect, possibly in imitation of metal vessels. In **slip decoration** the pot is dipped in or painted with a mixture of clay and water **(slip, engobe)** which forms an outer coat **(slip, colour coat, paint)** on firing, and is sometimes coloured. A **self-slip** uses the same type of clay as the pot itself. In **slip-painting** the slip is applied locally with a brush. **Gloss** is a mixture of very fine clay and water (similar to a slip) which produces a shiny surface when fired, resembling a glaze (for example, on samian pottery). **Barbotine decoration (en barbotine, slip trailing)** consists of piping a thick clay slip onto the surface of the pot, probably from a leather or skin bag, to produce relief decoration.

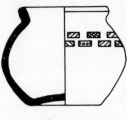

Roller Stamping

Rouletting

Barbotine

0   10cm

278

The pots are then left to dry carefully until tough and aplastic (**leather hard, green hard**) to prevent cracking and to prevent water in the pot forming steam in the kiln and shattering the pot. One or more of the following decorative techniques can be carried out when the pot is leather hard.

In **burnishing** a smooth tool (such as wood, bone, pebbles) is rubbed against the surface of the pot, either freehand or on a wheel or tournette; this produces a shiny surface. The term **polished** is often incorrectly used to describe this technique. **Ripple burnish** occurs when a pot which has become too dry is burnished, producing a ripple effect; this was sometimes a deliberate process. In **mineral surfacing** (such as **haematite coating** and **graphite coating**), powdered minerals (such as haematite or graphite) are rubbed onto the

Incised Decoration

0   5cm

surface of the pot to give it a distinctive colouring. It is then burnished. In **incised decoration (cut-glass decoration, grooving)** a pattern is cut with a sharp tool. When some of the clay is removed the correct term is **excised decoration**.

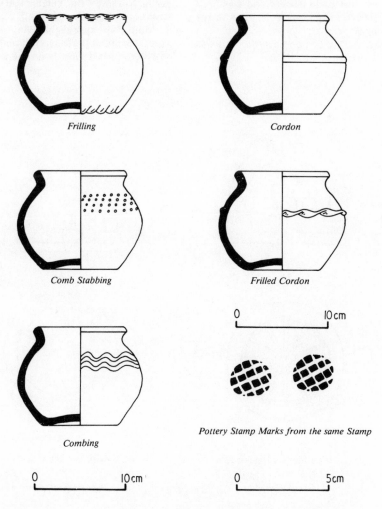

Frilling

Cordon

Comb Stabbing

Frilled Cordon

0   10cm

Combing

Pottery Stamp Marks from the same Stamp

0   10cm

0   5cm

Firing of the Pot

A pot is usually only fired once. The appearance and constituents of the fired clay are termed **fabric**. A glazed pot sometimes needs to be fired twice: the first firing cooks the pot, and is termed **biscuit firing (bisque firing)**, resulting in a **biscuit pot**; a glaze may then be applied, and a second firing fires the glaze (**glost firing**). In order to obtain a low temperature in firing the glaze, a **glost-oven** was sometimes used. This technique was introduced in the fifteenth century. **Sintering** is the firing of the clay to a particular temperature (**sinter point**), when the outer surfaces of the particles become soft and fuse together on cooling. If the particles are heated further and melt completely, the clay is said to be **vitrified** and collapses. Different clays have different melting points. **Terracotta** describes most early pottery and was fired below 1000°C. Pottery can be fired in the following ways:

1 Domestic fire or open hearth. This was mainly a prehistoric method.

2 **Bonfire kiln (clump kiln, clamp kiln).** The pots are stacked and baked in a pit under a bonfire. This method was in use in all periods for unglazed pottery.

3 **Single-flue updraught kiln (pit kiln).** The pots are placed inverted on clay **fire bars** supported on a column of tiles or clay (**kiln furniture**), with a fire underneath in a **fire-pit**, a covering dome with a vent for escaping gases and smoke, and a stokehole on one side. It was used in Roman times and again from about the seventh century.

4 **Parallel-flue kiln.** This was designed to fire building materials and large pots. Pots, bricks or tiles were stacked above tile arches which formed parallel flues. The front entrance was blocked on firing. These kilns were used in the Roman period and again from about the seventh century.

5 **Double-flue updraught kiln.** This was similar to a single-flue kiln but had two flues. It was used from the thirteenth century.

6 **Multi-flue updraught kiln.** This was used from about the thirteenth century. The pots were placed directly on the kiln floor.

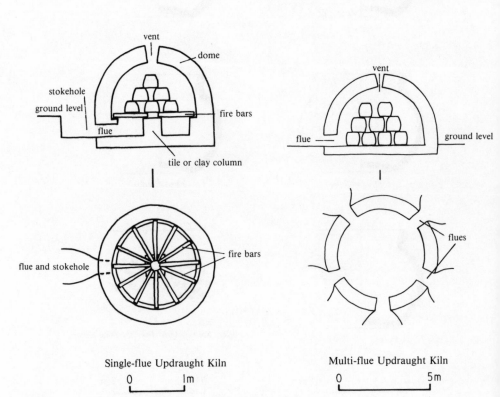

Single-flue Updraught Kiln

0   1m

Multi-flue Updraught Kiln

0   5m

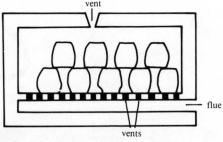

Longitudinal Section through one of the Flues

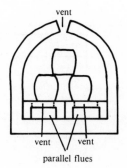

parallel flues

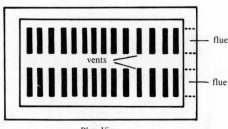

Plan View

Parallel-flue Kiln

0 ⎣_____⎦ 1m

Kiln coverings Domes were probably constructed of clay or cob. Permanent structures did not appear until the Post-Medieval period. **Kiln fuel** was probably wood, coal and peat. With a good draught in the kiln, oxygen remains present in the atmosphere, resulting in an **oxidizing atmosphere**. The pottery becomes **oxidized** and is usually light-red or orange in colour on the surface. When the air to the kiln is limited, the oxygen is used up, resulting in a **reducing atmosphere**. The pottery becomes **reduced** and is usually grey or black on the surface. Both effects can occur on the same pot in a bonfire kiln.

Glazes After a biscuit firing, a lead ore may be added to the surface of the pot, either dry or in a liquid form. This is then fired in a kiln or glost-oven. Colour may be applied to the biscuit pot before glazing **(underglaze colour)** or else to the glaze just before firing **(on-glaze or overglaze decoration)**. Glazes were commonly coloured green by the addition of copper compounds from the twelfth century. To prevent the pots from sticking together, they were fired in **saggers** (large cylindrical vessels). These were not used before the sixteenth century, and so many glazed pots could be ruined in firing. **Tin glazes** and **salt glazes** were not introduced until the Post-Medieval period. Glazes may be lightly **polished** with cloth or leather after firing to remove blemishes and increase the shininess.

Wasters are pots broken or misshapen in firing and subsequently discarded.

Reading for Techniques of Pottery Manufacture: Hodges, H. 1964; Musty, J. 1974; Shepard, A. O. 1956.

Pottery Forms

Rims

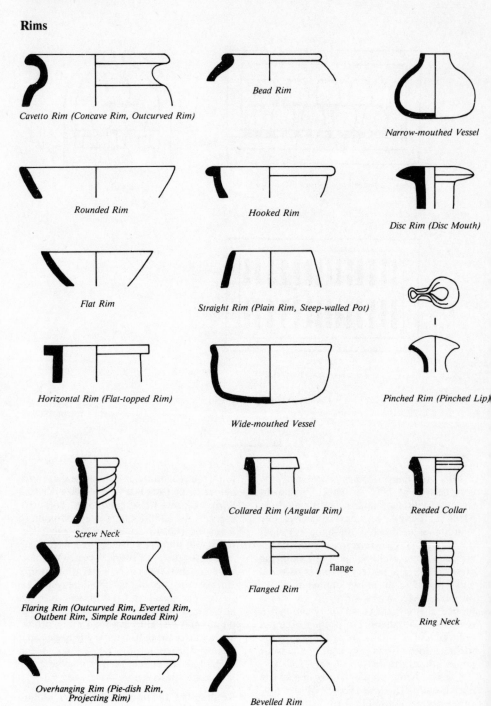

Cavetto Rim (Concave Rim, Outcurved Rim)

Bead Rim

Narrow-mouthed Vessel

Rounded Rim

Hooked Rim

Disc Rim (Disc Mouth)

Flat Rim

Straight Rim (Plain Rim, Steep-walled Pot)

Horizontal Rim (Flat-topped Rim)

Wide-mouthed Vessel

Pinched Rim (Pinched Lip)

Screw Neck

Collared Rim (Angular Rim)

Reeded Collar

Flaring Rim (Outcurved Rim, Everted Rim, Outbent Rim, Simple Rounded Rim)

Flanged Rim

flange

Ring Neck

Overhanging Rim (Pie-dish Rim, Projecting Rim)

Bevelled Rim

0   50cm

Bodies

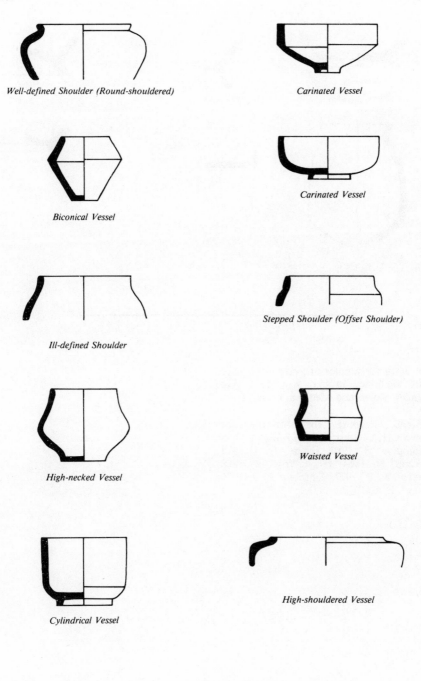

Well-defined Shoulder (Round-shouldered)

Carinated Vessel

Biconical Vessel

Carinated Vessel

Ill-defined Shoulder

Stepped Shoulder (Offset Shoulder)

High-necked Vessel

Waisted Vessel

Cylindrical Vessel

High-shouldered Vessel

0   50 cm

Bases

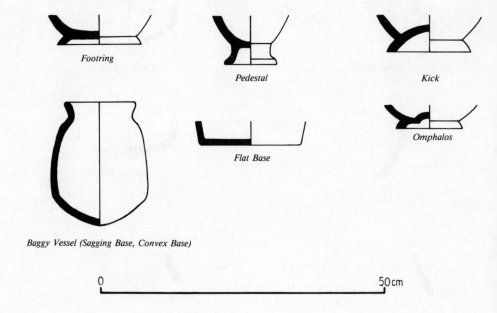

Footring

Pedestal

Kick

Omphalos

Flat Base

Baggy Vessel (Sagging Base, Convex Base)

0   50 cm

For further examples of pottery forms see also Neolithic, Bronze Age, Iron Age, Roman, Saxon and Medieval pottery.

General Reading for Miscellaneous: Bowen, H. C. 1961; British Museum 1968; Champion, S. 1980; Evans, J. G. 1975; Hodges, H. 1964; Hurst Vose, R. 1980; Oakley, K. P. 1972; Tylecote, R. F. 1976; Wood, E. S. 1979.

Bibliography

Abbreviations

Ant	Antiquity
Ant J	Antiquaries Journal
Arch	Archaeologia
Arch Camb	Archaeologia Cambrensis
Arch J	Archaeological Journal
BAJ	Bedfordshire Archaeological Journal
BAR	British Archaeological Report
CA	Current Archaeology
CBA	Council for British Archaeology
JBAA	Journal of the British Archaeological Association
LHA	Lincolnshire History and Archaeology
Med Arch	Medieval Archaeology
PHFCAS	Proceedings of the Hampshire Field Club and Archaeological Society
PPS	Proceedings of the Prehistoric Society
PSAS	Proceedings of the Society of Antiquaries of Scotland
RCHM	Royal Commission on Historical Monuments
SAF	Scottish Archaeological Forum
TLAMAS	Transactions of the London and Middlesex Archaeological Society

Two dates are sometimes given for journals, for example: '1943 (1944)' means that the journal was published in 1944, for the year 1943.

Abercromby, J., 1912 *A Study of the Bronze Age Pottery of Great Britain and Ireland and its associated grave-goods*

Aberg, F. A. (ed), 1978 *Medieval moated sites* (CBA Research Report no 17)

Åberg, N., 1926 *The Anglo-Saxons in England during the early centuries after the invasion*

Addyman, P. V. and Hill, D. H., 1969 'Saxon Southampton: A Review of the Evidence. Part II, Industry, Trade and Everyday Life', *PHFCAS* 26, 61–96

Adkins, R. A. and Jackson, R., 1978 *Neolithic Stone and Flint Axes from the River Thames. An Illustrated Corpus*

Aitken, M. J., 1974 *Physics and archaeology*

Alcock, L., 1971 *Arthur's Britain*

Aldsworth, F., 1979 'The Droxford Anglo-Saxon cemetery, Soberton, Hampshire', *PHFCAS* 35, 93–182

Allen, D. F., 1962 'Celtic coins', *Ordnance Survey 1962,* 19–32

——. 1967 'Iron currency bars in Britain' *PPS* 33, 307–35

——. 1971 'British Potin Coins: A Review' 127–54 in Jesson, M. and Hill, D., 1971

——. 1980 *The Coins of the Ancient Celts* (ed D. Nash)

Annable, F. K. and Simpson, D. D. A. 1964 *Guide Catalogue of the Neolithic and Bronze Age Collections in Devizes Museum*

Anstee, J. W. and Biek, L., 1961 'A study in pattern-welding' *Med Arch* 5, 71–93

Arthur, P. and Marsh, G. (eds), 1978 *Early Fine Wares in Roman Britain* (BAR 57)

Ashbee, P., 1960 *The Bronze Age Round Barrow in Britain*

——. 1970 *The Earthen Long Barrow in Britain*

Atkinson, R. J. C., 1955 'The Dorset Cursus', *Ant* 29, 4–9

——. 1978 *Stonehenge and Neighbouring Monuments*

——. 1979 *Stonehenge*

Atkinson, R. J. C., Piggott, C. M. and Sandars, N. K., 1951 *Excavations at Dorchester, Oxon*

Atkinson, R. J. C. and Piggott, S., 1955 'The Torrs Chamfrein', *Arch* 96, 197–235

Avent, R., 1975 *Anglo-Saxon Garnet Inlaid Disc and Composite Brooches* (BAR 11)

Bailey, D. M., 1976 'Pottery Lamps', 92–103 in Strong, D. and Brown, D., 1976

Bailey, R. N., 1980 *Viking Age Sculpture*

Baines, P., 1977 *Spinning Wheels, Spinners and Spinning*

Baker, D., 1974 'Excavations in the area of Mill Street, Bedford 1971', *BAJ* 9, 99–128

Baker, J., 1960 *English Stained Glass*

Bannister, B., 1969 'Dendrochronology', 191–205 in Brothwell, D. and Higgs, E. S., 1969

Barker, P., 1977 *Techniques of Archaeological Excavation*

Barley, M. W. (ed), 1975 *The plans and*

topography of medieval towns in England and Wales (CBA Research Report no 14)

Barley, M. W. and Hanson, R. P. C. (eds), 1968 Christianity in Britain, 300–700

Barrett, J., 1976 'Deverel-Rimbury: problems of chronology and interpretation', 289–307 in Burgess, C. B. and Miket, R., 1976

——. 1979 'Later Bronze Age Pottery in Southern Britain', CA 67, 230–1

Barton, K. J., 1979 Medieval Sussex Pottery

Bell, R. C., 1960 Board and Table Games from many civilizations

Beresford, G., 1975 The Medieval Clay-Land Village: Excavations at Goltho and Barton Blount

——. 1979 'Three deserted medieval settlements: a report on the late E. Marie Minter's excavations', Med Arch 23, 98–158

Beresford, M. W. and Hurst, J. G. (eds), 1971 Deserted Medieval Villages

Beresford, M. W. and St Joseph, J. K. S., 1979 Medieval England. An aerial survey

Biddle, M., 1976 'Towns', 99–150 in Wilson, D. M., 1976a

Birley, A. R., 1964 Life in Roman Britain

Blackmore, H. L., 1976 The Armouries of the Tower of London. I. Ordnance

Blagg, T. F. C., 1977 'The London Arch', CA 57, 311–15

Blair, C., 1958 European Armour circa 1066 to circa 1700

Blunt, C. E., 1960 'The Anglo-Saxon coinage and the historian', Med Arch 4, 1–15

Boardman, J., Brown, M. A. and Powell, T. G. E. (eds), 1971 The European Community in Later Prehistory

Boon, G. C. and Lewis, J. M. (eds), 1976 Welsh Antiquity

Bordaz, J., 1970 Tools of the Old and New Stone Age

Bordes, F., 1968 The Old Stone Age

Borg, A., 1979 Arms and armour in Britain

Bowen, D. Q., 1978 Quaternary Geology: A Stratigraphic Framework for Multi-disciplinary Work

Bowen, H. C., 1961 Ancient Fields

Bowen, H. C. and Fowler, P. J. (eds), 1978 Early Land Allotment in the British Isles. A Survey of recent work (BAR 48)

Bowen, H. C. and Wood, P. D., 1967 'Experimental storage of corn underground and its implications for Iron Age

settlements', Institute of Archaeology Bulletin 7, 1–14

Bowman, A. K. and Thomas, J. D., 1974 The Vindolanda Writing Tablets

Bradley, R. J., 1971 'Stock Raising and the Origins of the Hill Fort on the South Downs', Ant J 51, 8–29

——. 1978 The Prehistoric Settlement of Britain

Brailsford, J., 1975 Early Celtic Masterpieces from Britain in the British Museum

Brailsford, J. and Stapley, J. E., 1972 'The Ipswich Torcs', PPS 38, 219–34

Branigan, K. and Fowler, P. J. (eds), 1976 The Roman West Country

Braun, H., 1968 An Introduction to English Medieval Architecture

Breeze, D. J. and Dobson, B., 1978 Hadrian's Wall

Brewster, T. C. M., 1963 The Excavation of Staple Howe

British Museum, 1924 A Guide to the Medieval Antiquities and Objects of Later Date in the Department of British and Medieval Antiquities

——. 1968 Flint Implements: an account of stone age techniques and cultures (3rd edition)

Britnell, W. J., 1976 'Antler cheekpieces of the British Late Bronze Age', Ant J 56, 24–34

Brodribb, G., 1979a 'A Survey of Tile from the Roman Bath House at Beauport Park, Battle, E. Sussex', Britannia 10, 139–56

——. 1979b 'Tegulae mammatae', Ant J 59, 397–400

Brothwell, D. and Higgs, E. S. (eds), 1969 Science in Archaeology. A Survey of Progress and Research

Brown, D., 1974 'So-called "Needle Cases"', Med Arch 18, 151–4

——. 1976 'Bronze and Pewter', 25–41 in Strong, D. and Brown, D., 1976

——. 1978 Anglo-Saxon England

Brown, G. B., 1915 The Arts in Early England: Saxon Art and Industry in the Pagan Period

Brown, R. A., 1976 English Medieval Castles (3rd edition)

Bruce, J. C., 1978 Handbook to the Roman Wall (13th edition ed C. Daniels)

Bruce-Mitford, R., 1972 The Sutton Hoo Ship-Burial: A Handbook

——. 1975 The Sutton Hoo Ship-Burial Volume 1 Excavations, Background, the

Ship, Dating and Inventory

——. 1978 *The Sutton Hoo Ship-Burial Volume 2 Arms, Armour and Regalia*

Brunskill, R. W., 1978 *Illustrated Handbook of Vernacular Architecture*

Buckland, P., 1978 'A First-Century Shield from Doncaster, Yorkshire', *Britannia* 9, 247–69

Bulleid, A. and Gray, H. St. G., 1911 *The Glastonbury Lake Village* vol i

——. 1917 *The Glastonbury Lake Village* vol ii

Burgess, C. B., 1968a 'The later bronze age in the British Isles and north-western France', *Arch J* 125, 1–45

——. 1968b *Bronze Age Metalwork in Northern England c.1000 to 700 BC*

——. 1974 'The bronze age', 165–232 in Renfrew, C., 1974

——. 1976 'Burials with metalwork of the later Bronze Age in Wales and beyond', 81–104 in Boon, G. C. and Lewis, J. M., 1976

——. 1980 *The Age of Stonehenge*

Burgess, C. B. and Coombs, D. (eds), 1979 *Bronze Age Hoards. Some finds old and new* (BAR 67)

Burgess, C. B. and Miket, R. (eds), 1976 *Settlement and Economy in the Third and Second Millennia BC* (BAR 33)

Burl, A., 1976 *The Stone Circles of The British Isles*

——. 1979 *Prehistoric Stone Circles*

Butcher, S. A., 1976 'Enamelling', 43–51 in Strong, D. and Brown, D., 1976

Butler, L. A. S., 1974 'Medieval Finds from Castell-y-Bere, Merioneth', *Arch Camb* 123, 78–112

Butler, L. A. S. and Given-Wilson, C., 1979 *Medieval Monasteries of Great Britain*

Cameron, H. K., 1974 'Technical Aspects of Medieval Monumental Brasses', *Arch J* 131, 215–37

Campbell, J. B., 1977 *The Upper Palaeolithic of Britain: A study of man and nature in the late ice age*

Carver, M. O. H., 1979 'Three Saxo-Norman tenements in Durham City', *Med Arch* 23, 1–80

Casey, P. J., 1980 *Roman Coinage in Britain*

Champion, S., 1980 *A Dictionary of Terms and Techniques in Archaeology*

Chaplin, R. E., 1971 *The Study of Animal Bones from Archaeological Sites*

Charleston, R. J., 1975 'The glass', 204–25 in Platt, C. and Coleman-Smith, R., 1975

Charlesworth, D. and Thornton, J. H., 1973 'Leather found in Mediobogdum, the Roman fort of Hardknott', *Britannia* 4, 141–52

Cherry, B., 1976 'Ecclesiastical architecture', 151–200 in Wilson, D. M. 1976a

Christie, H., Olsen, O. and Taylor, H. M., 1979 'The Wooden Church of St. Andrew at Greensted, Essex', *Ant J* 59, 92–112

Christison, D., Barbour, J. and Anderson, J., 1898–9 'Account of the Excavation of the Camps and Earthworks at Birrenswark Hill in Annandale, undertaken by the Society in 1898', *PSAS* 33, 198–249

Clapham, A. W., 1934 *English Romanesque Architecture after the Conquest*

Clark, A. J., 1975 'Archaeological Prospecting: A Progress Report', *Journal of Archaeological Science* 2, 297–314

Clark, J. G. D., 1952 *Prehistoric Europe: The economic basis*

——. 1954 *Excavations at Star Carr*

——. 1960 'Excavations at the Neolithic site at Hurst Fen, Mildenhall, Suffolk, 1954, 1957 and 1958', *PPS* 26, 202–45

Clark, J. G. D. and Thompson, M. W., 1953 'The Groove and Splinter Technique of working Antler in Upper Palaeolithic and Mesolithic Europe with special reference to the material from Star Carr', *PPS* 19, 148–60

Clarke, D. L., 1970 *Beaker Pottery of Great Britain and Ireland*

——. (ed), 1972 *Models in Archaeology*

Clarke, D. V., 1970 'Bone Dice and the Scottish Iron Age', *PPS* 36, 214–32

Clarke, H. and Carter, A., 1977 *Excavations in King's Lynn 1963–1970*

Cleere, H., 1976 'Ironmaking', 127–41 in Strong, D. and Brown, D., 1976

Clephan, R. C., 1911 'The Ordnance of the Fourteenth and Fifteenth Centuries', *Arch J* 68, 49–138

Coles, J. M., 1972 *Field Archaeology in Britain*

——. 1973 *Archaeology by Experiment*

——. 1980 *Experimental Archaeology*

Coles, J. M., Heal, S. V. E. and Orme, B. J., 1978 'The use and character of wood in prehistoric Britain and Ireland', *PPS* 44, 1–45

Coles, J. M., Orme, B. J., Hibbert, F. A. and Wainwright, G. J., 1976 *Somerset*

BIBLIOGRAPHY

Levels Papers number 2

Coles, J. M. and Simpson, D. D. A. (eds), 1968 *Studies in Ancient Europe*

Collingwood, R. G. and Richmond, I., 1969 *The Archaeology of Roman Britain*

Collingwood, R. G. and Wright, R. P., 1965 *The Roman Inscriptions of Britain: I Inscriptions on Stone*

Collins, D., 1978 *Early Man in West Middlesex*

Collis, J. R. (ed), 1977 *The Iron Age in Britain — a review*

Collis, J. R. and Kjølbye-Biddle, B., 1979 'Early Medieval Bone Spoons from Winchester', *Ant J* 59, 375–91

Connolly, P., 1975 *The Roman Army*

Corcoran, J. X. W. P., 1952 'Tankards and Tankard Handles of the British Early Iron Age', *PPS* 18, 85–102

Corder, P., 1943 (1945) 'Roman Spade-irons from Verulamium, with some notes on examples elsewhere', *Arch J* 100, 224–31

Cordingley, R. A., 1961 'British Historical Roof-Types and their Members: a classification', *The Transactions of the Ancient Monuments Society* new series 9, 73–118

Cornwall, I. W., 1956 *Bones for the Archaeologist*

Cossons, N., 1975 *The BP Book of Industrial Archaeology*

Council for British Archaeology, 1970 *Handbook of Scientific Aids and Evidence for Archaeologists*

——. 1971 *Archaeological Site Index to Radiocarbon Dates for Great Britain and Ireland* and supplements

Cramp, R. J., 1976 'Monastic sites', 201–52 in Wilson, D. M., 1976a

Crowfoot, E., 1975 'The Textiles', 334–7 in Platt, C. and Coleman-Smith, R., 1975

Cruden, S. H., 1960 *The Scottish Castle*

Cunliffe, B., 1971 *Excavations at Fishbourne*

——. 1978 *Iron Age Communities in Britain* (revised edition)

Cunnington, M. E. and Goddard, E. H., 1934 *Catalogue of Antiquities in the Museum of the Wiltshire Archaeological and Natural History Society at Devizes*, part II

Curle, A., 1925–6 'Domestic Candlesticks from the Fourteenth to the end of the Eighteenth Century', *PSAS* 60, 183–214

Curwen, E. C., 1937 'Querns', *Ant* 11, 133–51

Davey, N., 1961 *A History of Building Materials*

Davidson, H. R. E., 1962 *The Sword in Anglo-Saxon England. Its Archaeology and Literature*

Dawson, E. W., 1969 'Bird Remains in Archaeology', 359–75 in Brothwell, D. and Higgs, E. S., 1969

Department of the Environment, 1976 *Crossbows*

Dickinson, J. C., 1961 *Monastic Life in Medieval England*

Dickinson, T. M., 1977 'Post-Roman and pagan Anglo-Saxon', in 'British Antiquity, 1976–77', *Arch J* 134, 404–18

——. 1979 'On the Origin and Chronology of the Early Anglo-Saxon Disc Brooch', 39–80 in Hawkes, S. C. et al, 1979

Dimbleby, G. W., 1967 *Plants and Archaeology*

Dix, B., 1979 'Roman lime-burning', *Britannia* 10, 261–2

Dolley, R. H. M., 1964 *Anglo-Saxon Pennies*

——. 1976 'The coins', 349–72 in Wilson, D. M., 1976a

——. 1978 'The Anglo-Danish and Anglo-Norse coinages of York', 26–31 in Hall, R. A., 1978

Doran, J. E. and Hodson, F. R., 1975 *Mathematics and Computers in Archaeology*

Douglas, R. W. and Frank, S., 1972 *A History of Glassmaking*

Down, A., 1978 *Chichester Excavations 3*

Drewett, P. C., 1977 'The excavation of a Neolithic causewayed enclosure on Offham Hill, East Sussex, 1976', *PPS* 43, 201–42

Dru Drury, G., 1926 'Thirteenth Century Steelyard Weights', *Proceedings of the Dorset Natural History and Antiquarian Field Club* 47, 1–24

Dunning, G. C., 1937 'A Fourteenth-century Well at the Bank of England', *Ant J* 17, 414–18

——. 1961 'Medieval Chimney-pots', 78–93 in Jope, E. M., 1961a

——. 1968 (1969) 'A Medieval Pottery Roof-finial Found at Portsmouth', *PHFCAS* 25, 95–101

——. 1974a 'The Horse and Knight Roof-finial, with a discussion of knight, finials and rider finials in England and on the Continent', 112–22 in Baker, D., 1974

——. 1974b 'The Medieval Buckler', 201–4

288

in Tatton-Brown, T., 1974

——. 1977 'Mortars', 320–47 in Clarke, H. and Carter, A., 1977

Dunning, G. C., Hurst, J. G., Myres, J. N. L. and Tischler, F., 1959 'Anglo-Saxon Pottery; A Symposium', *Med Arch* 3, 1–78

Dunning, G. C. and Jessup, R. F., 1936 'Roman Barrows', *Ant* 10, 37–53

Du Plat Taylor, J. and Cleere, H. (eds), 1978 *Roman shipping and trade: Britain and the Rhine Provinces* (CBA Research Report no 24)

Durham, B., 1977 (1978) 'Archaeological Investigations in St. Aldates, Oxford', *Oxoniensia* 42, 83–203

Eames, E. S., 1968 *Medieval Tiles. A Handbook*

——. 1980 *Catalogue of Medieval Lead-Glazed Earthenware Tiles in the Department of Medieval and Later Antiquities British Museum*

Elkington, H. D. H., 1976 'The Mendip Lead Industry', 183–97 in Branigan, K. and Fowler, P. J., 1976

Elliott, R. W. V., 1959 *Runes*

Ellison, A. and Drewett, P. C., 1971 'Pits and Post-holes in the British Early Iron Age: some alternative explanations', *PPS* 37, 183–94

Eogan, G., 1967 'The Associated Finds of Gold Bar Torcs', *The Journal of the Royal Society of Antiquaries of Ireland* 97, 129–75

Evans, J., 1881 *The Ancient Bronze Implements, Weapons, and Ornaments of Great Britain and Ireland*

——. 1897 *The Ancient Stone Implements, Weapons and Ornaments of Great Britain*

Evans, J. G., 1972 *Land Snails in Archaeology*

——. 1975 *The Environment of Early Man in the British Isles*

——. 1978 *An Introduction to Environmental Archaeology*

Everitt, B., 1975 *Cluster Analysis*

Evison, V. I., 1963 'Sugar-Loaf Shield Bosses', *Ant J* 43, 38–96

——. 1965 *The Fifth-Century Invasions South of the Thames*

——. 1968 'Quoit Brooch Style Buckles', *Ant J* 48, 231–49

——. 1975 'Pagan Saxon Whetstones', *Ant J* 55, 70–5

——. 1976 'Sword Rings and Beads', *Arch* 105, 303–15

——. 1978 'Early Anglo-Saxon Applied Disc Brooches. Part II: In England', *Ant J* 58, 260–78

——. 1979 *A Corpus of Wheel-Thrown Pottery in Anglo-Saxon Graves*

Evison, V. I., Hodges, H. and Hurst, J. G. (eds), 1974 *Medieval Pottery from Excavations. Studies presented to Gerald Clough Dunning*

Farmer, P. G., 1979 *An Introduction to Scarborough Ware and a Re-assessment of Knight Jugs*

Farrar, R. A. H., 1962 'A Note on the Pre-historic and Roman salt industry in relation to the Wyke Regis site, Dorset', *Proceedings of the Dorset Natural History and Archaeological Society* 84, 137–44

Feacham, R., 1977 *Guide to Prehistoric Scotland* (2nd edition)

Fitter, R. and M., 1967 *The Penguin Dictionary of British Natural History*

Fleming, A., 1978 'The prehistoric land-scape of Dartmoor Part I: South Dartmoor', *PPS* 44, 97–123

Fleming, S., 1976 *Dating in Archaeology: A Guide to Scientific Techniques*

Fletcher, J. (ed), 1978 *Dendrochronology in Europe. Principles, interpretations and applications to Archaeology and History*

Foard, G., 1978 'Systematic fieldwalking and the investigation of Saxon settlement in Northamptonshire', *World Archaeology* 9, 357–74

Forde-Johnston, J., 1976a *Prehistoric Britain and Ireland*

——. 1976b *Hillforts of the Iron Age in England and Wales. A Survey of the Surface Evidence*

——. 1977 *Castles and Fortifications of Britain and Ireland*

Foster, J. 1977 *Bronze Boar Figurines in Iron Age and Roman Britain* (BAR 39)

Fowler, E. 1963 (1964) 'Celtic Metalwork of the Fifth and Sixth Centuries AD', *Arch J* 120, 98–160

——. 1968 'Hanging bowls', 287–310 in Coles, J. M. and Simpson, D. D. A., 1968

Fox, C., 1946 *A Find of the Early Iron Age from Llyn Cerrig Bach, Anglesey*

——. 1955 *Offa's Dyke*

——. 1958 *Pattern and Purpose. A Survey of Celtic Art in Britain*

Fox, C. and Dickins, B. (eds), 1950 *The Early Cultures of North-West Europe*

BIBLIOGRAPHY

Frere, S. S., 1972 *Verulamium Excavations* vol 1
——. 1978 *Britannia*
Fry, D. K., 1976 'Anglo-Saxon lyre tuning pegs from Whitby, N. Yorkshire', *Med Arch* 20, 137–9
Fry, P. S., 1980 *The David and Charles Book of Castles*
Gailey, A. and Fenton, A. (eds), 1970 *The Spade in Northern and Atlantic Europe*
Galloway, P., 1976 'Note on descriptions of bone and antler combs', *Med Arch* 20, 154–6
Gentry, A. P., 1976 *Roman Military Stone-built Granaries in Britain* (BAR 32)
Gerloff, S., 1975 *The Early Bronze Age Daggers in Great Britain and a Reconsideration of the Wessex Culture*
Gibson, A. M., 1978 *Bronze Age Pottery in the North-East of England* (BAR 56)
Godfrey, W. H., 1955 *The English Almshouse*
Goodman, W. L., 1964 *The History of Woodworking Tools*
Goodyear, F. H., 1971 *Archaeological Site Science*
Graham-Campbell, J. and Kidd, D., 1980 *The Vikings*
Gray, H. St. G. and Cotton, M. A., 1966 *The Meare Lake Village* vol 3
Green, H. S., 1978 'Late Bronze Age Wooden Hafts from Llyn Fawr and Penwyllt', *Bulletin of the Board of Celtic Studies* 28, 136–41
——. 1980 *The Flint Arrowheads of the British Isles. A detailed study of material from England and Wales with comparanda from Scotland and Ireland* (BAR 75)
Green, M. J., 1975 'Romano-British Non-Ceramic Model Objects in South-east Britain', *Arch J* 132, 54–70
Greene, K., 1979 *The Pre-Flavian Fine Wares* (Report on the Excavations at Usk 1965–1976 ed W. H. Manning)
Grinsell, L. V., 1953 *The Ancient Burial-Mounds of England*
——. 1970 *The Archaeology of Exmoor*
——. 1979 *Barrows in England and Wales*
Guido, C. M., 1974 'A Scottish crannog re-dated', *Ant* 48, 54–5
——. 1978 *The Glass Beads of the Prehistoric and Roman Periods in Britain and Ireland*
Hall, R. A. (ed), 1978 *Viking Age York and the north* (CBA Research Report no 27)
Hamilton, J. R. C., 1956 *Excavations at*

Jarlshof, Shetland
——. 1962 'Brochs and Broch Builders', 53–90 in Wainwright, F. T., 1962
——. 1966 'Forts, brochs and wheelhouses in northern Scotland', 111–30 in Rivet, A. L. F. 1966
——. 1968 *Excavations at Clickhimin, Shetland*
Hampton, J. N., Palmer, R. and Clark, A. J., 1977 'Implications of Aerial Photography for Archaeology', *Arch J* 134, 157–93
Harbison, P. 1971 'Wooden and Stone Chevaux-de-Frise in Central and Western Europe', *PPS* 37, 195–225
Harbison, P. and Laing, L., 1974 *Some Iron Age Mediterranean Imports in England* (BAR 5)
Hardaker, R., 1974 *A Corpus of Early Bronze Age Dagger Pommels from Great Britain and Ireland* (BAR 3)
Harden, D. B., 1961 'Domestic Window Glass: Roman, Saxon and Medieval', 39–63 in Jope, E. M., 1961a
——. 1968 'Ancient Glass I: Pre-Roman,' *Arch J* 125, 46–72
——. 1969 'Ancient Glass II: Roman', *Arch J* 126, 44–77
——. 1971 'Ancient Glass III: Post-Roman', *Arch J* 128, 78–117
——. 1978 'Anglo-Saxon and later medieval glass in Britain: some recent developments', *Med Arch* 22, 1–24
Harding, D. W., 1974 *The Iron Age in Lowland Britain*
Harley, L. S., 1974 'A Typology of Brick', *JBAA* 37, 3rd series, 63–87
Harris, E. C., 1979 *Principles of Archaeological Stratigraphy*
Hartley, B. R., 1969 'Samian Ware or Terra Sigillata', 235–51 in Collingwood, R. G. and Richmond, I., 1969
Haseloff, G., 1974 'Salin's Style I', *Med Arch* 18, 1–15
Haslam, J., 1978 *Medieval Pottery in Britain*
Hatcher, J., 1973 *English Tin Production and Trade before 1550*
Hawkes, C. F. C. and Hull, M. R., 1947 *Camulodunum*
Hawkes, S. C., 1973 'The Dating and Social Significance of the Burials in the Polhill Cemetery', 186–201 in Philp, B., 1973
Hawkes, S. C., Brown, D. and Campbell, J. (eds), 1979 *Anglo-Saxon Studies in Archaeology and History I* (BAR 72)

290

Hawkes, S. C. and Dunning, G. C., 1961 'Soldiers and settlers in Britain, fourth to fifth century: with a catalogue of animal-ornamented buckles and related belt-fittings', *Med Arch* 5, 1–70

Henderson, I., 1979 'The Silver Chain from Whitecleugh, Shieldholm, Crawfordjohn, Lanarkshire', *Transactions of the Dumfriesshire and Galloway Natural History and Antiquarian Society* 54, 20–8

Henig, M., 1974 *A Corpus of Roman Engraved Gemstones from British Sites* (BAR 8)

Henshall, A. S., 1950 'Textiles and Weaving Appliances in Prehistoric Britain', *PPS* 16, 130–62

Hobley, B., 1971 'A Gyrus at the Lunt?', *CA* 28, 127–30

Hodder, I. and Hedges, J. W., 1977 '"Weaving combs": their typology and distribution with some introductory remarks on data and function', 17–28 in Collis, J. R., 1977

Hodder, I. and Orton, C., 1976 *Spatial analysis in archaeology*

Hodges, H., 1964 *Artifacts*

Holdsworth, P., 1980 *Excavations at Melbourne Street, Southampton, 1971–76* (CBA Research Report no 33)

Hull, M. R., 1958 *Roman Colchester*

Hunter, J., 1980 'The Glass', 59–72 in Holdsworth, P., 1980

Hurst, J. G., 1976 'The Pottery', 283–348 in Wilson, D. M., 1976a

Hurst Vose, R., 1980 *Glass*

Isings, C., 1957 *Roman Glass from Dated Finds*

Jackson, D. A., 1973 'A Roman Lime Kiln at Weekley, Northants', *Britannia* 4, 128–40

Jackson, K., 1950 'Notes on the ogam inscriptions of southern Britain', 199–213 in Fox, C. and Dickins, B., 1950

Jacobi, R. M., 1976 'Britain inside and outside Mesolithic Europe', *PPS* 42, 67–84

Jesson, M. and Hill, D. (eds), 1971 *The Iron Age and its Hill-Forts*

Jessup, R. F., 1959 'Barrows and Walled Cemeteries in Roman Britain', *JBAA* 22, 3rd series, 1–32

——. 1974 *Anglo-Saxon Jewellery*

Johnson, S., 1976 *The Roman Forts of the Saxon Shore*

Johnston, D. E., 1972 'A Roman Building at Chalk, near Gravesend', *Britannia* 3, 112–48

——. 1979 *An Illustrated History of Roman Roads in Britain*

Jope, E. M. (ed), 1961a *Studies in Building History*

——. 1961b 'Daggers of the Early Iron Age in Britain' *PPS* 27, 307–43

Jope, E. M., Jope, H. M. and Rigold, S. E. 1950 (1952) 'Pottery from a late 12th Century Well-filling and other Medieval finds from St. John's College, Oxford, 1947', *Oxoniensia* 15, 44–62

Kaye, W., 1914 *Roman (and other) Triple Vases*

Kennett, D. H., 1977 'Shale Vessels of the Late Pre-Roman Iron Age: Context, Distribution and Origins', *BAJ* 12, 17–22

Kent, J. P. C., 1975 'The coins and the date of the burial', 578–682 in Bruce-Mitford, R., 1975

Kenyon, G. H., 1967 *The Glass Industry of the Weald*

Kenyon, J. R., 1978 *Castles, town defences, and artillery fortifications: a bibliography* (CBA Research Report no 25)

Kilbride-Jones, H. E., 1937–8 'Glass Armlets in Britain' *PSAS* 72, 366–95

——. 1980 *Celtic Craftsmanship in Bronze*

Lacaille, A. D., 1954 *The Stone Age in Scotland*

Laing, L., 1975 *Settlement Types in Post-Roman Scotland* (BAR 13)

Lang, J. T. (ed), 1978 *Anglo-Saxon and Viking Age Sculpture and its Context: papers from the Collingwood Symposium on insular sculpture from 800 to 1066* (BAR 49)

Lanting, J. N. and Van Der Waals, J. D., 1972 'British beakers as seen from the Continent', *Helinium* 12, 20–46

Laver, P. G., 1927 'The Excavation of a Tumulus at Lexden, Colchester', *Arch* 76, 241–54

Lawson, A. J., 1976 'Shale and Jet Objects from Silchester', *Arch* 105, 241–75

Lawson, G., 1978, 'Medieval tuning pegs from Whitby, N. Yorkshire', *Med Arch* 22, 139–41

Leeds, E. T., 1945, 'The Distribution of the Angles and Saxons Archaeologically Considered', *Arch* 91, 1–106

——. 1946 'Denmark and Early England', *Ant J* 26, 22–37

——. 1949 *A Corpus of Early Anglo-Saxon Great Square-Headed Brooches*

Leeds, E. T. and Pocock, M., 1971 'A survey of the Anglo-Saxon cruciform brooches of florid type', *Med Arch* 15, 13–36

Lemmon, C. H. and Hill, J. D., 1966 'The Romano-British Site at Bodiam', *Sussex Archaeological Collections* 104, 88–102

Lewis, J. M., 1968 'Medieval church cruets in pottery', *Med Arch* 12, 147–9

——. 1973 'Some Types of Metal Chafing-dish', *Ant J* 53, 59–70

Lewis, M. J. T., 1966 *Temples in Roman Britain*

Limbrey, S., 1975 *Soil Science and Archaeology*

Liversidge, J., 1955 *Furniture in Roman Britain*

——. 1968 *Britain in the Roman Empire*

——. 1969 'Furniture and interior decoration', 127–72 in Rivet, A. L. F., 1969

——. 1977 'Recent Developments in Romano-British Wall Painting', 75–103 in Munby, J. and Henig, M., 1977

Lloyd-Morgan, G., 1977a 'Roman Mirrors in Britain', *CA* 58, 329–31

——. 1977b 'Mirrors in Roman Britain', 231–52 in Munby, J. and Henig, M. 1977

London Museum, 1940 *Medieval Catalogue*

Longworth, I. H., 1961 'The Origins and Development of the Primary Series in the Collared Urn Tradition in England and Wales', *PPS* 27, 263–306

Lowther, A. W. G., 1934 'The Roman "Chimney-Pots" from Ashtead, and Parallel Examples from other Sites', *Surrey Archaeological Collections* 42, 61–6

——. 1948 *Roman Relief-Patterned Flue-Tiles found in Surrey, and others of this Type found in Southern England*

——. 1972 'The Ventilator', 146–7 in Johnston, D. E., 1972

Lynch, F., 1972 'Ring-Cairns and Related Monuments in Wales', *SAF* 4, 61–80

Macalister, R. A. S., 1945 *Corpus Inscriptionum Insularum Celticarum* vol 1

McGrail, S., 1978 *Logboats of England and Wales with comparative material from European and other countries* (BAR 51)

McGrail, S. and Switsur, R., 1979 'Medieval Logboats', *Med Arch* 23, 229–31

MacGregor, A., 1975–6 'Two antler crossbow nuts and some notes on the early development of the crossbow', *PSAS* 107, 317–21

——. 1976 'Bone Skates: a Review of the Evidence', *Arch J* 133, 57–74

——. 1978 'Industry and commerce in Anglo-Scandinavian York', 37–57 in Hall, R. A., 1978

MacGregor, M., 1976 *Early Celtic Art in North Britain*

McInnes, I. J., 1968 'Jet sliders in late neolithic Britain', 137–44 in Coles, J. M. and Simpson, D. D. A., 1968

——. 1971 'Settlements in later Neolithic Britain', 113–30 in Simpson, D. D. A., 1971

McIntyre, J. and Richmond, I., 1934 'Tents of the Roman Army and Leather from Birdoswald', *Transactions of the Cumberland and Westmoreland Antiquarian Society* 34, 62–90

McK Clough, T. H. and Cummins, W. A. (eds), 1979 *Stone Axe Studies* (CBA Research Report no 23)

MacKie, E., 1965 'The Origin and Development of the Broch and Wheelhouse Building Cultures of the Scottish Iron Age', *PPS* 31, 93–146

Macklin, H. W., 1975 *Brasses of England*

Mackreth, D., 1973 *Roman Brooches*

McWhirr, A. and Viner, D., 1978 'The Production and Distribution of Tiles in Roman Britain with particular reference to the Cirencester region', *Britannia* 9, 359–77

Manby, T. G., 1974 *Grooved Ware Sites in Yorkshire and the North of England* (BAR 9)

Mann, J., 1962 *Wallace Collection Catalogues. European Arms and Armour Volume 1 Armour*

Manning, W. H., 1964 'The Plough in Roman Britain', *Journal of Roman Studies* 54, 54–65

——. 1970 'Mattocks, Hoes, Spades and Related Tools in Roman Britain' 18–29 in Gailey, A. and Fenton, A., 1970

——. 1976 *Catalogue of Romano-British Ironwork in the Museum of Antiquities, Newcastle upon Tyne*

Manning, W. H. and Saunders, C., 1972 'A Socketed Iron Axe from Maids Moreton, Buckinghamshire, with a note on the type', *Ant J* 52, 276–92

Margary, I. D., 1973 *Roman Roads in Britain*

Marsh, G. D., 1979 'Three "theatre" masks from London', *Britannia* 10, 263–5

Marshall, D. N., 1976–7 'Carved stone

balls', *PSAS* 108, 40–72

Maxwell-Irving, A. M. T., 1970–1 'Early firearms and their influence on the military and domestic architecture of the Borders', *PSAS* 103, 192–224

Mayhew, N. J., 1975 'A Tumbrel at the Ashmolean Museum', *Ant J* 55, 394–6

Mead, V. K., 1977 'Evidence for the Manufacture of Amber Beads in London in 14th-15th Century', *TLAMAS* 28, 211–14

Meaney, A., 1964 *Gazetteer of Early Anglo-Saxon Burial Sites*

Megaw, J. V. S., 1968 'An end-blown flute from medieval Canterbury', *Med Arch* 12, 149–50

——. 1971 'A Group of Later Iron Age Collars or Neck-rings from Western Britain', 145–56 in Sieveking, G. de G. 1971

Megaw, J. V. S. and Simpson, D. D. A., 1979 *Introduction to British prehistory*

Meirion-Jones, G. I., 1973 'The longhouse: a definition', *Med Arch* 17, 135–7

Mellars, P. A., 1974 'The palaeolithic and mesolithic', 41–99 in Renfrew, C. 1974

Metcalf, D. M. (ed), 1977 *Coinage in Medieval Scotland* (1100–1600) (BAR 45)

Michels, J. W., 1973 *Dating Methods in Archaeology*

Milne, J. G., 1948 *Finds of Greek coins in the British Isles*

Money, J. H., 1974 'Clay spacers from the Romano-British bath-house at Garden Hill, Hartfield, Sussex', *Ant J* 54, 278–80

Moorhouse, S., 1972 'Medieval distilling-apparatus of glass and pottery', *Med Arch* 16, 79–121

Morris, P., 1979 *Agricultural buildings in Roman Britain* (BAR 70)

Morris, R., 1979 *Cathedrals and Abbeys of England and Wales*

Muckelroy, K. W., 1976 'Enclosed Ambulatories in Romano-Celtic Temples in Britain', *Britannia* 7, 173–91

Munby, J. and Henig, M. (eds), 1977 *Roman Life and Art in Britain* (BAR 41)

Musty, J., 1974 'Medieval pottery kilns', 41–65 in Evison, V. I. et al, 1974

Myres, J. N. L., 1977 *A Corpus of Anglo-Saxon Pottery of the Pagan Period*

Myres, J. N. L. and Green, B., 1973 *The Anglo-Saxon Cemeteries of Caistor-by-Norwich and Markshall, Norwich*

Nash-Williams, V. E., 1950 *The Early Christian Monuments of Wales*

Neal, D. S., 1976 'Floor mosaics', 240–52 in Strong, D. and Brown, D., 1976

Newton, R. G., 1971 'The enigma of the layered crusts on some weathered glasses, a chronological account of the investigations', *Archaeometry* 13, 1–9

Newton, R. G. and Renfrew, C., 1970 'British Faience Beads Reconsidered', *Ant* 44, 199–206

Norman, A. V. B. and Pottinger, D., 1979 *English Weapons and Warfare 449–1660*

Oakley, K. P., 1972 *Man the Toolmaker* (6th edition)

Ordnance Survey, 1962 *Map of Southern Britain in the Iron Age*

——. 1966 *Map of Britain in the Dark Ages*

Orton, C., 1980 *Mathematics in Archaeology*

Oswald, F. and Pryce, T. D., 1920 *Introduction to the Study of Terra Sigillata*

Page, R. I., 1973 *An Introduction to English Runes*

Pantin, W. A., 1961 'Medieval Inns', 166–91 in Jope, E. M. 1961a

Patterson, R., 1956, 'Spinning and Weaving', 191–200 in Singer, C. et al, 1956

Payne-Gallwey, R., 1903 *The Crossbow*

Peacock, D. P. S., 1971 'Whetstones', 153–5 in Cunliffe, B., 1971

Phillips, C. W. (ed), 1970 *The Fenland in Roman Times*

Philp, B., 1973 *Excavations in West Kent 1960–1970*

Piggott, S., 1935 'Neolithic Pottery Spoon from Kent', *PPS* 1, 150–1

——. 1950 'Swords and Scabbards of the British Early Iron Age', *PPS* 16, 1–28

——. 1954 *Neolithic Cultures of the British Isles*

——. 1955 'Three Metal-work Hoards of the Roman Period from Southern Scotland', *PSAS* 87, 1–50

——. 1959 'The Carnyx in Early Iron Age Britain', *Ant J* 39, 19–32

——. 1968 *The Druids*

——. 1971 'Firedogs in Iron Age Britain and beyond', 245–70 in Boardman, J. et al, 1971

Pitts, M., 1980 *Later Stone Implements*

Platt, C., 1969 *The Monastic Grange in Medieval England. A Reassessment*

——. 1976 *The English Medieval Town*

——. 1978 *Medieval England*

Platt, C. and Coleman-Smith, R., 1975 *Excavations in Medieval Southampton 1953–1969 volume 2 The Finds*

Potter, T. W., 1979 *Romans in North-West England*

Pratt, P., 1976 'Wall painting', 222–9 in Strong, D. and Brown, D., 1976

Price, J., 1976 'Glass', 111–25 in Strong, D. and Brown, D., 1976

——. 1978 'Trade in glass', 70–8 in du Plat Taylor, J. and Cleere, H. 1978

Rackham, B., 1972 *Medieval English Pottery*

Rahtz, P., 1976 'Buildings and rural settlement , 49–98 in Wilson, D. M. 1976a

Rahtz, P., Dickinson, T. and Watts, L., 1980 *Anglo-Saxon Cemeteries 1979* (BAR 82)

Rainey, A., 1973 *Mosaics in Roman Britain*

RCHM, 1962 *Eburacum Roman York*

Reece, R., 1970 *Roman Coins*

——. (ed), 1977 *Burial in the Roman World* (CBA Research Report no 22)

Reed, R., 1972 *Ancient Skins, Parchments and Leathers*

Rees, S. E., 1979 *Agricultural Implements in Prehistoric and Roman Britain* (BAR 69)

Renaud, J. G. N. (ed), 1968 *Rotterdam Papers. A contribution to medieval archaeology*

Renfrew, C. (ed), 1974 *British Prehistory: a new outline*

Renn, D., 1973 *Norman Castles in Britain*

Reynolds, P. J., 1974 'Experimental Iron Age Storage Pits', *PPS* 40, 118–31

Richardson, K. M., 1961 'Excavations in Hungate, York', *Arch J*, 116, 51–114

Richmond, I., 1969 'The Plans of Roman Villas in Britain', 49–70 in Rivet, A. L. F., 1969

Riehm, K., 1961 'Prehistoric Salt-Boiling', *Ant* 35, 181–91

Rigold, S. E., 1975 'Structural aspects of medieval timber bridges', *Med Arch* 19, 48–91

Ritchie, J. N. G. and MacLaren, A., 1972 'Ring-Cairns and Related Monuments in Scotland', *SAF* 4, 1–17

Rivet, A. L. F. (ed), 1966 *The Iron Age in Northern Britain*

——. (ed), 1969 *The Roman Villa in Britain*

Robertson, A., Scott, M. and Keppie, L., 1975 *Bar Hill: A Roman Fort and its Finds* (BAR 16)

Robins, F. W., 1948 *The Story of the Bridge*

Robinson, H. R., 1975 *The Armour of Imperial Rome*

Rodwell, W., 1979 'Lead plaques from the tombs of the Saxon bishops of Wells', *Ant J* 59, 407–10

Rodwell, W. and Rowley, T. (eds), 1975 *Small Towns of Roman Britain* (BAR 15)

Roe, D. A., 1960 'Horn Cheek-pieces', *Ant J* 40, 68–72

Roe, F. E. S., 1966 'The Battle-Axe Series in Britain', *PPS* 32, 199–245

——. 1979 'Typology of stone implements with shaftholes', 23–48 in McK Clough, T. H. and Cummings, W. A., 1979

Ross, A., 1967 *Pagan Celtic Britain*

——. 1968 'Shafts, pits, wells — sanctuaries of the Belgic Britons?', 255–85 in Coles, J. M. and Simpson, D. D. A., 1968

Rowlands, M. J., 1976 *The Production and Distribution of Metalwork in the Middle Bronze Age in Southern Britain* (BAR 31)

Ryder, M. L., 1969 'Remains of Fishes and Other Aquatic Animals', 376–94 in Brothwell, D. and Higgs, E. S., 1969

Salmon, J., 1966 'A Note on early tower windmills', *JBAA* 29, 3rd series, 75

Schwarcz, H. P., 1980 'Absolute age determination of archaeological sites by uranium series dating of travertines', *Archaeometry* 22, 3–24

Sear, F., 1976 'Wall and Vault Mosaics', 231–9 in Strong, D. and Brown, D., 1976

Sedgley, J. P., 1975 *The Roman Milestones of Britain: their petrography and probable origins* (BAR 18)

Selkirk, A. and W. (eds), 1979 *CA* 57

Semenov, S. A., 1964 *Prehistoric Technology*

Shackleton, N. J., 1969 'Marine Mollusca in Archaeology', 407–14 in Brothwell, D. and Higgs, E. S., 1969

Shepard, A. O., 1956 *Ceramics for the Archaeologist*

Sherlock, D., 1976 'Silver and silversmithing', 11–23 in Strong, D. and Brown, D., 1976

Shortt, H. de S., 1959 'A provincial Roman spur from Longstock, Hants, and other spurs from Roman Britain', *Ant J* 39, 61–76

Shotton, F. W. (ed), 1977 *British Quaternary Studies. Recent Advances*

Sieveking, G. de G. (ed), 1971 *Prehistoric and Roman Studies*

Simpson, C. J., 1976 'Belt-Buckles and Strap-Ends of the later Roman Empire; a preliminary Survey of several new groups', *Britannia* 7, 192–223

Simpson, D. D. A., 1968 'Food Vessels: associations and chronology', 197–211 in Coles, J. M. and Simpson, D. D. A., 1968

——. (ed), 1971 *Economy and settlement in Neolithic and Early Bronze Age Britain and Europe*

Simpson, D. D. A. and Thawley, J. E., 1972 'Single Grave Art in Britain', *SAF* 4, 81–104

Simpson, M., 1968 'Massive armlets in the North British Iron Age', 233–54 in Coles, J. M. and Simpson, D. D. A., 1968

Singer, C., Holmyard, E. J., Hall, A. R. and Williams, T. I. (eds), 1956 *A History of Technology. Volume II. The Mediterranean Civilizations and the Middle Ages c. 700 BC to c. AD 1500*

Smith, D. J., 1969 'The Mosaic Pavements', 71–125 in Rivet, A. L. F., 1969

Smith, E., Cook, O. and Hutton, G., 1976 *English Parish Churches*

Smith, I. F., 1971 'Causewayed enclosures', 89–112 in Simpson, D. D. A., 1971

——. 1974 'The neolithic', 100–36 in Renfrew, C., 1974

Smith, M. A., 1959 'Some Somerset Hoards and their place in the Bronze Age of Southern Britain', *PPS* 25, 144–87

Southwark and Lambeth Archaeological Excavation Committee, 1978 *Southwark Excavations 1972–74 I & II*

Spencer, B. W., 1968 'Medieval pilgrim badges', 137–53 in Renaud, J. G. N., 1968

——. 1971 'A Scallop-Shell Ampulla from Caistor and Comparable Pilgrim Souvenirs', *LHA* 6, 59–66

——. 1975 'The ampullae from Cuckoo Lane', 242–9 in Platt, C. and Coleman-Smith, R., 1975

Spratling, M. G., 1979 'The Debris of Metal Working', 125–49 in Wainwright, G. J., 1979

Stanford, S. C., 1974 *Croft Ambrey*

——. 1980 *The Archaeology of the Welsh Marches*

Stead, I. M., 1979 *The Arras Culture*

Stevenson, R. B. K., 1976 'Romano-British Glass Bangles', *Glasgow Archaeological Journal* 4, 45–54

Stone, J. F. S. and Thomas, L. C., 1956 'The use and distribution of Faience in the Ancient East and Prehistoric Europe', *PPS* 22, 37–84

Strong, D. and Brown, D. (eds), 1976 *Roman Crafts*

Swan, V. G., 1978 *Pottery in Roman Britain*

Swanton, M. J., 1973 *The Spearheads of the Anglo-Saxon Settlements*

Tatton-Brown, T., 1974 'Excavations at the Custom House Site, City of London, 1973', *TLAMAS* 25, 117–219

Taylor, C. C., 1974 *Fieldwork in Medieval Archaeology*

——. 1975 *Fields in the English Landscape*

——. 1978 'Moated sites: their definition, form, and classification', 5–13 in Aberg, F. A. (ed), 1978

——. 1979 *Roads and Tracks of Britain*

Taylor, F. S. and Singer, C., 1956 'Pre-Scientific Industrial Chemistry', 347–74 in Singer, C. et al, 1956

Taylor, H. M., 1978 *Anglo-Saxon Architecture* vol III

Taylor, J. J., 1970 'Lunulae Reconsidered', *PPS* 36, 35–81

Thom, A., 1967 *Megalithic Sites in Britain*

——. 1971 *Megalithic Lunar Observatories*

Thomas, A. C., 1968 'Grass-marked pottery in Cornwall', 311–31 in Coles, J. M. and Simpson, D. D. A., 1968

——. 1970 'Bronze Age Spade Marks at Gwithian, Cornwall', 10–17 in Gailey, A. and Fenton, A., 1970

——. 1971a *Britain and Ireland in Early Christian Times AD 400–800*

——. 1971b *The Early Christian Archaeology of North Britain*

Thompson, F. H., 1976 'The Excavation of the Roman Amphitheatre at Chester', *Arch* 105, 127–239

Tite, M. S., 1973 *Methods of Physical Examination in Archaeology*

Tixier, J., 1974 *Glossary for the Description of Stone Tools with special reference to the Epipalaeolithic of the Mahgreb* (translated by M. H. Newcomer)

Todd, M. (ed), 1978 *Studies in the Romano-British Villa*

Toller, H., 1977 *Roman Lead Coffins and Ossuaria in Britain* (BAR 38)

Tonnochy, A. B., 1952 *Catalogue of British Seal-Dies in the British Museum*

Toy, S., 1966 *The Castles of Great Britain*

Toynbee, J. M. C., 1964 *Art in Britain under the Romans*

Turner, H. L., 1971 *Town Defences in England and Wales*

Turner, R. C., 1979 'The identification of

the game', 76–9 in Potter, T. W., 1979

Tylecote, R. F., 1962 *Metallurgy in Archaeology*

——. 1976 *A History of Metallurgy*

Vatcher, F. de M. and L., 1976 *The Avebury Monuments*

Wacher, J. S., 1971 'Roman Iron Beams', *Britannia* 2, 200–2

——. 1974 *The Towns of Roman Britain*

——. 1978 *Roman Britain*

Wainwright, F. T. (ed), 1962 *The Northern Isles*

Wainwright, G. J., 1971 'The Excavation of a fortified Settlement at Walesland Rath, Pembrokeshire', *Britannia* 2, 48–108

——. 1979 *Gussage All Saints: An Iron Age Settlement in Dorset*

Wainwright, G. J. and Longworth, I. H., 1971 *Durrington Walls: Excavations 1966–1968*

Ward Perkins, J. B., 1937 (1938) 'English Medieval Embossed Tiles', *Arch J* 94, 128–53

Waterer, J. W., 1956 'Leather', 147–90 in Singer, C. et al, 1956

——. 1968 *Leather Craftsmanship*

——. 1976 'Leatherwork', 178–93 in Strong, D. and Brown, D., 1976

Webster, G., 1955 'A note on the use of coal in Roman Britain', *Ant J* 35, 199–217

——. 1969 *The Roman Imperial Army*

——. 1974 *Practical Archaeology*

——. (ed), 1976 *Romano-British coarse pottery: a student's guide* (CBA Research Report no 6, 3rd edition)

Wheeler, R. E. M., 1929 (1930) 'The Roman Lighthouses at Dover', *Arch J* 86, 29–46

——. 1930 *London in Roman Times* (London Museum catalogue no 3)

——. 1935 *London and the Saxons* (London Museum catalogue no 6)

——. 1943 *Maiden Castle, Dorset*

Whimster, R., 1977 'Iron Age burial in southern Britain', *PPS* 43, 317–27

Whittle, A. W. R., 1977 *The Earlier Neolithic of S. England and its Continental Background* (BAR supplementary series 35)

Wild, J. P., 1970a *Textile manufacture in the Northern Roman Provinces*

——. 1970b 'Button-and-Loop Fasteners in the Roman Provinces', *Britannia* 1, 137–55

Williams, J. H., 1971 'Roman Building-

materials in South-East England', *Britannia* 2, 166–95

——. 1979 *St Peter's Street, Northampton. Excavations 1973–1976*

Wilson, D. M., 1965 'Some neglected late Anglo-Saxon swords', *Med Arch* 9, 32–54

——. (ed), 1976a *The Archaeology of Anglo-Saxon England*

——. 1976b 'Craft and industry', 253–81 in Wilson, D. M., 1976a

Wilson, D. R. (ed), 1975 *Aerial reconnaissance for archaeology* (CBA Research Report no 12)

Wood, E. S., 1979 *Collins Field Guide to Archaeology in Britain* (revised edition)

Wood, M., 1965 *The English Medieval House*

Wright, J. A., 1975 *Medieval Floor Tiles*

Wymer, J. J., 1968 *Lower Palaeolithic Archaeology in Britain: as represented by the Thames Valley*

——. (ed), 1977a *Gazetteer of mesolithic sites in England and Wales* (CBA Research Report no 20)

——. 1977b 'The archaeology of man in the British Quaternary', 93–106 in Shotton, F. W., 1977b

Index

In any sequence of page numbers, those printed in **bold** type refer to the clearest explanation(s) of the term.

abbeys, 173
abbots, 173
A, B & C beakers, 70
Abercromby, 70
Abingdon ware, 40
abrading, 257, **276**
abrasion, 257
abroad, 76, 80
absolute dates, 231
  magnetometers, 208
absolute pollen analysis, 217
  diagrams, 217
abutments, 110
acanthus ornament, 163
access holes, 269, 270
accessory vessels, 71-2, 164
Acheulian, 9, 10, 12, 13, **14-16**
  industries, 14-16
acid, 217, 223, 224, 230
acidity, 224
acid soils, 146, **227**
acorn derivative knops, 182
acorn knops, 182
Acton, Greater London, 17
Acton Park, Clwyd, 54
Acton Park phase, 54, 55
ad, 232
AD, 231
adzes, **21**, 25, 26, **37**, **85**, **117**, **149**, **150**, 255, **256**, 262
Aegean, 70
aeolian sediments, 223
aerial photographs, **205-6**, 216, 226
  photography, 205-6
aerobic, 228
Aethelraed II, 153
Africa, 164
Aftonian, 11
agger, 110
agglomerative techniques, 239
aggregate, 147
agricultural tools, **117-19**, **151**, **183**, 184, 188
agriculture (see also farming & cultivation), 216, 227, 241, **245-51**
  Bronze Age, 45-6
  Iron Age, 79
  Neolithic, 27-8
  Roman, 102, 107, 117
  Saxon, 143-4
aircraft, 206
air jets, 264
air photographs, 205
  photography, 205
aisled, 103, 169, 173
  houses, 107
  villas, 107
  wheelhouses, 76
aisle posts, 169
aisles, 105, **107**, 145, 169, 174, **175**

alchemists, 198
alchemy, 198
alcohol, 208
Aldbourne, Wiltshire, 48
Aldbourne cups, 48, **72**
Aldbourne-Edmonsham group, 48
alder, 11, 217
alembics, 198, 203, 204
algae, 219
Alice Holt pottery, 130
alkaline, **224**, 268
alkalis, 253
All Cannings Cross – Meon Hill group, 81
allerød, 12, 218
allochthonous deposits, 227
All Over Cord beakers, 70
all over cord decoration, 70
alloys, 84, 113, 114, 178, 207, 229, 264, 265, 267, 268
almond knob beakers, 127, 128
almshouses, 170
alphabets, 162
Alpha Omega, 104
Alps, 11
altars, **105**, 174, 175
alum, 252, 253
alum-dressing, 253
amalgam, 268
amber, **26**, 48, 64, **68-9**, **84**, 87, 88, 112, 116, 140, 153, 154, 157, **160**, **192**
ambulatories, 105
America, 11, 232
ammunition, 232
amphibians, 221
amphitheatres, 99, 103
amphorae, **83**, 96, 98, 130, **131-2**, **164**, **166**
Ampleforth Moor, North Yorkshire, 97
ampullae, 178, **180**
amulets, **66**, 115
anaerobic, 217, 219, 221, **223**, 224, 227, 228
anchor chapes, 90
ancient coastlines, 225
Andernach lava, 112
angle-backed blades, 19
Angles, 143
Anglesey, Gwynedd, 181
Anglian, 155, 156
Anglian Glaciation, **10**, **11**, 13
Anglo-Norman churches, 174
Anglo-Saxon period, 143
angular rims, 282
  spearheads, 151
animal
  bones (see also bones), 14, 28, 45, 79
  brains, 253
  dung, 253

figures, 201
hair, 252
  -like heads, 85
  motifs, 163
  patterns, 155
  remains, 215, **220-2**, 224
  skins, 253-4
  tissue, 220
animals, 13, 26, 28, 91, 95, 107, 110, 111, 112, 129, 130, **144**, 147, 156, 160, 161, 162, 170, 181, 182, 190, 197, 203, **216**, 219, **220-2**, 223, 224, 228, 233, 243, 245, 252, 253, 254
annealing, **265**, 266, 267, 268, **269**
  ovens, **269**, 270, 271, 272
annular beads, 87
  brooches, 155, 179
  loomweights, 157
antefixes, 110
Antepenultimate Glaciation, 11
Antepenultimate Interglacial, 11
antimonial bronze, 264
antimony, 264, **269**
antler
  artifacts, 9, **20**, **24**, **25**, 36, **44**, 66, **68**, 80, **83-4**, 91, 92, **115**, 116, **159-60**, 186, **192-3**, 257
  chisels, 25
  combs, 44
  handles, 44
  picks, 36, **44**, 83, 245
  rakes, 44
  sleeves, 21, **25**, 38
  wedges, 25
  working, 160, 192, 264
antlers, 25, **220**
Antonine Wall, 101
antoninianus, 136
anvil flaking, 14, **260**
  stones, 260
anvils, **117**, 149, 267
AOC beakers, 70
aplastic, 279
AP:NAP ratio, **11**, 217
apodyterium, 104
Apollo, 94
apostles, 196
apple, 73
applied, 81, 128
  brooches, 155
  clay, 72, 129
  decoration, 41, 71, **278**
  disc brooches, 155
  saucer brooches, 155
  strips, 201
appliqué decoration, 132, **278**
APs, 205
apses, 105, 173
apsidal, 104, 145, 174
aquamaniles, 203, 204

aquatic sediments, 222-3
aqueducts, 103
arable, 168, 241
  agriculture, 245
  farming, **46**, **79**, 219, 249
  land, 241
arboreal vegetation, 11, 218
archaeobotany, 217
archaeomagnetic dating, **233**, 234
archaeomagnetism, 233
archaeozoology, 220
arch buttresses, 175
arched, 103
  braces, 168
  fireplaces, 169
archers, 123
archers' equipment, 66
archery, 66, 68
arches, **106**, **174**, **175**, 176
archways, 145, 175
arcs, 165
arctic fox, 13
ard beams, 83
  heads, 246
  marks, 246
  points, 246, 247
ards, 245-8
area excavation, 210
arenas, 100, **103**
armatures, 196, 277
armets, 184, 185
armlets, **54**, **56**, **69**, 84, **87**, **88**, 147, 153, **154**
Armorica, 52
Armorican coins, 95
Armorico-British daggers, 48, **52**
armour, 90, **91**, 111, **123-6**, 178, **184-6**, 190
armourers, 184
arm-purses, 136
arm-rings, 84, 136-7
arms (see also weapons), 123
army, 100, 110, 132, 143, 156
Arras culture, 74
  group, 82
Arras type beads, 87
  burials, 97-8
Arretine ware, 83, **129**
Arreton Down, Isle of Wight, 54
Arreton Down tradition, **54**, **55**, 64
arrowheads, **22**, **23**, 26, **39**, 47-8, **54**, **65**, **90**, **123**, **124**, 153, **185**, **186**
arrow loops, **167**, 171
arrows, 21, 123, 153, 167, 185
arrowshafts, 26, 42, 153
arrow slits, 167
arsenic, 264
arsenical bronze, 264
art, 51, **95**, 143, **163**

artery forceps, 138
articulated inhumations, 32
  skeletons, 243
artifact analysis, 228-31
artillery, 102, **123**
  bolt-heads, 124
  machines, 123
aryballos, 127
as (pl asses), 136
ash, 46, 73, 151, 194, 217,
  218
ashes, 108, 120, 142, 251,
  268
ashlar, 112, 145
assarting, 251
assarts, 251
assemblages, 14, 15, 16, 19,
  21, 22, 23, **213**, 220, 235,
  236, 237, 243
asses, 123, 124, 136
association, **213**, 234, 242
ass skins, 253
astronomy, 50
Atlantic, 218
atomic absorption spectrometry, 231
atomic numbers, 231
atoms, 208, 230
Atrebates, 94
Atrebatic pottery, 82, 83
attached finials, 200
attributes, **235**, 236, 238
Aubrey Holes, 50
Auchterhouse, Tayside, 54
Auchterhouse phase, 54
Aucissa brooches, 140
auditorium, 103
augering, 207
augers, 183, **207**, **255**, 256
Augustinian order, 173
Augustus, 96
aureus (pl aurei), 136
Austria, 9
autochthonous   deposits,
  227
autumn, 254
auxiliaries, 124
auxiliary troops, 123
Avebury, Wiltshire, 29, 49
aventails, 184, 185
Avenue, the (Stonehenge),
  51
Avon, River, 51
awls, **19**, **21**, **25**, **39**, **44**, 47,
  52, **53**, **68**, **73**, 83, 84, **85**,
  117, 192, **193**, **254**, **255**,
  256, 257, 264
awnings, 103
axe-adzes, 117
axe factories, **36-7**, 38, 257
axe-hammers, **65**, 66, **67**,
  85, **86**, 146, 150
axes, 14, 242, **255**, **256**,
  257, 262
  Bronze Age, 48, **52**, **53**,
  54, **55**, **57**, **59**, **60**, **61**, **62**,
  63, **64**, 65
  Iron Age, 85, 86
  Medieval, **183**, 188
  Mesolithic, **21**, **22**, 25, 26
  Neolithic, **36-8**, 42, **43**
  Roman, **112**, **117**, **118**,
  183
  Saxon, **149**, **150**, 153
axle-caps, 91, 93, 111
axle ends, 92
axles, 83, 91
Aylesford, Kent, 98
Aylesford-Swarling ceme-
  teries, 98
  pottery, 82-3

backed blades, 19, 263-4
  knives, 17
backgammon, 137, 194
backing, 277
backyards, 168
badges, 180
bag beakers, 163
baggy vessels, 284
bags, 44, 83, 114, 146, 158,
  160, **191**, 216, 243, 278
bag-shaped chapes, 61
baileys, 171, 172
baked clay (*see also* clay),
  73, 80, 87, 90, 95, 116,
  123, 157, 178, 195, 199
baker's peels, 120
balance arms, 135, 181
balanced sickles, 27
balance pans (*see also* scale
  pans), 136
balances, **135-6**, **148**, **149**,
  178, **181**
balance scales, 136
balance weights (*see also*
  weights), 147
baldrics, 123
balks, 210
ballast, 75
Ballimore, Strathclyde, 62
Ballimore phase, 62
Ballintober, Ireland, 55
Ballintober swords, 55, 59
ballista balls, 123
ballistae, 123
ball knops, 182
ballock daggers, 187
balls, **43**, **51-2**, 66, **123**, 189,
  229, 251
baluster jugs, 202
baluster-moulded, 151
band pattern, 275
bangles, 84, **87**, 114, 126,
  139, **154**, 163
banjo enclosures, 79
bank barrows, 31
banks, 28, 29, 30, 31, 32,
  36, 45, 46, 47, 48, 49, 50,
  75, 76, 77, 79, 100, 101,
  102, 103, 147, 177, **206**,
  227, 228, 250, 251, 269
Bann culture, 27
baptism, 104
barbarous radiates, 136
barbed and tanged arrow-
  heads, 47-8, **65**, **67**
barbed arrowheads, 123,
  185, **186**
  spearheads, **24**, **25**, **62**,
  123, 124, 151
barbicans, 171
barbotine beakers, 130
  decoration, 278
barbs, 21, 25, 65
barb-spring padlocks, 121
bar charts, 235-6
barges, 112
bar hammer technique, **14-
  15**, 260
bark, 26, 232, 251, 253, 255
barked, 255
barley, **27**, 45, 46, 79, 117,
  144, 205, **206**
barns, 107, 168, 173
barrack blocks, 99, 100
barracks, 99, 100
barrel jars, 82
  jugs, 202, 203
barrel-padlock keys, 190
barrel-padlocks, 190
barrels, **115**, 158, 165, 188,

194
barrel-shaped, 79, **127**, **128**,
  203
barrel urns, 72
barrel vault ceilings, 174
barrel vaults, 175, 176
barrow burials, 98, 147
  cemeteries, 243
barrows, 177, 210, **243**, 245,
  246
  Bronze Age, **46-7**, 48, 49,
  50, 51
  Iron Age, 97, 98
  Neolithic, **30-6**, 43, 47, 48
  Roman, 142
  Saxon, 146
bar-shaped ingots, 113
bar shares, 246, 248
  torcs, 64
  tracery, 174
barter, 85
Barton Bendish, Norfolk, 54
basal-looped spearheads,
  54, 57, 58
basaltic rocks, 257
bascinets, 184, 185
baselards, 187, **188**
base lines, **213**, 214
  plates, 155
  rings, 272, 273
bases, of vessels, 40, 41, 71,
  81, 128, 131, 132, 165,
  181, 191, 197, 201, 270,
  272, **273**, 277, **278**, 284
basic soils, 227
basilards, 188
basilica exercitatoria, 99
basilicas, 102-3, 107
basinets, 184
basins, 147, 175
basketry, 80
baskets, 36, 158
basket-shaped earrings, 47,
  52, **64**
basketwork, 40, 73, 80, 83,
  114, 194, 211
bastard swords, 187
bastel-houses, 170
bast fibres, 251
bastles, 170
batches, **269**, 276
bath buildings, 100, 121
bath-houses, **99**, 121
baths, 102, 103, **104**, 110,
  113, 122
bath-shaped pits, 79
bath suites, **104**, 106, 107
bating, 253
bâtons-de-commandement,
  20
batter, 75
battered-back blades, 263
Battersea, 162
battle, 98, 150, 153
battle axes, 48, **65**, **67**, **183**,
  188
battlements, 101, **172**, **173**
baulks, 209, 210, 211
bayleaf-shaped   currency
  bars, 85
bays, **168**, **169**, 176
BB1, 131
BB2, 130, **131**
bc, 232
BC/AD system, 231
beaches, 114, 222, **225**, 227,
  257
beacon platforms, 101
  stands, 100
beaded rims (*see also* bead
  rims), 82

torcs, 86
bead rims (*see also* beaded
  rims), 83, **282**
beads, **26**, 44, 48, **52**, **53**, **64**,
  65, **68**, **69**, **70**, 83, 84, **87**,
  96, 114, 126, **140-1**, 151,
  153, **154**, 159, 160, 192,
  239, 270, **274-5**
Beaker
  bone and antler artifacts,
  68
  burial, 45, **47-8**, 50, 52,
  70
  culture, 45, 52, 64
  flint & stone work, 64-6,
  67
  metalwork, **52**, **53**, **64**
  pottery, 45, 47, 68, **70**
  settlement & economy, 45
beakers (*see also* Beaker
  pottery), 83, 122, **127**,
  128, 129, 130, 131, **132**,
  133, **163**, **164**, 198, 273
beaks, 221
beam ards, 246
  slots, **211**, 228
beaming knives, 253
beams, 83, **104**, **121**, 144,
  147, **177**, **211**, 230, 232,
  246, **249**, 252, **253**
beans, 117
bear, 13
bearded axes, 183
beasts, 196
beating, 113
Beaumaris castle, Anglesey,
  Gwynedd, 172
bedding trenches, **31**, **211**,
  228
bedehouses, 170
Bedfordshire, 81
bedrock, 207
beds, 28, 110, **189**
bed-sitting rooms, 169
beech, 43, 73, 218, 268
beehive bases, 203
  querns, 80, 112
  rotary querns, 80
beehive-shaped, 79
beetles, 221
belfries, 145
Belgae, 248
Belgic immigration, 74
  invasions, 78
Belgium, 143
bell barrows, 46, 47, 48
  beakers, 70, 163
  towers, 174
Belle Tout, Sussex, 45
bell-founding, 178
Bellovacian coins, 94
bellows, 266, 269
bells, 112, 114, 149, **178**
belt, attachment plates, 157
  buckles, 153, 156
  chapes, 178, **179**
  -end buckles, 179
  ends, 126
  fasteners, 44, 68
  fittings, **126**, 143, 153,
  156-7
  -hooks, 64, **65**, **68**
  mounts/mountings, **126**,
  128, 146, **157**
  plates, 125, 126, 156
  -rings, 48, **68**, **69**
  sliders, 44
  stiffeners, 125, 126, 157
belts, 66, 90, 96, 123, 126,
  158, 160, **179**, 191, 192,
  194

bench ends, 110
  marks, 214
benches, 105, 110, **253**
Benedictine order, 173
Berkshire, 25
  Downs, 82
bermed barrows, 46
berms, 46, **77**
beta-ray back-scattering, 231
beta-rays, 231
bevelled rims, 282
Bexley Heath, Greater London, 61
Bexley Heath tradition, 61
bezels, 141
biblical, 128, 181, 196
biconical
  beads, 141
  bowls, 132
  chopper-cores, 14
  chopping tools, 14
  jugs, 202, 203
  urns, 71, 165
  vessels, 283
bifaces, 14, 261
bifacially worked, 14
bifacial flaking, 261
bifid razors, 54, 58
bill heads, 188
  hooks, 85, 86
bills, 183, **188**
bindings, 64, 65, 85, 111, 194
biological, 207, 229
bipartite bowls, 81
  situlae, 81
birch, 11, 12, 25, 26, 46, 194, 217, 218
  bark, 26
bird bones, 40, 278
  remains, 221
birds, 13, 79, 144, 196, **221**, 228
biscuit firing, **280**, 281
  pots, **280**, 281
bishop's throne, 174
bison, 13
bisque firing, 280
bits, **92, 93, 111**, 149, **150**, 178, **190**, 255
bivalve moulds, 66, 264
bivalves, 222
black burnished 1, 131
black burnished 2, 131
black burnished wares, 81, **131**
Black Death, 168
blacksmiths' tools (see also smiths), 117, 119, 149
blade cores, 260, **261**
  cultures, 9
blades, 19, 21, 52, 54, 55, 56, 63, 85, 86, 90, 117, 118, 120, 123, 149, **151-2**, 169, 183, 184, 186, 187, 188, 246, 248, 253, 255, 260, **261, 263-4**, 266, 271
blanket bog, 46
  peat, 227
blanks, 94
Blattspitzen industries, 18
bleached, 252
blobs, 128, **197**, 270, 272, **274**
blockhouses, 75
block-on-block flaking, 260
blood-channels, 151
bloom, 266
blowing off-hand, 272
blown beads, 275

sand, 222, **225**
blowpipes, **270, 272,** 274, 275, 276
bluestones, 50, 51
Blunden's Wood, Surrey, 270
Blytt, 11
Blytt and Sernander zones, 11, 12, 218
boar figurines, **95, 148,** 149
boat-bowl, 69
boat burials, **146,** 243
boats, 47, 69, **73,** 146, 158, 243, 255
boat-shaped hollowed tree-trunk coffins, 47
boat shaped houses, 144
  pommels, 151
bobbins, 115, 116, 159, 251
bodkins, 178, 192
Bodvoc, 94
body, 277
  armour, 123-4, 125
  measurement, 50
body-yard, 50
bogs, 46, 79, 96, 218, 219, **227**
boilers, 104, 121
boiling pans, 254
bolt-heads, 123, **124**
bolts, 121, 178
bombards, 188
bonding courses, **100,** 109, 112
bone artifacts, **246, 247,** 253, 254, **257,** 258, 260, 262, 279
  Bronze Age, 45, 48, 66, **68,** 73
  iron Age, **80, 81, 83-4,** 87, **88, 89, 90, 92, 93**
  Medieval, 182, 186, 187, **192-3,** 194, 195
  Mesolithic, 24-5
  Neolithic, 36, **44**
  Palaeolithic, 9, 14, 15, **18,** 19-20
  Roman, 112, **115, 116,** 121, 122, 123, 135, 137, 138, 139, 140, 141
  Saxon, 146, 151, 154, **157, 158, 159-60**
bones, 14, 16, 19, 28, 30, 32, 45, 46, 79, 97, 136, 144, **220-1,** 224, 227, 228, **233,** 243, 245, 278
bone working, 144, 160, 167, 192, **257,** 264
bonfire fired, 131
  kilns, 81, 130, **280,** 281
bookbindings, 158
book clasps, 178
  covers, 194
  markers, 147
bootlace tags, 178
boots, 194
Borders, 54, 111, 114, 126, 170
boreal period, 218
borers, 83
boring-bits, 149, **150**
bosing, 207
Bos longifrons, 46, 79
bosses, 91, 109, **126, 152,** 164, **175,** 176, **190**
bossing tools, 266
boss ornament, 164
bottles, **127-8,** 134, 138, 163, **165, 166,** 194, 197, **198, 203, 204,** 208
bottle-shaped pits, 79

bouchers, 14
boulder clay, **223,** 224
boulders, 161, 223
boundaries, 45, 50, **79, 147,** 205, 211, 242, 249, 250
boundary effect, 240
  markers, 50, 101
bout coupé handaxes, 17
bow and fantail brooches, 140
bow ards, 246
  brooches, 155, 156
  drills, 255, 256, **262-3**
bowl barrows, **46, 47,** 48
  furnaces, 85, 114, 264, **266, 267**
bowls, 254, 271, 277
  Bronze Age, 69, 72, **73**
  Iron Age, **81, 82,** 83, 84
  Medieval, 180, **181,** 182, 194, **197,** 198, **201, 202**
  Roman, 113, 115, 122, **126, 127, 129,** 130, 131, **132, 133**
  Saxon, 146, **148, 149, 158,** 161, **163, 164,** 165, 166
Bowness-on-Solway, Cumbria, 101
bows, **26, 42, 43,** 73, 88, **89,** 153, **185-6,** 194, 255, **262**
bow saws, 117, 255
bow-sided houses, 144
bow steel, 185
bowstrings, 66, **185,** 186
boxes, 28, 47, 73, 115, 121, 130, 132, 141, 148, 149, 158, 160, 194, 203, 216
box flue tiles (see also box tiles & flue tiles), **108,** 120
box-frame construction, **168,** 169
box-style ramparts, 77
box system, 209, 210
  tiles, 120
Boyne culture, 27
bp, 232
BP system, 231
bracelets, **52, 53,** 64, **69,** 84, **87-8,** 114, 115, **139,** 153, **154,** 159, 160, 238
bracers, 48, 64, **66, 186**
braces, **168, 255,** 256
brachycephalic skulls, 221
bracing members, 169
brackets, 197
bracteates, 154
braid, 158, 252
brains, 221, 253
branding irons, 120
Brandwirtschaft, 27
brass, **114, 136, 178,** 180, **264**
brasses, **178,** 196
brass spelter, 267
brattices, 171
braziers, **108,** 144
brazil nut pommels, 186
brazing, 267
breast armour, 111
  augers, **255,** 256
  beams, 252
breccia, 223
breech-loaded cannons, 189
Breedon-Ancaster group, 82
Breton arrowheads, 65
Breton type arrowheads, 65, 67
bricks, 100, 106, 108, 109, **198-9,** 280
bridge-head villages, 168

bridges, 110, 168, **176,** 177
bridle, 111, **185**
  bits, **92, 93,** 111
  bosses, 190
Brigantes, 94
Brighton loops, 54
brine, 253
Brinell hardness number, 229
briquetage, 83, **114, 254**
bristlecone pine, 232
bristles, 149
Bristol Channel, 16, 62
Brittany, 50, 52, 95
British A-R coins, 94
British coins, 94
British X-Z coins, 94
broad-blade industries, 21
broad-butted flat axes, 52
broad-butt flat axes, 52, 53
broad rig, 250
  wall, 101
Broadward complex, 61, **62**
  group, 62
  tradition, 62
brochs, **75-6,** 144
Brockley Hill potteries, 130
broken ring brooches, 155
bronze, 45, 59, 64, 83, 84-5, 113, 114, 149, 178, 229, 241, **264-6,** 268
Bronze Age, 23, 27, 29, 30, 36, **45-73,** 74, 76, 79, 80, 81, 87, 90, 97, 218, 242, 246, 249, 251, 254, 256, 261, 264, 267, 283
bronze artifacts, 238, **264-6**
  Bronze Age, 46, **52-64,** 66, 73, 249
  Iron Age, 80, 81, 83, **84,** 86, 87, 88, 89, 90, 91, 92, 93, 94, 95, 96, 97
  Medieval, **178,** 179, 180, 181, 182, 188, 190, 191, 195
  Roman, **105,** 110, **111, 112,** 114, **116-17, 121, 122, 124, 126,** 128, 134, **135, 136, 137, 138, 139, 140, 141, 142**
  Saxon, 146, **148-9,** 152, **153, 154, 155, 156-7,** 158
bronze disease, 229
  ingots, 64
  sheet (see also sheet bronze), 83
bronzework, 84, 191
bronze working, 84-5, 149, **264-6**
brooches, 84, **88, 89,** 96, 117, 128, **140,** 143, 147, 149, 153, **154-6,** 164, 177, 178, **179,** 192
Broomend, Grampian, 68
brownearth soils, 224, 225
brow-reinforces, 185
Brundon, Suffolk, 13
brushes, **149,** 278
brushwood, 42, 73, 75
  peat, 223
  platforms, 25
Buckelurne (pl Buckel-urnen), 164, 165
bucket bindings, 85
  burials, 98
  urns, 71, 72
buckets, 62, 83, 95, **96, 98, 115,** 146, 149, 158, 194, **195**
Buckinghamshire, 81, 199
buckle plates, 156, 179

bucklers, **152**, **185**, 194
buckles, **92**, **125**, **126**, 143, 146, 149, 153, **156-7**, 159, 177, 178, 179
bugle-shaped objects, 61
buildings, 29, 42, 75, 99, 100, 101, **102-3**, 104, 106, **107**, 116, 158, 160, 162, 164, 168, 169, 170, 171, 173, 177, 199, 208, 211, 212, 254
building tools, 117
bulbar scars, 258, 259
surfaces, 258
bulb-headed pins, 52, 53
bulb pits, 258
bulbs, 14, **258**
of percussion, 15, **258**
bullets, 91, **95**, **123**, 124
bullet-shaped coins, 95
bulls, 95
bulls eye glass, 275
bulls eyes, 275, 276
bunghole jars, 203
pitchers, 203
bun-shaped loomweights, 73, 157, 158
Burghal Hidage, 145
burhs, 145
burial, 213, 221, 242, **243-5**
Bronze Age, 36, 45, **46-9**, 50, 51, 52, 66, 68, 69, 70, 71, 72, 73
Iron Age, 79, 84, 91, 96, **97-8**
Medieval, 175
Neolithic, 28, 29, **30-6**, 42, 43, 44, 46-9
Palaeolithic, 9, 18
Roman, 105, **142**
Saxon, **146-7**, 154, 165
Viking, 143, 146
burial chambers, 32, 51
rites, 31, 33, 71, **243**
buried channels, 226
burin blow technique, 264
burins, **18**, **19**, **21**, 263, **264**
burins busqués, 18
burin spalls, 264
burn-beating, 27
burning-on, 266
burnished, 40, 131, 178, 279
burnishers, 73
burnishing, 68, 83, **279**
Bush Barrow, Wiltshire, 48
Bush Barrow daggers, 52
group, 48
busked burins, 18
busqued burins, 18
butt beakers, 83, **132**, **133**
button-and-loop fasteners, 117
buttonholes, 117
buttons, 48, **68**, **69**, **88**, 115, **117**, 178, 192
button sickles, 54
butt purlin roofs, 169
buttressed buildings, 99
buttresses, 175
butts, **38**, 63, 123, **185**, **255**
byres, 107, 170

cabanes, 144
cable pattern, 275
cables, 139, 208
Caburn-Cissbury style, 82
Caereni, 94
Caesar, Julius, 99
cairnfields, 243
cairns, 29, 30, 31, 33, **34**,

35, **36**, 46, 47, **49**, 50, 51, 97, 226, **243**, 245
Caistor St Edmunds, Norfolk, 268
Caithness flagstone, 28
cake-moulds, 198
cakes, **64**, 138, **198**, 243
Calais Wold group, 65
calamine ore, 178
calcareous, 222, 223, 227
calceus, 114, 115
calcite, 131, 223
calcite-gritted wares, 131
calcite mineral grits, 131
calcium carbonate, 223
calculators, 241
caldarium, 104
Caledones, 94
calfskin, 254
calibrated dates, 232
calibrating, 232
caliga, 114
calipers, 183
calkins, 189
calmes, 277
calthrops, 123, 124
camber, 110
Cambridgeshire, 17, 59, 85, 165
cameo glass, 126, 128, 274
vessels, 126
cameos, 141
cameras, 206, **216**
Camerton, Somerset, 48
Camerton-Snowshill daggers, **48**, **52**, **53**, 54
cames, 178, **277**
campanulate bowls, 132, 133
camping sites, 26
camps, 28-9, 30, **100**, 143
Camulodunum, 132
numbers, 132
candelabra, 134
candle holders, 192
candles, 134, 191, 192
candlesticks, 129, **134**, 178, **191-2**
canes, **271**, 273, **274**
canisters, 142
cannon balls, 189
cannons, 167, **188-9**
canoes, **26**, **42**, **73**, 83, 112
canoe-shaped dugout tree-trunks, 47
canopies, 196
Canterbury, Kent, 180
Cantiaci, 94
cantonal capitals, 102
capes, 64
of mail, 184
capitals, 102, 105, 112
caps, **93**, 177
capstones, 32, 34
carbatina (pl carbatinae), 114
carbon, 219, 232, 266
carbonate organisms, 234
carbon-14 dating, 232
carbon dioxide, 223
carbonic acid, 223
carbonised grain, 219
carded, 195, **251**
carding combs, 115, 116
card weaving, 252
cargo, 112
carinated, 115, 116
jugs, 203
vessels, 283
carnivores, 220
Carnonacae, 94

carnyx (pl carnyxes), 91
carpenters' axes, 183
planes, 117, 118
tools, 117, 118, 149-50, 183
carpentry, 160, 169
carp's tongue complex, 61
sword complex, 61
swords, 61
carro-ballista, 123
cart burials, **97-8**, 243
fittings, 91, 93, 98
wheels, 115
Carthusian order, 173
carts, **91-3**, 97-8, **111**, 123, 243
carved, 96, 105, 110, 112, 156, 160, 161, 162, 174, 176, 199
figures, 42
stone balls, **51-2**, 66
carvel-built ships, 112
carvings, 40, 46, **51-2**, 112, 114, 161
cased glass, 126
cases, 159, 192, 194
casket fittings, 159
keys, 190
caskets, 128, 158, 159, 192
casks, 158, 194
cast, 84, 94, 95, 114, 126, 153, 155, 156, 181, 264, 265, 268
casting, **64**, 113, 127, 128, 149, 192, **264**, **265**, 266, **271**, 274, 275
flashes, 264
jets, 264
casting-on, 266
casting seams, 264
cast iron, 189, **266**
castle complex, 76
castles, 167, **171-3**
of enceinte, 171
Castor boxes, 130, 132
ware, 130
Castor ware boxes, 130
castra, 100
cast window glass, 275
catapulta, 123
catch joints, 86
caterpillar brooches, 155, 156
catgut, 185
cathedrals, 167, **174**, 196
cathode lamps, 231
cattle, 28, 46, 79, 117, 144, 192, 253
compounds, 28
enclosures, 45, 76
Catuvellauni, 94
cauldron chains, 85
hangers, 85
cauldrons, **63**, 84, 85, **181**, **182**, **201**, **202**
causewayed camps, **28-9**, 30
enclosures, 28
causeways, 28, 75, 177
cavalry, 123
sports' helmets, 124
cavea, 103
cave earth, 223
occupation, 46
Caverton, Borders, 54
Caverton phase, 54
caves, 13, 18, 19, **75**, 220, 223, 225, **227**
cavetto rims, 282
C-14 dating, 232
ceilings, 109, 169, 170, 171,

174, 175, 176
cella, 105
cellarium, 173
cellars, 109, **169**, **173**
cell enamel, 268
cells, 76, 173, 176, 219, 251, **268**
cellular plan churches, 145
Celtic, 144, 147, 149, 164
Celtic Britain, **143**, 144, 145, 146, 154, 156, 162
fields, 45, 79, **249**, 250, 251
Celtic-speaking people, 143
Celts, 143
cement, 108, 109, 277
cemeteries, **48**, 49, **97-8**, 142, **146**, 164, 213, **243**, 245
Central, 59
Central Gaulish colour coated pottery, 129
central place, 240
theory, 240
centurial stones, 101
centuriation, 102
centuries, 101
cephalic index, 221
ceramic, 103, 230
cereals, 28, 117, 218
cess pits, 104, 167, 168, 170, **211**, 228
chafing dishes, **181**, 202
chain mail armour, 146, **153**, **184**
chains, 84, 85, **121**, 140, 147, 149, 154, 155, 178, 197, 251
chairs, 110, 272
chalcolithic, 242
chalices, 146, **181-2**
chalk, 31, 36, 43, 73, 79, 80, 83, 96, 97, 107, 108, 110, 113, 114, 116, 157, 160, 167, 175, 195, 206, 208, 212, 224, 226, 257
balls, 43
cups, 43
drums, 43
figurines, 43
plaques, 43
chambered barrows, 30, **32-6**
long barrows, 30
round barrows, 30
tombs, 27, 30, **32-6**
chamber pots, 203
chambers, **32**, 33, 34, **35**, 51, **75**, **78**, 134, 142, 145, **169**, 189
chamfreins, 93
chamfrons, 114, **126**
chamoising, 253
champlevé enamel, 156, **268**
chancels, **145**, 170, **173**, 174, 175
changing rooms, 104
channel flaking, 261
channelled hypocausts, 107, 108
channels, 102, 103, 107, 177, **226**, 264
chapels, **170**, 171, 172, 173, 174
chapes, **59**, **60**, **61**, **62**, **63**, **90**, 149, 151, 178, **179**, **186**, 188
chape-shape ampullae, 180
chaplets, 265
chapter-houses, 173
charcoal, 109, 122, 177,

178, 181, **219**, 227, 266, 268
chariot equipment, 114
  fittings, 84, 85
  horn caps, 91, 93
  horns, 92
  racing, 127
chariots, **91-3**, 111
charms, 112
charred grain, 79
chartered towns, 102
charters, 205
chasing, 266
châtelaines, 149, 160
Cheddar, Somerset, 20
Cheddar Points, 19
Cheddar-type ware, 165
cheekpieces, **68**, 83, **92, 93, 111, 124, 125,** 149, **190**
cheese making, 132
  presses, 132
  wire marks, 278
  wrings, 132
Chelsea, Greater London, 55
Chelsea swords, 55, 59
chemical, 213, 223, 230, 253, 257, 269
  analysis, 230
  weathering, 222, **223**
chert, **257**, 262
Cheshire, 270
chessmen, 159, 160, 192, **194**
Chester-type ware, 165
chest handles, 178
  keys, 190
chests, **115**, 147, 194
chevaux-de-frise, 77
chevron ornament, 174, **275**
chewed, 253
Chichester, Sussex, 128
children, 49, 114, 134
Chilterns, 81
Chilterns and East Anglia style zone, 82
chimney pots, 134-5, **199-200**
chimneys, 135, 169, 200
Chinnor-Wandlebury group, 70
chip-carved, 156
chip-carving, 156
chipping floors, 263
Chi-Rho monograms, **104**, 113
chisel-ended arrowheads, 39
chisels, **25, 37, 39, 44, 54, 55,** 61, **62,** 117, **118,** 149, 183, 255, 256, 267
chloride corrosion, 229
choirs, 173, 174
chopper-cores, 13, 14, 16
chopping blocks, 83
  tools, **14,** 15
Christ, 196
Christian, 105, 108, 113, 142, 146, 161, 162
Christianity, **104-5**, 142, 143, 146, 164, 165
Christos, 104
chronology, 163, 225, **232**
chronometric dates, 231
church bells, 149, **178**
churches, **104-5, 145,** 164, 167, 169, **173, 174-5,** 195, 196, 203
churchyards, 146, 175
cill-beams, 211
cinerary urns, **71,** 164
cinquefoil heads, 196

circular brooches, 155
circus cups, 127
circuses, 103
Cirencester, Gloucestershire, 104
cire perdue, 84, 181, **176**, 271
Cistercian, 173
  wares, 202
cisterns, 203, 204
cists, 48, 49, 51, **97,** 142, 146, 175
citadels, 144
cithara, 137
civitates, 102
Clactonian, 9, **10, 13, 14,** 15, 16
  industries, 13-16
Clacton-on-Sea, Essex, 9, 13, 14
clamp kilns, 109, 164, 201, **280**
clamps, 85, 120
Clarke, D. L., 70
clasps, 146, 153, **154,** 178
Class I axe-hammers, 67
Class II axe-hammers, 67
Class I henges, 29
Class II henges, 29
classical, 84, 94, 95, 96, 103, 104, 105, 112, 163, 174, 181
  temples, 105
classification, 132, 151, **239**
classified, 129, 168, 195, 234, 243, 268
Class I stones, 161
Class II stones, 161
Clava group, 30, **35-6**
  passage graves, 30
clavicula, 100
claw beakers, **163,** 164, 273
claws, 164, 221
clay (see also baked clay), 28, 64, **69,** 72, 73, 79, **80, 83,** 84, 87, 90, **94, 95,** 100, 101, **107-8,** 110, 112, 113, 114, **116,** 123, 128, 129, 138, 141, 144, 153, 157, **164,** 169, 178, 195, 198, 199, 200, 208, 217, 219, 222, **223,** 224, 228, 229, 230, 233, 248, 252, 254, 264, 265, 266, 267, 270, 271, 277, 278, 279, 280, 281
  bars, 254
  cope, 178
  core, 178
  minerals, 223
  paste, 277
  shapes, 277
  slabs, 69
  spacers, 108
clearances, 27, 28, 46, 79, 218, 224, 251
cleats, 85, 120
cleavers, **15,** 123
cleaving, 255
clerestory windows, 105, 173
cliff-castles, 76
cliffs, 223, 227
climate, 9, 13, 26, 46, 216, 218, 220, 221, 222, 224, 225, 226, 227, 232, 253
climatic, 9, 11, 79, 218, 222, 245
  change, 76, 222, 234
clipeus, 124
clips, 85, 120

cloisonné enamel, 156, **268**
  jewellery, 128
  ornament, 156
cloisons, 268
cloister courts, 173
  walks, 173
cloisters, 173
closed base rings, 272, 273
cloth, 110, 149, 158, 176, 191, 252, 281
  seals, 178
clothes, 117, 140, 179
clothing, 83, 114, 140, 154, 180, 277
clubs, 38, **42, 43,** 73, 188
clump kilns, 280
cluster analysis, 239
clusters, 239
Clwyd, 54, 64
Clyde-Carlingford culture, 27
Clyde group, **34,** 35
Cnoc Sligeach, Oronsay, Strathclyde, 26
coal, 113, 114, 157, 281
  money, 114
coarse pottery, 82
  wares, 72, 82, 130-1, 132
coastal, 222, 228, 274
  blown sand, 225
coastlines, 222, **225,** 254
coasts, 25, 26, 83, 87, 100, 101, 272
coats of arms, 196
cob, 79, 80, **169,** 281
cobalt, 269
cobbled, 167, 169
cobblers' feet, 117
  tools (see also shoemakers' tools), 117
cobbles, 144, 169, 210, 213
cob-walled, **169,** 170
cocked hat shaped pommels, 151
Codford St Peter group, 65
coffins, **47, 48,** 73, 97, 113, 142, 158, 175, 182, 192, 255
coffin slabs, 162
coil bases, 272, 273
  building, 277
coiled finger-rings, 54, 56
coils, 277
coinage (see also coins), 75, 84, **94-5,** 113, 147, 178, 179
coin balances, 181
  hoards, 143, 153, **243**
coins (see also coinage), **94-5,** 114, **136,** 143, 146, 149, **153,** 154, 162, 177, **178-9,** 181, 212, 229, 243
Colchester, Essex, 129, 131, 132, 270
Colchester potteries, 130
Colchester type beads, 87
cold chisels, 149
cold-cutting, 271
cold working, **265,** 266, 267
collagen, 253
collared rims, 282
  urns, 71
collar-like torcs, 86
collar purlins, 168
collars, 64, **86,** 115, **121, 168, 249**
collateral flaking, 261
collective burial (see also multiple burial), 34
Cologne, 139
colonia, 102

colonnaded porticoes, 102
colourants, **268-9,** 277
colour charts, 224, 229
  coated wares, 129-30
  coats, 129, 130, **278**
  films, 216
coloured window glass, 145, 164, 196
colourless glass, 196
column bases, 112
columns, **105,** 174, 236, **280**
comb cases, **159,** 192
combed, 109, 251
  ornamentation, 40
combing, 251, 274, **278, 279**
combs, **44, 68,** 73, **80, 81,** 83, **89,** 115, **116, 138,** 146, 158, **159,** 160, 162, 178, **192, 193,** 194, 251, 257
comb stabbing, 278, 279
commandant's house, 99
  quarters, 99
commemorative stones, 160
common rafters, **168,** 169
compass-cut, 160
compasses, **117,** 213
composite
  barrows, 243
  bows, 186
  coffins, 47
  combs, 159, 192, **193**
  disc brooches, 155
  hypocausts, 107
  moulds, 175
  reaping knives, 27
compound pillars, 174
computers, 50, **241**
computer simulation, 241
concave bases, 272
  rims, 282
concentric circles, 49
  ring pattern, 275
conchoidal fractures, **258,** 260, 262
  rings, 258
  waves, 258
concrete, 147
conductivity, 208
cone beakers, 163
cones, 30, **52, 53, 54,** 257, 266
cones of percussion, 14, **257-8**
conical
  roofs, 74
  beads, 64
  bosses, 152
  buttons, 48, **68, 69**
  helmets, 184
  jugs, 202, 203
connecting plates, 192, **193**
conservation, 213
construction trenches, 211
containers, 113, 142, 243, 253
contexts, **213,** 220, **224-8**
context sheets, 216
Continent, the, 18, 22, 26, 27, 37, 51, 54, 63, 70, 74, 84, 87, 94, 95, 98, 126, 128, 143, 145, 163, 165
contour forts, 76
  maps, 241
contours, 76, 208, 241, 249
contracted burials, 97, **243**
  inhumations, 97, **243, 244**
contubernia, 99
convex bases, 284
  scrapers, 39
cooking, 28, 66, 69, 85, 132, 183, 198

INDEX

bowls, 166
pots, 130, 131, 132, 164, 165, 166, 201, 202
vessels, 181
Coolus jockey-caps, 124, 125
coordinates, 213
copper (*see also* copper artifacts), 45, 52, 64, 113, **114**, 149, 153, 178, 229, 242, 264, 265, 267, 268, 269, 277, 281
Copper Age, 242
copper artifacts, 47, **52**, 64, 180, 181
corrosion, 229
ores, **114**, 264
silicate, 109
Coptic bowls, 146
coracles, 112
coral, **84**, 87, 140, 234
corbelled roofs, 35, 76
corbelling, 32
corbels, 32, 168
cordate handaxes, 14, **15**
cordiform handaxes, 17
cordoned, 82, 83, 131
urns, 71
cordons, 71, 81, **133**, **278**, **279**
cords, 64, 141, 192, 255, 256, 263
corduroy foundations, 110
roads, 42
core casting, 265
core-dipping, 271
core rejuvenation, 261
flakes, 261
cores, 9, 10, **16**, **17**, **23**, **24**, 64, 102, 113, 114, 139, 181, 207, 234, 251, **258**, 260, **261**, 264, 265, **271**, **274**
core tablets, 261
tools, **14**, 23, **261**, 262
core-winding, **271**, 274
Coriosolites, 94
Coritani, 94
corium, 253
corn, **27**, 80, **107**, 112, 136
measures, 136
corn-driers, 107
corn-drying kilns, 168
ovens, 107
racks, 45
Cornish urns, 72
corn-milling, 176
Cornovii, 94
Cornwall, 37, 40, 46, 72, 75, 76, 113, 143, 161, 164, 214
corpses, 243
corridors, 78, 102, 106, 173
corries, 226
corrosion, 229
corrugated amphorae, 164
blades, 151
cortex, 257
cosmetic brushes, 149
brush holders, 146, **148**
cosmetics, 138
costrels, 165, 194, **203**, **204**
Cotswolds, 82
Cotswold-Severn group, 33
cottage houses, 106
cotton, 117
couches, 110
coulters, **246**, **247**, 248, **249**
counter relief tiles, 199
counters, 84, 114, 115, 126, **137**, 159, 179, 194

counterscarp banks, 77
country houses, 106
coups de poing, 14
coursed rubble, 145
stone, 145
coursing, 145
courtyard houses, 75, 102
inns, 170
villas, 102, **107**
courtyards, 75, 107, **170**, 171, 173
Coventry, 100
covered walks, 173
ways, 79
coversand, **223**, 226
Covesea Cave, Grampian, 62
Covesea phase, 62
cowrie shells, 26
cracked off, **272**, 276
rims, 272, 273
Crags, 10, 11
Crambeck ware, 130
cranes, 112
crannogs, **75**, 144
craticula, 122
Crayford, Kent, 13
Creffield Road, Acton, Greater London, 17
cremation cemeteries, **48**, **49**, 146
cremations, 30, 32, 44, 46, 47, 48, 49, 50, 71, 72, 73, 97, 98, **142**, 146, **243**, **245**
cremation urns, *see* urns
crenellated, 167, 172
crenellations, 172
crenelles, 172
crenels, 172
Creones, 94
crescentic-headed linch pins, 111
crescents, 22, 23
crescent-shaped linch pins, 91
cresset-lamps, **191**, 192, 198
crests, 124
Creswellian points, 19
Creswell points, 19
Crichie group, 65
Crickley Hill, Gloucestershire, 29
criss-cross pattern, 275
critical angle, 258
Croft-Ambrey-Bredon Hill style, 82
crofts, 168
Cromerian interglacial, 10, 11
cromlechs, 32
crook ards, 246
crop marks, 47, **205**, **206-7**
crops, 27, 144, 206, 207, 221, 245
cross bow bolts, 185
brooches, 140
nuts, **185**, **186**, 192, **193**
cross bows, 123, **185-6**, 189
cross-cut saws, **255**, 256
cross-dating, 234
cross-defences, 76
crosses, 149, **161**, 162, 167, 178, **179**
crossings, 174
cross-passages, 170
crosspieces, 89
cross-ploughing, 246
marks, 46
cross ridge dykes, **45**, 79
cross-roads villages, 168
cross-slab grave covers, 192

cross-slabs, 161
cross-trees, 176-7
cross-vaults, 176
crouched burials, 243
inhumations, 47, 48, 97, **243**, **244**
crowbars, 117
crowned urns, 71
crown glass, 128, **275**, **276**
crown method, 195
crown-posts, 168, 169
crowns, **105**, 136
crucibles, **84**, **85**, 149, 198, **203**, **204**, 264, 267, 268, **269**, 270, 271
crucifixes, 178
cruciform churches, 174
brooches, 155, 156
swords, 186-7
cruck construction, 168, 169
cruck-framed buildings, 169
crucks, 168, 169
cruets, 203
crutch-headed pins, 52, 53
cryptograms, 104
crypts, 145, **169**
crystal, 154, 231
cryoturbation structures, 226
cucurbits, 198, 203, 204
Cuerdale, Lancashire, 147
cuirass, 124
cuir bouilli, 194, **254**
cullet, **269**, 270
cultivated, 225, 248, 249, 250, 251
cultivation (*see also* agriculture & farming), 218, 224, 225, 245, 251
cults, 28, 43, 97
cultures, 234, **242**
Cumberland coast, 101
Cumbria, 49, 101
Cumbrian clubs, 38
Cumbrian type stone axes, 38
cumulative frequency polygons, 236
cumulative graphs, 236
Cunliffe, B., 81
cup-and-ring, 51
with gutter, 51
cupboards, 28, 110, 121
cupellation, 113, **267-8**
cupmarks, 51
cupped pebbles, 263
cupping, 126
cups, 36, **43**, 48, 64, **65**, **68-9**, **70**, **71-2**, 83, **95-6**, 113, **126**, **127**, 128, **129**, **130**, **132**, 158, **163**, **164**, 166, 194, **195**, **198**, **203**
curb-bits, **111**, 178, **190**
curfews, 203
Curle, 129
currency bars, 85
curry combs, 178
curses, 105, 113
cursive writing, 105
cursus (pl cursuses), **30**, 31
curved backed blades, 19
curvilinear plots, 249
cushions, 110
cut glass decoration, 279
cut-out bases, 272
flanges, 272
ridges, 272, 273
cut-stone floors, 108
cutting, 274
cuttlefish, 222

Cutts, Ireland, 54
Cutts dirks, 54
cutwaters, 176
cylinder beads, 141
glass, 128, **275**, **276**
method, 128, 164, 195, **275**, **276**
sickles, 54
window glass, 269
cylinders, 43, 91, **121**, 269, 272, 274, 275, 276
cylinder-segment beads, 141
cylindrical, 110, 114, 203
beads, 154
bottles, 127-8
loomweights, 73
-shaped pits, 79
vessels, 283

dagger
graves, 48
handles, 73
hilts, 68
pommels, 52, **68**
scabbards, 84
sheaths, 52, 73, **90**, 188, **194**
daggers
Bronze Age, 47, 48, **52**, **53**, 54, **55**, **64-5**, 67, **68**, 73
Iron Age, 90
Medieval, 187-8
Roman, 123
Saxon, 152
Dales, 34
Dales ware, 130
Dalriada, 143
Dalriadic Scots, 143
damascened swords, 152
damascening, 152
Damnonii, 94
Danegeld, 153
Danes' Camps, 143
Danes Graves, Humberside, 98
Danes Graves-Staxton style, 82
Danish raids, 153
Danish type flint axes, 38
Dark Ages, 143
Darmsden-Linton group, 82
Dartmoor, Devon, 45, 50
data, 235, 236, 237, 238, 239, 241
analysis, **235-8**, 241
banks, 241
matrices, 235
dates, **231**, 232, 233
dating, **9-12**, 128, 212, 213, **218**, 219, **232-5**
datum line, 214, 215
points, 214, 215
daub, 28, **144**, **169**
day rooms, 173
days, 174
debased coins, 136, 153
Deben, River, 146
débitage, 263
débris, 205
Decantae, 94
Deceangli, 94
deciduous woodland, 217, 224
de-colourants, 268-9
decorated Gothic, 174, 175
decorative windows, 196
dedicatory deposits, 30
deep-sea cores, **9-10**, 225, 234
sediments, 225

302

deer, 13, 45, 46, 79, 220
  parks, 177
Dee, River, 147
defences, 28, 76, 83, 99, 100, 101, 145, 167, 211
defensive enclosures, 144
Demetae, 94
denarius (pl denarii), **136**, 153
dendrochronology, 219-20, 232-3
dendrograms, 239
Denmark, 21, 143, 242
dentated bone mounts, 66, **68**
denticulate blades, 263
  flakes, 17, 263
depopulation, 79
depressors, 138
Derbyshire, 46, 49, 130, 146
Derbyshire Dales, 34
  ware, 130
Derby-type ware, 165
derma, 253
deserted Medieval villages, 144, **168**
deserted villages, 168
detergents, 219
detrital remanent magnetism, 234
developed group battle axes, 65
Devensian, 218
  glaciation, **10**, **11**, **12**, 17
Deverel, Dorset, 49
Deverel-Rimbury burial, 45, 49, 72
  culture, 45
  pottery, 45, **49**, **72**
  settlement, 45, 72
Devon, 45, 50, 76, 161
diadems, 105
diamond knops, 182
diatomaceous earth, 219
diatoms, 219
dice, 83, **84**, 114, 115, **137**, 159, 192, 194
dies, 94, 179, **180**, 199, 254
differential proton magnetometers, 208
differential weathering, 227
diffusion, 27, **242**
digging sticks, 245
diocese, 174
dipping ladles, 202
diptychs, 142
direct freehand flaking, 260
  percussion methods, 260
  rest flaking, 260
dirks, **54**, **58**, 59
disarticulated skeletons, 32, 97, **243**
disc
  attachments, 157
  barrows, **46**, **47**, 48
  brooches, 140, 154, 155, 179
  -headed pins, 52, 53
  heads, 88, 89
  mirrors, 138
  mouths, 282
  pins, 159
  pommels, 186, 187
  rims, 132, **282**
discoidal cores, 17
discs, 47, 64, 68, 84, 93, 129, 138, 158, **180**, 187, 275, 276
diseases, 220-1
dishes, **42**, **43**, 113, 122, 129, 130, **133-4**, 146, 165,

166, **181**, 194, **195**, **201**, **202**
Dis Manibus, 142
dismembered inhumations, 46
dispersed cemeteries, 48
Dissolution, of the Monasteries, 173, 174
distaff handles, 114
distaffs, 115-16, 195, 251, 252
distal ends, 259
distance slabs, 101
distilling bases, 203, 204
  equipment, 197, **198**, **203**, **204**
distribution, **239**, 241
  maps, **239**, 241
ditches, 28, 29, 30, **31**, 32, **45**, 46-7, 49, 50, 75, 76-8, 79, 97, 99, 102, 110, 145, 146, 167, 171, 177, 206, 208, **211**, 216, 219, 221, 222, **227-8**, 245, 249, 250
dividers, **117**, **136**, 183, 271
divining, 207
divisive techniques, 239
DM, 142
DMVs, 168
docks, 112
documentary evidence, 143, 145, 177, 270
  research, 205
dodecahedra, 137
dog dishes, 133
dogs, 79
dolabrae, 120
dolerite, 50
doliocephalic skulls, 221
dolmens, 32
Dolocauthi, Dyfed, 113
dolphins, **156**, 163
dolphin handles, 127, 128
Domesday book, 144
donjons, 171
donkeys, 112
door jambs, 121
  keys, 190
doorknockers, 178
doors, 83, 121
doorways, 77, **145**, **174**
Dorchester, Oxfordshire, 32
Dorchester culture, 27
dormitories, 146, 173
dorsal surface, **259**, 261
Dorset, 31, 48, 49, 73, 78, 82, 83, 84, 87, 98, 114, 131
dorters, 173
double
  -axe shaped ingots, 113
  buckles, 179
  -ended halls, 169
  -flue updraught kilns, 280
  houses, 146
  -light windows, 145
  linked chains, 147
  -looped Hallstatt razors, 63
  pedal drive, 256
  -ridged blades, 261
  -ring round-houses, 46, **74**
  roofs, 169
  -shelled lamps, 191
  -sided combs, 159, 192, 193
  -splayed windows, 145
  swag pattern, 275
  windows, 145

doughnut-shaped loom-weights, 158
dovecotes, 168
Dover harbour, 112
dowels, 256
dowsers, 207
dowsing, 207
Dr, 129
Drag, 129
Dragendorff, 129
dragonesque brooches, 140
drainage, 211, 223, 227, 250
  channels, 102
  gulleys, 74, 75
drains, 103-4
draught animals, 111
draughtsmen, 83, 146, **193**, **194**
drawbridges, 171, 172, 177
drawing frames, 213
draw-knives, 149, 253, **255**, 256
drawn beads, 274-5
draw-shaves, 255
dressed, 51, 112
Dressel, H., 132
Dressel numbers, 132
dress fasteners, **64**, 88
dressing, 37, **253**, 254
dress pins, 159, 160
drifts, 117, 267
drill halls, 99
drills, 183, 255, **262-3**
drill-tips, 262
drinking cups, 70
  horns, 93, 146, **163**
  vessels, 132, 146, 159, 181
drip-pans, 191
dripping pans, 202
drive mandrels, **255**, **256**
drop-hinges, 121
droppers, 138
dross, 264, **266**
droughts, 206
droveways, 79
Druidic cults, 97
drums, 43, 112
drying racks, 75
drystone, 45, 75
  walls, **32**, 33, **34**, 35, 74, 76
dry valleys, 226-7
dual-portal entrances (gateways), 77-8
Duddingston Loch, Lothian, 62
Duddingston phase, 62
dugout canoe coffins, 47
  canoes, **26**, **42**, **73**, 83
  coffins, 47
dumb-bell buttons, 88, 117
Dumfries and Galloway, 54, 93
dummy portals, 33
Dumnonii, 94
dump construction, 77, 145
  ramparts, 77
dunes, 225-6
dung, 224, 253
duns, **76**, 144
dupondius (pl dupondii), 136
duralumin, 207
Durham, 62
Durotriges, 94
Durotrigian pottery, 83
Durrington Walls, Wiltshire, 29
dusting, 278
dyed, 252, 254
dyeing, 195, 254

vats, 195
dyes, 252-3
Dyfed, 113
dykes, **45**, **75**, **79**, 102, **147**

Earlier Bronze Age, **45**, 46, 49, 51, 64, 66, 70, 71
  Mesolithic, **21-2**, **24-5**, 26
  Neolithic, 27
  Upper Palaeolithic, 9, 12, 13, 18
Early
  Acheulian, 14
  All Cannings Cross group, 81
  Bronze Age, 45
  Celtic art, 95
  Christian, 143
  English Gothic, 174-5
  Gothic, 196
  Iron Age, 74
  Last Glacial, 12
  Medieval, 143
  Neolithic pottery, 40-1
  Saxon, **143**, 149, **164**
  Saxon pottery, 164-5
early group battle axes, 65, 67
  stone circles, 30
ear-pendants, 52
ear-picks, 138
earrings, 47, **52**, **64**, **65**, 141, 153, **154**
ears, 248
ear-scoops, **138**, 146
earth, 79, 100, 144
earthen long barrows, 30-2
earthworks, 30, **45**, 78, 103, 147, 168, 176, 177, 206, 208, 227, 245, 251
earthworms (*see also* worms), 211, 224
East Anglia, 143, 145, 165
East Anglian Crags, 10, 11
East Midland burnished wares, 131
East Midlands, 82
Ebbsfleet pottery, 41
ecclesiastical, 176, 181, 191
éclats écaillés, 23
economy, 13, 26, **27-8**, **45-6**, 79, **117**, **143-4**, 222, 228
edge, of axe, 38
Edmonsham, Wiltshire, 48
Edward I, 171
Eemian, 11
eggshells, 221
eggshell ware, 130
egg yolks, 253
Egypt, 146, 268
einkorn, 27
electricity, 207
electron microprobe analysis, 231
  probe microanalysis, 231
electronic calculators, 241
electrons, 230, 231
electrum, **84**, 86, 264, **267**
elephant, 13, 160
elk, 13
elm, 73, 217, 218
  decline, 218
elongated points, 21
  wheel pommels, 186, 187
Elster, 11
émaillerie à jour, 268
émaux de basse taille, 268
embanked stone circles, 49
embossed leather, 194, **254**
embrasures, 167, **172**, **173**
Emertae, 94

emmer, **27**, 46, 79
emparking, 168, **177**
emperors, 99, 110, 136
enamel, 146, 156, **178**, 179, 180, 191, **268**
in openwork, 268
enamelled, 111, 117, 125, 126, 140, 146, 148
enamelling, **128**, 197, **268**, **277**
en barbotine, **129**, 130, 132, **278**
enclosed cremation cemeteries, 48-9
enclosed fields, 251
settlements, 77-9
enclosures, **28**, 30, **32**, 45, 46, 49, **76**, **77**, **79**, 97, **144**, 146, 171, 245, 250
encrustation, 229, 257
encrusted urns, 71
end-blown flutes, 192
end hall houses, 169
end-looped spearheads, 54
end scrapers, 18, 19, 21
end-winged axes, 61
English Gothic architecture, 174
engobe, 278
engraved, 89, 128, 141, 178, 181, 194, 274
bones, 19
engraving, 254, 266, 274
enlarged food vessels, 71
en taille d'épargne, 268
entrance graves, 34
entrenching tools, 120
environment, **9-12**, **26**, 46, 216, 217, 219, 221, 222, 226, 227, 229, 239
environmental evidence, 216-28
epidermis, 253
Epioti, 94
equal-arm brooches, 155, 156
equal-armed balances, 181
brooches, 156
equator, 9
erasers, 149
Erbenheim swords, 55, 59
erosion, 222, 223, 226, 227
escutcheons, 146, **148**, **149**
Eskimos, 253
Essex, 9, 13, 98, 129, 131, 132, 270
estuaries, 146, 225
estuarine, 219, 222, 225
Etruscan, 95
Europe, 11, 18, 40, 54, 55, 70, 197, 246
eustatic fall, in sea-level, 225
evaporation pans, 254
everted rims, 181, **282**
Ewart Park, Northumberland, 59
Ewart Park phase, 59, 61
swords, **61**, 63
ewers, 122, **181**, **203**
excavations, 30, 45, 50, 70, 76, 149, 164, 167, 178, 197, 205, 207, 208, **209-16**, 220, 221, 228
excised decoration, 279
exercise yards, 104
exotic barrows, 47
experimental archaeology, 216
experiments, 107, 112, 227
exposed burials, 243

exposure, 28, 32, 75, 97, **243**, 252
extended burials, 243
inhumations, 48, 97, 146, **243**, **244**
extensive excavation, 210
extra-revetment material, 33, 34
eye guards, 125, 126
motif patterns, 275
ointment, 138

fabric, 40, 41, 124, 128, 129, 130, 131, 164, 165, 166, 201, 202, **280**
fabricators, 39
fabricae, 99
façades, 31, 33, 34
faced, 102, 112, **255**
face jugs, 202
face-on-front jugs, 202
faces, **38**, 112, 132, 255, 267, 277
facet-cut glass, 126
facet-cutting, 126-7
faceted socketed axes, 62
facets, 126, 274
face urns, 132
facies, 242
factories, **26-7**, 38, 140
faience, **70**, 269
fairy ring champignon, 207
fairy rings, 207
fallow deer, 13
false-colour infra-red photography, 207
false portals, 33
fancy barrows, 47
fans, 138
fan vaults, 176
farmers, 36, 106, 117
farmery, 173
farmhouses, 28
farming (see also agriculture & cultivation), 46, **79**, 117, 219, 222, 249
farming estates, 107
farms, 28, 102, 106, 168, 173
farmsteads, 28
Farnham, Surrey, 130
Farnham pottery, 130
farriers' tools, 117
farthings, 179
fasteners, **44, 64, 68, 88, 89,** 117, 149
fastenings, 88
fast wheels, 165, 201, **277**
fat, 253
feather-edge flaking, 260
feathers, 221
features, 75, 207, 208, **209, 210,** 211, 213, 214, 216, 222, 224, 226, 228, 233
feature sheets, 216
Fécamp ramparts, 77
feeding bottles, 134
felling, 37, **255**
felloes, 91, 92
felt, 252
felted, 252
female burials, 97
fences, 28, 45, 249
Fengate-Cromer group, 82
Fengate pottery, 41
Fenlands, 102
fermenting, 253
ferrules, **54, 59, 60,** 62, **121, 123, 124,** 178
fertilisers, 168
fertility cults, 43

fibres, 251, 252
fibulae, 140
ficron handaxes, 15
field boundaries, 249, 250
fields, 45, 79, 168, 177, 205, 206, 213, **249-51**
field system, 46
fieldwalking, 205
fieldwork, 205-16
figure and canopy windows, 196
figures, 42, 95, 112, 129, 147, 178, 181, 196, 197, **198**, 201, 265
figure windows, 196
figurines, **43**, 83, **95**, **96**, 105, 112, **148**, 149
files, **85**, **86**, **117**, 149
filigree, 267
fill, 211, 222, **227**, **228**, 233
filler, 277
filling holes, 134, **135**
films (photographic), 207, 216
Findon type beads, 87
finds, 205, **210-11**, **213**, 216, 239, 241
sheets, 216
fine fabric, 164
fine ribbed bowls, 126
fine wares, 128-30
finger-rings (see also rings), **56**, 83, 84, **88**, 114, 153
finger tip decoration, 40, 81, **278**
finial knops, 182
finials, 134-5, **199-200**
finishing flakes, 15
fins, 274
fir, 11
fire, 28, 100, 104, 122, 181, 203, 253, 254, 255, 280
firearms, 167
fire bars, 114, **254**, **280**
fireclay, 269
fired, 81, 123, 130, 131, 164, 165, 185, 198, 201, 219, 233, 269, 280, 281
clay, 64, 69, 200, 208, 219, 229, 233, 280
fire dogs, 85, 86
fire-pits, 280
fireplaces, **169**, 170
fire-polished, 267
fire-rounded rims, 272, 273
firesteels, 149
firewood, 219
firing, 123, 128, 167, 189, 233, 269, 277, **280-1**
first brass coins, 136
first pointed style, 174
fish, 13, 25, 79, 113, 144, 177, 226, 228
Fishbourne villa, 107, 110
fish dishes, 202
gorges, 25
hooks, **25**, 114, 178
remains, 221
scale flaking, 260-1
scales, 23, 221
stews, 177
fishing, 26
nets, 80
fishponds, 177
fissures, 227, **258**
fittings, 84, 85, 91, 95, 98, 110, 111, 114, 115, 117, **120-1**, 126, 142, 143, 149, 152, 153, **156-7**, 158, 159, 178, 195
flagons, 95, **132**

flags, 169
flagstone, 28, 108
flake beds, 258
scars, **258**, 261
tools, 9, 13, **261**
flaked, 19, 37, 39, 65, 257, 262
flakes, **13**, **14**, **15**, **16**, **17**, 18, **21**, 27, **39**, 236, 237, 238, **258**, **259**, **260**, **261**, **262**, 263, 264
flaking, 13, 14, 17, 257, **258**, **260-1**, 262
platforms, 258
Flandrian, 10, 11, **218**
flanged
axes, 54, 55
maceheads, 188
neck flagons, 132
necks, 132
rims, 282
shares, 246
flanges, 54, **55**, 57, 131, 203, **272**, **274**, **282**
flanking towers, 171
flans, 153
flaring rims, 282
flashed, 267
glass, 276
flash glass, 276
flashing, 266, 276
flasks, 122, 127, 133, 180
flask-shaped ampullae, 180
flat
axes, 48, **52**, **53**, 64
bases, 41, 71, 181, **284**
blades, 151
bowed brooches, 87, 89
-butted cordate handaxes, 15
cemeteries, 49, **243**, 245
daggers, 52, 53
graves, 47, 48, **243**
rims, 272, 273, 282
riveted daggers, 52
tiles, 109
topped rims, 282
flattened hemispherical pommels, 186
flatters, 267
Flavian period, 99
flax, 73, 117, 144, 251
lint, 251
flesh, 222, 243
forks, 59, 60
goads, 59
hooks, 182-3
fleshing knives, 253
flexed burials, 243
inhumations, 243, 244
flint, 15, 16, 23, 24, 36, 37, 64, 100, 114, 229, 231, **257-64**, 268, 271, 277
artifacts, 239, 242, 249, 253, 254, 257, 262, 274
Bronze Age, 48, 50, **64-5**
Iron Age, 87
Mesolithic, **21-4**, 26
Neolithic, 21, **36**, **37**, **38**, **39**, **40**, 42
Palaeolithic, 9, **13-19**, 226
flakes, **21**, 27, **39**, 236, 237
-gritted vessels, 131
knappers, 36, **260**
knapping, **260**, 263
mines, **36**, 37, 43, 64, 245, 257
-mining, 36, 37

nodules, 37
  working, 15, 255, **257-4**
floating chronology, 232
floats, 117
flood plains, 226
floor inlay, 108
floors, 9, 28, 32, 100, 102, 106, **107, 108, 109,** 144, 145, 169, 210, **263,** 280
floor tiles, 198-9
florid cruciform brooches, 156
flot, 219
flotation, **219,** 220, 221
  tanks, 219
flour, 28, 40, 80, 112, 113
flower beds, 110
flowers, 196, 273
flower vases, 133
flues, 107, 269, **270,** 280, 281
flue tiles, 107, 108, **109**
fluorine analysis, 233
flushing, 104, **266**
  water, 170
fluted flaking, 261
flutes, 68, 137, 158, 192, **193**
flux, 268
fluxgate gradiometers, 208
flying buttresses, 175
flywheels, 251, 262, 263, 277
foederati, 143
fogous, 75
folded beads, 274
  beakers, 132, 133
folding
  arms, 181
  balance arms, 135
  knife blades, 149
  knives, 123
  spoons, 122
  stools, 110
Folkestone, Kent, 107
Folkton, North Yorkshire, 43
follis, 136
fonts, 105
food, 13, 26, 28, 79, 131, 132, 144, 177, 181, 202, 217, 220, 222, 228, 243, 245, 251
  offerings, 98
  vessels, 45, 48, **70, 71**
  vessel burials, 48
  vessel urns, 71
footings, 106
footplates, 189
foot-rests, 189
footrings, **197,** 272, **284**
footsoldiers, 188
footwear (see also shoes), 83, **114**
fora, 102
forceps, 138
force-pumps, 103
fords, 110
forecourts, 33, 34
foreshares, 246
forest clearance, 27, 79, 218, 224
  glass, 197, 198, **268**
  regeneration, 28
forests, 11, 218
forged, 152, 266
forgeries, 180
forging, 266, **267**
forked hoes, 117, 119
forks, **42, 182,** 188, **271**
former, 268

Forth-Clyde isthmus, 101
fortifications, 77, 102, 171
fortified, 75, 76, 102
fortlets, **100,** 101
fortresses, **99,** 100, 102
forts (see also hillforts), **76, 77, 78,** 99, **100,** 101, 102, 103, 104, **144,** 146
forum, 102-3
fossa, 99, **100**
fossil corals, 234
fossilised organisms, 234
fossil soils, 222
foundations, 110, 170, 211
foundation trenches, 45, 77, **211**
founder's barrows, 48
founders' hoards, 59, **243**
founding furnaces, 269
founding-pits, 178
fountains, 110
fourpence coins, 179
four-posters, 50
fowl, 226
foxes, 13
frames, 92, 138, 139, 169, **191, 213, 214,** 252, 253, 255, 277
frame saws, 117, **255**
frameworks, 9, 10, 11, 77, 109, 216, 231, 234
France, 14, 16, 17, 18, 22, 55, 74, 81, 95, 97, 129, 143, 166, 191, 202, 203
franciscas, 150, **153,** 183
Frankish denarius, 153
Franks, 143, 153
frater, 173
free-blowing, 272
free flaking, 261
freehand pressure flaking, 260
freshwater, 144, 219, 222
friars, 173
frigidarium, 104
frilled cordons, 133, 279
frilling, 201, **278, 279**
Frisians, 143
frit, 269
fritting furnaces, 269
  ovens, **269,** 270
frogs, 221
Frontinus bottles, 127, 128
frontlets, 25
frost action, 222
frost-pitting, 259, 260
frost weathering, 26, 227
froth flotation, **219,** 221
frying pans, 122, 202
fuel, 114, 267, 281
fullered blades, 151
  grooves, 186
  horsehoes, 189
fullers, 151, **152,** 189, **267**
fuller's earth, 252
fulling, 252
  mills, 176
  pits, 158
full last glacial, **9, 12,** 18
funerary deposits, 70
  enclosures, 49
  vessels, 72, 132, 165
fungus beakers, 164
funnel beakers, 164
funnel-shaped lamps, 191
furnaces, 85, 107, 108, 114, 149, 178, 264, **266-7,** 268, **269-70,** 272, 273, 275, 276
furniture, 110
furrowed bowls, 81
furrows, 245, 246, **250**

fused, 77, 267, 268, 269, 271, 273
fusing, 269
Fussell's Lodge, Wiltshire, 31
futhark, 162
futhorc, 162

gabled roofs, 28
gable ends, 199
gaffers, 272
galena, 113, **268**
Galicia, 51
Galician style, 51
galleried duns, 76
  promontory duns, 76
  shafts, 36, **37**
galleries, 32, 33, 34, 75, 76, 145, 169
gallery graves, 33-4
Gallo-Belgic, 83, 96, 130
  A-F coins, 94
  wares, 129
game pieces, 137
games, 137, **194**
gaming boards, **137,** 160, 192, 194
  counters, 84, 126, **137**
  pieces, 96, 160, 192, 194
gamma, 208
gamma-ray spectrometry, 230
Gangani, 94
gangue, 266
gapped concentric circles, 51
gardens, **110,** 177
gardrobes, 170
gardrobe towers, 170
garments, 117, 158
garnets, 146
gastropods, 222
gatehouse inns, 170
gatehouses, **170,** 171, **173**
gates, 78, **99,** 100, 101, 121
gateways, 78, 99, 100, **102,** 107, **167,** 170, **171, 172**
gathering, 13, 26, 79, 272
  ends, **270,** 272
gathers, 271, 272, 273, 274
Gaul, 83, 84, 95, 129, 130, 143
gauss, 208
gemstones, 126, 141
geological, 9, 11, 14, 207
geology, 216, 233
German armourers, 184
Germanic, 126, 143, 156, 162
Germany, 66, 143, 184, 198
ghost walls, 211
giant Irish deer, 13
gifts, 63, 95
gilded bronze, 141
gilding, 156, 254, **267**
gilt, 146
girdle-hangers, 146, **148, 149,** 160
girth beakers, 83, 132, 133
glacial deposits, 222, **223**
  features, 226-7
  periods, **9,** 12, 26
glacials, **9,** 10, 234
glaciations, 9, **10, 11, 12,** 13, 17, 225, 226
glaciers, 9, 12, 26, 222, 225, **226**
glacis ramparts, 77
gladiator beakers, 127, 128
gladiatorial contests, 127

gladius (pl gladii), 123, 124
glaives, 188
glandes, 123
glass, 228, **235,** 238, **268-77**
  armlets, 87, 154
  bangles, 87, 139, 154
  beads, **70,** 84, **87,** 96, **140-1, 154,** 239, 270, **274-5**
  Bronze Age, 70
  Iron Age, **84,** 96
  Medieval, 174, **195-8,** 203, 231
  Roman, 103, 108, 109, **117, 126-8, 137, 139, 140-1**
  Saxon, 145, 153, **154,** 156, 157, 158, **163-4**
glassblowers, 270, 272, 274
glassblowing, 126, **271-2**
glass canes, **271,** 273, **274**
  enamelling, 277
  founding, 269
  makers, 269
  making, 126, **269**
  melting, 269
  -metal, 269
  panes, 109
  shaping, 269
  slides, 229
  tubing, 274
  vessels, 84, 96, 103, **126-8,** 146, **163-4, 197-8,** 203, 243, 270, **271-4**
glasshouses, 139, 198
glass layer dating, 235
glassworking, **269-70,** 271, 272
  tools, 270-1
Glastonbury, Somerset, 75
Glastonbury Abbey, Somerset, 164
Glastonbury-Blaise Castle Hill style, 82
Glastonbury style, 82
glazed, 166, 199, 202, 280
glazes, 130, 166, 201, 202, 231, 268, 278, 280, **281**
glazing strips, 147
Glentrool, Dumfries and Galloway, 54
Glentrool phase, 54
  type pins, 54
gleys, 224
globe-headed pins, 52
globular flagons, 132
  bowls, 82
  jars, 82, 83
  ribbed jars, 127
  urns, 72, 165
glory holes, 269
gloss, 129, **278**
glossy, 128, 273, 275
glost firing, 280
glost-ovens, **280,** 281
Gloucestershire, 29, 48, 104
gloves, 158, 194
goads, 59, 249
goats, 28, 46, 83, 144, 253
goblets, 113, **197, 198**
gobs, 270, **272,** 274, 275
gods, 97, 104, 105, 243
gold, 47, 48, **52, 64, 65,** 68, 69, **84, 86,** 88, 94, 95, **113,** 136, 139, 140, 141, 146, **147,** 153, 154, 155, **177,** 179, 180, 264, **267,** 268
  -band glass, 126
  dust, 267
  foil, 126, 267
  leaf, 267
goldsmiths, 181

goose flesh petrified fabric, 130
gorges, 25
Gothic, **174**, **175**, 197
  architecture, **174**, 176
  style, 174
  vaults, 176
gouges, **37**, **39**, **44**, **61**, 62, 80, 83, **85**, **86**, **117**, 149, 255
Gough's Cave, Cheddar, Somerset, 20
gradiometers, 208
graffiti, 104, 105, 137
grain, **27-8**, **40**, 46, **79**, 107, 112, 113, 132, **145**, **219**, 228
  charcoal, 219
  impressions, 45, 46, 79, 219
  rubbers, 28, **40**, 45, 46
  storage pits, **27-8**
Grampian, 52, 62, 68
granaries, 75, 79, **99**, 107
granges, 173
granite, 95
granulation, 267
granules, 267
grape cups, 48, **72**
graphite coating, 279
graphs, 217, **236**, 238
grass, 73, 206, 207, 219
  impressions, 164
grassland, 11, **225**
grass-marked wares, 164
grave art, 51
  covers, **162**, 175, 192
  goods, 32, 45, **47**, **48**, 49, 52, **97**, **98**, 142, **146**, 163, 164, 213, **243**
  markers, 160, 162
  -pits, 47, 98
gravel, 108, 110, 113, 147, 208, 223, 226, 257
gravers, **21**, **22**, 263, **264**, **266**
graves (see also burial), 47, 48, 66, 97, 128, 146, 149, 151, 154, 155, 156, 158, 161, 163, 165, 175, 211, 213, 228, **243**, **244**
gravestones, 175
great chambers, 169
greater chambers, 169
Greater London, 17, 55, 61, 96
great helms, 184, 185
Great Ice Age, 9
Great Interglacial, 11
great square-headed brooches, 156
Greek, 94, 95, 104
green hard, 279
greens, 168
greensand, 108
gridded area, 207
grid frames, 213
gridirons, 122
grid method, 210
grids, 122, 167, 205, 207, 208, **213**, **214**
grid system, 205, 213
grilles, **109**, 171
Grimston ware, 40
grinding, **37**, 79, 80, 261, 262, 271
grips, 126, **151**, **152**, 158, 187
grisaille windows, 196
grit, 40, 131
grit-tempered fabric, 201

gritting, 277
groats, 179
grog, 277
groined vaults, 176
groin-vaults, 176
groove-and-splinter technique, 257
grooved bowls, 83
  decoration, 40-1
  sockets, 151
  ware, **41**, 70
grooving, 279
ground, 37, 66, 112, 126, 262, 272, 275
  -level, 99, 100, 167, 169, 171, 205, 211, 280
  -sills, 211
  -wrests, 248
growth rings, 219, 221, 232
grozing, **270**, 277
  irons, 270
grubenhaus (pl grubenhäuser), 144
grubhuts, 144
guano, 221
guard chambers, 75, 78
guards, 90, 151, **152**, **187**
guard towers, 99
guest houses, 146
Guido, C. M., 87
guisarmes, 188
gulleys, 74, 75, **211**
Gündlingen, West Germany, 63
Gündlingen swords, 63
gun loops, **167**, 171
  ports, 167
gunpowder, 189
guns, 167, 189
Gunz, 11
guttering, 109
gutters, 104
Gwithian, Cornwall, 46
Gwithian-style pottery, 164
Gwynedd, 36, 172
gypcières, 191
gypsum, 142
gyrus, 100

hackled, 251
Hadrian's Wall, **101**, 130
haematite bowls, 81, 82
  coating, 279
  slip, 81
hafted, 14, 21, 23, 52, 54, 188, 267
haft-flanged axes, 54, 55
hafting, 21, 25, **37**, **38**, **39**, **64**
hafts, **26**, **37**, **38**, **42**, **52**, **64**, 73, 83
hagioscopes, 174
hair, 44, 149, 154, 252, 253
hairpin decoration, 129, 130
hairpins, 140, 159, 192
halberd pendants, 48, **52**
halberds, 52, 53, 188
half groats, 179
half-life, 232
half-moon knives, 254
halfpennies, 179
half-timbered, 106, **169**
hall and cellar houses, 169
hall and cross wings, 169
halls, 99, **103**, **144**, **169**, **170**, 173
Hallstatt, **74**, 91
Hallstatt, Austria, 74
  brooches, 88
  daggers, 90
Hallstatt C culture, 74

Gündlingen swords, 63
  metalwork, 63
Hallstatt D daggers, 90
hammer-adzes, 117
hammer beams, 168, 169
  flaking, 260
  heads, 149
  stones, **14**, **15**, 260
hammers, **23**, **25**, **44**, **54**, **58**, 83, **85**, **117**, **118**, **149**, 183, 262, 267
Hampshire, 82, 87, 100, 103, 110, 144, 166, 269, 270
hand-and-a-half swords, 186, 187
handaxes, 13, **14**, **15**, **16**, **17**, 226, 235, 236
hand cards, 195
hand-drills, 183
hand guns, 189
handled beakers, 70, 132, 133
  combs, 159
  cups, 203
  ladles, 201, 202
  mugs, 70
handles, **42**, **44**, 64, 66, **68**, 72, 73, 80, 83, 85, 86, 89, 112, **113**, 114, 115, 116, 117, 120, **123**, **127**, **128**, 132, 134, **135**, 138, 159, 165, 178, 180, 181, 182, 183, 192, 194, **195**, **201**, **202**, 207, **246**, 255, **262**, 266, 267, 271, 272, 273, 278
hand-made, 81, 117, 130, 131, 157, 164, 165, 166, 178-9
hand mills, 112
  perforated beads, 275
  saws, 117, 118
handspindles, 251, 252
hanging bowls, 146, 148, **149**
  lamps, 135, 160, 197
Hanging Langford type beads, 87
hardness, 229
hardpan, 224
hard solder, 267
hares, 13
harness, 46, 83, 92-3, **111**, 114, 126, 180
  equipment, 114
  fittings, 84, 85, 95, 98, 117
  loops, **92**, 111
  mounts, 92
  rings, 92
harnessing, 249
harpoon heads, 25
harpoons, 19
harpoon shafts, 26
Harris-Winchester matrix, 214
Harrow Hill, Sussex, 46
harvesting, 27, 249
hauberks, 184
Hawkes, C. F. C., 74
Hawk's Hill-West Clandon style, 82
hazel, 11, 73, 153, 217, 218
head-dresses, 25
headed, 255
headlands, 251
headquarters-buildings, 99
heads, **19**, 84, 85, 87, **88**, **89**, 91, 92, 94, 95, 121, 126, 136, 140, 154, **156**, 160,

161, 181, 182, **188**, 195, 196, 221, 226, 266
headstalls, 111
hearths, 28, 75, 76, 85, 114, 144, 169, 170, 200, 208, 219, 270, 280
Heathery Burn Cave, Durham, 62
Heathery Burn tradition, 62
Heathrow, Greater London, 96
heaths, 224
heating, 102, 104, 106, **107-8**, 114, 169
heaumes, 184
heavy mineral analysis, 230
heavy ploughs, 245-6, 248
heckled, 251
heddle rods, 251, 252
hedgehogs, 220
hedgerow dating, 235-6
hedges, 110, **235-6**, 249, 251
Heel stone, 50
heirlooms, 153
helmets, 84, **91**, 93, **124**, **125**, 146, **153**, **184**
helms, 184, 185
Hembury ware, 40
Hemigkofen swords, 55, 59
hemispherical bowls, 132
hemp, 144, 251
henges, **29**, 30, 46, 49, **50**
Hengistbury, Hampshire, 87
heraldic, 181, 194, 196, 197
  discs, 180
  pendants, 178, **180**
  windows, 196
herbs, 218
Herd Howe group, 65
Herefordshire, 82
herringbone bricks, 108
  coursing, 145
Hertford Heath, Hertfordshire, 84
Hertfordshire, 84, 106
Heslerton ware, 40
hewing, 255
hewn timber, 115
hexagonal bottles, 127
hexagons, 240
hic situs est, 142
hides, 44, **253-4**
high-flanged palstaves, 54, 57
Highland, 52
Highland Britain, 245
Highland Zone, 48, 52, 79, **245**
high necked vessels, 283
High Peak, 34
high shouldered vessels, 283
Hiller borers, 207
hillforts, **46**, 75, **76-9**, 97, 102, 144, 145, 239
hillwash, **223**, 226
hilt guards, 90
hilts, 59, 68, 90, 115, **123**, 146, 147, **151**, **152**, 159, 184, 187, 188
hinge fractures, 258, 259
hinge-pivots, 178
hinges, 115, **121**, 178
hipped shafts, 159
hippo sandals, 111
histograms, 217, 222, **236-7**
historic period, 242
historical period, 242
  sources, 251
history, 242
hoarding, 171

hoards, 54, 59, 61, 62, 96, 143, 147, 153, **243**
of loot, 243
hobnails, 114
hoes, **27**, **117**, 119, 245
Hofheim cups, 126, 127
flagons, 132
hog-back grave covers, 162
stones, 162
tombstones, 162
hog's-backed tombstones, 162
hog's back knives, 61
holdfasts, 107-8
Holland, 143
hollow casting, 64, 265
cathode lamps, 231
cones, 52
ways, 168
Holocene, 9, 11
Holstein, 11
holy oil, 180
water, 180
homesteads, 76
hones, 123, 160, 192
honey jars, 132
Honorius, 99
hooded fireplaces, 169
hoods, 184
hooks and eyes, 154
hooked fasteners, 149
rims, 282
hooks, **25**, 114, **120-1**, 135, 136, 177, 178, **179**, **183**, 195, 271, 274
hook-tanged swords, 55
Hooper's hedgerow hypothesis, 235
hoops, of iron, 188, 189
hoop tyres, 91
horizons, **223**, 224, 225, 226, 227, 228
horizontal looms, 158, 195, **252**
rims, 282
stratigraphy, 213
horn, 68, 80, 91, 117, 137, 151, 159, 182, 186, 192, 257
hornbeam, 11, 218
horn caps, 91, 92, 93
horned helmets, 91
horns, 91, 93, 114
hornworks, 78
horrea, 99
horse
armour, **126**, 185, 190
bits, 92, 190
collars, 249
equipment, 59, 62
furniture, 180, **189-90**
harness, 46, 83, **92-3**, 114, 180
harness mounts, 63
horses, 13, 19, 46, 79, 91, 92, 94, 98, 100, 106, 111, 144, 180, 185, 192, 202, 249, 253
horseshoe, at Stonehenge, 51
horseshoes, **93**, **111**, 149, 178, **189**
Horsham, Sussex, 22-3
Horsham culture, 21, 23
points, 22, 23
hospitals, 99, **170**, 229
hostels, 170
hot springs, 223
hour-glass perforations, 23, 24, 262, 263
house platforms, 168

houses, **28**, **75**, **99**, **102**, 104, **106-7**, 108, **144**, 167, 168, **169-70**, 174, 177, 195
Housesteads, Northumberland, 120
Hoxnian Interglacial, **10**, **11**, 14
H-plan houses, 169
HSE, 142
hub linings, 91, 92, 111
rings, 91, 111
hubs, 91, **92**, 113
hulled barley, 46, 79
human bones, 28, 30, 97, **220-1**
Humber, River, 82
Humberside, 46, 48, 74, 82, 88, 97, 98, 130
humic acid, 223
horizon, 224
humidity, 222
humus, **223**, 224, 225
Hunsbury-Draughton style, 82
Huntcliff ware, 131
hunt cups, 130, 132
hunter-gatherers, 13, 26, 241
hunting, 13, 19, 25, 26, 28, 45, 46, 79, 128, 177, 186
spears, 188
hurdles, **42**, 73, 83
hut hollows, 144
huts, **45**, **46**, 73, **74**, 75, 76, 83, 144, 241
hyaline zones, 221
hydrogen atoms, 208
hydrolysis, 223
hypocaust heating, 102, 104, 106
hypocausts, 104, 106, **107-8**, 109

Iberian brooches, 88, 89
ice, 223, 225, 226
sheets, 9, 10, **226**
-skating, 192
wedge cracks, 207
wedges, 226
Ice Age, 9
Iceni, 94
ill-defined shoulders, 283
Illinoian, 11
imbrex (pl imbrices), 109, 110
imbrication, 34
imitation samian, **129**, 130
immigrants, 63, 74, 161, 164
immigration, 70, 74, 78
Imperial Cult, 104
imperial estates, **102**, 107
Imperial-Gallic helmets, 124, 125
importation, 84, 87
imported, 38, 40, 70, 75, 83, 84, 87, 88, 94, 95, 96, 98, 112, 126, 128, 129, 130, 131, 132, 139, 146, 147, 153, 164, 165, 166, 181, 184, 191, 197, 198, 202, 203, 253, 272
imports, 63, **95-6**, 197, 198
impressed, 109, 128, 129, 131, 180, 199, 254, **278**
decoration, 278
ware, 41
whipped cord ornamentation, 40
impulsive pressure flaking, 260
incense cups, 71, 132

incised, 41, 43, 54, 56, 70, 72, 81, 109, 137, 159, 160, 161, 192, 194, 199, **254**
decoration, 279
tiles, 199
inclusions, 229, **277**
indented axes, 59, 60
beakers, 130, **132**
indents, 275
independent invention, 242
indirect percussion methods, 260
individual burial (*see also* single burial), 146
industry, 242
infirmaries, 173
infirmary halls, 170
infra-red absorption spectrometry, 230-1
infra-red light, 207
photography, 207, 229
Ingleby, Derbyshire, 146
ingots, **64**, 85, **113**, 264, 268
inhumation cemeteries, 146
inhumations, 28, 30, 32, 46, 47, 48, 49, 71, 73, 96, 97, 98, **142**, 146, 164-5, **243-4**
inkwells, 129, **142**, 192, 194
inlaid, 150, 152, 159, 267, 268
tiles, 199
inlay, 84, **108**, 110, 113, 156, **266**
inlaying, 149
inner baileys, 171, 172
Inner Hebrides, 76
inns, 104, 106, 167, **170**
inscribed, 105, 110, 112, 161, 162, 179
stone pillars, 146
stones, 101, **161**, 162
stone slabs, 146
inscriptions, 104, **105**, 114, 131, **142**, 146, 152, 153, **161**, **162**, 178, 186, 197
insectivores, 220
insect remains, 228
insects, 196, 220, **221-2**, 227
inset, 96, 154, 155
in situ, 158, 161, 211, 227, **233**
insolation, 222
instrument pegs, 192
instruments, 137, 192
intaglios, 141
integrated plan churches, 145
interglacial periods, 9
interglacials, **9**, **10**, **11**, 12, 14, 225, 234
intermediate group battle axes, 65, 67
intermediate loomweights, 157-8
interments (*see also* burial), 32, **243**
interrupted ditch enclosures, 28
interstadials, **9**, 13, 234
intrusive burials, 243
interments, 243
inturned corridor entrances, 78
invasions, 74, 78, 84, 94, 98, 99, **142**, 167, 241, 242, 272
invasion theories, 74
invasive retouch, 261
Inverness area, 30, 36
circles, 49

ring cairns, 36
inverse retouch, 261
involuted brooches, 88, 89
involutions, 226
Ipswichian interglacial, 10, 11, 12
Ipswich spouted pitchers, 165
Ipswich-type ware, 165
Ipswich ware, 165
Ireland, 37, 51, 54, 55, 64, 71, 147, 154, 162
Irish, 143, 161, 164
bowl food vessels, 71
iron, 63, 74, 83, 85, 113, 114, **149**, 152, 171, **178**, 224, 225, 229, 241, 257, 264, **266-7**, 269, 271
beams, 104, 121
dogs, 85, 86, 120
grilles, 109
mail, 124
ores, **114**, 149, 266
oxides, 109, 224, 225, 233, 277
pans, **223**, 224
smelting, 178
Iron Age, 46, 51, 63, **74-98**, 102, 106, 111, 116, 118, 121, 131, 137, 140, 143, 183, 218, 241, **242**, 246, 247, 248, 249, 250, 256, 257, 266, 270, 283
Iron Age A, 74
Iron Age B, 74
Iron Age 'B' coarse ware, 82
Iron Age C, 74
iron artifacts, 270-1, 272, 274
Iron Age, **85-6**, 88, 89, 90, 91, 92, 93, 246, 247, 249, 257
Medieval, **178**, 179, 183, 184, 187, 188, 189, 190, 191, 194, 195, 196, 277
Roman, 107-8, 110, **111**, 112, 115, 116, **117-22**, 123, 124, 126, 134, 135, 136, 137, 138, 140, 141, 142, 246, 247
Saxon, 146, **149-51**, 152, 153, 155, **157**, **158**
ironworking, 168
Islamic glass, 197
Isle of Harris, Western Isles, 45
Isle of Wight, 54, 143
isolated burials, 97, 245
isosceles triangle microliths, 21, 22
isostatic recovery, 225
uplift, 26
isotopes, 230, 232, 234
Italy, 55, 95, 129, 184, 197, 198
Itford Hill, Sussex, 45, 73
itinerant smiths, 63
Ivinghoe-Sandy group, 81
ivory, 123, 138, 139, **160**, 180, **192**, 194, 257

jack planes, 255, 256
jade axes, 38
jambs, 121, 174
jangle-plates, 63
jar continuum, 82
Jarlshof, Shetland, 75
jars, 72, 81, **82**, 83, **127**, 129, **132**, **163**, 164, 165, 166, **201**, **202**, **203**, 271, **273**

javelins, 90, 123
jaw bones, 221
Jesse windows, 196
jet, **44, 48, 69, 84,** 87, 88, 112, **114,** 116, 137, 139, 140, 141, 153, 154, 157, **160,** 180, **192,** 194
jettied houses, 169
jetties, 112, **169**
jettons, 179, **194**
jewellery, 85, **86-9,** 95, 96, 113, 128, **139-41,** 146, 147, **153-6,** 163, **179,** 267
jewels, 154
Jews' houses, 169
jingle-jangles, 63
jockey-caps, 124, 125
joggle joints, 86
joiners' dogs, 120, 121
  tools, 117
joining, 256-7
joints, 51, 86, 169, 256, 267
jousting, 184
jugs, 95, 113, 122, 129, **132,** 165, **166, 181, 201, 202-3**
Julius Caesar, 99
juniper, 217
Jutes, 143
Jutish bottles, 165

Kansan, 11
keep-and-bailey castles, 171, 172
keeps, 171, 172
keep-towers, 171
Kent, 9, 13, 23, 94, 98, 104, 106, 107, 131, 143, 154, 155, 162, 163, 165, 180
kerb cairns, 48, 49
kerbs, 33, 34, 35, 36
key, 109
key-rings, 141
keys, **122,** 146, 149, **150,** 178, **190**
kicks, 198, **272, 273, 284**
kidney daggers, 187-8
kidneys, 187-8
kidney-shaped mirrors, 89
Kildale, North Yorkshire, 146
kiln coverings, 281
  floors, 280
  furniture, 280
kilns, 81, 109, **114,** 130, 147, 164, 165, 168, 177, 199, 201, 208, 233, **280-1**
Kimmeridge-Caburn group, 81
Kimmeridge shale, 110
  industry, 114
kingdoms, 147
king-posts, 168, 169
kings, 146, 196, 243
kitchens, 169-70, 173
kite-shaped blades, 54, 57
  shields, 152, 185
knappers, 36, **260**
knapping, **260,** 263
Knapton ware, 130-1
knee-hafts, 37
knee-shaft hafts, 37
knife blades, **86,** 255
  -daggers, **52, 64-5, 184,** 187, 194
  handles, 114, 115
  sheaths, 194
knight jugs, 202
knitting, 116
  needles, 251
knives, **17, 27, 39, 52, 61,** 62, **65, 67,** 80, **85, 123,** 146, **149,** 152, 183, **184,** 194, 242, 246, 249, 251, **253, 254, 255,** 264
knobbed sickles, 54, 56
knocked off, 272
knops, 182
Knorr and Walters, 129

labelling, 213
laboratories, 213, 221, 233
lace, 195
laces, 114, 158, 178
lace tags, 178
laconicum (pl laconica), 104
ladders, 36, 73, 83, 194
ladles, 68, 83, 201, 202
laeti, 143
La Fère-en-Tardenois, France, 22
lagenae, 132
Lake District, 37, 38, 49
lakes, 75, 219, 222, **226,** 227
lake villages, 75
Lambeth, Greater London, 55
Lambeth/Rosnoën swords, 55
Lambeth swords, 55
lamp chimneys, 135
lampfillers, 134, 135
lampholders, 134
lamps, 36, **43, 83,** 104, 132, **134, 135,** 160, **161,** 164, 165, 166, **191-2, 197,** 198, **203**
Lancashire, 147, 270
lances, 188
lancet windows, 174
landnam, 27
landscape, 222, 224, 226, 241, 245
languettes, 52
lanterns, 191-2
lantern towers, 174
Lanting and Van der Waals, 70
lapidary wheels, 126
large loop-headed pins, 54
lashing, 92, **256**
Last Glaciation, 11
  Interglacial, 11
lasts, 117
latches, 121
latchlifters, **85, 86, 121, 122,** 146, 149, **150, 190**
Late
  Acheulian, 14
  Bronze Age, 45
  Caburn-Saltdean style, 82
  Gothic, 196
  Last Glacial, **11, 12,** 18
  Middle Acheulian, 14
  Neolithic pottery, 40-1
  Saxon, **143,** 144, 149, 159, 160, 161, 163, 164
  Saxon pottery, 165-6
La Tène, 74, 81, 91
  art, 95
  bracelets, 87
  brooches, 88, 89
  culture, 74
  daggers, 90
La Tène I daggers, 90
late palstaves, **59, 60,** 62
Later
  All Cannings Cross group, 81
  Bronze Age, **45,** 46, 49, 64, 68, 69, 72, 250
  Mesolithic, **21, 22-3, 25,** 26

Neolithic, **27, 44,** 49, 50, 51
  Upper Palaeolithic, **9, 12,** 13, **18, 19-20**
lathes, 84, 114, 160, **255-6,** 265
lathe-turned, 114, 158, 194
laths, 169
Latin, 161
latrina (pl latrinae), 104
latrines, **99,** 103, **104,** 173
latten, **178,** 180, 181, 182, 184, 191, 264
lattice decoration, 131
lattimo decoration, 198
laurel leaves, 39
lava, 66, 112, 160
lavatories, 104, **173**
lavatorium, 173
lavatory seats, 194
lay brothers, 173
layers, **210,** 211, **212, 213,** 214, 216, 219, 222, 224, 226, **233,** 235
lazy bed cultivation, 245
leached, 224, 225
leaching, 223
lead, 80, **84,** 103, 104, 105, 112, **113,** 123, 134, 135, 136, 137, 139, 142, **147, 149,** 157, 158, 175, **177-8,** 180, 181, 195, 196, 201, 231, 264, **268,** 277
  bronze, 59, **264**
  glazed ware, 130
  ores, 281
  oxide, 268
  pigs, 113, 268
  working, 149
leaf, gold, 267
  -gilding, 267
  points, 18
  silver, 268
leaf-shaped currency bars, 85
  arrowheads, **39,** 123
  spearheads, **54, 58, 60,** 61, **151,** 188
  swords, 55
lears, 269
leather, 52, 66, 68, **73, 83,** 90, 91, 92, 110, **114,** 123, 125, **126,** 138, 141, 146, 152, **158,** 166, **179,** 180, 184, **186,** 187, 188, **191, 194,** 220, **253, 254,** 262, 278, 281
leather hard, 279
leather working, 145, 167, 245, **253-4**
  tools, 66, 73
leats, 177, 178
leaves, 129, 196, 219
leers, 269
legends, 94, 153
legionaries, 99, 123, 126
legs, 110, 114
lehrs, **269,** 275
Leicester ware, 165
leisters, 24, 25
Le Moustier, France, 17
lepers' windows, 174
lesser chambers, 169
letters, **104, 105,** 181, 197, 224
Levallois flakes, 16
Levalloisian, 9, 10, 12, 13, **16**
  industries, 16
  technique, 16
Levallois-Perret, France, 16

Levallois technique, 16
levelling staffs, 214
levels, 208, **214, 215**
lever locks, 121
levers, 36, 83
lewis, 112
  holes, 112
lewisons, 112
Lexden, Essex, 98
libra, 135
library, 173
lid mirrors, 138-9
lids, 79, 121, 130, 132, **133, 134, 138,** 146, 149, 166, 194, **203**
lierne ribs, 175
  vaults, 175, 176
lifting tackle, 112
lift keys, 121, 122
light, 207, 230, 231, 233
lighthouses, 112
lighting, 134, 191-2
light ploughs, 245-6
lights, **174,** 175, 192, 196
ligulae, 115, **138**
lime, 142, 238
lime-kilns, 114
lime putty, 147
limestone, 101, 108, 114, 116, 147, 224, 226, 268
Limoges, France, 191
limpet hammers, 23, 25
  picks, 23
  scoops, 25
limpets, 25
linch pins, 91, 92, 93, 111
Lincolnshire, 130, 131, 165
linear
  cellular churches, 145
  cemeteries, 48
  decorated tiles, 199
  ditches, 45
  earthworks, 45, 147
  patterns, 164, 165
  ranch boundaries, 79
line-impressed tiles, 199
linen, 73, 117, 158
  rubbers, **117,** 126
  smoothers, 158, 163, 198
linked pins, 154
lintels, 51, **75,** 76
liquids, 115, 131, 132, 230, 254
Lisburn, Ireland, 54
Lisburn dirks, 54, 58
litharge, 268
Little Paxton, Cambridgeshire, 17
Little Woodbury, Wiltshire, 76
living rooms, 169, 170
Llantwit Major, South Glamorgan, 62
Llantwit-Stogursey group, 62
  industry, **62,** 242
Llyn Fawr, Mid Glamorgan, 63
Llyn Fawr phase, 63
loam, 223
lobed cups, 203
  pommels, 151, 152, 186
locating sites, 205-9
locational analysis, 239
lochs, 75
locks, **121,** 149
loess, 222, **223,** 226
lofts, 170
logboats, **73,** 194, 255
London, 55, 61, 68, 106, 130

London ware, 130, **131**
long
  barrows, **30-5**, 47, 246
  bows, 43, 185
  cairns, **31**, 34
  cist cemeteries, 146
  cross coinage, 179
  cross pennies, 153
  fields, 250
  -headed skulls, 221
  -house form, of, 170
  -houses, 168, **170**
  mortuary enclosures, 32
  -necked beakers, 70
  tongue-shaped chapes, 59, 60
Long Wittenham-Allen's Pit group, 81
look-out posts, 101
loom-frames, 83
looms, 73, 116, 158, 195, **251-2**
loomweights, **73, 80,** 83, **116,** 147, **157-8,** 161, 164, **252**
looped socketed spearheads, 54
looped sockets, 183
  stirrups, 189
  studs, 88
loop fasteners, 88-9
loop-headed pins, 54
loop-hinges, 121
loopholes, 167
Loose Howe group, 65
lorica hamata, 124, 125
  segmentata, 124, 125
  squamata, 124, 125
lost wax casting, 264-5
  method, 114, 178, **264-5**
Lothian, 62
louvers, 200
louvres, 200
Low Countries, 198
Lower Nene valley ware, 130
Lower Palaeolithic, 9, 10, 13-17, 242
Lower Rhineland colour coated wares, **130,** 132
low-flanged palstaves, 54, 57
Lowland Britain, 106, 177, **245**
Lowland England, 199
Lowland Zone, 79, **245**
low relief, 206
low side windows, 174
lozenge pommels, 186-7
lozenge-shaped plates, 64
ludi, 103
Ludovici, 129
lugged chisels, 54, 55
Lugi, 94
lugs, 40, **55,** 71, 164, 165
lunate-opening spearheads, 59, 60
lunulae, 64, 65
lute, 198
lutes, 137
Lydney-Llanmelin style, 82
lye, 251
Lyles Hill ware, 40
lynchet banks, 79
lynchets, **228, 249,** 251
Lyon ware, 129
lyres, 137, 146, 158

maceheads, **23, 24, 39, 40, 44, 65, 66, 68, 69,** 188, 245, 257

macellum (pl macella), 103
maces, 188
McGrail, S., 73
machicolated parapets, 172
machicolations, 171, 173
Mâçon, France, 18
macroscopic examination, 229
  plant remains, 11, **219,** 227
Maes Howe group, 35
magical properties, 162
Maglemose, Denmark, 21
Maglemosian industries, 21
  culture, 21
magnetic anomalies, 208
  field, 208, 233, 234
  methods of detection, 208
magnetism, 233, 234
magnetometers, 208
magnetostratigraphy, 10, **234**
magnification, 229, 230
Maiden Castle, Dorset, 31, 78, 98
Maiden Castle-Marnhull style, 82
maidenhead spoons, 182
mail armour, 124, 184, 185
main flake surfaces, 258
main furnaces, 269
mainshares, 246
maisons-dieu, 170
maker's marks, 151
  names, 151
  stamps, 131, 134
mallets, 83, 183, 207, 251
malting floors, 107
  kilns, 168
mammae, 109
mammals, 79, **220-1**
mammoth, 13
Mam Tor, Derbyshire, 46
manacles, 121
Mancetter, Warwickshire, 270
mandrels, 255, 256, 265
mandrils, 265
manganese, 269
manhole covers, 103
manholes, 103
manor houses, 177
mansiones, 102, **106**
manuscripts, 191
maplewood, 146, 181
map-making, 216
maps, 205, 206, 216, 239, 241
marasmius oreades, 207
marble, 87, 108, 109, 140
Marches, the, 49, 62
marching camps, 100
marine, 108, 144, 219, 220, 222, 224, 225
  sediments, 224-5
markers, 50, 101, 142, 149, 175
market crosses, 167
  halls, 103
  places, 167
markets, 103
Marne district, 74, 95
Marnian invasions, 74
Marnoch, Grampian, 52
marsh, 25, 42, 110
martels-de-fer, 188
marver blocks, 270
marvered, marvering, 126, 128, 139, 198, **270,** 271, 272, 274, 275
marvers, **270,** 272

masks, 95, **103,** 126
masonry (see also stone), 172
Mass, 203
massage rooms, 104
massive armlets, 87, 88
  socketed axes, 63
MAT, 17
mathematical, 137, 232, 239, 241
mathematics, 50, **241**
matrices, **214, 216,** 223
matting, 80
mattock heads, 24, 25
mattocks, 25, **118,** 183
mattresses, 110
mauls, 51
mausolea, 142
Mayen lava, 160
mazer bowls, 180, **181**
mazers, **181,** 194
meadows, 207
Meare, Somerset, 75
Meare spiral type beads, 87
measured drawings, 208
measurement, **50,** 136, 208
measures, 135-6, 181
measuring rods, 50
  tapes, 208, 214
mechanical diggers, 209
  fractures, 257-8, 260
medallion and grisaille windows, 196
medallions, 96, 111, 196
medallion windows, 196
medical, 197, 229
medicaments, 138
medicine, 138
Medieval, 75, 130, **143,** 144, **167-204,** 205, 232, 233, 234, 248, 250, 251, 255, 256, 264, 266, 268, 269, 270, 274, 276, 283
Mediterranean, 112, 164
Medway group, 34
meeting places, 28, 76
megalithic burial chambers, 32
megalithic yard, 50
melon beads, 141, 154
memorials, 161
memorial stones, 161, 162
Mendips, 113
mercenaries, 126, 143, 164
Mercia, 143
mercury, 268
merlons, 172, 173
Merovingian Franks, 153
Mesolithic, **21-6,** 27, 36, **218,** 226, 238, **242, 256,** 257, 261, 264
metacarpi, 83
metal (see also bronze, gold, iron, lead etc), 207, 229, 230, 231, 243, 254, 257, 263, 264, 265, 266, 267, 268, 270, 271, 274, 278
  Bronze Age, 52, 59, 61, 63, 64
  Iron Age, 95
  Medieval, 181-2, 188, 191, 194
  Roman, 111, 115, 142
  Saxon, 154, 163, 178, 180
metal-framed purses, 191
metalling, 110
metallographic microscopy, 230
metallurgical microscopes,

230
metalwork, see metal
metalworking, 144, 167, **264-8**
metapodials, 192
metatarsi, 83
meurtrières, 167
mica, 278
micaceous schist, 192
  slip, 278
mica-dusted pottery, 129, 278
mica-dusting, 129
mica-gilt pottery, 278
Michelmersh ware, 165
microbial decay, 219
microburins, 23, 24, 263
microburin technique, 263
microliths, **21, 22,** 23, 263
microprocessors, 241
microscopes, 217, 229, 230, 269
microscopy, 229, 230
microscopic examination, 229
micro-trapezoids, 23
micro-triangles, 22
middens, 220, 222, 225, **228**
Middle
  Acheulian, 14
  Ages, 167
  Bronze Age, 45
  Gothic, 196
  Last Glacial, **12,** 18
  Palaeolithic, 9, 10, 13, 17, 242
  Saxon, **143,** 147
  Saxon pottery, 165
  Stone Age, 242
middle pointed style, 175
Mid Glamorgan, 63
Midlands, 79, 82, 131, 166
midribs, 52, 54
Migdale, Highland, 52
Migdale-Marnoch tradition, 52, 53
Migration, 143
Migration and Early Medieval, 143
migratory, 220, 221
Mildenhall ware, 40
milecastles, 101
miles, 101
milestones, 110
military, 99, 100, 101, 103, 104, 105, 114, 126, 136, 142, 187
  forks, 188
  spearheads, 188
  tools, 120
millefiori, 146, 156, **273**
milling, 112
milliprobe, 230
mill ponds, 177
millpools, 177
mill races, 113, 177
mills, 112, **145, 176-7**
millstones, **112,** 145, 160, 192
Mindel, 11
minerals, 223, 224, 228, 229, 230, 231, 233, 279
mineral salts, 207
  surfacing, 279
mines, **36-7,** 43, 64, 178, 245, 257
miniature cups, 71-2
  shears, 146
mini-hillforts, 46
minimissimi, 136
minims, 136

mining, 36, 37, 44, 102, 114, 147, 178, 264, 266
minted, 94, 179
mint marks, 136
mints, 94, 136
mirrors, 84, **89**, **138-9**
mithraeum, 105
Mithras, 105
mixed agriculture, 27, 28
farming, 46, 79, 117
moated sites, 177
moats, 171, 172, 177
model objects, 112
models, **43**, 84, 105, **112**, 178, **241**, **264**, **265**
of stone axes, 43
modius (pl modii), 136
Moh scale, 229
Mold, Clwyd, 64
molluscan, 227, 228
mollusc shells, 224, 227
molten metal, 178, 264, 265
monasteries, **145-6**, 167, 173
monastic, 163, 164, **173**, 177
money boxes, 203
monks, 146
monochrome films, 216
monoliths, **30**, **50**, 107
monoxylous coffins, 47
monumental arches, 106
brasses, 178
Monza, Italy, 55
moorland, 79, 224, 225
mordants, 253
mortar, 32, 101, 104, 108, 109, 114, 145, **147**
mortaria, 103, 129, 130, **131**
mortar mixers, 147
mortars, 160, **192**, **203**
mortise-and-tenon fastening, 88
joints, 51, 169, 256
Mortlake pottery, 41
mortuary carts, 97
crosses, 149
enclosures, 32
houses, 32
mosaic glass, 273
vessels, 271
mosaicists, 108
mosaics, 102, 103, 104, 106, 107, **108**, 109, 137
moss, 223
motte-and-bailey castles, 171
mottes, 171, 172
motto beakers, 130, 132
mould-blown vessels, 127
mouldboards, 118, 245-6, 248, 249
moulded, 115, 129, 174, 254, 271
sockets, 151
moulding, 277
planes, 255, 256
mouldings, 109, 112, **174**, 255
moulds, **64**, **66**, 84, 94, 95, 109, 112, 113, 114, 128, 153, 156, 164, 178, 180, 192, 198, 199, 254, **264**, 265, 266, 268, **270**, **271**, 272, 273, 274, 275, 277
mounds, 30, 31, 32, 33, 34, 46, 48, 171, 177, 205, 213, 243, 254
mountainous regions, 245
mounts, **63**, 64, 66, **68**, 89, 90, **91**, **93**, **126**, 146, 147, 157, 178, 179
Mousterian, 9, 10, 12

industries, 17
of Acheulian tradition, 17
points, 17
mouthpieces, 137, 190
Mucking-Crayford style, 82
mud, 169, 217, 221, 223
muff glass, 275
mugs, 70, 133, 203
mullions, **174**, 196
multi-flue updraught kilns, 280
multilobed circular pommels, 186
multiple burial (*see also* collective burial), 49
multiple wound beads, 274
multivallate hillforts, 76
multivallation, 78
mu-metal, 208
municipium, 102
Munsell colour charts, 224, 229
mural cells, 76
chambers, 75
towers, 167, 171
murder holes, 171
musical instruments, **137**, 192
mussels, 222
mussel-shells, 258
mutationes, 106
Mycenean culture, 70
Mynnydd Rhiw, Gwynedd, 36
mythological themes, 108
mythology, 141, 181

nail claws, 117
-cleaners, 138
holes, 189
nails, **85**, 109, **121**, 178, **257**
naked barley, **27**, 79
name-plates, 149
narrow
bladed palstaves, 54
-blade industries, 22
butted flat axes, 52, 53
-flake tools, 39
mouthed, 132, **282**
rig, 250
wall, 101
narthex, 105
nasals, 184
National Museum of Denmark, 242
natron, 268
natural shed, 251
nave bands, 62, **91**, **111**
bindings, 91, 111
hoops, 91, 92, 111
naves, 91, 107, 145, 173, 174, 175
Near East, 104, 171, 191
Near Eastern candlesticks, 192
nearest-neighbour analysis, 239-40
index, 240
Nebraskan, 11
neck guards, 91, 124, 125, 184, 185
necklaces, 68, **69**, 84, **87**, 140, 147, 154
neck-rings, 86
needle-cases, 146, **149**
needles, **19**, **68**, **80**, **81**, 83, 84, 115, **116-17**, 149, **158**, 159, 160, 178, 195, 251, 257
negative bulbs of percus-

sion, 258
flake surfaces, 258
lynchets, 249
negro-head beakers, 127
Nene Valley, 130
ware, **130**, 132
Neolithic, 21, 23, **27-44**, 46, 47, 49, 50, 51, 64, 65, 70, 218, **242**, 249, 256, 257, 261, 264, 283
'A' pottery, 40
nether stones, 112, 113
net rules, 66
sinkers, **80**, **84**, 160
weights, **80**, 83, 116
nets, 80, 116
netting needles, **80**, **81**, 83, **116-17**, 160
nettles, 251
network pattern, 275
neutral pH, 224
soils, 227
neutron activation analysis, 230
neutrons, 230
New Forest potteries, 130
Newlyn, Cornwall, 214
Newstead, Borders, 111, 114, 126
New Stone Age, 242
nibs, 142
Niedermendig lava, 66
niello, 113, 126, 156, 180, **268**
nine mens morris, 192, 194
nitrates, 207
nitrogen, 233
analysis, 233
nitrum, 268
nodular flint, 37
nomads, 45
Norfolk, 54, 82, 165, 180, 270
Norman, 174
Norman Conquest, 143, 171, 174
Normandy, 195
Norman invasion, 167
Norman Romanesque, 174
North America, 232
Northampton, 147
Northamptonshire, 82
Northampton ware, 165
Northern Ireland, 36, 37
Northern Isles, 75, 143, 144, 146, 161
North Italian colour coated wares, 130
red slip ware, 130
North Kent marshes potteries, 130
North Scottish spiral type beads, 87
Northton, Isle of Harris, Western Isles, 45
Northumberland, 59, 120
Northumbria, 143, 153, 165
North Yorkshire, 25, 26, 43, 48, 97, 114, 130, 131, 146
Norway, 143, 160
nosed scrapers, 18
notched-butt dirks, 54, 58
rapiers, 54
notches, 65, **263**
notching, 263
Nottingham splashed ware, 165
novacula, 138
Novantae, 94
nozzles, 134, **135**

nuclear cemeteries, 48
forts, 144
radiation, 233
reactors, 230
nucleated cemeteries, 48
settlements, 45, 75
nuclei, 208
nuggets of gold, 267
numerical taxonomy, 239
nuts, **185**, **186**, 192, **193**, 219

oak, 11, **43**, 73, **83**, **158**, 176, 194, 200, 217, 218, 253
oars, 115
oats, 117
Oban, Strathclyde, 23
Obanian culture, 21
industries, 23
oblique aerial photographs, 205
APs, 206
coursing, 145
flaking, 261
obliquely-blunted points, 21, 22, 23
observatories, 50
occupation debris, 225, 227
floors, 28
layers, **213**, 222, 224
O-C-H group, 35
ochres, 18, 109
octagonal bottles, 127
oculists' stamps, 138-9
OD, 214
oenochoe, 95
oersted, 208
Offa's Dyke, 147
officers' houses, 99
offices, 102, 103
offset method, 213, 214
planning, 213, 214
shoulders, 283
offshore sediments, 225
ogam, 161, 162
alphabet, 162
ogham, 162
oil, 36, 131, 134, 138, 164, 180, 191, 252, 253, 254
-dressed skins, 254
-dressing, 253
flasks, 122, **127**
lamps, 43
ointments, 133, 138
Oldbury type beads, 87
Old English, 162
Older Dryas, 12, 218
Old Stone Age, 242
olive oil, 131, 164
ombrogenous peat, 227
omphalos, 284
omphalos-based jars, 83
onager, 123
on-glaze decoration, 281
opaque zones, 221
open
base rings, 272, 273
bowl continuum, 82
-cast mining, 114, 266
-cast pits, 36, 37
excavation, 210
field system, 251
hearths, 280
lamps, 134, **135**, 191
moulds, 64, 66, 264
opening lehrs, **269**, **275**, 276
materials, 277
openwork, 93, 114, 156, 180
oppida, 75
optical emission spectrometry, **230**, 231

opus sectile, 108
 signinum, 108
 tessellatum, 108
oratories, 170
orchestras, 103
orders, 173
Ordnance Datum, 214
Ordnance Survey datum, 214
Ordovices, 94
ores, **114**, 149, 178, 264, 266, 267, 281
organic material, 12, 14, 26, 149, 211, 219, 223, 232, 243
 sediments, 223
oriel chambers, 169
oriels, 169
origin, 213
Orkney-Cromarty-Hebridean group, 35
Orkney Islands, 28, 35, 44, 75, 246
Ornament Horizon, 54, 56
ornaments, 85, 95, 98, 243
Oronsay, Strathclyde, 26
Orpheus, 104
orthostats, **32**, **33**, **34**, 35
ossuaria, 142
Otley-type ware, 165
otolith growth rings, 220
otoliths, 221
Our Lady of Walsingham, 180
outbent rims, 282
outbuildings, 106, **107**, 177
outcrops, 36, 51, 144, 257, 264
outcurved rims, 282
outer baileys, 171, 173
outhouses, 144
outpost forts, 101
outwash gravels, 223, 226
outwash sands, 223, 226
outworks, 171
ovate handaxes, 14, **15**
ovens, 28, 75, 83, **99**, **107**, 120, 233, **269**, 270, 271, 272, 275, 277, **280**, 281
overglaze decoration, 281
overgrazing, 222, 223, 226
overhanging rims, 282
overhanging-rim urns, 71
overlay, 266
ovoid beakers, 132, 133
oxen, 13, 27, 85, 91, 136, 144, 246, 249, 251
Oxford potteries, 130
Oxfordshire, 32, 140
ox-goads, 249
oxides, 233, 268
oxidized pottery, 281
oxidizing atmosphere, 128, **281**
ox-scapula shovels, 36, **44**
oxygen, 234, 281
 isotope analysis, 9, 220, **234**

pack-horses, 190
pad bases, 272, 273
paddles, **25**, **42**, **43**, 147
padlocks, **121**, 149, 178, 190
pagan, 104
 Saxon, **143**, 146, 147, 151, 154, 157
paint, 130, 196, 278
painted, 105, 109, 131, 194, 201, 278
 enamel, 268
 parchment ware, 130

painting, 254, 274, 277
palaeobotany, 217
palaeoecology, 216
palaeoethnobotany, 217
Palaeolithic, **9-20**, 226, 234, **242**, 257, 261, 264
palaeopathology, 221
palaeopedology, 222
Palaeozoic rocks, 245
palaestra, 104
palatial residence, 107
Palestine, 272
palimpsests, 178
palisade enclosures, 77
palisades, 28, 46, **77**, 100, 101, 145
palm cups, 163
palstaves, **54**, **57**, **58**, **59**, **60**, 62, **64**
palynology, 217
panes, 109, 126, 128, 275
pans, 95, 114, 135, **136**, 181, 202, **254**
parade helmets, **91**, **124**, 146
 shields, 91
paraisons, 272
parallel-flue kilns, 109, 130, 199, **280**, **281**
parapets, 101, 172, **173**, 176
parasites, 228
parchment, 253-4
 wares, 130
paring chisels, 118
Paris, France, 16
parish churches, 174
Parisi, 94
Parisian stamped wares, 131
Park Brow-Caesar's Camp group, 81
parks, 177
parrot beak jugs, **201**, 203
passage grave art, 51
 graves, 30, **33-6**, 51
passages, 32, 33, 35, 36, 75, 76
passageways, **102**, 167, 170
paste, 70
pastoral agriculture, 28, 245, 249
 enclosures, 79
pastoralism, 45, **79**, 245, 250
pastures, 168, 207, 251
Patch Grove ware, 131
patella (pl patellae), 95
patens, 182
paterae, 122, 123
patina, 229, 257
pattern-moulding, 274
pattern-welded swords, **151**, 152
pattern-welding, 149
pattern windows, 196
paved roads, 110
pavements, 199
Paviland Cave, West Glamorgan, 9, 18
Paxton stage, 17
pea grit, 225
Peak District, 49
Peak group, 34
pear-shaped spoons, 182
peas, 117
peat, 42, 207, 218, 219, 221, **223**, **227**, 281
 beds, 225
 bogs, 218, 219, **227**
 spades, 118, 119
pebble chopper-cores, 14
 chopping tools, 14
 maceheads with hour-

glass perforations, 23, 24
pebbles, 23, 157, 223, **262**, **263**, 279
pecked surfaces on stone, 262
pecking, 51
pedals, 255, **256**
pedestal bases, 81, 132
 beakers, 132
 urns, 82, 83
pedestals, 112, **284**
pediments, 105
pedology, 222
pegged socketed spearheads, 54
 spearheads, **54**, **58**, 59, **60**, 61, 62
peg-hole spearheads, 54
pegs, 42, 54, 64, 80, 83, 115, 121, 192, 193, 213, 256
peg-socketed spearheads, 54
pele-towers, 170
pellets, 221
pelts, 253
penannular armlets, 87
 bracelets, 64
 brooches, 88, 89, 140, 155, 156, 179
Penard, West Glamorgan, 54
Penard phase, 54-5, 58, 59
pendants, 26, **43**, **44**, 48, **52**, 64, **66**, **68**, **69**, 83, 84, 115, **140**, 153, **154**, 160, 178, **180**
pendents, 191
penknife points, 19
Penn, Buckinghamshire, 199
pennies, **153**, **178**, 179
Pennines, 19
pens, 142, 144
Penultimate Glaciation, **11**, 16
Penultimate Interglacial, 11
percussion flaking, **260**, 262
perforated
 animal teeth, 26
 antler hammers, 44
 antler maceheads, 44
 antler mattock heads, 24, 25
 antler sleeves, 25
 chalk blocks, 43
 clay plaques, 69
 lugs, 40, 71
 stone maceheads, **39**, **40**, **65**, 245
 teeth, 68
 whetstones, 192
perfumes, 133
periglacial area, 226
 features, 226
permafrost, 226
perpendicular Gothic style, 174, 175
personal hoards, 243
perspective drawing, 238
pestles, 83
pests, 222
Peterborough culture, 27
 pottery, 40-1
petit-tranchet arrowheads, 22
 derivative arrowheads, 39
petrological examination, 37, 66, 229
Pevensey ware, 130
pewter, 104, 113, 122, 141, **147**, 154, **177**, 178, 179, 180, 181, **182**, 264, **268**
pH, **224**, 227

phalerae, 62, **63**, **111**
phalli, 43
phallic symbols, 50
phosphate analysis, 224
photogrammetry, 216
photographs, 205, 206, 207, 216, 226, 229
photography, **205-6**, 207, 208, **216**, 229
photomicrographs, 229
physical examination, 229
 weathering, 222-3
phytoliths, 219
Picardy pins, 54
pickaxes, 120
picks, 21, **23**, **24**, 36, **44**, 83, **117**, **119**, **138**, 183, 245
Picti, 143
Pictish cross-slabs, 161
 stones, 161
 symbols, 161
 symbol stones, 161
Pictland, 143
Picts, 143
piece moulds, 198, **264**, 219, 220
pie
 charts, 217
 -crust decoration, 278
 diagrams, 217
 dish diagrams, 217, 218
 dishes, 133
 dish rims, 282
piers, 76, 110, 175, 176
pig-faced bascinets, 185
pig fibula pins, 159-60
Piggott, Professor S., 27
pigs, 28, 46, 79, **113**, 117, 144
pikes, 188
pilae, 107, 108
pila muralia, 100
piles, 73, 75
pilgrim bottles, 203
pilgrims' badges, 180
 signs, 177, 178, **180**
pillared hypocausts, 107-8
pillar-moulded bowls, **126**, **127**, 274
pillars, 146, 161, 174, **175**
pillar stones, 161
 mounds, 177
pillow-stones, 161
pilum (pl pila), 123
pilum muralium, 100
PIM, 208
pin beaters, **157**, **158**, 159, 192, 195
pincers, 270
pinched lips, 282
 projections, 127, 128, 274
 rims, 282
pine, 11, 73, 217, 218, **232**
pingos, 226
pins, 264
 Bronze Age, 48, **52**, **53**, **54**, 56, **63**, **68**
 Iron Age, 83, 84, **88**
 Medieval, 178, **186**, 192, 195
 Mesolithic, 25
 Neolithic, 44
 Palaeolithic, 18
 Roman, 113, 114, 115, 116, 117, **121**, 126, **140**
 Saxon, 146, 147, 149, 153, **154**, 155, 156, **159-60**
pipeclay figurines, 112
 figures, 198
pipes, **103**, 110, **115**, 121, 211

piping, 113
pipkins, 201, 202
piscina (pl piscinae), 175
pit alignments, 79
pitched roofs, 170
pitchers, 164, **165**, **166**, 201, 202, **203**
pitchforks, **118**, 183
pit-dwellings, 79
pit-head construction, 36
pit-huts, 144
pit kilns, 280
pit-props, 36
pits, 26, **27-8**, 29, 36, **37**, 46, 47, 48, 50, 74, 76, **79-80**, 97, 98, 104, 115, 144, 147, 149, 158, 167, 168, 170, 178, 194, 207, 208, 210, **211**, **212**, 213, 219, 222, **228**, 233, 253, 266, 280
pivot type hinges, 121
place names, 143
plague victims, 178
plaice, 221
plain rims, 282
plaited band ornament, 163
planes, **117**, **118**, 149-50, **255**, **256**
planishing, 265
plank-built boats, 73
plank coffins, 47, 48
planks, 83, 158, 255, 256
plank tracks, 42
planned street system, 167
planning, 213, 214
    frames, 213, 214
plano-convex knives, 65, 67
plans, 207, 208, 210, 213, 214, 216
plantain, 218
plant impressions, 219
    opals, 219
    remains, 11, **217-20**, 222, 223, 224, 227, 245
plants, 195, 207, **216-20**, 221, 223, 251
planum method, **210**, 253
plaques, **43**, **68**, **69**, 83, **105**, 159
plaster, 105, **108**, 109, 114, 117, 142, 145, 147, 174
plasterers' floats, 117
    trowels, 117
plastic, 219, 230, 277
plate armour, 184
plates, 64, **65**, 91, 105, 113, 114, 116, 122, 129, **133**, 140, 149, 156, 157, 159, 165, 168, 179, **181**, **182**, 184, 188, 192, **193**, 254
plate tracery, 174
platforms, **25**, 30, 32, 36, 46, 75, 97, 100, **101**, 112, **168**, 171, 177, 243, 269
platters, **133**, **134**, 194, **201**
Pleistocene, **9**, **10**, **11**, 218, 225, 234
plough beams, 246
ploughed-out, 47
plough handles, 83
    headlands, 251
ploughing, 206, 211, 224, **246**, 249, 250, 251
plough marks, 46, **225**, **246**
ploughs, 27, 79, 118, **245-9**, 250, 251, 260
plough scratches, 27, **246**
ploughshares, **85**, **118**, 151
plough share-shaped currency bars, 85
ploughsoil, 206

ploughwash, **223**, 227
plumbatae, 123
plumb-bobs, 123
plumping, 253
Plumpton Plain, Sussex, 45
plunge baths, 104
plunger moulds, 271
pockets, 191
podium, 105
podsols, 224, 225
pointed arches, 174, 175
    ferrules, **54**, 59
    handaxes, 15
    style, 174
    windows, 174
pointillé, 41, 72, **266**
point, of percussion, 258, 259
points, **17**, **19**, **21**, **44**, **68**, 257, 266
poker work, 254
polar ice sheets, 9
Poldar Moss, Central, 59
Poldar phase, 59
pole axes, 188
    lathes, 255, 256
    sheaths, 91, 92
    tips, 91, 111
polecats, 220
poled, 264
poles, 91, **92**, 172, **256**
polished, 37, 66, 69, 83, 129, 138, 152, 230, 262, 265, 271, 273, **279**, 281
polishers, 83
polishing, 37, 261, **262**, **281**
polissoirs, 262
political boundaries, 79
pollen, 11, **217-19**, 226, 227, 245
    analysis, 11, 12, **217-19**, 221, 236
    diagrams, **217**, 218, 222, 235
    grains, 217
    zones, 11, 12, 217, 218
polychrome jewellery, 156
    jugs and pitchers, 201, 202
polyptychon, 141
pommel bars, 90, **151**
    mounts, 64
    tangs, 63
pommels, 52, **68**, 146, **151**, **186-7**
Pompeian red pottery, 129
pond barrows, **46**, **47**, 48
ponds, 177
ponies, 64
pontil marks, 270
    scars, 270
    wads, 272
pontils, 270
pony caps, 93
Poole, Dorset, 87, 131
poppies, 132
poppy head beakers, 130, **132**, **133**
porches, 74
porta decumana, 99
    praetoria, 99
    principalis dextra, 99
    principalis sinistra, 99
portal dolmens, 32
    stones, 32, 34
portals, **33**, 102
Portchester, Hampshire, 100
Portchester-type ware, 165
portcullis, 167, **171**
porticoes, 105, 144

porticuses, 145
ports, 167
positive flake surfaces, 34, 258
positive lynchets, 249
posset, 203
pots, 203
post-and-panel technique, 34
post casts, 211
post-circles, 74
Post Deverel-Rimbury tradition pottery, 46, **72-3**
posterns, 172
Post-Glacial, 10, 11, 12
postholes, 28, 29, 42, 45, 47, 73, 74, 75, 78, 97, 100, 144, 158, **211**, 226, 228
posting stations, 106
Post-Medieval, 170, 189, 235, 250, 281
post-mills, 176-7
post packing, 211
post pipes, 211
post-rings, 74
posts, 29, 31, 46, 73, 74, 100, 107, 147, 176, 211, 271
Post Wilburton phase, 59
posy rings, 179
potash, 268
potash-lime glass, 268
pot boilers, 28, 66
potin coins, 94-5
pot-lid fractures, 259, 260
pot-metal, 276
pots, 203, 219, **269**, 270, 272, 277, 278, 279, 280, 281
potsherds, 80, 116, 137
potteries, 129, **130**, 201
potters, 164, 278
potters' stamps, 128, **278**
    tools, 83
    wheels, 82, 278
pottery, 167, 168, 205, 219, 228, 229, 230, 233, 235, 236, 237, 241, 243, **277-84**
    Bronze Age, 45, 46, 47, 48, 49, 64, 66, 68, **70-3**
    Iron Age, 79, **81-3**, 95-6
    Medieval, 167, 168, 177, 181, **191**, 197, **198**, **201-4**
    Neolithic, 28, **40-1**, **70**
    Roman, 103, 108, **128-34**, 140, 142
    Saxon, 145, 146, **164-6**
    spoons, 41
    stamps, 279
    working tools, 66, 68
pouch bottles, 163
pouches, 158, 194
pounds, 45-6
praetentura, 99
praetorium, 99
pre-boreal, 218
precious stones, 140, 155, 156, 179
precipitates, 223
prehistoric, 177, 192, 219, **242**, 245, 250, 253, 254, 277, 280
    fields, 249
prehistory, 241, **242**
prepared cores, 261
Preselay Mountains, 50
pressed beads, 275
press moulding, 277
pressure flaking, 260
pricket candlesticks, 191

pricket-spikes, 191
pricks, 111, 190
prick spurs, 149, **189-90**
priests, 175, 182
priests' regalia, 105
primary
    barrows, 48
    burial, 30, 32, 48, **243**
    fill, 227, 228
    flakes, 14, 15
    flaking, 260
    interments, 243
    silt, 227
    working, 260
Primary Neolithic, 27
principal rafters, **168**, 169
principia, 99
printed tiles, 199
priories, 173
priors, 173
prismatic cores, 17
prisms, 230
pritchels, 149, 267
pritchells, 267
privies, 170
probes, 138, 207-8
probing, 207
projecting rims, 282
    ring-headed pins, 88
promontories, 76
promontory forts, 146
prongs, 112, **179**, 183
protected looped spear-heads, 59
proto-handaxes, 14
protohistory, 242
proton gradiometers, 208
    magnetometers, 208
protons, 208
proto-pennies, 153
proto-Solutrean, 18
prototypes, 95, 166
proximal ends, 259
pruning knives, 184
prunts, 197, **270**, **273**
pseudo-mosaic tiles, 199
pseudo-samian, 129
P-shaped brooches, 140
P.T.D. arrowheads, 39
public baths, 103, **104**
    buildings, **102-3**, 112
    lavatories, 104
pucellas, 270
puddled clay, 100
pugio, 123
pulley rings, 68
pulpitum, 103
pulsed induction meters, 208
pump drills, 255, **262**
pumps, 103
punches, **54**, 61, **117**, 183, 254, 260, 266, 267
punch flaking, 260
puntees, 270
punty, 272, **276**
    irons, **270**, **272**, 275, **276**
    rods, 270
Purbeck, Dorset, 84
purlins, **168**, 169
purse frames, 178
    lids, 146
    -mounts, 146, **149**, **150**
purses, **136-7**, 158, **191**
put-log holes, 172
put-logs, 172
putty, 147
puzzle jugs, 202
pygmy cups, 71
pyramidal loomweights, 73

quadrangles, 170
quadrans (pl quadrantes), 136
quadrant method, **210**, 211
quadripartite rib-vaults, 176
quantification, 235
quantify, 235
quarrels, **185**, 189, **275**
quarried, 113, 114
quarries, 79, 196, **275**
quarry ditches, 31
  faces, 114
  pits, 211
  windows, 196
quarrying, 160
quarter bars, 176, 177
quartering, 260
quarter staters, 94
quartz, 268, 271
  crystals, 233
  sand, 277
quartzitic rocks, 257
Quaternary, 9
quatrefoils, 196
queen-posts, 168, 169
quenched, 266
quenching, 265
querns, **40**, **66**, **80**, 83, **112-13**, 145
quernstones, 79, 160, 192
quicklime, 147, 253
quillon daggers, 187
quillons, 186, 187
quoit
  beads, 70, 154
  brooches, 155-6
  -brooch style, 163
  -headed pins, 54, 56
  pins, 54
  -shaped beads, 70
  -shaped loomweights, 157
quoits, 156

rabbits, 177
race, 257
racquet pins, 53
radial striations, 112
radiate crowns, 136
radiated brooches, 155, 156
radiate head brooches, 156
radiates, 136
radiation, 230, 231, 233
radioactive isotopes, 230, 232
radioactivity, 230, 232
radiocarbon dating, 9, 10, 11, 27, 219, **232**, 234
  years, 232
radiographs, 229
radiometric assay, 233
radio transmitters, 208
rafter roofs, 169
rafters, **168**, 169
rafts, 83
raiders, 63, 100, 143
raids, 147, 153
rainfall, 219, 224, 227, 245
rainwater, 104, 223
raised beaches, **225**, 227
  granaries, 75, 79
raising, 265
rakes, **44**, **118**, 183, 269, 270
rammed chalk, 108, 110
  clay, 108, 110
  gravel, 108, 110
ramparts, 75, 76, **77-8**, 97, **99**, **100**, 101, 102, 145, 167, 171
rampart walks, 75
ranch boundaries, 25, 79, 250

ranches, 102
ranging rods, 208
rank-size rule, 241
rapid silt, 227
rapiers, **54**, **56**, 59
rapier sheaths, 73
raspberries, 129
raspberry cups, 129
rasps, 117
raths, **76**, 102, 144
rawhide, 254
ray beads, 87
  pattern, 275
razors, 52, 54, 58, 63, 138
reamers, 267
reaping hooks, 79, **85**, **86**, **118**, **119**, 183, 249
  knives, 27
reaves, 45
receivers, **198**, **203**, 208
reckoning counters, 194
recording, 205, 208, **213-16**
records, 209, 210, 214, 216, 234, 242
rectangular bottles, 127
rectification, 206
recumbent stone circles, 49
  stones, 49
recurrence surfaces, 227
red
  coated pottery, 128
  deer, 13, 45
  deer frontlets, 25
  gloss pottery, 128
  hills, 83, **254**
  ochre, 18, 109
Red Lady of Paviland, 18
reduced pottery, 281
reducing atmosphere, 128, **281**
reeded collars, 282
reed pens, 142
reeds, 109, 223
reedswamp peat, 223
refectories, 146, 173
Reformation, 181
refuse, 228
regalia, 105
reindeer, 13
reins, 92, 190
relative dates, **231**, 233
  dating, 11, 233, 234
release nuts, 186
relief, 110, 126, 180, 205, 206, 266, 268
  decoration, 109, 128, 278
  moulding, 129
  tiles, 199
religion, 33, **96-7**, **104-5**
remanent magnetism, 234
rendering, 108
rendsina soils, 224, 225
repoussé work, 266
reptiles, 221
reredorters, 173
rescue excavation, 209
research excavation, 209
resin, **22**, 26, 254
resinous, 253
resistivity, **207**, 208
  meters, 207
  surveys, 207
resolved flaking, 258
rest pressure flaking, 260
retaining kerbs, **33**, 34
  walls, 34
retentura, 99
retouch, 22, **260**, **261**
retouched, 19, 64
retouching, 23, 264
retractors, 138

retting, 251
revetments, 100, 102, 177
revetment walls, 45
revetted, 103
Rhenish wares, 130
Rhineland, 112, 129, 166, 181
rhinoceros, 13
Rhodian flagons, 95
ribbed, 53, 54, 198
  bowls, 126
  buckets, 95, 96
  cups, 64
  vaulting, 176
ribbon handles, 72
ribs, **175**, 176, 261
rib-vault ceilings, 174
rib-vaults, 175, 176
ricasso, 187
Richborough, Kent, 104, 106
riders, 80
ridge and furrow, 250-1
ridge purlins, 168
  ribs, 175
  tents, 114
  tiles, 200
ridges, 245, 250, 251, **259**, **261**, **272**, **273**, **274**
rig and furrow, 250
rilling, 81, **278**
Rimbury, Dorset, 49
rims, 40, 41, 71, 82, 83, 91, 118, 131, 132, 181, 197, 237, **272**, **273**, 274, 275, 278, **282**
ring-and-dot decoration, 160, 192
ring barrows, 36
  brooches, 155, 179
  building, 277
  cairns, 30, **36**, **48**, **49**, 226
  -coil method, 81
  ditches, **46-7**, 207
  -grooves, 74
  -headed pins, **52**, **53**, **54**, 68, **88**, **121**, **154**, 156
  necks, 132, **282**
  pendants, 68
  -pommels, 151
  -socketed sickles, 54, 58
  stirrups, 189
  swords, 151
  vases, 203
rings, **52**, **54**, **56**, 62, 64, **68**, **69**, 83, 84, **85**, **91**, **92**, 104, **111**, 114, 126, **141**, 147, 149, 151, **153**, 157, **160**, 162, 163, 177, 178, **179**, 184, 190, 197, **207**, 219, 220, 226, 232, 233, 265, **272**
ringwork-and-bailey castles, 171
ringworks, 171
Rinyo, Orkney, 28
Rinyo-Clacton culture, 27
  ware, 41
ripple burnish, 279
  flaking, 215
ripples, **213**, 258
rippling, 251
risers, 251
Riss, 11
rites, 31, 33, 71, 132, 135, 164, **243**
Ritterling, 129
ritual, **46**, 72, 95, 96, 97, 98, 103, 112, 175
  deposits, 46, 50, 59
  shafts, 46

River Avon, 51
  Deben, 146
  Dee, 147
  Humber, 82
  Thames, 21, 68, 257
  Welland, 82
  Wye, 147
rivers, 26, 96, 97, 104, 110, 112, 151, 167, 176, 222, 257, 260
river systems, 221, 226, 227
riveted flat daggers, 52
rivet holes, 52, 54, **55**
riveting, 266
rivet notches, 51, 54
rivets, **52**, **53**, 54, 64, 84, **86**, 111, 117, 149, 179, 184, 193, 266, 267
Rixheim, France, 55
Rixheim-Monza swords, 55, 59
Rixheim swords, 55
roads, **42**, 101, 106, **110-11**, 142, 168
robber trenches, 211
rock art, *see* stone carvings
rock outcrops, 36, 51, 144, 257
rocks (*see also* stone), 9, 50, 222, 223, 224, 225, 226, 229, 234, 245, 257, 262, 266
rock shelters, 227
rodents, 220
rods, **22**, **23**, 116, 207, 254, 265, 266, 267, 270, **271**
rod-tanged swords, 55
rod torcs, 86
rolled, 257
rollers, 278
roller stamping, 278
rolling, 257
Roman, 75, 76, 80, 84, 87, 88, 89, 91, 95, 96, 97, 98, **99-142**, 143, 150, 151, 153, 154, 156, 163, 164, 167, 183, 190, 246, 248, 249, 250, 251, 253, 255, 256, 266, 268, 269, 270, 272, 273, 274, 280, 283
  army, 110, 143, 156
  conquest, 126
  Empire, 140
  invasion, 74, 84, 94, 98, 142, 242, 272
  miles, 101
Romanesque architecture, 174
Romanization, 99
Romano-Celtic temples, 96, **105**
Romano-Saxon pottery, 134, **164**
Romans, 78, 99, 114, 123
Ronaldsway culture, 27
rondel daggers, 187
roof finials, 199
  flashings, 149
  furniture, 198, **199**
roofing, 109, 175, 199, 213
  slates, 200
roofs, 28, 31, **32**, 34, 35, 46, 74, 76, **109-10**, 144, 162, **168**, **169**, 170, 173, 175, 199-200, 223
root casts, 225
roots, **225**, 233, 251
rope, 36, **114**, 158, 195, 256
rose-water dishes, 181
rose windows, 196

Rosnoën, France, 55
Rosnoën swords, 55, 59
Rossington Bridge, South Yorkshire, 131
rotary hand-mills, 112
  keys, 122
  locks, 121
  querns, **80**, **112**, 113
roughcast, 129, 130, **278**
roughing-out, 14, 16
rough-outs, 36, 37, 160, **260**, 262
rouletted, 131
rouletting, 129, 130, **278**
round barrows, 30, 32, 34, **46**, 48, **49**, 50, 51, 210
  cairns, 34, **35**, **36**
rounded rims, 282
roundels, 111, 196
round-headed, 174, 221
round-houses, 46, **74**, **76**
rounds, 75, **76**, 102, 144
round-shouldered vessels, 283
rowels, 190
rowel spurs, 189-90
royal sites, 144
RSCs, 49
rubbers, 83
rubbing stones, 192
rubbish, 28, 97, 168, 208, 212, 213
  heaps, 228
  pits, 28, 79, 168, 169, **211**, 228
rubble, 33, 34, 36, 77, 102, 112, 145, 206, 223
rulers, **136**, 153
rules, 66, **255**, 256
rumbler bells, 178
runes, 162
rune-stones, 161
runic alphabets, 162
  inscriptions, 153, **161**, **162**
running-on, 266
rush-lights, 191
rush matting, 80
rustication, 278
ruts, 110
rye, 144
rynds, 113

Saale, 11
sacellum, 99
sacks, 142
sack-shaped bags, 191
  purses, 191
saddle bars, 196, **277**
  cloths, 111
  querns, 66, 80
  stones, 80
saddles, 114
saggers, 281
sagging bases, 165, 201, **284**
sails, 176, **177**
Saint-Acheul, France, 14
St Albans, Hertfordshire, 106
St Catherine's Hill-Worthy Down style, 82
St Neots, Cambridgeshire, 165
  dishes, 166
  spouted bowls, 166
  type ware, 165
St Rémy ware, 130
St Thomas à Becket, 180
salades, 184
salets, 184
salinity, 219

Salin's style I, 163
Salin's style II, 163
Salisbury Plain, Wiltshire, 50, 102
sallets, 184, 185
salt, **83**, **114**, **177**, 253, **254**
  glazes, 281
  pans, 254
  springs, 114
  working, 254
saltation, 223
salt-boiling kilns, 177
salt-dressing, 253
salterns, 177, 254
salvage excavation, 209
samian pottery, 83, 96, 103, **128-9**, 130, 142, 277, 278
samples, 207, 219, 220, 229, 230, 231, 232, 234
sampling, 228
sand, 64, 113, 114, 147, 169, 222, **223**, 224, **225**, 226, 230, 257, 262, 264, 268, 269, 271, 277, 278
  dunes, 225
sandals, 114
Sandhill culture, 27
sandstone, 51, 108, 246, 262
Sangamon, 11
sarcophagi, 142
sarsens, 51
sarsen stones, 51
satchels, 191
satellite burials, 243
  interments, 243
saucepan pot continuum, 82
saucepan pots, 82
saucepans, 122, 202
saucer barrows, **46**, **47**, 48
  brooches, 154, 155
  querns, 40
saucers, 177, **182**, 271
Sauveterre-le-Lemance, France, 22
Sauveterrian culture, 21
  industries, 22
Savernake ware, 131
saw blades, 255
sawing, 257, 263
saw-pits, 168
saws, **54**, **56**, **85**, **86**, **117**, **118**, 150, 183, **255**, **256**
Saxon, 99, 126, 128, 134, **143-66**, 167, 183, 195, 205, 243, 249, 250, 252, 256, 268, 269, 270, 274, 283
Saxo-Norman pottery, 165
Saxon shore defences, 100
  forts, 100
  signalling towers, 100
scabbards, 73, 83, 84, **90**, 114, 123, 149, **151**, **152**
scaena (pl scaenae), 103
scaffolding, 172
scaled, 23
scalene triangles, 22, 23
scale pans (*see also* balance pans), 135, 149, 181
scale plans, 207, 213
scales, 23, 124, **136**, 213, 214, 221, **229**
scallop-shells, 180
scalpels, 138
Scandinavia, 143, 147, 153, 162, 218
Scandinavian, 143, 160, 162
Scandinavian type flint axes, 38
scanning electron microscopes, 230

scaphopods, 222
scapulae, 83
scapula shovels, 36, 44
scatter diagrams, **236**, **237**, **238**, 241
scatters, 205
sceats, 153
sceattas, 153
scent stopper pommels, 186, 187
sceptres, 146
schist, 192
  hones, 160
Scilly/Penwith group, 34
scissors, **184**, 195
SCM, 208
scooped enclosures, 76
scoops, 25, **83**, **96**, 97
scored, 109, 128, 199
scores, 235
scoring, 199, 274
scorpers, 266
scorpion, 123
Scots, 143
Scotsburn group, 65
Scotti, 143
scour, 252
scrabble pattern, 275
scramasaxes, **152**, 162, 184
scrapers, **17**, **18**, **19**, **21**, **22**, 23, **39**, 64, 138, 242
scrap glass, 269
  metal, 59, 61, 243
  silver, 147
scraping, 257
scree, 36, **223**, 226, 228
  slopes, 77
screw necks, 132, **282**
scribers, 266
scrolls, 129, 130
scudding, 253
sculpture, **95**, 110, **112**, 137, 143, 146, **161-2**, 163
sculptured, 95, 160, 161
scutching, 251
scutum, 154
scythe-knives, 188
scythes, **118**, **119**, 151, 183, 188, 249
sea, 76, 177, 222, 225, 234
  buckthorn, 217
  caves, 227
  -level, 26, 214, 225, 226
seal boxes, 141
sealing compound, 198
seal matrices, 160, 177, 178, **180-1**
seals, 113, 141, **178**, **181**
seashore, 26
seasonal occupation, 220
seasoning, 255
seating, 103
seats, 103, 104, 110, 175, 194
seawater, 114, 254
seaweed, 268
seaxes, 152
secondary
  burials, 48, 49, **243**, 245
  fill, 227, 228
  flaking, 260
  interments, 47, **243**
  silt, 227
  working, 14, **15**, **260-1**
Secondary Neolithic, 27
  pottery, 40
second brass coins, 136
second pointed style, 175
section drawing, 214, 215
sections, **38**, 207, 210, **211**, **212**, **213**, **214**, 216

sector diagrams, **217**, 236
secular churches, 174
  plate, 181
sedilia, 175
sedimentary rocks, 234
sediments, 216, 217, 219, **222-8**, 234
seed beds, 245
  pods, 251
seeds, 73, 195, 219
segmental bowls, 132
  chopping tools, 15
segmented beads, 70, 141
  gallery graves, 34
self-coloured, 198, **273**
self-slip, 278
Selgovae, 94
semi-precious stones, 140, 141, 156
semisses, 136, 137
septal slabs, 34
serial flaking, 261
seriation, 213, **234**
Sernander, 11
sestertius (pl sestertii), 136
sets, **117**, 255, **267**
settlement, **26**, **28**, **42**, **45-6**, 69, **74-9**, 80, **102**, 143, **144**, 164, 224, 225, 239, 240, 241, 242
setts, 267
Severn-Cotswold chambered tombs, **33-4**, 47
Severn Valley ware, 130
sewers, **103**, 104
sewing, 44, 116, 158, 254
sewn, 256
sexpartite rib-vaults, 176
sgraffiato tiles, 199
shadow marks, **206**, 207
shaft furnaces, 114, 149, 264, **266**, **267**
  mining, 178
shafthole axes, 85
  battle axes, 48, **65**
  perforations, 263
shafts, 23, **26**, **36**, 37, **46**, 91, 97, 105, 112, 123, 145, 146, 151, 159, 170, **174**, 178, 188, 207, **228**, 255, 262, 263
shale, **26**, 44, 48, 64, **69**, 80, **84**, 87, 88, 108, 110, 112, **114**, 116, 139, 140
shallow flaking, 261
shanks, 190
shaping, of wood, 255-6
shaping tools, 271
shares, 118, 246, 247, 248, 249
shaving, 255
sheared, 80, 115, 251
shearing, 115, 195
Shearplace Hill, Dorset, 73
shears, 80, **115**, **118**, 146, 183, **184**, **195**, 251, **270**, 272
sheath chapes, 178
sheaths, 52, 73, **90**, **91**, **92**, 123, 158, 183, 184, 187, 188, **194**
shedding mechanism, 252
shed rods, 251, 252
sheds, 144, **251**, **252**
sheep, 28, 46, 79, 83, 115, 117, 144, 251
sheepskins, 253, 254
sheet bronze (*see also* bronze sheet), 105, 114, 149, 181

gold, 64, **267**
lead, 113
metal, 265
silver, 268
sheets, 153, 155, 166
shell, 140, 277
shellfish, 23, 26, 28, 45, 79, 122, 144, 228
shell-gritted wares, 131
shell-keeps, 171
shell middens, 228
shell-midden sites, 23, 25, 26
shells, 25, **26**, 131, 156, 220, 222, 224, 227, 258, 278
shell-tempered, 130, 165, 201
shelters, 13, 26, 227
shelves, 110
sherds, 229
Shetlands, 75, 246
shield bosses (see also bosses), 91, **152**
covers, 114
-pattern palstaves, 54, 55
shields, **54**, 83, 84, **91, 96, 124, 126**, 146, **152**, 178, 185, 196
shingles, **158**, 162, 169, 194, 200
ship building, 194
burials, 146
ships, 112, 146
shirts, 184
shivers, 253
shoemakers' tools (see also cobblers' tools), 117
shoemaking, 194
shoes (see also footwear), **114**, 115, **158, 194**
shops, **102, 103**, 167, 169
short cross coinage, 179
short-necked beakers, 70
short tongue chapes, 62
shot, 189
holes, 167
shoulder clasps, 146
shouldered points, 19
urns, 165
shoulders, 71, 81, 83, 283
shovels, 36, 44, **120**
shrines, 30, 75, 76, **96**, 99, 105, 140, 162, 180
Shropshire, 270
shrouds, 142, 175
shrubs, 217, 235, 253
shrunken villages, 168
shutters, 109, 172, **173**
shuttles, **80**, 83
sickle blades, 118
sickles, **27, 39**, 46, **54, 56, 58**, 79, **85, 86**, 183, 249
side
aisles, 145
chambers, 33
-looped kite-shaped spearheads, 54
plates, 184, **185**
-rings, 190
scrapers, 17
sieges, 171, **269, 270**
sieves, 219
sieving, 220, 221, 222
sights, 185
signacula, 180
signalling towers, 100
signal stations, 100
Silbury Hill, Wiltshire, 30
Silchester, Hampshire, 103, 110, 269, 270
silhouettes, 211

silica, 219, 238, **268**, 269
silk, 117, 158, 195
sill-beams, 211
sills, 109
silt, 211, 223, 227, **228**
silted up, 211, 216, 226, 228
Silures, 94
silver, **84**, 88, 94, 95, 96, 105, 112, **113**, 116, 122, 136, 138, 139, 140, 141, 146, **147**, 152, 153, 154, 155, **177**, 178, 179, 180, 181, 182, 229, 264, **267-8**, 277
chloride, 277
leaf, 268
sulphide, 268, 277
silvered, 139, 155
silvering, 156, 178, **268**
simple combs, 192, **193**
ring-post houses, 74
rounded rims, 282
shafts, 37
simulation, 241
sinew, 186
single
buckles, 179
burial (see also individual burial), 46, 47, 48, 49
combat, 184
-edged, 152, 187
-flue kilns, 130, **280**
-flue updraught kilns, 280
grave art, 51
looped spearheads, 59
-piece brooches, 140
-piece reaping knives, 27
-piece sickles, 27, 39
-portal entrances (gateways), 77, 78
-ridged blades, 261
-ring round-houses, 74
-riveted tanged daggers, 52
roofs, 169
-sided combs, 159, 192, **193**
-splayed windows, 145
valve moulds, 264
valve stone moulds, 66
sinking, 265
sintered glass, 70
sintering, 269, 280
sinter point, 280
site catchment analysis, 240-1
situlae, 81, **98**
situlae-type pottery, 81
Skara Brae, Orkney, **28**, 44
skates, **159**, 192, **193**
skeletons, 79, 211, 221, 243
skeuomorphs, 166
skewer pins, 44
skewers, 192
skillets, 113, 128, 181, 201, 202
skins, 44, 126, **253, 254**, 257, 278
skulls, 9, 25, **185**, 220, **221**
slabbing, 277
slab forming, 277
slag, 178, **266**
heaps, 178
slaked, 147
slash-and-burn, 27
slate, 192
slates, 106, 109, 169, 199, 200
slave chains, 85
Sleaford-Dragonby style, 82
sleeper beams, 211
sleeve clasps, 154

slide keys, **121, 122**, 190
sliders, 44
sling bolts, 123
bullets, 91, 123, 124
shots, 91
stones, 83, **90, 91**
slingers, 123
slip, 81, 128, 129, 130, 199, 201, **278**
decoration, 278
-painting, 278
trailing, 278
slopes, 223, 226, 249
slopewash deposits, 222, **223**
slots, 37, 38, 59, 99, 113, **211**, 228, 255
slotted tangs, 59
slow silt, 227
slow wheels, 165, 199, 201, **277**
slug knives, 64
slugs, 222
slypes, 173
small finds, **213**, 216
small-long brooches, 155, 156
small towns, **102**, 106
smelted, 114, 264, 266, 268
smelting, 85, 114, 149, 178, **266**, 268
furnaces, 178
smiths, 63
smiths' tools, 149
smoke, 107, 170, 199, 253, 280
hoods, 169
turrets, 200
smoking, 253
smoothing planes, 255, 256
snaffle-bits, 149, **150**, 178, **190**
snaffles, 111
snails, 222
snakes, 87, 139, 221
snake thread decoration, 127, 128
snaps, 266
snout-faced bascinets, 185
snow, 206
Snowshill, Gloucestershire, 48
Snowshill group, 65
Soay sheep, 79
soccus (pl socci), 114
socketed, 85, **90, 117**, 118, 123, 182, 246
arrowheads, 185, 186
axes, **54, 57**, 59, 60, 61, **62, 63, 64, 86**
candlesticks, 192
chisels, **54**, 61, 62
gouges, **61**, 62, **86, 117**
hammers, 54, 58
punches, **54**, 61
reaping hooks, 85, 86
shares, 246, 247
socket-looped kite-shaped spearheads, 57
spearheads, 54, 57
sockets, **38**, 54, 64, **80**, 121, **183**, 188, 191, **201**, 264
soda, 238, **268**
soda-lime glass, 197, 198, **268**
sods, 246, 248, 250
soil, 26, 79, 146, 177, 206, 207, 208, 210, 211, 212, 213, 216, 217, 219, 220, **222-8**, 233, 245, 246, 248, 249, 250, 257, 266

conductivity meters, 208
crumbs, 223
erosion, 222
marks, **206**, 207, **209, 210**
profiles, 223, 225
samples, 220
stability, 222
solarium, 169
solars, 169
solar years, 231, 232
soldered, 138, 277
soldering, 266, 267, 268
soldiers, 102, 111, 120
solea, 114
sole ards, 246
solers, 169
soles, **114**, 115, 117, 194, **246**
solid lugs, 40
solidus (pl solidi), **136**, 153
solifluction, **223**, 226
solifluxion, 223
sols lessivés, 224
Solutrean industries, 18
Solutré, Mâcon, France, 18
Somerset, 20, 48, 54, 62, 75, 82, 164
Sompting, Sussex, 63
Sompting axes, 63
sondage, 209
sorting, 223
souterrains, **75**, 144
Southampton, Hampshire, 144
Southcote-Blewburton Hill style, 82
south eastern B, 82
south-eastern type axes, 61
southern British saucepan pot style, 82
southern third B, 82
South Gaulish colour coated pottery, 130
South Glamorgan, 62
South Harting type beads, 87
South Street long barrow, 246
South Welsh socketed axes, 62
south-western palstaves, 54
South Yorkshire, 131
spacer beads, 48, **68, 69**
spacer-plates, 68
spacers, 107-8
spade-irons, 118
spade marks, 46, 245
spades, **27**, 46, 79, **118, 119, 183**, 194, 245
spade-shoes, **118, 119**, 151
Spain, 51, 88, 95, 96
spalls, 264
Spanish colour coated wares, 130
spathae, 116, 123, 151
spathomelae, 138
spatial analysis, 239-41
patterns, 239
spatulae, 66, 68
spatula-probes, 138
spatulate blades, 246
linch-headed pins, 111
spearheads, 24, 25, 54, 55, 57, 58, 59, 60, 61, 62, 90, 123, 124, 151, 188
spear-points, 9, 14
spears, 59, 112, 121, 123, 146, 151, **188**
spearshafts, **26**, 54, 73, 123
spear-shaped currency bars, 85

spectrometers, 230, 231
spectrometry, 230-1
speculum, 264
    coins, 94-5
spelt, 79, 144
spelter, 267
sphagnum moss, 223
    peat, 223
spherical beads, 154
    pommels, 186, 187
spindles, 80, 112, **113**, 115,
    116, 121, 194, **195**, **251**,
    252, 255
spindle whorls, **73**, **80**, 83,
    84, 113, 114, **116**, 146,
    147, 157, 159, 160, 163,
    164, 192, **195**, 198, **251**,
    252
spinning, 80, 116, **251-2,
    265**
    wheels, 251
spiral beads, 274
    knobbed bracelets, 87, 88
    pattern, 275
    snake bracelets, 87
spires, 174-5
spirit levels, 214
spital houses, 170
spits, 85, **210**
spit-shaped currency bars,
    85
spittle houses, 170
splayed, 109, 117, 118, 167,
    272
splinters, 257
split pea, 225
    pins, 121
splitting, 257
spokes, **92**, 113
sponge-finger stones, 66
spoon augers, 183
    burials, 97
    knops, 182
spoons, **41**, **96-7**, 104, 113,
    115, **122**, 146, 158, 159,
    177, 178, **182**, 194, 271
spotted dolerite, 50
spouted bowls, 166
    jugs, 202
    pitchers, **165**, 166, **167**,
    201
    strainers, 132, 133
spouts, **131**, **132**, 165, 181,
    202, **203**
springs, 96, 114, 223
spuds, 118, 119
spun glass, 275
spur dykes, 45, 79
spurs, 79, **111**, 149, 178,
    189-90, 261
spur-trimming scars, 261
square
    bottles, 127
    -ended chancels, 145, 174
    -headed brooches, 155,
    156
    -headed fireplaces, 169
    -sectioned beads, 141
    stirrups, 189
squat jars, 163
squints, 174
stabbing, 266, 278, 279
stabilisers, 268
stables, 107, 170
stabling, 106
stadials, 234
staffs, 68, 194, **214**, **215**
stage-buildings, 103
stages, 103
stained glass windows,
    195-7, 276-7

staining, 196, 277
stains, 211
staircases, 75, 101, 103, 169,
    170
stairs, 75, 76, 171, 173
stakeholes, 47, 74, **211**
stakes, 73, 74, 75, 83, 100,
    211, 213
stake-wall round-houses, 74
stalagmite, 219, **223**
stalled cairns, 35
    chambers, 35
Stamford, Lincolnshire, 165
Stamford jugs, 166
Stamford spouted pitchers,
    166
Stamford-type ware, 165-6
stamped, 109, 194, 254, 278
    ornamentation, 40, 165,
    201
stamping, 198
stamps, 113, 128, **131**, 134,
    138, **139**, 164, 194, 199,
    266, 267, **279**
stanchions, 277
standard deviation, 232
standard jugs, 202
standing monuments, 208
    stones, 29, **30**, **36**, 46, 48,
    49, **50**, 51
Stanton Harcourt-Cassing-
    ton style, 82
staples, **85**, **120**, 178
star beads, 70
Star Carr, North Yorkshire,
    25, 26
starch fracture, 259, 260
stars, 50
star-shaped beads, 70
statera, 135
staters, 94
statistical, 232, 240, 241
statistics, 241
statues, 110, 112, 114
statuettes, 83, **95**, 96, 112,
    192
stave-built, 73, 194, **195**
stave construction, 158
steatite, 160
steel, 149, 152, **185**, 186,
    207, 208, 229, 266
steelyards, 135, 136, 181
steelyard weights, **135**, **136**,
    178, **181**
steep-walled pots, 282
stehende bogen, 165
stemmed beakers, 163
    glasses, 197
stems, 122, 182, 197, 251
step-flaking, 258
stepped-blade spearheads,
    59, 60
stepped shoulders, 283
steps, 105, 169
stereoscopes, 206
stereoscopic pairs, 205-6
sterlings, 179
stewponds, 177
stick pins, 154
sticks, 121, 138, 192, **245**,
    251, **255**, 264
stills, 198, 203
stilts, 32, **246**, **249**
stilus (pl stili), 141-2
stirrups, 149, **150**, 178, **189**
stockaded enclosures, 77
stock enclosures, 245
    raising, 250
stocks, 185, 255
Stocton Heath, Lancashire,
    270

Stogursey, Somerset, 62
stokeholes, 104, **107**, **108**,
    269, **280**
stone (see also stone arti-
    facts & masonry), 211,
    213, 229, 230, 241, 249,
    251, **262-3**, 267
    Bronze Age, 47, 48, 49,
    66
    Iron Age, 74, 75, 76, 77,
    97
    Medieval, 167, 168, 169,
    170, 171, 174, 175, 176,
    177, 196
    Neolithic, 30, 32, 33, 34,
    35, 36
    Roman, 99, 100, 101,
    102, 103, 104, 106, 107,
    108, 109, 110, 112, 114,
    142
    Saxon, 144, 145, 146,
    160-1
Stone Age, 242
stone ard points, 246
    shares, 246
stone artifacts, 229, 230,
    245, **246**, **247**, 253, 257,
    258, **260**, **262-3**, **264**, 268,
    270
    Bronze Age, 48, 50, 51-2,
    64-7, 73
    Iron Age, **80**, 83, 90, 91,
    95
    Medieval, 180, 189, 191,
    192, 195
    Mesolithic, 22-3, 24, 25
    Neolithic, 21, **28**, **36-40**,
    42, 43, **51-2**, **65**
    Roman, 105, 112, 113,
    123, 135, 137, 138, 140,
    142
    Saxon, 157, 158, **160-2**,
    163
stone axe factories, 36-7
    trade, 37
stone balls, **51-2**, 66
    carvings, 40, 46, **51**
    circles, **29-30**, **35**, **36**, 46,
    49-50, 51
    guard chambers, 78
    line, 224, 225
    packing, 45
    pads, 144
    rings, 226
    rows, 50
Stonehenge, Wiltshire, 30,
    46, **50-1**
stoneware, 130
stoneworking, 255, 257,
    262-3
stools, **110**, 112
stoppers, 83, 194
stop-ridges, 54, 55
storage, **79**, 132, 169, 213,
    228
    jars, 132, 201, 202
    pits, **28**, 76, **79-80**, 97,
    168, **211**, 228
    storerooms, 169
    stores, 100
Strabo, 84
straight backed blades, 19
straight-based basal-looped
    spearheads, 54
straight rims, 282
straight-sided angular
    spearheads, 151
straight-sided cups, 198
strainers, 95, 122, **132**, **133**,
    181
strakes, 91

strandlooping, 26
strap buckles, 92
    distributors, 62, **92**
strap-end buckles, 179
    hooks, 177, **179**
strap-ends, 146, 149, 156,
    157
strap handles, 72
strap-hinges, **121**, 178
strap junctions, 92
strap links, 92
straps, 92, 111, 126, 149,
    179, 194, 208
strap suspension, 90
    unions, 92, 93
strapwork, 196
Strathclyde, 23, 26, 62
stratified layers, 233
    deposits, **211**, 216
stratigraphy, 210, **211-13**,
    214, **233-4**
straw, 109, 169
stray finds, 25, 213
streaming, 178
streets, 103, 167, 168, 169, 170
street-villages, 168
striations, 112
strigils, 138
strike-a-lights, 149
strikers, 258
striking planes, 258
    platforms, 15, 16, 17,
    258, **259**, **261**
string, 141, 158, 191, 195,
    213, 214, 262, 278
stringed musical instru-
    ments, 192
stringers, 42
string marks, 278
strip handles, 181
    lynchets, 251
    tangs, 184
stroke alphabet, 162
strongrooms, 99
struck, 94, 153, 178, 257,
    258, 260, 261, 264
struts, 92, 168
stucco, 109, 114
studs, 64, 69, 84, **85**, **88**,
    121, **125**, **128**, 149, 178,
    180
stycas, 153
style I, 163
style II, 163
style zones, 81-2
styli, 109, **141**, **149**
stylised, 94, 95, 156, 163,
    174, 273
sub-Atlantic, 218
sub-boreal, 218
sub-cordate handaxes, 15
subject and canopy win-
    dows, 196
subject windows, 196
sub-Roman, 143
subsequent primary burials,
    243
    interments, 243
subsidiary burials, 243
    interments, 243
subsoils, 206, 207, 208, 212,
    223, 224, 227, 228
sub-triangles, 23
sudatorium, 104
Suffolk, 13, 146
sugar-loaf bosses, 152
sugar-tongs, 571
sunflower pins, 63, **88**
sunken droveways, 79
sunken-featured buildings,
    144

sunlight, 206
surface enrichment, 229
surgical instruments, 138
Surrey, 23, 82, 130, 202, 270
  white wares, 201-2
surveyed, 207, **208**
surveying, 205, **208**
surveyors, 110
surveys, 207, 208
Sussex, 22, 23, 45, 46, 63, 73, 82, 128, 130
  loops, 54, 56
Sutton Hoo, Suffolk, 146
Sutton Hoo ship burial, 146
swages, 267
swans, 68
Swanscombe, Kent, 9
swan's neck pins, 88
  sunflower pins, 63, 88
Swarling, Kent, 98
sweating rooms, 104
Sweden, 143
Swedish parade helmets, 146
swidden agriculture, 27
Switzerland, 74
swollen necked pins, 54, 56
sword blades, 186
  grips, 158
  hilts, 115, 147, 159
  -shaped currency bars, 85
  sheaths, 73, 158, 187, 194
swords
  Bronze Age, **55, 59, 60, 61,** 62, **63,** 64, 68
  Iron Age, 90, 96, 116, 123
  Medieval, **186-7,** 251
  Roman, 123
  Saxon, 146, 149, **151-2, 157, 158, 159**
symbols, 104, 113
symbol stones, 161
Syria, 197, 272
Syro-Frankish glasses, 197
system walking, 205

tables, **110,** 114
tablets, **105,** 113, 114, 141-2, 149, 159, 192, 252, **261**
tablet weaving, 116, 252
  plates, 115, **116**
tablewares, 83, 95, 98, 104, 114, 126, 128, 130, 164, 197, 268
tabular flint, 37
Taezali, 94
tag ends, 148, 149, 178
tags, **149,** 178
tail poles, 176
talismans, 180
tallow, 253
tally, 137
  sticks, 194
tanged
  -and-collared spearheads, 54, 55
  and lugged chisels, 55, 62
  arrowheads, **54, 90,** 185, **186**
  chisels, 62
  daggers, 52
  flat daggers, 52, 53
  knives, **52, 123,** 184
  points, 19
  razors, 52
  shares, 246, 248
  spearheads, 54, 55
  spearheads, with a separate collar, 54
tangs, **52,** 54, **55,** 59, 62, 63, 65, **95,** 123, 151, 183,

184, 187, **246**
tankards, 83, **133, 134,** 194
tanks, **103, 104,** 113, **219**
tanned, 220
tanneries, 222
tanning, 79, 222, **253**
  pits, 158, 194, **253**
tannins, 253
tan pits, 253
tapered segmented beads, 274, 275
tapes, 208, 214
tap handles, 178
Tardenoisian culture, 21
  industries, 22
Taunton, Somerset, 54
Taunton-Barton Bendish phase, 54
Taunton-Hademarschen socketed axes, 54, 57
Taunton phase, 54, 56-7
tawing, 253
taxonomy, 239
Tayside, 54
tazze, 132, 133
teardrop decoration, 129, 130
teased, 195, **251**
tectonic uplift, 225
teeth, **26,** 68, 84, 87, 193, 220, 255
tegulae, 109, 110
  mammatae, 108, **109**
telescopic sights, 214
tempered, 40, 130, 131
tempering, **266,** 277
temples, 29, 96, **104-5**
tension pins, 186
tent pegs, 115
tents, 99, 100, 114
tepidarium, 104
terminals, 59, 86, 87, **91, 126,** 149, 155, 189, **190**
terminus ante quem, 205, **233**
  post quem, 212, 233-4
ternary diagrams, 238
terrace fields, 251
terraces, 226
terracotta, 198, **280**
terra nigra, 83, **129,** 131
  rubra, 83, **129**
  sigillata, 128
terrestrial sediments, 223
terret rings, 92, 93, 111
terrets, 92
Tertiary, 10, 11
tertiary fill, 228
  silt, 228
tessellated floors, 102, 106, **108**
tesserae, 108
test pits, 209
textiles, **73, 80-1, 115-17,** 144, **157-8, 195,** 245, **251-3**
texture, 223
Thames, 21, 68, 81, 82, 91, 95, 98, 257
  Battersea, 162
  estuary, 82
  patina, 257
  picks, 21
  type swords, 63
  Valley, 62, 94, 143
thatch, 116, 169, 199
Thatcham, Berkshire, 25
thatched roofs, 28, 46, 74, 109
thatch weights, 116
theatre masks, 103

theatres, 103
The Lunt, Coventry, 100
thermal fractures, 260
thermoluminescence, 233
thermoluminscent dating, 233
thermo-remanent magnetism, 208, **233, 234**
Thetford, Norfolk, 165
Thetford cooking pots, 166
Thetford-type ware, 165
Thiessen polygons, 240
thimbles, 113, **116, 117,** 178, 195
thin-butted axes, 54
thinned-out, 255
thin sections, 229
third brass coins, 136
third pointed style, 175
thistle brooches, 140
Thom, Professor, 50
Thomsen, Christian Jurgensen, 242
thongs, 64, 114, 141, 194, 255, 256
thread, 149, 158, 251, 252, **274**
  boxes, **148, 149,** 158
  pickers, **158,** 159
threading, 274
threads, 80, 158, 251-2
three age system, 242
three-dimensional pollen diagrams, 218
three-dimensional recording, 210-11, 213, **216**
three-link bridle bits, 93
three-piece bridle bits, 93
three-pole triangular graphs, 238
three-ribbed daggers, 54, 55
threshed, 27
threshing, 79
  floors, 107
through purlin roofs, 168, 169
throwing axes, 150, 153
  spears, 123
thrymsas, 153
Thwing, Humberside, 46
tie-beams, 168, 169, **177**
tierceron ribs, 176
  rib-vaults, 175
  vaults, 176
tiercerons, 175
tile clamps, 109
tiled floors, 169
tile mosaic, 199
tiles, 100, 104, 106, **107, 108, 109-10,** 112, 120, 137, 142, 169, **198-9, 200,** 213, 219, 280
till, 223
tillage, 223, 226, 227
tillers, 185
timber (*see also* wood), 29, 31, 37, 45, 74, 76, **77,** 99, 100, 101, 102, 103, 108, 109, 112, 115, 145, 168, 169, 171, 175, 227, 232, 233, 254, 255
  -framed, **75,** 76, 102, 103, **169,** 170
  guard chambers, 78
  halls, 144
  -laced, 76, **77**
  -lacing, **77,** 102
  revetments, 102
  slots, 211
tin, 52, **84,** 94, **113, 114, 178,** 264, 267, 268

-bronze, 59
coins, 94-5
glazes, 281
mines, 178
tinder-pouches, 149
tinning, 149, 156, 178
tiplines, 213
tippets, 64, 184
tituli picti, 131
TL dating, 233
toads, 221
toe-rings, 88
tofts, 168
toggles, **68,** 83, **88, 89,** 159
toilet combs, 115
  instruments, 138
  sets, 89, 146
toilets, 170
tokens, 179
tolls, 167
tomb chambers, 142
tombs, 27, **30-6,** 196
tombstones, 110, **142, 161, 162**
tongs, 62, **85, 86, 119, 149,** 183, **267,** 271
tongue-and-groove joints, 51
tongue chapes, 59
  -shaped chapes, 59, 60
tooling, 254
toolmaking, 14
tools, 230, 242, 243, 245, 253, 254, 255, 256, 257, 260, 261, 262, 263, 265, 266, 270-1, 272, 274, 275, 279
  Bronze Age, 59, 62, 63, 64, 66, 68, 73, 256
  Iron Age, 74, 83, 84, 85, 256
  Medieval, 178, **183-4,** 188, 192, 194, 199, 256
  Mesolithic, 23, 256
  Neolithic, 27, 36, 37, 39, 42, 256
  Palaeolithic, 9, 13, 14, 15, 19, 256
  Roman, 114, 115, **117-120,** 123, 256
  Saxon, **149-51,** 160, 162, 256
tooth picks, 138
  segments, 192
topogenous peats, 227
topography, 224, 227
topsoil, 224
torches, 134, **203**
torcs, **54,** 56, **64,** 84, **86-7**
Torksey-type ware, 165
torques, 86
Torrs, Dumfries and Galloway, 93
Torrs chamfrein, 93
tortoise brooches, 156
  cores, 16
tortoises, 156
tournaments, 184
tournettes, **277,** 278, 279
tower houses, 170
tower-keeps, 171
tower mills, 177
towers, 75, **99, 100, 102, 145,** 167, **170,** 171, **172, 174,** 175
town defences, 167
  houses, **102,** 104
  walls, 102, 167, 172
towns, **102-3,** 104, 105, 106, 108, 142, **144-5,** 146, **167,** 170, 173, 176, 228, 240

TP:NTP ratio, 11
trace elements, 229
  loops, 92
tracers, 54, 266
tracery, 174
  lights, 196
tracks, **42**, 110
trackways, **42**, 45, 50, **73**, 83
trade, 28, 37, 40, 65, 70, 95, 99, 145, 153, 160, 243
  goods, 63, 95
trading centres, 102
tradition, 242
trailed slip, 201
trails, 126, 128, 197, 198, 272, 274
training, 100, 103
  grounds, 100
trains, 208
tranchet adzes, 21
  axes, 21, 22
  flakes, 21
transepted gallery graves, 33
transepts, **33**, 145, **173**, 174
transhumance, 79
transitional Gothic, 174
  palstaves, **54**, **58**, 59
  phase, 174
translucent enamels, on sunk relief, 268
transmission electron microscopy, 230
transmitter coils, 208
transmitters, 208
transport, **112**, 131, 224, 240
transverse arrowheads, 22, 23, 39
  flakes, 21
  flaking, 261
  ribs, 175
trapezes, 22, 263
trapezoids, 22, 23
travelling pricket candlesticks, 191
travertine, 222, **223**
trays, 114
treads, 251
treasury, 173
treenails, 256-7
tree of Jesse windows, 196
tree-ring analysis, 219
tree-rings, 232, 233
trees, 11, 27, 46, 217, 219-20, 225, 232, 233, 253, 255
tree-trunk coffins, **47**, **48**, 255
tree-trunks, 36, 42, **47**, 73, 219, 220, 253, **255**
trefoil-mouthed flagons, 95
trefoil pommels, 186
trefoil-shaped brooches, 156
tremisses, 136, 153
trenails, 256
trenches, 31, 45, 77, **209**, **210**, **211**, 228
trend surface analysis, 241
Trent Valley style zone, 82
  ware, 131
trepanation, 221
trephination, 221
trephining, 221
trial excavation, 209
  pieces, 159, 160
  trenching, 208, **209**
triangular basal-looped spearheads, 54, 58
  loomweights, 80
  perforated knives, 61

triangulation, 213, 214
tribal centres, 75
  groups, 143
tribes, **94**, 95
tricephalos, 95
trientes, 153
triggers, 185
trilithons, 51
trimming, 14, 255, 260, 277
Trinovantes, 94
tripartite urns, 71
triple dykes, 45
triple-tailed horses, 94
triple vases, 133, 134
tripod bowls, 132, 133
  cauldrons, 201, 202
  pipkins, 201, 202
  pitchers, 166, 201, **203**
tripods, 85, **110**, 214, **215**
triptychs, 141
triskele designs, 93
  mounts, 93
trituration, 131
triumphal arches, 106
trivets, 178
troops, 99, 100, 101, 123
troughs, 28, 147
trowels, **117**, 183
trueing planes, 255
trumpet brooches, 140
trumpets, 91, 137
trunks, 220, 255
trusses, 169
trying planes, **255**, 256
T-shaped axes, 150, 183
T-staples, 120, 121
tubas, 137
tubes, 149, 270, **274**, 275
tubing, 198, 213, **274**
tubs, 73, 83
tubular beads, 52, 53
  ferrules, **59**, **60**, 62
  rims, 272, 273
  spouts, 132
  torcs, 86
tubuli, 109
Tudor green, 202
tufa, 219, 222, **223**, 226
tumbler locks, 121
tumbrels, 181
tumuli, 243
tundra, 12, 26, 217, 218
tuning pegs, 192, **193**
tunnel vaults, 175
turf, 28, 76, 100, 101, 144, 212, 225, 227, 228
  cutters, 118, 119
  line, **224**, 233
  wall, 101
  -walled long-houses, 170
turfed roofs, 74
Turkish baths, 104
turning, 265
turnips, 117
turnshoe construction, 158, **194**
turntables, 277
turrets, **101**, 167
turves, 245
tutulus, 100
tuyères, 267
tweezers, 48, **68**, 84, **89**, **138**, 146, 149, 178
twigs, 219
twine, 158
twin loop suspension, 90
twisted torcs, 86
twisted wire bracelets, 139
two-link bridle bits, 93
two-piece bridle bits, 93
two-piece moulds, **64**, **66**,

134, **264**
Tyne and Wear, 101
type 1 alembics, 203, 204
type 2 alembics, 203, 204
type 1 glass bangles, 139
type 2 glass bangles, 139
type 3 glass bangles, 139
types, 239
type-sites, 98, 165
typology, 163, 234, **239**
tyres, 91, 92

ultimate Deverel-Rimbury culture, 81
ultra-narrow tranchets, 23
umbo (pl umbones), 126, 152
unchambered barrows, 30-2
  long barrows, 30-2
  long cairns, 31
  round barrows, 30
  tombs, 30-2
unctoria, 104
undercrofts, **169**, 170, 173
undercutting, 227, 228
underglaze colour, 281
undergrowth, 245
unenclosed settlements, 46, **74-6**
unguent bottles, **127**, **128**, 138
  flasks, 133
uniface gold staters, 94
unifacial flaking, 261
units, 99, 101, 123, 136, 208, **235**, 236
univallate hillforts, 76
unlooped socketed spearheads, 54
unsorted sediments, 223-4
unurned cremations, 49, 97, **243**
updraught kilns, 280
upholstery, 110
upper hall houses, 169
Upper Palaeolithic, **9**, **10**, **18-20**, **218**, 242, 253
upper stones, 112, 113
upright looms, 73, **251**
uranium, 233
  analysis, 233
  dating, 233
  nuclides, 234
  series dating, 9, 10, **234**
  series disequilibrium dating, 234
urinals, 197-8, 203
urine, 252, 253
urn covers, 51
urned cremations, 49, 97, **243**
urnfield cultures, 54
urnfields, 49
urns, **83**, 97, 98, 243
  Bronze Age, 48, **49**, **71**, **72**
  Saxon, 164, 165
U-shaped valleys, 226
  wall hooks, 120-1
U-shouldered swords, 55, 59
utensils, 182-3

Vacomagi, 94
valetudinarium, 99
valley glaciers, 226
valleys, 222, **226**, **227**
vallum, 99, 101, 146
  monasterii, 146
vases, 95, **133**, **134**, **203**
  carénés, 81

piriformes, 81
vase-shaped linch pins, 91, 93
vats, 79, 195, 253
vaulted, 103, 110, 142, 170, 173, 174
vaults, 175-6
vegetables, 13, 26
vegetable tanning, 253
vegetation, 11, 12, 26, 216, 217, **218-19**, 220, 222, 225
vellum, 254
Venice, 197, 198
Venicones, 94
ventilation, 99
ventilators, 135, 200
ventral surfaces, **258**, **259**, 261
vents, 264, 280
Venus, 112
vertical aerial photographs, 205
  APs, **205**, 206
vertical looms, 251
vertically faced ramparts, 77
Verulamium, Hertfordshire, 106
via decumana, 99
  praetoria, 99
  principalis, 99
vici, 102
Viking, 143, 144, 145, 146, 147, 156, 160, 163, 186
Vikings, **143**, 146, 161, 242
villages, 28, 75, 102, 144, **168**
villa outbuildings, 107
villas, 102, 104, **106-7**, 108, 109
vines, 196
vine scrolls, 163
viscous liquid, 230
visors, 184, **185**
vitrified, 76, **77**, **280**
  forts, 77
volcanic rocks, 234
Votadini, 94
votive
  deposits, 243
  hoards, 243
  lamps, 134-5
  offerings, 96, 112, 140
  plaques, 105
  shields, 96
  swords, 96
  tablets, **105**, 113, 114
voussoirs, 110
V-perforated conical buttons, 68, 69
V-shouldered swords, 59

waisted type flint axes, 38
waisted vessels, 283
waldglas, 268
walkways, 103, 110
wall-brackets, 191
wallets, 158, 191
Wallington, Northumberland, 59
Wallington tradition, 59, 60
wall-paintings, 102, 104, 106
wall plaster, **108**, **109**, 174
  plates, 168
  walks, 167, 172
walls, 32, **33**, 34, 74, **75**, **76**, 77, **100**, **101**, **102**, 107, **108**, **109**, 112, 142, 144, **145**, 147, 162, **167**, 168, **170**, **171**, **172**, 174, 175, 206, 207, 210, **211**, 213,

249, 251, 270, 271, 274, 277
Wallsend, Tyne and Wear, 101
walrus, 160
Walsingham, Norfolk, 180
war cemetery, 98
  games, 95
wardrobes, 169
wards, 171
warp beams, 252
  threads, 251, **252**
  -weighted looms, 116, 158, **251**
warrens, 177
warrior burials, 97
war trumpets, 91
Warwickshire, 270
Wash, 16, 82
washing, 104, 173, 175, 203
waste, 266
  flakes, 14, 15, 18
  flint, 23, 36
  fragments, 263
wasters, 281
watchtowers, 75, 171
water, 28, 103, 104, 114, 115, 147, 170, 177, 178, 180, 203, 207, 208, 219, 222, 223, 226, 227, 233, 234, 251, 252, 253, 254, 257, 262, 265, 272, 278, 279
  -divining, 207
  fowl, 226
  pipes, 110
  storage pits, 168
  supply, 103
  tanks, 104
  wheels, 113
waterlogged, 114, 115, 194, 219, 220, 222, 223, 224, 228
waterlogging, 224
watermills, 113, 145, 176
wattle, 73, 83, 144, **169**
  and daub, 74, 144, 147, **169**
wave pattern, 275
wax, 84, 141-2, 178, 181, 192, 264, 265
  seals, 141
  tablets, 149
weapons, 59, 62, 63, 64, 66, 74, 84, 85, **90-1**, 95, 96, 97, 114, **123-4**, **126**, 149, 150, **151-3**, 162, 178, 184, **185-9**, 242, 243
weapon training grounds, 100
wear marks, 230
weasels, 220
weather, **46**, 168, 257
weathered, 224, 225, **277**
weathering, 26, **222-3**, **227**, **235**
weaving (see also textiles), **80**, **116**, **157-8**, 195, **251-2**
  batons, 158
  combs, 73, **80**, **81**, 83, 115, **116**
  implements, 73
  sheds, 144
  swords, 68, 116, 149, **157**, **158**, 159
  tablets, **80**, 83
wedges, **25**, 36, **44**, **117**, 150, 255
weeds, of cultivation, 218
weft, 158, 252
  threads, 80, 116, 252

Weichselian, 11
weights, 43, **80**, 83, 113, **116**, **135-6**, 147, 149, 177, 178, **181**, 207, 245, 262, 263
welded, **151-2**, 189, **267**
Welland, River, 82
well defined shoulders, 283
wells, 97, 115, 158, 167, 194, 221, 222, **228**
well-sorted sediments, 223
Welsh Marches, 49, 62
welting-off rings, 272
Welwyn burials, 98
Welwyn Garden City, Hertfordshire, 84
Welwyn Garden City type beads, 87
Wessex, 47, 48, 54, 70, 79, 81, 83, 143, 145
Wessex I, 48, 52, 68
  flint and stone artifacts, 66
Wessex II, 48, 52, 68
  flint and stone artifacts, 65, 66
Wessex culture, **45**, 52, 68, 70
  bone and antler artifacts, 68
  burials, 45, **48**, **68**, 69
  gold, 64
  metalwork, 52, **53**
Wessex grog tempered wares, 131
West Country, 45, 113, 178
Western Isles, 45, 75
Western Neolithic pottery, 40
West Germany, 63
West Glamorgan, 9, 18, 54
West Harling-Staple Howe group, 81
wet sieving, 222
whalebones, 28
wharves, 167
wheat, 27, 46, 79, 117, 144
wheel-cut lines, 127
wheelhouses, **76**, 144
wheel pommels, 186, 187
wheel-rowels, 190
wheel ruts, 110
wheels, 82, 83, **91**, **92**, 111, 112, 113, 115, 123, 126, 165, 199, 201, 273, 274, **277**, **278**, 279
wheel throwing, 277
wheel thrown, 83, 128, 131, 164, 165, 166, 278
whelks, 222
whetstone pendants, 66
whetstones, **66**, 83, **123**, 146, **160**, **192**
whirl beads, 87
  pattern, 275
whistles, 137, 194
Whitby, North Yorkshire, 114
Whitby-type ware, 165
wickerwork, 79, 92, 110, **257**
wicks, 36, 134, 191
wide mouthed, **132**, **133**, 201, **282**
Wilburton, Cambridgeshire, 59
Wilburton leaf-shaped swords, 59, 60
Wilburton phase, 59, 60
Wilderspool, Cheshire, 270
wild ox, 13

willow, 73, 217
Wilsford group, 65
Wilsford shaft, Wiltshire, 46
Wiltshire, 29, 30, 31, 43, 46, 48, 49, 50, 51, 76, 82, 131, 246
Winchester, Hampshire, 166
Winchester bottles, 166
Winchester ware, 165, 166
wind-blown, 219, 223, 225
wind instruments, 137
Windmill Hill culture, 27
  pottery, 40
  ware, 41
windmills, 145, **176-7**
window-coverings, 253
  frames, 174
  glass, 128, 145, **164**, **195-7**, 269, 270, **275-7**
  grilles, 109
  jambs, 174
  leading, 178
  panes, 126, 128
windows, 105, **109**, **145**, 167, **169**, 170, 173, **174**, **175**, **195-7**, 275, **276-7**
wine, 83, 95, 96, 131, 132, 164, 203
  amphorae, 98
  strainers, 95, 122
winged chapes, 63
  corridor houses, 106
  corridor villas, 102, **106**
  houses, 102
  hunting spears, 188
  sockets, 183
  spearheads, 188
wing-flanged axes, 54, 57
wings, 106, 246, **248**
wing-shaped chapes, 63
wing walls, 171
winnowed, 27
wire, 86, 139, 140, 141, 195, 197, 267, 274, 278
Wisconsin, 11
withies, 28, 42
woad, 144
Wolstonian glaciation, **10**, **11**, 16
wood, wooden (see also timber), 211, 219, 227, 233, 251, 253, **254-6**, 281
  Bronze Age, 46, 47, 48, **73**
  Iron Age, 75, 76, **83**, 96
  Medieval, 167, 170, 171, 172, 173, 176, **194-5**
  Neolithic, 36, **42**
  Roman, 100, 101, 104, 107, 109, 110, 111, 121, 142
  Saxon, 144, 145, 146, **158**
wood-ash, 268
Woodeaton, Oxfordshire, 140
wooden artifacts, 207, **245**, **246**, 248, 251, 254-5, **256**, 260, 262, 264, **270-1**, 275, 279
  Bronze Age, **47**, **48**, 52, **64**, 66, 68, **73**
  Iron Age, 83, 86, 90, 91, 92, 96, 97, 98
  Medieval, 175, **180**, **181**, **182**, **183**, **185**, **186**, **187**, **188**, **189**, **194-5**, 199, 202, 246, 277
  Mesolithic, 25-6
  Neolithic, **27**, 28, 36, **38**, **42-3**

Palaeolithic, 9, **14**, 15
Roman, **103**, 109, **110**, **111**, 112, 113, 114, **115**, **116**, **117**, 121, 123, **126**, **137**, **138**, **141-2**, 246
Saxon, 146, **151**, **152**, **153**, **158**, 165
wooden forks, 271
Woodhenge, Wiltshire, 29, 43
Woodhenge group, 65
woodland, 11, 26, 217, 224, 225, 245
woodman's axes, 183
woods, 12, 26, 96, 218
woodwork, 120
woodworking, 144, 156, **254-7**
wool, 46, 73, 80, 110, 115, 116, 195, 251, 252
woollen, 80, 117, 124, 158, 252
woolly rhinoceros, 13
word squares, 104
work boxes, **149**, 160
working floors, 263
  hollows, 79
workshops, 99, 144
worms (see also earthworms), 225, 233
wound beads, 274
woven, 116
  grasses, 73
  wicker lining, 158
Wraxall class torcs, 86
wrist clasps, 153, **154**
wristguards, **66**, **186**, 194
writhen, 198
writhen knops, 182
writing, 105, **141-2**, 253
  implements, 146
  tablets, 105, **141-2**, 159
wrought iron, 266
  nails, 266
Wroxeter, Shropshire, 270
Würm, 11
Wye, River, 147
Wymer, J. J., 14

X-ray diffraction analysis, 231
  fluorescence spectrometry, 230
  microscopy, 229
  milliprobe, 230
  photographs, 229
X-rays, 230, 231

yards, **50**, 167, 169, 213
Yarmouth, 11
Yarnbury-Highfield style, 82
yellow ochre, 109
yew, 11, 43
Y holes, 51
yoke mounts, 91
yokes, 91, **92**, 115, 249
yoke terminals, 91
York, 138, 165
Yorkshire, 32, 49, 54, 114
Yorkshire axes, 62, 63
  vase food vessels, 70-1
  vases, 64, **70**
York-type ware, 165
Younger Dryas, 12, 218

Z holes, 51
zinc, 114, 264, 267
zonation, 11
zoomorphic, **140**, 149, 154, **163**, 200